PARTY, PROCESS, AND POLITICAL CHANGE IN CONGRESS, VOLUME 2

SOCIAL SCIENCE HISTORY

Edited by

Stephen Haber and David W. Brady

Anne G. Hanley, *Native Capital: Financial Institutions and Economic Development in São Paulo, Brazil, 1850–1920*

Fernando Rocchi, *Chimneys in the Desert: Argentina During the Export Boom Years, 1870–1930*

J. G. Manning and Ian Morris, *The Ancient Economy: Evidence and Models*

Daniel Lederman, *The Political Economy of Protection*

William Summerhill, *Order Against Progress*

Samuel Kernell, *James Madison: The Theory and Practice of Republican Government*

Francisco Vidal Luna and Herbert S. Klein, *Slavery and the Economy of São Paulo, 1750–1850*

Noel Maurer, *The Power and the Money*

David W. Brady and Mathew D. McCubbins, *Party, Process, and Political Change in Congress*

Jeffrey Bortz and Stephen Haber, *The Mexican Economy, 1870–1930*

Edward Beatty, *Institutions and Investment*

Jeremy Baskes, *Indians, Merchants, and Markets*

PARTY, PROCESS, AND POLITICAL CHANGE IN CONGRESS, VOLUME 2

Further New Perspectives on the History of Congress

Edited by

DAVID W. BRADY AND

MATHEW D. MCCUBBINS

STANFORD UNIVERSITY PRESS

Stanford, California

2007

Stanford University Press
Stanford, California

Printed in the United States of America on acid-free, archival-quality paper

Library of Congress Cataloging-in-Publication Data

Party, process, and political change in Congress : further new perspectives on the history of Congress / edited by David W. Brady and Mathew D. McCubbins.

v. cm.—(Social science history)

Includes bibliographical references and index.

Contents: American political geography / David Brady and Mathew D. McCubbins—External influences on Congress—Progressive Era—What did the direct primary do to party loyalty in Congress? / Stephen Ansolabehere, Shigeo Hirano, and James M. Snyder—The effects of presidential elections on party control of the Senate under indirect and direct elections / Erik J. Engstrom and Samuel Kernell—The dynamics of Senate voting: ideological shirking and the 17th Amendment / William Bernhard and Brian R. Sala—The electoral connection: career building and constituency representation in the U.S. Senate in the age of indirect elections / Wendy J. Schiller—The first "Southern Strategy": the Republican Party and contested-election cases in the late 19th-century House / Jeffery A. Jenkins—Postwar period—Explaining the ideological polarization of the congressional parties since the 1970s / Gary C. Jacobson—One D is not enough: measuring conditional party government, 1887–2002 / John H. Aldrich, David W. Rohde, and Michael W. Tofias—Who parties? Floor voting, district ideology, and electoral margins / Brandice Canes-Wrone, Julia Rabinovich, and Craig Volden—Internal changes in Congress—19th-century development of Congress—Architect or tactician? Henry Clay and the institutional development of the U.S. House of Representatives / Charles Stewart—Committee composition in the absence of a strong speaker / Chris Den Hartog and Craig Goodman—Roll-call behavior and career advancement: analyzing committee assignments from Reconstruction to the New Deal / Craig Goodman and Timothy P. Nokken—The evolution of agenda-setting institutions in Congress: path dependency in House and Senate institutional development / Jason M. Roberts and Steven S. Smith—Progressive Era—Filibuster reform in the Senate, 1913–1917 / Gregory Koger—Cloture reform reconsidered / Gregory J. Wawro and Eric Schickler—Candidates, parties, and the politics of U.S. House elections across time / Jamie L. Carson and Jason M. Roberts—Speaker David Henderson and the partisan era of the U.S. House / Charles J. Finocchiaro and David W. Rohde—Postwar period—The motion to recommit in the House: the creation, evisceration, and restoration of a minority right / Donald R. Wolfensberger—The motion to recommit in the U.S. House of Representatives / Gary W. Cox, Chris Den Hartog, and Mathew D. McCubbins—The motion to recommit: more than an amendment? / D. Roderick Kiewiet and Kevin Roust—An evolving end game: partisan collusion in conference committees, 1953–2003 / Robert Parks Van Houweling—Postbellum trends—Bicameral resolution in Congress, 1863–2002 / Elizabeth Rybicki—The electoral disconnection: roll-call behavior in lame-duck sessions of the House of Representatives, 1879–1933 / Timothy P. Nokken—Policy—Measuring significant legislation, 1877–1948 / Joshua D. Clinton and John S. Lapinksi—The Fugitive Slave Act of 1850: an instrumental interpretation / Jeffrey Rogers Hummel and Barry R. Weingast—Power rejected: Congress and bankruptcy in the early republic / Erik Berglöf and Howard Rosenthal—Afterword / David Brady and Mathew D. McCubbins—Notes—References—Index.

ISBN 978-0-8047-5590-0 (cloth : alk. paper)

ISBN 978-0-8047-5591-7 (pbk. : alk. paper)

1. United States. Congress—History. 2. United States—Politics and government. I. Brady, David W. II. McCubbins, Mathew D. (Mathew Daniel), 1956–

JK1021.P36 2007

328.7309—dc22 2007004609

Typeset by Newgen in 10½/13 Bembo

This book is dedicated to Joseph Cooper and Nelson Polsby, who were here before us

CONTENTS

CONTRIBUTORS

John Aldrich is Pfizer-Pratt University Professor of Political Science at Duke University. He has authored or coauthored *Before the Convention, Linear Probability, Logit and Probit Models, Why Parties?* and a series of books on elections, the most recent of which is *Change and Continuity in the 2004 Elections*. His articles have appeared in *American Political Science Review, American Journal of Political Science, Journal of Politics, Public Choice*, and other journals and edited volumes.

Stephen Ansolabehere is the Elting R. Morison Professor of Political Science at the Massachusetts Institute of Technology. He studies elections, democracy, and the mass media. He is coauthor (with Shanto Iyengar) of *The Media Game* and *Going Negative: How Political Advertising Alienates and Polarizes the American Electorate*. His articles have appeared in *American Political Science Review, British Journal of Politics, Journal of Politics, Legislative Studies Quarterly, Public Opinion Quarterly, The Quill*, and *Chance*.

Eric Berglöf is chief economist and special advisor to the president at the European Bank for Reconstruction and Development. He is a widely published and internationally respected specialist in the field of transition economics. His focus has been on policy-related issues in transition economies, and he has frequently provided advice to national governments and international institutions, including the International Monetary Fund and the World Bank. Before his current position, he was director of the Stockholm Institute of Transition Economies (SITE) and professor at the Stockholm School of Economics from 2000 to 2005.

William Bernhard is an associate professor of political science at the University of Illinois at Urbana-Champaign. His work has appeared in *American Journal of Political Science, American Political Science Review, International Organization, International Studies Quarterly, Journal of Politics*, and the *Quarterly Journal of Political Science*. His most recent book, *Democratic Processes and Financial Markets*, examines the conditions under which political events affect the behavior of asset prices.

David W. Brady is deputy director and senior fellow at the Hoover Institution. He is also the Bowen H. and Janice Arthur McCoy Professor of Political

Science and Leadership Values in the Stanford Graduate School of Business and professor of political science in the School of Humanities and Sciences at Stanford. He is an expert on the U.S. Congress and congressional decision making and has authored *Congressional Voting in a Partisan Era* and *Critical Elections in the U.S. House of Representatives.*

Brandice Canes-Wrone is an associate professor of politics and public affairs at Princeton University. Her interests include political institutions, representation, and formal and quantitative methods. She is the author of *Who Leads Whom? Presidents, Policy, and the Public* and numerous articles in the leading journals of political science including *American Journal of Political Science, American Political Science Review,* and *Journal of Politics*. She is currently on the editorial boards of *American Journal of Political Science, American National Election Studies, Presidential Studies Quarterly,* and *Public Choice.*

Jamie L. Carson is an assistant professor of political science at the University of Georgia. He received his Ph.D. from Michigan State University in 2003. His research interests include congressional politics and elections, American political development, and separation of powers. He has published articles in a number of scholarly journals, including *American Journal of Political Science, Journal of Politics, Legislative Studies Quarterly, Political Analysis, Political Research Quarterly,* and *Public Choice.*

Joshua D. Clinton is an assistant professor in the Department of Politics at Princeton University. His research interests largely focus on the incentives for position-taking and lawmaking activity in the legislative and electoral arenas. A sample of published work includes "Representation in Congress: Constituents and Roll Calls in the 106th House" in *Journal of Politics*; "The Statistical Analysis of Roll Call Voting (with Simon Jackman and Doug Rivers) in *American Political Science Review*; "Testing Accounts of Legislative Strategic Voting" (with Adam Meirowitz) in *American Journal of Politics*; and "Integrating Voting Theory and Roll Call Analysis: A Framework" (with Adam Meirowitz) in *Political Analysis.*

Gary W. Cox is Distinguished Professor of Political Science at the University of California at San Diego. In addition to numerous articles in the areas of legislative and electoral politics, he is the author of *The Efficient Secret* and *Making Votes Count* and coauthor of *Elbridge Gerry's Salamander, Legislative Leviathan,* and *Setting the Agenda.*

Erik J. Engstrom is an assistant professor of political science at the University of North Carolina. His research focuses on American national institutions and political development. His current projects include research on the politics of congressional redistricting during the 19th century and an examination of the impact of presidential coattails on party control of the U.S. Congress.

Charles J. Finocchiaro is an assistant professor of political science at the University of South Carolina. He received his Ph.D. from Michigan State University, where he was a fellow in the Political Institutions and Public Choice Program. His research interests include political parties and legislative organization, congressional elections, and institutional development. His published work has appeared in outlets such as *Political Research Quarterly* and *American Politics Research.*

Craig Goodman is an assistant professor of political science at Texas Tech University. He is a coauthor of "Lame Duck Legislators and Consideration of the Ship Subsidy Bill of 1922," which was published in *American Politics Research.* Currently he is working on several projects examining legislative behavior in the United States Senate and redistricting in Texas.

Chris Den Hartog is an assistant professor of political science at Cal Poly, San Luis Obispo. His research deals primarily with how the interaction between political parties and congressional institutions affects policy decisions made by Congress, in both historical and contemporary periods. Current projects include a study of the role of the majority party in the contemporary Senate and a study of the development of the modern legislative process in the 19th-century House of Representatives.

Shigeo Hirano is an assistant professor of political science and a faculty fellow at the Institute for Social and Economic Research and Policy at Columbia University. His research focuses on issues related to elections and representation in both the United States and Japan. His current projects are related to the incumbency advantage, electoral institutions, intraparty competition, and minor political parties.

Jeffrey Rogers Hummel is an assistant professor of economics and history at San Jose State University. He is the author of *Emancipating Slaves, Enslaving Free Men: A History of the American Civil War.*

Gary C. Jacobson is a professor of political science at the University of California at San Diego. He is the author of *Money in Congressional Elections*, *The Politics of Congressional Elections*, and *The Electoral Origins of Divided Government* and coauthor of *Strategy and Choice in Congressional Elections*, *American Parties in Decline*, and *The Logic of American Politics*. His latest book is *A Divider, Not a Uniter: George W. Bush and the American People*. He is a fellow of the American Academy of Arts and Sciences.

Jeffery A. Jenkins is an assistant professor of political science and a faculty fellow in the Institute for Policy Research at Northwestern University. He works in the areas of American political institutions, representation, and American political development. His work has appeared in *American Journal of Political Science*, *Journal of Politics*, *Legislative Studies Quarterly*, *Political Analysis*, *Electoral*

Studies, *Studies in American Political Development*, and *Journal of Economic History*, as well as peer-reviewed outlets. He is currently finishing a book manuscript with Charles Stewart III titled *Fighting for the Speakership: The House and the Rise of Party Government.*

Samuel Kernell is a professor of political science at the University of California at San Diego. He is the author of *Going Public: New Strategies of Presidential Leadership* and coauthor of *The Logic of American Politics*, *Strategy and Choice in Congressional Elections*, and *Chief of Staff: Twenty-five Years of Managing the Presidency*. He has edited or coedited three books: *The Politics of Divided Government*, *Parallel Politics: Economic Policymaking in the United States and Japan*, and *Principles and Practice of American Politics*.

D. Roderick Kiewiet is a professor of political science at the California Institute of Technology. He is the author of *Macroeconomics and Micropolitics* and coauthor of *The Logic of Delegation* and *Legislatures: Comparative Perspectives on Representative Assemblies*. He has authored or coauthored articles on several subjects, including the effects of economic conditions on voting behavior, congressional elections, legislative politics, Russian politics, ethnic politics in California, state and local government, public school finance, and American political history.

Gregory Koger is an assistant professor of political science at the University of Montana. He earned his Ph.D. from University of California at Los Angeles in 2002, and he has published articles on cosponsoring in *Legislative Studies Quarterly* and institutional change in the *Journal of Politics*. His research focuses on filibustering, institutional change, and political parties. He is currently preparing a book manuscript on the history of filibustering in the U.S. House and Senate.

John S. Lapinski is an assistant professor of political science at Yale University and a resident fellow in the Institute for Social and Policy Studies. His research concerns the Congress, political parties, elections, history, and quantitative methods. His publications have appeared in *American Journal of Political Science*, *Journal of Politics*, *Perspectives on Politics*, and *British Journal of Political Science*. He is also coeditor of *The Macropolitics of Congress*.

Mathew D. McCubbins is the Chancellor's Associates Chair VIII in the Department of Political Science at the University of California at San Diego. He is the coauthor of five books, *The Logic of Delegation*, *Legislative Leviathan*, *The Democratic Dilemma*, *Stealing the Initiative*, and *Setting the Agenda: Responsible Party Government in the U.S. House of Representatives*. He is also editor or coeditor of eight additional books and has authored more than 75 articles.

Timothy P. Nokken is an assistant professor in the Department of Political Science at Texas Tech University. He received his Ph.D. from the University of Illinois at Urbana-Champaign in 1999. His research investigates roll-call voting behavior and the role of parties in agenda development in the U.S. Congress. His work appears in *Legislative Studies Quarterly*, *American Politics Research*, and *Journal of Theoretical Politics*.

Julia Rabinovich is a Ph.D. candidate in the Political Science Department at Northwestern University. Her interests include political behavior and the impact of public opinion on public policy. Her current research focuses on the impact of public opinion on the policy-making decisions of unelected officials, especially in the areas of regulatory policy and foreign trade policy.

Jason M. Roberts is an assistant professor at the University of Minnesota. His research interests include American politics, the U.S. Congress, elections, and Supreme Court nominations. He has published articles in *American Journal of Political Science*, *Journal of Politics*, and *Congress and the Presidency*.

David W. Rohde is a professor of political science at Duke University and director of the Political Institutions and Public Choice Program. He received his Ph.D. from the University of Rochester. He was editor of *American Journal of Political Science* and chair of the Legislative Studies Sections of the American Political Science Association. He is the author of books and articles on various aspects of American national politics (most dealing with elite behavior in institutional contexts), including a series of 13 books on national elections since 1980 coauthored with Paul Abramson and John Aldrich.

Howard Rosenthal is a professor of politics at New York University and Roger Williams Straus Professor of Social Science, Emeritus, at Princeton University. He previously served on the faculty of Carnegie Mellon University for 27 years. He is an author of *Polarized America: The Dance of Ideology and Unequal Riches; Congress: A Political Economic History of Roll Call Voting*; and *Partisan Politics, Divided Government, and the Economy*. He is a member of the American Academy of Arts and Sciences and has served as a fellow of the Center for Advanced Study in the Behavioral Sciences, a visiting scholar at the Russell Sage Foundation, a national fellow at the Hoover Institution, and Sherman Fairchild Distinguished Scholar at the California Institute of Technology.

Kevin A. Roust is a visiting assistant professor of political science at Duke University. His research broadly addresses institutions, with a particular focus on the effects and stability of endogenous institutions such as constitutions or parliamentary rules. His dissertation, "Minority Rights in Majoritarian Institutions," considered the role of the minority party in the U.S. House of Representatives. He received his Ph.D. from the California Institute of Technology in 2005.

Elizabeth Rybicki is an analyst in American national government at the Congressional Research Service and a Ph.D. candidate in political science at the University of Minnesota.

Brian R. Sala is an assistant professor of political science at the University of California at Davis. His research focuses on applications of positive political theory to the study of congressional behavior and has appeared in *American Political Science Review*, *American Journal of Political Science*, and *Journal of Politics*. He is currently studying the relationship between bill cosponsorship and corporate campaign contributions in the Senate.

Eric Schickler is a professor of political science at the University of California at Berkeley. He is the author of *Disjointed Pluralism: Institutional Innovation and the Development of the U.S. Congress* and coauthor of *Filibuster: Obstruction and Lawmaking in the U.S. Senate* and *Partisan Hearts and Minds*.

Wendy J. Schiller is an associate professor of political science and public policy at Brown University. She is the author of *Partners and Rivals: Representation in U.S. Senate Delegations* and coauthor of *The Contemporary Congress*. Before coming to Brown, she held fellowships at the Brookings Institution and Princeton University, and she worked as a legislative staff member to Senator Daniel P. Moynihan and Governor Mario M. Cuomo.

Steven S. Smith is the Kate M. Gregg Professor of Social Sciences and the director of the Murray Weidenbaum Center on the Economy, Government, and Public Policy at Washington University. He is the author or coauthor of *The American Congress*, *Committees in Congress*, *Call to Order: Floor Politics in the House and Senate*, *Managing Uncertainty in the House of Representatives: Adaptation and Innovation in Special Rules*, *Politics or Principle: Filibustering in the United States Senate*, *The Politics of Institutional Choice: The Formation of the Russian State Duma*, and two forthcoming books, *Parties in Congress: Essays on the Study of Party Influence on Legislative Outcomes* and *Steering the Senate: The Development of Party Leadership in the U.S. Senate*.

James Snyder is the Arthur and Ruth Sloan Professor of Political Science and Economics at the Massachusetts Institute of Technology. He has published over 50 articles in political science and economics, mainly on questions of legislative representation.

Charles Stewart III is professor and head of the Department of Political Science at the Massachusetts Institute of Technology. He has written extensively about congressional elections, committees, leadership, and budgeting, often from a historical perspective. His most recent books are *Analyzing Congress* and *Fighting for the Speakership*.

Michael Tofias is an assistant professor of political science at the University of Wisconsin at Milwaukee. He received his B.A. from Cornell University in 2000 and his Ph.D. from Duke University in the summer of 2006. He has previously published in *Public Choice*. While working on the study for this volume, he was supported in part by Duke's Social Science Research Institute.

Robert Parks Van Houweling is an assistant professor in the Charles and Louise Travers Department of Political Science at the University of California at Berkeley. His work has been published in *American Political Science Review* and *American Journal of Political Science.*

Craig Volden is an assistant professor at Ohio State University. He pursues research and teaching interests in American politics and quantitative and formal methods. His work explores coalition formation and the interaction among political institutions, with a specific focus on legislative-executive relations and on federalism. He is coauthor of *Revolving Gridlock: Politics and Policy from Jimmy Carter to George W. Bush* and has published numerous articles in *American Journal of Political Science, Journal of Politics, Journal of Law, Economics and Organization*, and *Publius: The Journal of Federalism.*

Gregory Wawro is an associate professor of political science at Columbia University. He is the coauthor of *Filibuster: Obstruction and Lawmaking in the U.S. Senate.*

Barry R. Weingast is a senior fellow at the Hoover Institution as well as the Ward C. Krebs Family Professor in the Department of Political Science at Stanford University. He is a fellow of the American Academy of Arts and Sciences and is coauthor of *Analytic Narratives.*

Donald R. Wolfensberger has been director of the Congress Project at the Woodrow Wilson International Center for Scholars since 1999. He initially came to the center in 1997 as a guest scholar and then a public policy scholar, during which time he wrote *Congress and the People: Deliberative Democracy on Trial.* He is a 28-year staff veteran of the U.S. House of Representatives, culminating as chief of staff of the House Rules Committee in the 104th Congress. He earned a B.A. in English from North Central College and successfully completed the course work toward an M.A. in political science at the University of Iowa.

LIST OF EQUATIONS

(unless otherwise noted, ** = significant at 0.01 level, * = significant at 0.05 level)

LIST OF FIGURES AND TABLES

PARTY, PROCESS, AND POLITICAL CHANGE IN CONGRESS, VOLUME 2

Chapter 1

American Political Geography

DAVID BRADY AND MATHEW D. MCCUBBINS

I. Economic and Social Determinants of Political Divisions

The compromise that brought the diverse American colonies together into a union reflected the divisions among the colonies at the framing of the Constitution. As a result of this division, legislative power was to be twice checked, first by a division of the Congress into a House and Senate and then by granting the executive a correctable veto over legislation. Representatives would be apportioned by population in the House and by state in the Senate, which served to create a different distribution of power in each representative body. The Electoral College, responsible for electing the president and vice president, combined these two forms of representation. Further, congressional districts would be drawn by states.

Under some circumstances regional differences in the economy and society may be amplified by a system of representation; under others the system of representation may mute these differences. For much of American history regional differences have been amplified, driving American politics and shaping our national assembly.

Since the conclusion of the American Revolution the nation has, in fact if not in name, been the union of two quite different countries: the Northern states and the Southern states.[1] The differences between these two regions manifested themselves economically, socially, and politically. We now consider a variety of economic and social topics to demonstrate that the much-discussed contemporary division between red and blue states has roots that may be traced back to before the founding of the Republic.

AMERICAN ECONOMIC GEOGRAPHY: A BRIEF HISTORY

There have long been considerable economic differences between the Northern and Southern states. These divisions began before the Republic itself. Shortly after the American Revolution, the North's economy had moved toward small, relatively productive farming and to fishing, trade and commerce, and industry (Margo 2000; Atack, Bateman, and Parker 2000; Walton and Rockoff 1990). Helper (1857) argues that, although the North and South were relatively equal in economic production at the time of the American Revolution, the South fell considerably behind as early as the 1850s. Helper compares Virginia and New York to show that in 1791 Virginia had more exports than New York but by 1850 New York's exports were more than 40 times those of Virginia. A similar discrepancy in wealth shows up in a variety of forms by 1850.[2]

Economic differences also manifested themselves in agricultural output. Each region grew a different assortment of products, as might be expected on the basis of different types of soil, weather, and slaveholdings. However, one way to examine production is to compare each region's total production and its value as Helper (1857) does. In 1850 he finds that the Northern states produced a total of 17,423,152 bushels more agricultural product than did the Southern states and that the value of the North's agriculture exceeded the South's by $44,782,636. Further, he shows that "the annual hay crop of the free States is worth considerably more in dollars and cents than all the cotton, tobacco, rice, hay, hemp and sugar cane annually produced in the fifteen slave states." The value of Northern agriculture is not simply a function of greater acreage farmed, either. Helper argues that the North also had greater productivity of its land, which is reflected in the difference in value of farms and animal stock between the two regions. The combined value of the North's farms and animal stock in 1850 is estimated to be $2,576,425,397 and the South's is $1,492,107,338, which gives the North an advantage of more than $1 billion in the value of agricultural products.

These statistics partially obscure the massive role that cotton played in the economy of the South. The productivity of Southern land began to decline at the end of the 18th century because of a reduction in the soil's productivity (Walton and Rockoff 1990). However, after the invention of the cotton gin (1794), agricultural productivity in the South spiked upward. In 1790 American production of cotton totaled 3,135 bales, by 1830 production had grown to 731,452 bales, and by 1860 cotton production had climbed to 3,837,402 bales (Gray 1933; see also North 1961 for a discussion of the significance of cotton in American economic growth from 1800–1850). The increase in cotton production caused a simultaneous increase in the value of slaves, especially with the embargo on the importation of new slaves, and led to a period during which most of the South's wealth was in slaves (Weingast [2003] estimates that the value of slaves was equivalent to U.S. gross domestic product [GDP] at this time). Not only was the South's wealth largely tied up in a single asset but the North had about one-third more total wealth than the South (Helper 1857), and if we exclude the value of slaves, the North's wealth was about three times greater than the South's.

The data presented demonstrate that Northern states had considerably more value in their agricultural products than Southern states. The North held a distinct advantage over the South, as measured by numerous economic indicators. A comparison of the value of the products of manufacturing in 1859 reveals that the North produced just over $840 million in manufacturing to the South's $165 million. Northern states possessed considerably greater infrastructure in the form of both canals and railroads than the South. In 1854 the North had 3,682 miles of canals compared to 1,116 miles in the South. Additionally, by 1857 the North had nearly 18,000 miles of railroads, while the South had just under 7,000 miles. This infrastructure, in turn, allowed Northern states to be connected both internally and to foreign markets, which is reflected in the greater extent of imports and exports. The differences in infrastructure and manufacturing, when combined with the agricultural data, also show Northern states to be considerably more diversified, with agriculture and manufacturing comprising a significant portion of the total economic activity. Northern and Southern states clearly had different economies, and as Helper (1857) argued, the North was pulling away from the South with regard to each region's economic fortunes.

Although the discussion to this point has centered on Northern and Southern states, the West also played an important role in the development of U.S. politics. While the West's economic structure never exactly matched either the North or South, income levels in the West look more like those found in the North than the South (see Heim 2000 for a discussion of various perspectives on regional economic convergence). The West, in both its early form (as western Pennsylvania, West Virginia, Kentucky, Ohio, Michigan) and later form (as Arizona, California, Colorado, Idaho, Montana, New Mexico, Nevada, Oregon, Washington, and Wyoming), featured economies based on farming and resource extraction as in the South (California, and perhaps the entire West Coast, has since evolved an economy and politics that look more like the Northern states). However, in 1900, per capita GDP in the South was just more than 50 percent of the U.S. average, whereas incomes in the West were more than double those of the South and greater than the U.S. average. Incomes in the North were about twice the incomes in the South (Barro and Sala-i-Martin 1995). By 1990 the South had made considerable economic gains, drawing nearly even with the West in terms of per capita GDP to equal 76 percent of the North's per capita figures (Barro and Sala-i-Martin 1995).

These data make it clear that, although all the regions of the country have experienced economic gains, the South is still economically distinct from the rest of the country in income levels. This is a distinction that goes back at least as far as the 1850s and also demonstrates the long-standing geographic differences in the economies of the states in the Union.

AMERICAN SOCIAL GEOGRAPHY

In addition to differences in economic structure, output, and wealth between the North and South, the two regions differ along a number of social dimensions. In this section we consider the educational attainment of citizens of the different U.S. regions and differences in immigration across the country.

In 1870 school enrollment continued to show definite regional differences. For instance, 73 percent of the total 5–18-year-old population (both black and white) was enrolled in school in the Northeast. In the South, this population's enrollment totaled only 30 percent; in the Midwest, 67 percent; and in the West, 53 percent (U.S. Census 1870[3]). The West at this time had just barely come into existence, and only three states today considered Western were included in the 1870 census. These divisions in school attendance are reflected in regional literacy rates of the 19th century. According to the 1870 census, 25 percent of the South's population could not read and 29 percent could not write. By contrast, in the North 4.1 percent could not read and 6 percent could not write. In the West, about 8 percent of the population could not read and about 9 percent could not write. As is quite clear, the South was significantly different from the rest of the country in terms of the educational attainment of its residents. Similar to the economic trends, there has been considerable convergence in educational levels, but the South still lags behind the rest of the country in many indicators of educational attainment. According to the 2000 census, the South has the highest percentage of the population without a high school diploma and the lowest percentage of the population with a bachelor's degree or higher. This suggests that the gap between the Northern and Southern educational systems evident in the 1870 census have not been completely eliminated, even after nearly 140 years.

The social composition of the U.S. states has also been greatly affected by immigration. Although almost all regions of the United States have been affected by immigration, the regions have been affected at different times. According to U.S. census data, in the Western states 22 percent of the population was foreign-born in 1870 and 18.6 percent in 2000. In the Northeast 18 percent of the population was foreign-born in 1870, declining to 13.5 percent in 2000. The Midwest has seen a much more precipitous decline in foreign-born population. In 1870 foreign-born made up 20 percent of Midwesterners but only 9 percent by 2000. The area that has not seen much change is the South, which has always had the smallest percentage of foreign-born among its population.

The population in the South has undergone dramatic increases over the last 130 years. The South is now the most populated region of the country. During this same time the West has experienced nearly a tenfold increase in population. The political result of these population trends is that a greater number of members of the House of Representatives now come from the West and South, which is a decided change from over a century ago. While the historical differences in education and immigration have become muted over time, they are still clearly present. Moreover, the overall distribution of the U.S. population has clearly shifted to the South and West.

II. Regional Political Divisions

The regions, particularly the Northern and Southern, of the United States have been divided along economic and social lines since early in the Republic's history. One consequence of this division has been the creation of political fracture lines between the different regions of the country. Although the regions have not always been solidly Democratic or solidly Republican, they have almost always been divided into separate partisan camps.[4] The 1792 election featured every state voting for Washington, but the nonpartisan nature dissolved by 1796 when the North and South voted for different candidates and Adams (a Federalist) won the election. The North versus South division, with Republicans representing the North and Democrats the South, persisted in the 1828 election, where Jackson (Democrat) beat Adams (Northern Republican). In 1860 the partisan divisions underlying the Civil War were apparent as Lincoln (Republican) won the North and the election, beating Breckenridge (Southern Democrat). In 1892 a solid Democratic South combined with a few Northern states to give Cleveland

(Democrat) the victory. In 1896 the South and North continued their division in presidential voting; however, the Midwest voted with the South and the West split its vote, which led to a win for McKinley (Republican). In 1904 the North and West voted as a bloc against the South and sent Roosevelt (Republican) to the White House. In the 1916 the South and West voted together, leading to a Democratic victory for Wilson. In 1932 only the northernmost states voted for a Republican, and Roosevelt (Democrat) won across the rest of the country. In the 1960 election the North, South, and Midwest voted for Kennedy (Democrat), and he won the election. The last election featuring a solid Democratic South was the 1976 election in which Carter (Democrat) won the Southern states and the election. By the 2004 election, the South had become solidly Republican, the North solidly Democratic. The Midwestern and Western states also divided, with the West voting Democratic and the Midwest Republican. The end result of the various divisions was a Bush (Republican) victory, with the Midwest playing the pivotal role in elections. This brief review of U.S. presidential elections demonstrates the consistent partisan and geographic divisions among the states.

Before the American Revolution, all of the British North American colonies permitted slavery. Sentiment during the American Revolution led Vermont, Pennsylvania, Massachusetts, New Hampshire, Connecticut, Rhode Island, and New York to abolish slavery before the 18th century. States admitted before 1800 were divided, roughly, between slave states (Kentucky in 1792 and Tennessee in 1796) and a nonslave state (Vermont in 1791). Following the War of 1812, one of the critical political issues was the admission of new states in a manner acceptable to both the North and the South, which essentially meant balancing the admission of slave and free states (Sundquist 1983; Weingast 1991; McCarty, Poole, and Rosenthal 2002). The state-based representation in the Senate made it possible to balance political power by simply considering the number of states supporting slavery and abolition rather than considering the population of the states as the House of Representatives would require. To balance power between 1812 and 1850, six slave states and six free states were admitted. The slave states were Mississippi (1817), Alabama (1819), Missouri (1821), Arkansas (1836), Florida (1845), and Texas (1845). The free states were Illinois (1811), Indiana (1816), Maine (1820), Michigan (1837), Iowa (1846), and Wisconsin (1848). After 1850 all of the states that were admitted entered the Union as free states. The issue of slavery created a political division from early in the Republic's history, and the institution of the Senate ensured that this division was carried forward with the admission of new states.

In addition to the issue of slavery, the political demands of the U.S. regions reflected their economic and social differences. The commercial interests of the North demanded protection from English imports and English shipping and thus favored high tariffs on manufactured goods and special privileges in banking, printing, and shipping (Bensel 2000; Studenski and Kroos 1952, chapter 5). Northerners also wanted a larger banking system and expansion of markets into new territories (see Poole and Rosenthal 1997a, chapter 5, and McCarty, Poole, and Rosenthal 2002 for a discussion of how these trends reveal themselves in congressional voting patterns).

While the North was moving toward an economy structured around industrial production, the South had large, relatively unproductive plantations, with the principal input to production being slaves. The tremendous value of slaves at this time made the subject of runaway slaves an important political issue to Southerners (see chapter 25 in this volume).

Southerners, first as Democrat-Republicans under Jefferson and later as Democrats under Jackson, sought states' rights, the maintenance of the Missouri Compromise across the Louisiana Purchase, and relatively low tariffs. Northerners, beginning as Federalists, later becoming National Republicans and members of various other small parties, and eventually calling themselves Whigs, sought higher tariffs, which they imposed when they had power, and advocated a national banking system, stable currency, and special privileges for shipping. In short, they pushed for policies associated with manufacturing and commerce. These Northern political parties sought to expand government and the boundaries of free soil (Sundquist 1983).

The Whigs could not sustain a unified national political party, and eventually the Republicans picked up the Northern Whig banner. The election of Lincoln in 1860 precipitated a series of events that quickly led to the secession of Southern states and civil war. The Civil War and its aftermath ended the debate on some issues (e.g., slavery), but it did not change the fact that parties and the economy were still divided geographically. Indeed, the Civil War and Reconstruction only exacerbated the economic differences for the next 50 years, as the North's industry developed while the South stayed principally agricultural, relatively poor, and highly susceptible to the panics that emanated from Wall Street. While financial panics led to widespread bankruptcies, unemployment, and business defaults in the North, the duration of these ills there was relatively short. On the other hand, in the South, financial disruptions were more widespread and their effects were felt for much longer periods (Studenski and Kroos 1952, chapter 25).

During the 1920s and the early part of the Great Depression, Northern industrialists and workers sought protection from foreign competition. Together they sought unemployment insurance, old-age pensions, health care, and other nonwage benefits (Gordon 1994; Klein 2003). Industrial flight to the South and West exacerbated the migration trends that were already under way at this point (see Polsby 2004 for an elaboration of the causes of this migration). The population trends discussed in the previous section gave ever greater political weight to the South and West. One result of this is the West's continuing role as the critical balancing role in national elections. The importance of the Western vote can be seen in the maps that show the 1896, 1916, and 2004 elections, in which Western states played the key role in determining who won the presidency.

Democratic control of political power during the 1930s led to the passage of policies collectively known as the New Deal, which was based on an implicit bargain within the Democratic Party to require uniform taxes and benefits (exempting sectors of the economy most prevalent in the South) across the country so that the South and West did not have a wage advantage relative to the North. Tax surpluses were then to be used toward improvements (e.g., public works projects), principally in the South. This held the New Deal together as long as the Northerners did not press for further political reconstruction in the South (i.e., greater civil rights). However, once the deal frayed, in 1937, an implicit three-party system between the Republicans, Northern Democrats, and Southern Democrats resulted (Rohde 1991; Cox and McCubbins 1993; Poole and Rosenthal 1997a). During the 1960s this three-party system began to return to a more traditional two-party system as the Warren Court's political reconstruction of the South, waged principally through the redistricting cases, changed the basis of representation in the Southern states. Once congressional districts were redrawn, urban districts located in both the North and the South came to be represented mostly by liberal Democrats; rural and suburban districts were represented by Republicans. In both cases the representatives of the Democratic and Republican parties grew ever more polarized (see chapter 7 in this volume). However, the polarization and regional divisions of 21st-century American politics are yet another chapter in the history of regionalism in the United States.

III. 20th-Century Trends

The basic regional fissures in American politics existed at the founding of the Republic and have persisted over nearly 225 years. In this section we review a few significant social and economic trends of the 20th century to highlight ones that seem to affect all the regions of the country. These trends have had a considerable effect on the social and economic composition of the American polity. However, they have not fundamentally altered the regional political divisions, as the discussion of American presidential elections made clear. We offer this discussion because an overarching theory of Congress must incorporate both historical and contemporaneous circumstances. Further, these current trends seem liable to affect politics into the future.

Demographic changes are likely to affect political behavior, such as individual partisan identification and voting (Campbell et al. 1960; Berelson, Lazarsfeld, and McPhee 1954; Fiorina 1981; Zaller 1992; Bartels 2000). Furthermore, scholars have shown that constituents affect representatives' voting decisions in Congress (Burnham 1975; Erikson and Wright 2000, 2001; Ansolabehere, Snyder, and Stewart 2001b; Canes-Wrone, Brady, and Cogan 2002). Taken together, these findings suggest that changes in electoral constituencies are likely to affect the policies and votes of political representatives. Two of the most significant causes of demographic and constituent change in the United States over the last century are the aging of the population and the increase in the income and wealth of Americans.

Another significant change across the states is the substantial aging of the U.S. population, a trend that is occurring in nearly all advanced industrial democracies (Kinsella and Velkoff 2001). Over the last 100 years the proportion of the population over age 65 has increased consistently. The increase in the age of the American population will have profound effects on American politics, effects foreshadowed by the current debates over public and private pension plans, Social Security, and Medicare and that will only increase as the population continues to age.

Perhaps the most dramatic changes over the last 100 years are the increases in the economic fortunes of Americans and the emergence of an American middle class. According to U.S. census data, the average real income of Americans has increased nearly five-fold in the last 70 years. The research on income, wealth, and politics suggests that wealth affects the types of political activities in which individuals engage (Rosenstone and Hansen 1993). Moreover, it is likely that the change in economic status of Americans over the last century has had considerable effect on their political behavior and policy preferences. Indeed, the rise of the American middle class, in many states but principally in the Midwest and West, was a factor in the Progressive movement (Hofstadter 1955; Wyman 1974) and its many political reforms. These reforms and their effects on congressional elections, organization, and behavior are the topic of many of the chapters in this volume.

The distribution of income, or income equality, has also changed over the last century. Income equality increased during the early part of the 20th century, decreased during the middle of the century, and has increased over the past few decades (Levy and Murnane 1992; Jones and Weinberg 2000). In part, these trends are the result of how we count income (Rector and Hederman 1999), changes in tax policy (Auten and Carroll 1998), and the introduction of Social Security and Medicare (Liebman 2002). But they are largely the result of changes in households (Karoly and Burtless 1995; Weinberg 2004). Whatever the cause, these differences cause political rifts and policy changes.

We must take account of the aforementioned demographic changes when we seek to understand why political parties and politicians behave as they do. Furthermore, we must examine how political decisions affect these demographic changes rather than viewing politicians as simply responding to the changes.

IV. Conclusion

The foregoing suggests that understanding the nation's politics requires knowledge of the country's economic and social background. A political economy approach to understanding American politics must account for the way that social and economic changes affect politics and the effect politics has on society and the economy. The alignment of economic and political divisions, for example, has made partisan polarization the norm and partisan comity the exception. Periods of tight party competition, alternating party government, frequent divided government, and overlapping regional, economic, and social divisions leads to what is called polarized politics. This was true in the 1820s, 1850s, 1870s, 1880s, and 1930s and has been the norm since the late 1960s.

Although recognition that the economic and social system affects politics is by no means new, this volume aims to contribute to a theory of politics that is, at its core, about the decisions of political actors. Throughout the ebbs and flows in politics and economics, we typically view members of Congress as responding to the demands of their constituents and party (Mayhew 1974a). The chapters in this volume examine how the organization, behavior, and policies produced by Congress have evolved with the corresponding evolution of social and economic factors.

Scholars concerned with the history of institutions, including those who focus on the U.S. Congress, have often viewed institutional change as a teleological process in which history inevitably marches forward (Chiu 1928;

Cooper 1970; Polsby 1968; Polsby, Gallagher, and Rundquist 1968; Abram and Cooper 1968; Price 1975). According to this view, there is an almost unavoidable move from less to more efficient institutions, from high to low transaction costs, from little to big government, from part-time to professional legislators, from generalists to specialists, from low to high legislative productivity (for examples, see North and Wallis 1986; Polsby 1968; Polsby, Gallagher, and Rundquist 1969; Lipset 1959; Skowronek 1982; Weingast and Marshall 1988). While these theories have been valuable in directing our attention to changes in society, economy, and politics, some of this work is grounded in theories devoid of politics and does not take into account the strategic actions of politicians. Theories that do not incorporate actors' strategies lack in some important manner an understanding of why, when, and how individuals take actions that lead to the outcomes we observe. Ultimately, approaches that favor an inevitable march of history teach us a great deal about empirical conditions but are less use in understanding political history and creating robust congressional theory.

A brief consideration of three topics familiar to congressional scholars should make it clear that politics involves interaction between external factors and the decisions of political actors. For instance, consider the scholarship on the "solid South" (Key 1949) that largely presumed Democratic domination of the Southern states was an unvarying fact. Shortly after much of this literature was published, the South began to switch to Republican presidential candidates, and now Republicans dominate Southern states. It seems difficult to believe that this shift was inevitable, because specific congressional decisions began the transition from Southern Democratic to Republican control of the South (Sundquist 1983), and decisions by the Warren Court finally finished the task of reconstructing the South. This example suggests that we must be careful to avoid developing theories that are specific to a particular period of congressional history, and we must further strive to construct more general theories that have the ability to incorporate period effects.

Another example is Mayhew's (1974b) observation about the decline of marginal seats in congressional House races. As Jacobson (1987) demonstrated, the famous decline in the number of marginal House seats was simply an artifact of incumbents winning by a larger margin. Jacobson showed that incumbents also faced a larger possible seat swing, which in the end left unchanged the probability of an incumbent losing any given election. The change in incumbent vote share has been traced to constituency service (Fiorina 1977), dealignment (Mayhew 1974a; Ferejohn 1977), and candidate quality (Jacobson 1990; Cox and Katz 1996, 2002). The most compelling of these explanations, candidate quality, integrates external changes in the political environment (redistricting and realignment) with the strategic decisions of politicians and campaign fund-raisers. Jacobson's (1987) work demonstrates the importance of fully understanding the phenomenon to be examined, and his work, as well as Cox and Katz's (1996, 2002) research, shows the importance of considering the role strategy plays in politics.

One consequence of the interaction between external conditions and political strategy is the level of congressional party voting, as measured by party-unity scores. Analysis of certain periods, for instance, 1940 to 1970, would lead one to the conclusion that parties were less cohesive and weaker (see, for instance, Brady, Cooper, and Hurley 1979). However, if the analysis is extended to the 1990s, such a conclusion appears flawed, and it becomes clear that the decline in party unity was not part of an inevitable trend but rather a temporary dip in party voting sandwiched between two periods of much higher party voting. Observing the long-term movement of party voting reveals the difficulty in developing a general theory or conclusion based on a subsample of the time periods; it is likely that such a theory will be inaccurate if we go far enough backward or forward in time.

These examples demonstrate the substantial variation in political trends and the errors that we can make if we draw our understanding of Congress and American politics only from the most modern era or fail to appreciate the interaction between social and economic conditions and political changes. We realize that our short discussion of the history of political and economic divisions in the United States is not new. Rather, we offer it as a way to explain what we see as the goal of a satisfying theory of U.S. Congress, which is to connect the type of external influences exerted on the strategies of political actors, on congressional activity, and eventually on policy outcomes. The chapters in this volume take a first step in that direction by examining a historical period and giving serious consideration to the underlying politics that affect congressional behavior. In their analyses of history and institutional change, the authors in this volume all take a rationalist approach to the study of Congress. That is, they study the reasons why people do what they do. They follow the strategies people take to reach their ends. A strategic approach places people in relationships with other people who may have different ends. It is this difference in means and ends that leads to political competition and the resolution of that competition that sets the path of Congress in America. This volume seeks to move away from a teleological view of congressional history and examine how and why congressional institutions change. Accordingly, the focus in this volume is on the changes that have occurred within Congress and how political actors have structured institutions to achieve certain ends.

V. Plan of the Book

This book has three parts. Part 1 examines how external influences in the last 125 years, such as changes in party competition that resulted from westward expansion during the Progressive Era or changes in the economy and society that arose after World War II, affected the organization and behavior of Congress and its individual members. Part 2 looks at how the internal activity of Congress has changed and discusses the consequences, for policy making, of changes in the internal organization and procedure of the House and Senate. Part 3 examines how the titanic partisan and economic divisions in the country have been played out in national policy making. We will now briefly review each part in turn.

PART I: EXTERNAL INFLUENCES ON CONGRESS

The chapters in part 1 examine how the external political, economic, and social environment shapes the behavior of congressional actors. This part is itself divided into two sections. The first focuses on the effects of Progressive Era reforms in the states on congressional elections and organization. The second section considers the postwar era and the changes wrought by the Warren Court on state politics and congressional elections as well as the political consequences of these changes in Congress.

Section 1: Progressive Era. The chapters in section 1 focus on explaining the effects of a variety of changes that occurred during the Progressive Era. The ostensible goal of these reforms was to remove political power from the party machines and economic elites and place it in the hands of ordinary citizens. To that end, the favored reforms included direct election of politicians (especially U.S. senators), initiative and referendum processes, campaign-finance reform, direct election of judges, nonpartisan political races, primary elections, recall processes, women's suffrage, and civil service reform. The progressive reformers placed varying levels of importance on these goals, and there were considerable regional differences in support for each policy; however, what united all of the reformers was a desire to realign power (Sundquist 1983). Chapters by Stephen Ansolabehere, Shigeo Hirano, and James M. Snyder Jr.; Erik J. Engstrom and Samuel Kernell; William Bernhard and Brian Sala; Wendy J. Schiller; and Jeffery A. Jenkins explore how various of these progressive reforms affected the behavior of congressmen. Luckily, from the point of view of social science, the implementation of these reforms was often staggered and did not occur across all states at the same time. This interrupted pattern of policy change allows scholars the opportunity to parse out the effects of individual policy changes. Together these chapters suggest that the Progressive reformers' hopes for dramatic reforms in Congress have gone largely unrealized.

Section 2: Postwar Period. The second section of part 1 highlights changes in the external environment of Congress that have occurred since World War II. This is a period marked by two significantly different relations between political parties. In the early part of the postwar period, the division of the parties did not follow the traditional geographic focus. Instead, the Democratic Party straddled the traditional North-South divide. As is widely known (Sundquist 1983), this system eventually collapsed and the parties realigned along geographic lines, with the North being the province of Democrats and the South serving as the base of the Republican Party. The Western states played the balancing role, and as they have swung between Republicans and Democrats, so has control of the federal government. It is against this backdrop that Jacobson; Aldrich, Rohde, and Tofias; and Canes-Wrone, Rabinovich, and Volden explore different indicators of party activity in Congress. The findings from these chapters suggest that external factors have a profound connection to the activities of political parties within Congress.

PART II: INTERNAL CHANGES IN CONGRESS

The chapters in part 2 examine internal changes in Congress and how political actors structure the institutions in which they serve. Of particular interest to the scholars in this part are institutions related to the control of the congressional agenda such as committees, filibuster and cloture, and the motion to recommit. One of the central theoretical puzzles these authors seek to answer is Why, if these institutions constrain the majority party, do they continue to exist? The general answer is that these institutions may not significantly affect the majority party's ability to enact its goals and that the institutions may improve bargaining power with the president or the other branch of Congress. This part is divided into four sections focusing on the early 19th century, the Progressive Era, the postwar era, and the somewhat longer time span running from the Civil War to the present. We now turn to discuss each section.

Section 1: 19th-Century Development of Congress. Section 1 focuses on congressional changes during the 19th century, when slavery, tariffs, hard versus soft money, and territorial expansion were key political issues. Despite dramatic changes in the political issues over the last 200 years, the authors in this section all find that the seeds of many of the institutions and practices we observe in the contemporary Congress began during this period. Congressional institutions, therefore, appear to be well-suited to the needs of strategic politicians, even as the issues they face change. This suggests that political actors will often find ways to adapt or manipulate institutions to serve their interests, and when we examine the function of an institution we must be cautious about interpreting our findings as related to the institutional origins. Of particular interest to the authors in this section, Charles Stewart, Chris Den Hartog, Craig Goodman, Timothy P. Nokken, Jason M. Roberts, and Steven S. Smith, is the evolution of the committee system and how politicians use committees to further their strategic goals.

Section 2: Progressive Era. The works by Gregory Koger, Greg Wawro and Eric Schickler, Jamie L. Carson and Jason M. Roberts, and Charles J. Finocchiaro and David W. Rohde address internal changes in Congress that occurred during the Progressive Era. This period is marked by significant changes in the relationship between voters and politicians, and the prominent reforms of the period aimed to give voters a greater ability to affect public policy. At the same time that these changes were occurring in the relationship between voters and politicians, the U.S. Senate, in particular, was also revisiting and changing some of its central institutions such as the cloture rule. These chapters offer a preliminary step at understanding the origins of institutional changes within Congress.

Section 3: Postwar Period. The postwar period featured two distinct political periods. The first involved the New Deal and the politics that followed it for over 20 years, in which Southern and Northern Democrats were able to hold their coalition together despite differences over civil rights. This coalition broke down in the 1960s as the Northern Democrats pushed forward legislation that was designed to address racial inequities. As a result of the decision of Northern Democrats to change the terms underpinning the New Deal, the South slowly became the base of the Republican Party's support. During most of the postwar period, the Democrats held a considerable advantage in the House and also typically controlled the Senate. The West during this period typically determined whether the Republicans or Democrats controlled the Senate. This period of Democratic dominance characterized most of the postwar period until 1994, at which point the Republicans claimed control of the House. Against this backdrop of political party change, the chapters by Donald R. Wolfensberger; Gary W. Cox, Chris Den Hartog, and Mathew D. McCubbins; D. Roderick Kiewiet and

Kevin Roust; and Robert Parks Van Houweling explore how the majority and minority parties used the tools at their disposal to affect legislation.

Section 4: Postbellum Trends. Over the last 150 years the United States has seen dramatic growth. The number of states increased from 33 to 50, which added 34 seats to the Senate. The increase in the size of the United States was matched by its population growth, which grew from 31 million in 1860 to 296 million in 2004. The key policy issues changed as well. The gold standard, tariffs, and hard versus soft money all disappeared from the agenda during this period. Likewise, government intervention in the economy became accepted and the political debate centered on the extent and beneficiaries of the intervention. New issues such as civil rights and health and welfare programs became important in politics.

At the same time that political issues were changing, the United States was growing, expanding westward, and becoming predominantly urban as laborers moved away from the farms and toward cities. The movement of the population, coupled with court-ordered redistricting of the 1960s (e.g., *Westberry v. Sanders*), made the House increasingly urban, and representatives accordingly focused more on issues of interest to urban residents (McCubbins and Schwartz 1988; Ansolabehere, Gerber, and Snyder 2002). The addition of Western states made the Senate more rural than the House, and as a result of the greater Western presence, the Senate supported farm subsidies (Thies 1998), reclamation and mining policies, and added pork to appropriations bills. The divergence in each institution's constituency led to conflicts in the goals of legislators in the House and Senate. Rybicki's chapter explores how these institutions reconciled their differences and how this varies over time as the actors and their strategies change. Nokken studies changes in the behavior of congressmen with the removal of electoral constraints in lame-duck sessions of Congress.

PART III: POLICY

The chapters in this part trace out the ultimate policy effects of internal congressional changes and the external social dynamics. Hummel and Weingast and Berglöf and Rosenthal analyze specific policy decisions that are historically important, and in both works, explore how legislation reflects the forces acting on Congress and the political strategies of members of Congress. Clinton and Lapinski analyze a broad swath of legislation to create a dataset of significant legislation that can be used to study the effects of internal and external change on congressional output.

Part I

External Influences on Congress

Part I is divided into a section addressing the Progressive Era and one considering the post–World War II period. The first section examines the reforms of the Progressive Era, which occurred during the late 19th and early 20th centuries and were designed by their proponents to change who held political power in the country. As such, many of these reforms aimed to wrest power away from political machines. At the national level the reforms included the passage of the Interstate Commerce Act (1887) and the Sherman Antitrust Act (1890), direct election of senators enshrined in the 17th Amendment, and passage of early regulation of railroads and food and drugs. Progressive reforms also targeted state and local political power. At the state and local levels, the reforms included the direct primary, secret ballot and the initiative, referendum and recall, civil service reforms, and adoption of city-manager systems of government. Despite the ambitions of Progressive Era reformers, the actual effect of these reforms is unclear, and the chapters in this section examine the interaction between reforms and behavior of political actors.

The second section of part I examines the politics of the postwar period. At the end of World War II the New Deal alliance between Northern and Southern Democrats was still firmly in place without any obvious sign that it would fall apart within the next 30 years. The major external changes that affected Congress and the balance of power within and between the political parties during this period were a series of court decisions by the Warren Court that required redistricting of congressional districts to enforce a one-person, one-vote rule. The first two of these decisions, *Baker v. Carr* (1962) and *Westberry v. Sanders* (1964), precipitated a rash of state redistricting. Eight states were redistricted for the 89th Congress, 24 for the 90th, 17 for the 91st, and 6 for the 92nd. One effect of this was that Democratic districts became increasingly urban and Republican districts increasingly rural, which realigned the nation's historical geographic and political divisions. The chapters in this section all consider how politics changed throughout the postwar era.

Part I, Section 1: Progressive Era

In "What Did the Direct Primary Do to Party Loyalty in Congress?" Stephen Ansolabehere, Shigeo Hirano, and James M. Snyder Jr. examine the panel of elections and roll-call votes from 1890 to 1920 and find evidence that loyalty in Congress fell among a state's congressional delegation following the introduction of the primary. Also, incumbent defeat rates for renomination and split-ticket voting increased in states that introduced the primaries compared with states that did not. The data, however, suggest that the primaries were not transformative. The largest effect of the direct primaries on disloyalty occurred within the Congress elected in 1908, which ultimately revolted against Speaker Cannon.

Erik J. Engstrom and Samuel Kernell examine presidential coattails in "The Effects of Presidential Elections on Party Control of the Senate under Indirect and Direct Elections." They find a strong role for presidential elections under both indirect and direct elections, but one subject to the mediating influence of state electoral laws and institutions. They also find that passage of the 17th Amendment further tightened the responsiveness of the Senate to presidential elections and reduced the anti-Democratic bias of indirect elections.

William Bernhard and Brian R. Sala examine the effects of the 17th Amendment in "The Dynamics of Senate Voting: Ideological Shirking and the 17th Amendment." They show that the likelihood of extreme, or polarizing, shifts declined significantly after 1913. Conversely, the likelihood of moderating shifts increased. The post–17th Amendment patterns of legislative voting are remarkably similar to findings from the modern period.

The relationship between constituents and politicians is also the focus of Wendy J. Schiller's "The Electoral Connection: Career Building and Constituency Representation in the U.S. Senate in the Age of Indirect Elections," which delves deeper into the dynamics of Senate representation at the individual level between 1880 and 1913. Of primary interest here is how a candidate won a Senate seat, the strategies that he employed to try to retain it, and whether his institutional behavior influenced his electoral success in subsequent elections. To win and keep a Senate seat, U.S. senators had to consolidate power within their own party organizations and send continual signals from Washington that they were both loyal partisans and attentive to constituents in the districts of state house and state senate members.

The strategic actions of political actors and their relationship to the larger electoral environment take center stage in Jeffery A. Jenkins's "The First 'Southern Strategy': The Republican Party and Contested-Election Cases in the Late 19th-Century House." He argues that the Republican Party strategically used House contested-election cases in Southern states as a systematic response to the changing political climate in the mid-1870s. Although the Republicans were relatively weak in the South, they used contested-election cases to ensure that the entire section of the country would not be completely lost as national electoral politics tightened.

Part I, Section 2: Postwar Period

Gary C. Jacobson undertakes an analysis of one of the oft-noted political trends of the last 30 years in "Explaining the Ideological Polarization of the Congressional Parties since the 1970s." He finds that the electoral connection explains a substantial portion of the division between the parties because their bases of support have changed and politicians have reacted to those changes. At the same time, Congress appears to be more polarized than the electoral connection can directly explain, and he argues that actions within the House and Senate contributed to the polarizing trend not only indirectly, by shaping electoral politics, but also directly, by altering the formal and informal political environment within Congress itself.

John H. Aldrich, David W. Rohde, and Michael W. Tofias, in "One D Is Not Enough: Measuring Conditional Party Government, 1887–2002," argue that analysis that takes into account only the first dimension from an ideal-point estimation procedure may be missing important information regarding the underlying structure of politics. Specifically, the addition of a second dimension to our understanding of conditional party government allows us to better see the effects of shifts in congressional opinion, such as that caused by racial issues during the 20th century.

In "Who Parties? Floor Voting, District Ideology, and Electoral Margins," Brandice Canes-Wrone, Julia Rabinovich, and Craig Volden examine the relationship between electoral safety and legislative voting, particularly the "marginality hypothesis," which states that members with safe seats are more likely to vote with their party. Their analysis is consistent with the marginality hypothesis for the 1980s and 1990s, especially for members from moderate districts. However, consistent with claims in the literature on the rise of the personal vote, they find that the opposite of the marginality hypothesis more accurately characterizes legislative behavior in the 1960s.

Chapter 2

What Did the Direct Primary Do to Party Loyalty in Congress?

STEPHEN ANSOLABEHERE, SHIGEO HIRANO, AND JAMES M. SNYDER JR.

1. Introduction

The direct primary stands as one of the most significant and distinctive political reforms of the Progressive Era in America. Within a relatively short period— roughly 1896 to 1915—all but a handful of states adopted the primary as the chief method of nominating candidates for federal, state, and local offices.[1] Among the world democracies, only the United States has made regular use of primary elections to nominate candidates at all levels of government. All other democracies rely on party or private organizations to select candidates for the general election. In this chapter we estimate the effects of introducing the direct primary on party loyalty in the U.S. Congress from 1890 to 1920.[2] If the primaries weakened the party organizations and parties in the electorate, then they should have weakened the parties in government as well. Did party loyalty fall with the introduction of the direct primary, and if so, by how much?

2. Arguments and Conjectures

At the turn of the 19th century, progressives had high hopes for the primary, expecting that it would reduce the power of party machines and bosses, help more independent-minded, honest, and progressive politicians win office, increase voter participation and give voters a greater sense of political efficacy, and generally help reduce corruption in government. A few quotes are revealing.

> The direct primary will lower party responsibility. In its stead it establishes individual responsibility. It does lessen allegiance to party and increase individual independence, both as to the public official and as to the private citizen. It takes away the power of the party leader or boss and places the responsibility for control upon the individual. It lessens party spirit and decreases partisanship. These are some of the reasons why the primary should be retained and extended. (Senator George W. Norris of Nebraska)[3]

> The power has been taken out of the hands of those few men who formerly dictated the list of candidates and made the platform. . . . A man to be nominated now must be worth while and offer something for the good of the state, instead of his chief qualification being whether or not he can be handled. (Governor Walter R. Stubbs of Kansas)[4]

> [The direct primary makes] the elective officer more independent of those who would control his action for their own selfish advantage and enables him to appeal more directly to his constituency upon the basis of faithful service. (Governor Charles Evans Hughes of New York)[5]

> The direct primary was carried forward in New York politics when the insurgent forces in the Republican party felt that there was no other way of capturing the established organization which had been discredited by the insurance investigation, the legislative scandals, and other serious exposures during the first years of the new century. (Historian Charles A. Beard)[6]

Over the past 100 years, political scientists and historians have assessed the consequences of the direct primary and made a variety of claims about its impact on political life. Overall, the general assessment seems to be that primaries transformed the parties from disciplined organizations up and down the ladder—from voter to boss to legislator—into collections of like-minded but independent politicians and voters operating without the assistance of bosses and machines as intermediaries. The ratio of conjecture to hard evidence in this literature is quite high, however, and the evidence that exists is decidedly mixed.

In one of the earliest analyses, Millspaugh (1917, 173) writes that the direct primaries "had taken from him [the party professional] his most prized powers and have made him the appointee of the candidate, thus reversing the former relation." This caused a breakdown on discipline: "Since the candidate is simply a self-assertive individual who steps out of the ranks and gathers around him a following which is one of the several factions and often merely a minority of the party membership, his control is ephemeral and decentralizing and encourages insubordination." Another early assessment, by Brown (1922, 246), is similar: "The primary had made the Congressman an individualist and had deadened the old sense of clanship." Therefore, "with party lines weakened the tendency was for each man to think and act for himself. He was no longer coerced or instructed by the caucus, and the restraining influences of that instrument of stern discipline no longer held his intellectuality in check. Inevitably a candidate for reelection, he outlined his own campaign, and paddled his own political canoe. Gradually he committed himself to his constituents on an increasingly large number of issues" (245–246).

Later scholars largely concur with this view, although there is some dissent and attention to variation. V. O. Key (1964, 342) writes, "The adoption of the direct primary opened the road for disruptive forces that gradually fractionalized the party organization. By permitting more effective direct appeal by individual politicians to the party membership, the primary system freed forces driving toward disintegration of party organizations and facilitated the construction of factions and cliques attached to the ambitions of individual leaders. The convention system compelled leaders to treat, to deal, to allocate nominations; the primary permits individual aspirants by one means or another to build a wider following within the party." In a similar vein, Ranney (1975, 129) argues, "The direct primary in most instances has not only eliminated boss control of nominations but party control as well. Whatever may have been the case before the La Follette revolution, there are today no officers or committees in the national parties and very few in the state and local parties who can regularly give nominations to some aspirants and withhold them from others." And Galderisi and Ginsberg (1986, 116) claim, "The primary can be seen as an antiparty reform on three separate counts. First, by weakening party leaders' capacity to control nominating processes, primary elections undermine the organizational coherence of established parties. Second, primaries tend to direct the attention of voters and political activists toward the nominating contests of the party most likely to win the general election, and away from the interparty race. Over time, primary elections have probably helped to erode two-party competition in at least some states. Last, and most interesting, primary elections have the effect of inhibiting the formation of new parties."

Swenson (1982, 24–25) makes some of the strongest claims, arguing that not only did the direct primary lead to less party loyalty, but it was also a major driver of "professionalization" and "institutionalization" in Congress. The logic is as follows: Party organizations were weakened, causing candidates to rely more on their own personal resources and supporters to win nomination and election contests. Combined with civil service reforms and other reforms, the weaker party organizations were also unable to continue serving "as an immense employment agency for defeated congressmen." Members of Congress therefore began to see Congress itself as a career: "Thus the 20th century congressman, lacking easy mobility within as well as outside politics, at the mercy of a relatively unpredictable electorate in direct primary elections, sought to turn the occupation of congressman into a protected profession. Thus we see after the 1920s increasing evidence of behavior and arrangements in the House that have been called 'legislative professionalism' (Price 1975). Where once congressmen were usually career politicians, they were by the 1930s becoming career legislators, or more precisely, professional congressmen."

On the other hand, others argue that the primary did not live up to its promise. In an early analysis of the situation in Missouri, Loeb (1910, 171) states, "The direct nomination system has not weakened the party organization nor lessened the influence of the professional politician." McKenzie (1938, 318) argues, "Designed originally to eliminate the evils of a party machine under the convention system, it is doubtful if the direct primary has accomplished as much as its supporters claimed for it. Certainly the machine continues to exist in undiminished prestige." Beard's (1924, 551) assessment is similar: The direct primary "has not fulfilled all the hopes of its advocates. It has not destroyed party bosses, eliminated machines, or led to radical changes in the character of the men nominated. Its actual achievements are difficult to measure. In fact no searching examination has yet been made into the operations of the direct primary throughout the Union." Ranney and Kendall (1956, 284) agree: "Few attempts have been made to measure precisely what effects the direct primary has actually had on the control of nominations. What evidence we have on this point consists of statements made by students on the subject on the basis of personal observation of the general workings of the system over a number of years. But certainly the consensus among these students is that the party organizations or 'machines' put forward slates of carefully selected candidates, back them in the primaries, and elect them, often with little or no opposition." Pollack (1943, 61–62) provides a more mixed assessment: "I do not find that the party system in Michigan has been weakened by the primary system. I do not find that party responsibility is any weaker today than it was in 1909. . . . I do find that the primary system has broadened the control over nominations and the control of political parties, although politics is still pretty much of an insider's game even today. . . . The failure of the rank and file of the parties to participate in large numbers in the primary . . . has made it easier for organization leaders to control nominations in the primary. But this control has not been absolute, nor steady, and it has always been subject to popular revolts."

Ware (2002) concurs in the notion that primaries had limited effects and offers a revisionist view of the history of the adoption of the primaries in the first place. He argues, contrary to the traditional and dominant view, that many party loyalists and "machine" politicians actually supported the primaries. After all, how could the primaries be adopted by party organizations and state legislatures if the machines opposed their introduction? Under this view, we might not expect primaries to hurt the parties much, if at all.

Much of the progressive and revisionist history concerns the Northeast, Midwest, and West. Southern politics presents a noticeably different story but provides lessons that may have general application. Ranney and Kendall (1956, 284) argue, "In the 'multifactional' one-party areas especially, the direct primary has undoubtedly lessened the power of the few leaders at the top of the party hierarchy to make nominations; so that the Democratic primaries in such states as Arkansas, Florida, and Mississippi probably resemble more closely the utopia of the partisans of the direct primary than those in the two-party states or the bifactional states."

While it would be unfair to term it a consensus, the dominant view is certainly that the primaries were expected to decrease party strength in the electorate and create a new class of independent representatives. Loyalty rates in Congress should have declined, unless, of course, the revisionist view of the history holds.

3. Introduction of Primaries

During the first two decades of the last century, almost all U.S. states changed their method of nomination, abandoning conventions and caucuses in favor of direct primaries. Merriam and Overacker (1928) describe the relatively rapid adoption of this mechanism throughout the country. While progressives led the way, the reform was chosen in both progressive and conservative states. Ware (2002) offers an excellent analysis focused on a puzzling question: if party regulars controlled the electoral and legislative processes in most states, then why were primaries adopted in the first place? Key (1949) and Kousser (1974) argue that the primaries in the

Southern states were designed to preserve one-party rule by white elites and middle-class citizens. Elsewhere it is generally believed that the primary reflected the rise of progressivism.

As noted previously, we exploit the variation in the pattern of adoptions to estimate how much primary elections affected the loyalty of members of Congress to their parties within the legislature and of voters to the parties in congressional elections. Within a state the adoption of the primary may have had two effects on representatives. It may have turned out representatives who were unpopular or out of line with their party's electorate. It may also have changed the incentives facing sitting incumbents, making them less reliant on local party officials and more attuned to their electoral base. By examining behavior before and after the adoption of the primaries, we can assess whether popular control of the nominating process affected roll-call voting in Congress and general-election competition. We can also exploit variation across states to examine how behavior within specific Congresses is affected, because not all states adopted primaries at the same time. Within a given Congress, we expect that legislators from states with primaries will be less loyal to their party than legislators from states with convention or committee nomination procedures.

Somewhat surprisingly (to us), one of the most difficult problems is determining when and where the direct primary was actually used. In this respect, two features of the direct primary in the early 20th century complicate the coding. First, primaries were mandatory in many states, but in some states they were optional, and in some cases they were used only to "advise" a convention or nominating committee (sometimes the party delegation in the state legislature). Second, although some states immediately codified the primaries in statute, in others the primary emerged as a regular party practice that was not enshrined in state law until later.

Using a variety of sources, including historical works, state manuals, and election results, we coded the dates and types of primary elections used in each state and year. In some cases the coding is difficult and involves an element of judgment. The most difficult cases are those where the primary is optional but appears to be used routinely as a matter of party practice. The white primaries in the South are particularly difficult to date since many of these were allowed by law or party rules and used at the discretion of the party leaders. Further complicating the coding, some states use primaries for only some offices—e.g., for many years, Indiana and New York used primaries to nominate candidates for the U.S. House but not for the U.S. Senate.

The dates we chose for our analysis reflect the date the law was passed. We use the dates to identify which candidates had to run for election under a primary system and when in the panel the change occurred. We do not consider our dates definitive and appreciate comments and corrections. We have inspected tables published in other works, such as Merriam and Overacker (1928), Galderisi and Ezra (2001), Ware (2002), and Harvey and Mukherjee (n.d.), and find noticeable discrepancies. We have built on these tables and have done our best to resolve discrepancies, but some questions remain.[7]

In the analysis below we restrict our definition of primaries to mandatory primaries, or cases where optional primaries were used every year (e.g., Kentucky) and would therefore appear to be effectively mandatory from the point of view of individual House candidates. We omit cases where the coding of the primary election law is unclear or contradictory.[8]

As always, a major methodological concern is omitted variables. In particular, our analysis must somehow incorporate unmeasured characteristics of a state's politics—a strong progressive ideology, for example—that influence both party loyalty in the state's congressional delegation and the introduction of the direct primary in the state. Omitting these characteristics could lead us to infer a causal link between party loyalty and the direct primary, even when none exists. The panel structure of the data alleviates this problem to a large degree. We can include state fixed effects and even district fixed effects, which will capture the underlying unmeasured state characteristics.

Even fixed effects will fail us, however, if the unmeasured factors are trending rather than fixed. Suppose, for example, that a state party is trending away from the national party. Then its congressional delegation might have decreasing loyalty rates. In addition, it might adopt the primary, perhaps to guarantee its independence from the national party in the future (as Ulysses lashed himself to the mast to hear the sirens sing). The result would be a spurious positive correlation between the use of the primary and party disloyalty—reflecting the changing nature of the state's politics—even with the inclusion of state and year fixed effects.

We do not have sufficient data to estimate a trend for each district or state. However, we can assess whether short-run changes in loyalty of a state's delegation explain which states adopt primaries and when. We find that loyalty rates and changes in loyalty rates do not provide any leverage in explaining the timing of the adoption of primaries. This is consistent with Ware's (2002) description of how and why the direct primary was adopted. He attributes it to a practical, problem-solving approach—the "problem" being how to nominate and elect candidates in a large and growing society with highly decentralized political parties and a participatory culture—together with a variety of idiosyncratic factors including personal goals and rivalries, factional battles, and interparty conflict. He notes that the pattern of timing across states cannot be explained by conventional arguments. And he describes a number of cases, including Illinois, Massachusetts, Missouri, and Pennsylvania, where party loyalists and party regulars were instrumental in passing primary laws. As he and others have observed, states with strong party organizations were just as likely and almost as quick to adopt the direct primary as states with a progressive or populist streak.

4. Primaries and Loyalty in Congress

The main dependent variable of interest in this study is party loyalty within Congress. We measure this in two ways: (1) the percentage of times that members of Congress vote in the same direction as a majority of the members of their party, and (2) the percentage of times that members of Congress vote in the same direction as a majority of the leadership of their party.

As noted previously, some scholars speculate that the introduction of primaries would lead to the selection of more extremists within parties, while others argue that introduction of primaries might lead to policy moderation as legislators must attend more to voters and less to party elites. To test these hypotheses, in future work we will study ideological measures, such as Poole and Rosenthal's (1997a) NOMINATE scores and "pro-progressivism" roll-call scores.

In formulating the dependent variable, one question is, What population of roll-call votes ought to be included in the analysis? A large number of roll-call votes are nearly unanimous or very lopsided and reflect grandstanding or symbolic politics. These carry little information about the influence of party in government. To capture the issues where party loyalty likely matters, we study all roll-call votes decided by less than 80 percent. We also examine the subset of very close votes—those with a division of 60 – 40 percent or less.

A second methodological question is, What to do about the optional primaries, especially in the South? In most Southern states primaries were optional, but they were used so regularly by the Democratic Party that they probably appeared mandatory, at least from the point of view of the individual member of Congress. For the purposes of this chapter we omit the Southern states—we will study them in the future once we determine when a state's use of the primary is de facto mandatory. This has the unfortunate effect of limiting the inferences that we can draw about Democrats, because most of them came from Southern states in this period.

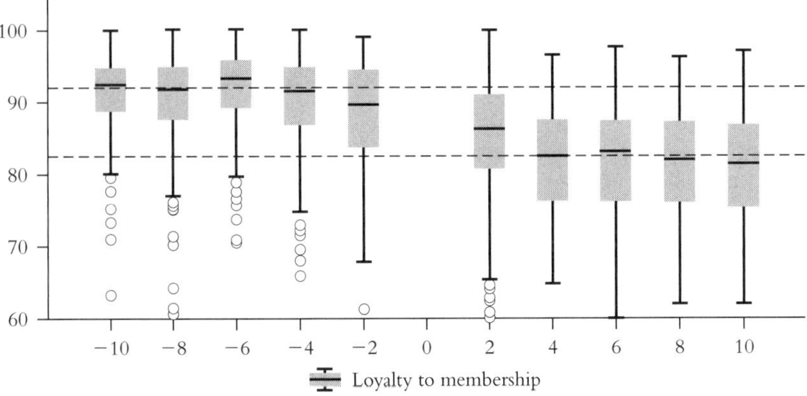

Figure 2.1 Distribution of party loyalty

A simple before-and-after analysis suggests that direct primaries lowered party loyalty rates somewhat. Consider all states that passed primary laws during the period of intense activity, 1904–1917, and consider the loyalty scores of their congressional delegations before and after the change. Using the "loyalty to the party membership" variable (previously defined as the percentage of times that members of Congress vote in the same direction as a majority of the members of their party), the average loyalty rate across the five preprimary Congresses is 90 percent and the median is 92 percent. For the five postprimary Congresses, the corresponding average and median figures are 81 percent and 82.5 percent, respectively. Thus, there was a 9-point drop in the mean loyalty rate and a 9.5-point drop in the median. Figure 2.1 shows the distribution of loyalty rates for each of the 10 pre- and postprimary Congresses. There is a clear drop between the pre- and postprimary periods. Importantly, the series is not simply trending downward.

To exploit all of the available data and to control for district preferences and year effects, we employ standard panel-data methods. We regress loyalty rates on an indicator of primary election in addition to fixed effects for years and fixed effects for either districts or members. When using district effects, we include a separate effect for each district for each decade. This captures the partisanship of the district within the decade, as well as other factors, such as state-level factors.

The choice of district or member fixed effects reflects two possible ways that primaries might affect loyalty. Primaries might create less loyalty either by replacing one legislator with another, or they might increase the responsiveness of the existing member to the partisans in the district.

Estimates using member-specific fixed effects capture the latter. Specifically, member-specific effects hold constant the preferences of the individual legislator. Any change in loyalty attributable to the introduction of the primary reflects a change in the individual legislator's roll-call voting behavior. Estimates using district-specific fixed effects capture both channels of influence—turnover and responsiveness. The district-specific fixed effect holds constant the district's preferences as well as features of the state. Any change in loyalty attributable to primaries may reflect either a change in who represents the district or the behavior of a single representative over time. The difference in the direct primary effect between these two analyses, then, is substantively meaningful as it reflects the change attributable to turnover and the change attributable to responsiveness.

Equations 2.1–2.4 present the estimated effects of the direct primary on party-loyalty rates of the House of Representatives. The analyses show Democrats and Republicans separately, and two different dependent variables: loyalty to the party membership as well as loyalty to the party leadership. The model contains district fixed effects and several control variables drawn from the literature. The controls are (1) the share of seats held by the member's party (*Seats Held by Member's Party*), (2) whether the member is in the majority party (*Member Maj Party*), and (3) whether the member is of the same party as the president (*Member President's Party*). We compute clustered standard errors, where each cluster is a representative.

$$\begin{aligned}\textit{Republican Loyalty to Membership} = {} & -5.69(1.35^{**})\textit{Direct Primary} \\ & - 28.71(2.17^{**})\textit{Seats Held by Member's Party} \\ & + 3.82(0.62^{**})\textit{Member Maj Party} + 7.15(0.48^{**})\textit{Member President's Party} \\ & - 0.04(0.08)\textit{Year}\ (\text{Adj. } R^2 = 0.46,\ N = 2{,}836) \qquad \textbf{(2.1)}\end{aligned}$$

$$\begin{aligned}\textit{Democratic Loyalty to Membership} = {} & -1.94(1.59)\textit{Direct Primary} \\ & - 20.35(4.74^{**})\textit{Seats Held by Member's Party} - 0.38(1.08)\textit{Member Maj Party} \\ & - 0.87(1.15)\textit{Member President's Party} \\ & + 0.00(0.15)\textit{Year}\ (\text{Adj. } R^2 = 0.63,\ N = 1{,}352) \qquad \textbf{(2.2)}\end{aligned}$$

$$\begin{aligned}\textit{Republican Loyalty to Leadership} = {} & -6.56(1.37^{**})\textit{Direct Primary} \\ & - 33.61(2.35^{**})\textit{Seats Held by Member's Party} + 4.61(0.60^{**})\textit{Member Maj Party} \\ & + 9.59(0.52^{**})\textit{Member President's Party} \\ & - 0.15(0.08)\textit{Year}\ (\text{Adj. } R^2 = 0.50,\ N = 2{,}816) \qquad \textbf{(2.3)}\end{aligned}$$

$$\begin{aligned}\textit{Democratic Loyalty to Leadership} = {} & -3.02(1.63)\textit{Direct Primary} \\ & - 31.29(5.29^{**})\textit{Seats Held by Member's Party} - 0.52(1.17)\textit{Member Maj Party} \\ & - 2.56(1.46)\textit{Member President's Party} + 0.08(0.16)\textit{Year} \\ & (\text{Adj. } R^2 = 0.64,\ N = 1{,}318) \qquad \textbf{(2.4)}\end{aligned}$$

Overall, the results are consistent with the claims that moving to direct primaries reduced party loyalty, especially for Republicans. For Republicans there is a drop of 3–5 percentage points in loyalty rates overall, attributable to the introduction of primary elections. The results for Democrats do not show an effect for the introduction of the primary.[9] The results suggest that the direct primaries had less of an impact on the party loyalty of Democratic members of Congress.

While generally statistically significant, the effect is of a modest size. For example, consider a Congress with 235 Republicans and 220 Democrats and suppose party loyalty falls by 5 percentage points, from 85 percent to 80 percent. On average, this will lead to almost 12 additional Republican defections. If the Democrats suffer equally, then this would be offset by an average of 11 defections by Democrats, leading to an expected net loss of just one Republican vote. On the other hand, the loss could loom large for a risk-averse leadership. If majority-party leaders want to be certain they have enough votes to pass a bill, then the 5-percentage-point decline in loyalty means that the leaders must plan on spending resources to persuade 12 additional members to vote with them. Even in this context, however, our findings imply that the direct primary hardly produced the transformation that many Progressives imagined and many commentators feared.

How robust is the effect? We checked robustness in two ways. First, we considered how the effect varied across regions. Second, we considered how specific years in Congress affected the estimates.

Region appears to be quite important. We divided the nation into West (all states west of the Mississippi other than South or border states) and nonwest (east of the Mississippi but outside the South). Prior commentary and research argues that the Westerners were more likely to break from their party, because the Progressive movement was much stronger in the upper Midwest and far West than in the East (e.g., Nye 1951; Sanders 1999). Indeed, the data bear out the distinctiveness of the West.

Equation 2.5 shows the estimated effect of the introduction of the direct primary on Republicans in the West and in the nonwest when we estimate the relationship with district fixed effects. The difference between the regions' coefficients is statistically significant at the 1 percent level. When we estimate the regression with member-specific fixed effects we do not find much difference between regions. The results are similar for loyalty to the party leadership.

Republican Loyalty to Leadership, 1890–1920

$$\begin{aligned}&= -11.73(2.35^{**})\textit{Direct Primary West} - 2.99(1.15^{**})\textit{Direct Primary Nonwest}\\&- 28.73(2.16^{**})\textit{Seats Held by Member's Party} + 3.79(0.61^{**})\textit{Member Maj Party}\\&+ 7.12(0.49^{**})\textit{Member President's Party}\\&- 0.03(0.08)\textit{Year}\ (\text{Adj. } R^2 = 0.47,\ N = 2{,}836) \qquad \textbf{(2.5)}\end{aligned}$$

The variation across years is also interesting. (Note that we do not present the year fixed effects, to conserve space.) One way that year matters is through the direct effect on loyalty rates. Party loyalty may be lower in some years than others. Indeed, some of the years do stand out—party loyalty rates are much lower, on average, in the 54th Congress (1895–1897) and 61st Congress (1909–1911). The 1894 election brought into Congress a large number of Populists and new Republicans. This election heralded the realigning election of 1896. The 61st Congress experienced one of the most dramatic events in the early 20th-century Congress—the revolt against Speaker Cannon. Both years saw somewhat lower rates of loyalty overall. Even controlling for these facts, the introduction of the primaries significantly affects loyalty.

As a further test of the importance of years, we omitted each year from the data and reestimated the effect of primaries on loyalty. The effects are unchanged across the analyses run with one of the years dropped, with one exception.

The exception is the 61st Congress. When we omit this Congress from the data, the estimated effect of primaries on loyalty falls by nearly 50 percent. The large difference suggests that most of the observed effect of the primaries on loyalty was manifest in the 61st Congress. Specifically, this result means that in 1909 and 1910 representatives subject to primary elections were especially disloyal, relative to those not subject to the primary. This is clear from the marginals: the average party-loyalty score among Republicans in the 61st Congress who were not yet subject to primary elections was 90 percent, while the average party-loyalty score for those who faced primaries was just 72 percent.

The 61st Congress is historically very important. It is the Congress that revolted against Speaker Cannon. Indeed, the direct primaries might have contributed to the insurgency against the old order. Primaries might have sufficiently freed members from control by local political organizations to allow them to oppose the Speaker without fear of electoral retribution. Some evidence of this is found using the analysis in J. Baker (1973). Baker identifies the insurgent legislators who led the attack on Cannon and further classifies them as Progressive or non-Progressive on the basis of their voting records on Progressive issues. The Progressive Insurgents were William Cary (Wis.), Henry Cooper (Wis.), Charles Davis (Minn.), Asle Gronna (N.Dak.), Gilbert Haugen (Iowa), Elbert Hubbard (Iowa), Irvine Lenroot (Wis.), Charles Lindbergh (Minn.), E. H. Madison (Kans.), Eben Martin (S.Dak.), Clarence Miller (Minn.), Elmer Morse (Wis.), Victor Murdock (Kans.), John Nelson (Wis.), George Norris (Neb.), and Miles Poindexter

(Wash.) (J. Baker 1973, 680). All of the Progressive Insurgents either won nomination in a primary or would have to run in a mandatory primary in 1910. Of the 27 non-Progressive Insurgents, 15 faced primary elections. Thus, 72 percent of the 43 Insurgents faced primaries. This compares with just 45 percent for non-Insurgents.

Finally, we should point out that our results might either overstate or understate the importance of the direct primary, because we have not attempted to weight the various roll calls in terms of their importance. It is possible the reduction in loyalty mainly took the form of defections on symbolic votes—it is even possible that the agenda changed to incorporate more such votes, in response to a demand by members of Congress seeking to signal back to their primary constituencies. This requires careful study and coding of the votes, and we leave it for future research.

One thing we can say for certain: it is not simply the case that the effect of the primary appears only on lopsided roll calls. If anything, the opposite is true. When we restrict the sample to the set of close roll calls—with a vote division of 60 – 40 percent or less—and reestimate the regression, we almost always find even stronger effects of the direct primary.

5. Primaries and Loyalty in the Electorate

Elections are the mechanism through which primaries affect loyalty within the Congress. Primaries may affect loyalty by changing people or by changing the incentives of those in office. Voters might use primary elections to remove party stalwarts and replace them with representatives who are more responsive to voters. Candidates might realize that without party organizations controlling nomination they need to act more independently and establish a personal base. The first effect would be evident in turnover rates: renomination rates should be lower with primaries. The second effect would be evident in voters' loyalty rates: split-ticket voting in general elections should grow in states with primaries. To our knowledge, no study has looked at the first sort of effect; a small literature examines the effects of primaries on party voting in general elections.

We first consider the effects on renomination. For every member of Congress, we used Inter-university Consortium for Political and Social Research (ICPSR) study 7803 and primary election returns, to determine whether the member ran for reelection and won or lost the nomination. In the decade before a state adopted the primary, about 2.6 percent of U.S. House members were not renominated. In the decade after a state adopted the direct primary, about 4.5 percent of U.S. House members lost in a primary election. The difference between these proportions is significantly different from 0 at the 0.05 level.

To control for state and year effects, we estimated a conditional logit model (G. Chamberlain 1980). This procedure adjusts for systematic variation in renomination rates across states and within years. The results are shown in equations 2.6 and 2.7. Holding constant the state and year, the estimated coefficient on the indicator of whether the state has a primary election was 1.94. This is statistically significant at the 5 percent level. The estimate implies that in a typical state few stalwarts were actually replaced as a result of the introduction of the primary, which produced at most a few additional replacements a year within each party.

Member Renominated (all states) = 1.94(0.51**)*Direct Primary*
(Pseudo $R^2 = 0.06$, $N = 2{,}399$) **(2.6)**

Member Renominated (by region) = 2.26(0.59**)*Direct Primary West*
+ 1.74(0.54)*Direct Primary Non-West* (Pseudo $R^2 = 0.07$, $N = 2{,}399$) **(2.7)**

Viewed from another perspective—the congressional career—the effect might be a bit more important. While the magnitude of this effect is modest, if legislators are highly risk averse, then the primary potentially represented a nontrivial increase in the risk of defeat. Over the course of five elections, an increase in the probability of defeat in renomination from 0.04 to 0.046 would increase the probability of defeat at some point from about 0.185 to 0.21, a 14 percent increase.

A second way that the electoral connection is manifest is through the party loyalty of voters. The primaries, it was widely argued at the time of their adoption, were expected to make politicians freer agents. While we cannot observe directly how independent they were of the party organizations, general elections do provide indirect evidence of the independence of politicians. If politicians indeed became less tied to their parties and their campaigns more personalistic, then party-line voting within elections should have declined.

We measure the split-ticket voting in U.S. House elections using the absolute difference between the Democratic vote share for the U.S. House candidates and for governors. Our specification differs from that in Harvey and Mukherjee (n.d.), in four respects. First our analysis is at the county level so we include county-level fixed effects instead of state- or district-level effects. Second, we include only House races where the partisan affiliations of the House candidates match the partisan affiliations of the gubernatorial candidates. Third, we include year fixed effects to take into account national shifts in split-ticket voting. Finally, we disaggregate the effect of the direct primaries on split-ticket voting in the Western (again, all states west of the Mississippi other than South or border states) and nonwestern (east of the Mississippi but outside the South) states.

Equations 2.8 and 2.9 present the regression results including both county and year fixed effects. The estimates reveal that the introduction of the primaries is associated with an increase in the difference between the partisan vote in House and gubernatorial elections. Introducing direct primaries increased the difference between the Democratic vote share in the House and gubernatorial elections by 0.7 percentage point.

$$\begin{aligned} \textit{Split-Ticket Voting} \text{ (all states)} &= -3.90(0.28^{**})\textit{Party Ballot} \\ &- 2.19(0.18^{**})\textit{Straight Ticket} + 1.02(0.29^{**})\textit{Direct Primary} \\ &(\text{Adj. } R^2 = 0.09,\ N = 6{,}643) \end{aligned} \qquad \textbf{(2.8)}$$

$$\begin{aligned} \textit{Split-Ticket Voting} \text{ (by region)} &= -3.49(0.29^{**})\textit{Party Ballot} \\ &- 1.98(0.18^{**})\textit{Straight Ticket} + 1.60(0.31^{**})\textit{Direct Primary West} \\ &+ 0.31(0.32)\textit{Direct Primary Nonwest} \text{ (Adj. } R^2 = 0.10,\ N = 6{,}643) \end{aligned} \qquad \textbf{(2.9)}$$

The results suggest there is a modest increase in personalistic voting and a drop in party line voting, which is consistent with findings in Harvey and Mukherjee (n.d.). The overall effect of the direct primary on split-ticket voting is less than a third as large as the effect of the party ballot and about half as large as the effect of having a straight-party-ticket circle or lever. Again, the effects are much more pronounced in the West. There, the effect of the direct primary is nearly as large as the effect of the party ballot, and larger than the effect of the straight-ticket level. The estimates suggest that the direct primary had no effect in the nonwest or might even have led to a slight decline in split-ticket voting.

Primaries might have contributed to increases in governor-House ticket-splitting in several ways. One possibility is that individual politicians asserted their political independence and developed a personal vote. Interestingly, there was a small increase in the incumbency advantage in this period, but it is never more than 2 percentage points (e.g., Gelman and King 1990).

Another important possibility is that the institution of primary elections weakened party organizations. Party organizations no longer had the function of nomination and recruitment, and they may have lost some of the reward that they could offer loyalists within the organization. In New York, for example, Thomas Platt was a longtime Republican party boss and, at the end of his career, was rewarded with a U.S. Senate seat. Without the ability to assign loyalists to posts, the party organizations lost a valuable reward that they could offer in exchange for the effort local leaders exerted on behalf of the state and local machines. Split-ticket voting and variance in electoral returns might have grown not because politicians were more assertive and independent but because parties were simply weaker. Party nominees, then, became a more heterogeneous lot. Voters responded in turn. And election results became more variable.

6. *Conclusions*

Contrary to the revisionist view, the introduction of the primary decreased loyalty in Congress, especially in the Congress that revolted against Speaker Cannon. And the primaries lowered party loyalty within the electorate, producing higher levels of split-ticket voting, more variability in election results, and slightly lower renomination rates for incumbents. The traditional view, however, grossly exaggerates the importance of the primary. While the reform did affect party loyalty, it was hardly the transformative electoral institution that many envisioned. The effects on party loyalty in Congress and on split-ticket voting are statistically significant but seem substantively modest.

Chapter 3

The Effects of Presidential Elections on Party Control of the Senate under Indirect and Direct Elections

ERIK J. ENGSTROM AND SAMUEL KERNELL

In devising the U.S. Senate, the framers intentionally sought to create an institution insulated from transient popular passions. Indirect elections and staggered terms would create a body capable of "cool" (Madison's phrasing) deliberation of policy. Yet there is evidence that Senate elections in the 19th century were not so insulated from national political forces as previously believed. Throughout this era Senate seats consistently tracked the presidential vote, and the party winning the White House almost always also won control of the Senate. How and why could indirect Senates elections be so responsive to national political forces? We argue that, much like House elections during this era (Engstrom and Kernell 2005), the mass mobilization of state electorates and party-strip balloting meant state legislative elections closely tracked presidential elections. In turn, so did Senate elections.

At the same time victory in the statewide presidential vote did not necessarily guarantee control of a state's Senate delegation. Biases in both the election of state legislators and the subsequent selection of senators by bicameral legislatures contributed to a pro-Republican structural advantage in the Senate. The passage of the 17th Amendment cleared away these biases and increased the responsiveness of Senate elections to national forces.

Pre- and Post-reform Senate Elections

Certainly indirect elections, along with the Senate's longer and staggered terms and malapportioned seats, provide ample reason to suspect that this chamber's party ratios would have been much less responsive to presidential elections than were those for the House of Representatives. Unsurprisingly, after adoption of the 17th Amendment, the electoral connection between the presidency and the Senate strengthened significantly as party ratios in the Senate began to more "tightly" track the national presidential vote (Crook and Hibbing 1997). In all eight presidential elections from 1913 through 1940, the party winning the presidency also captured or retained majority control of the Senate, and in three of these contests the out party simultaneously took away control of both the presidency and the Senate. Yet, as noted at the outset, even when state legislatures were electing the Senate, one can find traces of presidential elections in that chamber's changing party ratios. The party winning the presidency won or retained control of the Senate in 17 out of the 19 presidential results between 1840 and the first direct election in 1914. On four of the six occasions where an out party won the White House and also sought to take away the Senate, it succeeded.

As suggestive as these results are, the fact that only a third of the seats are up for election during any given election year means that overall seat shares are bound to understate the actual responsiveness of both direct and indirect Senate elections to national forces. Also, the Senate's party ratios included a large block of seats from the South that after the 1850s were impervious to national swings in party fortunes. Including this electorally insulated region both understates the responsiveness of Senate to presidential elections for the rest of the country and muddles the prospect of identifying the underlying mechanisms that generate this electoral connection. Hence, as important as the South was for deciding the partisan balance of power at both ends of Pennsylvania Avenue, we shall exclude this region from our investigation of the electoral connection between presidential and Senate elections before and after the 17th Amendment.

In figure 3.1 we have plotted for non-Southern states the Democratic share of the in-play Senate seats against the Democratic presidential vote. Clearly, the highly responsive Senate elections after direct elections confirm the observation (Crook and Hibbing 1997; Wirls 1999) that the 17th Amendment effectively nationalized Senate elections. Two other patterns for indirect elections can also be discerned in figure 3.1. First, throughout the 19th century Democrats ran stronger in presidential than Senate elections, as measured by seat shares. Others have noted and offered various explanations for

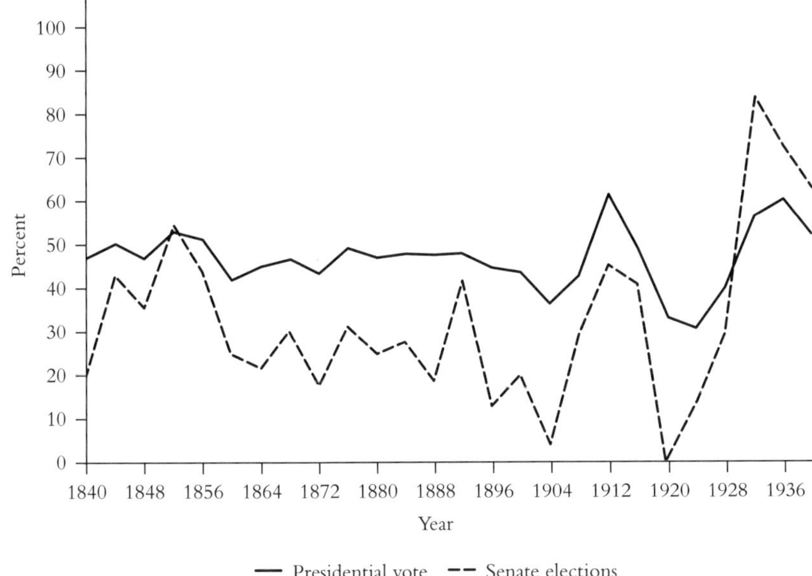

Figure 3.1 Democratic shares of vote in presidential and Senate elections: Non-South, 1840–1940

the Senate's anti-Democratic bias (King and Ellis 1996; Stewart 1991; Stewart and Weingast 1992). The second, less pronounced pattern is the distinct correlation of Democratic seat shares with the party's presidential vote before as well as after 1914.

To see this better, from these data we have calculated separately the familiar vote-seat relationship for elections under the direct and indirect election systems. The results are displayed in figure 3.2, where both bias and the swing-ratio coefficients are significant components of Democratic seat shares. Under indirect elections there is a 17-point anti-Democratic bias; when the Democratic presidential candidate won 50 percent of these states' vote, his party managed to capture only 33 percent of the Senate seats up for grabs. After passage of the 17th Amendment, bias is reduced nearly to zero. Clearly, a major accomplishment of the 17th Amendment was to eliminate bias—not an obvious outcome given the population differences across the states—and to bring the swing ratio into the region of the cube-rule norm (equivalent to a logistic coefficient of 3; Kendall and Stuart 1950; Butler 1951; Tufte 1973).

With national forces passing through state legislative filters, it is unsurprising that presidential voting had a weaker impact on Senate races during

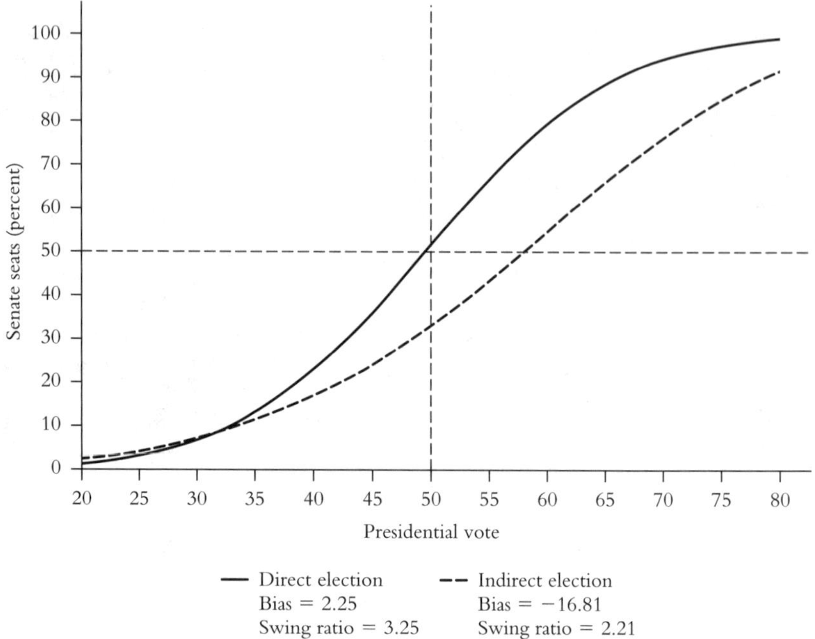

Figure 3.2 Presidential vote: Senate seats curve under indirect and direct elections

the regime of indirect elections. In this era when most state constitutions followed the national Congress in modeling representation in their bicameral chambers and the "one person, one vote" standard applied only to a state's lower chamber, if at all, the natural malapportionment of county-based seats in the upper chamber and the opportunities for gerrymandering the lower chamber allowed great differences between partisan shares of the votes and seats in the state legislature. Moreover, even where representation was fair, the joint election of senators by coequal chambers, frequently occupied by factitious partisans, made for unpredictable and occasionally manipulated outcomes.

Before exploring the complex and extended linkages between presidential voting and Senate elections, we first need to assess an altogether different explanation for the less responsive and biased outcomes we observe. During the Civil War and early Reconstruction, Republican Congresses engaged in a concerted practice of carving out new, safely Republican states to ensure their majority control after the presumably Democratic South reentered the Union. In the next section, we test this argument and conclude that, while those states admitted after 1860 did add critical Republican votes to the Senate, the presence of these new "rotten boroughs" does not fully account for the pronounced anti-Democratic bias and weaker responsiveness of the indirect election era.

The Statehood Admissions Strategy

According to both contemporaneous accounts and historians' assessments, the Republicans exploited their near supermajority control of the Civil War Congresses to secure future success by stacking the Senate with new Republican seats. More than avaricious partisan greed was at work here. Republicans had good reason to fear an ultimate Confederate victory when the Southern states were readmitted and this region's representation in the House of Representatives and Electoral College would no longer be discounted by the Constitution's three-fifths rule for counting slaves. So Republicans embarked on a "rotten borough strategy" of admitting sparsely populated, staunchly Republican states to guarantee control into the foreseeable future of at least one institution of the national government. In 1861 Kansas was admitted. During the next 4 years, another 14 different laws redrew territorial boundaries and admitted new states. By 1868 sparsely populated Nevada, Nebraska, and West Virginia had entered the Union, and only a veto by Southern-sympathizing President Andrew Johnson kept Colorado out a few more years. Stewart and Weingast (1992) argue persuasively that these and subsequent admissions succeeded in preserving a Republican Senate and with it a veto over the efforts of a Democratic-leaning House of Representatives to undo the nation's wartime policies. By Stewart and Weingast's calculations, in the absence of stacking, the Democrats would have won Senate majorities for 9 of the next 11 Congresses after 1876 instead of the 2 that actually occurred.

Evidence of the pronounced effects of these new, sparsely populated states on the presidential vote–Senate control relationship is displayed in equations 3.1 and 3.2. If one limits the relationship to states admitted after 1860, the Republican bias is an extraordinary 24 percentage points. Even had Democrats received 50 percent of the non-Southern presidential vote, they still would have commanded no more than a quarter of these states' Senate seats. Moreover, befitting their characterization as rotten boroughs, these states' Senate elections were less responsive to the presidential vote. Unsurprisingly, from the date of admission until the switch to direct election, 80 percent of the senators these states sent to Washington were Republican.

$$\textit{Republican Bias}, \text{ pre-1860 Admits} = 2.53(0.68^*)\textit{Responsiveness} - 14.50(3.82^*)\textit{Bias} \text{ (Log-likelihood} = -155.28, N = 268) \quad \textbf{(3.1)}$$

$$\textit{Republican Bias}, \text{ post-1860 Admits} = 1.54(1.04)\textit{Responsiveness} - 24.46(7.49^*)\textit{Bias} \text{ (Log-likelihood} = -37.04, N = 72) \quad \textbf{(3.2)}$$

Yet equation 3.1 also shows that the admissions strategy is not the only source of the anti-Democratic bias in Senate elections. Even for non-Southern states that entered the Union before 1860, Senate elections exhibit a 14-percentage-point bias and, compared to subsequent direct elections, a weaker swing ratio. These relationships add weight to the argument (King and Ellis 1996) that elections in non-Southern state legislatures inherently favored Republicans. Clearly, leveling the playing field for Democrats was an important effect of direct election reform. One might be tempted to conclude from the relationships in equations 3.1 and 3.2 that the same level of vote-seat bias occurred within the states. Reports of the notoriously maldistricted, anti-Democratic New England state legislatures during the late 19th century would seem to square much of the state-level histories with the national vote-seat relationships. Connecticut (Argersinger 1992; McSeveney 1972) offers an especially egregious instance where town-based legislatures managed repeatedly to frustrate the claims of popular Democratic pluralities and majority-elected governors to control state government and with it the state's Senate delegation. Yet other history points to highly competitive state politics elsewhere, especially throughout the Midwest, in which political control of state government swung with the ebb and flow of national elections. In fact, these case histories remind us that national elections in this era were largely the sum of disparate state-level events.

An Institutional Model of Presidential Effects on Senate Elections

When 19th-century voters cast their party-supplied ballots for president, to what degree, if any, did their presidential votes spill over on their preferred party's success in capturing a Senate seat in the next state legislative session? In answering this, one must consider how a state's political and institutional features might facilitate or impede the conversion of presidential preferences into state legislative elections. Political parties represent an obvious source for coordinating votes across offices. A strong party could bind its candidates to pursue a common campaign strategy and solve the legislators' collective-action problems. Less well understood, a state's electoral institutions could have had a similarly centripetal influence on the behavior of voters and politicians. Institutional mechanisms might have tied the fortunes of party politicians together across offices and connected popular votes for the president to legislative votes for senators. These mechanisms can be best examined through the following causal sequence:

1. Presidential coattails: presidential vote → state legislative vote
2. Vote-seat conversion: state legislative vote → partisan composition of legislative chamber
3. Indirect elections: party ratios of upper and lower chambers → Senate elections

For presidential preferences to influence indirect Senate elections via coattails, presidential and state legislative elections needed to occur contemporaneously. If the election calendars of these politicians were much different because of staggered terms, odd-year state elections, or even simply different polling dates for state and presidential elections as was commonplace during the first half of the 19th century, the party's candidates for these lower-level offices could not have benefited either from mobilization of the presidential vote or partisan enthusiasm generated by the national campaigns. Similarly, legislative districts needed to be configured in ways that fairly and closely reflected swings in popular support. When one or both chambers were gerrymandered into safe seats, statewide variations in popular voting for legislative candidates might not influence the aggregate partisan division of seats. With two chambers jointly electing the senator, bicameralism further served to filter the coattail connection. Divided party control of these legislatures frequently resulted in stalemated elections and occasionally led to a minority-party winner. Again, pervasive institutional rules govern outcomes. In the next section we test the first two stages of this process, estimating the impact of presidential voting on the partisan composition of state legislatures. We then turn to the effects of bicameral decision making.

The Presidential Vote–State Legislative Seats Relationship

Two prominent features of the states' 19th-century electoral systems that might well have mediated presidential elections' impact on state legislative elections, and in turn, on Senate elections, are ballot form and electoral calendar. Both features appeared in a variety of configurations across the states and time periods of our data. Until the 1890s, states employed the party-strip ballot, binding candidates vertically from the presidency down to the state legislator (and beyond). Parties would print and distribute these ballots, listing only their candidates on the ticket. By consolidating voters' choices on a single ballot, voters had little opportunity to split their ticket had they been so inclined; coattail voting occurred as the default outcome. As a result, the electoral fortunes of state legislative candidates, and any politician who aspired to the Senate, depended on the success of the presidential standard bearer at the top of the ticket.

The adoption of Australian ballot reform throughout the states from 1888 to 1911 (Evans 1917; Fredman 1968) dismantled the party-ticket system and weakened the connection between presidential and state legislative elections. By placing candidates of both parties on a single state-supplied ballot and removing voters from under the watchful eye of party workers, the Australian ballot made it easier for voters to split their tickets (Rusk 1970). Some states opted for the office-bloc ballot, while many more initially chose the party-column format. The former required voters to separately designate their candidate preference for each office. This ballot form was intended to discourage straight-ticket voting. The party-column ballot, by comparison, facilitated straight-ticket voting by aligning candidates in columns by party or even supplying a party box in which a single check indicated a straight-ticket vote. Since states adopted ballot reform at different times over a 23-year period, and some would periodically revise them even after adoption of the 17th Amendment, this state-level variable might have mediated responsiveness during both the indirect- and the direct-election eras.

Another potentially important mediating feature was a states' electoral calendar. States adopted numerous combinations of term lengths for the two chambers of their state legislatures. Some states elected all legislative seats during presidential election years, while others contested half, a third, or even none. In 1876, for example, 19 of the non-Southern lower chambers had all of their seats up for election, 3 had half, and 5 had none since they held state elections in odd-numbered years. In addition, some states elected their legislative (and gubernatorial) officers at times other than during the November presidential election. In some cases, state elections occurred months earlier. In testing for the effects of presidential voting, we shall distinguish those state elections held simultaneously with the presidential election from those held on separate dates.

Another ballot reform of special significance for Senate elections allowed voters to express their candidate preferences for the Senate. Some states with this precursor to direct election instituted nonbinding nomination primaries that presumably guided, if not dictated, the nomination of a party's state legislative caucus. In 1901 Oregon went one step further, creating a binding, "straw" Senate election. Here, voters selected among competing candidates across the parties. Prescriptive elections patterned on the Oregon plan were soon adopted by 13 other states and continued until direct election. The presence of senatorial candidates on the ballot might well have altered coattail voting up and down the ballot. In reminding voters of the broader implications of their state legislative vote, and in promoting particular candidates to the legislature, the Oregon plan might have forced partisan legislators to surrender their discretion and become merely electoral colleges registering popular preferences. Where present, this reform could have mitigated the relationship between presidential voting and Senate election.

A full analysis of the relationship between the presidential vote and state legislative seat shares requires systematic voting data for state legislative elections. Unfortunately, these data are currently unavailable for the 19th and first half of the 20th centuries. Unable to separate the effects of presidential coattails from those of vote-seat conversion, we must settle for estimating the overall relationship between states' presidential votes and the partisan composition of their state legislatures. To test this relationship we have collected all of the relevant institutional variables for every non-Southern election-state pair for 1840 (or date of admission if later) through 1940. This gives us an unbalanced, time-series cross-sectional data structure. The dependent variable is the Democratic percentage of state legislative seats; the key treatment variable, the Democratic percentage of the presidential vote. We then interact the presidential vote with those institutional variables hypothesized to mediate the impact of the coattail. To control for stable state partisan differences, we estimate an ordinary least squares (OLS) model with state fixed effects. Also, as is appropriate for time-series cross-sectional data, the model is estimated with panel-corrected standard errors (Beck and Katz 1995).

Table 3.1 presents the coattail effects of the state's Democratic vote share under various institutional constraints for the lower and upper chambers during presidential-election years when there is a true coattail potential. The analyses were performed using OLS with panel-corrected standard errors. State fixed effects were also used but not reported. Although not reported here, we also analyzed midterm elections. The pervasive absence of significant relationships for all of the coattail coefficients in the midterms reassures us that the significant relationships for the on-year elections represent the hypothesized treatment effects of the states' election institutions and are not an artifact of the distribution of states on these institutional variables. In both chambers' elections the presidential vote appears to have been a major determinant of the legislatures' partisan makeup. When presidential and state legislative elections were held on the same day under a party ticket,

TABLE 3.1
Impact of presidential vote on state legislative seats as a function of electoral laws, 1840–1940

Variable	Lower House seats	Upper House seats
Presidential vote (% Democratic)	1.02**	1.04**
	(0.17)	(0.14)
Ballot Form		
Non-November election (intercept)	18.88**	14.82**
	(6.73)	(6.79)
Non-November election∗presidential vote	−0.38*	−0.36*
	(0.16)	(0.16)
Office bloc ballot (intercept)	24.54**	29.36**
	(7.69)	(5.88)
Office bloc ballot∗presidential vote	−0.57**	−0.71**
	(0.19)	(0.14)
Party column ballot	16.96*	24.17**
	(7.64)	(6.66)
Party column ballot∗presidential vote	−0.27	−0.50**
	(0.18)	(0.15)
Senate preference (intercept)	−8.72	−3.00
	(6.87)	(5.79)
Senate preference∗presidential vote	0.33*	0.16
	(0.15)	(0.13)
Lag of Legislative Seats		
Lag of legislative seats	0.55**	0.63**
	(0.05)	(0.05)
Lag of legislative seats∗half up for reelection	0.09	0.02
	(0.05)	(0.05)
Lag of legislative seats∗one-third up for reelection		−0.10
		(0.07)
Lag of legislative seats∗one-fourth up for reelection		0.03
		(0.06)
Constant	−34.08**	−36.13**
	(7.16)	(6.86)
N	659	657
R^2	0.70	0.77

$*p < 0.05$; $**p < 0.01$.

NOTE: OLS with panel-corrected standard errors and state fixed effects. DV = % of Democratic seats in state legislature.

there is nearly a one-to-one relationship (1.02 and 1.04 percentage points in the lower and upper chambers, respectively).

Table 3.1 also allows us to test the potential mediating effects of institutions on the president's coattail. The first three institutions—electoral calendar, office-bloc ballot reform, and party-column ballot reform—were hypothesized in the preceding to weaken the party ticket's strong coattail effect.[1] Our expectations are less clear for the fourth institutional variable, *Senate Preference*. The presence of Senate candidates on the ballot might additionally nationalize the issues and strengthen party labels, and if so, might incline voters to incorporate this information into their state legislative choices. Conversely, the availability of Senate-preference choices on the ballot might have reduced the significance of using the state legislative vote as a vehicle for expressing one's preference for the upcoming legislative selection of the next senator.

The significant interactive relationships for the lower and upper chambers confirm the hypothesized effects of a split election calendar. Separating these elections pared the coattail effect by about a third. As expected, the ballot form also mitigated the coattail effect. The office-bloc reform weakened the coattail more (significantly more for the lower chambers' elections) than did party-column reform. These results accord closely with those reported elsewhere for coattails in congressional elections (Engstrom and Kernell 2005). The presence of a senatorial candidate on the ballot during the pre-direct-election era appears to have strengthened presidential coattails, although the relationship does not reach significance for the upper chambers.[2]

The last four variables in these equations represent the Democratic shares of the current chamber's membership under four different reelection settings. Not only is the lag term a suitable control for our analysis but variations in term lengths across chambers and states offer a rich variety of settings for examining the impact of election exposure on the continuity of party strengths in the face of presidential coattails. The first term is the standard lag term where all seats are elected at once (either annually or biennially). These term lengths applied to 75 percent of lower chamber elections and 26 percent of upper chamber elections. The coefficients for these variables rank in strength just as we would expect: the smaller the share of members exposed to election, the stronger the lag term. In the lower house, for example, this impact rises from only 0.55, when every seat is up for grabs, to 0.64, when only half of the legislature is up for election.

These findings show that partisan composition of state legislatures was highly responsive to the short-run national forces that decided presidential elections. This is all the more impressive, since presumably our inability here to separate coattails from the vote-seat function only serves to understate the underlying coattail effect. Moreover, most of the states' electoral institutions mediate the influence of presidential voting in the direction hypothesized. Ballot reform weakened but did not sever the connection. The presence of Senate candidates on the election ballot strengthened the association between presidential and state legislative voting.

Throughout the era of indirect elections, unified party control of state legislatures was the norm, in part reflecting the impact of presidential elections on both chambers' partisan composition. In those elections in which the full membership of each chamber stood for reelection, unified government resulted 93 percent of the time. When the state senates were not wholly elected in tandem with the lower chamber, the incidence of unified party control dropped to approximately 80 percent. Finally, in those few periods when no more than a quarter of either chamber was elected during the presidential election, a divided legislature was nearly as likely as unified party control. And in cumulative percentages we find that unified party control mostly meant Republican control. Here, then, might be a source of the Republican structural advantage identified in figure 3.2. Although the national Democratic Party remained surprisingly competitive outside the South from the Civil War until the end of the 19th century, Democratic competitiveness rarely translated into victory (Silbey 1977, 1991). Small but pervasive and persistent Republican pluralities across the states sufficed to assure the party's control of non-Southern Senate delegations.

Indirect Elections of Senators

Throughout the 19th century, Republicans enjoyed a distinct advantage in state legislative seats. This alone foretold the party's success in indirect elections. In the preceding we found that state legislative party ratios swung with the presidential vote but in such a way to overcome the large Republican bias that dominated state legislative elections outside the South throughout the 19th century. We now consider another potential source of bias—the high threshold of representation presented by bicameralism.

State legislative election of a senator is akin to a single-member district, winner-take-all election, but with an important difference: bicameralism. The election of a senator required the mutual agreement of constitutionally independent legislatures. Occasionally, the lower and upper chambers could not agree on a candidate, even after prolonged negotiations and numerous votes. During these sometimes lengthy gridlocks, the seat remained vacant. Between 1891 and 1905, factional and interparty divisions caused 14 states to fail to elect a senator (Haynes 1938, 92). Delaware's factional battles within the majority Republican Party were so fierce the state forfeited Senate representation for the entire 58th Congress.

In 1866 Congress intervened and attempted to resolve bicameral gridlocks (and ward off gubernatorial appointments) with legislation mandating rules that would allow the election of a senator even where majorities in the two chambers could not agree. Initially, each chamber was to vote separately. If no candidate received an absolute majority in both houses, the legislature then had to vote at least once a day in joint session until a candidate received an absolute majority. Despite the law's stated purpose to resolve bicameral gridlock and standardize election procedures across the states, deadlocks actually increased after passage (Haynes 1932; Hall 1936). The provision requiring a majority (rather than a simple plurality) in both chambers, or on joint ballot, meant that determined factions could prevent the party caucus from unifying around a single candidate. As a result elections sometimes stretched over months and consumed hundreds of ballots.

All of the states in this analysis followed the federal model with larger lower chambers—a mean of 115 members compared to 31 for the upper chamber. After federal law mandated joint elections to break deadlocks, legislators presumably looked down the decision tree as they separately nominated and voted on Senate candidates. Their individual and collective decisions whether to accommodate or stonewall the other side were determined by the numbers of supporters each candidate could anticipate in the joint session (along with the uncertain prospects of getting the two chambers to assemble such a session). Nonetheless, the federal law presumably shifted the balance of power to the lower chamber. Later we incorporate this chamber's potentially greater clout in the analysis.

Of course, when the same party controls both chambers the difficulty of electing one of their own is dramatically reduced.[3] Indeed, 96 and 98 percent of Democratic- and Republican-controlled legislatures, respectively, elected a member of their party. And with presidential coattails at work in both arenas, unified control was the norm throughout this era.

Another feature of indirect Senate elections that may have altered the calculations of state legislators was the opportunity for voters to formally register their opinion for senatorial candidates. As noted in the previous section, some states created binding straw elections or nonbinding preference primaries to select party nominees. State politicians appeared inclined to defer to popular preferences; the Republican Oregon legislature elected the Democratic candidate to the Senate after a majority of the state's voters supported him in the 1908 election.

To test the effect of state legislative composition, along with environmental features that represent expressions of voter sentiment in their states, on the likelihood of electing a Democratic senator, we estimate a logit equation with a Democratic victory as the dependent variable. We model this likelihood of a Democratic victory as a function of the partisan composition of the state legislature; this variable is scored as 1 if the Democrats control both chambers, 0 for a divided legislature, and −1 if Republicans control both chambers. We also include two measures of voter sentiment. These are the Democratic share of the state's presidential vote (along with an intercept for presidential-election years) and a variable scored 1 for an Oregon-plan victory for the Democratic candidate for the Senate and −1 for a Republican victory.[4]

Election of a Dem. Senator = 3.61(0.30**)*Partisan Control of Legislature*
+ 0.08(0.03**)*Presidential vote* − 3.56(1.39*)*Presidential election year*(Intercept)
+1.85(1.76)*Preference vote winner* − 0.14(0.24)
(Pseudo $R^2 = 0.58$, $N = 648$) **(3.3)**

It comes as no surprise, of course, to find in equation 3.3 party control of the legislature trumping other potential influences on Senate elections. The presence of a significant presidential-vote term suggests that 19th-century legislators were as responsive to the current political breezes as were the swing ratios that allowed many of them to ride into office on the president's coattails. (The same rationale does not extend to the preference-vote winner, however.) Converting the logit coefficients into probabilities reveals the contingent, marginal direct effects of the presidential vote on the legislature's choice. Where control is unified, a swing of 20 percentage points (from 40% to 60%) in the state's presidential vote altered the chances of winning the seat by less than 5 percentage points. Where party control was divided, however, consideration of the presidential election could prove decisive on the choices of the politicians in the legislature. When the Democratic presidential candidate won 40 percent of the popular vote, the Democratic Senate candidates' prospects were a dismal 39 percent—again, even though Democrats controlled one of the chambers. At 50 percent, the candidate's prospects improved to a 62 percent probability. At 60 percent presidential vote, the candidate's prospects of winning the seat soared to 81 percent.

Additional evidence of the importance of institutional rules in deciding Senate elections can be found in the federal mandate of a joint ballot. Since the most decisive partisan impact of this law occurred during divided party control of the legislature, we narrowed our analysis to these instances of divided control. Specifically, we estimate the probability of electing a Democratic senator, in divided legislatures, as a function of the joint combined number of Democrats in the state legislature. We also interact this with a dummy variable indicating whether the election was held before the 1866 law went into effect, and as in the previous equation, include the state presidential vote and an Oregon-plan winner variable. (This latter variable perfectly predicted the outcome where present and so was dropped from the final analysis.)

Not surprisingly, the combined Democratic share of both chambers is significant after the federal government mandated joint sessions to resolve deadlocked elections but not before. Converting these coefficients into probabilities, when the Democratic share was 60 percent rather than 40 (and all other variables set to their means), the probability of selecting a Democratic senator increased by only 11 percentage points before 1866 but by 53 points after implementation of the joint ballot requirement.

Institutional Mediation under Direct Election

The 17th Amendment brushed aside the role of state legislatures and with it the complex set of coattail and vote-seat linkages that determined the impact of presidential voting on Senate elections. With statewide popular election of a senator, the formerly complex relation between votes and seats became a highly responsive, winner-take-all relationship. The only uncertainty concerned the length of presidential coattails for Senate candidates on the ballot. The literature suggests two possible sources of mitigation of presidential coattails in post-1912 elections. First, the Senate gradually evolved into an institution of career-oriented politicians who tenaciously sought to win reelection even in the face of stiff, contrary political breezes (Hall 1936; Daynes 1971). Second, ballot form remained a major potential source of mitigation. The party ticket had everywhere been replaced by secret voting of state-supplied ballots by the time of adoption of the 17th Amendment, but states still differed and occasionally changed their ballot form from the party column, which facilitated coattail voting, to the office bloc, which was designed to discourage it (Evans 1917; Rusk 1970; Fredman 1968).

In equation 3.4 we test the impact of presidential voting on Senate voting. The analysis is performed using OLS with fixed effects. Note that the Democratic percentage of the statewide Senate vote is now the dependent variable. To test for institutional mediation, we interact presidential vote with differences in ballot structure. Recall that by 1914 all of the states had implemented the secret ballot; thus only the office-bloc format is included, leaving the party column as the base category. We expect the office-bloc interaction to significantly reduce the impact of coattail voting. Moreover, we include a variable indicating the presence of an open seat (scored 0) or an incumbent on the ballot (1 for Democrat, −1 for a Republican).

$$\begin{aligned} &\textit{Dem. Share of Statewide Senate Vote} = 0.46(0.08^{**})\textit{Presidential Vote} \\ &\quad + 3.04(1.15^{**})\textit{Incumbent Senator} - 7.635(6.803)\textit{Office Bloc Ballot} \\ &\quad - 0.22(0.15)\textit{Pres Vote} \times \textit{Office Bloc Ballot} + 26.10(5.79^{**}) \\ &\quad (R^2 = 0.50, N = 178) \end{aligned} \qquad \textbf{(3.4)}$$

These results demonstrate the close connection between presidential and direct Senate elections. An increase of 1 percentage point in the presidential vote boosts the Senate vote by 0.46 percent. The incumbency variable is positive and significant, demonstrating a small vote boost (3%) when an incumbent is running.[5] Finally, the interaction between presidential vote and office-bloc ballot is in the expected direction but not significant ($p < 0.13$).

Conclusion

In designing the Senate the framers sought an institution insulated from transient public opinion. Staggered, 6-year terms, statewide constituencies, and above all, indirect election served this common purpose. The analysis presented here indicates that the framers never wholly succeeded in their goal. By the 1840s mass mobilization of electorates behind party-nominated tickets meant that political recruitment for the state house as well as the White House tracked the party success in presidential elections. This list of party-aligned offices, indirectly, included the Senate. As a consequence, unified party control of the national government was the norm.

Indirect election had its effects, but they assumed more the form of partisan bias rather than unresponsiveness. If the Democrats had a lock on the Southern seats, the Republicans had at least a distinct competitive advantage in the rest of the country. In part this reflected the Republican party's "rotten borough" strategy of carving out and admitting staunchly Republican states. The analysis here finds a Republican bias also embedded in the vote-seat relationships that determined the composition of state legislatures and in the joint-agreement requirement that meant that the smaller, predominantly Republican upper chambers could block Democratic majorities in the lower chambers. After implementation of direct election in 1914, the bias disappeared and party control of the Senate more closely tracked presidential elections, a pattern that continues to the present day Senate (Erikson 2002; Alford and Hibbing 2002).

Chapter 4

The Dynamics of Senate Voting: Ideological Shirking and the 17th Amendment

WILLIAM BERNHARD AND BRIAN R. SALA

The 17th Amendment, ratified in 1913, compelled the popular (direct) election of senators. Few scholars have argued that it had much independent effect on the composition of the Senate or the nature of senatorial representation, however. Riker, for example, opined that

> the system of pledging [state] legislators, the direct primary, and finally the Oregon system, had each formalized the role of the voters a little more, until finally it seemed likely that the legislatures would select senators as mechanically as the electoral college selected the President. Thus these earlier reforms both occasioned the Seventeenth Amendment and *anticipated its effects*. . . .
>
> The Seventeenth simply universalized a situation which a majority of state legislatures had already created. (1955, 467–468; emphasis added)

We find, contra Riker, strong evidence that senators' intraterm legislative voting patterns *did* change after 1913. The 17th Amendment subtly, yet fundamentally, changed the representational focus of U.S. senators from the interests of party elites toward those of the statewide median voter.

Estimating Senators' Ideal Points

In this chapter we rely on a scale derived from annual, static W-NOMINATE scores, which we generated using Poole and Rosenthal's publicly available program (Poole and Rosenthal 1997b). Using the observed yeas and nays cast by senators, we estimated one ideal point for each senator in each session for the 45th (1877–1879) through 72nd (1931–1933) Congresses.[1]

RESCALED ANNUAL W-NOMINATE SCORES

We linearly transformed our annual W-NOMINATE scores to lie between 0 (most conservative or Republican) and 100 (most liberal or Democratic), echoing the approach typically taken by the Americans for Democratic Action (ADA). The relative distances between pairs of individuals are unchanged by this transformation. These W-NOMINATE scores are not technically comparable over time, unlike D-NOMINATE scores, because legislators do not vote on identical agendas from year to year. We therefore applied Groseclose, Levitt, and Snyder's (1999b) procedure for "inflation-adjusting" interest-group-like scores. The Groseclose, Levitt, and Snyder routine estimates "stretching and shifting" parameters that to some degree adjust legislators' voting scores for changes in the sets of scaled votes and distributions of voters over time.[2] We refer to the output as rescaled annual W-NOMINATE (RAW) scores. The unadjusted and inflation-adjusted scores correlate at 0.99.

The average RAW score of the Democratic and Republican parties drew much closer during the 1920s, after the adoption of the 17th Amendment. The main driving force for this convergence between party means seems to have been divisions within the Republican Conference between regulars, on the one hand, and farm-bloc and progressive members, on the other (Brady, Brody, and Epstein 1989). For example, the estimated standard error of the distribution of Republican scores during 1921–1932 was roughly 22 percent larger than it had been during 1911–1920. The variability of Democrats' scores in the 1920s increased only about 7 percent, in contrast, even though they were more tightly distributed to begin with. These observations are consistent with those of conventional histories of the Republican party (e.g., Mayer 1967). For the whole sample period, the median Democratic RAW score was 85.1 with an interquartile range of 70.9 to 95.6. The median Republican score was 18.0 with an interquartile range of 5.9 to 35.2.

Our analysis focuses on major-party members serving at least the first five session-years of their respective terms and participating frequently enough to generate usable W-NOMINATE scores in each of those years. A total of 551 senator observations satisfied this full-term criterion, 468 of whom were coded as seeking reelection to the Senate. In most years, we obtained usable observations for at least two-thirds of the senators whose seats were up for reelection in that Congress. Because so few recorded votes were held in the middle 1900s, however, we have very little coverage in those years: only one observation for the class up for reelection in 1904 and seven for the class up in 1906. We also dropped nine senators from third parties, retaining 459 total cases.

Strategic Shifting and the 17th Amendment

We want to evaluate whether direct election induced senators to change their patterns of legislative voting during their terms. To do so, we compare senators' late-term voting scores to their respective early-term averages. As we have noted, the literature on post–World War II Senate voting argues that senators enjoy considerable representational slack early in their terms (Levitt 1996; Wood and Andersson 1998). But because each senator-year score is an estimate, it is measured with error. The postwar literature's slack argument implies that the set of early-term scores for each senator can be used to get a better handle on both a senator's "unconstrained" ideological position and the scope of measurement error.

Thus, to test whether a senator's late-term score reveals an intentional change in ideological positioning, we compare each reelection-seeking senator's voting to the mean of his early-term scores. We can then use the observed variation in early-term scores to construct a standardized measure of early- to late-term movement and define a threshold size of standardized movement that will distinguish between significant (intentional) and insignificant (random noise) changes in position. Specifically, we compare a senator's score in the final long session of his term (year 5) to his average behavior in years 1 through 4. The final short session in a senator's statutory term was held after the fall elections, which generally determined whether an incumbent could win reelection. Since it is not clear that short-term reelection incentives would influence voting in this 6th year, we do not include them here.

The alternative arguments we test are that direction and average magnitudes of shifts changed after the amendment. Reformist critiques of indirect election suggested that postbellum senators were insufficiently responsive to popular preferences (Haynes 1960). Hence, one possibility is that the 17th Amendment reduced the degree of representational slack senators enjoyed. This would be consistent with a finding that the average shift became smaller in absolute value after 1913. We refer to this as the *populist hypothesis*. Second, the switch from indirect to direct election also changed the focal point for reelection-seeking behaviors. If the ideological preferences of pivotal voters in state legislatures were systematically different from those of pivotal voters in the general electorate during our study period, the *direction* of ideological shifts could have changed. We refer to this as the *directional hypothesis*.

To evaluate these alternatives, we first examine the magnitudes of nominal changes in a senator's inflation-adjusted RAW score between the 5th year and the average of the senator's first 4 years. This is a simple, one-tailed t test, comparing the mean (absolute value) shifts by senators in the two periods. The Rikerian no-effect null is that there should be no difference between the two means; the populist alternative is that postamendment shifts should be *smaller* on average. We group senators running for reelection in 1882–1914 for the preamendment period and those running in 1916–1932 for the postamendment period. The preamendment period starts with the 1882 election, because we need to observe senators over a full term and our ideal-point estimates begin with 1877. It ends with the 1914 election on the logic that the senators running in these inaugural direct elections had been elected under the prior regime and did not have the benefit of seeing the new regime in action before choosing their electoral strategies. The U.S. Secretary of State declared the amendment ratified on May 31, 1913 (U.S. House).

Our first test found no significant difference in (absolute) shifts between the two periods. On average, 249 reelection-seeking, preamendment senators moved about 14.1 points on our scale, while 210 postamendment senators moved about 12.9 points from their respective, early-term averages, a difference of only 1.1 points ($t = 1.01$). Thus we cannot reject this null hypothesis of no effect for the 17th Amendment. By this measure, the 17th Amendment had no effect on the degree of ideological slack enjoyed by incumbents early in their terms.

The picture changes when we look at direction of movement as well as magnitude, however. Because large shifts in each direction tend to cancel each other out in calculating the mean movements, these averages are much smaller. On average, preamendment senators *polarized* by 1.9 points while postamendment senators *moderated* by 3.4 points, clearly significant in a two-tailed test ($t = 3.18$).

When we plotted the distributions of score changes before and after 1913 for all Democrats and Republicans coded as having served a full term and running for reelection, the data clearly indicate that the two distributions differ. Before 1913 Democrats and Republicans tended to move away from one another in the reelection campaign sessions. Out of 249 cases, 149 (59.8%) polarized nominally and 100 (40.2%) moderated nominally.

After the adoption of the 17th Amendment, the general pattern is reversed. Only 84 of 210 postratification senators (40.0%) polarized, whereas 126 (60.0%) moderated. Clearly, the *typical* pattern of behavior changed from before to after ratification of the direct-election amendment.

This transition affected incumbents of both parties. Preamendment Democrats polarized by 3.1 points on average, while the typical post-amendment Democrat moved 1.4 points in the moderating direction, a difference of almost 4.5 points ($p < 0.01$). For Republicans, direct election changed their average shift from a small polarizing movement (1.2 points) to a relatively large moderating movement (5.4 points), a difference of over 6 points ($p < 0.008$) on our scale. The initial results, therefore, appear to reject the no-effect null model in favor of the directional alternative, while showing little support for the populist hypothesis that average movements should be smaller in magnitude.

To better deal with this issue, we standardized changes in a senator's inflation-adjusted RAW score by each senator's early-term variance. Thus,

$$\textit{Democratic StdChange}_{i,5} = (RAW_{i,5} - RAW_{i,1-4})/\mathrm{SD}(RAW_{i,1-4}) \qquad \textbf{(4.1)}$$

$$\textit{Republican StdChange}_{i,5} = (RAW_{i,1-4} - RAW_{i,5})/\mathrm{SD}(RAW_{i,1-4}) \qquad \textbf{(4.2)}$$

where $RAW_{i,5}$ is Senator *i*'s RAW score in the 5th year of his term, $RAW_{i,1-4}$ is *i*'s year 1–4 average RAW score, and $\mathrm{SD}(RAW_{i,1-4})$ is the standard deviation of that average. Because Republican scores tend toward the minimum of the scale and Democratic scores tend toward the maximum, the numerators for the two parties differ by a factor of -1. A standardized change indicates a *polarizing shift* (away from the likely location of a major-party opponent), and a negative value indicates a *moderating shift* (toward the likely location of a major-party opponent), regardless of party.

Our approach thus seeks to distinguish *intentional* changes in position from background noise, under the assumption that early-term variability is primarily noise rather than systematic. The standardized scores provide a more complete account of the information contained in the revealed-preference data history available to us than the simple change measure we used earlier. They measure a late-term change in the senator's public ideology measured against early-term behavior, discounting the political valence of late-term score changes by senators whose early-term behavior was highly variable.

Early-term variability changed little over the two periods. The median Democrat's year 1–4 standard deviation was 11.8 before 1913 and 12.8 afterward. For Republicans, the early-period median was 13.4 and the late-period median 14.2. The comparable figures in the post–World War II era are 9.8 for Democrats and 9.0 for Republicans, reflecting the generally higher numbers of votes per year and lower levels of absenteeism that have characterized contemporary Senates.

Using this standardized measure, we again tested the populist and directional hypotheses against the Rikerian null. Again, we were unable to confirm the populist alternative—the average, absolute standardized shift in the early period was 1.37 standard deviations, compared to 1.32 standard deviations in the postamendment period ($t = 0.31$).

On the other hand, we confirmed our support for the directional hypothesis. The average senator polarized by 0.02 standard deviations before the 17th Amendment, but moderated by 0.55 standardized units afterward ($t = 2.85$). Democrats polarized more aggressively than did Republicans in the earlier period, averaging 0.26 units.

Republicans actually *moderated* on average in the preamendment period, driven by a cluster of large, moderating shifts in the 1891 session-year. On average, the other 133 Republican observations in the preamendment era polarized by 0.29 standard deviations. In contrast, the 10 Republican senators seeking reelection in 1891–1992 each moderated by between 2.7 and 9.3 standardized units.

Two features of this data are remarkable. First, there are two obvious outlier years in our data, corresponding to the elections of 1892 and 1918, respectively. We will have more to say about those elections shortly. The other feature of the graph is the distributions of points above and below the zero line before and after 1913. Eleven of the 15 election years during 1881–1913 yielded average movements toward the poles of the ideological scale (we dropped the observations for 1903 and 1905 owing to low numbers of observations—one and seven, respectively). Conversely, after 1913, six of nine elections saw moderating average movements. This change in tendencies—treating each election year as a case, coded as "moderating" or "polarizing," depending on the within-year mean shift—is not significant ($\chi^2 = 0.155$, 1 degree of freedom), but it is at least suggestive.

Additionally, note the pattern of average shifts—or rather, their lack—within each period. Our Rikerian null hypothesis of no significance for the 17th Amendment argued for, at best, a gradual transition toward a "modern" pattern of voting dynamics throughout the three decades preceding ratification. But the 1881–1913 data in fact show no evidence of any withering of its characteristic polarizing tendencies.

A third way to evaluate the effect of direct election is to examine the distribution of large movers over time. The data further demonstrate that large polarizing movements were considerably more common than large moderating ones before the 17th Amendment but less frequent than large moderating shifts afterward.[3] A chi-square test of the trichotomized data comparing the frequencies of large polarizers, large moderaters, and small shifters (regardless of direction) shows that the differences across periods are highly significant. That is, the change in average and modal behaviors we discussed earlier persists when we trichotomize the movements. Ratification of the 17th Amendment is associated with a significant decline in the propensity with which reelection-seeking senators polarized ideologically in the 5th year of their terms.

Most of this decline is absorbed by the residual, small-shifter category, which pools small moderating and small polarizing moves. This result is consistent with our populist hypothesis—the first bit of evidence we have found to suggest that the 17th Amendment may be associated with a decrease in the representational slippage criticized so heavily in calls for popular election. Second, in both periods there appear to have been elections dominated by either moderating movements (e.g., 1892, 1918) or polarizing movements (e.g., 1888, 1914, 1922). This suggests that we need to take a closer look at the data to better grasp what is going on in the two periods. We turn next to a brief discussion of two of these apparently anomalous years and of the facts surrounding some of the largest ideological shifts we found in the data.

Reconsidering Significant Shifting

A key question for our analysis is whether the year-by-year results we observe within each period are generated by some relatively stable data-generating process or are themselves more noise than signal. This is a very difficult question to answer. Our voting scores are, of course, derived from roll-call behavior, which is itself a product of the choices senators made in each year about what questions deserved recorded votes. As yet, we lack a general theory capable of explaining the evolution of policy agendas over time in a legislature. We have instead worked within a framework that implicitly assumes that senators respond independently to exogenously determined agendas of votes.

The elections of 1892 and 1918 stand out as by far the strongest outliers in our data. In each case, the average standardized shift was roughly 3.95 standard deviations in the moderating direction. The first case seems strongly contradictory to the general pattern of behavior we observe in the preamendment era. The second, conversely, seems to evoke exactly what we expect to find in the modern Senate. In this section, we dig a little deeper in the roll-call data and historical evidence to better explain these outcomes.

MODERATION IN A PARTISAN ERA: THE ELECTION OF 1892

The 52nd Senate (1891–1893) accounts for 16 of the 49 preamendment cases of moderating shifts larger than a standardized unit. Overall, the average reelection-seeking senator in this session moderated by 30.9 points on our roughly 100-point scale. This stands in sharp contrast to the average 4.6 point *polarizing* move of other preamendment observations in our sample. Senators' scores in the 1891 session-year were affected in every region of the country. Southern- and border-state senators moderated about 21.35 points, on average, while senators in the rest of the country averaged 36.8. What accounts for these movements?

In this section, we account for the anomalous results in the 1891–1892 session by identifying one key factor. The legislative agenda in the 1891 session-year was significantly affected by a critical, crosscutting issue—the coinage of silver. Other issues, such as tariff reform and railroad regulation, gained considerable press coverage. But the silver issue generated over 10 percent of the recorded votes held in the session. This issue served to bridge the gap between Eastern, hard-money Democrats and the majority of Republicans in bipartisan opposition to Western and Midwestern Republicans and Populists.

Because we fitted the voting data to a two-dimensional space, the consequence of this block of votes seems to have been to push the first-dimensional scores of *all* Republicans closer to those of the Democrats, while stretching Republicans (and to a lesser extent, Democrats) on the second dimension. The votes received ample play in the national press that summer (see, e.g., "Silver Men Are Joyful," *New York Times*, July 2, 1892, p. 1). Defeat of the free coinage bill in the House a few days later caused Eastern Democrats and Republicans alike to declare that it removed silver as an issue in the presidential election ("Effect of the Vote," *New York Times*, July 14, 1892, p. 5). But it seems to have hardened the case in favor of third-party candidates in Western states.

Adding to the effects of the 1891 silver votes on our ideal-point estimates was an unusually high level of bipartisanship, or "hurrah," voting. Whereas 80 percent of the roll calls in the 51st Senate had been party votes, only 63 percent made the 50 percent or higher Democratic versus the 50 percent or higher Republican threshold in the 1891–1892 session-year.

Despite the best efforts of Western Republicans to co-opt Populist issues, the party's candidates struggled in the 1892 elections in the region.

The Populists elected enough state legislators and statewide officers to play an important role in Senate elections in a number of states, although they failed to win unified party control of any state governments (Hicks 1961, 274). For example, both the Populists and the Republicans claimed to have won majority control of the Kansas house, going so far as to elect rival Speakers in January 1893. The Kansas Populists fell just short of a majority of the combined membership of the state legislature. Consequently, they agreed to support Democrat John Martin to complete the term of the late Republican Preston Plumb (Hicks 1961, 278).

In Nebraska a handful of Democrats held the balance of power in each chamber of the state legislature after the 1892 election. Only after 3 weeks of wrangling were the Populists and Democrats able to forge an agreement to supplant incumbent Algernon S. Paddock with William V. Allen, a former Republican who had been elected a district judge under the Populist banner in 1891 (Hicks 1961, 282). Paddock's voting scores in 1887–1890 were 5.2, 3.6, 9.3, and 17.4, respectively. His score jumped to 55.0 in 1891, as he voted with the silver bloc on seven of the nine ballots on S 51. This score placed him just below the overall mean score of 58.2 for the session, before falling back to 14.1 in his 1892 lame-duck session.

Populists and Democrats made common cause in North Dakota as well, ousting Republican Lyman Casey in favor of Democrat William Roach. Casey had earned the opposition of the Northern Pacific Railroad Company by advocating "hasten[ing] the taxation of the railroad's earned lands east of the Missouri," ("Senator Casey's Opponents," *New York Times*, January 28, 1892, p. 2). At the same time, however, Casey was conspicuously absent on all nine votes relating to the silver bill, S 51. Thus he seems to have alienated hard-core Republicans without winning over Farmers' Alliance–friendly voters and legislators.

Overall, these elections were disastrous for Republicans. Whereas they had easily controlled most non-South state legislatures in 1889–1890, capturing on average 52.4 percent of available seats (55.9% in states with Senate elections), they won only 50.3 percent of the seats on average in 1891–1892, including 48.3 percent in non-South states with Senate elections.[4]

Despite the convergence in Democratic and Republican RAW scores we observe for the 1891 session-year, then, this case offers only mixed support for a "Downsian" interpretation of electoral competition before 1913. Closer inspection of the roll-call agenda reveals that the apparent increase in bipartisanship during the session is better explained as an episode of *intraparty* heterogeneity on a single crosscutting issue. We are thus inclined to discount the significance of our results for this election—thereby implying that the case for election-year polarizing behavior is even stronger than it initially appeared for the preamendment era.

POLITICS IS ADJOURNED? THE ELECTION OF 1918

The other outlier Congress is the 65th (1917–1919), which accounts for 19 of the 33 postamendment moderating shifts. The nine reelection-seeking Republicans moved from their early-term average of 9.5 to about 42.5 in 1917–1918, while the 14 Democrats averaged 88.8 in their early period and 64.8 in the pre-election sessions of the 65th Senate. Should we discount the aggregate evidence from this election as well?

The 65th, of course, was the World War I Congress—and the last with a Democratic majority in both chambers under President Woodrow Wilson. The 64th Senate had closed with a 23-day filibuster against a bill to arm American merchant ships, led by Robert La Follette (R-Wis.) and George Norris (R-Neb.). In contrast, the 65th Congress opened with Senate adoption of a cloture rule to limit filibusters. Standard historical treatments imply that politics was adjourned—and bipartisanship ruled—for at least the early part of U.S. involvement in the war (Livermore 1966). After a crushing defeat for the Democratic candidate in an April 1918 Senate by-election in Wisconsin, President Wilson went so far as to propose "a moratorium on politics until the end of the war," to quote historian George Mayer (1967, 351).

However, the roll-call data do not entirely support this claim that politics was adjourned *after* the Wisconsin by-election. Over half of the roll calls held from mid-April to November of 1918 pitted at least a majority of Republicans against at least a majority of Democrats, compared to only 38 percent of the roll calls held in the 65th Senate before the by-election. Further, both parties *increased* their cohesion levels on party votes after the by-election. Democrats raised their average agreement on party votes to 81.5 percent for the period from mid-April to November of 1918, compared to 73.2 for party votes before the by-election. Republicans raised their average agreement to 79.8 percent (from 72.9%). Both changes were statistically significant at the 0.05 level in two-tailed tests. These numbers suggest that the ideological distance between the two parties probably *increased* after Wilson's call for a moratorium on politics, rather than decreased.

Thus the rash of moderating movements we observe for the 1917–1918 session-year must have been driven by voting in calendar-year 1917 and the first 3 months of 1918. According to Mayer, Democratic tactics in 1917 and early 1918 "had driven the Progressive Republicans and the standpatters to make common cause, despite their differing attitudes toward taxes on war profits and other issues" (351). Inspection of the actual votes cast suggests a somewhat different explanation, however. The key to this minor mystery probably lies in Senate consideration of HR 4280, the war-revenue measure. Senators held 38 recorded votes on this bill between August 18 and September 10, 1917. Of these votes, nearly half were hurrah votes, matching large majorities of Democrats with large majorities of Republicans. Most of these were motions offered by progressive or isolationist Republican senators, such as Robert La Follette (R-Wis.), Hiram Johnson (R-Calif.), and Porter McCumber (R-N.Dak.), then defeated by large, bipartisan majorities. For example, senators voted down by large margins seven separate amendments offered by La Follette, most of which proposed increases to individual income taxes or to taxes on war profits. La Follette was strongly opposed to U.S. entry into the war, to the point of driving Democrats and regular Republicans to oppose him and his "little group of willful men," as President Wilson termed the antiwar faction.

The degree of systematic, ideological change implied by our results for the 65th Senate is, therefore, probably overstated. While large majorities of senators did band together to "rally around the flag" in opposition to La Follette and the isolationists, this seems conceptually distinct from the Downsian, moderating shifts contemplated by the post–World War II Senate literature. Politics hardly seems to have been adjourned in 1918.

Our inspection of the two major outlier years in our data thus seems to suggest that both episodes probably overstated the degree of strategic shifting (in the modern sense) that occurred in each. If, however, we drop the 1891–1892 and 1917–1918 observations from our analysis, our main results hold in support of the directional hypothesis. The average preamendment senator polarized just over a third of a standard deviation—or 4.6 points, whereas the average postamendment senator moderated slightly—0.14 standard deviations and 0.4 points. Both of these differences were statistically significant.

Additionally, we find weak support for the populist hypothesis when we omit the 1892 and 1918 elections. In absolute-value terms, the average preamendment senator ran for reelection by adjusting his ideological position by 1.15 standard deviations, compared to only 0.99 standard deviation for the postamendment group. This difference falls short of the 0.05 significance level criterion but meets the standard for the 0.10 level.

Conclusion

Taken together, our results show fairly compelling evidence that senators' voting patterns were different after 1913 compared to before. Before 1913 the average reelection-seeking senator became slightly more extreme in his reelection year and large polarizing shifts were considerably more frequent than large moderating ones. After 1913 the average reelection seeker tended to moderate roll-call behavior toward the end of his or her term and the relative frequency of large polarizing shifts fell sharply. These results are consistent with our interpretation that the 17th Amendment fundamentally changed the electoral connection between senators and the mass electorate.

Chapter 5

The Electoral Connection: Career Building and Constituency Representation in the U.S. Senate in the Age of Indirect Elections

WENDY J. SCHILLER

Introduction

In Federalist 63, Madison wrote the following about the Senate: "Such an institution may be sometimes necessary as a defense to the people against their own temporary errors and delusions" (Rossiter 1961, 384). Underlying this "defense" is the supposition that indirect elections, combined with a 6-year term, would create a different electoral environment for senators than for their counterparts in the House and would thus produce a legislator who would not be directly responsive to individual constituents.

This work delves deeper into the dynamics of Senate representation at the individual level between 1880 and 1913. Before 1913 the basic model for the election of senators was to have state legislatures serve as intermediaries between the people and their senators. Of primary interest here is how candidates won a Senate seat, the strategies they employed to try to retain it, and whether their institutional behavior influenced their electoral success in subsequent elections. With the exception of works by George Haynes (1938), David Rothman (1966), and Douglas Price (1977), few authors have systematically explored individual U.S. Senate behavior, from the perspective of responsiveness to constituent interests, during this period.

The strong state-level party system that existed in this era meant that party control of both houses of the legislature would usually guarantee a candidate of the majority party a Senate seat; however, from election to election, it was never certain that there would be one candidate who could easily garner a majority of party members' votes. There was a great deal of turnover in state legislatures at that time, so when senators sought reelection, they frequently faced a different set of legislators from the group that had elected them previously. As George Haynes (1906) wrote,

> Suppose that a senator were elected, for the first time, by the legislature of a given State . . . years before the question becomes imminent whether he shall be returned, or shall be replaced by another, the body of men which elected him has been dissolved, never to meet again. In some States, five other legislatures may have intervened, and only a small remnant—and, it may be, no saving remnant—of the original legislature will survive in the one which is in session as the end of his term approaches, and thus be in position to pass a verdict upon his service. (166–167)

Who was holding senators accountable if the state legislators who initially elected them were no longer in office? How could senators anticipate the composition and preferences of state legislators who had yet to be elected? How much control did senators have over their own electoral fate?

During this era, a winning strategy required that an incumbent senator's party retain majority control of the legislature and that the incumbent was the majority choice within the party. Support in the state party was essential to securing victory in the legislature, but it was not a sufficient condition. To win and keep a Senate seat, senators had to construct both a state-based strategy and a Washington strategy using all the tools that the U.S. Senate had to offer. U.S. senators had to consolidate power within their own party organizations, and they had to send continual signals from Washington that they were both loyal partisans and attentive to constituents in the districts of state house and state senate members.

Research Design and Methods

To study the interaction between indirect elections and U.S. senators' behavior, I randomly selected 10 states that varied by region and population size. Those states are Delaware, Kentucky, Louisiana, Maryland, Nevada, North Carolina, North Dakota, Pennsylvania, Washington, and Wisconsin.[1] Data on election returns in state legislatures were collected using yearly editions of the *Tribune Almanac* from 1880 to 1914 and supplementary archival newspaper articles. Using the *Congressional Record Index* and *The Congressional Directory*, I collected data on committee assignments and public bills, private bills, and petitions sponsored by each senator from these states in the 51st (1889–1891), the 55th (1897–1899), the 57th (1901–1903), and the 60th (1907–1909) Congresses. In addition to quantitative data, I also use secondary sources and newspaper articles to construct brief case studies of senators' careers.

Senate Elections and Party Politics

By most accounts, the U.S. Senate began to reflect the effects of a solidifying two-party system in the latter part of the 19th century; some historians argue that the Senate was strongly partisan as early as the 1870s (Shade et al., 1973). As political party organizations strengthened at the state level and voters began to associate policy platforms with parties, contests for the Senate moved outside the state legislature to a wider public audience (Rothman 1966). In many states, the public canvass emerged, which tied voters' choices of state legislators to their subsequent votes for senators (Riker 1955, 463). For example, T. D. Hughes, a candidate for the House of Representatives from the 27th North Dakota district, announced similar support in the *Bismarck Daily Tribune* (February 27, 1908, p. 6): "I am for the election of C.B. Little of Bismarck for United States Senator," he wrote, "because he is a resident of my district and his past political record for 18 years in the senate of North Dakota has amply demonstrated that he has always stood for the best interests of the Missouri Slope." The practice of the public canvass, as illustrated by Mr. Hughes, presented a stronger public link to voters between state legislators and Senate candidates before an election.

However, as political party entrepreneurs harnessed the powers of federal, state, and local patronage, the spoils increased, and existing rifts and conflicts within parties intensified and were reflected in Senate elections in state legislatures (Haynes 1906). Despite some legislators announcing their preferences before an election, there were usually multiple candidates from the same party running for the Senate. Although a party majority in the state house and state senate would often guarantee the election of a U.S. senator of that party, it did not guarantee agreement around a single candidate because the majority party could comprise several factions supporting different U.S. Senate candidates. Moreover, state legislators who had professed support for a specific candidate would frequently have to abandon that candidate if it became clear the candidate could not attract a sufficient number of votes to reach a majority.

The typical state legislature was bicameral, and the house and senate met separately to choose a U.S. senator; to win the seat, the candidate had to have a majority of votes in each chamber. A candidate might win a majority in one chamber but only a plurality in the other chamber; if no candidate won a majority in both chambers, the election went to a joint session where the outcome was frequently not determined until after multiple ballots were cast. In this sample, 65 elections were decided by majority votes in the state house and state senate, and 48 elections were decided in joint session. If no candidate secured a majority of votes, the state legislature would declare a deadlock, and the Senate seat would remain vacant until the legislature elected a majority candidate.

In some cases, a candidate for the U.S. Senate could win a plurality in each chamber, but not a majority, and then go on to lose the election in the joint session, when the majority party would turn to a compromise candidate who could win a majority of the vote. Statistics about the Senate elections that occurred in the states in the sample follow.[2]

Descriptive Statistics about Indirect Senate Elections in 10 States, 1884–1913	*Total*
Elections in state legislatures	113
Initial candidates	457
Legislative ballots	1,311
Party ballots	203
Repeat challengers	76
Incumbents seeking reelection	46
Incumbents unopposed	5
Percentage incumbents reelected	65
Democratic candidates	242
Republican candidates[3]	191
Final-ballot candidates	305
Republican-controlled legislatures	49
Democratic-controlled legislatures	37
Split-party-controlled legislatures	17
Legislatures controlled by Populists (2), silver Republicans (3), or silver Democrats (1)	6

Several preliminary conclusions can be drawn from the data displayed here. First, Senate elections were hotly contested, *as much within parties as between them*. Majority parties frequently disagreed on whom to nominate for a Senate seat, and if the legislature was under divided party control, deadlock was more likely. Second, incumbent senators sought reelection with relative frequency across the states in the sample. Unfortunately for incumbent senators, state legislatures appear to have drawn from a small but consistent pool of politicians in the state when choosing senators, and the men in this pool posed a constant threat to incumbent senators over time within their own party and, of course, in the opposite party. Even incumbents who lost their bids for reelection would return 2, 4, or 6 years later to contend for a Senate seat; in this sample nine incumbent senators who lost a reelection bid came back to challenge for a subsequent seat—five senators were successful.

To test for the impact of the factors previously discussed, I constructed a regression model where the *dependent* variable is measured as the *percentage margin of victory* (*PMV*), which is how many more votes the winning senator received than did his opponents, divided by the overall size of the legislature. I use the *percentage margin of victory* for each senator in the election preceding the first Congress in the sample in which he served. The set of independent variables includes *percentage seats held by a senator's party* (*PSEAT*; in the joint legislature), the *number of majority-party candidates* (*MAJC*), the *number of party ballots* (*PBAL*), the *number of legislative ballots* (*LEGB*), *shared party affiliation with other senator* (*SPART*; coded 1 or 0), and *primary* (*PRIM*), which is coded 1 if there was a primary before the election and 0 if not. It should be noted here that only two elections in the set of prior elections had primaries.[4]

This model is simply designed to identify the component variables that explain winning Senate candidacies in the era of indirect elections, and the dependent variable is designed to reflect the ease or difficulty that a senator had in securing election, with the expectation that senators who had differing margins of victory in the election to the Senate might adopt different career-building strategies once inside the Senate. The model yields the following results:[5]

$$\begin{aligned} PMV = {} & -0.13(0.15) + 0.85(0.19^{**})PSEAT - 0.02(0.007^{**})MAJC \\ & - 0.0001(0.0011)PBAL - 0.002(0.002)LEGB + 0.12(0.06^{*})SPART \\ & + 0.37(0.11^{**})PRIM\ (R^2 = 0.52,\ F = 11.96) \end{aligned} \qquad \textbf{(5.1)}$$

PSEAT was one of the major predictors of the winner's percentage margin of victory. However, party discord could erode a senator's margin of victory; for every additional *MAJC*, the margin of victory decreased by 2 percent. In closely competitive legislatures where the majority party had a small margin, the elections were obviously closer, but they could be made even more precarious by intraparty fighting. Such was the case in 1893 in North Dakota, when the majority Republican legislature ended up choosing a Democrat, William Roach, because they were divided among themselves. Close

Senate races were sometimes as much about challenges within the majority party as they were about competition between the two parties. At the very least then, senators had a strong incentive to solidify their foundation within their party in the legislature, even if they could not control the partisan balance in the state legislature when they sought election.

Constructing Successful Legislative Portfolios in the Senate

Candidates for the Senate in the era of indirect elections faced stiff competition from multiple opponents within their own party, as well as opponents from the opposing party. The challenge facing candidates who did manage to get elected by their state legislature was to carve out powers within the Senate itself that would solidify their electoral base in the next election. Senators who served from 1880 to 1913 were faced with a balancing act—their national policy positions were often delineated by their party affiliation, but their electoral fate frequently rested on the strength of their party organization or faction in their home state. In the electoral environment in most states during this era, men who wished to be elected to the Senate—and reelected—had to be political entrepreneurs, vowing to protect specific interests in their states and cultivating strong ties with state party organizations.

Unlike modern-day senators, who have a personal staff, their own media operation, and numerous offices in their home state, senators who served a century ago had few if any of these advantages to help them construct their own individual portfolio of accomplishments. Senators did have a set of tools with which to construct their agendas, including records of roll-call voting, patronage, committee assignments, bill and amendment sponsorship, and the presentation of petitions to the Senate. Roll-call voting was heavily influenced, if not dominated, by party affiliation and the Senate displayed relatively strong party unity within each major party from 1870 to about 1906 (Shade et al. 1973; Poole and Rosenthal 2001). Key to understanding the role of party at this juncture in the Senate's history is to recognize that the strong ties that senators had to their *state* party organization translated into strong party unity in the Senate on roll-call votes. Bernhard and Sala (chapter 4 in this volume) find that senators who were seeking reelection in the pre-direct-election era did try to use their roll-call votes to attract support from state legislators in their political party. They find that senators voted in a highly polarized fashion in their 5th year to appease strong party regulars at the state level. After direct elections, they find that senators tended to vote in a more centrist direction to attract the median voter in their state.

For the most part, as it is in today's Senate, U.S. senators in the late 19th century voted with their party when there was a stated party position; the more closely aligned the state party was to the national party, the more senators voted consistently partisan.

From the Civil War to the early 1880s, senators tightly controlled federal patronage and used it to build state party organizations and demonstrate a commitment to individual constituents in terms of jobs and funding for the state (Fish 1904; White 1958). Senators used patronage to shore up their political base in the state and cultivate their successors. Senator Arthur Gorman (D-Md.), who was first elected in 1880, rose to power through the combination of the party and patronage system:

> As a member of the ruling party in Maryland, Gorman was in line for the appointment to the presidency of the internal improvement company, a traditional political plum. As the current favorite of William P. Whyte [the sitting senator], the leader of the dominant faction within the Democratic Party, he was the logical choice to carry out the political purposes for which canal patronage was used. From his control of the waterway, he gained the skill, experience, and personal following necessary to give him powerful influence in state politics. He used this influence to consolidate his own position in the Assembly. Domination of the legislature in turn made possible his election to the United States Senate, thus providing the springboard which launched him on his public career in national politics. (Sanderlin 1947, 337)

Senators' direct control of federal patronage began to decline after the infamous Custom House incident, when President Hayes refused to appoint the person preferred by Senator Rosco Conkling (N.Y.) in 1878. When he took over in 1881, President Garfield continued the trend of asserting executive control over what were essentially executive-branch appointments. Senators still had influence over the distribution of federal jobs, but only in cooperation with the president.

Over the course of the 1880s, senators' direct control of federal patronage declined, and therefore it became more efficient for them to rely heavily on legislative tools, such as committees and bill sponsorship, to appear attentive and deliver benefits to their states.[6] Committee assignments were for the most part controlled by parties in the Senate in the late 19th century and were made by each party's steering committee (Canon and Stewart 2002b). On average, senators had six committee assignments per session during the period studied here.[7] Senators from the same state and the same party (the bulk of all senators at this time came from same-party delegations) were generally not assigned to the same committees by party leaders (Swift 1996). During this period, senators were serving longer and had longer tenures on the same committees, so seniority started to become a larger factor in committee assignments and in the selection of committee chairs by party leaders (Price 1975, 1977). Senator Gorman, for example, served in the Senate from 1881 to 1898 and from 1902 to 1908, and he retained seats on the Commerce, Appropriations, Interstate Commerce, and Printing committees for most of that time.[8]

State newspapers took note of senators' committee assignments, especially when there was a state interest at stake, as this quote from the *Nevada State Journal* from December 18, 1906, illustrates:

> Senator Charles Dick of Ohio will continue to be chairman of the Senate committee on mines and mining. The committee assignments were made public today. Senator Nixon of Nevada, now chairman of the committee on national banks will be chairman of that on coast defense in addition. Senator Newlands of Nevada remains a member of the committee on mines and mining with Senator Nixon, so that Nevada still has two of the nine members of this important committee.

Senators sought out membership on committees that dealt with their state's specific economic and geographic interests, and senators used their work on committees as evidence of their legislative accomplishments in the Senate. For example, in a long campaign stump speech in 1912, Senator Furnifold Simmons (D-N.C.) emphasized his power as a member of the Senate Commerce Committee:

> For a long time we did not get our part of the money the Government was spending on rivers and harbors. For over six years I have been a member of the Committee on Commerce having these appropriations in charge. I have not been asleep. We are getting our share now, and so long as I am on that committee and in the Senate I promise you we are going to get our share or there is going to be a row. In the last river and harbor bill . . . we got a million four hundred thousand ($1,400,000). In the Senate, out of about six million ($6,000,000) added to the House bill, North Carolina got seven hundred thousand dollars ($700,000). . . . Do you want these appropriations to continue, or do you want them to stop?[9]

Committee assignments served as one element of a senator's "toolbox," and if used properly, one might expect the number of committee assignments to have a positive impact on a senator's electoral margins in the state legislature.

Senators also used bill sponsorship and the presentation of petitions to demonstrate their legislative activism in the Senate. Bill sponsorship serves as a good measure of attentiveness to constituents because most of the bills that senators introduced at this time were individual pension or relief bills, and they were an efficient way of establishing a direct link to individual constituents. Of all the legislative tools available to them, bills were the only way that a senator could set an individual agenda for himself and claim total credit for the outcome. All other tools, from voting to patronage and committee assignments, were in part controlled by other political actors. Moreover, because each senator was forced to share the state with a same-state Senate colleague, individual bill sponsorship was even more important in cultivating distinct coalitions within their party and in local constituencies (Schiller 2000, 2003).[10]

During the period after the Civil War, bill sponsorship had become an increasingly popular legislative activity in both the House and the Senate as a means of demonstrating attentiveness to constituency concerns (Cooper and Young 1989; Cooper and Rybicki 2002). According to Cooper and Rybicki, senators used bill sponsorship to "publicize themselves for their own personal and political gain" (198). Senators introduced public bills on both national and constituent or local issues, and they introduced private bills for pensions and general relief of individual constituents. Following are 5 of the 79 bills that Senator Gorman introduced in the 55th Congress, when he sat on the Commerce, Appropriations, Interstate Commerce, Printing, and Organization of Executive Departments committees:

S 710—Baltimore, Maryland, to erect public building at.
S 1202—Emily M. Tyler, to increase pension
S 3121—Glen Echo Railroad, granting right of way to.
S 5049—Government Printing Office, to regulate salaries
S 5458—Executive departments, for renewal of bonds by officers and clerks in

This list is a just a small selection, but it suggests that senators used bills to confer direct benefits on constituents and localities in the state, and that committee assignment influenced bill sponsorship.

To identify the patterns of behavior of senators who served during this era, I constructed a regression model that uses bill sponsorship as the dependent variable for the following set of reasons. First, the voluntary nature of bill sponsorship makes it a more sensitive measure of a senator's individual efforts to cultivate a power base and reputation. Second, prior work has shown that committee assignments, committee positions (e.g., chair), and state population size interact with bill sponsorship in that senators tend to sponsor bills in the areas of jurisdiction of the committees that they sit on (Schiller 1995). By looking at patterns of bill sponsorship, therefore, we can also learn more about how committee assignments, and positions, influenced individual agenda setting. In terms of state population size, since senators were using bill sponsorship to address individual constituent needs, larger numbers of constituents should yield higher levels of bill sponsorship. We can also use bill sponsorship to investigate the electoral connection by using the senator's prior margin of victory to see whether senators rewarded constituents who elected representatives and senators who had voted for the senator. Since the legislators themselves were unlikely to be in the state legislature when the senator ran for reelection, it made much more sense to use bill sponsorship to directly reward constituents in their state house and state senate districts. An increase in the margin of victory should yield higher bill sponsorship.

In this sample, on average, senators introduced 76 bills per Congress, consisting of essentially three types: relief (41%), pension (37%), and legislative (22%).[11] I constructed a regression model to predict the number of bills sponsored (*BILLS*) as a function of *number of committee assignments* (*NCOM*); *majority party* (*MAJP*), which is coded 1 if the senator was in the majority party and 0 if not; *chair* (*CHAIR*), which is coded 1 if the senator was a chair and 0 if not; *years in Senate* (*YEARS*), which is measured as the absolute number of years a senator has served in the Senate; *state population* (*POP*; in millions), *reelection cycle* (*REELECT*), coded 1 if the senator was in a reelection cycle and 0 if not; the *senator's margin of victory in the prior election (logged)* (*MAJV*); and *other senator's bills* (*OSENBILLS*), which is the number of bills introduced by the other senator from the state. Because bill sponsorship is the dependent variable, an event-count model is appropriate, and I use a negative binomial regression model with Huber-White standard errors. The results are the following:

$$\begin{aligned} BILLS = {} & 0.70(0.48) + 0.29(0.07^{**})NCOM + 0.40(0.17^{*})MAJP \\ & + 0.019(0.019)YEARS + 0.22(0.05^{**})POP - 0.05(0.16)REELECT \\ & + 0.33(0.09^{**})MAJV - 0.0018(0.0007^{**})OSENBILLS \\ & (\text{Pseudo } R^2 = 0.07,\ N = 74) \end{aligned} \qquad \textbf{(5.2)}$$

NCOM, *MAJP*, *POP*, *MAJV*, and *OSENBILLS* all increase the number of bills sponsored by senators.[12] Senators who were in the majority and held chairs introduced 25 more bills than senators who were in the minority. When the model is run with *CHAIR* instead of *MAJP*, the coefficient for *CHAIR* is 0.41 (0.17) and the rest of the coefficients are relatively unchanged. On average, each additional committee assignment increased bill sponsorship by 17 bills, although the effect is greater for senators who held six or more committee seats. State population has a generally linear relationship with bill sponsorship, except for the very largest states in the sample. On average, an increase of 1 percent in margin of victory yields an increase of 20 bills. The numbers of bills sponsored by senators from the same state are negatively correlated, albeit weakly, which suggests that two senators from the same state did not use bill sponsorship equally to cultivate constituencies.[13]

The remaining piece of the puzzle is to establish a link between institutional behavior, as measured through bill sponsorship, and senators' electoral margins in reelection campaigns. Are senators rewarded for bill sponsorship in terms of state legislators' votes? The third model is applied only to those senators that sought reelection, and it includes senators who won and senators who were defeated. I regress *percentage margin of victory* (*PMV*) on the *percentage prior margin of victory* (*PPMV*); *percentage seats held by a senator's party* (PSEAT); *number of majority-party candidates* (*MAJC*); *retained support* (*RETSUP*), which is the prior percentage margin of victory interacted with the number of majority-party candidates in the current election; the *number of party ballots* (*PARB*); the *number of legislative ballots* (*LEGB*); *years in office* (*YEARS*); *number of committee assignments* (*NCOM*); *chair* (*CHAIR*; coded 1 or 0); *shared party affiliation with other senator* (*SPART*; coded 1 or 0); the *number of bills introduced* (*BILLS*); and *primary* (*PRIM*), which is coded 1 if there was a party primary preceding the election and 0 if not. In the set of postelections, there were seven senators who faced a primary before the election, all in the last period of the sample.

I ran two different models using combinations of these variables; the statistically significant coefficients are listed in the following for each model:

$$PMV = -0.02(0.34) + 0.79(0.26^{**})PPMV - 0.12(0.05^{**})MAJC - 0.011(0.003^{**})PARB + 0.0012(0.006^{*})BILLS\ (R^2 = 0.67, N = 44) \quad \textbf{(5.3)}$$

In the second model, I replaced *PPMV* and *MAJC* with *RETSUP* with the following results:

$$PMV = 0.11(0.63) - 0.16(0.03^{**})RETSUP - 0.009(0.003^{**})PARB + 0.55(0.18^{**})PRIM + 0.0014(0.0005^{**})BILLS + 0.032(0.14^{*})YEARS\ (R^2 = 0.47, N = 50) \quad \textbf{(5.4)}$$

The party variables demonstrate that if an incumbent senator can ward off competition within his own party before the legislature meets, he stands to win much more easily. Once the legislature begins voting, the higher the number of majority-party candidates considered, the lower the margin of victory for the senator, which could sometimes result in his defeat at the hands of a fellow partisan. Prior margin of victory is significant, and since we know that the legislature contained a different set of individuals when a senator ran for reelection, (the percentage of seats held by the senator's party in the first set of elections and the second set of elections is 0.28), it may reflect the success of senators in retaining general support within their own party over time. To try to unpack the effect of prior margin of victory, I included the prior percentage margin of victory interacted with the number of majority-party candidates that the senator faced in the subsequent election (*RETSUP*). This interactive variable is statistically and substantively significant; this suggests that prior margin of victory in this analysis is a proxy for retaining the support of the party rank-and-file members in the state, as filtered through a freshly elected crop of state legislators, and simultaneously warding off challenges from political elites within the majority party.[14]

Bill sponsorship was the only institutional tool that yielded any return in terms of margin of victory. For every 10 additional bills introduced, electoral margin of victory increased by 1 percent. Senators very likely calculated that if they served, or appeared to serve, constituent interests through bills (e.g., individual pension or relief bills), they could attract constituent support in the home districts of the state legislators, which could produce reelection support.

Implications and Future Research Directions

In the age before the adoption of the 17th amendment, Senate elections were very contentious and hard fought within the party as much as—if not more than—between parties. Senators could not simply rely on the public nature of party campaigning in state legislative elections because there could be several factions within their state party in the legislature and even differences within the party in the state house and state senate. Because of the 6-year term, senators would frequently outlast most of the members of the state legislature who initially voted for them. Consequently, senators had to construct a new winning coalition in their own majority party before their reelection, and they did so using strategic roll-call voting, patronage, and benefits delivered to individuals and districts through committee work and bill sponsorship. All this work was designed to cultivate a sufficiently strong "personal" vote among constituents in state legislative districts such that the legislators themselves felt pressured to support the senator, so much so as to deter any intraparty challenge to the senator. In sum, the conditions for getting elected to the Senate in the late 19th century may have been mechanically different, but senators' own reelection-seeking behavior looks quite similar to their modern-day successors.

Chapter 6

The First "Southern Strategy": The Republican Party and Contested-Election Cases in the Late 19th-Century House

JEFFERY A. JENKINS

I. Introduction

In this chapter I focus on a strategic initiative adopted first by the Republican Party and used in House politics throughout the late 19th century, one that has not received nearly as much attention in the scholarly literature—contested-election cases.[1] By a "contested election," I refer to an election result that is disputed; specifically, the loser in a congressional race contests the validity of the election outcome on the basis of any number of charges (but often relating to fraud, corruption, or other electoral irregularities). While quite rare today, contested-election cases were a normal extension of the electoral process from Reconstruction through the turn of the 20th century, and a veritable staple of late 19th-century partisan politics.

The remainder of the chapter is organized as follows. After a short history of contested elections in the House, emphasizing trends over time, I describe the Republicans' use of contested-election cases during and after Reconstruction, respectively. I then step back and probe more generally the data surrounding contested elections in the late 19th century, before examining why contesting elections ceased to be an overt partisan strategy as the 19th century was coming to an end. I investigate why a similar contested-election strategy was not used by Senate Republicans in the late 19th century, and then summarize my findings in the final section.

II. Contested House Elections: A Short History

The possibility of a dispute arising over the outcome of an election to Congress was a contingency recognized by the framers during the Constitutional Convention. As a result, guidelines for dealing with such a contingency are laid out explicitly in Article I, Section 5, Clause 1 of the Constitution: "Each House shall be the Judge of the Elections, Returns, and Qualifications of its own Members." With this simple statement, each chamber of Congress is granted complete authority over the composition of its membership. Thus, when the result of a given election is contested, each chamber acts as the sole arbiter without executive or judicial constraint. This constitutional guarantee was an artifact of English and colonial rule, as fear of executive authority led the House of Commons and nearly every colonial legislature to adopt similar protections (Dempsey 1956, 12–20, 25–28).

The contested-election process in the House was institutionalized fairly early on. By the First Congress, a standing committee—the Committee on Elections—was established to handle contested-election cases. And, after various temporary laws were tried throughout the late 18th and early 19th centuries, a uniform mode of procedure in contested-election cases was adopted in 1851, which established guidelines for the development of a contest.[2] This statutory framework, with minor revisions, would last for more than a century.[3]

There have been 601 contested-election cases in the House between the 1st and 107th Congresses (1789–2002), or an average of just over 5.6 per Congress.[4] During the antebellum era, the House dealt with relatively few contested-election cases—only 107 over the first 36 Congresses, or an average of just under 3 per Congress. A significant jump occurred with the Civil War, however, as 19 and 17 cases were considered in the 37th and 38th Congresses (1861–1865), respectively. The number of cases remained relatively high for the next 35 years, alternating between 5 cases in the 49th Congress (1885–1887) and 38 cases, the high-water mark for contested-election cases, in the 54th Congress (1895–1997). In all, between the Civil War and the turn of the 19th century, the 37th through 55th Congresses (1861–1899), the House considered 262 contested-election cases, or an average of nearly 15 per Congress. A gradual decline began with the 56th Congress (1899–1901); since then, the number of contested-election cases has reached double digits only twice, 12 in the 62nd Congress (1911–1913) and 17 in the 73rd Congress (1933–1934), and no more than one case has been considered in 16 different Congresses. In total, the House dealt with 212 contested-election cases between the 56th and 107th Congresses (1899–2002), or an average of just over 4 per Congress.

Across time, the ruling in contested-election cases has mostly favored the contestee (i.e., the individual holding the election certificate, who is typically seated). Of the 601 contested-election cases, the contestee has emerged victorious in 407 cases (or 67.7%), the contestant (i.e., the individual contesting, or disputing, the election) has won 128 cases (or 21.3%), and the election has been voided, and the seat vacated, in 66 cases (11%). Thus, in just over 2 of every 3 cases, the contestee has retained his or her seat.

Historically, these percentages have fluctuated. During the antebellum period (1st–36th Congresses), contestees won nearly 62 percent of contested-election cases. From the Civil War through the turn of the 19th century (37th–55th Congresses), contestees fared less well, winning just over 57 percent of contested-election cases. This period also represents the high point for contestant success, as nearly 29 percent of cases resulted in seatholder replacement. Since the beginning of the 20th century (56th–107th Congresses), contestees have fared exceedingly well, winning over 85 percent of contested-election cases. Thus, while contestants at one time stood a reasonable chance of winning an election contest, this has not held true in the modern period.[5]

Overall, less than one-third of all contested-election cases have been decided by roll call, with the remaining cases dealt with by voice vote or by the House taking no action (and thereby accepting the outcome from the initial election).[6] Of those election cases determined by roll call, partisanship has typically determined the voting: 87 percent of such cases can be classified as party votes, i.e., votes in which at least 50 percent of one major party opposed at least 50 percent of the other major party.[7] And just over one in seven roll calls is a perfectly aligned party vote, in which all voting members of one major party oppose all voting members of the other major party. A cross-period breakdown reveals that these aggregate results are in fact driven by results from the late 19th century—nearly 95 percent of election-contest roll calls in the late 19th century were party votes, and more than one of every five roll calls was a perfectly aligned party vote. This compares to the other two periods, in which less than 80 percent of election-contest roll calls were party votes.[8]

Thus, the late 19th century clearly stands out amid a historical overview of contested House elections. It produced the largest per-Congress ratio of election contests, the highest proportion of seat changes (or "flips"), and the highest levels of party voting in case outcomes. I now turn to a systematic analysis of contested-election cases during the late 19th century and examine the role election contests played in the Republicans' party-building efforts.

III. The Rise and Fall of the Southern Republicans during Reconstruction

After the Civil War, the Republicans shed their label as a sectional party and emerged as a true national force. Thanks to newly enfranchised African American voters, an "occupying" army of Union troops, and no general amnesty for former Confederate combatants, the South would quickly become fertile ground for a Southern Republican organization. For example, of the 41 former-Confederate House seats in the 40th Congress (1867–1869), 36 were controlled by the Republicans. Shortly thereafter, however, a Southern Democratic Party began to revive, and growing violence toward and intimidation of African American voters threatened the electoral process (Trelease 1971; Perman 1984). The Republican-controlled Congress responded quickly with two reform efforts. First, a series of enforcement acts (or force bills) was passed to protect the voting rights of African Americans and ensure the sanctity of the electoral process in the South (Gillette 1979, 25–27; Foner 1988, 454–459, 528–531).[9] Second, contested-election cases were used to remedy the current electoral situation. In all, 10 apparent Democratic seats in the 41st Congress (1869–1871) were either successfully contested or vacated on the basis of charges of fraud and corruption and subsequently became Republican seats.

For the next two Congresses, the 42nd (1871–1873) and 43rd (1873–1875), the Republicans did not use contested elections as an overt partisan tool, relying instead on the army to oversee Southern elections in keeping with the various Enforcement Act provisions. While the Democrats were making steady inroads in the Deep South as well as the border states, the Republicans downplayed their growing strength, as they still enjoyed unified control of the national government. This was to change very quickly, however, owing to two factors. First, the political context changed: in 1873–1874 the Midwest suffered a serious economic depression, and the larger Northern electorate was becoming disenchanted with Southern Reconstruction and demanding new economic policies. Second, the Union army was slowly being withdrawn from the South, leaving African American voters vulnerable to violence and intimidation.[10] As a result, the Democrats erupted in the 1874 congressional midterms, dominating the South, winning a majority of seats in the border states, pulling even with the

Republicans in the Great Lakes states, and capturing a sizable number of seats in the Northeast (Stewart 1991); in doing so, the Democrats won majority control of the House in the 44th Congress (1875–1877). Moreover, in that and the succeeding Congress, the Democrats used the contested-election process to their advantage, adding a total of nine seats to their ranks.

Thus, the Republicans found themselves in a position that they had not experienced for over a decade—as a chamber minority. For a time, the Republicans could afford to discount the South and any attempts by the Democrats to revive a Southern organization, as they could count on a substantial House majority simply from dominating the Northern states. However, with their recent successes, the Democrats had reestablished themselves as a national power. Consequently, the Republicans had to devise a "[S]outhern strategy" if they hoped to vie consistently for House control (De Santis 1959, 12; Valelly 1995).

The problem was *how* to make inroads in the South. Many of the strategic tools that Republicans used effectively throughout the late 19th century, like admittance of Western states, deployment of federal election officials, and redistricting, were not effective in maintaining a Republican presence in the post-Reconstruction South. And with federal troops no longer stationed in the South, per the implicit agreement underlying the Compromise of 1877, no credible enforcement mechanisms were in place to ensure fair elections.[11] Contested-election cases, therefore, became the chief means by which the Republicans would fight Democratic-sanctioned fraud, intimidation, and violence in the South and promulgate hopes that a Southern wing of the Republican Party could be resuscitated.[12]

IV. The Post-Reconstruction Southern Strategy

Initially, however, it appeared that the new contested-election strategy was finished before it started. That is, by the 46th Congress (1879–1881), the Southern component of the Republican Party was virtually eliminated—only three Republican seats remained, one each in Florida, Tennessee, and Virginia. Moreover, a new mobilization and recruitment campaign was attempted as the liberal element within the Republican Party, led by President Rutherford Hayes, undertook a "new departure" in the South, courting white Southern Democrats with Whiggish persuasions while denying patronage to the carpetbaggers, scalawags, and African Americans who made up the Southern Republican rank and file (Hirshson 1962, 25–26; Woodward 1966, 22–50; Hoogenboom 1988, 51–78).

This strategy of conciliation would prove disastrous: white Southerners accepted Hayes's patronage positions while gleefully rejecting Republican principles, and the "regular" Southern Republicans and their local organizations were left to slowly wither away (De Santis 1955; 1959, 99–103, 135–136; Summers 2000, 30–39, 45–45).

Yet the Southern Republican organization was afforded new life when the Republicans regained control of the House in the 47th Congress (1881–1883). And with Hayes now out of the picture, and the new-departure policy an unmitigated failure, they labored to keep their Southern pulse alive. Contested elections would be the vehicle; six Southern Democrats—one each in Alabama, Florida, Mississippi, and Missouri and two in South Carolina—would be unseated in favor of Republicans.[13] These institutional seat gains provided the Republicans with some leeway in constructing their policy agenda because they commanded only a bare majority when the House convened and, combined with seven seats captured outright in the general congressional elections—one each in Louisiana and North Carolina, two in Virginia, and three in Tennessee—gave the Southern Republican organization newfound hope.

This was not to last, however, as the Democrats would seize control of the House for the next three Congresses, effectively eliminating election contests as a means to prop up the fledgling Republican organization in the South. By the late 1880s, the Democrats had completely swept the Republicans from Alabama, Arkansas, Florida, Georgia, Louisiana, Mississippi, South Carolina, and Texas. The only remaining Republican foothold was in the hill country of eastern Tennessee, western North Carolina, and southwestern Virginia.

The Republicans regained the House in the 51st Congress (1889–1891), and with the backing of President Benjamin Harrison and a small group of congressmen sympathetic to the party's radical roots, they resumed their Southern mission (De Santis 1959, 195–197; Hirshson 1962, 200–214; Welch 1965; Socolofsky and Spetter 1987, 60–65). A new force bill would be introduced, this time advocating the federal courts rather than the army as the guardian of Southern elections,[14] and election contests would continue to be wielded as the great "equalizer." In all, five Democrats from the former Confederate South—one each in Alabama,[15] Arkansas, and South Carolina and two in Virginia—and three Democrats from the former border slave states—one from Maryland and two from West Virginia—would be unseated and replaced by Republicans.[16] After a two-Congress switch in control, the Republicans took back the House in the 54th Congress (1895–1897), and their Southern efforts continued. Four Democrats from the former Confederate South—one each from South Carolina and Virginia, and two from Alabama—and two Democrats from the former border slave states—Missouri and Kentucky—were unseated in favor of Republicans.[17]

At that point, the Republicans' use of election contests as a means of securing a Southern base began to slow. Three Democrats from the Deep South in each of the next two Congresses, the 55th (1897–1899) and 56th (1899–1901), were unseated in favor of Republicans. But while the Republicans would control the House for the next five Congresses, no additional Democrats from the former Confederate South would be unseated and replaced by Republicans. Meanwhile, the Republicans' electoral success in Southern congressional elections left little doubt that the party's Southern base was essentially dead. Except for occasional Republican successes in eastern Tennessee, southwestern Virginia, and western North Carolina, the South became a one-party Democratic state.[18]

V. Examining the Data

In this section, I pull back a bit and examine more generally the data on contested-election cases across the late 19th and early 20th centuries. Between the 40th and 61st Congresses (1867–1911), generally considered the most partisan period in American history, there were 270 contested-election cases in the House,[19] of which 162 (or 60%) dealt with seats from the former Confederate South.[20] This is an exceedingly high ratio, as the former Confederate states only made up, on average, around 25 percent of the entire House during this period. If the term *South* is expanded to include all former slave states, then 188 contested-election cases (or 69.6%) dealt with Southern seats.[21]

A significantly greater number of elections were contested when the Republicans controlled the chamber—more than 14 per Congress, compared to fewer than 9 per Congress under Democratic control. In addition, a larger proportion of the Republicans' caseload dealt with seats from the former Confederate South specifically—nearly 66 percent, relative to less than 44 percent under the Democrats—and the former slave states more generally—nearly 83 percent, relative to less than 51 percent under the Democrats. This suggests a selection effect, that is, amid the Democratic-sanctioned fraud and corruption that typified Southern elections during this time, losing Republican candidates likely believed that their chances of a successful contest were higher if the Republicans controlled the House; thus, more cases involving Southern seats were considered under Republican rule.

Of the 270 cases of successful election contests and vacated seats between the 40th and 61st Congresses (1867–1911), 80 (or 29.6%) resulted in seat flips. Of those 80 seat changes, 70 (or 87.5%) favored the majority party. And of those 70, almost half (34, or 48.6%) were seats from the former Confederate South. And finally, if *South* is expanded once again to include all former slave states, then 46 pro-majority-party seat flips (or 65.7%) were Southern seats.

As discussed previously, before the enforcement acts being adopted and fully implemented between 1870 and 1872, the Republicans used election contests to combat Democratic fraud and intimidation in Southern elections. Once the enforcement acts were in place, the army and federal election officials took over monitoring Democratic electoral impropriety; as a result, Republican leaders no longer employed election contests in an aggressively partisan way. In fact, in the 42nd (1871–1873) and 43rd (1873–1875) Congresses, the Republicans would apply the contested-election procedure in a very evenhanded manner, awarding five seats to Democrats in the former Confederate South but just two seats to their own partisans.[22]

This evenhandedness would not last for long, as the changing political climate led the Republicans to rethink their use of contested-election cases. Once the Democrats regained control of the House in the 44th Congress (1875–1877), combined with the Southern withdrawal of the Union army and the subsequent emasculation of the enforcement acts, Republican leaders realized that the party's foothold in the South was slipping away. As a result, during the next five Congresses in which they controlled the House, the 47th (1881–1883), 51st (1889–1891), 54th (1895–1897), 55th (1897–1899), and 56th (1899–1901), the Republicans behaved much more parochially, seating 20 of their own partisans in the former Confederate South, while seating *no* Democrats. Moreover, the Republicans now used the contested-election process almost exclusively as a means of maintaining a Southern presence: of the 29 Republican seats added via contested-election cases in these Congresses, only *3* were located outside the former slave states.

When the Democrats were the majority party in the House, they pursued a different strategy. They did not add many Southern seats via contested elections, relying instead on strong-arm tactics to influence the electoral process in the South.[23] Rather, contested-election cases were a means by which the Democrats expanded *outside* the South. In the eight Democratic Houses between the 44th and 53rd Congresses (1875–1895), 13 of the 21 Democratic seats (or 61.9%) added via election contests were located outside the former slave states.

Between the 40th and 43rd Congresses (1867–1875), the Republicans controlled a majority of House seats in the former Confederate South, which was accomplished almost wholly through the standard electoral process: only 7 of the 150 Republican seats (or 4.7%) resulted from contested elections. Beginning in the 44th Congress (1875–1877), with the Democrats' resurgence, the Republicans' share of seats dropped off substantially. It soon became clear that without the help of contested elections, the Republicans could count on only single digits in the former Confederacy. Thus, on the next five occasions when the Republicans controlled the House, contested elections became a major tool to boost the party's Southern seat totals. Of the 58 seats that the Republicans controlled during these five Congresses, 20 (or 34.5%) came directly via election contests.

VI. The End of Contested Elections as a Partisan Strategy

After the 56th Congress (1899–1901), the strategic use of contested elections ended quite abruptly. Despite retaining majority control of the chamber, the Republicans did not use election contests to add a single Southern seat over the next five Congresses. What accounts for this change?

Three complementary explanations can be provided. First, while contested elections had added Republican seats in the South and were supported by prominent party leaders like President Harrison, many Republicans were not enthusiastic about their continued use as a partisan device. One very vocal opponent was Thomas B. Reed, Republican Speaker of the House in the 51st (1889–1891), 54th (1895–1897), and 55th (1897–1899) Congresses. Reed believed that the contested-election process was incredibly costly, requiring committee members to read thousands of pages of testimony and the House as a whole to spend weeks and sometimes months each session considering arguments and rendering decisions (Robinson 1930, 76, 85).[24] His principal concern was the Republican Party agenda, which was often put on hold for contested-election cases. As Reed (1890, 114–115) stated, election contests "consume the time of the House to the exclusion of valuable legislation." Thus, in Reed's mind, the Republicans had become too fixated on adding Southern seats; in the meantime, valuable time was wasted and the party's legislative agenda had stagnated. Consequently, the party suffered, as the Republicans had managed to capture the House only 2 of 10 times between the 44th (1875–1877) and 53rd (1893–1895) Congresses.[25]

Second, the strategy of using election contests to maintain a Republican presence in the former Confederate South was largely a failure. Most of the Republicans who successfully unseated Democrats via election contests were unable to build a base of support and maintain control of their districts. Of the 15 successful Republican contestants in the Republican-controlled 47th, 51st, 54th, 55th, and 56th Congresses who ran for reelection to the subsequent Congress, only *6* were reelected. And of those 6, only *2* were elected outright. The other 4 gained their seats via *another successful election contest.*[26] More generally, of the 20 Republican seats achieved via election contests in these five Congresses, only *8* would be controlled by the Republican Party in the next election. And only *3* of those 8 would be won outright.

Moreover, the *loyalty* of these successful Republican contestants left much to be desired. For each of the five Congresses in question, Southern Republicans elected outright were significantly more supportive of the party than were Southern Republicans seated via election contests. Thus, in addition to being unable to maintain control of contested seats across Congresses, Republicans received very little bang for the buck from those members who held contested House seats. As a result, it was in many ways a no-win strategy: it was a time-consuming process to flip a seat, and the ensuing benefit was minimal.

Third, and finally, the changing electoral landscape in the late 1890s made the continued use of election contests unnecessary. To reiterate, after the Democrats had reemerged as a national power in the mid-1870s, the Republicans endeavored to maintain a Southern presence because it was necessary to do so. That is, the two congressional parties were running neck and neck in their competition for voters for the next 20 years; thus, if they cared about capturing and maintaining control of the House, the Republicans could not afford to ignore the South entirely. Contested elections provided them with an opportunity to add Southern seats, despite the Democrats' iron grip on the electoral process in the South.

This all changed, however, with the congressional elections of 1894, which produced a national electoral realignment. Battling over industrial, agrarian, and monetary issues, the Republicans and Democrats emerged from the 1894 elections with a new distribution of solid, lasting constituencies—and the Republicans were the better for it. As Brady (1988, 61) states, these elections "converted competitive two-party states in the industrial East and Midwest into solid Republican regions and made the Border states . . . [which] were solidly Democratic before 1894 . . . into a competitive two-party region."[27] In effect, the two parties offered distinct economic platforms in the mid-1890s, and the electorate (outside of the South) overwhelmingly supported the Republican agenda. The 1894 elections produced a sizable Republican uptick in every region of the nation. For the next decade and a half, this surge would either be maintained or increase in every region outside of the South, leaving the Republicans firmly in control of New England, the mid-Atlantic, the Midwest, and the West and battling for control of the border South.

As a result of this electoral realignment, the Republicans would reassess their partisan strategies. In effect, as Valelly (1995, 208) states, the South became "superfluous to Republican Party interests," as the Republicans no longer needed Southern representation to maintain a working majority in the House. Consequently, they could heed Reed's advice by dropping their (largely unsuccessful) contested-election strategy and focusing their energies on their policy agenda. This did not happen immediately, however, as it was not initially clear whether their electoral victories in the mid-to-late 1890s reflected a temporary swing or a more general, lasting movement. Hence, the Republicans proceeded cautiously and continued using election contests to add Southern seats—four in the 54th (1895–1897) Congress, and three each in the 55th (1897–1899) and 56th (1899–1901) Congresses. After President William McKinley's reelection in 1900, however, Republican Party leaders were confident in their newfound electoral success, and the partisan use of election contests (and the Republican presence in the South) vanished.

VII. Examining the Senate

In examining the Republicans' use of contested elections as a partisan strategy in the late 19th-century House, a natural question emerges: was a similar strategy employed in the Senate? The answer is no. While contested elections in the Senate reached their high point during Reconstruction, they all but dried up by the late 1870s. In fact, between the 46th and 56th Congresses (1879–1901), only two contested-election cases from Southern states were considered in the Senate.[28]

This divergence can be explained in part by an institutional difference. That is, state legislatures were an additional component of the contested-election process in the late 19th-century Senate—before the adoption of the 17th Amendment, senators were elected by state legislatures, rather than directly by the people. And while the Republican Party possessed majorities in many Southern state legislatures in the decade after the Civil War, the subsequent situation mirrored that of the national level: the reemergence of the Democratic Party in the early-to-mid 1870s combined with the gradual withdraw of Union troops from the South ended the Republicans' Southern ascendancy very quickly. By 1877 the Republicans had lost majority control of every state legislature. And with threats and violence toward African Americans continuing unabated and the rise of Jim Crow laws, the Republican Party disappeared in all practical terms from many states. Between 1877 and 1900, the average Republican seat share across state legislatures in the former Confederate South was 11.1 percent in the lower chamber and 9 percent in the upper chamber. In 8 of the 11 states, the average Republican seat share was below 12 percent in both chambers. And even in states like North Carolina and Tennessee, where the Republican organization remained active, the average Republican seat share was less than 30 percent.

As a result, adding Southern seats via contested elections was problematic for the Republican Party after Reconstruction. Since senators were elected by state legislatures and the Republicans had such a small share of seats in Southern state legislatures, each Senate contest would require an investigation into *many* state-level elections. That is, to generate a state-legislative majority so that a Republican senator could be elected, a substantial number of seats would need to be flipped, which would require investigating a substantial number of state-level elections. For the Senate Republicans, this was simply not worth the effort, especially since, despite the Democrats' resurgence, the Republicans still controlled the Senate 8 of 10 times between the 44th (1875–1877) and 53rd (1893–1895) Congresses.

For House Republicans, on the other hand, election contests *were* worth the effort. This was because a simple, direct link existed between a district election and a House seat. Stated another way, while each Senate seat was tied to *multiple* state-level elections and thus required *multiple* coordinated investigations, each House seat was tied to *one* district election and thus necessitated *one* basic investigation. At a time when every seat mattered and the Republicans were struggling electorally, losing majority control of the House to the Democrats 8 of 10 times between the 44th (1875–1877) and 53rd (1893–1895) Congresses, election contests as a partisan strategy made sense. Thus, variance in the electoral connection between the House and Senate and a different sense of Republican urgency across the two chambers in the late 19th century led to different patterns of election contests.

VIII. Conclusion

I have argued in this chapter that Republicans in the late 19th-century House used contested-election cases as an overt partisan strategy to combat the illegal electoral practices by white Southern Democrats. Specifically, after the Democrats' resurgence in the mid-1870s, the Republicans, who enjoyed little meaningful opposition going back to the Civil War, quickly found themselves in an electoral dogfight for national supremacy. To stem the tide, the Republicans realized that they could not cede control of the South completely to the Democrats; yet with the Union army no longer stationed in the former Confederacy, no enforcement mechanism was present to ensure fair elections. Thus, the Republicans turned to an institutional mechanism, election contests, when they controlled the House, unseating Southern Democrats and replacing them with Republicans. This strategy continued through the mid-to-late 1890s, when the Republicans realized that the 1894 electoral realignment was a permanent one; as a result, they could afford to ignore the South because they were highly competitive or dominant in every other region of the country, and thus the active pursuit of election contests came to an end.

Chapter 7

Explaining the Ideological Polarization of the Congressional Parties since the 1970s

GARY C. JACOBSON

Introduction

The sharp increase in the ideological polarization of the congressional parties since the 1970s has naturally attracted a good deal of scholarly attention. In this chapter I examine competing explanations for the rise in partisanship. Poole (2003) claims, "Based on the roll call voting record, once elected to Congress, members adopt a consistent ideological position and maintain it over time. They may be changing minds, but not in Congress." This is a bold claim with important implications. If Poole is right, then not only have the bitter partisan fights within Congress contributed nothing (at least directly) to partisan polarization but the changing electoral environment is reflected only in the replacement of moderate by more extreme partisans, not by continuing members who adapt to new electoral realities—an important limitation on the electoral connection's influence. The work of other scholars (Berard 2001; Theriault 2003a; Stonecash, Brewer, and Mariani 2003; Roberts and Smith 2003a), as well as the broader assumptions underlying the electoral connection and conditional-party-government literature, implicitly or explicitly challenge Poole's conclusion. My purpose in this chapter is to examine Poole's claim and its competitors as part of a broader review of evidence regarding the sources of increasing partisan polarization in Congress over the past three decades.

Partisan Polarization

By every observed measure, the distance between the congressional parties has been growing steadily since the 1970s. The widening gap appears in party loyalty on roll-call votes (Rohde 1991; Aldrich 1995; Deckard [Sinclair] 2000; Roberts and Smith 2003a), adjusted Americans for Democratic Action (ADA) scores (Groseclose, Levitt, and Snyder 1999b), and presidential-support scores (Fleisher and Bond 2000; Jacobson 2003) as well as, most prominently, in Poole and Rosenthal's first-dimensional DW-NOMINATE scores (Poole and Rosenthal 1997a; McCarty, Poole, and Rosenthal 1997).[1] The Poole-Rosenthal data show that the wide ideological gap between the congressional parties observed in recent Congresses is by no means unprecedented; the parties were even further apart in the latter half of the 19th century than they are now, and the recent increase in polarization followed a period in which the congressional parties were, by historical standards, unusually close to one another on this dimension (Poole 2003; Theriault 2003b). Nonetheless, the steep increase in polarization since the Nixon administration is unprecedented, and by the 107th Congress the parties in both chambers had moved further apart than they had been at any time since before World War I.

Between the Nixon administration's first Congress and the George W. Bush administration's first Congress, party differences in mean DW-NOMINATE scores grew from 0.54 to 0.87 in the House and from 0.47 to 0.80 in the Senate on this 2-point scale. As the parties pulled apart ideologically, they also became more homogeneous internally; the standard deviations of each party coalition's DW-NOMINATE scores and adjusted ADA scores have declined among both parties in both chambers since the early 1970s.[2] These changes had, by the 107th Congress, left the House and Senate with the most divergent and homogeneous party coalitions in more than 50 years.

Polarization and Electoral Change

The ideological polarization of the congressional parties parallels changes in the parties' respective electoral constituencies. Two major trends have given the congressional parties increasingly divergent electoral coalitions. First, the partisan, ideological, and policy views of voters have grown more internally consistent, more disparate, and more predictive of voting in House and Senate elections (Jacobson 2000b, 2001). Second, electoral units into which voters are sorted have become more homogeneously partisan (Stonecash,

Brewer, and Mariani 2003; Carson et al., 2003). That is, changes in both the preferences and the distribution of congressional voters have given the congressional parties more divergent and polarized electoral bases.

A principal source of both trends has of course been the partisan realignment of the South (Black and Black 1987; Frymer 1995; Nadeau and Stanley 1993; Wattenberg 1991; Stanley 1988; Hood, Kidd, and Morris 1999, Jacobson 2000a, 2004). The civil rights revolution, and particularly the Voting Rights Act of 1965, brought Southern blacks into the electorate as Democrats, while moving conservative whites to abandon their ancestral allegiance to the Democratic Party in favor of the ideologically and racially more compatible Republican Party. In-migration also contributed to an increasingly Republican electorate, which gradually replaced conservative Democrats with conservative Republicans in Southern House and Senate seats. The constituencies that elected the remaining Democrats became more like Democratic constituencies elsewhere, giving the House and Senate parties more homogeneous (and more liberal) electoral coalitions (Jacobson 2000a). As a consequence, the ideological distinctiveness of Southern Democrats in both chambers has been diminishing for three decades, although Southerners remain a bit more conservative than other Democrats. This change has helped move the party' mean ideological location to the left in both houses, an effect compounded by compositional trends: since the 1950s the proportion of Southerners among Democrats has fallen from 41 percent to 25 percent in the House and from 42 percent to 18 percent in the Senate.

Compositional changes have also contributed to the rightward drift among Republicans. Southern Republicans have been consistently more conservative than other Republicans, and Republicans from states in the Northeast consistently more liberal, for several decades. Since the 1950s the proportion of Southerners among House Republicans has grown from 3 percent to 34 percent, while the proportion from the Northeast has fallen from 37 percent to 17 percent. In the Senate, Southerners have increased from zero to 26 percent of the Republican membership, while Northeasterners have fallen from 35 percent to 16 percent.

Compositional changes are clearly not the whole story, however. Both DW-NOMINATE and ADA measures of ideology indicate that Republicans from all regions have become increasingly conservative, and Democrats from all regions have become increasingly liberal, over the past three decades. Thus partisan polarization in Congress is by no means explained entirely by the Southern realignment or regional changes in the partisan distribution of House and Senate seats.

This should not be surprising, because the South is not the only region where electorates have been changing. Party loyalty among congressional voters has also increased since the 1970s (Jacobson 2004), so the relationship between ideology and voting has become notably stronger. The shift among conservatives is particularly notable, as is the pivotal role of the 1994 election in solidifying support for Republican candidates among conservatives. In the most recent election, 80 percent of self-identified liberals voted for Democrats, while 80 percent of conservatives voted for Republicans.

These changes in voting behavior have left the congressional parties with increasingly divergent electoral coalitions. For analytical purposes, we can represent each congressional party's electoral coalition by the National Election Studies respondents who voted for its successful candidates. The proportion of the Republican electoral coalition supplied by conservatives has been growing in both chambers, while the share supplied by liberals has fallen. Back in 1972, for example, the Republican Senate electoral coalition was composed of 43 percent conservatives and 20 percent liberals; in 2002 the comparable percentages were 67 and 9, respectively. The opposite is true for the Democrats's electoral coalitions, which were once evenly balanced but now contain a substantial preponderance of liberals.[3]

Aggregate electoral data also show a widening disparity between the congressional parties' electoral bases. In 1972, for example, George McGovern's vote was, on average, only 7.6 percentage points higher in Democratic than in Republican House districts; in 2002 Al Gore's vote (in 2000) was an average of 19.2 percentage points higher in districts won by Democrats. The aggregate electoral bases of the Senate parties have also become more divergent by this measure, though in absolute terms the differences are considerably smaller than in the House.

Polarization through Selection

Electoral and congressional polarization increased in tandem, just as assumptions about the electoral connection's potency would lead us to expect. It is also evident that the electoral connection operated mainly via selection. In theory, selection could work several ways to increase ideological polarization. Moderates might select themselves out by choosing to leave more frequently. They might also be more liable to defeat. Voters might select generations of progressively more extreme members to replace whoever leaves for whatever reason. All three patterns might, of course, occur simultaneously. As it happens, both selection in and selection out (voluntary and involuntary) contributed to partisan polarization, although to varying degrees depending on the party, chamber, and measure of ideology.

The DW-NOMINATE scores of entering and departing Republicans and Democrats in each chamber in elections from the 93rd to the 107th Congresses show that, among Republicans, newcomers have been more conservative than departing members in all but a couple of Congresses over the past three decades.[4] In the House, entering Republicans were an average of 0.068 units more conservative (on the 2-point DW-NOMINATE scale) than departing members (as well as 0.042 more conservative than continuing members, who were thus themselves 0.026 more conservative than departing members). Entering Senate Republicans were 0.042 more conservative than departing Republicans (and 0.060 more conservative than continuing Republicans).

The pattern among House Democrats is not so regular, although on average, departing Democrats were more conservative than either entering or continuing Democrats during this period. Departing Democratic senators were an average of 0.047 more conservative on the DW-NOMINATE scale than entering Democrats and 0.031 more conservative than continuing Democrats; Democrats who left the House were an average of 0.037 more conservative than newcomers and 0.058 more conservative than continuing members. Thus among Democrats, the departure of conservatives made a larger contribution to their leftward drift than the entrance of liberals.

The 1994 elections produced the largest change, as the Democrats who departed either voluntarily or involuntarily came disproportionately from the party's moderate-to-conservative contingent, most of whom had been representing Republican-leaning districts (Jacobson 2004). The Republican class of 1994 was also the most conservative of the entire period, highlighting the crucial contribution the 1994 election made to the ideological polarization of Congress. It made no difference for either party if departure was voluntary or involuntary; mean DW-NOMINATE scores do not differ significantly between losers and those who did not seek reelection.

The evidence from the DW-NOMINATE points to the influx of conservative Republicans as the most important generational source of partisan polarization in Congress, although the departure of more conservative Democrats also contributed to the trend. What is behind the increasing conservatism of successive Republican cohorts? Change in the composition of the Republican House and Senate coalitions is one likely source. One major compositional change has already been noted: a growing portion of congressional Republicans were from the South, and Southern Republicans are typically more conservative than Republicans from other regions. The proportion of Republicans who can be considered members or allies of the conservative Christian movement, which has emerged as a core component of the Republican coalition since the 1970s, has also grown.[5] Because such Republicans are far more conservative than their more secular colleagues (by an average of 0.17 in the House, 0.29 in the Senate), their growing presence in the coalitions should have pushed congressional Republicans to the right. An additional generational factor may be at work in the Senate. As Rae and Campbell note, many recently elected Republicans "came from the House, after having been baptized by . . . Newt Gingrich (R-Ga.) into relentless and combative partisanship" (2001, 8).[6] I will have more to say about these potential sources of ideological change after reviewing the case for an additional source: adaptation.

Adaptation

Clearly, partisan polarization in the House and Senate has been driven by a process of generational turnover and the resulting electoral selection of ideologically more extreme members. The idea that selection has been the sole source of change is, however, challenged by the Southern realignment scenario itself. If Southern Democrats moved toward the party mainstream in response to the growing proportion of African American voters in their electoral constituencies, continuing as well as newly elected members should have been affected. Berard (2001, 151) presents compelling evidence that they were in fact affected, at least as measured by their rising party-support scores. Nor does according exclusive agency to selection allow for developments internal to Congress—specific fights, newly divisive issues, the sharpening of party tools for enforcing discipline—to exercise an independent influence on partisan behavior. If these things matter, then, contrary to Poole and Rosenthal's conjecture, party polarization in Congress may be the product of adaptation as well as selection.

Theriault (2003a), using DW-NOMINATE scores, finds evidence that congressional polarization has been driven by adaptation, or as he specifies it, "conversion," as well as by selective replacement. Theriault is onto something here, but his methodology (summing changes in DW-NOMINATE scores between one Congress and the next among members serving in both and comparing similar calculations among replacements) makes it difficult to estimate the net effect or statistical significance of adaptive changes. Moreover, his analysis does not distinguish conversion induced by electoral change from conversion induced by internal congressional politics.

Brady, Han, and McAdam (2003) show that redistricting as well as replacement moved Democrats to the left and Republicans to the right, again suggesting adaptive behavior on the part of continuing members; they do not, however, consider whether endogenous sources of ideological polarization were also at work.

Poole's claim that members do not change their ideological locations rests primarily on a rank-ordering technique (optimal classification); his estimates of members' ideological locations are highly correlated with, but not identical to, their DW-NOMINATE scores (2003, 22). If we examine the DW-NOMINATE scores directly, however, we find that members who are in Congress for at least five terms do change their ideological location over time. In any given Congress over the period in question, a large majority of such members are more liberal or conservative than they were in their initial Congress. More important, since the 1970s, Democrats in both chambers are much more likely to have moved left than right, and Republicans in both chambers have been much more likely to have moved right than left (Jacobson 2004).

A more complete view of patterns of individual change in DW-NOMINATE scores is determined by regressing the cumulative change in a member's DW-NOMINATE score on the member's initial score in his or her first Congress, by a trend term, and by count of the number of Congresses in which the member has served. The results show that, with each passing Congress, Democrats have tended to move further to the left of their initial ideological location, and Republicans have tended to move further to the right. Moreover, the longer House members have served, the further they have moved (this variable is unrelated to change among Senators). According to the coefficients, a Democrat who served 20 years in the House during this period would, on average, have moved −0.078 units left on the DW-NOMINATE scale, while a Republican with the same career would have moved 0.085 units to the right.[7] The equivalent estimates for senators are −0.033 and 0.040, respectively.

If members have changed their ideological locations over time, have they merely adapted to a changing electoral environment or have they also responded to endogenous forces (strengthened party leadership, specific electoral events)? To address this question, I estimated a series of regression models designed to clarify the sources of ideological change among members of each party in each chamber. The dependent variable is the member's DW-NOMINATE score in each Congress from the 96th (1979–1980) through the 107th (2001–2002).[8] We can use the results of these regressions and their equivalents from analyses of adjusted ADA scores to estimate the

TABLE 7.1
Summary of ideological polarization since the 96th congress

	DW NOMINATE SCORE		ADJUSTED ADA SCORE	
	House	Senate	House	Senate
Estimated polarization since 96th Congress (1979–1980)[a]	0.351	0.338	30.2	32.0
Estimated polarization with electoral forces controlled[b]	0.182	0.169	10.8	17.4
Percent of polarization not explained by electoral forces	51.9	50.0	35.7	54.4

[a]Estimated from the following equation for House and Senate Democrats and Republicans: ADA or NOMINATE = β_1*Constant + β_2*Trend. For House Democrats $\beta_1 = -0.231(0.01^{**})$, $\beta_2 = -0.011(0.001^{**})$. For House Republicans $\beta_1 = 0.227(0.01^{**})$, $\beta_2 = 0.016(0.001^{**})$. For Senate Democrats $\beta_1 = -0.242(0.019^{**})$, $\beta_2 = -0.011(0.00^{**})$. For Senate Republicans $\beta_1 = 0.187(0.027^{**})$, $\beta_2 = 0.015(0.003^{**})$.

[b]Estimated from the following equation for House and Senate Democrats and Republicans: ADA or NOMINATE = β_1*Constant + β_2*Trend + β_3*Entered + β_4*Departed + β_5*South + β_6*(South × Trend) + β_7*Dem_presidential_vote. For Senate Republicans the equation includes β_8 × Elected_to_House_during_GingrichEra. For House Democrats $\beta_1 = -0.314(0.009^{**})$, $\beta_2 = -0.001(0.001)$, $\beta_3 = 0.007(0.008)$, $\beta_4 = 0.013(0.007)$, $\beta_5 = 0.308(0.017^{**})$, $\beta_6 = -0.019(0.002^{**})$, $\beta_7 = -0.0086(0.0002^{**})$. For House Republicans $\beta_1 = 0.121(0.009^{**})$, $\beta_2 = 0.013(0.001^{**})$. $\beta_3 = 0.051(0.007^{**})$, $\beta_4 = 0.016(0.008^{*})$, $\beta_5 = 0.001(0.007)$, $\beta_6 = 0.138(0.006^{**})$, $\beta_7 = -0.0072(0.0004^{**})$. For Senate Democrats $\beta_1 = -0.320(.018^{**})$, $\beta_2 = -0.005(0.002^{**})$, $\beta_3 = -0.002(0.016)$, $\beta_4 = -0.013(0.016)$, $\beta_5 = 0.302(0.037^{**})$, $\beta_6 = -0.013(0.004^{**})$, $\beta_7 = -0.0096(0.0009^{**})$. For Senate Republicans $\beta_1 = 0.103(0.019^{**})$, $\beta_2 = 0.008(0.002^{**})$, $\beta_3 = 0.024(0.018)$, $\beta_4 = 0.033(0.019)$, $\beta_5 = 0.092(0.015^{**})$, $\beta_6 = 0.227(0.013^{**})$, $\beta_7 = -0.0118(0.0009^{**})$, $\beta_8 = 0.047(0.018^{*})$.

proportion of the polarizing trend that remains to be explained. The full cumulative effect of the trend can be calculated by multiplying the difference between the Republican and Democratic trend coefficients (estimated by regressing the DW NOMINATE and ADA scores on a time trend) by the number of years in the time series (the first row of table 7.1). Repeating this calculation using the trend coefficients from an equation that also controls for dates of entry and exit, the adjusted district-level presidential vote, South, and South multiplied by time provides an estimate of the cumulative effect of changes not explained by these factors (the second row of table 7.1). The third row indicates that from one-third to one-half of the widening ideological gap between the House and Senate parties cannot be explained by selection or adaptation alone.

These results do not prove that events and developments endogenous to Congress contributed directly to partisan polarization, but they certainly leave that possibility wide open. They are fully consistent with Roberts and Smith's (2003a) analysis of sources of changes in House party unity, which attributes the rise in Democratic Party unity in part to "the more aggressive strategies of the late O'Neill and Wright years of the 1980s" and attributes the later rise in Republican Party unity to the Republican members adopting Newt Gingrich's strategy of confrontation for winning control of the House (2003a, 315). Roberts and Smith are justifiably cautious in their discussion of just how the various endogenous factors operated and how they interacted with exogenous electoral forces, and I share their caution. The data at hand do not allow us to untangle the effects of stronger party leadership from particular controversies and events that sharpened partisan divisions. But they do support an account of partisan polarization in which the cumulative impact of events and experiences on the Hill itself played an important part in this historically remarkable transformation of national politics.

A stylized summary would go something like this: Since the 1970s both new and continuing members have experienced galvanizing incidents and broader patterns of conflict that manifestly ratcheted up partisan tensions. In the House, rules changes adopted by the Democratic caucuses in the 1970s strengthened the hand of the party leadership, enhancing the party's capacity to act collectively (Rohde 1991). The more unity the Democratic majority achieved, the easier it was to cut Republicans out of the legislative process. The more they were cut out of the process, the more disgruntled Republicans of all ideological stripes became and the more inclined they were to support the disruptive guerrilla tactics of conservative insurgent Newt Gingrich (Koopman 1996). The more disruptive the Republican minority, the more Democratic leaders resorted to manipulations of the rules to control the agenda and to produce desired outcomes (Deckard [Sinclair] 2000). The more Democratic leaders used rules to thwart Republicans, the more resentful the minority became.

This self-reinforcing spiral continued from the late 1970s until the Republicans finally took control of the House, whereupon their leaders adopted many of the same tactics to stifle Democrats (Deckard [Sinclair] 2000). It was punctuated by specific events that deepened partisan bitterness. In the spring of 1984, for example, Speaker Tip O'Neill, reacting angrily to the Republicans' use of "special orders" (speeches delivered at the end of the legislative day intended for C-SPAN viewers) to attack the patriotism of House Democrats, ordered the TV cameras to pan the empty chamber to show that no one was listening. This violation of House rules led to a shouting match on the floor between O'Neill and Gingrich, described as "the most venomous floor exchange observers had seen in years," after which O'Neill was officially reprimanded for using derogatory language about another member.[9] A year later, a party-line vote in the House to award Indiana's disputed Eighth District to the Democrat sparked a Republican walkout and protest on the steps of the Capitol, during which Republicans sang "We Shall Overcome" and proclaimed a "unanimous declaration of war" against the Democrats (Uslaner 1993, 32). Gingrich managed to drive O'Neill's successor, Speaker Jim Wright, from the House in 1989 on ethics charges; in retaliation, House Democrats mounted ethics charges against Gingrich, leading to an official reprimand in 1997. Finally, of course, the parties faced off in what turned out to be a ferociously partisan battle over Bill Clinton's impeachment in 1998 (Jacobson 2000c).

Polarizing events and developments were not confined to the House. Although the Senate's rules make it more difficult for the majority party to impose its will unilaterally, the Senate, too, experienced increasing tactical maneuvering for partisan advantage. Majority leaders have taken to "filling the amendment tree" to keep minority alternatives off the agenda and to invoking Senate rule 14 to bypass committee and thus maintain maximum control over the content of proposals most important to the party. Senate minorities have increasingly resorted to the filibuster, to the point where it now takes 60 votes to enact any controversial measure except the budget resolution, which cannot be filibustered. In response, majority leaders have resorted to early cloture motions to preempt filibusters and avoid unwanted amendments (Evans and Oleszek 2002).[10]

Specific battles also exacerbated partisan divisions in the Senate. The Democratic Senate's rejection of Supreme Court nominee Robert Bork in 1987, for ideological reasons and largely along party lines, helped set the tone for future struggles over judicial appointments. The Republican Senate majority after 1994 dragged its feet on Clinton's nominees; the Democrats retaliated in kind against George W. Bush's nominees after Jim Jefford's switch gave them control of the Senate in 2001 and continued to filibuster some of them after Republicans retook the Senate in 2002. In 1996 Minority Leader Tom Daschle "held the Democratic minority together behind a series of dilatory floor tactics to stall the Republican legislative agenda, to effectively bring the Senate to a halt, and to force the resignation of Republican presidential candidate Bob Dole as majority leader" (Rae and Campbell 2001, 11).

All of these incidents occurred against a background of the widening partisan division on basic political issues discussed earlier. Conflicts that raised the partisan temperature inside the Beltway were echoed in the wider political world. The effect was most pronounced among political activists, the people who pay the most attention and care the most about what is going on (Jacobson 2000a). Political battles not only mobilized activists but also helped create them in the first place. The abortion issue, for example, brought new people into electoral politics on both sides, inspiring political careers that contributed to the generational changes observed in roll-call ideology. Similarly, Ronald Reagan's opposition to taxes and Newt Gingrich's loathing of the welfare state became orthodoxy among Republican activists and thus among aspiring Republican congressional candidates.

Voters responded to the increasingly distinctive party positions and images by sorting themselves into increasingly coherent and divergent party coalitions. Parties and candidates, meanwhile, adopting positions and projecting images strategically, created and exploited openings in the evolving configurations of popular opinion on issues and leaders in an effort to expand their coalitions. The electoral connection, continually renewed through this interactive process, moved the congressional parties steadily apart. But actions within the House and Senate contributed to the polarizing trend, not only indirectly by shaping electoral politics but also directly by altering the formal and informal political environment within Congress itself.

Chapter 8

One D Is Not Enough: Measuring Conditional Party Government, 1887–2002

JOHN H. ALDRICH, DAVID W. ROHDE, AND MICHAEL W. TOFIAS

Introduction

In this chapter we develop a general, multidimensional extension of the original conditional party government (CPG) measure (Aldrich, Berger, and Rohde 2002) and apply it to the same historical period as the earlier measure. In doing so we also modify the specific measurement techniques employed. Substantively, 1877 to 2002 covers the Democratic-Republican period from the full reentry of white Southern Democrats at the end of Reconstruction through the most recent available date. We hope to show that there is real value in considering partisan politics as basically (or at least often enough) multidimensional, and that doing so yields a measure of CPG that reflects not only the one "big" historical dynamic (giving justification to W. E. B. DuBois' claim that the 20th century indeed was the century of race, at least in partisan congressional politics) but also other important historical aspects of the Congress. We also offer a theoretical exposition of CPG to aid understanding of what the model implies by suggesting that a majority party will "act in ways to empower its leadership" when the conditions are met.

Conditional Party Government

The basic notion underlying CPG begins with the emergence of candidates for a legislative office (whether voluntarily choosing to run purely on their own instigation or being recruited by parties or others), the screening of primaries or conventions that select a single party nominee, and the general election that chooses between the two resulting party nominees.[1] This set of electoral mechanisms, we assume, selects members and induces in them policy preferences that they bring with them to the Congress and that they would choose to reveal in voting and other policy-making actions. These preferences may be shaped by legislators' personal views as well as the consequences flowing from the reelection incentive. Members' behavior, we further assume, may also be shaped to a considerable degree by the legislative party. While parties as electoral institutions likely have the larger impact on behavior, we do assume that the parties may have considerable effect on members' behavior through their partisan legislative institutions. Further, the relative importance of the party as a legislative institution is a consequence of the degree to which the *condition* in CPG is satisfied. By *satisfaction of the condition,* we mean the degree to which the preferences of party members are similar within each party (particularly the majority), and different between the parties. Because the degree of satisfaction is partially due to electoral forces, the electoral party and the internal legislative party are closely related.

Three sets of consequences flow from the increasing degree to which the condition is satisfied. First, the greater the degree to which the condition is met, the more likely that members of a party choose to provide their legislative party institutions and party leadership with stronger powers and with greater resources. Second, the greater the satisfaction of the condition, the more often the party will be expected to employ those powers and resources. Third, legislation should reveal whether the majority party has (by virtue of its being the party that organizes the legislature) more powers and resources to employ than the minority party. In particular, the greater the degree of satisfaction of the condition in CPG, the farther or more frequently the policy outcomes should be skewed from the center of the whole Congress toward the center of opinion in the majority party. This policy consequence can be seen as a tug-of-war between the chamber and the majority party within it, contesting over the pull of the policy center of the legislature and the push toward the center of the majority party.

Historical Variability of CPG

Poole and Rosenthal (1997a) are correct when they argue that most Congresses are able to be estimated in a unidimensional manner since it is a relative handful where the overall fit of the model is greatly improved with the addition of a second dimension in the ideal-point estimation analysis. However, this view becomes problematic if one is interested in studying Congress across time. Longitudinal analysis will typically include at least one period of Congresses when the second dimension matters. Instead of ad hoc fixes to deal with this problem, we develop a single-scored latent measurement of CPG from two-dimensional estimates of ideal points (and develop it for the general, *n*-dimensional data-input case). Our technique allows for a more textured understanding of Congress compared to the previous one-dimensional measurement, one that is more congruent with the inherited explanations of the historical Congress.

The Use of Voting Data and Scaling

SCALING AS DATA REDUCTION

All scaling procedures end up having the (intended) consequence of data reduction. That is, they yield a small number of dimensions, or they end up using fewer parameters to describe a portion of the information originally available. In general, of course, this is a good thing and emphasizes what is common and general over what is unique and idiosyncratic.

One of the key differences between majoritarian and partisan theories of Congress is the way that each deals with the shape of preferences of those members who make up a given session. These differences are not merely theoretic in nature; they each imply that different information be considered when describing a Congress. In fact, the theories each imply a different data-reduction scheme in aggregating from 435 members to a single Congress to study such things such as historical variability. In Krehbiel's majoritarian theory (see Krehbiel 1998), Congress can be described by studying the preferences of the *pivotal members;* the median voter; the two-thirds, or veto-override, voter; and so on. Furthermore, one of the assumptions of Krehbiel's models is unidimensionality of the preference space, potentially making certain questions or eras difficult to study.

Both partisan and ideological models (including most forms of informational models) anticipate that the major space of policy competition will be one of low dimensionality. Indeed, in our case, we believe that the space in which actual partisan policy voting takes place is of low dimensionality precisely because of partisan influence over the agenda. The Cox-McCubbins-Kiewiet account (see Cox and McCubbins, 1993; Kiewiet and McCubbins, 1991), for example, is that the majority party exerts great control over the agenda. While negative agenda control is generally an option for a majority party, when CPG is high, positive agenda control becomes more likely. Cox, McCubbins, and Kiewiet do not develop this particular point, but it seems likely that they would expect a space of low dimensionality for most policy purposes. Our account also anticipates a small-dimensional space over which parties contest (in addition to being at least consistent with a lot of "small" dimensions, akin to distributive policy).

The actual policy fight is over the common partisan reputations as well as what is unique to the particular needs of each member of Congress (MC) seeking to satisfy their district constituency. Thus, while some information is lost when using lower-dimensionality spaces, we will be picking out the areas over which partisan competition is most keen—and over which public dialogue is most intense. It is, however, our contention that important information is lost when reducing the space from two dimensions to one.

The CPG variant of partisan theory implies knowledge of the entire shape of preferences of a Congress. Specifically, CPG uses the heterogeneity of the two parties and the homogeneity of the majority party. CPG theory assumes an n-dimensional preference space. However, one cannot proceed with 435 pieces of information even if members of Congress were to arrive in Washington with their ideal points stamped on their foreheads. As with many other studies of Congress, ours is forced to use ideal points estimated from roll-call data to describe the members of Congress. The question for the measurement of the conditions of CPG becomes how to measure interparty heterogeneity and intraparty homogeneity. This measurement is a theoretically required data reduction from the estimated ideal points.

We proceed in a second-level data reduction, the data reduction of a data reduction. The *CPG* measure is a data reduction of size M members' estimated ideal points to a single *CPG* measure per Congress from a data reduction on a roll-vote matrix of M members by N votes. Both data reductions (our *CPG* measure and the DW-NOMINATE reduction) take advantage of changes (and the lack thereof) over time. Poole and Rosenthal use time to anchor each Congress to a common space; we use time to exploit the commonality of the components of measured *CPG*. This process allows us to assign values to the shape of preferences in a Congress. While the value for a given Congress may mean nothing in absolute terms, when we compare the historical variability of the *CPG* measure we are able to get a better handle on the changing nature of Congress. Furthermore, we have developed a measurement technique that is extensible to n-dimensions. CPG as a theory is not limited to a single dimension or even to two dimensions. Therefore we have extended our measurement theory to be flexible in case researchers someday, for some Congress, recover a third, or more, dimension. It is not clear what happens to majoritarian theory in a multidimensional space.

DATA AND MEASUREMENT

In earlier work Aldrich and Rohde used a mixture of D-NOMINATE and W-NOMINATE ideal-point estimates to develop a number of measures used to analyze the structure of both the House and the Senate (in this chapter, we look only at the analysis of the House for purposes of clarity and exposition). After constructing their four measures of partisan ideal-point structures, they ran a principal-component analysis and found support for the thesis of a single underlying variable. In engaging the two-dimensional Congress, we wed ourselves to the original methodology but consider the four aspects that are changing in the new analysis:

1. We extend the time series used to include the 107th Congress;
2. we use two estimated dimensions, with input data from
3. the DW-NOMINATE procedure; and
4. we develop new component measures to accommodate two-dimensional ideal-point estimates.

The first three changes are straightforward as item 2 is the focus of our current analysis and DW-NOMINATE has supplanted the D-NOMINATE and W-NOMINATE procedures. Item 4 demands some understanding of the original component measures.

To tap different aspects of CPG, four separate measures were developed previously (Aldrich and Rohde 1998; Aldrich et al. 2002; descriptions taken from the 1999 paper): the difference between the location of the Democratic and Republican parties' medians; the ratio of the majority-party to floor standard deviations in ideal points; the extent of overlap between ideal points in the two parties; and the R^2 of the ideal-point location of all M members and their party affiliation.

These measures had to be reconceived to truly account for the two-dimensional nature of the DW-NOMINATE ideal-point estimates. The concept of *median* becomes problematic, as there is not likely to be a median in all directions for the majority party. Similarly, the score based on the standard deviation (SD) was measured as deviation about this same median. Overlap becomes similarly problematic to calculate, as the overlapping area in two dimensions becomes difficult to identify. Perhaps the most puzzling would be the ordinary least squares (OLS) regression used to calculate R^2. To proceed, we faced a research decision on how to incorporate the second dimension. We chose to develop truly two-dimensional measures, as opposed to creating eight separate measures, by merely carrying out on the second dimension what had already been done on the first. The new measures, based on both dimensions of DW-NOMINATE (with the second dimension weighted by 0.3 per Keith Poole's instructions, see http://voteview.com), are as follows:

1. **Interparty heterogeneity** was calculated by finding the Euclidean distance between the intersection of both party medians. For each party the intersection of the two medians in DW-NOMINATE space (*dwnom1, dwnom2*) was identified. The Euclidean distance between the median point of each party was calculated.
2. **Intraparty homogeneity**, a measure of dispersion, was calculated by measuring the spread of the majority party around its median (using the same intersection technique as we previously described for identification). The Euclidean distances are calculated for each MC in the majority party to this median point. We take the median distance to get a measure of *majority spread*, which is used for the factor analysis. For graphical purposes we calculate a measure of intraparty homogeneity by subtracting *majority spread* from 1. (Checking this measure of spread against a similar measure where the central-tendency statistic of distance from the median is the mean distance shows it to be quite similar, and the correlation coefficient between the two measures is around 0.94.)
3. **Party separation** was measured by the percentage of MCs correctly predicted by a discriminate function analysis that is performed with party affiliation as the group variable and has both dimensional scores of DW-NOMINATE used as predictors. As the percentage of MCs correctly predicted increases, overlap decreases, making this really a measure of party separation.
4. **Party-label fitness** was determined by using the (pseudo) R^2 from the discriminate function analysis just described. We interpret a higher R^2 to be associated with a goodness of fit between the party label of an MC and his or her two-dimensional DW-NOMINATE scores.

We discuss the nature of these changes later.

CPG as a Latent Factor

As the earlier papers held, we consider the four component measures to be generated by an underlying latent *CPG* variable. This variable is generated by conditions in the electorate but should be observable in the actions (voting records) of members of Congress since their voting records are used to further their reelection goals. Therefore, we engage in a principal-factor analysis to perform a confirmatory-factor analysis.

Using an eigenvalue of 1 as the standard for accepting a factor, the first factor clearly should be accepted and the second factor discarded as not having the information contained in even one variable. Roughly speaking, the first factor accounts for nearly 90 percent of the variation in the matrix. We regard this as being strongly suggestive of the existence of a single latent factor that can be used to describe our four component measures of the underlying ideal-point structure of the House. The factor loadings on the first two dimensions further support this view.

We find that all four component measures of *CPG* load onto the first factor but do not load onto a second factor, further suggesting the appropriateness of the first factor. Also, each of the four strongly loads on the dimension (rather than it being asymmetrically dominated by one or two variables). Therefore we consider the first component to be our estimate of *CPG*. We think that the ability of the four measures to load onto a common factor suggests that some latent variable drives the components in the predicted directions. Without such a variable, there is no good reason to expect that interparty heterogeneity and intraparty homogeneity would move in similar directions. Second, we are less concerned with the specific values of *CPG*; instead we are concerned with its variation over time. Therefore we present a standardized factor (mean = 0, SD = 1) to facilitate analysis and comprehension of the variation in *CPG* over this time period.

Two-Dimensional CPG

If we examine the estimated *CPG* measure based on two-dimensional distributions of Poole-Rosenthal ideal points, we can see that the *CPG* measure was high in most Congresses from 1877 through about 1910, where by *high* we mean in comparison to other Congresses in this historical period, since these have been normed to have a mean of 0 and a variance of 1 over the full set of Congresses included. The measure appears to have declined around that time to a moderately high level (above the mean, or 0) through the 1920s. While there was fluctuation, the *CPG* level was at a below-average level from the 1930s through about 1970. At that point, it declined sharply until about 1980, and then rose to above-average levels similar to those around 1920 or so in the last four Congresses. When we compare this two-dimensional measure with what arises from using only the first-dimensional estimates of ideal points, we can see that the one-dimensional measure overstates the level of *CPG* around 1980, in comparison to the two-dimensional version, while understating the level of *CPG* around 1960.[2] The single-dimensional measure also overstates the level of *CPG* during the New Deal and World War II eras. It is interesting to note the differences between the two versions of *CPG* scores. They seem to differ in a predictable way, not as normally distributed errors around zero, that is, not being independent and identically distributed. Rather, they seem to form a pattern based on the ebb and flow of partisan strength and how it relates to the effect of the second DW-NOMINATE dimension. We therefore turn first to examine why, in the cross section, the two-dimensional results are more informative. We then return to the time series to provide a second argument about the value of this two-dimensional version, and we conclude with a consideration of the relationship between this measure and well-known historical cases.

Why Two-Dimensional Ideal Points Are Needed

What we hope to show in this section is that in some cases ideal points in two dimensions reveal much more of the nature of the partisan structuring of estimated congressional preferences, that there seem to be two different reasons for this, and finally that there are important, systematic occurrences of these reasons in the historical period under consideration. Consider first the distribution of Poole-Rosenthal estimated ideal points in one and two dimensions for the 107th Congress, a Congress that is relatively high on the *CPG* measure. In this case, one dimension appears to capture the single most important fact, that affiliates of the two parties stand for very different things, and thus, there is very little overlap between the two parties. To be sure, the second dimension reveals a great deal of nuance to this story, and it shows considerable spread within each party (with each party roughly comparable in that spread) on the second dimension, but one can hardly miss the degree of partisan polarization in either version.

Compare those figures to the comparable ones for the 96th Congress, one quite low in *CPG* score. Here, the one-dimensional distribution of ideal points illustrates a great deal of overlap. Looking at the two-dimensional distribution, however, one can see that there is uniqueness to the two parties. Both have their own, nearly non-overlapping clouds of ideal points. Still, in many respects they do overlap on both dimensions. Thus, we would say that the two parties are (still) quite similar and highly dispersed on the second dimension. There is more separation between the two parties on the first dimension, but there is a reasonably high degree of variation within each party and there are conservative Democrats (compared to the most liberal Republicans) on it, and vice versa. The line of division between the two parties appears to be more or less 45 degrees, or more accurately, something clearly between 0 and 90 degrees. Thus, how important polarization versus overlap is depends on how the two dimensions are invoked in any given alternative and whether preferences between the two dimensions are separable or nonseparable.

From the preceding discussion, it appears that we might be interested in the relative balance of the two dimensions in distinguishing between the two parties. The discriminant function analysis used in defining *CPG* provides relevant information. In particular, it estimates coefficients for each dimension in the discriminant analysis. The ratio of, say, the second to the first dimension will vary from 0 to the absolute value of 1. When 0, the second dimension does not contribute at all to the categorization. When 1, its coefficient has the same effect relative to the Poole-Rosenthal scales, whose second dimension is set at 0.3 when the first is set at 1. When the ratio exceeds the absolute value of 1, its effect is larger than the first dimension. Note that this analysis differs from the one comparing the first and second dimensions of the ideal-point estimates themselves. Here the question is, How strongly does each dimension help us distinguish Republicans from Democrats? The answer helps us see whether partisan affiliation is unidimensional (when the ratio is near 0) or whether it requires at least two dimensions to characterize well.

The data are quite clear. For the latter part of the 19th and the early part of the 20th centuries, the second dimension is relatively unimportant, with a ratio of discrimination less than 20 percent that of the first dimension. Beginning in the late 1930s, the ratio climbs smoothly and continuously until it reaches half the size of the first-dimensional effect at the beginning of the 1970s. After persisting at that level for a few Congresses, it begins to decline steadily and smoothly, dropping back in the 107th Congress to approximately the range of values it achieved in the 19th century.

This makes it apparent that what we had described in our earlier paper (Aldrich, Berger, and Rohde 2002) as the civil rights era's impact on the division of the Democratic Party in one dimension is less the failure of the condition in *CPG* to be satisfied as it is to a substantial degree the importance of viewing party affiliation as combining two-dimensional preferences, with the second dimension reaching historical highs in relative importance in distinguishing between the two parties' members. It is this dynamic that made the one-dimensional view so regular in its V-shape decline and return of one-dimensional *CPG*. Correcting for this fact by including the two-dimensional nature of preferences makes the divisions within the Democratic Party less severe than they would be by viewing only a part of apparently relevant preferences. There is a decline in the *CPG* measure in the 1950s and 1960s, but a less severe one. The collapse of the measure of *CPG* therefore was particularly stark only in the late 1970s, especially during the Carter and first couple of years of the Reagan administrations.

Conclusion

One way of summarizing these data is to look at the two-dimensional-based measure of *CPG* over the full time period, overlaid with speakership tenures (see figure 8.1). This helps us observe that this measure of *CPG* does provide a richer and more nuanced account. For example, many of the eras we think of as relative highs in party strength seem to be reflected as relatively high in *CPG* too. Perhaps most notable are the highest scores being concentrated in the czar speakerships (especially the dramatic jump

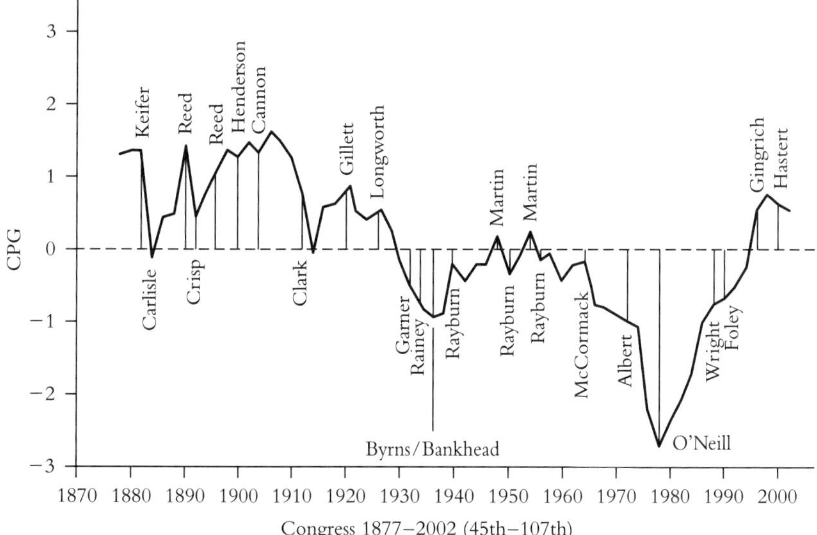

Figure 8.1 Conditional party government in the House, 1877–2002, with changes in the speakership

in the first Reed Congress), the decline and partial resurgence at the revolt in 1910, and then the coming of the short-party caucus era. Thus, unlike the one-dimensional case, the measure based on two dimensions of preferences seems to reflect a *CPG* that appears at least broadly and perhaps quite closely reflective of the usual story about party and division at the turn of the 20th century.

Chapter 9

Who Parties? Floor Voting, District Ideology, and Electoral Margins

BRANDICE CANES-WRONE, JULIA RABINOVICH, AND CRAIG VOLDEN

In this chapter we examine the relationship between electoral safety and legislative voting. We examine the methodological challenges encountered in trying to assess the validity of the marginality hypothesis and personal-vote perspective—theoretical frameworks that link electoral performance and legislative voting. Next, we explore the empirical support for these claims from the 1960s through the 1990s. Finally, we test whether the relationship between electoral safety and legislative voting differs between members from moderate districts and those from conservative Republican or liberal Democratic districts.

To do so, we analyze how a member's electoral safety affects what we call his or her *relative ideological voting extremity*, which reflects the degree to which the member votes more with his or her party than district opinion predicts. In other words, we are looking to capture the difference between a member's district preferences and how that member actually votes on the floor of the House. In conducting this analysis, we account for the potential endogeneity between electoral safety and ideological extremity. In addition, we control for a variety of factors such as challenger quality, committee assignments, and seniority.

The empirical analysis suggests that the relationship between electoral safety and legislative voting has changed over time. In the 1960s and 1970s, the results indicate that higher vote shares resulted in more moderate behavior on the floor of the House. Consistent with the personal-vote account, members developing a personal incumbency advantage appear to have been liberated from voting consistently with the party, allowing moderation toward their districts' preferences. This relationship is stronger in the 1960s than in the 1970s, however, and by the 1980s, the marginality hypothesis receives corroboration. In both the 1980s and the 1990s, larger vote shares are shown to lead to more extreme legislative voting relative to district preferences. Moreover, especially for the 1980s and 1990s, these effects are strongest for members from moderate districts, who face the greatest cross-pressures from parties and constituents. Taken as a whole, this chapter illustrates the evolution of the relationship between electoral margins and voting in Congress over the past four decades.

Theoretical Perspectives

The literature contains two main lines of thought about the relationship between a member's electoral safety and the tendency to vote with his or her party. The first, which is associated with the marginality hypothesis, suggests that safe members are more likely to support their party because they can hope to do so without losing their seat (e.g., Turner 1951; MacRae 1952). The second perspective, which derives from work on the personal vote, indicates that electoral safety may actually decrease a member's propensity to vote with his party because the member is no longer as beholden to party leaders for electoral assistance (e.g., Cain, Ferejohn, and Fiorina 1987). These schools of thought depend on divergent assumptions about the incentives of parties and candidates.

The divergence in the assumptions between the marginality hypothesis and the personal-vote account underscores the possibility that the applicability of the perspectives may vary over the course of American history. In other words, the expected relationship between electoral safety and legislative voting in a given era will depend on one's assumptions about members' incentives. Only if incumbents have policy motivations that are independent of the desire to be reelected and correlated with those of their party does the marginality hypothesis hold. When, instead, incumbents are primarily motivated by reelection and the primary purpose of parties is to aid them in the general election, then electoral safety may decrease a member's tendency to vote with his or her party.

METHODOLOGICAL CHALLENGES

The theory and prior literature present several challenges to testing the marginality hypothesis and personal-vote perspective. We outline four major ones before describing our efforts to resolve them.

First, one must distinguish between party voting aligned with district opinion and party voting that diverges from it. The theoretical foundations of the marginality hypothesis highlight the importance of focusing not simply on party voting but on the potential tension between party and district. The personal-vote account of Cain, Ferejohn, and Fiorina (1987) likewise rests on this tension. Accordingly, empirical investigation of these perspectives must analyze the extent to which a member will vote with his or her party above and beyond what district opinion would predict, not simply the overall likelihood of voting with the party. A few early works recognized this issue (e.g., Kuklinski 1977). Most, however, did not, and as a result, the divergence of findings in the literature may derive at least in part from the tendency to presume that party voting pulled members from representing their district.

Second, one must account for the potential endogeneity between legislative voting and electoral performance. Both the marginality hypothesis and the personal-vote perspective predict that electoral safety affects voting in Congress. Typically, empirical studies have estimated safety or marginality on the basis of previous vote share. However, the literature suggests that vote share is in turn influenced by a member's prior voting and policy positions (e.g., Erikson 1971a; Deckard [Sinclair] 1976; Canes-Wrone, Brady, and Cogan 2002). Simple correlations among such measures can be quite misleading. For example, a negative correlation between vote share and the degree of floor voting with one's party (rather than one's district) could indicate that higher vote shares encourage members to vote against their district, *or* that such party voting harms a member's electoral prospects. Some early studies of the marginality hypothesis recognized this problem (e.g., Deckard [Sinclair] 1976), but no study thus far has attempted to resolve it.

Third, one must be historically sensitive to the possibility that the relationship between floor voting and electoral safety may have changed over time. The theoretical discussion emphasized that any prediction about the relationship between electoral safety and party voting depends on assumptions regarding the motivations of parties and incumbents. The literature indicates that these incentives may have varied over the course of American history because of a variety of factors, such as developments in recruitment efforts. For example, the roles of local party organizations, activists, direct primaries, television, and other phenomena have changed over time (e.g., Swenson 1982; Fiorina 1999). Fiorina suggests that in recent decades candidates have become more likely to arise out of social movements and single-issue organizations, and they are accordingly more likely to be policy-motivated than candidates of earlier eras, who were selected by local party organizations largely on the basis of electability. Assuming he is correct, then we would expect the marginality hypothesis to be more germane in recent decades than in prior eras.

Finally, one must control for factors other than electoral safety that may influence a member's likelihood of voting with his or her party. Several scholars have noted that simple correlations between legislative voting and electoral safety may be misleading because each of these variables may be influenced by yet other factors (e.g., Fiorina 1974; Deckard [Sinclair] 1976). For instance, members' committee assignments may help their electoral prospects by giving them an opportunity to claim credit for legislation pertinent to district interests (e.g., Mayhew 1974a) as well as influence their likelihood of voting with their respective parties (Cox and McCubbins 1993). Controlling for such factors is thus an important component of estimating the direct relationship between legislative voting and electoral safety. In addition, the analysis of such factors contributes to our broader goal of understanding why some incumbents are more likely than others to favor the party over district opinion.

Data

Our dataset includes members of the House of Representatives from the 88th through 106th Congresses (1963–2000) who faced a contested race in their most recent election. We analyzed these data by decade to allow for the possibility that the relationship between electoral safety and party voting has changed over time. This chronological analysis has the advantage of addressing the third methodological issue previously identified, the need to be historically sensitive.

Addressing the first methodological challenge, which was distinguishing party voting that aligns with district preferences from party voting that diverges from them, required constructing a measure of how each member would vote if he or she were concerned only with representing the district. To accomplish this end, we ran an initial regression of each member's Americans for Democratic Action (ADA) score on the vote share that the Democratic candidate for president received in the district in the most recent election as well as a dummy variable for whether the member hailed from a Southern state.[1] The use of presidential vote to capture district ideology follows numerous earlier studies (e.g., Erikson 1971a; Canes-Wrone, Brady, and Cogan 2002) arguing that this variable is the best available measure of voters' ideology at the district level over this time period.[2] We include the South indicator because of the well-known fact that, during much of our time series, Southern Democrats tended to vote in a systematically more conservative fashion than their fellow partisans.

Based on those regression results, we generated predicted district-based ADA values for each member in each Congress. Our main dependent variable, *ADA Voting Extremity Relative to District*, reflects the divergence between these predicted scores and the actual ADA scores. Because Democrats are unlikely to face general election competition from the left and Republicans are unlikely to face competition from the right, we define ideological extremity by conservative voting for Republicans and liberal voting for Democrats. Specifically, for Democrats *ADA Voting Extremity Relative to District* equals the value of the actual ADA score minus the predicted district-based ADA score, while for Republicans the variable equals the district-based ADA score minus the actual ADA score. In each case, a higher value reflects greater ideological extremity than predicted for the district.

The dependent variable has a good degree of variance, with a low value of about −70 ranging up to about +80. The mean is 18.2, providing preliminary evidence that members on average vote at least somewhat more ideologically than we would expect based solely on district preferences.

The independent variables of key interest are those that pertain to the marginality hypothesis and the personal-vote perspective on the relationship between electoral safety and legislative voting. To test the predictions from these schools of thought, we constructed the measure *Vote Share*, which captures the proportion of the two-party vote garnered by the member in his or her most recent election. As highlighted by the above discussion of our second methodological challenge, there is a great deal of potential endogeneity involved with this measure. Not only might electoral safety influence voting, but research indicates that the latter influences the former (e.g., Brady, Canes-Wrone, and Cogan 2000; Canes-Wrone, Brady, and Cogan 2002). To overcome the challenge of disentangling these effects, we use an instrumental variable approach, as described in the next section.

The final methodological challenge identified in the previous section concerns the need to control for factors that may influence a member's voting other than electoral safety. We accordingly include a number of control variables in the empirical analysis. The first of these variables, *Seniority*, reflects the possibility that members' voting is influenced by their legislative life cycle. It could be that members in their first few terms are interested in building up their reputation as being willing to vote with their party. Alternatively, senior members of Congress may be in a better position to vote with their party against their district because they have a long voting record and significant name recognition that they can rely on to secure their reelection.[3] We coded seniority as the number of preceding terms consecutive to the current one that the member has served in the House. We would expect a negative coefficient on this variable if junior members were more likely to vote in a more extreme fashion and a positive coefficient if more senior members were to vote in a more extreme manner than suggested by their districts.

Another reason that a member might vote with his or her party when doing so conflicts with district opinion is that party leaders may have created some sort of reciprocity system. For instance, members who are willing to vote with the party and against their districts may be rewarded with better committee assignments (e.g., Cox and McCubbins 1993), which may help these legislators secure distributive benefits for their districts and enable credit claiming (Mayhew 1974a). These district benefits may then free these members to vote on key liberal-conservative measures in a manner that is somewhat out of step with their districts. To explore this possibility, we created a measure of committee assignments.

Groseclose and Stewart (1998) assign an attractiveness value to every committee based on transfers and the presumption that members will move over time to more attractive committees. For two different eras of their analysis (81st–93rd Congresses and 94th–102nd Congresses), values are assigned for every House committee except Rules, Appropriations, and Ways and Means, when no members transferred off these three prestige committees. Our committee variable reflects the revealed preference for these committees. Specifically, we code *Committee Value* to take a value equal to the Groseclose and Stewart coefficient for the member's best committee assignment in the respective era, with higher values reflecting a better assignment. Outside of the prestige committees, the highest estimated coefficients are 2.85 for Foreign Affairs in the earlier era and 2.28 for Armed Services in the later era. The lowest value is −0.31 for Small Business in the later era. For members of the prestige committees that were not given a coefficient by Groseclose and Stewart, we set the *Committee Value* equal to 5.[4] If members on highly valued committees vote in a manner more extreme than their districts dictate, we would expect positive coefficients on these variables.

Our third control variable, *Challenger Quality*, reflects the possibility that the type of challenger a member has recently defeated may affect legislative voting. As do others in the literature (e.g., Jacobson and Kernell 1983), we define a challenger who previously held an elective office as high quality; the variable is accordingly coded 1 if he or she has and 0 otherwise. If a member has recently defeated a challenger with electoral experience, the member may feel safer than an incumbent who has the same vote share but did not face a challenger with such experience. Thus if the marginality hypothesis is correct, we would expect a positive coefficient on this variable. Alternatively, if the personal-vote account is correct, we would expect members who have recently defeated a high-quality challenger to feel secure enough to moderate their positions away from the party more than would their counterparts who faced low-quality ones.

Beyond these effects we may find a different degree of voting extremity between Democrats and Republicans and between members of the president's party and members of the out party. If Democrats tend to vote in a more extreme fashion than dictated by their districts, relative to Republican extremity, we would see a positive coefficient on *Democrat*, which equals 1 if the member is in the Democratic party and 0 otherwise.[5] Likewise, if members of the president's party tend to be more ideologically extreme, we would expect a positive coefficient on *President's Party Member*, which equals 1 if the member is in the president's party and 0 otherwise.[6]

Specification and Estimation

To account for the potential endogeneity created by our use of *Vote Share* as an explanatory variable, we adopt an instrumental variable approach.[7] Specifically, our regression equations are as follows for each member i in Congress t, with the primary equation of interest listed first. The β and α represent coefficients to be estimated; γ and δ represent a set of district-specific random effects that control for the possibility that certain voting patterns are unique to a district; and ε and ν are error terms.

$$\begin{aligned} \textit{ADA Voting Extremity Relative to District}_{it} &= \beta_0 + \beta_1 \textit{Predicted Vote Share}_{it} \\ &+ \beta_2 \textit{Seniority}_{it} + \beta_3 \textit{Committee Value}_{it} + \beta_4 \textit{Challenger Quality}_{it} \\ &+ \beta_5 \textit{Democrat}_{it} + \beta_6 \textit{President's Party Member}_{it} + \gamma_i + \varepsilon_{it} \end{aligned} \quad \textbf{(9.1)}$$

where *Predicted Vote Share*$_{it}$ is equal to the predicted values from

$$\begin{aligned} \textit{Vote Share}_{it} &= \alpha_0 + \alpha_1 \textit{Midterm}_{it} + \alpha_2 \textit{Midterm}_{it} \times \textit{President's Party Member}_{it} \\ &+ \alpha_3 \textit{President's Party Member}_{it} + \alpha_4 \textit{Seniority}_{it} + \alpha_5 \textit{Committee Value}_{it} \\ &+ \alpha_6 \textit{Challenger Quality}_{it} + \alpha_7 \textit{Democrat}_{it} + \delta_i + \nu_{it} \end{aligned} \quad \textbf{(9.2)}$$

Beyond the independent variables from the primary equation, the secondary equation includes two instruments: *Midterm*, a dummy variable for whether the previous election was a midterm election, and *Midterm* × *President's Party Member*. The *Midterm* variable along with the interaction account for the midterm-loss phenomenon, in which members of the president's party typically lose seats in the midterm election. We would expect this phenomenon to be reflected in a member's vote share but not to otherwise influence the likelihood of voting with the party. The system of equations was estimated using the Generalized Least Squares random-effects command of Stata.[8]

Results

The results of this analysis are shown in equations 9.3–9.6. For purposes of investigating the intertemporal trends, we present the results by decade, beginning after the bulk of the redistricting following each census. Thus the 1960s encompass the 88th through 92nd Congresses (1963–1972), the 1970s the 93rd through 97th Congresses (1973–1982), the 1980s the 98th through 102nd Congresses (1983–1992), and the 1990s the 103rd through 106th Congresses (1993–2000).

$$\begin{aligned}\text{1960s: } & \textit{ADA Voting Extremity Relative to District}_{it} = 139.7(16.4^{**}) \\ & - 177.9(27.7^{**})\textit{Predicted Vote Share}_{it} - 0.087(0.233)\textit{Seniority}_{it} \\ & + 2.24(0.473^{**})\textit{Committee Value}_{it} - 3.54(1.38^{**})\textit{Challenger Quality}_{it} \\ & - 21.0(1.42^{**})\textit{Democrat}_{it} - 6.50(1.05^{**})\textit{President's Party Member}_{it} \\ & + \gamma_i + \varepsilon_{it}\ (N = 1{,}474) \end{aligned} \qquad \textbf{(9.3)}$$

$$\begin{aligned}\text{1970s: } & \textit{ADA Voting Extremity Relative to District}_{it} = 77.0(17.6^{**}) \\ & - 83.4(28.1^{**})\textit{Predicted Vote Share}_{it} - 0.285(0.179)\textit{Seniority}_{it} \\ & + 0.430(0.327)\textit{Committee Value}_{it} + 0.239(1.41)\textit{Challenger Quality}_{it} \\ & + 0.002(1.21)\textit{Democrat}_{it} - 14.8(0.755^{**})\textit{President's Party Member}_{it} \\ & + \gamma_i + \varepsilon_{it}\ (N = 1{,}823) \end{aligned} \qquad \textbf{(9.4)}$$

$$\begin{aligned}\text{1980s: } & \textit{ADA Voting Extremity Relative to District}_{it} = -34.1(21.5) \\ & + 75.1(34.0^{*})\textit{Predicted Vote Share}_{it} - 0.539(213^{**})\textit{Seniority}_{it} \\ & + 0.230(0.427)\textit{Committee Value}_{it} + 2.66(1.43)\textit{Challenger Quality}_{it} \\ & + 14.0(1.24^{**})\textit{Democrat}_{it} + \gamma_i + \varepsilon_{it}\ (N = 1{,}421) \end{aligned} \qquad \textbf{(9.5)}$$

$$\begin{aligned}\text{1990s: } & \textit{ADA Voting Extremity Relative to District}_{it} = -2.53(10.1) \\ & + 55.1(16.1^{**})\textit{Predicted Vote Share}_{it} - 0.553(0.135^{**})\textit{Seniority}_{it} \\ & + 0.715(0.285^{*})\textit{Committee Value}_{it} + 2.61(1.04^{*})\textit{Challenger Quality}_{it} \\ & - 16.4(1.09^{**})\textit{Democrat}_{it} + \gamma_i + \varepsilon_{it}\ (N = 1{,}171) \end{aligned} \qquad \textbf{(9.6)}$$

A notable time trend exists in the relationship between a member's electoral support and legislative voting. In the 1960s and 1970s, increased vote shares were associated with more ideological moderation relative to district preferences. Thus, consistent with the personal-vote account of Cain, Ferejohn, and Fiorina (1987), the development of the personal vote in the 1960s and 1970s appears to have freed members from a need to support their party when doing so conflicts with district preferences. Specifically, in the 1960s, a Democratic incumbent with 50 percent of the two-party vote had an ADA score approximately 33 points higher on the 100-point ADA scale than a fellow partisan from the same district who had recently won with 68.6 percent of the two-party vote (the mean vote share).[9] This effect is highly significant ($p < 0.01$). In the 1970s, the magnitude of the impact is lower but still significant at conventional levels ($p < 0.01$); a Democrat with 50 percent of the two-party vote had an ADA score approximately 16 points more extreme than a Democrat from the same district with a vote share of 68.6 percent.

By the 1980s and 1990s, the effect of higher vote shares had reversed. Indeed, the marginality hypothesis receives strong support in this era. In other words, in recent years higher electoral margins have made members more likely to vote with their party relative to district ideology. In the 1980s a Democrat with 50 percent of the two-party vote had an ADA score about 14 points more moderate than an otherwise similar Democrat (from the same district) who had recently won with 68.6 percent of the two-party vote. The impact in the 1990s is similar; the Democrat with 50 percent of the vote had an ADA score 10 points more moderate than the one with 68.6 percent of the vote.

These results indicate that some of the recent rise in party voting that others have observed (e.g., Cox and McCubbins 1993; Aldrich 1995) may be associated with changes in the electoral environment. Likewise, the findings suggest that, if electoral safety were to increase in the near future owing to exogenous factors such as redistricting, this development would increase party voting. It is worth highlighting, however, that we cannot distinguish between ideological extremity resulting from party pressure and that resulting from members' personal preferences. Thus while our results are consistent with accounts that argue parties have been "strong" within the legislature in recent decades, the results are also consistent with research that suggests recruitment efforts have produced candidates who are stronger partisans.

It is also worth noting that our results are robust when conducting the analysis without any observations of Southern members. Regardless of whether the Southern members are included, the personal-vote account receives support in the 1960s and 1970s and the marginality hypothesis in the 1980s and 1990s. The results without the Southern members are available upon request.

Returning to equations 9.3–9.6, one can see that the effects of the control variables do not present surprises. The effect of seniority on ADA extremism is consistent with the argument that junior members vote more frequently with the party to gain a reputation of loyalty early in their careers. In each decade, the coefficient on seniority is negative and of at least marginal significance beginning in the 1970s. The magnitude of the effect increases across time, indicating that the impact of seniority on legislative voting has increased gradually since the 1960s.

The coefficients regarding committee assignments do not exhibit any clear intertemporal trend but on the whole suggest that valued committee assignments are associated with ideological extremity. These coefficients are all positive and for two of the decades, the 1960s and 1990s, achieve conventional levels of significance. The coefficient for the 1990s indicates that a member whose best assignment is highly valued, like Rules or Ways and Means, votes about four points more extreme than a similar member on the Small Business Committee, relative to what would be predicted by the member's district preferences alone.

Challenger quality is also found to affect legislative voting, and in the manner expected. Recall, we suggested that the impact would be similar to that of increased vote shares; a member who had recently defeated a high-quality challenger would feel safer than an otherwise similar member who had defeated a low-quality challenger. Consistent with this logic, in the 1960s when the personal-vote account received its strongest support, members who had recently defeated a high-quality challenger were more ideologically moderate, relative to their districts, than incumbents who had recently defeated a low-quality challenger. Likewise, during the decades in which the marginality hypothesis receives support, members who had recently defeated a high-quality challenger were more ideologically extreme relative to district preferences than were other members.

The effects of the final controls, which account for differences between the major parties as well as between members of the president's party and out-party members, are not consistent across time. One limitation of these variables is that they are relatively collinear with each other, as well as with majority-party status. (As mentioned in a previous note, we could not include a separate variable for majority-party status due to this collinearity.) Indeed, in the two most recent decades, separate effects could not be estimated for the member's party versus whether he or she was a member of the president's party.[10] Because of these limitations, we do not make much of the effects of these control factors.

Moderates versus Extremists

The predictions of both the marginality hypothesis and the personal-vote perspective are based on the assumption that district preferences and party preferences differ from one another. Absent such an assumption, neither the marginality hypothesis nor the personal-vote perspective has much bite. If a legislator's partisan, personal, and district incentives are all aligned, he or she will clearly vote with these preferences regardless of the margin of electoral victory. We might expect some legislators to be torn to a greater or lesser extent between district and party (or other) pressures on the basis of preferences of the voters back home. Specifically, Democrats from very liberal districts and Republicans from very conservative districts are less often conflicted in voting with the district or the party than are those from moderate districts. Indeed, consistent with the marginality hypothesis, it is the moderates who, when holding a safe seat, would be much more willing to vote with the party than when their seats are at risk. Likewise, members who are liberated from partisan voting through the establishment of a personal vote are more likely to moderate their voting behavior if they come from moderate districts than if they come from those more closely aligned with party interests.

To test whether support for the personal-vote perspective in the 1960s and 1970s (and for the marginality hypothesis thereafter) is due mainly to voting behavior of members from moderate districts, we divide our sample between moderates and extremists and rerun the analyses presented earlier. Specifically, we note that the presidential vote share for the party of a member elected to Congress averaged 55.76 percent between 1962 and 2000. This means that Democrats were, on average, elected from districts that gave the Democratic presidential candidate a vote share of just under 56 percent; and, likewise, Republican members hailed from districts that leaned toward the Republican in the presidential race. More-partisan districts showed even greater support for the congressional member's presidential candidate. And less-partisan (more moderate) districts found less support for the presidential candidate from the same party as the member of Congress. Using this criterion, we labeled the less-partisan-aligned districts "Moderate," and the more-partisan-aligned districts "Extreme." We then reran our instrumental variable models on these two groups of members, pooling the personal-vote era and the marginality era.

Moderates 1960s–1970s: *ADA Voting Extremity Relative to District*$_{it}$
$$= 121.2(19.1^{**}) - 142.4(32.1^{**})\textit{Predicted Vote Share}_{it} - 0.338(0.212)\textit{Seniority}_{it} + 0.929(0.416^{*})\textit{Committee Value}_{it} - 1.24(1.32)\textit{Challenger Quality}_{it} - 8.50(1.3^{**})\textit{Democrat}_{it} - 13.7(0.969^{**})\textit{President's Party Member}_{it} + \gamma_i + \varepsilon_{it}\ (N = 1{,}711) \quad \textbf{(9.7)}$$

Extremists 1960s–1970s: *ADA Voting Extremity Relative to District*$_{it}$
$$= 110.3(21.7^{**}) - 145.4(34.6^{**})\textit{Predicted Vote Share}_{it} + 0.206(0.212)\textit{Seniority}_{it} + 1.49(0.377^{**})\textit{Committee Value}_{it} - 5.65(1.80^{**})\textit{Challenger Quality}_{it} - 10.9(1.62^{**})\textit{Democrat}_{it} - 5.34(1.03^{**})\textit{President's Party Member}_{it} + \gamma_i + \varepsilon_{it}\ (N = 1{,}586) \quad \textbf{(9.8)}$$

Moderates 1980s–1990s: *ADA Voting Extremity Relative to District*$_{it}$
$$= -90.5(38.0^{*}) + 205.7(62.9^{**})\textit{Predicted Vote Share}_{it} - 1.19(0.348^{**})\textit{Seniority}_{it} + 0.979(0.415^{**})\textit{Committee Value}_{it} + 7.97(2.72^{**})\textit{Challenger Quality}_{it} - 7.22(1.94^{**})\textit{Democrat}_{it} - 8.39(2.28^{**})\textit{President's Party Member}_{it} + \gamma_i + \varepsilon_{it}\ (N = 1{,}343) \quad \textbf{(9.9)}$$

Extremists 1980s–1990s: *ADA Voting Extremity Relative to District*$_{it}$
$$= -2.25(14.8) + 39.3(22.0)\textit{Predicted Vote Share}_{it} - 0.624(0.144^{**})\textit{Seniority}_{it} + 0.597(0.271^{*})\textit{Committee Value}_{it} + 3.53(1.44^{*})\textit{Challenger Quality}_{it} - 0.242(1.13)\textit{Democrat}_{it} - 7.36(1.04^{**})\textit{President's Party Member}_{it} + \gamma_i + \varepsilon_{it}\ (N = 1{,}249) \quad \textbf{(9.10)}$$

Equations 9.7–9.10 report the results of these analyses. Once again we find strong support for the personal-vote perspective in the 1960s and 1970s, and for the marginality hypothesis starting in the 1980s, with the control variables taking values consistent with those above. Of greatest interest to us here is whether the main relationship between vote share and legislative ADA voting extremity is related to the placement of the legislative district. The first two columns show no such effect for the 1960s and 1970s. Here, for members from either moderate or extreme districts, an increase in the vote share by 10 percent is associated with a moderation of about 14 points (or 3 of the 20 key ADA votes per year). Although all of the previous results were unchanged upon excluding Southern districts, in this early era excluding the South changes the results dramatically. Specifically, for non-Southern moderate districts, the coefficient on the *Vote Share* variable for the 1960s and 1970s is −189.7, while it is −103.3 for non-Southern extreme districts on the basis of separate regression results available from us. Thus, outside of the South, the personal-vote perspective receives significantly stronger support among members from moderate districts. Given that moderate Democrats held the majority of the Southern seats, and given that most faced few significant general-election threats, it is understandable that their inclusion would weaken the finding of a stronger personal-vote effect in moderate districts outside the South.

For the 1980s and 1990s, there is far stronger evidence that the marginality hypothesis is explained by the actions of members from moderate districts. Specifically, according to the preceding results, a member from a moderate district receiving 50 percent of the two-party vote share will vote nearly 40 points more moderately than would the same member who receives the average 68.6 percent vote share. For a member from a more extreme district, a similar rise in vote share leads to much less moderation—merely 7 points. In sum, consistent with theoretical underpinnings, both the personal-vote perspective in the earlier era and the marginality hypothesis in more recent years appear to be driven significantly by members facing conflicting pressures between their parties and their districts.

Conclusion

Our empirical results indicate that relationships among members, parties, and voters have changed substantially over time. In the 1960s House members appear to have been primarily motivated by reelection and relied on their parties for electoral support. As they acquired a personal vote, they were able to become more moderate than their party and vote with district opinion. By the 1990s, parties played a smaller role in the electoral security of members, who possessed an incumbency advantage based on name recognition, the personal vote, and responsiveness to district preferences. However, our results indicate that these more current members of Congress have cared not only about office holding but also about various policy goals. As their vote margins have increased owing to factors other than their legislative voting, they have moved away from those district positions toward party-aligned ones. These effects are found to be most dramatic for legislators from moderate districts, who are often torn between district and other pressures.

Part II

Internal Changes in Congress

Some of the earliest scholarly literature on changes in congressional structure argued that the increase in workload was the driving force behind congressional change (Polsby 1968; Cooper 1970; Sait 1938; Skladony 1985). The increase in legislative workload, driven by changes in social and economic conditions in the country, led to new legislative structures that facilitated the increasing demand for political action. While this perspective took seriously the role of the external environment, it largely ignored why politicians made their specific decisions. Thus it could not explain why particular institutions were adopted, even if it could provide a general explanation for the necessity of change.

An alternative approach to the study of institutional development in the House has focused on how political actors shape political institutions to meet their needs and preferences (Gamm and Shepsle 1989; Jenkins 1998; Rohde and Shepsle 1987). This approach focuses on the microlevel foundations of change and considers how the demands of political actors lead to changes in congressional structure (Stewart 1989; Binder 1999; Dion and Huber 1997; Dion 1997). These scholars typically look at external conditions as affecting the demands of politicians and then study how those demands are translated into institutional change.

Both the external and the internal approach to congressional change have at their heart the development of new institutions and changes in existing institutions. Accordingly, the chapters in part II seek to place the behavior of politicians into the larger political context in a way that provides useful insights about how the internal structure of Congress changes. Section 1 considers institutional change in the 19th century. Section 2 looks at the Progressive reforms and their effects on Congress. The postwar period is the subject of Section 3. The entire postbellum period is addressed by the chapters in Section 4.

Part II, Section 1: 19th-Century Development of Congress

In "Architect or Tactician? Henry Clay and the Institutional Development of the U.S. House of Representatives," Charles Stewart III offers an analysis of the role that Clay played in congressional history. Stewart concludes that, although some have seen Clay as an institutional architect, it is more accurate to consider him a tactician who worked within the institutional structure to advance his goals.

Chris Den Hartog and Craig Goodman argue in "Committee Composition in the Absence of a Strong Speaker" that, in the antebellum United States, House majority party members who exhibited higher levels of party loyalty were more likely to be appointed to Ways and Means than were less loyal members of the party. However, they find that majority-party members' loyalty does not appear to have been an important determinant of assignment to other top committees, or to committees generally, during this era. Their results are consistent with previous work indicating that congressional parties played important roles in legislative organization in the antebellum period, but that this role was limited compared to the role that they play in the contemporary House.

In "Roll-Call Behavior and Career Advancement: Analyzing Committee Assignments from Reconstruction to the New Deal," Craig Goodman and Timothy P. Nokken analyze partisan differences in party loyalty by examining committee assignments. They find significant differences between the parties' assignment practices: Republicans placed a premium on party loyalty, while the Democrats did not. They conclude that important differences in the constituencies of Democrats and Republicans best explain the different effects.

Jason M. Roberts and Steven S. Smith explore how the majority party came to control the agenda in the House and Senate in "The Evolution of Agenda-Setting Institutions in Congress: Path Dependency in House and Senate Institutional Development." They argue that, although the majority parties in both the House and the Senate have worked to structure debate to their advantage, the avenues for doing so were affected by conditions established in the 19th century. They observe that the presence of a motion for the previous question in the House and the absence of such a motion in the Senate has been responsible for major differences in procedural development between the two houses.

Part II, Section 2: Progressive Era

In "Filibuster Reform in the Senate, 1913–1917," Gregory Koger argues that the Senate's choice of a cloture rule with a two-thirds-majority requirement reflected senators' weak incentives to restrain obstruction and their concerns about presidential and partisan influence.

In another chapter that examines cloture, "Cloture Reform Reconsidered," Gregory J. Wawro and Eric Schickler argue that cloture reform is best thought of as an insurance mechanism for risk-averse legislators who trade off some of the benefits of passing legislation against the probability of its passage. Their analysis of the rule suggests that the cloture rule promoted efficiency in the appropriations process and refutes the contemporary conventional wisdom that cloture was merely a symbolic reform with little impact.

Jamie L. Carson and Jason M. Roberts analyze the incumbency advantage in the late 19th and early 20th centuries in "Candidates, Parties, and the Politics of U.S. House Elections across Time." They find strong evidence of a quality effect in several elections from this era, but they do not find corresponding levels of incumbency success either in presidential or midterm elections.

In "Speaker David Henderson and the Partisan Era of the U.S. House," Charles J. Finocchiaro and David W. Rohde argue that the role Speaker Henderson played is central to models of conditional party government (CPG), which argue that high party homogeneity (present during Speaker Henderson's tenure) is related to strong party leadership. Finocchiaro and Rohde find that although Speaker Henderson has not claimed a central position in our stories of House leadership the evidence indicates that, as expected by CPG theory, his actions were largely partisan in nature, even if he was more personable in his pursuit of the strategy than were other well-known speakers of the same time.

Part II, Section 3: Postwar Period

Donald R. Wolfensberger traces the various changes related to one of the House's central rules in "The Motion to Recommit in the House: The Creation, Evisceration, and Restoration of a Minority Right." He concludes that the changes to and usage of the motion to recommit are conditioned by the power relationships between the majority and minority parties.

In "The Motion to Recommit in the U.S. House of Representatives," Gary W. Cox, Chris Den Hartog, and Mathew D. McCubbins argue that House rules and practice constrain the use of recommittal motions to a far greater extent than has been recognized. Using data on recommittal motions and other legislative behavior, they provide evidence that casts doubt on claims that the minority party gains substantial policy influence via the motion to recommit.

In "The Motion to Recommit: More Than an Amendment?" D. Roderick Kiewiet and Kevin Roust trace historical changes in the motion to recommit to discover whether offering an amendatory motion to recommit (AMR) is more valuable to the minority party than offering an amendment in the Committee of the Whole. The data indicate that the minority party rarely uses its right to offer motions to recommit. Ultimately, they cannot reject the null hypothesis that AMRs and ordinary amendments are of equal value.

In "An Evolving End Game: Partisan Collusion in Conference Committees, 1953–2003," Robert Parks Van Houweling argues that conference committees are used strategically by the Senate majority to advance policy goals. He finds that bicameral majorities use conference proceedings to enable majority senators to enact extreme policies that they could not vote for on the open floor.

Part II, Section 4: Postbellum Trends

Elizabeth Rybicki explores "Unresolved Differences: Bicameral Negotiations in Congress, 1863–2002" and argues that the House and Senate have adopted flexible negotiation rules to encourage agreement rather than stalemate. Furthermore, the necessity of bicameral negotiation affects the actors' decisions about how to invest their legislative time and constrains the policies that the House and Senate can pursue independently.

Timothy Nokken uses the natural experiment afforded by lame-duck sessions that took place before the 20th Amendment to study how constituency and electoral forces influence the activities of members of Congress.

The lame-duck session provides an environment to study how the removal of constituency constraints influences the voting behavior not just of those who depart voluntarily but also those who lost their reelection bids. He finds that departing members of Congress exhibit significant ideological changes in their roll-call behavior in addition to the expected increased abstention. He also finds find that returning members increase their participation rates in lame-duck sessions.

Chapter 10

Architect or Tactician? Henry Clay and the Institutional Development of the U.S. House of Representatives

CHARLES STEWART III

Introduction

Henry Clay is widely regarded to be the most significant personality in the antebellum House of Representatives. He is the only pre–Civil War Speaker to be subjected to major biographies, and the *only* Speaker whom each generation of American historians feels compelled to reexamine (Schurz 1898; Clay 1910; Mayo 1937; Van Deuzen 1937; Eaton 1957; Peterson 1987; Remini 1991). To students of congressional history, Clay is most importantly remembered for transforming the office of Speaker into a partisan one. Mary Parker Follett wrote,

> As a presiding officer Clay from the first showed that he considered himself not the umpire, but the leader of the House: his object was clearly and expressly to govern the House as far as possible. In this he succeeded to an extent never before or since equalled by a Speaker of the House of Representatives. Clay was the boldest of Speakers. He made no attempt to disguise the fact that he was a political officer. (Follett 1896, 71–72)

The primary theme that emerges in scholarship about Clay's House experience is his role as an institutional innovator and tactician. No doubt betraying their professional proclivities, political scientists have tended to emphasize his institutional innovations, while historians have tended to emphasize his tactics. The earliest appreciation for Clay's role as an institutional innovator came from Harlow (1917, 199–219). Binder's research systematically confirms Harlow's characterization of Clay, by demonstrating convincingly that the adoption of the previous-question motion by the House in 1811 was a Clay-led effort at "choosing war and choosing rules" (Binder 1997, 58–60).

Another institutional stream flowing within political science has focused more specifically on committee development than on rules of debate and floor procedure. Gamm and Shepsle (1989) argued that Clay's desire to keep together his fragile War Hawk coalition after the War of 1812 prompted Clay to innovate in the use of standing committees as a tool for keeping his coalition together. This argument is amplified by Jenkins (1998), who maintains that Clay's manipulation of the House committee system in the early 1820s was a result of his vying for advantage in the upcoming presidential election of 1824. Strahan et al. (1998, 2000) argue for a more complex understanding of Clay's committee-appointment strategies, but they nonetheless consider the committees the primary source of Clay's strategic maneuvering once the war was over.

Of Clay as a skilled legislative tactician, many stories abound. Some of Clay's tactics amount to an implementation of grand strategy. The best-known case of Clay as a grand strategist concerns his leading the House to declare war on England in 1812. Getting the House to this point of declaring war necessitated his stacking the committee system with War Hawk supporters, buying off pivotal old-line Republicans (like former Speaker Nathaniel Macon) with attractive committee assignments, and then commanding the House floor so that the renegade John Randolph could not filibuster the Clay-stacked legislative process from doing its will (Remini 1991, 78–80; Fritz 1977, 5:25–42).

It is indisputable that Clay was *the* legislative personality in the antebellum House of Representatives. Yet an important question remains about how best to partition this dominance between his skills as a *legislative tactician* and his skills as an *institutional architect.* In making this distinction between Clay as tactician and as architect, I am distinguishing between two general lines of attack that a leader such as Clay can use to achieve his goals. Basically, he could take the rules as given, using them to his advantage by creative manipulation (tactician), or he could change the rules, not only allowing short-term political victory but also helping to perpetuate those victories (architect). As tactician, he had a range of options at his disposal, such as "stacking" committees to his liking and using the Speaker's right of recognition to control the direction of floor action. As architect, his range of options was more limited, involving essentially the formal amendment of the House's rules.

The rest of this chapter provides a glimpse into how one would approach the role of Henry Clay in the House's early institutional development by focusing on three well-known episodes in Clay's House career—first, the declaration of war against England in 1812; second, the transformation of the House committee system from select- to standing-committee dominated; and third, the passage of the first and second Missouri Compromises in 1820 and 1821. Preceding these cases, I examine the empirical difficulties that are inherent when political scientists take on such a task.

Henry Clay and the Problem of Evidence

Even if students of Congress do not know from firsthand experience how difficult it is to assemble evidence when researching political history, they can probably intuit that the chasm of time separating 2006 from 1812 is vast and that the instruments available to bridge the gap are crude. Doing modern research is hard, too. Equivalent historical research is just harder. For every modern social science technique, there is an unsatisfactory historical analogue. Moderns can rely on interviews; historians rely on diaries and letters. Modern congressional students readily peruse newspapers (*New York Times*, *Washington Post*, etc.) and specialized publications (*CQ Weekly Report*, *Roll Call*, etc.). Historians can use newspapers and specialized publications (*Nile's Weekly Register*), too, but access to them is limited and indexing is even worse. The business of the modern Congress is recorded verbatim (plus or minus some redaction) in the *Congressional Record* and televised via C-SPAN. The earlier Congress was also reported, though not verbatim and not always by congressional-employed reporters.[1] Once a session is completed, original documents and records are available for research at the National Archives. Older records are available, too, but much more sketchily (see National Archives 1987a and 1987b). The class of evidence that is most comparable across time is the roll-call record, which has been put to creative use by scholars such as Poole and Rosenthal (1997a). Even here the evidence is shakier in past years, due to the paucity of roll-call votes, particularly at the amendment stage, before the onset of recorded teller votes in Committee of the Whole in 1973.

Moving back in time, it grows increasingly difficult to acquire high-quality and reliable evidence about congressional behavior *in general*, since the general sources such as newspapers and congressional records grow spotty, even when well-preserved. Evidence about *individual* legislators does not monotonically grow worse, however, since significant effort has gone into preserving the records of prominent individuals who participated in formative historical moments. Thus, acquiring evidence about the activities of the most prominent legislators, such as Henry Clay, John C. Calhoun, and Daniel Webster, is orders of magnitude easier than acquiring the same evidence about an average House member in the 1810s and 1820s.

Still all is not rosy, however. In the particular case of Henry Clay, for instance, the primary documentary evidence is uneven. The historiography of Clay was not created with the institutional development of the House high on the priority list. Students of American history are mostly interested in Clay for two reasons. First, he was the Speaker who led the nation into the War of 1812. Second, later in his life he was one of the nation's most prominent politicians. Clay was the Harold Stassen of antebellum America. He was also a pivotal player in the stories of regional crisis until his death in 1852. He was, after all, one-third of the Great Triumvirate, along with Daniel Webster and John C. Calhoun, who so dominated American politics for half a century.

Unfortunately, students of American history have been much more interested in Clay for the latter part of his official life than the early part. Of his speakership, scholars tend to be much more interested in the strategic maneuvers of the War Hawks or in the blow-by-blow unfolding of the Missouri crisis than in the nitty-gritty work of how Clay might have behaved as an institutional innovator. Clay's first serious biographer, Carl Schurz, spent 122 of his 797 pages on Clay's speakership, focusing almost exclusively on Clay's contribution to the War of 1812 and to the Missouri Compromise. Remini's 800-page biography of Clay spends only 83 pages on his speakership, attending to more of Clay's foreign policy interests and his designs on the presidency. Peterson's (1987) collective biography *Great Triumvirate* contains even less about Clay's speakership: 6 pages. All of these histories are primarily interested in painting a portrait of Clay the tactician, not Clay the architect.

Lest we blame historians for overlooking obvious material about Clay's institutional engineering, it is important to note that this imbalance starts with Clay himself. Of the 10,000 pages contained in the *Papers of Henry Clay*, only about 1,500 cover the period when he was Speaker. Most of that material pertains to his personal affairs, not his official duties. Virtually all of the material that addresses his official acts was culled from published sources, particularly the *National Intelligencer*, so there are few fresh insights to be gleaned about Clay's speakership from Clay's private correspondence.[2]

Scholars trying to assess the role of Clay in either transforming or manipulating the House as an institution have to contend with the historical inheritance from Clay's biographers. Looking for a strong political figure on which to focus the story of the War of 1812, 19th-century historians lionized Clay for his decisiveness and cunning, particularly in light of the reluctant and indecisive James Madison. However, a major problem with telling a convincing story of Clay's decisive legislative hand during the war is that he left no clear fingerprints on the institution. This is the "no smoking gun problem" that Gamm and Shepsle (1989) refer to in constructing their interpretation of Clay's role in the development of the House committee system. Neither newspaper accounts (such as *Niles' Register* or the *National Intelligencer*) nor Clay's papers comment directly on his personal role in either developing the standing-committee system or in manipulating the committees, or about his direct role in reforming the rules of floor debate. Even reporters in the House chamber were so lax in recording Clay's speeches for posterity that Remini (1991) had to reconstruct indirectly several of Clay's most important speeches on the House floor by using Clay's *opponents'* responses to Clay.

We are sometimes left with the papers and remarks of Clay's contemporaries to gain insights into his actions and motivations. Here we have to proceed with extreme caution. For instance, the best-informed and most prolific contemporary diarist was John Quincy Adams who, while clearly respecting Clay's abilities, held him in personal contempt.

If we are to understand the significance of Clay's House activities from the perspective of contemporary political science, we need (1) a theoretical framework that allows us to put broad historical claims about Clay's behavior into some sort of tractable system (so that we might generate hypotheses, null and maintained) and (2) strategies of measuring the variables we need to test these hypotheses. In the following three sections, I will suggest how Clay's behavior, as specified by traditional historians, can be cast in contemporary political science terms. In each of those cases, it will be necessary to characterize carefully Clay's preferences, the preferences of those around him (inside and outside the House), and the policy instruments he was attempting to manipulate. That is because all claims about Clay's legislative and institutional prowess can be reduced to claims that he was able to affect the quality of the policies chosen. Thus, we need some way of characterizing a counterfactual—what would have happened had Clay not acted?—and of characterizing how Clay intended to perturb policy away from this counterfactual.

Coming up with good quantitative measures of Clay's goals and behavior as Speaker is particularly vexing, for two reasons. The first is because Clay was House Speaker virtually nonstop from the moment he walked into the House chamber in 1811 until he left for the last time in 1825. Except for the second session of the 16th Congress, when he was a (mostly absent) rank-and-file member, Clay almost never took the opportunity to vote on the floor. The one exception was the fateful 12th Congress, where Clay voted 12 times (out of a total of 314 roll calls). He voted only once in each of the 14th, 15th, and 17th Congresses and never cast a recorded vote in the 13th (ICPSR Study 0004). There is consequently no reliable roll-call record with which to anchor more qualitative descriptions of Clay's goals and behaviors while he was a House member.

Historians have been diligent about identifying the issues Clay cared about throughout his career. During the House years, those issues included war with England (of course), support for internal improvements and a protective tariff (the embodiment of Clay's "American System"), moderate opposition to slavery restrictions, and support for American recognition of newly liberated Latin America.

Historical research into Clay's political endeavors has been useful to political scientists in placing Clay's behavior in broad political context. Beyond that, though, the standard biographies are not particularly useful for shining light where most political scientists are interested in looking. The first scholar to pick up on this was James Sterling Young (1966), who noted that, although Clay held an iron grip on the Speaker's chair, he had a terrible batting average getting the House to do his bidding once the war was under way. Even more embarrassing is the fact that Clay could not translate the virtually unanimous margins by which he was elected Speaker into a simple majority of votes for president when the election of 1824 was thrown into the House of Representatives, over which he presided.

Why was Clay so unsuccessful? Was it because, as Young speculated, Clay distributed committee assignments to members of too many boardinghouse groups? Or was it something else? Absent an equally rich analysis of the political stances and skills of the other 708 House members Clay served along with, assessing the significance of Clay's poor legislative track record after 1813 and placing it alongside the heady days of the 12th Congress is virtually impossible.

Research by Strahan and collaborators has revisited Young's dismissal of Clay as an effective party leader after 1812 (Strahan 1994; Strahan et al. 1998, 2000). Using the accumulated historical record, they have reconstructed

Clay's policy positions on important issues of the day, mapping those positions onto roll-call votes, so that they can create Clay-support scores for the rank-and-file House members he led. On the basis of this technique they discover that Clay was able to exercise strategic leadership on a limited range of issues, notably the tariff. On issues where he just could not prevail, he allocated committee resources simply to maintain his procedural majority.

Strahan's research is an important step forward in more rigorously assessing the independent contribution of Clay to House decision making during his speakership. But because Clay took so few positions on contemporary political questions, compared to the total roll-call record he presided over, these Clay-support scores must be particularly noisy. It would be preferable to map Strahan's analysis onto more robust measures of House member preferences, such as D-NOMINATE or Heckman-Snyder linear factor scores (Poole and Rosenthal 1997a; Heckman and Snyder 1997). There we run into a new problem, however.

In addition to the fact that we cannot directly calculate D-NOMINATE scores for Clay during most of his House service, due to a lack of roll-call votes, Clay's House tenure also perfectly coincides with the most "spatially chaotic" period of American history. Before the 15th Congress, the House and Senate can be easily arrayed along a single dimension, mostly on account of attitudes toward belligerents in the Napoleonic conflicts (see Poole and Rosenthal 1997a, chapter 3). After the 18th Congress, a left-right structuring reemerges, now based mostly on attitudes toward federal government activism in the economy. In the interim, the best-fitting scalings still do not predict roll-call votes very well. For these Congresses of the transitional era—the 16th, 17th, and 18th Congresses—the primary political cleavage was regional, reflecting the animosity stirred up by the Missouri controversy.

Furthermore, while the research of Poole and Rosenthal reveals that legislators tend to have stable preferences throughout their careers, the major exception is the Clay era, at least as far as methods like NOMINATE are concerned. An examination of graphs of estimated ideal points from consecutive Congresses during this period reveals that the space was rotating, with representatives who had previously favored internal improvements and government activism (the primary issue structuring the second dimension) moving rightward year to year, and those who had previously opposed governmental activism in this realm moving leftward (see Jenkins and Stewart 2002).

This rotation of the space is demonstrated by examining D-NOMINATE scores for a select few House members—those who had House service *both* before the 13th Congress and after the 25th.[3] Erstwhile Republicans who later became Whigs (such as Clay) were a diverse lot before the 13th Congress, spanning the entire ideological spectrum. Following the 25th Congress, those same House members were somewhat more to the right, but more importantly, they had become ideologically cohesive. Republicans who later emerged as Democrats shifted a bit to the left, while old-line Federalists who eventually took on the Whig moniker moved even further (and more cohesively) to the right.

Can we place Clay more precisely within this pattern of ideological migration? The qualitative historical record is consistent with the notion that Clay, himself, migrated across the ideological map during this period. He started off as an orthodox small-government Jeffersonian, in the bosom raised, and ended his life as the best-known antebellum Hamiltonian except, of course, for Hamilton.[4] The sketchy D-NOMINATE record we have is also consistent with this movement. Clay's late-career House spatial location is in the middle of the ideological space. By the time he had acquired a Senate roll-call record in the 22nd Congress, he had clearly taken up residence on the right.

It might be possible to fill in this measure of Clay's ideological positioning through a deft combination of historical analysis and quantitative research. For instance, support for declaring war against England is almost perfectly predicted by first-dimensional D-NOMINATE scores in the 12th Congress. Thus, it would be safe to place Clay somewhere in the far left of the issue space for that Congress. Regression of Strahan's Clay-support scores on the first two dimensions of the D-NOMINATE scores reveals that in the interim Congresses Clay's strongest supporters tended to be in the northwest quadrant of the ideological space, which is what we would expect if Clay were traversing the space from left to right.

Thus, surveying both qualitative and quantitative data, the best we can say about Henry Clay is that he was an ideological moving target for all of his House career. That makes drawing general conclusions about Clay's behavior during these years dicey. Nonetheless, it may be possible to inquire into Clay's motives and behavior at particular times in congressional history. In the following sections I turn my attention to the integration of qualitative and quantitative data about Clay, his followers, and the policy environment at important moments in Clay's House career in an attempt to build a general conclusion about Clay's legacy from the ground up.

Clay and the War Hawks

Scholars trying to assess the role that Clay himself played in bringing the nation to war against England face the same problems that any scholars face in assessing the independent role of great men in times of crisis. Crises tend to focus the attention of scholars on the principal dramatis personae. The danger of this type of selective attention, of course, is that it may blind us to the pursuit of similar strategies by leaders in less crisis-filled times. In the case of Clay, for instance, his attention to using the House rules to pursue his policy ends has been regarded as precedent-setting by his biographers. Yet Clay was not the first avowedly partisan Speaker. Theodore Sedgwick Sr. (6th Congress, 1799–1801) claims that prize, for his attempts to use the Speaker's prerogatives to serve majoritarian ends. Follett notes that Sedgwick "made many enemies by decided and even partisan acts. . . . So great was the feeling against him that the customary vote of thanks at the end of Congress recorded the names only of his party associates" (Follett 1896, 67–68).

What were Clay's parliamentary tactics as Speaker in the 12th Congress? Which were architectural? Which tactical? What were their effects? Harlow (1917, 219) claimed that "the man who made the speakership was concerned primarily with improvements in the methods of transacting business, and it is in this field that Clay made his great contributions." Binder (1997), through her quantitative study of minority procedural rights in the House, has confirmed Harlow's claims about Clay's attentiveness to expediting the House's business.

The best measures of legislative pace that we can construct confirm Harlow's and Binder's conclusions. I say the "best" we can construct because it is impossible to reconstruct Committee of the Whole proceedings in the House—where most legislative work was actually done—with any accuracy in the 12th Congress. We are left, therefore, with the records of the formal House proceedings, about which there are no reliable, contemporaneous verbatim accounts. However, one indirect measure of legislative delay is simply the number of recorded roll-call votes on the floor, both the number in general and the number associated with parliamentary maneuvers. To test whether Clay was successful in putting down dilatory tactics in the 12th Congress, I examine both the total number of roll-call votes in the House and the fraction of roll calls that were held on the question of adjourning the House.

The total number of roll-call votes had been increasing secularly from the 1st Congress, until free-falling in the 12th. Adjournment roll calls had been rare until the 11th Congress, when it became a motion frequently made by

Federalists to bottle up consideration of measures intended to show contempt or resolve toward England. Such roll-call votes again became relatively infrequent in the 12th Congress. Both time series began to march upward following Clay's departure from the House, reaching record levels once regional animosities began to boil again toward midcentury.

The other tactic Clay reportedly employed to his advantage as Speaker was the manipulation of the House committee system. One manifestation of this manipulation was his stacking of House committees with War Hawks in the 12th Congress, which I will examine here. The other manifestation, his willingness to expand the range of the standing-committee system to bolster his political support, will be examined in the next section.

Remini (1991, 80) writes that, upon ascending to the Speaker's chair,

> In a bold and determined move he started off by assigning all the War Hawks to the important committees, and he saw to it that they held control of each one. Peter B. Porter, a House veteran of two years, was named to head the Committee on Foreign Relations. Clay also assigned Calhoun, Harper, Joseph Desha, and Grundy to that committee.

In documenting Clay's stacking of the Foreign Affairs Committee, most historians rely on an identification of War Hawks—Clay's anti-English ideological cadre—that is based on John Randolph's attack on pro-war Republicans. Since Randolph was by far the most outrageous member of the small band of "quids" who clung to the most conservative principles of Jeffersonianism, one should take with a grain of salt Randolph's attempts at ideological scaling (Cunningham 1963; Carson 1986). Furthermore, upon surveying the historical literature, it appears that identification of the War Hawks is largely inferred from the institutional position of people like Porter, Harper, and Desha, making the whole business of assessing Clay's behavior prone to tautology.[5] Because Clay was such a skilled parliamentary manipulator, he certainly would not appoint people to the critical Foreign Affairs Committee who were not ideological soul mates! Hence if Porter, for example, was appointed to *chair* this committee, he certainly must have been in the pocket of Clay. Conversely, anyone who did not bear the stigmata of being a War Hawk—principally, being a freshman from the West or South—must not have been an ideological true believer and therefore does not count as evidence of Clay's stacking of Foreign Affairs.

Fortunately, social scientists have made tremendous strides over the past decade, empirically and theoretically, in developing ways to assess whether committees are stacked in nonmajoritarian ways. Taking a cue from Krehbiel's (1991, 1993) critique of the outlier view of congressional committees, a committee should be called *stacked* only if it is actually composed of members who have atypical preferences with respect to the whole chamber. Relying on the empirical work of Poole and Rosenthal (1997a) and their D-NOMINATE scores, we have one objective measure of the underlying preferences of House members in the 12th Congress. Was Clay's Foreign Affairs Committee composed of outlying fire-breathers?

Yes and no. I begin to demonstrate this point using the first-dimensional Poole-Rosenthal scores, comparing the distribution of ideal points among committee members with that of the whole House.[6] Using these scores, we see that Clay appointed a majority of Foreign Affairs Committee members from among the anti-English side of the Republican party. Note that three committee Republicans are virtually on top of each other in figure 10.1. These three members constituted the median of the committee. They occupied a position close to the most anti-English quartile of the Republican party. Thus, it is fair to say that the Foreign Affairs Committee, which bore the responsibility of reporting most of the legislation leading up to the war, was more anti-English than even the majority of Republicans.

Clay's tactic of stacking the Foreign Affairs Committee with anti-English House members is put into context if we widen our focus a bit, peering back to the 11th Congress, when belligerent rhetoric was heating up, and comparing House behavior with the Senate—which is where Clay had first observed deadlock over relations with England. I do this by examining D-NOMINATE scores in the two chambers for the 11th and 12th Congresses—both the scores of the chambers themselves and the scores of the two chambers' committees on Foreign Affairs.[7]

The D-NOMINATE technique makes it impossible to compare scores across chambers, but it is possible to compare the movement of scores within each chamber across Congresses. Note that the elections of 1810 and 1811 changed the ideological compositions of both chambers only slightly from the 11th to 12th Congresses: the Senate became a little bit less anti-English and the House became a little more anti-English. Therefore, it is inaccurate to conclude that the movement to war in 1812 was due to a sea change in the ideological compositions of the two houses.

The ideological composition of the Senate Foreign Affairs Committee that was appointed in the second session (no single committee was appointed in the first session to consider foreign affairs) had a much more pro-English cast than the Senate as a whole. While the composition of the committee moved against England in the third session, this much smaller committee was at most representative of the Senate on only the most pressing foreign policy questions. On convening in the 12th Congress, with the War Hawks

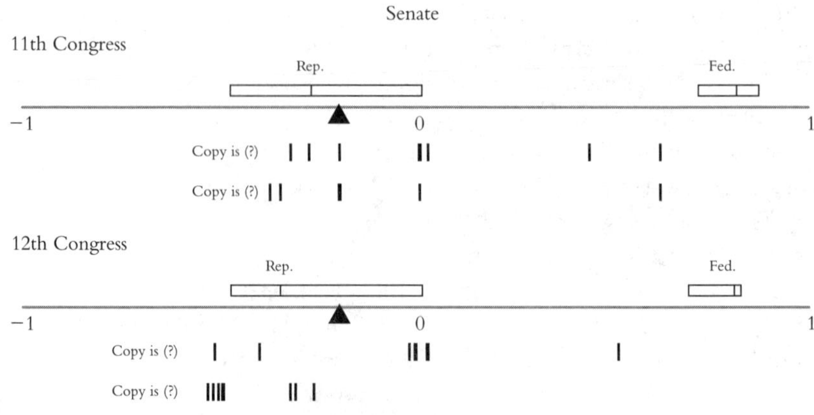

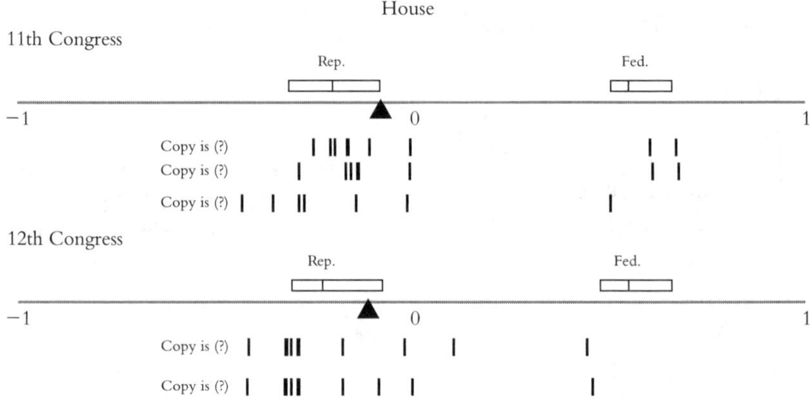

Figure 10.1 Comparison of ideological (D-NOMINATE) locations of House and Senate members of foreign affairs committees, 11th and 12th Congresses

in the House agitating for war, the Senate appointed a select committee on relations with England and France that was considerably more amenable to conciliation with England than even the Senate chamber as a whole. It was to *this* committee that most of the House-passed war measures were referred and, not surprisingly, it was in this committee that so many measures languished, including the ultimate declaration of war. Once war had been declared, in the second session the Senate appointed a staunchly anti-English committee to oversee the war's conduct.

Unlike the Senate, the House Foreign Affairs Committee was more anti-English than the whole chamber throughout the 11th Congress. Indeed, *in the third session Speaker Varnum appointed a select committee that was just as anti-English as the one Speaker Clay appointed in the first session of the 12th Congress.* Hence, the stacking of the House Foreign Affairs Committee was not a War Hawk innovation but a strategy that had been tried in the previous Congress.

The strong anti-English cast of the House Foreign Affairs Committee in the 12th Congress is only part of the story about Clay's construction of that committee. Even though he appointed a comfortable anti-English majority to the Foreign Affairs Committee, Clay also appointed two Republicans who did not share their copartisans' revulsion toward England, along with one Federalist who was outright pro-English.

The two outlier Republicans are particularly noteworthy: The first was John Randolph, easily the most hated Republican to the fire-breathers, who eventually led the effort to apply the brakes in declaring war on England. The second was Peter Porter, the chair of the committee, who is often identified by historians as a fire-breathing War Hawk, by virtue of his formal position. Porter was in fact one of the *least* loyal Republicans on issues of foreign policy during the 12th Congress, dutifully voting to declare war on England but opposing the fire-breathers on other matters (see Hatzenbuehler 1972, 377; 1976, 6). Porter's ambivalence about a war with England was honestly acquired: He had begun his political life as a Federalist and represented a district with Federalist leanings. Porter's support for war against England elicited strong reactions from his constituents. Feeling the political heat, he declined to run for reelection and instead entered the military service during the War of 1812. Porter's successors in the House from his upstate New York district, Samuel Hopkins and Nathaniel Howell, were both Federalists.[8]

With a more accurate understanding of Porter's ambivalence about declaring war on England, Clay's political genius may even be clarified. In addition to providing the Foreign Affairs Committee with a strong anti-English majority, Clay also used the leadership of this important committee to reach out to more moderate members of his party, in an attempt to assemble a coalition in favor of his hard-line agenda. The final vote in favor of declaring war illustrates the success of Clay's tactic.

One of the things that this analysis makes clear is that histories of Clay's activities in moving the country toward war in 1812 have failed to appreciate the opposition that Clay faced *from the Senate.* The Senate, like the House, contained a clear anti-English majority in both the 11th and 12th Congresses. Unlike the House, the Senate had weaker mechanisms to convert policy majorities into policy. It lacked a motion to cut off debate, as did the House. But Clay's first procedural move as Speaker was to change the House's rules to add the motion for the previous question. Likewise, the Senate's rules at that time provided for the appointment of committees by ballot. Balloting for committee allowed cohesive minorities to do better in setting the composition of committees than if the majority party strictly controlled the appointment of committees. Clay did not have to change the rules to be able to construct a clear anti-English majority on the House's Foreign Affairs Committee. Of course, neither did his predecessor, Speaker Varnum, who employed a similar committee-packing strategy himself.

Taken as a whole, then, Clay's activities as Speaker were aimed at reducing delay as much as possible, rather than at manipulating agenda-setting mechanisms to coerce a reluctant House into a war it did not want. In his activities in changing the House rules, he was an architect, insofar as he was the champion of the rule that most distinguishes the House from the Senate—the motion for the previous question. In his activities in stacking the Foreign Relations Committee, he was a tactician, following the lead of Speakers before him who had also crafted committees to their liking.

Clay and the Committee System

Recent scholarship about the development of the standing-committee system in the early 19th century has taken it as axiomatic that Henry Clay was the political figure around whom the committee system's transformation revolved. This plausible assumption arises because of Clay's leadership of the War Hawks. If there were only 9 standing committees in the House when Clay arrived in 1811 and 24 when he finally left in 1825, he must have been the principal champion not only of using standing committees but of manipulating them to achieve his policy goals.

Because "Congress in committee is Congress at work," the remarkable transformation of the congressional committee system in the early 19th century demands an accounting.[9] Within the past decade, at least three explanations have emerged for the change that occurred in the House, associated with Gerald Gamm and Kenneth Shepsle (1989), Jeffery A. Jenkins (1998), and Randall Strahan (1994). While each of these has important and subtle differences, they are unified by at least one characteristic: Speaker Henry Clay is the chief protagonist.

For Gamm and Shepsle, the supplanting of select with standing committees was related to Speaker Clay's political situation.[10] The end of the war with England removed the unifying impulse of the ideologically diverse Republicans. The committee system amounted to a convenient political stockpile that could be looted for Clay's advantage. In particular, by shifting legislative work from ad hoc select committees to more permanent standing committees, Clay discovered how to distribute the work of the chamber to also shore up his political support. He relinquished to the new standing committees detailed control over legislation. In return, he got from his followers continued support for reelection as Speaker.

For Jenkins the logic of committee development is similar in spirit to Gamm and Shepsle's, though different in particulars. Jenkins takes note of Clay's presidential ambitions, suggesting that by creating politically valuable property rights in committee assignments and distributing those rights widely throughout the chamber, Clay was essentially buying support within the House in his quest for higher office.

Finally, taking a fundamentally different route, Strahan suggests looking at Clay's speakership in "political time." By focusing on political time, Strahan argues that political institutions periodically face critical moments (or crises), which are mostly defined by developments outside the institutions themselves. In these moments, institutions may have at their helm either innovators or traditionalists. The period surrounding the War of 1812 was one such critical moment in congressional history. Clay, an innovator, was endowed with certain legislative skills and je ne sais quoi. He used his considerable political talents to seize control of the House, transforming it in the process.

These accounts of and explanations for the transformation of the House committee system in the early decades of the 19th century have been good starting points, but they have been incomplete for at least two reasons. First, by focusing on Henry Clay they have tended to overly personalize the transformation of the committee system during this era. Clay was an important player in the early institutional development of the House, but he was not alone, even among his contemporaries. Clay served in the House with 708 different men. Some of them—such as John C. Calhoun, John Quincy Adams, John Tyler, and Daniel Webster—are remembered in American history books for deeds other than serving in the House. Scores of others were important national and regional politicians, adept at manipulating the electoral and legislative mechanisms of their day. Thus, it is certainly a mistake to overly credit the political ambitions and genius of a single individual when we could easily develop counterfactuals, with others of Clay's contemporaries taking the lead in his stead.

Stated another way, recent accounts of the evolution of the early House committee system have tended to be "supply-driven," with Clay providing entrée into the benefits of a standing-committee system in return for political support. There is likely a "demand-side" half of this story that demands at least equal emphasis.

Second, virtually all accounts of the rise of standing committees seem to take a rather simple view of the House and, consequently, a simple view of how the standing committees were used. It is usually enough simply to note that the number of standing committees grew and, with them, the amount of legislation considered by committees. Yet committees—then as now—were useful for more than writing legislation. They were convenient graveyards for bothersome constituents claiming special government benefits.[11] They formed a base for harassing executive-branch officials (White 1951). In the immortal words of David Mayhew (1974a), they were used to "take positions, take credit, and advertise." In the words of Richard Fenno (1973), they were used to pursue "good public policy, power within the House, and reelection."

Many of the committees created during the Clay years, from the 12th to the 18th Congress, did not consider legislation at all, but were instead a way for the House to scrutinize the actions of bureaucrats. Some committees considered legislation of sweeping national importance. Others adjudicated disputes over land titles. The transformation of the committee system that was contemporary with Henry Clay did more than simply rechannel the flow of legislation within the House. It also provided new constituency service opportunities, on the one hand, and a new capacity to affect the implementation of legislation, on the other. Therefore, a full accounting of why standing committees eventually dominated the organizational landscape of Congress must appreciate the full range of uses to which legislative majorities can put their committees.

While it is true that Clay was a master parliamentarian who used the tools at his disposal to the utmost, in extolling the virtues of Clay as an institutional innovator, it is important to keep his contributions in perspective.[12] In the case of the evolution of the committee system into one dominated by standing committees, the drift in favor of standing committees began before Clay assumed the speakership, made important gains during his occasional absences from the Speaker's office, and did not reach equilibrium until Clay had left the House for good.

This point is illustrated by data that summarize the drift toward the use of standing committees in the early years of the 19th century. Between 1800 and 1981, 24 standing committees were created in the House. The data prompt two preliminary remarks about the development of the committee system during this time. First, the lion's share of committees created in the House from 1800 to 1831 pertained to internal housekeeping matters, private claims, and military pensions. Committees overseeing significant policies of national scope were clearly in the minority. Second, while many new standing committees were created during the years of the Clay speakership, it is important to note both what types of committees were created and which standing committees were delayed in their creation during Clay's leadership. Of the 11 new committees created during Clay's tenure, only 2 handled substantive policy—Manufactures and Agriculture.[13] One of these, Manufactures, was created via a motion from the floor when the committees were being appointed in the early days of the 16th Congress. The rest were either aimed at overseeing expenditures within the executive branch (the 6 expenditure committees assigned to individual agencies in the 14th Congress) or private claims.

The motion to create a Committee on Manufactures provoked opposition from the chair of Commerce and Manufactures and two supporting floor speeches that survive. The yeas and nays were not taken on the vote to amend the rules but on a division the motion carried by 88–60 (*Annals of Congress*, 16th Cong., 1st sess., pp. 708–710). The *Annals of Congress* and the *House Journal* both report that the committee was appointed immediately on the passage of the resolution. It is noteworthy that, using the D-NOMINATE metric, the newly constituted Manufactures Committee was a significant outlier on the second dimension, which Poole and Rosenthal report is associated with votes on the tariff during the 16th Congress (Poole and Rosenthal 1997a, 49). The Commerce Committee membership was uniformly distributed across the second dimension. Hence, Clay stacked the committee once it was created, but he was not clearly responsible for its creation.

Only one resolution was submitted during the Clay speakership to significantly expand the number of standing committees with substantive legislative jurisdictions. It died in the Rules Committee (*Annals*, 14th Cong., 1st sess., pp. 380–381; Harlow, 1917, 215–216). Thus, the most important expansion of the standing-committee system in the realm of substantive legislation occurred in the 17th Congress, when Clay was a thousand miles away from the House.[14]

As the number of standing committees grew, so too did the fraction of the House that was assigned to them. Two trends stand out in this relationship. First, the fraction of the House assigned to at least one standing committee rose at a steady clip throughout this entire period. By comparison, changes in the Senate came more abruptly. Second, while the transformation of the House as a standing-committee-dominated legislative body continued under the speakership of Henry Clay, it was not until the 23rd

Congress, during the Speakership of Andrew Stevenson, that standing-committee membership was finally universal.

While some scholars have described the committee system during the Clay speakership as undergoing a sea change, it is not obvious that the changes wrought by Clay (or at least under the sufferance of Clay) were entirely discontinuous. If one desires a look at significant and abrupt change in the congressional committee structure during the Clay years, the place to look is the Senate, not the House. At the very least, it is ironic that in a literature that claims to examine Clay's transformation of the system of *standing* legislative committees, the most prominent stories of his manipulating committees to his advantage are in his appointments to *select* committees in the 12th Congress.

Consistent with Clay's behavior preceding the War of 1812, his use of the committee system during the 1810s more generally was one of tactician rather than architect. He was associated directly with no major reform of the committee system during his reign as Speaker. Others around Clay, fellow leaders and the rank and file, were the ones more interested in the transformation of the committee system into one dominated by a small number of standing committees with fixed jurisdictions. And it was they, not Clay, who accomplished this important work of institutional reform.

Clay and the Two Missouri Compromises

On February 13, 1819, less than a month before the expiration of the 15th Congress, a bill reached the House floor providing for the admission of Missouri to the Union. During its consideration, James Tallmadge, simultaneously a rookie and lame-duck congressman from New York, moved an amendment to prohibit the further introduction of slaves into the territory and to free those born in the territory on their 25th birthday.[15] When Tallmadge made his motion, few apparently realized that before the month was out the old organization of national politics, which took much of its structure from how elites thought America should respond in the face of the Napoleonic wars, would be replaced with a new fundamental cleavage, organized regionally and taking most of its energy from the slavery issue. Tallmadge's motion shifted the primary axis of political conflict in Congress so that it became regional, leaving a second dimension that split North and South along questions of internal improvements and the tariff.

The central role of Henry Clay in eventually resolving the Missouri question marked him as one of the leading spokesmen for national union, earning him the nickname Great Compromiser. Research into Clay's activities over the 2 years in which the question was burning makes it clear that he was a determined worker on behalf of compromise. *How* did he achieve this compromise? Was it sheer skill as a legislative draftsman and coalition builder? Or was Clay able to convert his powers as Speaker to his advantage? The major powers at Clay's disposal were two: first, the appointment of committees; second, the right of recognition. In the end, the many committees Clay had a hand in appointing were powerless in setting and controlling the agenda on the Missouri question. Thus Clay's influence lay in his ability to push the issue to the eve of adjournment, where the option of not acting at all proved unacceptable to a small number of pivotal House members.

Even though the interjection of slavery into congressional debate brought national politics to a high boil and upset established ideological coalitions, the House as an organization did not disintegrate immediately. Debate on the Tallmadge amendment in the 15th Congress quickly grew sharp and divisive, still proceedings on the Missouri statehood bill were expeditious in the House. Both sections of Tallmadge's amendment (prohibiting the importation of new slaves and the emancipation of existing slaves at age 25) passed the House, 87 to 76 and 82 to 78, respectively, and the bill was sent to the Senate in less than a week (Spann 1957, 169–195). The bill failed when the conference report, which omitted the Tallmadge amendment, was rejected by the House (*Journal*, 15th Cong., 2nd sess., pp. 335–339; *Annals*, 15th Cong., 2nd sess., pp. 1436–1438).[16] The 15th Congress then adjourned.

On the opening of the 16th Congress, the Missouri question, and the new, related question about whether to admit Maine as a free state, hung over the Congress. When the House organized itself at the start of the 16th Congress, appointing the standing committees and typical select committees, it also created two new selects, one to bring in a bill admitting Missouri, the other for Maine (*Journal*, 16th Cong., 1st sess., pp. 18–19). The next day the Missouri bill was reported back almost immediately with no mention of slavery, and the furor began again. John W. Taylor, a representative from New York who had spoken in favor of the Tallmadge amendment the previous Congress, moved that the Missouri bill be tabled and that a select committee on the issue of slavery in the territories be appointed (*Journal*, 16th Cong., 1st sess., p. 44; *Annals*, 16th Cong. 1st sess., pp. 732, 734–735). The Select Committee on Slavery in the Territories was unable to reach an agreement on whether or how slavery should be restricted in the territories, prompting Taylor to ask for the committee to be discharged on December 28, 1819 (*Journal*, 16th Cong., 1st sess., p. 82; *Annals*, 16th Cong., 2nd sess., pp. 801–804).

As Missouri and the slavery issue were being debated, the Select Committee on the Admission of Maine was grinding along, finishing its work on December 21 (*Journal*, 16th Cong., 1st sess., p. 60). Although the House eventually passed the Maine bill 2 weeks later, Clay was the first to note publicly that the issue of Maine's admission would likely be paired with Missouri's in the near future (*Annals*, 16th Cong., 1st sess., p. 841).

With Maine out of the way for the moment, the House returned to the issue of Missouri and slavery. The House was in the midst of a renewed Missouri debate when the Maine bill, having been amended to admit Missouri as well, arrived from the Senate on February 19, 1820. The House immediately took up the Senate bill, removed all mention of Missouri, sent the bill back to the Senate, and then returned to work on the House Missouri bill again. When word reached the Senate of the House's action, the upper chamber asked for a conference committee, which was granted (*Annals*, 16th Cong., 1st sess., p. 1558). Deliberation on the Missouri bill still continued in the House, even though a conference committee was working on a bill to admit both Maine and Missouri. For a short while, statehood politics seemed to be a three-ring circus, with separate statehood bills for Missouri and Maine still being debated in the House and Senate and a conference committee trying to arrive at a compromise.

By early March, the House had passed a bill admitting Missouri with a prohibition of slavery west of the Mississippi (this prohibition was termed the "Taylor amendment"), the Senate had passed a bill admitting Missouri with a prohibition of slavery north of the 36″30′ parallel, excepting Missouri (this form of the prohibition was labeled the "Thomas amendment"), and the conference committee submitted a report that was essentially the Senate position on both slavery and the Maine-Missouri linkage (*Annals*, 16th Cong., 1st sess., pp. 430, 472, 1572–1573, 1576). In the end, enough erstwhile restrictionists in the House changed their votes to side with the Senate, so that on March 3, 1820, the Missouri Compromise, admitting Missouri and Maine and restricting slavery above the 36″30′ parallel (excepting Missouri), was passed and sent to President Monroe for his signature. All that was left was for Missouri to write a constitution and report back to Congress.

During the second session of the 15th Congress and the first session of the 16th, the House created four select committees, charging them with the task of crafting a statehood compromise and reporting back to the House. Under the rules of the House, this gave the Speaker, Henry Clay, four chances to manipulate the agenda by his appointment of the committees.

What course did Clay pursue in his committee appointments? How successful were these committees in achieving Clay's goals?

Evidence of Clay's appointment strategy is contained in the preferences of the members of these select committees: he stacked them with pro-slavery majorities. Unlike the committees, the House majorities were moderately pro-restrictionist. Therefore, it is not surprising that each time one of the committees reported a bill without a slavery restriction, the restriction was added to the bill by the floor, which added the strongest versions of slavery restrictions then under consideration. The only pro-slavery committee that prevailed was not a select committee, but the final *conference* committee, which operated under special rules that allowed it to offer the House a take-it-or-leave-it proposition: a weak restriction or no bill at all. Only then could the restriction most palatable to Southerners pass, presumably because the pivotal restrictionist preferred a weak form of slavery restrictions to protracted debate over Missouri and the uncertainty that would have flowed from that.

After the completion of the first session of the 16th House, Clay resigned from the speakership, unable to the maintain this position because of financial problems brought on by the Panic of 1819 (Peterson 1987, 66–68; Remini 1991, 176–177; cf. Adams 1875, 5:59). It appears that Clay favored John W. Taylor as a successor, figuring that the Missouri question was behind the House and that Taylor was the most able House leader on the issue of the protective tariff—which interested Clay more than slavery restrictions (Ravenal 1901, 208–209; Spann 1957, 224).

The battle to replace Clay at the start of the second session rapidly became structured along regional lines. Taylor emerged as the predominant Northern candidate, but support was sufficiently split among others that repeated balloting proved inconclusive. After 2 days and 22 ballots, Taylor was eventually elected Speaker by a margin of one vote. Critical to Taylor's election was support from the Bucktail (anti-Clinton) faction from his home state, which had been a major source of Northern opposition to Taylor in the early balloting, but which eventually swung to Taylor after he pledged to Bucktail supporters his neutrality in New York politics (*Annals*, 16th Cong., 2nd sess., pp. 434–438; Spann 1960, 384; Leintz 1978, 69–71).

Clay's earlier prediction that Missouri was behind the House—and that Taylor therefore was a safe successor—proved immediately wrong. As soon as Taylor was elevated to the speakership, the House received the Missouri constitution, which included a provision excluding free blacks from entering the new state. The Missouri constitution rekindled debates that many had thought had been put to rest only a few months before. The presidential election of 1820 only stoked the flames higher: with the Missouri constitution the center of congressional debate, a constitutional crisis was nearly created over the question of whether Missouri's electoral votes should be counted (Peterson 1987, 64; Remini 1991, 188–190).

Preoccupation with the Missouri constitution caused virtually all other lawmaking to grind to a halt. Immediately upon receiving the Missouri constitution, Taylor appointed a three-person committee to examine it and report to the House. Consisting of two moderate slavery expansionists (William Lowndes of South Carolina and Samuel Smith of Maryland) and one moderate restrictionist (John Sergeant of Pennsylvania), the committee split on the propriety of restricting the movement of free blacks into Missouri (*Annals*, 16th Cong., 2nd sess., p. 440). The report back was only the prelude to a 3-month debate.

As the debate stretched into January and toward February, patience began to wear thin. Clay, who had been absent from the House all this session, returned in late January and was immediately drawn into efforts to extricate the House from endless debate (Brown 1926, 35–43, 65; Peterson 1987, 62–66; Remini 1991, 185). Now a rank-and-file member, Clay stepped into the leadership position on Missouri. Adopting a similar tack to the one he had attempted as Speaker, Clay moved that the resolution admitting Missouri be referred to a select committee. The House complied and Taylor proceeded to appoint 13 representatives to the committee, selecting from a list that Clay had prepared (Spann 1957, 241; Remini 1991, 187). Unlike the earlier committees on Missouri that Clay had a role in appointing, this one was a surprisingly faithful representative sample of the entire House. Still, the relationship between Clay's committee and the floor was similar to past episodes. The committee recommended the acceptance of the Missouri constitution, on the condition that the Missouri legislature pledge "by solemn public act . . . never to pass any law preventing any description of persons from coming to or settling in said State, who are or hereafter may become citizens of any State of this Union" (*Annals*, 16th Cong., 2nd sess., p. 1080). However, the restrictionists on the committee were all indisposed toward the proviso, favoring instead a rejection of the Missouri constitution altogether. The proviso favored by the select committee was interpreted by Northern restrictionists as a victory for the South, and it was defeated by a close vote, 82 to 88 (*Annals*, 16th Cong., 2nd sess., p. 1146).

The session dragged on with no resolution to whether Missouri "was a river, an Indian tribe, a territory, or a state" (Spann 1957, 240). Finally,

Clay moved again to appoint a committee on the Missouri question, this time as a joint committee with the Senate, referred to as the "Committee on Compromise." The House acceded to this request, with the House members this time selected by ballot (Spann 1957, 244; Remini 1991, 190–191). The ballot suggests that the slavery expansionists were more united in their preferences for joint committee members than restrictionists, since the ranking of the committee (which was based on number of ballots received) tended to have expansionists on the top and restrictionists on the bottom (*Annals*, 16th Cong., 2nd sess., pp. 1219–1220).[17] However, the overall membership of the committee again closely mirrored that of the House. And yet again, the committee recommended the admission of Missouri under essentially the same conditions that the House had rejected before. This time, under the pressure of adjournment, the bill passed, 87–81 (*Annals*, 16th Cong., 2nd sess., p. 1239).

According to Spann (1957), whose study of Speaker Taylor's actions during the Missouri debate constitutes the most extensive institutional analysis of the controversy, the House agreed to the eventual passage of the Missouri resolution because "the House was now ready to vote for almost anything and . . . rushed it through." (245). In fact, the two votes on Missouri's constitution were virtually identical, and thus closure on the Missouri question did not come through the wholesale conversion of House members. Nine House votes, out of a membership of 186, shifted over the course of the debate on whether to accept the Missouri constitution—five were originally abstentions and four had been restrictionists.

Spann's interpretation of the outcome of the final vote is correct in noting the importance of one strategic detail, however: The final vote on Missouri was held 5 days before the 16th Congress adjourned. Failure to resolve Missouri's status in the Union threatened Western violence and continued secessionist rhetoric from the South. Thus, just like the end of the first session, closure on the Missouri issue in the second came not because a committee had induced stability to a chaotic debate but because looming adjournment was what mattered.

Yet again, Clay's behavior during the Missouri controversy saw him operate in a formal setting of rules and committees, and in a more rough-and-tumble tactical setting of trying to work a political coalition so that a small number of pivotal voters came his way. Using what was by now a well-worn strategy of stacking committees, Clay was a failure. Clay was much more successful, however, in using the flow of the legislative calendar—in particular, the deep, dark night of adjournment—to his advantage.

Conclusion

The purpose of this chapter has been two-fold. First, I have attempted to supplement traditional historiography about the legislative legacy of Henry Clay through the use of political science data and analytical techniques. Doing so casts some new light on the legislative moments in the House that have been closely associated with Clay. The research of Poole and Rosenthal and their construction of estimated ideal points allows us to understand more precisely when and how Clay attempted to stack committees to his advantage. Clay, it turns out, was a committee stacker. He did not invent the practice, however, nor was he especially successful when he did it.

The second purpose of this chapter has been to assess more broadly the nature of Clay's contribution to the institutional development of the House. In this review, the bottom-line conclusion seems clear: Clay was a brilliant and dogged tactician but not an institutional architect. Others in the House served the architectural role. None of them shone as brightly in the antebellum firmament as Clay, and therefore we may never know, with any satisfaction, the details of why the House evolved as it did.

Chapter 11

Committee Composition in the Absence of a Strong Speaker

CHRIS DEN HARTOG AND CRAIG GOODMAN

Introduction

Budgeting is at the heart of policy making. Legislative spending and revenue committees thus play important roles in policy making. Studies of the House show that, since World War II, more-loyal members of the majority party are more likely to be appointed to key committees than less-loyal members. However, there has been little systematic analysis of committee appointments or composition in earlier periods. In fact, there is limited work of any type on the role of committees during the decades immediately following the emergence of the standing committee system. We take a step toward filling in this gap by examining whether party loyalty affected appointments to the House's antebellum revenue and spending committee, the Ways and Means Committee. We examine committee assignments from the 20th through 36th Congresses (1827–1861). We find that majority-party members who had shown higher levels of loyalty to the party *were* more likely than less-loyal party members to be appointed to Ways and Means.

Parties, Committees, and Appointments

PARTISAN-APPOINTMENT INCENTIVES

The institutional and political environments of the antebellum House were very different from those of the modern House. Mass politics, as well as mass parties, emerged during this era; the advent of sharp partisan competition—in both the electoral and the legislative arenas—would seem to have created incentives for party leaders to be strategic when making committee assignments. Indeed, various accounts suggest that antebellum party leaders were acutely aware of the relationship between legislative outputs and the likelihood of retaining the majority at the next election, and that they therefore had reasons to care about whether committees served the interests of the party. Also, it is clear that, in ways other than committee assignments, party leaders used institutional rules to prevent debate on issues (such as slavery) that would not be beneficial to the electoral prospects of either party.

On the other hand, there is also evidence that Speakers sometimes refrained from using House rules for their party's advantage, as when Speakers refused to count a quorum in cases in which the minority party used disappearing quorums to block bills (Alexander 1916; Hinds 1907; Luce 1922). Moreover, before the collapse of the party system in the 1850s, both parties were national and drew support in all areas of the country (Fogel 1989), meaning they faced significant internal sectional divisions that decreased incentives to create strong party leadership.

Various historical accounts of the period suggest anecdotally that party loyalty *was* an important consideration in committee assignments (cf. Alexander 1916; Hinds 1907; McConachie 1898). Most research on antebellum committees, however, focuses either on the first decades of House history (Cooper 1970) or on the initial emergence of the standing-committee system circa 1816–1823 (Cooper 1970; Gamm and Shepsle 1989; Jenkins 1998; Jenkins and Stewart 2002). Considerably less attention has been given the role of committees in the years and decades following the initial creation of the standing-committee system.

Background: The Growth of Standing Committees

When the First Congress convened, prevailing political wisdom feared the centralization of power in the hands of a few legislators (Alexander 1916) and wanted to ensure that committees were responsive to the wishes of the chamber (Canon and Stewart 2001). As a result, select committees were chosen to handle the details of legislation after general debate in the Committee of the Whole (Alexander 1916; Canon and Stewart 2001; Cooper 1970; McConachie 1898).

The growth of standing committees occurred gradually. By 1795 there were still only five standing committees. Most legislation was referred to select committees after general debate; most committees did not exercise the institutional prerogatives associated with modern committees (Canon and Stewart 2001); and there was still a strong norm for the chamber to make decisions before sending proposed legislation to a select committee for finalizing the details (Smith and Deering 1990). However, dramatic changes in the internal organization of the House occurred around the time of the War of 1812.

The most significant institutionalization of congressional committees occurred between 1811 and 1865 (Smith and Deering 1990). The system of standing committees emerged between 1812 and 1823, and by the 1830s they were an important part of the legislative process. They were no longer reconstituted during each session of Congress (Canon and Stewart 2001), and legislation was typically referred to standing committees before consideration in Committee of the Whole (Cooper and Young 1989). Moreover, they could introduce new legislation and report it to the floor (Smith and Deering 1990). Scholars have suggested a number of possible reasons for why they emerged during this particular period. The most common reasons are the increased workload associated with the War of 1812 (Cooper 1970), the political and partisan ambitions of House leaders (Cooper 1970; Gamm and Smith 2000), and the demands of House members more generally (Jenkins 1998; Jenkins and Stewart 2002).

Committee Appointments

Before the emergence of the standing-committee system, ad hoc committees were appointed for most legislation. From early in House history, Speakers were responsible for making all committee appointments (Alexander 1916; McConachie 1898). There is little systematic evidence about what factors influenced appointments to select committees during this era, but geographic balance, seniority, partisanship, and members' individual skills have been listed as important factors (Alexander 1916; Canon and Stewart 2002a).

There is a variety of anecdotal and historical evidence regarding partisanship as the basis for committee appointments once the standing committee system emerged. Cooper (1970) notes that seniority was not as well-established as a basis for committee appointments as it would later become. He also notes that party leaders often used committee assignments to cement political alliances, as well as to help their party develop a collective reputation.

Cooper's hypothesis about the political and partisan goals of Speakers has received considerable attention from subsequent scholars. Gamm and Shepsle (1989) suggest that particular individuals' decisions played an important role in the development of the standing-committee system. Although there is no smoking gun showing that Henry Clay deliberately used committee assignments to produce specific outcomes, Gamm and Shepsle suggest there is enough circumstantial evidence of the importance of partisanship.

Alexander (1916) argues that committees evolved quickly into partisan panels working to safeguard party policies. Many accounts of congressional committees during the antebellum era point to the high levels of bargaining that occurred over committee assignments. Most commonly, committee assignments were currency that could be traded to secure the support of some faction for a particular candidate for Speaker (Smith and Deering 1990). Other accounts indicate that party leaders were concerned with whether potential committee leaders could be counted on to support partisan interests during committee deliberations.

Hypothesis: The Effect of Loyalty on Ways and Means Appointments

We explore the extent to which loyalty affected appointments in the antebellum House by testing the hypothesis that antebellum Speakers used their committee-appointment power to selectively reward or punish members' loyalty or disloyalty to the party. We focus on the Ways and Means Committee, which served as the focal point for much of the legislative activity in the House of Representatives before the Civil War. Unlike Ways and Means in the contemporary House, the antebellum Ways and Means Committee's jurisdiction included both revenue *and* appropriations measures as well as other matters. In fact, Ways and Means exercised so much control over the floor schedule of the House that its chairman became a de facto floor leader, with substantial responsibility for the order of business (Alexander 1916). There is therefore ample reason to believe that it played a paramount role in shaping the majority party's reputation, which would give Speakers a strong reason to stack it with loyal party members.[1]

For the antebellum period, since Speakers were always members of the majority party, we expect to find that loyalty affected the committee assignments of majority-party members; but it is unclear what effect, if any, one would expect loyalty to have on minority-party members' assignments. We therefore focus on the effect of loyalty on majority-party members' committee assignments.

In addition, our analysis includes only House members who were not already members of Ways and Means to control for the possibility that members enjoyed property rights that gave them some level of entitlement to a committee slot once they were appointed to that slot (Jenkins 1998). Thus, we test the hypothesis

> H_{party}: Majority-party backbenchers with higher party loyalty were more likely to be appointed to the Ways and Means Committee, all else constant.

In other words, we examine the extent to which party loyalty affected the probability that a majority-party member who was not already on the Ways and Means Committee would be appointed to that committee. We test this hypothesis against the null hypothesis that loyalty is unrelated to majority members' probability of being appointed to Ways and Means.

Testing Our Hypothesis

Our research design is analogous to an experiment on the effects of a drug, in which we first observe that a subject is ill (in our study, *ill* translates to not being a member of Ways and Means), then observe the amount of the drug administered to the subject (a member's party loyalty), then observe whether the subject recovers (is appointed to Ways and Means). Our implementation of this research design is straightforward: for Congresses between 1827 and 1861 (20th through 36th Congresses), we identify which majority-party members of the House were on the Ways and Means Committee in each Congress.[2] Using a member of Congress as the unit of observation, and pooling observations for members across our time series, we limit our analysis to members who were *not* appointed to Ways and Means *at the start* of Congress $t - 1$. We then perform a probit analysis of a dummy variable for whether each member i was appointed to Ways and Means *at the start* of Congress t on a measure of i's loyalty to the party *during* Congress $t - 1$ (we also include a variety of controls, discussed below).[3] Like previous studies of loyalty's effects on committee appointments (Cox and McCubbins 1993; Rohde and Shepsle 1973; Smith and Ray 1983), this research design has the advantage of neatly capturing *changes* in whether members were on

Ways and Means that occurred between the time immediately before the "treatment"—that is, a member's level of loyalty—and the time immediately after the treatment.[4]

Formally, the model that we estimate is

$$WaysandMeans_{it} = \alpha + \beta_1 Loyalty_{it-1} + \beta_2 Tenure_{it} + \beta_3 WMopen_t + \beta_4 LagTop3_{it} + \beta_5 DWDistpty_{it} + \beta_6 South_i + \beta_7 Margin_{it} + \beta_8 Nvotes_t + \varepsilon_{it},$$

where

$WaysandMeans_{it}$ is a dummy variable coded 1 if *i* was on the Ways and Means Committee in Congress *t* and 0 otherwise; and

$Loyalty_{it-1}$ is the standardized proportion of key votes on which *i* voted with the party position in Congress $t - 1$.[5]

The rest of the right-hand-side variables are controls for various other factors that might also affect appointments to Ways and Means:

$Tenure_{it}$ is the number of congressional terms that *i* has served (including *t*) during his or her career;

$WMopen_t$ is the number of open seats on Ways and Means in Congress *t* (that is, the total number of seats on Ways and Means, minus the number of returning members on Ways and Means);

$LagTop3_{it}$ is a dummy variable coded 1 if member *i* was appointed to any of the three most-sought-after committees in Congress $t - 1$ and 0 otherwise;

$DWDistpty_{it}$ is *i*'s ideological distance from the majority-party median on the first dimension of DW-NOMINATE (McCarty, Poole, and Rosenthal 1997; Poole and Rosenthal 1997a), for Congress *t*;

$South_i$ is a dummy variable, coded 1 if *i* is from a Southern state (defined as the 11 Confederate states, plus Tennessee) and 0 otherwise;

$Margin_{it}$ is *i*'s margin of victory in the election for Congress *t*; and

$Nvotes_t$ is the mean number of party leadership votes on which party members participated in Congress $t - 1$, included to account for possible heteroscedasticity arising from the variable number of party leadership votes in each Congress.

As an additional safeguard against heteroscedasticity, we estimate the model using robust standard errors (Huber 1967; White 1980). We also estimate the model with and without fixed-effects dummy variables for each Congress—which, as it turns out, does not affect our results substantively.

Results

We now turn to the results of our probit estimation, shown below (the numbers in parentheses are the standard errors [SEs] of the coefficients). We remind the reader that the results presented here were estimated using standardized loyalty scores, as well as fixed-effects dummy variables for each Congress, with the 21st Congress as the omitted category.[6]

$$\begin{aligned} WaysandMeans_{it} = \alpha &+ 0.214(0.095)Loyalty_{it-1} + 0.136(0.043)Tenure_{it} \\ &+ 0.100(0.059)WMopen_t + -0.692(0.414)LagTop3_{it} \\ &+ 0.984(0.508)DWDistpty_{it} + -0.194(0.198)South_i \\ &+ 0.001(0.002)Margin_{it} + -0.002(0.003)Nvotes_t \end{aligned} \quad \textbf{(11.1)}$$

As hypothesized, the coefficient for loyalty is significantly positive (coefficient = 0.214; SE = 0.095; one-tailed *p* value = 0.013), indicating that, among majority-party members who were not assigned to the Ways and Means Committee at the outset of the previous Congress, the probability of being appointed to Ways and Means in the present Congress increased along with members' loyalty to the party in the previous Congress, all else constant.[7]

To illustrate the substantive impact of loyalty, we begin by reminding the reader that the standardized loyalty scores measure each member's loyalty relative to copartisans in the same Congress, and they do so in terms of how many standard deviations above or below the party mean a given member's level of loyalty is. For a member with the mean level of party loyalty, the probability of being appointed to Ways and Means is 0.039 (the 95% confidence interval ranges from 0.027 to 0.052).[8] As loyalty drops one and two standard deviations *below* the mean, the probability drops to 0.016 (0.005 to 0.034) and 0.025 (0.013 to 0.041), respectively. As loyalty increases to one and two standard deviations *above* the party mean, however, the probability increases to 0.061 (0.040 to 0.085) and 0.093 (0.048 to 0.151), respectively. Thus, as loyalty goes from one standard deviation below the mean to one standard deviation above, the probability of being appointed to Ways and Means increases by 0.036; as loyalty goes from two standard deviations below the mean to two standard deviations above, the probability of being appointed to Ways and Means increases by 0.077.

Though we do not discuss the results in detail, we note briefly that the coefficients for some of our control variables were also at least marginally significant. The most noteworthy is members' tenure in the House; as tenure increases, majority-party members are significantly more likely to be appointed to Ways and Means. The coefficients for the number of open seats on Ways and Means, and for members' ideological distance from the party median, were positive at significance levels between 90 and 95 percent. And members who were assigned to one of the other top three committees in the previous Congress were less likely to be appointed to Ways and Means, at a significance level of just over 90 percent.

These findings suggest that *ex ante* stacking of this powerful committee was one way that antebellum majority parties attempted to influence House decision making. We also point out, however, that this is only one aspect of the legislative process—and that we do not see our findings as evidence that antebellum majority parties were akin to the types of well-organized, influential party organizations we see in the modern House. Rather, we see our findings as filling in one small part of an overall picture (i.e., the role of antebellum parties) that remains largely incomplete. Our findings can thus be reconciled with other recent studies that, in broad strokes, paint a picture of antebellum House legislative parties and party organization as being nontrivial but being in early stages of development (Binder 1997; Dion 1997; Maltzman 1997).

Conclusion

In this chapter, we have examined antebellum House committee appointments, with an eye toward discerning whether the majority party systematically tried to stack the Ways and Means Committee—the antebellum House's lone "power committee"—in its own favor. We found that, as is the case in the modern House, antebellum majority parties did indeed systematically stack the Ways and Means Committee. Among party members who were not on the Ways and Means Committee in the previous Congress, the probability of being appointed to it in a given Congress was significantly higher for members who had demonstrated higher loyalty to the party on key votes and lower for members who had exhibited lower loyalty.

Chapter 12

Roll-Call Behavior and Career Advancement: Analyzing Committee Assignments from Reconstruction to the New Deal

CRAIG GOODMAN AND TIMOTHY P. NOKKEN

Introduction

In this chapter, we investigate the theoretical importance of partisan polarization and party unity in the U.S. House of Representatives. More specifically, we seek to apply the notions of conditional party government (CPG) to two important eras in the House: that of the strong Speaker and the era following the revolt against Speaker Joe Cannon. We investigate the linkage between internally homogeneous and cohesive parties and committee assignments for members of the majority party from the end of Reconstruction to the beginning of the New Deal era (1877 to 1933, or the 45th to 72nd Congresses). A number of scholars look to the era of Republican Speakers Thomas B. Reed and Cannon to investigate strong parties and powerful leaders. We take a different tack in this chapter. We analyze the characteristics of the Democratic Party to see if the notion of CPG can apply. As we will show, an important condition needed for CPG during Congresses with Democratic majorities is met, yet many seem not to think of CPG with respect to congressional Democrats of the era. While Democratic Party unity appears to have been impressive, party leaders apparently were unable to translate high levels of party unity into a coherent legislative program because the party contained two distinct factions. The problems that emerged following the end of Reconstruction would persist for nearly a century.

This chapter proceeds as follows. We provide a brief overview of political history of the period we examine in this chapter. Next, we survey the literature on House committee assignments during the strong-Speaker era and the changes that occurred following the revolt against Cannon. We describe how high levels of polarization generated periods of strong parties. In particular, we focus on work by Cooper and Brady (1981) to explain Republican strength in the late 19th and early 20th centuries and the works of Aldrich and Rohde (1997, 2000b, 2001) that provide the theoretical underpinnings of the CPG argument. On the basis of these theoretical expectations, we formulate a series of hypotheses about party differences in terms of cohesion and committee-assignment strategies. Finally, we specify a series of models to test our hypotheses and discuss the results.

Historical Background

Most consider the period from the end of Reconstruction until the revolt against Speaker Joe Cannon in 1910 as the high point of party government in the United States. Such assumptions require greater scrutiny as many of the claims of party government rely solely on analyses focusing explicitly on the Republican Party. The parties had substantial differences between them on any number of issues, but there were internal divisions within the parties as well (Schickler 2001; Wiebe 1967). Majority margins in the House were often very narrow and rather fluid, resulting in a number of close votes that required cross-party coalitions to form majorities. The intraparty heterogeneity persisted until the critical election of 1896. During the elections of 1894–1896, dramatic changes in the constituency bases of each party occurred. As a result, party homogeneity was significantly higher than in previous decades (Jenkins, Schickler, and Carson 2005). The levels of polarization would then decline following the 1910 congressional elections as both parties struggled with competing constituencies: the Republicans with the agrarian insurgents and the Democrats with sectional differences.

The evidence suggests that the Republican Party was more successful in overcoming internal differences, exhibiting high levels of agreement on a series of important economic policies of the day (Bensel 2000). One key characteristic of the Republican Party was its ability to maintain a cohesive majority on procedural matters. Despite occasional internal division within the party, Republican leaders could usually count on the support of the rank-and-file members on final-passage votes (Schickler 2001). Such strong Republican unity eventually collapsed as Midwestern insurgents grew dissatisfied with a tariff policy that failed to help agrarian constituents as well as with the strong speakership (Barfield 1970). The revolt of Midwestern insurgents was an important development in the Republican Party, and from 1910 until 1932, the party faced internal divisions between Old Guard Republicans and Progressives that made governing a difficult task.

The situation was very different for the Democratic Party. The party often represented an unwieldy coalition of Southerners and machine politicians from the East (Barfield 1970; Bensel 2000) that hindered the development of a common party platform. On tariff issues, for instance, a number of Democrats, including Samuel Randall (Pa.) who eventually became Speaker, were fierce protectionists who joined Republicans in support of tariffs. Following the election of 1896, the Democrats had largely been reduced to a parochial party, one concerned more with dispensing political favors than anything else, and possessed few tools to secure party loyalty on key votes. As the majority party from 1911-1919, Democrats failed to foster party loyalty even with the use of the binding caucus (Green 2002). Despite the increasing levels of party polarization that characterized American politics at the turn of the century, the Democratic Party struggled with internal divisions and would continue to struggle with competing interests through the New Deal. The presence of strong parties suggests that one would observe more distinct differences in House proceedings than one would expect during periods of weak parties and low levels of polarization. One area in which party strength might serve as an important explanatory variable was in the politics of committee assignments during the era of the strong Republican Speakers.

House Committee Assignments in the Strong-Speaker Era

The rise of the strong speakership is well documented in both historical and political science works (Alexander 1916; Hasbrouck 1927; Chiu 1928; Binder 1997). The strong-Speaker era is closely associated with two prominent Republican speakers of the late 1800s and early 1900s. The era began with Speaker Thomas B. Reed's (R-Maine) successful effort to revise House rules and essentially eliminate dilatory tactics used by the minority party to tie up House business and frustrate the majority. While the era has its roots in Reed's actions, Speaker Joseph Cannon (R-Ill.) is the figure most closely associated with the dominating, even dictatorial, speakership of the era. Cannon's willingness to use his position of power to further the Republican cause was widely known, as was the overthrow of Cannon that effectively ended the era of the strong Speaker. During his reign, the tool most closely associated with Cannon's rule over the House and the Republican Party was his power to appoint members to the standing committees, to name committee chairs, and his willingness to use these powers to reward supporters and severely punish opponents (Chiu 1928; Hasbrouck 1927; Jones 1968; Polsby, Gallagher, and Rundquist 1969; Abram and Cooper 1968; Cooper and Brady 1981; Lawrence, Maltzman, and Wahlbeck 2001; Krehbiel and Wiseman 2001; Finocchiaro 2001).

A number of studies in the aforementioned citations investigate the generally accepted statement that Cannon used the committee system to further Republican objectives by appointing allies to the power committees and by demoting the less supportive members of the party, namely, the more liberal Insurgents who later contributed to his downfall.

Polarization and Party Government

The last decade of the 19th and first decade of the 20th centuries mark an era of powerful congressional leaders. The dramatic events that surround the inception of the era of the strong Speaker (adoption of the Reed rules), the ruthless implementation of those rules by Speaker Joseph Cannon, and the revolt against Cannon in 1910 are interesting events in and of themselves.[1] These events also speak to the importance of political parties in shaping legislative institutions and member behavior. Cooper and Brady (1981) use Cannon's reign as Speaker to investigate whether political context of individual style best explains why some congressional leaders are able to exert power and why some are not. Cooper and Brady argue forcefully that the Speaker's ability to invoke party discipline stemmed not from Cannon's personal leadership qualities but from high levels of Republican Party unity during the era. Had the Republicans not been a unified, ideologically homogeneous party, Cannon would not have been able to administer House rules as forcefully as he did. Generally, then, the party composition and the cohesiveness of the party coalition are important determinants of party strength.

Recent treatments of party government argue that the influence of parties is contingent on two factors, the level of intraparty homogeneity and interparty heterogeneity. Rohde (1991) and Aldrich and Rohde (2000b, 2001) argue that the level of within-party agreement coupled with stark differences between the parties creates the "condition" that leads to CPG. More simply, when the parties are ideologically polarized, the majority party can build on its internal agreement on policy matters to carry over to procedural matters and subsequently delegate significant powers to its leadership team. Party leaders can, in turn, use their powers to pursue aggressively a highly partisan agenda supported by their strong majority-party procedural coalition. Should the procedural coalition prove reliable, the power of the majority party is further enhanced at the expense of the minority party, which is essentially irrelevant since it is not needed to construct majority coalitions.

While Rohde (1991) and Aldrich and Rohde (2000b, 2001) use the theory to explain events in the post-reform-era House, the theory can be applied to investigate partisanship during the strong-Speaker era and even across institutions to investigate the possibility of CPG in the Senate (Forgette and Sala 1999; Smith and Gamm 2001). Again, as this literature review illustrates, efforts to study CPG in the late 19th and early 20th centuries apparently begins and ends with the Republican Party. Most studies seem to imply that even during periods of extreme party polarization, the Democrats were hopelessly divided. On the basis of the distance between the parties' NOMINATE scores, the period in question is marked by historically high levels of partisan polarization. Such polarization implies at least some significant intraparty agreement among Democrats. Indeed, high levels of partisan polarization could not exist without intraparty cohesion. In support of our contention, the high level of polarization results from high levels of intraparty agreement, as indicated by low levels of average within-party differences.

The low levels of within-party differences strongly suggest that one of the key conditions needed for Democratic CPG is met. As an additional check, we calculated the average cohesion scores for each party. Both Democrats and Republicans exhibit high levels of cohesion on the roll-call votes that divide the parties. Coupled with the evidence from the NOMINATE polarization measures, high levels of party cohesion suggest that the Democrats, much like their Republican counterparts, possessed an important component needed to implement CPG. Why, then, do scholars focus primarily on the Republican Party as an example of CPG during this era?

The easy answer to the question is that Republican Speakers obtained and wielded significant powers. Simply, there just are not as many telling anecdotes of Democratic Party leaders exercising near-dictatorial powers. In fact, Democrats were so disgusted with the effectiveness with which the Reed rules eliminated dilatory tactics that they refused to use the powers the rules granted the Speaker to push through their agenda even though Reed, as a member of the minority, encouraged them to do so (Schickler 2001, 49). Somewhat ironically, however, at least one important component of the strong speakership can be traced back to Democratic majorities in the 1870s. It was the Democrats, under Speaker Samuel Randall, who asserted the Speaker's right of recognition (Peters 1997; House 1935).

While intraparty homogeneity and cohesion would be a necessary condition for CPG, it is not necessarily a sufficient condition. In the modern era, high levels of agreement within each party's primary election constituencies prove to be an important component of CPG (Aldrich and Rohde 2001). It is obvious that this was not the case in the late 1800s because the time period preceded the use of primary elections. The apparent high levels of Democratic agreement may actually be ephemeral. The conventional wisdom of the time posits a divided Democratic Party despite the evidence of cohesiveness we report. The illusory nature of the cohesion is certainly plausible when one considers the primary components of the Democratic coalition: the solid South and scattered pockets of strength in the industrial Northeast most commonly associated with party-machine politics. Furthermore, it is fairly safe to assume that a Tammany Hall Democrat did not share many of the same policy views as his fellow partisans from the former Confederate states. This rather incongruent coalition highlights another important condition needed for CPG, ideological homogeneity among the party in the electorate.

Consistent with Aldrich and Rohde (2001), we too contend that heterogeneity in the electoral coalition of the Democratic Party from Reconstruction to the New Deal did reduce the likelihood they implemented CPG. That heterogeneity coexisted with high levels of cohesion, not because of widespread agreement among Democrats on a proactive policy agenda, but because the coalition was more unified in its opposition to the Republicans and their agenda. If that is a correct characterization of the political context of the times, one would expect to see higher unity among Democrats when they were in the minority and lower levels of cohesion when serving as the majority. We label this scenario the *negative cohesion hypothesis*. Simply put, Democrats could agree on the things they opposed (namely, the Republicans) but would be less unified when it came to identifying matters on which they agreed. In the next section, we will specify a model and test the negative cohesion hypothesis.

A second facet of CPG that is especially relevant for the period we analyze, is ability of party leaders to exercise power. One area in which leaders, notably Republican Speakers, were especially active was in the appointments of members of Congress (MCs) to committees. In sum, if CPG characterizes Republican House regimes, but not Democratic majorities, we should observe predictable party-based differences in committee assignments. Furthermore, we should expect to see shifts in both parties' strategies as a result of the revolt against Cannon and universal acceptance of a seniority norm.

The results presented in the next section test these hypotheses about the relationship between party loyalty and committee assignments.

Party Leadership and Party Loyalty

While political forces such as high levels of ideological polarization and party loyalty are offered to account for strong congressional leadership, an alternative explanation will stem from different styles of leadership or the talent of specific leaders. The abilities or ineptitudes of individual leaders certainly can contribute to the level of party cohesion. We tend to agree with scholars like Cooper and Brady (1981) who trace much of the power of strong congressional leaders to political context rather than personality traits. That said, leaders who exercise poor judgment or who fail to act even during periods in which the political context is conducive to strong leadership will appear to be less able than those who can successfully navigate their party and the House during such times. One rather simplistic characterization of the leadership qualities of the individual Speakers of the time period we analyze tends to equate strong leaders with the Republican Party, weaker leaders with the Democratic Party. While this is arguably too simplistic, there are indeed some poignant examples highlighting why scholars tend to make such a generalization.

The exploits of the strong Republican Speakers Reed and Cannon are well known, while scholars have been less interested in investigating the machinations of Democratic leadership practices of the time. One reason for the lack of interest in Democratic leadership of the House is that, unlike Cannon and Reed, Democratic leaders simply refused to run Congress with an iron fist. Two explanations can account for Democratic unwillingness to bring heavy-handed leadership tactics to the House during their time as majority party. First, and perhaps most idealistically, they proclaimed to value minority rights, including obstructionism. In the 53rd House, during debate on the coinage of silver, Reed continually used the disappearing quorum in an effort to goad Speaker Crisp and the Democrats into using the rules of the House to overcome that dilatory tactic (Peters 1997, 72).[2]

A second, possibly more plausible reason Democratic leaders shied away from strong-arm leadership tactics stemmed from the nature of their coalition. One obvious reason, as we stated earlier, was the strange cross-regional coalition of urban, machine-oriented Democrats with those representatives from the solidly Democratic South. The party system of the time (from post-Reconstruction to the New Deal) was characterized by strong division between the parties, but that division was not necessarily the result of divergent stands on important issues. Those few issues that did serve to divide the two parties also created stresses within the Democratic coalition. Tariff policy, perhaps the most divisive of the substantive policy issues that divided the two parties, also created stress within the Democratic Party.

Early indications of cross-regional stresses over the tariff appear during the leadership of Democratic Speaker Randall from Pennsylvania. Randall was a strong supporter of the tariff and actually used his leadership position, namely, as chair of the Appropriations Committee, to gain passage for a protectionist tariff in 1884 (Peters 1997). Disarray within the Democratic Party became evident in subsequent pieces of tariff legislation. During the debate over the Payne-Aldrich Tariff in 1909, House Republican leaders successfully wooed Southern Democrats to support a protective tariff with promises to protect specific goods of great importance to Southern Democratic constituencies. Such Republican efforts "revealed dramatically the vulnerability of Democratic congressmen to various economic pressure groups and interests and concomitantly the lack of control of the minority organization exercised when such pressure was applied" (Barfield 1970, 311).

Successful Republican efforts to exploit disunity within the Democratic Party on the tariff may also provide some basis for additional party disunity within different policy areas. Democrats, for instance, may well have faced similar internal stresses over pension policies. The Northern, urban wing of the party may well have faced pressures to support pensions owing to the fact that a number of their constituents were Civil War veterans receiving a pension, while the Southern members faced no such demands. The parties might well have faced pressures on other fronts such as tax policy, commercial policy, and banking policy. In other words, the high levels of partisan conflict and polarization that are traditionally thought to characterize the era may be illusory. In the next section, we investigate further the notion that Democratic and Republican party cohesion differed in predictable ways. We then move from aggregate measures of party cohesion to party cohesion within specific policy areas to determine whether the parties were susceptible to internal division on specific issue areas. We then seek to address questions of how members' party loyalty influenced their advancement within the institution.

Data and Methods

We test our hypotheses about the relationship between party loyalty and committee assignments using data from the 45th through 72nd Congresses.

We address two separate, but related questions. First, we investigate the total value of a member's committee portfolio, which allows us to compare the quality of committee assignments loyal partisans received compared with those considered less loyal. Second, we explore whether there is any systematic relationship between serving on a top committee and party loyalty. For both questions, we expect that party loyalty will be positive and statistically significant. However, we also believe that the clearest relationships between party loyalty and committee assignments will be confined to Republicans before the revolt against Speaker Cannon. Given what we know about the Democrats, we do not expect to find evidence of a strong relationship between party loyalty and committee assignments.

Our negative cohesion hypothesis predicts that party-cohesion levels were affected by majority-party status. To test this notion, we estimate a series of regression models with a dependent variable taking the value of each party's average cohesion within a Congress. The independent variables include the absolute difference in the number of seats held by each party and a dichotomous variable indicating whether the party was in the majority. If our hypothesis is correct, we expect to observe a significant and negative coefficient on the majority-party variable for Democrats but a significant and positive coefficient for Republicans. Consistent with our hypothesis, party cohesion among Democrats is lower when the party is in the majority. Conversely, when the Democrats were in the minority, their party-cohesion scores were higher. Among Republicans, party cohesion was higher when their party was in the majority, which lends further support to our hypothesis.

$$\textit{Democratic Party Cohesion, 45th–61st Cong} = -0.117(0.03^{**})\textit{Abs Diff in Seats} - 0.069(0.007^{**})\textit{Maj Status} + 0.857(0.006^{**})\text{Constant} \quad (R^2 = 0.039,\ N = 2{,}877) \tag{12.1}$$

$$\textit{Democratic Party Cohesion, 62nd–72nd Cong} = 0.045(0.03^{**})\textit{Abs Diff in Seats} - 0.050(0.008^{**})\textit{Maj Status} + 0.742(0.006^{**})\text{Constant} \quad (R^2 = 0.018,\ N = 2{,}345) \tag{12.2}$$

$$\textit{Republican Party Cohesion, 45th–61st Cong} = -0.171(0.028^{**})\textit{Abs Diff in Seats} - 0.016(0.007^{**})\textit{Maj Status} + 0.873(0.006^{**})\text{Constant} \quad (R^2 = 0.012,\ N = 3{,}057) \tag{12.3}$$

$$\textit{Republican Party Cohesion, 62nd–72nd Cong} = 0.250(0.03^{**})\textit{Abs Diff in Seats} - 0.040(0.008^{**})\textit{Maj Status} + 0.778(0.008^{**})\text{Constant} \quad (R^2 = 0.032,\ N = 2{,}503) \tag{12.4}$$

Having established that Democratic and Republican patterns of party cohesion differ, we turn to the analysis of committee appointments. We first estimate majority-party MCs' committee portfolio values using ordinary least squares (OLS) regression. We estimate separate models for each party given our expectation of different results for the two parties. Additionally, we estimate separate models for pre- and post-Cannon-overthrow Congresses to account for the importance of institutional changes that stemmed from that event. We generate our committee portfolio based on the Grosewart scores (Groseclose and Stewart 1998). More desirable committees (such as Ways and Means or Public Buildings) receive higher values, and less desirable committees (such as Insular Affairs or Mines) receive lower values and can take on negative values. We create an aggregate committee portfolio for each member during each Congress to measure the total value of a member's assignment. As a further test of our hypothesis regarding committee assignments, we investigate how the two parties went about distributing seats on especially valuable committees. We specify a series of probit models to estimate the probability a member receives a seat on one of the committees ranked in the top 10.[3]

Our major independent variable of interest is each member's party-cohesion score. We calculated members' abstention-adjusted party-cohesion scores for each Congress.[4] Committee assignments take place at the start of each Congress, which requires us to think about how cohesion scores can influence the assignment process. We contend that members' most recent cohesion scores, those from the preceding Congress, are the most appropriate for our estimation. That coding choice, however, requires us to drop freshman members from the analysis. Our expectation is that higher levels of party cohesion should lead to more-valuable committee portfolio assignments for Republicans, especially before the 1910 revolt. Democratic cohesion, on the other hand, is not expected to have a statistically significant effect on portfolio values.

To discern how cohesion influences committee assignments, we control for a series of electoral and member-specific variables. Seniority becomes a more important factor during the period we study, especially after the overthrow of Cannon in the 61st Congress (Abram and Cooper 1968; Polsby 1968; Schickler 2001), and we include a seniority variable that takes the value of the number of terms a member served. As an additional control, we include a squared measure of seniority to account for members' incentives to remain on a committee in an effort to ascend to the chairmanship. We have no clear expectations about the effects of seniority on committee portfolios and assignments on top committees except that seniority should become a more important factor following 1910.

Given the relatively close partisan divisions of the late 19th century, we include each member's margin of victory as a control variable. The data on margin of victory was drawn from Dubin's (1998) compendium of congressional elections. The preferred strategy for congressional parties is to maintain as many seats as possible, and one strategy might be to place those MCs most at risk on valuable committees. Placing marginal members on more valuable committees might allow MCs to direct projects to their districts and enhance their prospects of winning reelection, especially as the value of a seat in Congress increased as more members began to serve more terms (Kernell 1977) and members began to build personal constituencies (Katz and Sala 1996; Kernell and McDonald 1999).

Another mechanism for members to use to increase the size of their committee portfolio is simply to serve on more committees. However, serving on more committees does not necessarily translate into an enhanced committee portfolio and could be construed as a sort of punishment. Hence, we include a variable to account for the total number of committees in a member's portfolio to capture possible decreasing marginal returns from additional committee assignments. We include controls for the size of the majority-seat share in the House, coded as the percentage of seats held by the majority party in a given Congress. Our expectation is that narrow majorities may well lead to majority-party committee stacking and increased portfolio values for majority-party members (Binder 1997). Finally, we include a dichotomous variable for the South, which we define as the 11 former states of the Confederacy, for the regression equations for the Democratic Party to see whether there was a regional bias in Democratic assignments.

As we noted earlier, we estimate separate regressions for the Democratic and Republican parties because we have different expectations about the impact of party cohesion on committee assignments. Different eras within the House also generate different expectations about the committee-assignment process. To account for these temporal differences, we estimate separate regressions for the period between the 45th and 61st Congresses (1877–1910, the strong-Speaker era) and the period between the 62nd and 72nd Congresses (1911–1933, the emergence of the "textbook Congress" [Shepsle 1989]). Our first set of regressions estimates the total value of committee portfolios for the members of the majority party from the 45th to 61st Congresses, estimating separate models for Democrats and Republicans. Our results, presented in equations 12.5 and 12.6, support our conjecture that majority-party status had differential effects in the Republican and Democratic parties. Despite the relatively high levels of party cohesion within both parties, the coefficient on the cohesion variable is statistically insignificant for the Democrats. On the other hand, party cohesion is an important determinant of committee assignments within the Republican Party. More substantively, a Republican MC who is more than half a standard deviation above the party mean might be rewarded with a seat on a committee such as Public Lands or Military Affairs, for example.

$$\begin{aligned}&\textit{Maj. Party Committee Portfolio Values, Republicans, 45th–61st Congresses}\\&\quad = 0.493(0.196^{*})\textit{Party Cohesion} + 0.266(0.038^{**})\textit{Seniority}\\&\quad - 0.015(0.002^{**})\textit{Seniority}^2 + 0.241(0.590)\textit{Maj Seat Share}\\&\quad + 0.00(0.001)\textit{Margin} + 0.068(0.042)\textit{Num of Committees}\\&\quad - 0.280(0.419)\text{Constant } (R^2 = 0.05,\ N = 1{,}463)\end{aligned} \tag{12.5}$$

$$\begin{aligned}&\textit{Maj. Party Committee Portfolio Values, Democrats, 45th–61st Congresses}\\&\quad = 0.228(0.19)\textit{Party Cohesion} + 0.212(0.072^{**})\textit{Seniority}\\&\quad - 0.013(0.007)\textit{Seniority}^2 + 1.58(0.444^{**})\textit{Maj Seat Share}\\&\quad - 0.02(0.074)\textit{South} - 0.001(0.001)\textit{Margin} + 0.193(0.063^{**})\textit{Num of Committees}\\&\quad - 1.09(0.372^{**})\text{Constant } (R^2 = 0.05,\ N = 781)\end{aligned} \tag{12.6}$$

The coefficient on the seniority variable was significant and positive for members of both parties. Longer terms of service produced more valuable committee portfolios. For the Democrats this result is not surprising since seniority represented an objective criterion for distributing congressional committee assignments. The results for the Republicans were more surprising given all the attention received by Czar Cannon and his iron-fisted rule of the House. It appears that during the era of strong Republican speakers the longest-serving MCs received the most valuable committee assignments. For Democrats, it appears that large majorities enabled the party to favor its members when doling out committee assignments. There is no evidence that marginal MCs were favored with more-valuable committee portfolios in either party.

The results from the 45th to the 61st Congress clearly support our argument that party cohesion played differing roles in structuring the committee-assignment process for the two major parties. Next, we turn our attention to the post-revolt Congresses to determine whether and how cohesion influenced assignments in the beginnings of the textbook Congress. We estimate models for the 62nd to 72nd Congresses: the first Congress following Cannon's demise up until the first New Deal Congress. The results, presented in equations 12.7 and 12.8, mirror those from our previous era. Interestingly, while party cohesion remains a positive and statistically significant factor in determining Republican portfolio values, its effect is half as large as it was in the strong-Speaker era. Republicans with cohesion scores half a standard deviation greater than the mean could expect to be assigned to a committee such as Irrigation or Invalid Pensions, both of which rank much lower in the committee hierarchy. Seniority, on the other hand, exhibited a significant and positive effect for Republicans, while electoral margins only slightly assisted Republicans who won by large margins.

Republican Maj. Committee Portfolio Value, 62nd–72nd Congresses

$$= 0.260(0.140)\textit{Party Cohesion} + 0.097(0.02^{**})\textit{Seniority} - 0.004(0.001^{**})\textit{Seniority}^2 + 0.260(0.328)\textit{Maj Seat Share} + 0.002(0.000^{**})\textit{Margin} - 0.032(0.016^{*})\textit{Num of Committees} - 0.349(0.231)\text{Constant } (R^2 = 0.05,\ N = 1{,}355) \quad \textbf{(12.7)}$$

Democrat Maj. Committee Portfolio Value, 62nd–72nd Congresses

$$= 0.235(0.22)\textit{Party Cohesion} + 0.078(0.046^{**})\textit{Seniority} - 0.004(0.003^{**})\textit{Seniority}^2 + -1.01(0.482)\textit{Maj Seat Share} - 0.020(0.074)\textit{South} - 0.103(0.092)\textit{Margin} - 0.032(0.016^{*})\textit{Num of Committees} - 0.349(0.231)\text{Constant } (R^2 = 0.02,\ N = 702) \quad \textbf{(12.8)}$$

The committee-assignment process for the Democrats from the 62nd to the 72nd Congress is somewhat more difficult to explain. Despite attempts to use the binding caucus, our results provide additional confirmation of Green's (2002) argument that the Democrats were unsuccessful in enforcing party discipline because they were unwilling to penalize members who did not support the party position. Seniority had a positive impact on the total value of committee portfolio values, but the impact was marginal. The only other statistically significant variable was the size of Democratic seat share, and the negative coefficient suggests that the Democrats stacked more valuable committees when they had a narrow majority.

Consistent with our expectations, the results illustrate the differences between Democrats and Republicans with respect to meting out committee assignments. The results show that the two parties viewed party cohesion differently. Clearly, the Republican Party was more willing to use party cohesion as requirement for better committee assignments. The internal factionalization of the Democratic Party, on the other hand, made it much more difficult to employ such a strategy. To investigate further the importance of party cohesion, we look at appointments to specific committees to determine whether the parties reserved the most important and most valuable seats for their stalwart supporters.

To gain additional insight into the relative value of party cohesion for Democrats or Republicans, we use probit models to estimate the probability that a member receive an appointment to one of the 10 committees with the highest Grosewart scores. The results for the 45th to 61st Congresses, displayed in equations 12.9 and 12.10, lend additional supporting evidence that Democrats and Republicans used different committee-selection criteria. Republicans who exhibited higher levels of party loyalty had a much greater likelihood of receiving a spot on a top-10 committee. Holding each of the independent variables at their means, we can vary cohesion scores to determine the marginal effect. We find that Republicans who demonstrated perfect party cohesion were three times more likely to receive an assignment to a top-10 committee than a Republican who tallied a party-cohesion score of 0. Seniority also contributed to winning a spot on one of the more valuable committees. Republicans in their second terms had approximately a 1 in 10 chance of landing a place on one of the top committees. That probability approached 1.0 for Republicans who served 20 years.

As expected, Democrats did not use party loyalty as a condition for service on a top committee. The coefficient for party cohesion is insignificant and negative. Among Democrats, seniority appeared to be the driving force behind committee assignments, which represents a relatively neutral criterion favoring Southern and Eastern Democrats, who were the backbone of the party.

$$\begin{aligned}&\textit{Top-10 Committee Assignments, Republicans, 45th–61st Congresses}\\&\quad= 0.832(0.254^{**})\textit{Party Cohesion} + 0.371(0.056^{**})\textit{Seniority}\\&\quad- 0.029(0.004^{**})\textit{Seniority}^2 + 0.584(0.686)\textit{Maj Seat Share}\\&\quad+ 0.001(0.002)\textit{Margin} + 0.039(0.049)\textit{Num of Committees}\\&\quad- 2.14(0.507^{**})\text{Constant } (\chi^2 = 73.86^{**},\ N = 1{,}464) \qquad \mathbf{(12.9)}\end{aligned}$$

$$\begin{aligned}&\textit{Top-10 Committee Assignments, Democrats, 45th–61st Congresses}\\&\quad= -0.191(0.276)\textit{Party Cohesion} + 0.251(0.105^{*})\textit{Seniority}\\&\quad- 0.018(0.01)\textit{Seniority}^2 - 0.308(0.643)\textit{Seat Share}\\&\quad+ 0.009(0.107)\textit{South} + 0.001(0.001)\textit{Margin} + 0.073(0.091)\textit{Num of Committees}\\&\quad- 0.601(0.54)\text{Constant } (\chi^2 = 12.89,\ N = 781) \qquad \mathbf{(12.10)}\end{aligned}$$

As we did previously, we divide our observations into two periods to distinguish between the rise of stronger parties in the House and the post-revolt era, which was characterized by lower levels of party polarization and cohesion. Focusing on top-10 committee assignments, the patterns in the 62nd to 72nd Congresses (displayed in equations 12.11 and 12.12) are similar to the value of committee portfolios that we discussed previously. The impact of party cohesion was reduced by nearly half, which is consistent with our OLS estimates. Members who had higher levels of party cohesion were still more likely to receive an assignment to a top committee, but seniority plays a more influential role. Not surprisingly, members who served on more committees were less likely to receive an assignment to one of the top-10 committees. Republicans with the highest cohesion scores had a slightly better than 50–50 chance of being assigned to a top-10 committee. Interestingly, a Republican who had a cohesion score of zero still had a better than 1 in 3 chance of receiving such an assignment. Compared to what transpired in the late 19th and early 20th centuries, party loyalty was a considerably less important consideration for the most valuable committees.

$$\begin{aligned}&\textit{Top-10 Committee Assignments, Republicans, 62nd–72nd Congresses}\\&\quad = 0.443(0.254)\textit{Party Cohesion} + 0.098(0.035^{**})\textit{Seniority}\\&\qquad - 0.004(0.002)\textit{Seniority}^2 + 0.490(0.570)\textit{Maj Seat Share}\\&\qquad + 0.004(0.001^{**})\textit{Margin} - 0.207(0.208^{**})\textit{Num of Committees}\\&\qquad + 0.582\ (0.403)\text{Constant}\ (\chi^2 = 95.71^{**},\ N = 1{,}355)\end{aligned} \quad \textbf{(12.11)}$$

$$\begin{aligned}&\textit{Top-10 Committee Assignments, Democrats, 62nd–72nd Congresses}\\&\quad = 0.125(0.359)\textit{Party Cohesion} + 0.113(0.076)\textit{Seniority}\\&\qquad - 0.005(0.006)\textit{Seniority}^2 - 1.64(0.781^{*})\textit{Maj Seat Share}\\&\qquad - 0.115(0.151)\textit{South} + 0.000(0.001)\textit{Margin}\\&\qquad - 0.176(0.04^{**})\textit{Num of Committees} + 0.986(0.584)\text{Constant}\\&\qquad (\chi^2 = 35.52^{**},\ N = 702)\end{aligned} \quad \textbf{(12.12)}$$

Majority-party committee assignments for the Democrats in the post-revolt Congresses reveal no clear pattern. Party cohesion has no effect on committee assignments, and while seniority is properly signed, it does not reach conventional levels of statistical significance. The statistically significant and negative coefficient on the seat-share variables provides some indication that the Democrats attempted to stack key committees during those Congresses in which they held slim majorities. It is no surprise that Democrats receiving more committee assignments were less likely to receive a seat on one of the top committees in the House during this era.

ISOLATING POLICY EFFECTS

The overall pattern of results we have presented suggests that greater levels of party cohesion among Republicans contributed to a more valuable committee portfolio. On the other hand, we find little evidence that the Democratic Party used party loyalty as an important criterion for making congressional committee assignments. As we indicated previously, most observers noted that the Democratic Party was composed of competing factions while the Republican Party was more unified. Some, however, argue that despite high levels of competition between the two parties, partisan divisions were not based on any sort of programmatic policy differences (Sundquist 1983) but quibbles over a small subset of issues that traditionally separated them, like the tariff. To determine how specific policy areas influenced party cohesion, we focus our attention on five particularly important policy areas that were critical components of the legislative agenda from 1877 to 1932: banking and finance, interstate commerce, military pensions, income taxes, and tariffs and trade.[5] The number of votes in each Congress that fell into one of these five areas varied significantly and the range of votes for our modified party-cohesion scores ranged from as few as three votes in the 69th Congress (1925–1927) to 139 votes in the 52nd Congress (1891–1893). In some Congresses no votes were taken on some of the issue areas. For example, there were no tariff votes in either the 54th or the 65th Congress. After identifying the sets of votes in each of these issue areas, we calculated individual party-cohesion scores from votes in all five issue areas as well as issue-specific cohesion scores.

Somewhat contrary to our expectations, the issue-specific cohesion scores closely resemble the aggregate-level scores. Once again, we find that Republicans were slightly more cohesive than Democrats. The average party cohesion for Republicans was 89.9 percent; for Democrats, 87.1 percent. More significantly, when we divide the Democrats into their Northern and Southern wings, we see that Southern Democrats were more cohesive (91.2%) than Northern Democrats (83.8%). Turning our attention to each of the specific policy areas, we find Republicans more cohesive on each of the issues in question.

The aggregated scores show Republican cohesion generally exceeds Democratic cohesion by approximately 2 to 3 percentage points. The largest gap between the parties occurs on pension votes, a result that is not surprising given the importance of pensions to Union veterans as an important aspect of maintaining the Republican coalition (Bensel 2000).[6] Northern Democrats were likely less supportive of their party position because they were able to provide some constituency benefits that might pay off during the next campaign. Since former Confederate veterans did not receive benefits, Southern Democrats opposed any expansion of pension funds. Both parties were cohesive on tariff votes, although it is important to note that Southern Democrats were considerably more cohesive than Northern Democrats on such votes. Most of the attention on tariff votes focuses on a small number of Southern Democrats who defected, but it is important to note that many Northern Democrats who represented industrial districts were more likely to favor the protective tariff.

The most significant issue is whether party loyalty on this subset of votes affected the value of a legislator's committee portfolio and the probability of receiving a top-10-committee assignment.[7] Estimating a fixed-effects regression model,[8] we find that party loyalty on the limited set of issues was a significant and positive predictor of the value of committee portfolios for Republicans. For Democrats, the effect was not statistically significant. Given the importance of the tariff for both parties, we estimated a regression model using party loyalty on tariff votes as the key independent variable and found that it was significant and positive for Republicans but nearly zero for the Democrats. The findings of these additional analyses are certainly consistent with the findings we reported in the previous section. Ideological heterogeneity among the Democratic Party, even on subsets of issues thought to divide the parties, meant that criteria other than party loyalty dictated committee assignment practices.

Conclusion

The analyses we devised for our hypotheses, based on the pattern of congressional committee assignments, provide confirmation for the differences between Democrats and Republicans. Party loyalty did not have an influence on Democratic committee assignments when the party was in the majority. This result is robust across two distinct periods in time and two different measures of committee assignments. The patterns among Republicans stand in sharp contrast to the Democrats. Republicans place greater emphasis on party loyalty when doling out valuable committee assignments. Even following the revolt and the rise of the seniority system, party loyalty still exerted an important and independent effect on Republican committee assignments.

Chapter 13

The Evolution of Agenda-Setting Institutions in Congress: Path Dependency in House and Senate Institutional Development

JASON M. ROBERTS AND STEVEN S. SMITH

Introduction

Scheduling legislation is one of the most vexing collective-action problems faced by a legislative body. When the combination of must-pass legislation and legislation wanted by individual members exceeds the available time and resources, choices among alternatives must be made. These choices about the form and content of the legislative agenda create winners and losers, so it is important that we understand how these agenda-setting institutions emerge and develop. In this chapter we focus on the two most important agenda-setting institutions in the U.S. Congress—special rules in the House and unanimous-consent agreements (UCAs) in the Senate.

From the 1880s on, the House of Representatives and the Senate took different procedural paths in addressing the problem of setting the floor agenda. In the House, the resolutions reported by the Committee on Rules that eventually became known as "special rules" took form in the 1880s. At about the same time, complex UCAs became a common way to limit debate and schedule votes in the Senate. In both chambers, management of burgeoning workloads and the evolving partisan conflict appear to have motivated innovations in the mechanisms of setting the floor agenda.

We know something about the path taken by each house. Bach (1990) provides the first account of the changing strategies reflected in the House Committee on Rules resolutions, a transformation he describes as a shift from special orders to special rules, while Bach and Smith (1988) note the increasing sophistication of special rules in the late 1970s and 1980s. Gamm and Smith (2000) report on the transformation of UCAs from informal arrangements among senators to formal orders of the Senate, while Smith and Flathman (1989) track the changing content of UCAs in the last decades of the 20th century.

Missing from previous studies is a systematic account of the acquisition of the multiple functions served by special rules and UCAs. Explanations of institutional development cannot be tested without a more systematic account that identifies the timing of key changes in rules and practice. We seek to demonstrate how and when each chamber adopted innovations in the use of these agenda-setting tools.

Equally important, existing studies of scheduling mechanisms do not provide a direct comparison of House and Senate institutional development. Comparison of the House and Senate gives us useful analytical leverage. The two houses, facing broadly similar workload and partisan pressures but starting from different initial procedural conditions, evolved very different rules and practices to manage the floor agenda. These differences had important consequences for the distribution of procedural advantages and the development of legislative parties.

Setting the legislative agenda became the primary responsibility of majority-party leadership. Consequently, an examination of the evolution of agenda-setting mechanisms yields insights about two of the leading views of congressional parties. One view, the conditional-party-government thesis of Aldrich and Rohde (2000b), proposes that legislative parties are policy coalitions whose cohesiveness varies in response to the degree of homogeneity of the local electorates that elect their members. Legislators' willingness to delegate power to the party leadership—over the agenda and other matters—varies directly with the homogeneity of their electorates and, therefore, their own policy preferences. A second view of legislative parties is that of Cox and McCubbins (1993, 2005), in which parties are considered to be electoral coalitions that form procedural cartels. A legislative party exists to enhance its members' electoral prospects, and it does so primarily by asserting control over the legislative agenda. Agenda control is used to preserve the party's "brand name," by preventing measures from moving to the floor that would divide the party. On floor votes, at least final-passage votes, agenda control produces a united majority party.

Both of these theories posit, either explicitly or implicitly, that parties seek to control outcomes by shaping the legislative agenda, suggesting that both chambers would seek to develop similar, if not identical, agenda-control mechanisms. Yet, as we demonstrate below, in the late 19th and early 20th centuries, the inherited procedural and workload differences between the chambers promoted contrasting approaches to floor scheduling and generated different incentives for the delegation of power to the majority-party leadership. The House of Representatives, starting with a previous-question motion in its rules and a presiding officer elected from its membership, acquired the means for the chamber's majority party to assert procedural control over the floor agenda whenever it could muster a simple majority.[1] The Senate, which did not have a previous-question motion or a presiding officer elected from its membership, lacked the means by which a majority party could assert control over the floor agenda. Instead, it evolved mechanisms that, under most circumstances, require the consent of both majority and minority members to organize floor debate and amending activity. Further, the Senate's majority party took much longer than its House counterpart to place responsibility for floor-agenda setting in a floor leader.

The Motion on the Previous Question and Path Dependency

A potentially strong path dependency exists in the development of congressional agenda-setting mechanisms. This path-dependent process is stronger than those usually encountered in processes of institutional change. Pierson (2000) describes path-dependent processes that are a product of the increasing returns of an institutional arrangement. In fact, increasing returns are a common, maybe the most common, form of path-dependent processes. With little difficulty, we can see this form operating in Congress, too. But what we see in the contrasting paths of House and Senate development is a stronger form.

Both the House and the Senate rules contained a previous-question motion from the First Congress; however, the motion had not yet been transformed into a tool to end debate. The question took the form of "shall the main question be now put," which was the traditional parliamentary means of putting off discussion on a controversial measure. If the motion failed, discussion was put off; if it passed, discussion continued. The early Senate rarely invoked the motion, and eliminated it from its rules in 1806. The House overturned a ruling of the Speaker in 1807 that a successful previous-question motion ended debate on a bill before reversing this precedent in the face of obstruction in 1811. Thus, from 1811 forward, the House had an effective means for a majority to end debate on a bill or proposed rule change, while the Senate, bound by its lack of a previous-question motion, has never been able to develop an efficient means of ending debate.

Our working hypothesis is that the presence or absence of a motion for the previous question played a pivotal role in the development of House and Senate rules. As Binder (1995, 1094) notes, "The emergence of a majoritarian chamber by the end of the nineteenth century was contingent on the majority's ability to force votes on proposed rules changes . . . without a previous question rule, a simple majority has no such power to direct the course of institutional change." House majority parties have regularly modified and elaborated on their chamber's rules, while Senate majority parties seldom seek, let alone achieve, a change in their chamber's rules. As a consequence, modern House rules are several times as long as Senate rules. When the House and Senate have determined that some limitation on debate is desirable, as for budget measures and trade agreements, special provisions have been written for the Senate to guarantee that debate could be closed (Binder and Smith 1997). But this has happened only when supermajorities favor the change and often has happened as a part of a much larger legislative package.

The Senate's history appears to share features of increasing-returns processes identified by Arthur (1994, 112–113) and reviewed by Pierson (2000, 253). The initial event (dropping the little-used previous-question motion from the rules) seemed unimportant at the time but had lasting effects. The long-term effects were unpredictable because they depended on so many other unpredictable events, the procedural change proved very difficult to reverse (and has not been fully reversed), and the long-term consequence was inefficiency for an institution in which the constitutionally specified decision-making process was no different than that of the House. Because reform of debate-closing rules can be filibustered, this feature of Senate procedural history surely is a self-reinforcing process that can be characterized as path dependent.

Nevertheless, the story of path dependency in Senate procedure is special. Many of the factors—collective-action hurdles, transaction costs, vested interests, accumulated social capital, and so on—cited by Pierson, North (1990), and others that contribute to institutional persistency are not the primary forces underlying the path dependency of Senate procedure. In contrast to the increasing-returns process, the Senate's basic decision rule has not been changed even under conditions of dramatically *decreasing* returns for the majority of senators. On only rare occasions have the costs of the inherited rules proved so high for a large enough number of senators to produce reform that reduced the threshold for cloture, itself an unwieldy procedure in comparison to House mechanisms for limiting debate, and even then the reforms have been modest. This is the product of the threshold itself and the infrequency with which large majorities arise that may find their enduring interests subverted by the threshold.

Recognition of potentially path-dependent features of congressional procedure is essential to a comparison of House and Senate agenda-setting mechanisms and their implications for the development of legislative parties. House rules have been adopted, modified, or eliminated many times with little or no support from minority-party legislators; Senate rules seldom have. The consequence is a different blend of procedures and parties in the two houses and a different dynamic to the changing role in policy making of the parties of the two houses.

Efforts to Modify the Order of Business

In the late 19th century, the House and Senate faced similar, although certainly not identical, logistical problems in the decades following the Civil War. By the 1880s, both houses faced serious obstacles to the completion of even routine legislative business. Our hypothesis is that two problems—an expanding legislative workload and renewed, sharp partisan conflict—were the mutually reinforcing motivations for change. A large legislative workload reflected an expanding nation, new demands for federal programs, and an increasingly complicated tariff code. The revival of the Democratic Party as Reconstruction ended generated intense competition for control of Congress and eventually yielded very polarized parties, particularly at the turn of the century. Minority obstructionism, made more damaging by the time pressures of a large workload, became a serious problem in both houses.

Before inventing more flexible agenda-setting devices of special rules and UCAs, both houses of Congress addressed the challenges of scheduling with changes in the order of business provided in their standing rules. Over the course of the 19th century, both chambers created special times and days for the transaction of particular kinds of legislative business and identified classes of legislation that could be reported and considered at any time (privileged measures). The daily schedule and classification of legislation were changed frequently, sometimes in response to abusive practices of the membership and sometimes in response to the burden of legislative business (Alexander 1916; Rybicki n.d.).

The challenges were not identical in both houses. The size of the House grew far more rapidly than the Senate as the nation's population grew faster than states were added to the Union. The House was quicker to elaborate a complex order of business and create a set of floor calendars. For example, the House went further than the Senate in limiting certain kinds of motions to specified times or days and eliminating the requirement of gaining recognition on the floor to submit petitions, bills, and reports. In 1890 the regular tinkering with the order of business was overcome by a sweeping set of changes proposed, and later imposed, by Speaker Thomas Brackett Reed (R-Maine). The rules assigned to the Speaker several powers previously reserved for the House (referring bills to committee and disposing of business on the Speaker's table such as executive messages). More important, the Reed rules made it easy for a House majority to continue deliberating on a measure in the "morning hour," which could be stretched to any length, thus undermining a common source of obstructionism in the House.

Ultimately, changes in the formal order of business proved inadequate to the challenge of scheduling important legislation for floor consideration. In both chambers, debates about what to consider next and ad hoc motions from bill managers or sponsors to create special orders were common, often generating confusion about the schedule as well as tension within and between the parties. As we detail in the following sections, the struggle to solve this problem was addressed in fundamentally different ways in the two houses.

The House of Representatives and Special Rules

The House Committee on Rules first gained power to report to the House at all times in 1841, but it would take decades for the committee to begin to play a major role in shaping the agenda and floor debate in the chamber through the use of what we now refer to as special rules. The Committee on Rules quickly moved from reporting "special orders," which provided that measures be considered on the floor outside the regular order, to "special rules," which added limitations on debate or amendments (Bach 1990). By the time of the revolt against Speaker Joseph Cannon during the 61st Congress, the House had almost completely discontinued use of special orders in favor of special rules, and it had developed many of the components of modern-day special rules, including amending restrictions, waivers of points of order, and self-executing provisions.

First Uses of Special Order: Resolutions from the Committee on Rules

The first documented instance of the Committee on Rules attempting to alter the rules for consideration of a specific bill occurred in the 47th

Congress during consideration of the Tariff Act of 1883. The original bill sought to lower the sales tax on tobacco, matches, and medicine and easily passed the House in mid-1882. The Senate took up the bill in early 1883 and made radical changes, striking out all but the enacting clause and transforming the measure into a general tariff-reduction bill (Stanwood 1903, 209). The Senate bill was not wholly acceptable to the Republican leaders in the Senate, but Senators Morrill (R-Vt.), Sherman (R-Ohio), and Aldrich (R-R.I.) allowed the bill to pass with the understanding that they would be able to alter it in conference (McCown 1927, 109). Simultaneously, the House was trying to pass a tariff bill, but a sharply divided Republican caucus was unable to come to agreement on a bill. The result was a House bill with the same title as the Senate measure but one that dealt only with internal taxes, in contrast to the exclusive focus on tariffs in the Senate version. The House Republicans caucused on this issue and voted to disagree with the Senate amendments and request a conference. However, close to 40 members of the Republican caucus were absent from the meeting and presumably would have voted to accept the Senate bill if given the opportunity.

Republican leaders of both chambers sought to pass a bill with significantly higher tariffs than the bill passed by the Senate and decided that the best approach was to get the bill to a conference committee where the provisions of the bill could be amended to provide for higher tariff rates. The House leadership could bring up a motion to disagree with the Senate amendments and go to conference, but under House rules a motion to agree with the Senate amendments would have taken precedence and likely would have passed. An alternative approach was to consider a motion to disagree and request a conference under suspension of the rules, which would require a two-thirds vote of the chamber—a margin that was likely unattainable. A third approach was taken. Representative Reed, who had recently become a member of the Committee on Rules and became Speaker a few years later, authored the following resolution, which was reported from the committee:

> *Resolved,* That during the remainder of the session it shall be in order at any time to move to suspend the rules, which motion shall be decided by a majority vote, to take from the Speaker's table House Bill Number 5538, with Senate amendment thereto, entitled "A bill to reduce internal-revenue taxation," and to declare a disagreement with the Senate amendments to the same and to ask for a committee of conference thereon, to be composed of five members on the part of the House. If

> such motion shall fail, the bill shall remain upon the Speaker's table unaffected by the decision of the House upon such motion. (*Congressional Record*, February 24, 1883, p. 3259)

The resolution was adopted. It is the first known instance of the adoption of a special order to supplant or supplement the standing rules by a simple majority rather than a two-thirds majority. The episode also demonstrated the potential of the Committee on Rules to augment the power of House majorities by limiting the House to a vote to disagree with the Senate amendments. The rule did not provide for a motion to agree with the Senate amendments, thus forcing a vote between going to conference or not passing a tariff bill. This use of the Rules Committee to shape the agenda allowed majority-party Republicans to ensure that their preferred outcome—a bill with higher tariffs—was adopted while also preventing a vote on the Senate bill, which was preferred by most Democrats and moderate Republicans.

The House was slow to repeat this use of the Committee on Rules. The resolution providing for consideration of the tariff bill was the only one reported by the committee during the 47th Congress; none were reported during the 48th Congress. When interjections into the order of business by the Committee on Rules reappeared during the 49th Congress, they all took the form of special orders—they provided for the consideration of a particular bill or bills from a committee but did not alter the procedures by which the bills were considered. Although the wording of these special orders was not consistent, the following order from the 49th Congress (1885–1887) is typical:

> *Resolved*, That on Tuesday, February 1, 1887, the House will take a recess at 5 o'clock p.m. until half past 7 p.m., and that the evening session shall be devoted exclusively to the consideration of such measures as may be presented by the Committee on Military Affairs. (*Congressional Record*, January 29, 1887, p. 1156)

Special orders were not new features of House procedures, but the ability to change the order of business through a majority rather than supermajority vote was an innovation. The debate on these orders suggests that special orders were not particularly partisan in effect. Minority members still held all parliamentary rights under the "regular order," including the right to offer amendments and dilatory motions. With the burgeoning workload, the House simply needed a more efficient means of reaching bills that were unlikely to be reached by taking bills off the calendar in order. Special orders served this role quite well, often designating days for multiple bills or committees in the same order.

Members soon recognized that the occasional special order was a harbinger of things to come from the Committee on Rules. During debate on a special order in the 49th Congress (1885–1887), Representative Bayne (R-Pa.) observed,

> if the powers of the Committee on Rules, with its special prerogatives and special powers, are to be perverted to the mere object of fixing a night or day for the consideration of special bills to be reported from some particular committee . . . there soon will cease to be any respect for the rules of the House at all. (*Congressional Record*, July 19, 1886, pp. 7156–7157)

The Early Special Rules

The transformation of special orders into special rules began in the 51st Congress (1889–1891), the first with Reed as Speaker. Traditional special orders were still employed, but 7 of the 11 interjections into the regular order by the Committee on Rules in that Congress were special rules. All 7 limited the time for either general debate or amendments under the 5-minute rule, while two of the rules barred all amendments—the first "closed" rules.

The 51st Congress also marked a shift to partisan debate over the content of reports from the Committee on Rules. During debate on the rule for considering the currency bill, a minority party legislator, Representative James Blount (D-Ga.), called attention to the power of special rules to restrict policy alternatives and provide political cover for the majority party:

> If it was permissible for me to state what occurred in the Republican caucus last night, I could show an infinite amount of division; I could show just such a division on other side of the House as makes it necessary to put the whip of this order upon them to save them from such a record as would be terrible to them. . . . Your Republican platform declared for silver coinage. In your secret councils many of you have recognized the importance of some sort of coinage of silver, yet here is an order changing the rules of this House to escape that issue in the Congress of the United States. (*Congressional Record*, June 5, 1890, p. 5646)

The use of special rules to prevent cross-party coalitions from amending or even overturning the legislation of a majority of the majority party has come to be recognized as a vital source of influence for majority-party leaders (Bach and Smith 1988; Sinclair [Deckard] 1983).

While the 51st Congress marked the beginning of the transformation from special orders to special rules, it would take several Congresses for practices to settle into a predictable form. In the next Congress, with the Democratic party back in the majority, most rules resolutions were special orders. Some were proposed and adopted after a consideration of a bill had begun on the floor and served only to provide for an end to the debate. In the following Congresses, the House adopted hybrid orders that had components of both special rules and special orders, such as the following:

> *Resolved*, That immediately upon the adoption of this order the Committee of the Whole be discharged from the consideration of House bill 1217, and the same be considered in the House as in Committee of the Whole; that only an hour's general debate be allowed, and then said bill shall be considered under the five-minutes' rule [*sic*] for amendment until the hour of 4:30 o'clock p.m., when the previous question shall be considered as ordered on pending amendments and the bill to its passage, when the vote shall be taken without delay or other motion.
>
> That Thursday, the 12th instant, after the second morning hours [*sic*], be assigned to the consideration of business reported by the Committee on Foreign Affairs.
>
> This order not to interfere with the consideration of conference reports or revenue or appropriation bills. (*Congressional Record*, July 11, 1894, pp. 7335–7336)

By the 54th Congress (1895–1897), Reed was back in the Speaker's chair and legislators referred to reports from the Committee on Rules as "rules." The use of special rules began to grow and the rules became increasingly restrictive of amending activity. Some began to streamline activity by including "self-executing" previous-question orders in special rules that had the effect of closing or restricting amending opportunities in the House under the hour rule, such as in this rule:

> *Resolved*, That immediately after the adoption of this resolution it shall be in order in the House to call up for debate, the previous question being considered as ordered, a bill reported by the Ways and Means, entitled "A bill to temporarily increase revenue to meet the expenses of Government and provide against a deficiency;" that at 5 o'clock, without delay or other motion, the vote shall be taken. General leave to print is hereby granted for ten days. (*Congressional Record*, December 26, 1895, p. 305)

This rule eliminated amending opportunities by embedding the previous-question motion in the rule, limited the time for general debate to less than 1 day, and precluded "other motions," such as the motion to recommit.

Thus, over the course of only a few Congresses, the House moved from a body that had a difficult time transacting any business to a body with the means to dispose of major legislation in less than a day. Commenting on this transformation, Representative Bailey (D-Tex.) warned, "It was foolish, I grant you, to debate without deciding; but it is dangerous to decide without debating. . . . This error, sir, is more mischievous than the one which we have abandoned" (*Congressional Record*, December 27, 1895, p. 344). The phrase was borrowed from Senator Henry Cabot Lodge, who had used a different version to criticize the Senate filibuster.

Innovations in special rules were not always restrictive in nature. During consideration of an appropriations bill, members discovered that many of the salaries funded in the bill had not been authorized and were subject to successful points of order raised by minority-party members. The Committee on Rules responded by reporting a rule that read,

> *Resolved*, That hereafter, in consideration of the bill [HR 16472] making appropriations for the legislative, executive, and judicial expenses of the Government, and for other purposes, in the Committee of the Whole House on the state of the Union, it shall be in order to consider, without intervention of a point of order, any section of the bill as reported, except section 8; and upon motion authorized by the Committee on Appropriations it shall be in order to insert in any part of the bill any provision reported as part of the bill and heretofore ruled out on a point of order. (*Congressional Record*, March 28, 1906, p. 4398)

The 1906 special rule appears to have been one of the first rules to waive points of order. This waiver did not have profound policy consequences, but the incident was important for two reasons. First, the rule expanded the repertoire of special rules to supplant a new class of standing rules. Rather than merely limiting debate or amendments, the rule showed that a House majority also could set aside any restriction in the standing rules, which eventually would include germaneness and many other important restrictions. Second, the rule was adopted in response to unanticipated developments on the floor, which in the future would limit the effectiveness of innovative minority tactics.

The ability of majorities to streamline floor action on legislation is one of the defining characteristics of the modern House of Representatives. However, this has not always been the case. Before the development of the special order and the institution of the Reed rules, the House was chaotic with members regularly obstructing business and arguing over the order of business. The special order and later the special rule developed as means for the House to legislate efficiently and for majority parties to gain control of the agenda. These developments would have been much more difficult, if not impossible, without a previous-question motion. The previous-question motion not only provided a means for the House to close debate on substantive legislation but it allowed a majority to close debate and prevent amendments to special orders and special rules. In less than two decades the House developed many of the features of modern-day special rules, including debate and amendment restrictions, waivers, and self-executing provisions, and often used them for partisan purposes, especially on tariff legislation. Despite the development and innovation of special rules in the late 19th and early 20th centuries, the use of this new procedural tool was limited. It would be decades before the House permitted the Committee on Rules to be the primary agenda setter in the House.

The Senate and Unanimous-Consent Agreements

The term *complex* has sometimes been applied to the important class of UCAs that interests us—those that limit debate or amendments in some way (Keith 1977; Smith and Flathman 1989). In the modern Senate, most complex UCAs are negotiated by, or under the supervision of, the majority leader and are offered by him, but the floor leaders' responsibility for agreements took decades to emerge after UCAs became a regular feature of floor action.[2]

Pre-1914 Period

Although the Senate has always been less formal and more leisurely than the House in floor procedure, the first, and somewhat isolated, use of a unanimous-consent request to limit debate or amendments occurred in 1846 (Keith 1977). Not surprisingly, the 1846 agreement was raised in a most casual way (*Congressional Globe*, April 13, 1846, p. 659). A senator observed that the debate on the Oregon resolutions seemed to be winding down after more than 2 months and that "it would be an accommodation to many Senators to have an understanding as to the exact day" the Senate would vote. The agreement was quite informal—merely to vote on the resolutions in 3 days. A senator noted that the chamber could not be sure that debate on amendments would end by then; another assured him that the remaining debate would be brief. Notably, one senator said that he "had not the slightest objection to fixing upon some day for terminating the debate, provided it was not to be regarded as establishing a precedent." On the appointed day, the debate lasted longer than some senators had expected, but they brought the resolutions to a vote.

Identifying complex UCAs in the mid-19th century is difficult. As informal agreements, UCAs were not reported or indexed in the *Senate Journal* or other official publications. Perusal of the *Congressional Globe*, which does not provide reliable coverage of all procedural action, indicates that by 1870 UCAs were being used with some frequency. As many are today, the UCAs were time-limitation agreements that provided for disposal of a measure by a specified time. The typical UCA provided for a vote on a bill by a certain time, usually 4 or 5 o'clock, 1 or 2 days in the future. The presiding officer usually repeated the agreement once offered so that senators could hear and understand it.

As early as 1870 the Senate found itself bound by an interpretation of the parliamentary status of UCAs that made them difficult to enforce. On Saturday July 4, 1870, with many senators losing patience as their summer stay in Washington was extended, the hour for a final vote on a naturalization bill under a UCA passed, with opponents continuing to press amendments and debate the bill. Senators observed that the debate continued in violation of the UCA. John Sherman, in fact, complained that it was the first violation of a UCA in the history of the practice (*Congressional Globe*, July 4, 1870, p. 5152). When a point of order was raised by another senator, the president pro tempore, Henry Anthony, stated that the chair did not have the power to enforce the agreement. "The agreement under which the Senate came to an understanding to vote at five o'clock on Saturday was by unanimous consent," Anthony declared. "It was not an order entered on the *Journal*, but merely an understanding among Senators. The Chair has no power and no right to enforce an agreement of that kind" (*Congressional Globe*, July 4, 1870, p. 5150). Anthony's repeated rulings established a precedent that UCAs could not be enforced by the presiding officer, a precedent that led to much confusion over the next four decades.

Anthony's interpretation appeared to be based on the casual nature of UCAs in the years before the Civil War, when UCAs were viewed as mere gentlemen's agreements. The argument was based on two premises—that UCAs were not recognized in the Senate's rules and that the presiding officer had no authority except that granted explicitly by the rules or an order of the Senate. After Anthony left the Senate, Henry Cabot Lodge

(R-Mass.) became the Senate's unofficial parliamentarian-in-residence and frequently articulated this rationale.

In practice, presiding officers after Anthony were not entirely consistent in their approach to UCAs in the late 19th century. Most presiding officers contributed to the implementation of UCAs by noting that the time had arrived to call up or vote on a measure subject to a UCA. But senators varied in their understanding of the role of the presiding officer, and the role of presiding officers in facilitating the UCA process was not settled before the century ended. Most presiding officers routinely refused to enforce UCAs, but others chose to go their own way and their colleagues tolerated their choices. In 1888 Senator John Ingalls (R-Kans.), then president pro tempore, interrupted a senator who exceeded the 5-minute limit for a speech under a UCA and asked if there was objection to allowing the senator to continue (*Congressional Record*, 1888, p. 1848). Ingalls was not alone in enforcing the UCA limits on speeches (*Congressional Record*, 1908, p. 3615). President Pro Tempore William Frye (R-Maine) once took the initiative to note that debate was not in order under a UCA and ruled on a point of order raised against amendments based on provisions of the same UCA (*Congressional Record*, 1900, pp. 2448–2449). And Vice Presidents Charles Fairbanks and James Sherman were not timid about enforcing UCAs at times (*Congressional Record*, 1908, p. 3602; *Congressional Record*, 1909, pp. 549–550; *Congressional Record*, 1912, p. 10974; *Congressional Record*, December 8, 1913, pp. 423–426).

Responsibility for negotiating UCAs appears to have rested primarily on the shoulders of bill managers until the second decade of the 20th century. The *Congressional Record* is replete with long exchanges among senators about a bill manager's unanimous-consent request. Confusion about the provisions of UCAs was common, with senators sometimes quoting the *Record* to prove a point. Senators sometimes complained that they were not present when unanimous consent was granted.

Further complicating the use of UCAs after the turn of the century was the thesis that UCAs could not be modified, even by unanimous consent. Lodge made this argument in 1907 (*Congressional Record*, January 10, 1907, pp. 878–879) and consistently maintained the position (*Congressional Record*, January 10, 1913, pp. 1389–1390) along with the view that the presiding officer could not enforce UCAs. Lodge's theory was that a UCA, as a gentlemen's agreement, created an obligation that could not be violated at a later time by senators who happened to be on the floor and were seeking a modification. Lodge argued, as Sherman had maintained in 1870, that modifications in UCAs, even by unanimous consent, would eventually undermine confidence in UCAs. Although presiding officers were not consistent on this matter, the Lodge thesis was the prevailing interpretation during the first decade of the 20th century.

Agreements that provided for a vote on a bill and pending amendments at a certain time were a regular part of floor-management practice at the turn of the century. Although compliance with UCAs was generally good, critical features of modern floor practice were not in place. No formal party floor leaders were present to orchestrate agreements and oversee their implementation. The thesis that UCAs could not be modified by unanimous consent made them inflexible tools for scheduling. Presiding officers enforced agreements sporadically, whether because of the ignorance of precedent or the forbearance of senators.

In the first years of the 20th century, the Senate adopted practices that reduced confusion about UCAs. Senators began to submit unanimous-consent requests in writing to the desk. UCAs were often read by the secretary at the request of the presiding officer. UCAs that were intended to govern the conduct of business on subsequent days were printed on the title page of the daily Calendar of Business as long as they were operative. And the secretary appears to have reworded numerous agreements so that they would conform to what had become the "usual form," as some senators noted on the floor. These innovations occurred without any official recognition of the UCAs in the standing rules of the Senate.

Arguments about the twisted logic in Senate precedents on UCAs came to a head in January 1913 (*Congressional Record*, January 10–11, 1913, pp. 1324–1329, 1354–1356, 1388–1395). After having failed in previous days to gain unanimous consent for consideration and a vote on a prohibition bill, Newell Sanders (R-Tenn.) asked for unanimous consent once again and, probably much to his surprise, received it. Reed Smoot (R-Utah) quickly inquired, "Was there a unanimous consent agreement just entered?" When the substitute presiding officer indicated that there was, Smoot immediately asked that it be reconsidered, to which the presiding officer responded that "it is beyond the power of the Senate to change or interfere with a unanimous consent agreement after it is made." Several senators insisted that they had not heard the request and that previous practice in such cases was to have the request submitted to the Senate again. Others, including Lodge, had to confess that a UCA must be observed. One senator, Joseph Bristow (R-Kans.), proclaimed that he was free to violate the UCA. The next day, Smoot suggested that the request be resubmitted to the Senate. Over the strong protest of another Republican, New Hampshire's Jacob

Gallinger, President Pro Tempore Augustus Bacon (D-Ga.), now back in the chair, indicated that he had no power to rule on the matter and allowed the issue to be decided by the Senate. A large majority voted to have the request resubmitted, which it was, and Smoot promptly objected to the request. Gallinger then restated the request—with a different date for action on the measure—and it was accepted.

By the beginning of the next session, a committee recommended the adoption of a new rule, an additional paragraph for rule 12. The rule provided that

> no request by a Senator for unanimous consent for the taking of a final vote on a specified date upon the passage of a bill or joint resolution shall be submitted to the Senate for agreement thereto until, upon a roll call ordered for the purpose by the presiding officer, it shall be disclosed that a quorum of the Senate is present; and when unanimous consent is thus given, the same shall operate as the order of the Senate, but any unanimous consent may be revoked by another unanimous consent granted in the manner prescribed above upon one day's notice. (Rule 12 [4])

The requirement for a quorum call was not controversial. Even the provision for UCAs to be considered orders of the Senate, enabling the presiding officer to enforce them, received little discussion. Lodge and Smoot complained about the ability to modify UCAs by unanimous consent but appeared to accept the logic once the proponents of the rule accepted an amendment that required 1 day's notice of a request to modify such a UCA (one providing for a final vote). Later rulings would allow the 1-day notice requirement to be waived by unanimous consent (Riddick 1992, 1354). A bipartisan majority supported the proposal, as amended (*Congressional Record*, January 16, 1914, pp. 1756–1759).

Post-1914 Period

With the new rule, UCAs became formally recognized as orders of the Senate. As such, a UCA supersedes Senate rules and precedents that are contrary to its provisions. Presiding officers began to exhibit consistency in their interpretation of the parliamentary status of UCAs and their power to implement them. They would enforce UCAs as all other orders of the Senate and, over time, a large body of precedent accumulated in support of the proposition that presiding officers were obligated to take the initiative in enforcing the provisions of UCAs (on interpretations of UCAs under rule 12, see Riddick 1992, 1311–1369).

By the early 1920s, central features of modern Senate floor practice were in place. As orders of the Senate, UCAs began to be reported faithfully in the *Journal*. It took a few years for floor leaders to assume primary responsibility for negotiating UCAs and managing their approval on the floor. By 1921 party leaders were actively engaged in the process (*Congressional Record*, July 20, 1921, p. 4115, and August 1, 1921, p. 4480). In the 1910s and 1920s, as party leaders assumed control of the Senate floor, the presiding officer's role as neutral arbiter and enforcer of UCAs was settled.

Practices surrounding UCAs were not entirely settled in the mid-20th century. In the last half of the 20th century, the majority leader became more inventive in designing agreements to limit debate and amendments (Smith and Flathman 1989). Just as the House majority leadership began to craft limits on debate and amendments in special rules to the political situation of each bill, Senate majority leaders acquired a larger repertoire of UCA provisions. This process took place in stages.

For more than 30 years, nearly all UCAs propounded were of a standard form. The form is recorded in former Senate parliamentarian Floyd Riddick's *Senate Procedure*:

> Ordered, by unanimous consent, that on the calendar day of _______, 19_______, at not later than _______ o'clock p.m. the Senate will proceed to vote, without further debate, upon any amendment that may be pending, any amendment that may be offered, and upon the bill (*bill number and name*) through the regular parliamentary stages to its final disposition; and that after the hour of _______ o'clock p.m., on said calendar day, no Senator shall speak more than once or longer than _______ minutes upon the bill, or more than once or longer than _______ minutes upon any amendment thereto. (Riddick 1992, 1312)

The purpose of these UCAs was to gain final disposition of a bill, including any action on amendments, by a certain time and to divide time for debate equitably in the meantime.

To see how the content of UCAs evolved since the 1930s, we have coded the provisions of UCAs for selected Congresses. Nearly all complex UCAs were offered by the majority leader so we can safely characterize UCA provisions by leader. The percentages in the table refer to the percentage of all complex UCAs—those that limit debate or amendments in some way—adopted under each leader.

Under Joseph Robinson (D-Ark.), who Gamm and Smith (2002) characterize as the first modern floor leader, and Albin Barkley (D-Ky.), UCAs remained of the traditional form. Their successors, Ernest McFarland

(D-Ariz.), Robert Taft (R-Ohio), and William Knowland (R-Calif.), were not particularly innovative but occasionally singled out one or more amendments for special debate limits. For the most part, these leaders offered time-limitation agreements after debate on a measure had consumed considerable time and as their colleagues came to recognize the importance of moving on to other legislation.

Robinson is noteworthy for another reason vital to the modern use of UCAs. During his tenure, with a friendly vice president presiding, the precedent was established that, when more than one senator seeks recognition, priority of recognition is given to the majority leader.[3] This precedent allows the majority leader to gain recognition to address the Senate, make a motion before another, or ask for unanimous consent. With the right of first recognition, the majority leader is given an opportunity to propound UCAs.

Lyndon Johnson (D-Tex.) has been given credit for great innovation in Senate leadership, including his use of UCAs. Caro (2002), following on Evans and Novak (1966), argues that Johnson was far more aggressive in seeking unanimous consent, and when he overcame objections he immediately went to the floor, gained consent for a time limitation, bullied colleagues into withholding amendments, and rammed the bill through the Senate. More frequently than his predecessors, Johnson successfully propounded time-limitation agreements before the motion to proceed on a measure was offered. Then, much more frequently than earlier UCAs, Johnson's UCAs divided control of time for general debate on a bill between the floor leaders, giving Johnson more control over the flow of debate and an opportunity to offer amendments of his own in a timely way. Moreover, Johnson sought to keep the Senate focused on the bill at hand by barring nongermane amendments when he could. Finally, Johnson's UCAs were more likely to provide for special treatment of one or more amendments than were his predecessors' UCAs (see Smith and Flathman 1989 on UCAs since the early 1950s).

Mike Mansfield (D-Mont.) was far less aggressive than Johnson, but at least at first, the mix of provisions changed little under Mansfield. This did not last long. As senators became more assertive and amending activity expanded, a more tactical, flexible approach to setting the floor agenda was required. This flexibility wasn't always a matter of choice. Under Mansfield, senators often objected to unanimous-consent requests that required amendments to be germane and the use of germaneness provisions dropped (Smith and Flathman 1989, 360).

Robert Byrd (D-W.Va.), who took over routine floor duties for Mansfield in the late 1960s and early 1970s, instituted innovations in UCA practice. Most obviously, Byrd frequently offered multiple UCAs during the course of debate on a single measure. UCAs became far less comprehensive and frequently dealt with a single amendment or short period of time. To be sure, UCAs providing for time agreements on a bill were offered before the debate on the measure began, but they were regularly supplemented during the course of debate. The lower relative frequency of certain kinds of UCA provisions was due to the limited or tactical purpose of many of Byrd's UCAs.

Bryd's successors were not quite so quick to offer UCAs, but they did continue to use the full array of UCA provisions. Omnibus measures—particularly budget measures, which were debated under time limitations established by statute—reduced the number of UCAs propounded by leaders. Beginning in the mid-1980s, UCAs providing for the consideration of a single amendment were more common. The greater frequency of provisions barring second-degree amendments reflected the leaders' efforts to more fully structure the floor agenda when possible. Such provisions were almost always accompanied by provisions barring other motions, appeals, and points of order. At times, although for only a small fraction of bills, amendments to certain sections of bills were barred by UCAs.

Modern UCAs come in all sizes, big and small. While UCAs are often tailored to individual measures and often to brief periods of debate and a single amendment, they also have been used to establish a comprehensive floor agenda for a measure, or even a set of measures, in delicate legislative situations. UCAs have the virtue of being difficult to modify (only by unanimous consent, of course) so they provide a particularly useful means for cementing arrangements intended to guarantee votes on certain measures or amendments or preclude votes on others.

A Still Unsettled Practice

The Senate remains a legislative body with inherent inconsistencies in its rules. Unanimous-consent, supermajority requirements for cloture and other motions, and the constitutional requirement of a simple majority for approving legislation live side by side. On occasion, these inconsistencies surface and senators are confronted with difficult parliamentary choices.

For example, among the issues raised but still not resolved is whether the Senate should, by majority vote, overturn rulings of the presiding officer based on UCAs. A common situation is one in which the presiding officer rules that an amendment is out of order because it violates a UCA that requires amendments to be germane. Should the Senate majority overturn a ruling that an amendment is out of order? The power to appeal a ruling to the Senate may undermine senators' confidence that a UCA will be observed and threaten the entire practice of operating by unanimous consent. But to back away from appeals when proceeding under a UCA hands to the presiding officer a source of influence over outcomes that the Senate has not been explicitly granted.

Lessons from the History of House Special Rules and Senate UCAs

The remarkable parliamentary ingenuity that is reflected in modern House special rules and Senate UCAs reflects the common purposes of these agenda-setting mechanisms. In both chambers, majority-party leaders seek to structure debate and amending activity to improve legislative efficiency and to the advantage of their parties. Yet the differences in the tools available to set the agenda are one of the most prominent and visible differences between the contemporary House and Senate. The House is often considered a model of legislative efficiency, while legislating in the Senate is often an arduous, if not impossible, task. That these differences persist over time is quite remarkable, given that both chambers respond to similar external forces that shape the public agenda and that the chambers themselves determine their floor procedures. Differences in their decision rules (simple majorities vs. unanimous consent) and the inherited body of floor procedures, themselves in part a product of the long-standing decision rules, have generated different paths of development in agenda setting and a different repertoire of strategies for floor leaders.

Path Dependency: The Previous-Question Motion and Agenda Setting

The presence or absence of a motion for the previous question has played a pivotal role in the development of House and Senate rules. Reducing opportunities to speak, offer legislation or amendments, and obstruct action is the essence of efforts to improve efficiency in legislative agenda setting and related decision-making processes. Such efforts generally serve the interest of the majority more than the minority. Consequently, the minority often argues that efficiency-improving changes undermine a fair, deliberative process and opposes the changes. In the House, majority support for a previous-question motion allows the majority party to get a vote on a rules change and impose its will on the minority. In the Senate, organized minority-party opposition is generally enough to prevent a vote on a rules change. The consequence is that the House has a body of rules and precedents that allow a simple majority to set its agenda. The Senate never has, even though Senate majorities have sometimes expressed an interest in efficiency-improving reforms (Binder and Smith 1997).

Path Dependency: Institutional Constraints on Party Development

While agenda-setting mechanisms reflect early procedural choices of the two houses, legislative party development is influenced by development of agenda-setting institutions. In the House, with its effective means of agenda control—perhaps most important, the ability to bring a matter to a vote—the incentive exists to devise the means to coordinate party strategy in setting the agenda and enhancing the ability of leaders to induce cooperation for fellow partisans. In the Senate, the majority party can do little to structure the agenda and get votes without the cooperation of the minority. As a consequence, strong central leadership serves less purpose and may even be more dangerous. Majority-party senators would be suspicious of a leader who can impose discipline on them while making necessary concessions to the minority to acquire unanimous consent or supermajorities to limit debate and amending activity.

The contrasts between the House and Senate give us perspective on two contending views of legislative parties—Aldrich and Rohde's conditional-party-government thesis (also see Cooper and Brady 1981, and Sinclair [Deckard] 1983) and Cox and McCubbins's procedural cartel thesis—both of which largely ignore the Senate (Gamm and Smith 2001).

The conditional-party-government thesis treats legislative parties as policy coalitions—although legislators' policy preferences are largely a product of ebb and flow of election outcomes. The degree of polarization in the policy preferences of members of the two legislative parties determines the powers and aggressiveness of party leaders. Two issues are raised about the conditional-party-government thesis from the record of innovation in House special rules and Senate UCAs.

First, the thesis fails to capture the sometimes one-directional process of innovation in House special rules. While the majority party sometimes redistributes influence over the design of special rules among members of the party, the majority party has not given up its control over special rules and, in several stages, improved special rules as a tool of agenda management. At least some core features of majority-party leadership powers are not wholly cyclical but rather seem to have cumulative elements.

Second, applications of the conditional-party-government thesis have little to say about the Senate. In fact, nothing in this chapter contradicts

Gamm and Smith's (2001) claim that the conditional-party-government thesis does not fit the Senate, where little phasing in the power delegated to central leaders is detectable. The inability of the Senate majority to impose rules changes that disadvantage the minority limits the degree to which even a cohesive majority can empower its leadership and centralize decision making in the chamber. Thus, while the thesis may capture an important tendency in legislative bodies, the variation in centralized decision making is likely to be conditional on the procedural context.

The electoral coalition hypothesis provides the foundation for the procedural cartel thesis. While the procedural cartel model is developed entirely in the context of House decision making, it too should apply to the Senate. There is no apparent rationale for separate House and Senate theories of legislative parties. For the House, Cox and McCubbins place substantial emphasis on the majority party's control of the agenda through the speakership, Committee on Rules, special rules, and other key features of floor procedure. These features are missing in the Senate, so perhaps the procedural alliance represented by the parties is less conspicuous there, but the general underlying logic—electoral concerns motivate cooperation among party members on agenda strategy—should fit the Senate too.

Senate parties seek to structure the floor agenda to their liking even if the chamber lacks rules allowing a simple majority to force action on legislation. Many of the early features of Senate party organization, the caucuses and steering committees, were used to arrange the agenda (Gamm and Smith 2002). Moreover, the history of the Senate is replete with cases of majority party efforts to change the rules—usually to no avail when the proposals disadvantaged the minority. As we have described, the majority-party leaders have been forced to pursue innovative approaches to crafting time agreements and seeking unanimous consent to implement them. Indeed, negotiating UCAs to structure the agenda is probably the single most important legislative task assigned to modern Senate leaders. Furthermore, around UCAs have emerged other practices, such as bill-clearance processes and holds, that represent leaders' efforts to respond to fellow partisans' expectations for floor scheduling while pushing measures vital to the party's collective interests.

In our view, legislative parties are both electoral coalitions and policy coalitions. Resolving conflict between electoral and policy objectives is the everyday burden of parties and their leaders. In fact, we would assert that balancing collective electoral and policy goals is a public good for legislative parties that leaders are asked to provide in the form of legislative strategies.

Both perspectives appear to be essential to understanding legislative parties. On the one hand, the history of House special rules and Senate UCAs indicates that majority parties consistently seek to *create* procedural tools to manage the agenda in their interest and that a certain minimum level of support for efforts to set the agenda are expected of rank-and-file members. Legislative parties surely are, in major part, procedural cartels. On the other hand, the *use* of procedural tools may reflect the extent of agreement about the policy purposes to which partisans hope that they are put. This would be reflected more in the timing and content of special rules and UCAs than in their frequency or, in the case of special rules, the vote margins by which they were adopted.

Different Responses to Similar Conditions

The late 19th century proved to be a critical period for both House and Senate parliamentary practice. Developments common to the two houses—a sizable increase in the legislative workload and the renewal of sharp partisan conflict—led to nearly continuous conflict about the floor agenda and a search for new rules to allow the majority party to get action on its legislation. Modifications of the formal order of business and competing special-order motions were typical of both House and Senate sessions.

We have observed that a critical difference in initial conditions—the presence of a motion for the previous question in the House and the absence of such a motion in the Senate—has been responsible for major differences in procedural development between the two houses since the late 19th century. These institutional features pre-date the modern party system and are clearly rooted in the nature of the two bodies in their formative years (Binder 1995, 1997; Binder and Smith 1997). They created a procedural status quo that was impossible to dislodge. In the House, majorities have no incentive to give up the motion for the previous question because it is the means by which a majority is able to get a decisive vote on a pending question. In the Senate, minorities have no incentive to reinstate a previous-question motion and have managed to retain supermajority rules for closing debate.

Chapter 14

Filibuster Reform in the Senate, 1913–1917

GREGORY KOGER

Introduction

This chapter analyzes the adoption of the first Senate cloture rule in 1917. This institutional change marked the end of the Senate's era of unregulated debate and the beginning of a long struggle over formal constraints on Senate minorities. The basic story of the 1917 rules change is familiar to most congressional scholars: in March 1917, a handful of senators filibustered a bill that authorized antisubmarine weapons on U.S. merchant ships during the waning hours of the 66th Congress. Furious, President Wilson publicly excoriated the Senate and called it back into session to adopt a rule limiting obstruction, which it did. Even though the Senate cloture rule is a central feature in American politics (Krehbiel 1998; Sinclair 2002b), there has been relatively little research on its adoption beyond early descriptive accounts (Burdette 1940; Haynes 1938; Luce 1922) and brief discussions in broad analyses of congressional history (Binder 1997; Binder and Smith 1997; Dion 1997). Ryley (1975) is an exception, but this book-length work devotes little attention to the Senate rule change itself.

Two elements of the basic story are curious. One puzzle is the content of the rule: why did the Senate adopt a two-thirds threshold rather than a simple majority? A second puzzle is the timing of the cloture rule change: why did these events occur in 1917 rather than earlier or later? This chapter proposes new answers to these questions. The two-thirds threshold reflected the de facto balance of power in the 1910s; with or without a cloture rule, a filibuster could not last long without the cooperation of at least one-third of the chamber or an artificial time constraint. The timing of the change is explained by the emerging role of a policy-oriented, media-swaying presidency (Tulis 1987). Woodrow Wilson's aggressive use of the bully pulpit provided the additional incentive for senators to codify the status quo as a formal cloture rule. This analysis of events is based on analytical narratives of seven institutional choices regarding obstruction from 1913 to 1917, many of which illustrate senators' ambivalence about restricting debate. These case studies are guided by an underlying model of institutional choice summarized in the next section.

Frameworks for Analyzing Institutional Choice

There are four basic steps to analyzing legislators' choices. First, identify what the status quo rules are. This includes both the threshold for limiting debate (if one exists) and the price of filibustering for both the obstructionists and the supporters of the filibustered bill. The price will depend on how difficult it is to filibuster under the rules—Do obstructionists have to stand and speak? Can they read from texts? Do their speeches have to be germane?—and on how expensive it is for the antifilibuster coalition to wait until the obstructionists are exhausted. Waiting out a filibuster is increasingly expensive when time is scarce and many other bills await chamber consideration (Oppenheimer 1985). In the next three steps an entrepreneur, the minority party, and the majority party choose whether to support or oppose institutional change.[1]

Each actor considers two types of rewards or costs for institutional change: utility attached to *outcomes* and utility attached to *acts*. The former is easier to understand: if the chamber rules are changed, how does that affect the flow of legislation? Actors might consider whether a reform will generally make a chamber more efficient and whether it will facilitate the passage of controversial legislation. Legislators may also weigh short-term and long-term implications of a rule change, since a reform that benefits them now may cost them later when they are on the losing side.

Second, actors receive *transaction payments* based on their positions for or against institutional change. Transaction payments include the *effort* required to develop a proposal and form a reform coalition; the *external rewards* from voters, interest groups, presidents, or other outside players; and the *internal sanctions* imposed by other legislators who oppose reform.

I consider two veto points for institutional change: reform does not occur if no entrepreneur proposes a change or if the majority party opposes reform. The first condition can be met with relative ease since there must be merely one senator who cares enough about reform to make a proposal. However, it is worth noting that, given sufficient internal or external sanctions for proposing reform, institutions may remain unchanged even if a majority of the Senate is willing to vote for it.[2]

The minority party cannot directly veto reform, but it is able to influence the majority party's transaction payments. Senators and scholars sometimes suggest that a supermajority is required to change Senate rules since it takes 67 votes to invoke cloture on a rule change. While it is true that a supermajority may be necessary using rule 22, the majority party can overcome filibustering if it is willing to utilize unconventional tactics like revising Senate precedents (Binder and Smith 1997; Burdette 1940, 216–220; Haynes 1938, 420–426; Koger 2003; Wolfinger 1971).[3] This may be a costly strategy, so the transaction payments for unconventional tactics are much higher than for conventional, bipartisan reform, but it is not *impossible* for a simple majority to achieve success. The cases that follow illustrate this point; in three instances (one in 1914, two in 1915), narrow Senate majorities could have limited obstruction despite minority opposition but did not.

In this framework, the primary claim is that institutional change occurs when the payoffs for reform are, on balance, positive for both the entrepreneur and the majority party, with prior procedural choices and the minority party having a significant influence on whether these two conditions can be met. In the following I specify how this claim can be evaluated within the context of the early 20th-century Senate. I should note, however, the scenarios that can arise when actors are influenced by both transaction payments and outcome preferences *and these goals are conflicted*. First, an actor may expect that reform would have positive policy benefits but that change would be costly. Then the actor will propose or support reform only if the effort will succeed and if the policy benefits outweigh the political costs. Second, a reform may be politically beneficial but have negative policy consequences. In these cases actors will either support reforms only if they are likely to fail or will support reforms that have minuscule policy consequences but reap political gains for action.

Data and Methods

I evaluate these claims using theoretically guided case studies, or analytical narratives. This approach is useful for testing models because one can evaluate not only the central prediction but also the assumptions and structure of a complex model (Bates et al. 1998; Buthe 2002). For example, we can evaluate whether the framework adequately summarizes the decision to propose a reform or whether the minority party's choice influences the majority party's transaction payments.

I use seven cases of institutional choice from 1913 to 1917 in the U.S. Senate. The best known of these is the adoption of the first Senate cloture rule in 1917, but the preceding choices help us evaluate the theory and explain the 1917 rule. By focusing on this time span I am able to hold constant important historical factors: the party in control of the White House and Congress, the general political and institutional climate, and the identity of most of the major actors. While these cases are from a limited time span, they include meaningful variation in the tactics used by would-be reformers and the outcomes of institutional choices. This is preferable to a study that selects on the dependent variable (i.e., that looks only at cases of successful reforms) because we have the leverage to distinguish the conditions for change from the conditions for stability (Geddes 2003).

How do we measure the policy and transaction payoffs for the key actors? The following studies make use of news reports, party caucus records, floor statements, and legislators' actions to make inferences in specific instances. Additionally, there are some general indicators that we can apply to most cases:

- *Agenda-setting sequence* is usually a signal of the majority party's outcome preferences. All else equal, the majority typically schedules its top priorities early, while low priorities are deferred until a later time—or never.
- The benefits of restricting obstruction probably increase with overall *inefficiency* in chamber decision making and with the value members attach to *legislation targeted for obstruction*.
- *Public presidential actions* (speeches to Congress, press releases) typically influence transaction payoffs by drawing media attention to the legislative process (Wolfinger 1971). Public positions may be supplemented by presidential influence over patronage jobs, distributive benefits, and campaign funds.
- *Party platforms* are also indicators of transaction payoffs. If Senate rules are explicitly mentioned in a party's platform, senators of that party have an incentive to publicly conform to party preferences. Also, if reform is necessary to realize a policy promise in a party platform, that may increase the transaction payoffs for reform.

The next section uses these expectations to evaluate institutional choices during the 1910s Senate.

Institutional Choices in the Senate, 1913–1917

This section analyzes seven cases of institutional choice: (1) the Democrats' decision to not challenge the right to filibuster at the start of the 63rd Congress; (2) prohibiting and then reinstating the right to yield for questions during debate; (3) raising the threshold for suspending Senate rules from simple majority to two-thirds; (4) a cloture proposal during the 1915 ship-purchase debate; (5) the Democrats' failure to propose a cloture rule at the start of the 64th Congress; (6) a Rules Committee cloture proposal in June 1916; (7) the adoption of the first cloture rule in 1917. The central narrative of these cases is that the majority-party Democrats were initially unconcerned that obstruction would inhibit their agenda. The 1915 ship-purchase-act debate crystallized senators' view of obstruction; many senators came to see minority obstruction as a necessary check on majority-party domination. Thus the 1917 rule, adopted in a firestorm of public criticism, was designed to satisfy public demands for a cloture rule while minimizing its effect on the Senate's balance of power. These choices are best understood against the backdrop of presidential and party politics during the Wilson administration.

Responsible Democratic Party Government, 1913–1919

Democrats won a complete but precarious victory in the election of 1912. Owing to a split in the Republican Party, the Democratic Party gained control of Congress and the presidency with a plurality of the popular vote. Woodrow Wilson won the White House with 41.8 percent of the popular vote, with Roosevelt and Taft splitting 50.5 percent of the votes. Similarly, House Democrats won 41.1 percent of the votes in congressional elections outside the South. Future success or defeat for the Democrats depended on the party's ability to appeal to the progressive voters who bolted the Republican Party in 1912; they constituted a national swing group crucial to almost every state outside the South (Bowers 1918, 282–283; James 2000, 132–137).

Although the Democratic Party was, like the Republicans, split into conservatives and progressives (Oleszek 1991), Wilson sought to rule as the leader of a president-dominated responsible party (Link 1956).[4] Wilson worked closely with party and committee leaders who, in turn, met frequently with party caucuses in both chambers (Bowers 1918; Link 1956). Wilson worked to muster media attention and public support for his policy proposals, including frequent addresses to Congress (Kernell 1997, 261–262; Link 1956, 79–85, 152–153; Tulis 1987, 117–144). Finally, Wilson used patronage appointments to reward and punish members of Congress, as Arthur Link summarizes:

> [Wilson] controlled the [Democratic Party] not merely by strong postures and a bold voicing of public opinion but also by using the immense patronage at his command as an instrument of effective government. Confronted by no entrenched national party organization and no body of officeholders loyal to another man, he was able to build from the ground up and to weld the widely scattered and disparate Democratic forces into nearly as effective a political organization as one can build in the United States. (1956, 157)

Senate Democrats even filibustered several of Taft's nominations after the 1912 election so that they would receive the maximum benefits from presidential appointments (Burdette 1940, 93–94).

To ensure that the Senate would faithfully pass the party agenda, the progressive faction of the Senate Democrats replaced their current leader, Thomas Martin (Va.), with John Kern (Ind.), who had helped write the party platform. Since 30 of 51 Democrats were pledged to Kern, Martin conceded the position without a vote (Oleszek 1991). The next step was new caucus rules weakening the power of committee chairs so that senior conservatives could not stifle party legislation. On April 8, 1913, the Democratic caucus adopted rules allowing the majority-party *members* of a committee to call committee meetings, select conference committee members, and appoint subcommittees, all by majority vote (Bowers 1918, 293–295; *Minutes of U.S. Senate Democratic Conference* [*Democratic Minutes*] 1998, 74–76; Oleszek 1991). The most significant rule, however, had already been adopted. In 1903, trying in vain to organize a united front against the Panama Canal treaty, the Democratic caucus adopted a rule allowing two-thirds of the caucus to bind all party members to vote the caucus position, provided that members would not have to violate instructions from a state legislature, pledges to constituents, or their interpretation of the Constitution (Lambert 1953, 303–304; *Democratic Minutes* 1998, 3–4). According to the minutes of the Democratic caucus, this rule was not used from 1903 to 1913; the new majority revived the rule to commit members to New Freedom legislation and, in the process, made the rule a lightning rod for criticism of party government.

What Were the Status Quo Filibuster "Rules"?

Even without a formal rule for ending obstruction, Senate majorities were not powerless to stop obstruction. In the 19th-century House and Senate, the classic solution to a filibuster was to wait it out in the hopes that the obstructionists would become too tired to fight anymore. Furthermore, Senate rules limit members to two speeches per topic per legislative day; if a majority keeps a bill on the floor continuously, obstructionists run out of opportunities to speak.[5] A waiting strategy was often accompanied by strict enforcement of existing rules limiting debate.

Senators had recently acted to increase the costs of obstruction. In 1897 the presiding officer refused to recognize a quorum call (i.e., counting members to ensure that at least 50 percent of the Senate is in attendance) when no debate or vote had occurred since the last quorum call (Burdette 1940). In 1908 the Senate approved 35–13 a precedent that further restricted quorum-call use by requiring some business other than debate to come between quorum calls. During the same vote, the Senate renewed the practice of counting nonvoting members toward a quorum, much as House Speaker Reed did in 1891. At the time, Senator Burkett (R-Neb.) called these reforms "the greatest evolution in facilitating legislation since [the Reed rules of 1890]" ("Filibuster Is Doomed," *Washington Post*, June 1, 1908, p. A4).

One reason the Senate needed no formal cloture rules before 1913 was that the Senate's overall efficiency reduced the payoffs for obstruction. The majority party's opportunity costs of waiting out a filibuster increase with the backlog of legislation waiting for chamber consideration (Oppenheimer 1985). An efficient legislature, therefore, can afford to wait out a filibuster. In other work, I find that a backlog of workload during the 1880s House created the conditions for effective obstruction (Koger 2002). For example, during the 1880s the House passed only about 35 percent of its committee reports, while the 62nd Senate approved 71.0 percent of the bills reported out of Senate committees. In fact, the 62nd Senate took some floor action (passing, tabling, recommitting) on 90.3 percent of all bills reported from its committees, so the Senate chamber was usually able to register some opinion on most committee recommendations.[6]

The Senate's effectiveness coincided with a low level of obstruction from 1891 to 1913. According to a compilation of filibusters (Beth 1994), there were 11 recorded filibusters between 1895 and 1913, averaging 1.2 per Congress.[7] This represents a mild acceleration over the previous period; from 1875–1895 there were 7 filibusters, 0.7 per Congress. Ten of the 11 filibusters occurred during "short" sessions of Congress, i.e., the 3 months of legislating after the fall elections. During short sessions, the combination of a fixed end date and an accumulation of reported legislation increased the value of floor time and, therefore, the effectiveness of obstruction.

The combination of high chamber efficiency and low obstruction rates suggests that the potential policy rewards for reform were generically low for senators as the 63rd Congress began. Few bills were killed by filibusters and reducing obstruction would probably have a marginal effect at best on the Senate's overall effectiveness. Of course, legislators could have strong feelings about a single obstructed bill (or a few key bills) such that a rule change could realize a significant change in policy outcomes.

CASE 1: ORGANIZING THE 63RD CONGRESS

In our initial case, nothing happens—*and that's interesting*. At the beginning of the 63rd Congress, no member of the Democratic majority in the Senate proposed a new restriction on obstruction. This inaction occurred despite the Democrats' interest in forcing their party-platform legislation through the Senate and the interest of some Democrats in suppressing obstruction.[8]

In two scenarios no member proposes a reform: either there is simply no policy or political reward for institutional change or the costs of proposing one outweigh the likely gains—especially if reform is likely to fail. Both explanations are possible in this case, but the first scenario seems more likely—costs exceed any possible benefits. First, as previously noted, it is not clear that there were any policy benefits to reducing obstruction rights. Even though a couple of Democratic agenda items were later filibustered—the Federal Trade Commission and Clayton Antitrust bills (Beth 1994)—the Democrats were still able to pass these bills. Second, nothing indicates there were political rewards for supporting reform; no primary source mentioned presidential interest in changing Senate rules, and the 1912 Democratic Party platform did not mention Senate rules reform. On the other hand, Democratic efforts to restrict obstruction would have probably been politically costly. Assaulting the practice of filibustering just weeks after obstructing Republican nominations and legislation would have invited public ridicule. Furthermore, the Democratic progressives had just seized control of the party apparatus; pushing for a major rules change might have driven Democratic conservatives into open revolt. *Summary: low policy payoffs deter entrepreneurs.*

CASE 2: YIELDING DURING DEBATE, SEPTEMBER 1914

During September 1914, Democrats briefly attempted to reduce obstruction by restricting the practice of yielding during a speech.[9] In mid-

September a bill appropriating funds for rivers and harbors reached the Senate floor. This bill was a Democratic agenda item and especially important to Southern Democrats (*Democratic Minutes* 1998, 169–171). Several Republicans objected to the $53 million funding level and obstructed passage by prolonged speaking. After a week of debate and 2 consecutive days of speaking by William Kenyon (R-Iowa), Nathan Bryan (D-Fla.) objected to Kenyon yielding to other members for comments or questions without obtaining unanimous consent. The Senate sustained this objection 28–24, with Republicans (and one Progressive) opposing the ruling 0–18 and Democrats supporting it 28–6. Note that the majority was, as assumed, able to restrict obstruction despite minority-party opposition.

The effect of this precedent was to increase the physical cost of filibustering, since speakers would have to deliver uninterrupted speeches, but the ruling also reduced discussion and interchange during debate. The next day, however, the Senate held a second vote on the same question and reversed the precedent, 15–35. No Republican switched positions on the ruling, but 10 Democrats changed their positions from yea to nay, including Kern. What changed overnight? The historical record is scanty, but the best explanation is that the Democrats reevaluated whether the policy payoffs for the institutional change were worth the costs of reduced deliberation and obstruction rights. In this case, the reform had already been accomplished and the transaction payments seemed to be minimal, so most of the reevaluation was probably tied to policy effects. One consideration was that reducing obstruction rights affected Democrats as well as Republicans; Democrats continued to filibuster while in the majority, including two Democratic filibusters in the final weeks of the 1914 session. Second, the immediate object of the reform—pushing the rivers and harbors bill through the Senate—became an untenable goal during the course of the Republican filibuster. Republicans linked this "extravagant pork barrel bill" to the Democrats' imposition of "war taxes" during peacetime, suggesting that a military buildup could be funded by government belt-tightening instead. Days later, a coalition of Republicans and Northern Democrats reduced the bill to $20 million so it would pass (*New York Times*, September 23, 1914, p. 9). *Summary: minority and majority parties reject reform because of low policy payoffs.*

CASE 3: SUSPENSION OF THE RULES, JANUARY 1915

A third notable event was an extraordinary reinterpretation of a Senate rule. During consideration of an appropriations bill for Washington, D.C., the Senate Rules Committee reported a proposal by Morris Sheppard (D-Tex.) to suspend the rules of the Senate and consider an amendment banning saloons in the nation's capital. Sheppard needed to suspend the rules because policy amendments were (and are) prohibited by Senate rules. Rule 40 (now 5) of the Senate allows senators to suspend, modify, or amend rules after a 1-day wait, but in 1915 no senator could remember an attempt to suspend the rules. The rules of the Senate did not (and do not) specify what proportion of the chamber must approve a motion to suspend the rules, implying that a simple majority was sufficient; the previous precedent was an 1861 suspension of the rules by simple majority. However, the Senate voted 41–34 on January 15, 1915, to require a two-thirds majority to suspend the rules.

This decision was a clear opportunity to end obstruction in the Senate. Motions to suspend the rules can include the restrictions now included in unanimous-consent agreements or House special rules—restrictions on amendments; time limits on speeches; and most important, definite times for votes on final passage (Beth 1993). Furthermore, this precedent demonstrates the ability of a simple majority of the Senate to alter the practical meaning of standing rules by establishing new precedents. The imposition of a two-thirds threshold was contrary to the previous (if rare) practice of the Senate and the general norm of parliamentary construction: unless specified otherwise, all decisions are based on simple-majority rule. The best argument the majority could muster was that the House of Representatives requires a two-thirds majority to change its rules, but this is only because House rules specify this threshold, and resolutions reported from the Rules Committee in the House require only a simple majority to pass.[10]

Gilbert Hitchcock (D-Neb.) raised the point of order against Sheppard's motion. Hitchcock's floor speech argues against the practice of appending policy riders to appropriations bills (*Congressional Record*, January 13, 1915, pp. 1504–1505). Other advocates for reinterpreting the Senate rule stressed that simple-majority suspension could be used on a variety of different issues (see Senator Stone's speech, ibid.). Hitchcock may have been especially motivated to propose this change by his frequent disputes with the party caucus and Wilson administration over patronage, tax policy, and banking; simple-majority suspension of the rules would empower a party he frequently opposed.

Curiously, the coalitions supporting and opposing the precedents were not based on any obvious cleavage: Democrats split 24–18, Republicans 17–15. While Republicans divided basically along progressive (simple majority) and conservative (two-thirds) lines, Democrats cleaved neither along ideological or regional lines.[11] Nor is the precedent vote strongly correlated with key upcoming votes on the ship-purchase act. The cross-partisan nature of the coalition and the absence of overt presidential or party interest in the precedent suggest that the transaction payments were minimal for all concerned. In short, preferences on alcohol seem to have influenced senators' votes, but so did the prospect of simple-majority rule on other issues (*Congressional Record*, January 13, 1915, pp. 1503–1512). *Summary: legislators' general policy interests motivated institutional change to further* restrain *majority action.*

CASE 4: THE SHIP-PURCHASE BILL, FEBRUARY 1915

The final institutional choice of the 63rd Congress was a rejected cloture rule that would have obtained the passage of a shipping bill. After the November 1914 elections, the Wilson administration proposed a ship-purchase act that would have established a government corporation to purchase and operate merchant ships. The purpose of this bill was to alleviate a shortage of ocean transportation after the outbreak of World War I. A coalition of regular Republicans and renegade Democrats filibustered the bill to oppose the creation of a government enterprise and the provocative steps of giving cash to Germany (in exchange for German ships) and increasing trade with Germany (Garraty 1953, 308–311; *Congressional Record*, June 8, 1918, p. 7537).

While Democrats loyal to the Wilson administration tried to exhaust bill opponents on the Senate floor, they met in caucus six times January 16–23, debating and resolving their internal differences. At the conclusion of these meetings, the caucus voted to bind all Democrats to support the bill as a party measure. This vote, however, became a source of controversy. Since there were 53 Democrats in the Senate, 36 votes were required to bind a caucus. The initial vote was 35–3, other Democrats being absent, but Charles Thomas (Colo.) agreed to switch his vote so the caucus would be bound (*Democratic Minutes* 1998, 191–193). On this basis the caucus expected every Democrat to support the bill once the Republicans grew tired of talking.

On January 25, Duncan Fletcher (D-Fla.) introduced the caucus bill as a substitute amendment. Over the next 7 days, Republicans used every obstructive tactic—dilatory motions, prolonged speaking, and disappearing quorums—to prevent a final vote on the Fletcher substitute. Of the 19 votes during this week, most Republicans were absent from 12; on 8 of these 12 votes a quorum was "broken." Six amendments to the underlying bill were tabled by almost perfectly party-line votes, demonstrating to Republicans the futility of deliberation. Finally, on February 1, several Democrats allied with the Republicans to support recommitting the bill to committee (Burdette 1940, 107). On the crucial vote to table the motion to recommit, seven Democrats opposed the party and the motion failed

42–44. However, another five Democrats had supported the rebels on at least one of two preceding procedural votes, suggesting even broader discontent within the majority party.[12]

At this point the Democrats, instead of conceding defeat, began filibustering while rounding up absent members from around the country and negotiating with dissident Democrats and progressive Republicans (*Democratic Minutes* 1998, 194; Burdette 1940, 107). A week later, three returning senators had reinforced the Democrats and the roles reversed again—Republicans obstructing, Democrats pushing for a vote. Four days later (February 12) the Democrats began to press for a new cloture rule.

The primary Democratic proposal was the equivalent of a special rule in the House: it added a clause to the *standing rules* of the Senate requiring a vote on the shipping bill at 2 p.m. on February 19, 1915. On February 13, the Democratic caucus met and formally approved (no vote is recorded) a resolution supporting "modified cloture" enabling a majority to reach a final vote and, specifically, "a rule which would terminate the filibuster on the shipping bill" (*Democratic Minutes* 1998, 199). The targeted nature of this "rule" underscores senators' apparent belief that obstruction rights generally served their policy interests. Despite this action, votes on the cloture resolution revealed an even divide, with seven Democrats consistently voting with the Republicans and the outcome heavily contingent on turnout.

Throughout this debate, Republicans voiced traditional arguments for obstruction, but their primary focus was a new target: the institution of the caucus. Their specific complaint was that 35 senators were using the caucus to dictate outcomes to the remaining 61 senators, when clearly a majority of the Senate opposed the bill. More generally, Republicans claimed that the president used the caucus (backed by discretion over patronage) to pressure Senate Democrats, and thus the Senate, to adopt his legislation hastily and without change. Gilbert Hitchcock (D-Neb.) noted, "There would have been no Democratic caucus [on the shipping bill] if it had not been for outside influences." George Norris (R-Neb.) replied, "That is the case nine times out of ten" (*Congressional Record*, February 16, 1915, p. 3849). Theodore Burton (R-Ohio) noted that the party pressure on Democrats was greater on the shipping bill than on any of the significant New Freedom bills—tariff reform, antitrust bills, and the Federal Reserve Act. Albert Cummins (R-Iowa) cited this pressure as a justification for obstruction:

> Whenever the Chief Executive of the country attempts to impose his will upon the Senate, and thus to preclude or prevent that fair and open mind to which all discussion ought to be directed, when senators

> do not feel that they are at liberty to vote upon a particular measure in any way which their judgment and their conscience direct them to vote, then a rebellion in the form of a filibuster is not only justified but, I think, it is absolutely required if we would preserve the freedom and the Senate of the United States. (*Congressional Record*, February 16, 1915, p. 3840)

The Republican critique was an innovation on classic arguments for obstruction. Since many Democrats faced severe conflicts between their policy views and political interests, minority obstruction was necessary to realize the true preferences of most Senators.

The unpopularity of caucus power may have contributed to the defeat of the Democratic cloture proposal. Cummins offered an amendment invalidating the cloture rule on any issue on which a party caucus had bound its members' votes. An attempt to table this amendment failed 45–47, with Robert La Follette (R-Wis.) defecting from the pro-shipping-bill coalition to oppose caucus rule. Rather than take a direct vote on Cummins's amendment, Democrats conceded defeat on both the proposed cloture rule and the shipping bill—not because obstruction prevented a final vote, but because the votes indicated that they would lose.[13] In other words, the cloture-reform effort failed because the near-term marginal change in outcomes, passing the ship-purchase act, was not a sufficient inducement to motivate a partisan reform coalition.

Had the Democrats not conceded defeat, they had a majoritarian strategy prepared to force a vote on the shipping bill and, in the process, transform the Senate. Ollie James (D-Ky.) suggested during Senate debate that any member could move the previous question on the bill. Once the chair ruled this motion out of order, any member could appeal the ruling. James promised to force a vote on his ruling if he were the presiding officer. Democrats seriously considered the strategy but abandoned it because they did not have the votes to win.[14] *Summary: there were insufficient policy payoffs to adopt a targeted cloture rule.*

CASE 5: THE DEMOCRATIC CAUCUS DEBATES REFORM, DECEMBER 1915

When the Senate Democrats, strengthened by a net gain of four members, met to organize their caucus in November–December 1915, their first act was to reelect Kern as majority leader; their second act was to begin debating cloture reform (*Democratic Minutes* 1998, 201–213). The caucus met five times in 6 days but eventually decided not to attempt a rule change.

Senators had a significant policy stake in these procedural questions. The *New York Times* claimed,

> The proposed cloture rule is regarded as more important in its bearing on general legislation than any constitutional amendment that has been considered in recent years. If the caucus finds a way to have the rule adopted, opponents of the measure say, the doors will be thrown open to radical legislation in the years to come. Of more immediate interest . . . the adoption of the rule might make it possible for the President's program to be enacted in most of its particulars. (November 29, 1915, p. A1)

Wilson's policy agenda included increasing military troop levels, raising revenues, a ship-purchase bill, allowing corporations to cooperate in foreign trade, a rural loan system, Philippines autonomy, and Latin American treaties (ibid.).

The caucus appointed an ad hoc committee to propose changes in the Senate rules; the committee proposed a simple-majority cloture process that Democrats would push through by moving the previous question (*New York Times*, December 1–4, 1915). The caucus, however, took no action on the proposed cloture rule. The death knell for the reform effort was a caucus vote against making cloture reform a "party measure." This vote is unrecorded in the caucus minutes, while the *New York Times* reports that only three senators supported this approach (December 5, 1915, p. 22). Further caucus debate revealed dissent over whether a simple-majority or two-thirds supermajority should be sufficient to limit debate, how much time should be allotted for postcloture debate, and what tactics should be used to push the rules change (ibid.; *Democratic Minutes* 1998, 201–213). Reform advocates proposed that the Democrats deny that the Senate is a "continuous body" with permanent rules. If the Senate does not have permanent rules, then the majority has increased latitude to push through rules changes at the beginning of a Congress while the chamber operates under general parliamentary law. This would make it easier to overcome an expected Republican filibuster against a rule change. Once it became clear to Democrats that they lacked the internal unity necessary to adopt a cloture rule, the caucus shelved the issue.

Why didn't some entrepreneur attempt reform anyway? The primary reform advocate was Robert Owen (D-Okla.; *New York Times*, December 2, 1915, p. 10), who considered a serious attempt on the floor. In the end, however, the expectation that the attempt would consume time, prevent President Wilson from addressing the Senate, and intensify Democrats' internal conflicts deterred a floor effort (*New York Times*, December 2–3, 1915). President Wilson took no overt position on cloture reform. *Summary: Entrepreneurs were deterred by the transaction cost of proposing and anticipated failure. The majority party supported reform weakly, so the additional transaction costs imposed by minority-party obstruction meant that the proposal would die.*

CASE 6: A REFORM PROPOSAL DIES, JUNE 1916

On March 16, 1916, the Democratic caucus expressed vague support for cloture reform and requested the Senate Rules Committee to report a rule allowing the Senate to defeat determined obstruction (*Democratic Minutes* 1998, 215). This request went unanswered until the June 1916 Democratic Convention approved a party platform stating "We favor such alteration of the rules of procedure of the Senate of the United States as will permit the prompt transaction of the Nation's legislative business." The Democratic platform was mostly written by President Wilson, and this plank presumably had his blessing (*New York Times*, June 12, 1915, p. 3). Days after the convention, Hoke Smith (D-Ga.) of the Rules Committee dutifully reported a rule that, at the petition of 16 senators, allowed a two-thirds majority to impose a 1-hour debate limit per senator—essentially the rule later adopted by the 65th Congress (*Congressional Record*, June 20, 1916, 9637–9638). However, Republicans expressed interest in discussing the proposal at length, and the Democratic caucus prioritized other issues during agenda-setting discussions (*Democratic Minutes* 1998, 217–231). Once again, the caucus's failure to develop a joint strategy on cloture reform or prioritize Smith's cloture proposal suggest both intraparty divisions on institutional change and low interest in reforming the Senate. *Summary: increased publicity motivated a proposal, but the majority party was deterred by the transaction costs of overcoming minority opposition.*

CASE 7: THE SENATE ADOPTS A CLOTURE RULE, MARCH 1917

On February 1, 1917, Germany resumed unrestricted submarine attacks on ships headed for Britain; Wilson broke relations with Germany on February 3. On February 26, only 7 days before the mandated end of the session, Wilson addressed Congress to request legal authority to arm merchant ships. It was clear to most senators that the president already possessed the authority to arm ships; Wilson's real intent, they feared, was to obtain a broad grant of power to pursue a policy of "armed neutrality" (Ryley 1975, 74). To do so, Congress would have to write, debate, and pass a law during the most hectic, time-pressured week of the Congress. On March 1, the House approved its version 413–13. The same day, the White House made public Germany's "Zimmerman note" to Mexico, which proposed a Germany-Mexico alliance in the event that the United States entered the war against Germany.

The armed-ship bill came up in the Senate on March 2 amid the public firestorm over the Zimmerman note. Notably, the Democrats did *not* meet in caucus to discuss the bill. An organized group of senators then began to obstruct the bill with William Stone (D-Mo.), chairman of the Senate Foreign Relations Committee, giving the longest speech (4 hours) against the bill (Burdette 1940, 118–123; Ryley 1975). Since time was short and the Senate had to interrupt the armed-ship bill to conduct other end-of-session business, the filibuster succeeded easily.

Wilson and the general public did not see the bill's failure as the predictable outcome of trying to pass a new, controversial bill in a work-clogged system within a week. In a famous phrase, Wilson blasted the "little group of willful men" who had blocked his bill, and he called for reform of the Senate rules (*New York Times*, March 5, 1917, p. A1). Most major newspapers expressed similar outrage against the filibuster and those who had spoken against the bill (Ryley 1975, 132). Citizens held rallies criticizing the obstructionists, senators were burned in effigy, and some senators' lives were threatened (Ryley 1975, 134–135). Public pressure to change the rules of the Senate was probably greater than at any other time in Senate history.

President Wilson reconvened the Senate in executive session on March 5, 1917, for the primary purpose of adopting a cloture rule. On March 6, both party conferences appointed committees to negotiate and agree on a cloture rule (*Democratic Minutes* 1998, 259; Wolff and Ritchie 1999, 67); this bipartisan committee played the role of entrepreneur. The Democrats appointed five senators who advocated simple-majority rule (Owen, James, Reed, Walsh, and Swanson) and one senator who preferred supermajority rule: Hoke Smith, the senator who reported and defended the Rules Committee proposal in 1916. The Republican negotiators included Henry Lodge (Mass.), a defender of obstruction, and Cummins, a participant in the filibuster against the armed-ship bill who supported cloture but opposed caucus rule. A day later, the negotiators reported to their respective parties a rule much like Hoke Smith's 1916 proposal: a 16-signature petition would trigger a vote and, if two-thirds of those voting supported cloture, each senator was limited to an hour of debate time. The Republicans endorsed the proposal by a vote of 30–2; the Democrats unanimously adopted the report after rejecting a proposal to further limit postcloture debate in the last 2 weeks of the session and after referring a previous-question proposal to the bipartisan negotiators (Wolff and Ritchie 1999, 68–70; *Democratic Minutes* 1998, 262–263).

On March 8, the Senate adopted the new rule 76–3 after brief debate. The bipartisan agreement on cloture included mutual restraint; members opposed to cloture would not obstruct the proposal or offer weakening amendments. Since the 1915 cloture proposal had been killed when a "caucus exemption" amendment had split the reform coalition, this was a significant concession. On the other hand, cloture proponents agreed not to try to strengthen the proposal; thus Thomas Martin persuaded Henry Hollis (D-N.H.) to withdraw an amendment lowering the threshold for cloture to a simple majority (Burdette 1940, 128).

Consequences. What was the effect of this rule on Senate policy making? First, had the rule existed a month earlier, it would have been ineffective against the ship-arming-bill filibuster. There was not enough time for the cloture petition to ripen and bill opponents to exhaust their debate time, especially since opposition to the bill may have been broader than the 10 or 11 members labeled as the obstructionists (Ryley 1975). More generally, the rule essentially codified the status quo, since a prolonged filibuster already required a significant number of active participants. For example, it took careful preparation to plan the 2-day filibuster against the armed-ship bill (Ryley 1975, 73–78). A year later, Lawrence Sherman (R-Ill.) would argue, "A few members here can not carry on a filibuster. . . . In fact, if there was not a considerable number, or nearly a united minority, the minority had as well not undertake to carry on the filibuster for practical results; and even then it is limited to a certain time" (*Congressional Record*, June 11, 1918). When Hoke Smith first introduced the cloture proposal in 1916, his statements suggested its primary use would be to make the Senate more efficient by depriving small groups of their ability to delay business and block unanimous-consent requests, rather than to suppress a sincere filibuster (*Congressional Record*, June 20, 1916, pp. 9637–9638). It is no surprise, then, that the new rule had little marginal effect on organized obstruction (Burdette 1940); it was not intended to.

Why, then, didn't the Senate adopt a stronger cloture rule, e.g., a simple-majority process for ending debate? The simplest explanation is that, transaction payments aside, only a minority of the Senate personally preferred majority rule. As described above, the Democrats were deeply divided on cloture reform. Even in the midst of the ship-arming firestorm, only a minority of the Senate expressed support for simple-majority rule. As the 64th Congress drew to a close, Senator Owen (D-Okla.) circulated a letter pledging its signers to support a rule change that would "enable the majority to fix an hour for disposing of any bill or question." Thirty-three of 96 senators signed the petition, while 7 more did not sign but supported the "movement," including Hoke Smith (*New York Times*, March 5, 1917, p. A1). Since a separate petition pledging support to the armed-ship bill had circulated simultaneously and received 75 signatures (and only 10 senators were unable to sign it), we can infer that many members—probably more than 33—had an opportunity to sign Owen's letter and refused.

Could a determined majority have adopted a stronger cloture rule? It seems unlikely that the Democratic majority proposed a weak cloture rule for fear of a filibuster. The Republicans did not seem willing to obstruct the cloture rule; it was the Republicans who had first proposed bipartisan reform. Furthermore, given the public mood, the Republicans would have suffered a disastrous political cost for obstructing cloture reform. As Ryley notes, "The nature of public opinion was such that most people, who knew very little about the complexity of Senate rules, would accept virtually anything. They equated the filibuster with obstructionism and treason, and that was enough for them" (1975, 148). Second, if Republicans (or a cross-party coalition) had filibustered, the Democrats could have easily waited it out as they had on the ship-purchase act and other party agenda bills. The cloture proposal was introduced in the Senate on March 8; the next Senate vote was April 4, so there was ample time to exhaust the minority if a majority was willing to wait. The Democrats' acceptance of a weak, negotiated outcome suggests that there was insufficient support for majority rule to ensure its adoption.

Evaluating the Alternatives. An alternative account of the 1917 cloture rule by Gregory J. Wawro and Eric Schickler (chapter 15 in this volume) suggests that the rule *did* significantly affect Senate decision making. It would be rational, they suggest, for a legislative entrepreneur to trade off the possibility of passing controversial legislation (i.e., bills supported by a near-majority coalition) for increased certainty that one's bill will not be killed by a filibuster.[15] Thus the cloture rule aids bill sponsors by ensuring that bills appealing to two-thirds of the Senate will pass.

Wawro and Schickler predict that (1) coalitions supporting legislation on final passage will be larger and more uniform after adoption of the cloture rule and (2) appropriations bills should be more likely to pass after the adoption of the cloture rule. They test these claims with a dataset of 29 significant bills from 1881 to 1946 and appropriations bills from 1890 to 1946, finding support for their hypotheses. Their tests for coalition size mean and variance are bivariate comparisons, while their test for appropriations success includes seven control variables.

Wawro and Schickler employ long time series to increase the power of their tests, but their predictions can be tested more precisely using data from immediately before and after the 1917 rule change. If we are to judge the motives for reform, we should look for short-term effects traceable to the new rule rather than the long-term or unintended consequences of the rule. Thus I gathered data on all final-passage votes for legislation requiring a simple majority from the last 3 months (i.e., the short sessions) from the 64th–67th Congresses (1917, 1919, 1921, and 1923).

If we compare distribution of coalition sizes on final passage votes for the 64th (no cloture rule) and 65th (cloture just adopted) Congresses, the variance of the coalition sizes does decrease as predicted—but so too does the average size of coalitions, contrary to prediction. Data from the 66th and 67th Congresses do little to clarify the picture. Using a student's *t* test for samples with unequal variance to compare the 64th Congress to each subsequent Congress, only the shift from the 64th to the 65th Congress is statistically significant—but this is a significant decrease, not the predicted increase.[16] The pattern of coalition size diversity is also interesting; if we compare the standard deviation of the 64th Senate (13.4) with the standard deviation of passage votes pooled from the 65th to 67th Congresses (15.6) we find, contrary to prediction, an increase. A Conover parametric test of equal variances does not reject the hypothesis of equal variance ($p = 0.378$ for a two-tailed test), but we can confidently reject the claim that variance decreased after the adoption of the cloture rule.

A short-term analysis of the appropriations process also suggests a null effect for the cloture rule. Wawro and Schickler endeavor to distinguish the effects of the cloture rule from the 1921 Budget Act and the 20th Amendment. We can avoid this difficulty by comparing the fate of appropriations bills during each session of the precloture 64th Congress and the postcloture, pre–Budget Act 65th Congress.[17] These two Congresses shared several relevant features: the same president, same majority party, same Senate Appropriations Committee chair, and many of the same legislators and issues. For each bill, we are curious whether it was reported by committee, passed the Senate, and eventually made it to the president for signature or veto.

During both Congresses, every bill considered during long or special sessions made it to the president. For the short session of the 64th Congress, it is not surprising that 4 of 14 bills failed to pass since the filibuster against the ship-arming bill occupied the Senate floor. The record of the 65th Congress, however, was worse; four reported bills failed to pass the Senate and another two bills died after passing the Senate. The cause of this attrition was a general Republican filibuster led by Robert La Follette (R-Wis.; Burdette 1940, 128–131), who wanted to force an early session of the Republican-controlled 66th Congress. In the end, La Follette was aided by less than a third of the Senate; the Republican Conference voted 15–14 against a strategy of blocking appropriations bills (*New York Times*, March 2, 1919, p. A1). The new rule offered little help; with 3 days left in the short session, Democrats found it easier to wait out a filibuster than to attempt cloture (*New York Times*, March 3, 1919, p. A1) and never attempted a cloture vote. The short-term effects of the cloture rule thus seem to be minimal.

What should we infer from these results? *Nothing*. Wawro and Schickler clearly acknowledge the limitations of inferences based on small samples. This limitation is highlighted by employing alternative samples and finding different results. Yet if analyses of different samples yield contrasting results, we should infer, in the absence of more powerful tests, that the immediate effects of the cloture rule were . . . nothing. That does not mean that the cloture rule would never be influential; as the Senate agenda grew and time became more scarce, senators eventually preferred to attempt cloture rather than wait out filibustering. This transition, however, would not occur for decades (Oppenheimer 1985), so the minimal short-term effects of the cloture rule are probably a better indication of senators' expectations and preferences in 1917. *Summary: an exogenous shock increased the transaction payoffs for both parties. Legislators supported reform to reap these gains yet designed this new rule to have minimal effects on policy outcomes.*

Discussion

This chapter first developed a framework for studying institutional choices in which both legislators' preferences and the decision-making process are influential. I then applied this framework to senators' institutional choices from 1913 to 1917 to better understand the adoption of a weak cloture rule in 1917. The role of entrepreneurship is highlighted by two cases of inaction: the Democrats' decision to not propose a rule change at the beginning of the 63rd and 64th Congresses. Second, the claim that the majority party can impose reforms despite minority-party opposition is supported by several cases. Together, these cases demonstrate the weak incentives to restrain obstruction during the 1910s Senate. It is not surprising, therefore, that the 1917 cloture rule included a two-thirds majority requirement that made it almost inconsequential. In the midst of a firestorm of public concern about Senate obstruction, senators chose to codify the status quo balance of power (it took at least a third of the Senate to sustain a prolonged filibuster) rather than push for simple-majority cloture. This case demonstrates the potential for positive transaction payments to motivate a rule change that legislators would not otherwise adopt for policy reasons.

Chapter 15

Cloture Reform Reconsidered

GREGORY J. WAWRO AND ERIC SCHICKLER

Introduction

This chapter investigates the impact of the adoption of cloture by the U.S. Senate in 1917, assessing the degree to which the rule affected lawmaking in the institution. In previous work, we found that, before the adoption of cloture, the Senate was for the most part a majoritarian body (Wawro and Schickler 2004). The main exception was that larger coalitions appeared to have been necessary to overcome obstruction toward the end of a Congress in lame-duck sessions, when severe time constraints gave minorities a particular advantage. Given the success that slim majorities had in passing legislation before 1917, it is puzzling why senators adopted a cloture rule that required coalitions to be *larger* than what was generally necessary at the time. We develop a model that shows how senators might have benefited from a supermajority procedure for shutting off debate even though it was still possible to pass legislation with narrower majorities. The model also shows how the rule could have had an impact even though senators rarely resorted to it. We consider how legislative entrepreneurs might trade off a decrease in the uncertainty of passage of legislation for an increase in the size of coalitions necessary to pass it. The model is tested by examining coalition sizes on the passage of significant legislation and on appropriations bills. We also consider how the adoption of cloture affected the efficiency of the Senate in processing appropriations bills, which was a major area of concern when it came to the lack of rules limiting debate. We find evidence that cloture was more than just a symbolic reform and had a real and discernible impact on lawmaking in the Senate.

Alternative Views of Cloture Reform

Even though the 1917 cloture rule was far from the previous-question rules that existed in the House of Representatives and many other legislatures (Luce 1922),[1] some observers at the time thought it would be an effective solution to the problems presented by unlimited debate. The *Washington Post* claimed that, as a result of the amendment to the rules, "the organized filibuster of a few men as recognized in the Senate is dead."[2] While acknowledging that the rule "probably cannot be successfully used to prevent the spectacular one-man filibusters by which senators have talked bills pending in the closing hours of a session to a legislative grave" unless they are foreseen, the *Post* contended that "an organized affair which must be planned two days or more ahead of a session's end can be disposed of easily." The *New York Times* argued, "It is difficult to overestimate the importance of the new rule, both on measures of immediate interest and on the general course of legislation," adding that "the real importance of the rule lies in its almost unlimited potential effect on future legislation" (March 9, 1917, p. 1). In the floor debate on the amendment to rule 22, a few senators even argued that the new rule would be too effective, limiting debate to such a degree that it would diminish the Senate's role in the separation-of-powers system (ibid.).

Woodrow Wilson, who is credited with mobilizing mass opinion to bring about the adoption of cloture, is reported to have "expressed warm support for the proposal" (*New York Times*, March 8, 1917, p. 2). Wilson's reaction is telling. For a president, he had gone to unprecedented lengths to vilify senators on the issue of the filibuster, launching an all out public relations campaign against those who defeated the armed-ship bill and the rules of the Senate that allowed them to do so. For example, at a luncheon for the Democratic National Committee at the White House, Wilson "threw aside all reserve in expressing his opinion of those Senators who blocked passage of the Armed Neutrality bill." The *New York Times* characterized Wilson's remarks as an "outburst" that "both surprised and pleased" the attendees, as the president "castigated those Democrats who joined with Republicans in the Senate to embarrass the Administration at a time when the highest order of patriotism was necessary to enable the Government to cope with a delicate situation" (March 7, 1917, p. 1). The fact that Wilson did not push for a more stringent rule suggests he thought it would be effective.[3]

In the aftermath of the cloture reform of 1917, the rule has been almost universally denigrated by close observers of the Senate. Byrd (1988, 124) claims that as early as November 1918, "it was becoming clear that the cloture rule was not going to be effective." White (1968, 60–61) argued that "the rule bore within itself the seeds of its own nullification" because it could be applied only to halt debate on a "measure" but not a "motion."[4] Although the Senate reformed its rules in 1949 to apply the cloture rule to motions as well as measures, this change was part of a compromise that raised the threshold to alter the rules to two-thirds of the entire Senate, and therefore it meant that "cloture was in practical fact at least as far off as ever, and the Senate in plain fact retained what amounts to unlimited debate" (White 1968, 64). Rogers (1926, 177) argued that the cloture procedure was "so cumbersome as to be possible only in emergencies." During the debate on anti-poll-tax legislation in 1948, President Pro Tem Arthur Vandenberg declared that "in the final analysis, the Senate has no effective cloture rule at all . . . a small but determined majority can always prevent cloture, under the existing rules" (U.S. Senate Committee 1985, 20). Luce (1922, 295) also expressed doubts about the rule's effectiveness, since "very rarely does either party control two thirds of the votes of the Senate." Haynes's (1938, 1:420) views on the impact of cloture in the decade after it was adopted are mixed, but he nevertheless claims that the rules still lent themselves to "practices which have been injurious to legislation and have greatly discredited the Senate in the opinion of the public," and he noted that there were "hopeful signs of co-operation to remedy these evils." In an interesting point that he does not develop but one we view as crucial to this debate, Haynes (1938, 1:405) argues that "the efficacy of this rule for the most part inheres in the consciousness that it is available rather than in its actual use." Still, the gist of these views is that legislation that could be killed with a filibuster before the reform could still be killed by a filibuster after the reform.[5]

Other critics of the cloture rule note the infrequency with which it was applied at all, let alone applied successfully. From the 66th to the 86th Congresses (1919–1960), only 23 cloture votes took place, and of those, only 4 were successful (Oppenheimer 1985, 398). Between 1927 and 1962, the Senate had an unbroken string of unsuccessful cloture votes—14 in all. By these measures, the 1917 rule did not appear to arm senators with a practicable weapon against obstruction.

If these views are correct, why did senators even bother to amend rule 22? To be sure, the reform apparently served to placate a public incensed about the successful end-of-session filibuster of the widely popular armed-ship bill. It was also viewed at the time as a necessary first step toward majority cloture. The *New York Times* reported, "But everyone believes, and many Senators said on the floor of the Senate today, that before long the rule inevitably will be amended so as to give to a bare majority the power now given to two-thirds. Then a direct vote in the Senate can be obtained almost as easily and quickly as in the House" (March 9, 1917, p. 1).

The symbolic importance of the cloture reform is unassailable, yet the perspective that its substantive impact was nil is questionable. If that view is correct, why did Wilson, who so masterfully marshaled public opinion to change rules that had gone unreformed for over 110 years, settle for the two-thirds rule rather than support the majority cloture provision that was considered in the Democratic caucus?[6] Although Wilson, the political scientist, had lauded the Senate's rules protecting unlimited debate in *Congressional Government* ([1885] 1956), Wilson, the president, vigorously opposed them and would be plagued by the obstruction they allowed throughout his presidency.[7] Perhaps he was simply being a practical politician and knew that there was not support for a more severe cloture rule. But this raises the question of why more support did not develop in the Senate, given that filibustering allegedly became a more serious problem (Burdette 1940, chapters 5–6).

In the years following the reform, the Senate did not reduce the threshold further as many had thought it would. This was not for lack of trying. Shortly after the reform was adopted, the Senate in 1918 considered a resolution by Senator Oscar Underwood (D-Ala.) to reintroduce the previous-question motion and limit debate during the conduct of World War I. Although the resolution was reported out favorably by the Rules Committee and a unanimous-consent agreement was adopted to bring it to a vote, it was rejected by the Senate on a vote of 41 nays to 34 yeas. In the 67th Congress (1921–1923), five resolutions for limiting debate were introduced, yet none made any headway beyond the committee stage (U.S. Senate Committee 1985, 17).

A Simple Model of Cloture

Our reconsideration of the cloture rule begins with the puzzle of why members would have maintained a procedure that critics have charged offered no real benefits to them. We develop a simple model that shows how senators might have benefited from a cloture rule even though they rarely resorted to invoking the procedure. The model contemplates how senators can trade off a decrease in the uncertainty of passage for an increase in the size of coalitions necessary to pass legislation. In this sense, cloture may have constituted a kind of insurance policy for risk-averse legislators, which protected them from the risk they faced when considering legislation late in the session, when obstructionists had a particular advantage.

This trade-off can be modeled by considering a legislative entrepreneur's expected utility from passing legislation with and without cloture. The legislative entrepreneur (LE) can add individuals to the coalition, which increases the probability that the proposal will pass, but this comes at the cost of receiving fewer benefits from the legislation if enacted. The decrease in benefits can be viewed in terms of having to share with each additional legislator some piece of a fixed-size pie. The LE may have to provide a project to a senator's state, which means fewer funds for projects in the LE's own state. Or the decrease in benefits may be thought of as a spatial adjustment of the proposal that moves the policy outcome in a direction closer to the ideal point of a senator who is hesitant to join the coalition but away from the LE's ideal point. The question then is to what extent is the LE willing to compromise on the substance of the proposal to enhance its prospects for passage?

Let π denote coalition size (as a proportion), such that $\eta \in [0.5, 1]$. We restrict η to this range because values of η below 0.5 are not relevant for our purposes, since we are interested only in coalitions that meet the necessary, but possibly not sufficient, threshold of a majority for passage.[8] Define π as the probability of passage of a piece of legislation, and B as the benefit obtained from passing legislation.[9] Both π and B are functions of η. Specifically, let

$$\pi(\alpha) = \left(\frac{\eta - 0.5}{0.5}\right)^{\alpha} \qquad \textbf{(15.1)}$$

This gives nonlinearly increasing π, with the α parameter indicating how much an additional coalition member beyond 51 percent of the chamber contributes to the probability of passage. We assume $\alpha \in [0, 1]$, such that as α approaches 1, the marginal increase in probability from adding a legislator to the coalition increases. This form for π has properties that are intuitively appealing for representing the functional relationship between coalition sizes and probabilities of passage. When $\eta = 0.50$, $\pi = 0$ (i.e., you need at least a minimum majority to have any chance of passing legislation) and when $\eta = 1$, $\pi = 1$ (i.e., you are assured of passing legislation when all members of the chamber are part of the supporting coalition). Having a minimum majority does not guarantee passage because various (unmodeled) factors may affect a bill's chances for passage, such as obstruction by opponents or being crowded out by other items on the agenda.

In this model, we let

$$B = \frac{1 - \eta}{0.5} \tag{15.2}$$

This gives linearly decreasing *B*, such that *B* is maximized at a coalition of 0.51 and $B = 0$ when the coalition is unanimous. We also assume $B = 0$ if the legislation fails to pass.

The expected utility for the LE can then be written as

$$EU = \pi B + (1 - \pi)0 = \pi B \tag{15.3}$$

There is a clear trade-off of the utility the LE expects between coalition size and benefits.[10] With α set at 0.1, the baseline probability for a coalition size of 0.51 is fairly high, and the marginal increase in probability from adding new coalition members is fairly small after 0.6. Expected utility (EU) is maximized at 0.55, which should lead the LE to put together close to minimum-majority coalitions. As α increases, it is more beneficial to build bigger coalitions. For $\alpha = 0.5$, a coalition of 0.67 maximizes the EU for the LE, and thus we should expect to see supermajority coalitions. For higher values of α, coalitions are predicted to be oversized—EU is maximized at 0.71 for an α of 0.75. Note that the loss in benefits from adding another member to the coalition is the same across these different scenarios; all that changes is the contribution of each coalition partner to the probability of passage.

One way to think about the 1917 cloture rule is that it makes the probability function π jump upward at $\eta = 0.67$. That is, building a coalition that exceeds the supermajority threshold specified by the rule makes it sharply more probable (although not certain) that the legislation will pass. By building a supermajority coalition, LEs insure themselves against some of the malevolent vicissitudes of the legislative process. Should a filibuster develop against the legislation, the LE has the votes to invoke cloture. However, being able to invoke cloture does not guarantee that the legislation will pass, since obstructionists may be able to run out the clock, depending on how much time is left in the legislative session and how many other pieces of legislation that are more salient to legislators remain to be addressed.

In the presence of the cloture rule, the EU would be

$$EU_c = \pi(\alpha)B \cdot 1[\eta < 0.67] + \pi(\alpha^*)B \cdot (1 - 1[\eta < 0.67]) \tag{15.4}$$

where $1[\cdot]$ is the indicator function and $\alpha^* < \alpha$, which serves to scale up the probability, making it more likely for the bill to pass if the coalition supporting it exceeds the two-thirds threshold. When $\alpha = 0.1$, there is very little gain from having a two-thirds cloture rule. The jump that occurs in π does not produce a big enough increase in πB to exceed the maximum that existed without cloture.

However, for the other values of α^*, the maximum of πB is greater than the maximum without cloture. When $\alpha = 0.25$ and $\alpha^* = 0.1$, an LE realizes a gain in EU when the size of the coalition increases to two-thirds. The prediction for this situation then is a larger coalition than what the LE would have put together without a cloture rule. When $\alpha = 0.5$ and $\alpha^* = 0.25$, we do not expect to see any difference in the LE's behavior. The utility for the LE is maximized with a two-thirds coalition now as it was before. The model predicts a *decrease* in coalition sizes when $\alpha = 0.75$ and $\alpha^* = 0.5$, since the maximum of the EU function drops to 0.67 with cloture, down from 0.71.

While it is difficult to tell which situations best characterize lawmaking in the late 19th and early 20th centuries, the analysis of significant legislation and tariff bills in Wawro and Schickler (2004) indicates that the one represented by α in the vicinity of 0.25 was fairly common. There are numerous cases where legislation passed with coalitions below the threshold established by the 1917 cloture rule. The increase in the average coalition size after the adoption of cloture that we found in previous work is consistent with this view. While we acknowledge that other factors might have contributed to this increase, no one has yet offered a theoretical framework that explicitly demonstrates how these factors operate.

Another important point that emerges from the model is that the number of times cloture was sought and invoked successfully is not necessarily a good indicator of the impact of cloture reform (cf. Beth 1995). Once the cloture rule establishes a threshold for passage, EU-maximizing LEs have a clearer target to aim for and should adjust their coalition-building behavior accordingly. In many cases, this would mean building bigger coalitions in an attempt to preempt obstructive efforts. Would-be obstructionists have less incentive to filibuster if they know that cloture can be invoked on them. While there are various benefits to filibustering, the price that legislators have to pay to engage in this activity in terms of effort, opportunity costs, and the loss of good will may be too dear if there is a good chance the filibuster will be defeated without changing policy substantively. Thus, the cloture rule alters the strategic calculations of legislators so that LEs should build bigger coalitions to head off potential filibusters and those who might have engaged in obstruction before instead channel their resources into other activities that have more promise of a substantive return.

Our model then provides theoretical underpinning for Haynes's assessment that the cloture rule was efficacious because legislators knew they could credibly resort to it if they built large enough coalitions, not because they actually had to apply it.

An additional prediction that emerges from the model is that the variance of coalition sizes should decrease after the adoption of cloture. This would hold if values of $\alpha > 0.25$ generally represent the lawmaking situations that LEs face and if members in a specific situation know the distribution—but not actual value—of α. We believe that such uncertainty is particularly likely near the end of a Congress. The time constraints imposed by the automatic adjournment deadline of March 4 for each pre-1933 Congress and the rush to address pending items during lame-duck sessions should have made it more difficult for LEs to ascertain how much support was necessary to gain passage. The availability of the cloture procedure reduced this uncertainty.[11]

Coalition sizes on significant legislation offer a way to test this prediction. While the change in the first moment in the distribution of coalition sizes noted earlier supports our theoretical conjectures, if the point about uncertainty is correct, then we should also see a change in the second moment. That is, the variance of coalition sizes on significant legislation should be smaller after 1917 than it was before enactment of the cloture rule. We expect this to hold only for lame-duck sessions, given the heightened threat that obstruction presented then.

The data do support this prediction, although we need to be careful about our inferences because of small sample sizes. The variance of coalition sizes in lame-duck sessions before cloture reform was 0.017 (for 6 bills) but then decreased to 0.013 (for 4 bills) after cloture reform. Although this difference is small, a nonparametric test of equal variances based on squared ranks, which is particularly well suited for samples of this size (Conover 1999, 300–303), indicates the difference in variances is significant at the 0.1 level.[12] If we include voice votes taken at the end of a Congress and treat them as unanimous, this increases the sample size to 21 in the precloture period (with coalition-size variance equal to 0.025) and 8 in the postcloture period (with coalition-size variance equal to 0.01). The nonparametric test with the larger sample size also leads us to reject the null of equal variances (at the 0.01 level).[13] These results are consistent with the argument that a goal of cloture reform was to reduce the uncertainty created by obstruction toward the end of a Congress, particularly as norms of restraint started to break down at the turn of the 19th century (Wawro and Schickler 2006, chapter 2).

Since coalition sizes are bounded above by 1.0, one might worry that an increase in the average coalition size would necessarily lead to a reduction in the variance. But our argument implies that this would happen to a significant degree only at the end of a Congress. We should not see a significant difference in the variance of coalition sizes for legislation passed *earlier* in precloture versus postcloture Congresses.[14] Consistent with our hypothesis, the precloture and postcloture variances differ only to the fourth decimal place, with the former equaling 0.0174 and the latter equaling 0.0171. Conover's (1999, 301) T_1 statistic is only -0.04, which has a p value of 0.484. We clearly cannot reject the null of equal variances across the two periods (even though coalitions on average became larger for legislation considered before the end of the Congress).

This analysis supports our arguments about the impact of cloture reform. While our model is relatively sparse, we believe that it illuminates one of the central strategic features of the cloture rule. By providing a sufficient—but not strictly necessary—condition for passing legislation, it allowed legislative entrepreneurs to reduce the uncertainty posed particularly by late-Congress filibusters by building a larger supportive coalition. The result was an increase in the average coalition size and a reduction in the variance when bills came up for consideration near final adjournment.

It is important to note that other theories exist that offer explanations for supermajority coalitions. These theories show how governing by supermajorities, while undoubtedly more burdensome, has potential advantages. Groseclose and Snyder (1996) demonstrate formally that a vote-buying strategy that involves putting together supermajorities can be less costly than a strategy of building minimal winning coalitions. Caplin and Nalebuff (1988) show that majorities of 64 percent (or greater) can solve problems of cycling and unraveling of legislative bargains. Yet these theories do not offer explanations as to why we would observe the variation in coalition sizes that exists historically.

The Impact of Cloture on the Appropriations Process

We pursue this issue further by examining the effects of cloture on the appropriations process in the Senate. The failure to pass appropriations bills, especially because of obstruction, was a major concern of senators in the period under examination. They perennially confronted the problem of passing appropriations before the fiscal year expired, which was necessary to keep the federal government operating.

In debates about obstruction, concerns about appropriations were constantly expressed. In his campaign in 1925 against the rules that allowed filibusters, Vice President Charles Dawes asked whether "the power to kill legislation providing the revenues to pay the expenses of government should, during the last few days of a session, ever be in the hands of a minority, or perhaps one senator? Why should they ever compel the President of the United States to call an extra session of Congress to keep in functioning activity the machinery of the Government itself?" (*Congressional Record*, 69th Cong., special sess., March 4, 1925, pp. 3–4). According to Haynes (1938, 1:395), "Appropriations bills engrossed so much of the Senate's time that the necessity of some limitations on debate first became convincing in regard to them." The death of appropriations bills at the hands of obstructionists often prompted calls for cloture reform. For example, a cloture proposal introduced by Senator Platt (R-Conn.) in 1901 was alleged to be in response to the successful filibuster of a rivers and harbors appropriations bill in the previous Congress (*New York Times*, March 6, 1901, p. 5). Rogers (1926, 183–184) argued that the power of the filibuster came through its effects on the appropriations process: "It is through their ability to hold up the appropriation bills that a filibustering minority can win a victory." It is important to note that these concerns were not just about filibusters of appropriations bills but also about how filibusters of any legislation would affect the Senate's ability to pass spending measures.[15] The filibuster that defeated the armed-ship bill took with it several regular appropriations bills and a general-deficiency bill, which amounted to about $511,000,000 worth of lost funds ("$511,000,000 in Bills Blocked by Senate," *New York Times*, March 5, 1917, p. 2).

In a series of articles on the failure to pass appropriations bills by the fiscal-year deadline in 1912, the *New York Times* painted a dire picture of the resulting disruption. The *Times* contended that government departments would be in violation of the law if they continued to operate without the passage of appropriations bills that provided them with funds ("Convention Halts Department Funds," July 1, 1912, p. 4). It was noted how the "most serious phase of the situation is the prospect that all the letter carriers and the rural free delivery carriers . . . may have to stop work until Congress acts . . . the 28,000 letter carriers in cities, 41,000 rural carriers, 33,000 clerks in post offices, 16,000 railway mail clerks, and upward of 8,000 other clerks in the service will be out of work and the public service will be prostrated" ("Dilatory Senate Halts Money Bills," June 27, 1912, p. 1). The need to work through the summer on the appropriations bills was also problematic because it would keep members of Congress from the "pressing political business for most of them at home" ("The Delays in Congress," *New York Times*, July 9, 1912, p. 8).

The uncertainty that filibusters presented to the appropriations process was a major concern of efforts to reform Senate procedure. If our arguments about the cloture rule serving as an uncertainty-reducing mechanism are correct, then this should be reflected in the Senate's ability to process appropriations bills. We investigate whether the cloture rule led to increased efficiency in the appropriations process by more clearly prescribing a threshold for bringing debate to an end and legislation to a vote. We argue that cloture was an important component in a set of reforms enacted during this period that helped the Senate deal with problems that obstruction presented in the enactment of fiscal policy.

An examination of Senate action on appropriations is important beyond our interest in filibuster politics because, while several studies have undertaken historical analyses of the appropriations process in the House (e.g., Stewart 1989 and Kiewiet and McCubbins 1991), the process in the Senate has received little scholarly attention. In part because of its traditional role of moving first in the process, the House has been seen as the dominant congressional partner in spending decisions. The Senate is seen as reactive, serving as a "court of appeals" for claimants on the federal treasury who seek more funds than provided in the legislation initially passed by the House (Fenno 1966). Yet the role of the Senate in the appropriations process is far from secondary. This chapter helps to illuminate the part that the Senate's unique rules and procedures have played in spending decisions and the ability of the federal government to meet its fiscal obligations.

Studies of obstruction have paid little attention to its effects on Congress's power over the purse strings of government. Yet one of the factors that is most important for understanding obstruction—time constraints—are particularly relevant for spending bills. Appropriations presented deadline problems beyond those associated with lame-duck sessions. The beginning of the fiscal year, which occurred on July 1 during the period we examine, required that appropriations bills be passed by then for the government to meet its fiscal obligations and maintain operations. Congress would typically not be in session when the deadline passed for fiscal years that began in odd-numbered years. After adjourning on March 3 in odd-numbered years, Congress would usually not meet again until December of that year. As a result, Congress had to pass appropriations bills by the March 3 adjournment date if it was to provide funds before the new fiscal year started. Since

Congress did not start considering appropriations bills for even-numbered fiscal years until the lame-duck sessions, this made time constraints especially relevant.[16]

For fiscal years that began when Congress was conducting its regular session, the Senate nonetheless often struggled to complete work on spending bills. In fact, Congress was less likely to meet the fiscal-year deadline for these years. Although members may have been less concerned about failing to meet the deadline when they knew they would still be in session to rectify the problem relatively quickly, it is worth noting that such failures were by no means costless. The failure to meet the deadline would still mean that the relevant government entities would run out of money to fund their operations and Congress would have to go through the effort of passing continuing appropriations in addition to regular appropriations to keep these entities functioning. While this has become an annual ritual in today's Congress, continuing resolutions were more unusual and appear to have been less acceptable in earlier periods of congressional history.[17]

We posit that the cloture rule should have made the Senate better able to meet the relevant deadlines that it faced for passing spending bills. Although cloture was rarely invoked, we have presented evidence that senators built bigger coalitions after the rule was adopted, possibly with the intention of preempting filibusters. If such preemption was occurring, then it should have been easier for the Senate to pass appropriations in a timely manner. We can investigate systematically whether this is the case.

However, such an analysis needs to be sensitive to other institutional changes that might have affected the appropriations process during this period. These include some of the most important institutional changes involving the appropriations process in Congress's history. The two main changes include the passage of the Budget Act of 1921 and the decentralization and recentralization of committee jurisdictions over appropriations.

While studies that focus on the appropriations process in the House and how these institutional changes affected it are plentiful, almost no systematic research has been conducted on the appropriations process in the Senate during this period—or for subsequent periods for that matter. Fenno's (1966) landmark work, *The Power of the Purse*, is one of the only studies that has examined the process in the Senate in any depth. Although Fenno's analysis is fairly time bound, covering the Senate only in the mid-20th century (1947–1965), a few major themes emerge from his work that have theoretical relevance for the study of obstruction in earlier periods and point to important factors that any empirical model of the appropriations process should account for. It is important then to assess whether the features that Fenno saw as central to the process in the Senate in the mid-20th century mattered in earlier periods.

One of Fenno's major conclusions was that the most important part of the appropriations process was the committee stage, since the overall parameters of debate and deliberation were set in committee, and primarily in the House Appropriations Committee (HAC). The Senate Appropriations Committee (SAC) was also important in the process, but less so than HAC. A key difference between HAC and SAC, however, concerns the relationship between the committees and their parent chambers. The relationship between HAC and its parent chamber was characterized by tension, predominantly because of the committee's exclusivity, isolation, and tight-fisted control over the government's purse strings. Many House members complained about HAC's refusal to fund projects or programs that they believed were meritorious—or at the very least electorally beneficial.

The relationship between SAC and its parent chamber was much more cordial. Fenno hypothesized that this difference was rooted in both the greater openness of the committee in the Senate and the fact that a higher percentage of senators held seats on SAC, making it more representative. This made the committee much more accessible and rendered committee and chamber preferences over appropriations much more consonant than in the House. To paraphrase Fenno (1966, 614), SAC is the Senate.

This observation has theoretical relevance for our investigation of the Senate's ability to process appropriations. The greater representativeness of SAC should lead to less conflict on the Senate floor, since the bill that the committee reports is more likely to be in line with the preferences of noncommittee members. Although the standard rules of floor debate grant substantial leeway to noncommittee members to amend or obstruct SAC's proposals, it may be that senators see little need to do so because of their agreement with the committee. The greater representativeness of SAC should mean that it better anticipates what latent obstructors would object to once the bill reaches the floor and preempt them by making adjustments to the bill in committee.

This raises two important questions about SAC during the period we are interested in: First, how representative was SAC? Second, to what extent were the committee's proposals amended on the floor? The answers to these questions are complicated because of shifts in committee jurisdictions over spending bills that occurred in 1899 and 1922. In 1899 the Senate carved up most of SAC's jurisdiction and redistributed it to other committees. A similar devolution had taken place in the House in 1885 (Brady and

Morgan 1987; Stewart 1989). This decentralization of appropriations stood in contrast to the centralizing efforts of party leaders that took place about the same time (Rothman 1966). The institutional change was largely driven by younger, less senior senators who sought more power over the Senate's proceedings (Schickler 2001; Schickler and Sides 2000).

In early March 1922, the Senate reversed course and reinstated SAC's jurisdiction over all spending bills. However, committees that had appropriations jurisdiction after the 1899 divestiture were allowed to have three members serve ex officio on SAC when bills that had been on their legislative committee's turf were under consideration at SAC. They also could send one conferee to take part in conference-committee deliberations.[18] The ex officio provision contributed considerably to the representativeness of SAC that Fenno reported. One of the questions for our analysis then becomes to what degree were the committees that received parts of SAC's jurisdiction representative of the larger chamber? The question of the representativeness of committees, especially those that craft spending bills, has garnered considerable attention in the congressional literature. Proponents of the distributive perspective of legislative organization contend that committees are generally unrepresentative of their parent chambers. According to this work, committees consist of homogeneous preference outliers, which is the result of a system of self-selection to committees that enables those with the greatest electoral stake in the committees' jurisdictions to obtain their preferred assignments (Shepsle 1978, 1979; Shepsle and Weingast 1987a; Weingast and Marshall 1988). This view has been challenged by both the informational and the partisan perspectives of legislative organization. The former argues that committees should be microcosms of the parent chamber to facilitate the communication of policy-relevant information (Krehbiel 1991), while the latter argues that committees should be representative of the (majority) party caucus so that committees will be more effective and loyal agents of the party (Cox and McCubbins 1993; Kiewiet and McCubbins 1991). This dispute launched many empirical efforts using different measurement approaches to try to determine just how representative committees are (Krehbiel 1990; Groseclose 1994; Hall and Grofman 1990; Maltzman 1997).

The studies of representativeness have focused mainly on the post–World War II period. Unfortunately, we are limited by existing data with regard to how we can address the issue of SAC's representativeness in earlier periods. Most importantly, existing data on committee rosters for the period under investigation does not include the names of the ex officio members of SAC. This makes it difficult to determine without possible error the ideological makeup of the panels making spending decisions. However, since we know the number of ex officio members from each of the legislative committees, we can compute the percentage of the chamber that is eligible to participate in SAC deliberations.[19] While this measure is undoubtedly a crude one, it seems to fit well with the notion of representativeness that Fenno discussed, long before more sophisticated measures of committee ideology were developed. The key idea of interlocking committee memberships is still tapped by this measure and addresses our concern about conflict on appropriations bills between committee and floor.

The time series for the percentage of the Senate's membership that was involved in spending decisions for devolved and nondevolved appropriations bills indicates there was a general upward trend in the representativeness of the funding committees by this measure, and the trend appears to have picked up with the recentralization of appropriations. Thus, the interlocking memberships that Fenno discussed appear to have extended back to the recentralization, and given the proximity of this institutional change to the enactment of cloture, it is imperative to account for these changes to the committee system in our analysis.[20]

By comparison, the percentage of House members involved in appropriations decisions at the committee stage was much smaller both before and after the recentralization in that chamber. The legislative committees that lost jurisdiction to HAC when appropriations were recentralized in 1920 were not compensated as in the Senate, resulting in much grumbling and resentment of the committee (Stewart 1989, 205). As a consequence, the relationship between HAC and its parent chamber continued to be problematic after the committee regained its lost authority.

The degree of harmony between the appropriating committees and the Senate should be reflected in the degree to which committee proposals were amended on the floor, and the degree to which conflict spills out onto the floor should affect the Senate's ability to process legislation. Much has been made of the extent to which HAC recommendations remained intact once the committee reported out bills. Fenno (1966) examined appropriations for 36 bureaus from 1947 to 1962, finding that HAC's recommendations were accepted without alteration in the overwhelming majority of cases. The same seemed to be true of SAC. Kiewiet and McCubbins (1991, 149–152) extended Fenno's analysis to cover fiscal years 1947 to 1985 and found that the appropriations committees "appear to get most of what they want on the floor," since "amendments tend to be small in percentage terms" or "lacking in substance." A key difference between the appropriations process during the postwar period and the period we cover is that unanimous-consent agreements had become a much more common way of doing business in the Senate and may have limited the range of amendments that could have been offered on the floor (see Fenno 1966, 591).

But one major issue was that the Senate almost invariably raised the dollar amount included in House bills. Anecdotal evidence indicates this tradition extends far back into congressional history. MacNeil (1963, 394) notes that House members complained of the Senate's additions to appropriations bills as far back as the 1860s, and that by the end of the 19th century, this tradition appears to have been well established (see also Reinsch [1907, 112], and Rogers [1926, 111]).

For our analysis, it is important to know whether this was the case systematically, and if so, whether the increases occurred during committee deliberations or during the amendment process on the floor. If they occurred during the latter stage, then this may have made it difficult for the Senate to process bills by the relevant deadlines. The wide-open floor procedure in the Senate would have provided ample opportunity for senators to try to insert pork barrel projects into a bill through floor amendments. Indeed, the threat of obstruction may be one of the causal factors behind the more generous bills that came out of the Senate. The first reported case where a senator explicitly threatened to filibuster an appropriations bill to increase spending was when Ben "Pitchfork" Tillman (D-S.C.) claimed he would talk a 1903 deficiency bill to death unless funds to reimburse the state of South Carolina for expenses incurred during the War of 1812 were reinserted into the bill. His successful threat prompted Joseph Cannon—then House Appropriations chair—to deliver a rousing speech on the floor, charging that the rules of the Senate subjected the House to "legislative blackmail" ("Mr. Cannon Stirs the House," *New York Times*, March 5, 1903, p. 2; Burdette 1940, 72). Rogers (1926, 170–171) discusses this and one other incident where senators successfully had items inserted into appropriations bills in response to their threats of obstruction, and he cites a statement made in 1913 by Senator Charles Thomas (D-Colo.) in which he claimed there were "scores of others which have disfigured our consideration of appropriations bills" during his service in the chamber (see also Matthews 1960, 259).

The degree to which the Senate alters House bills might have been particularly problematic after the passage of the Budget Act. Kiewiet and McCubbins (1991, 172–173) argue that the Budget Act was largely prompted by a new interest in economy that stemmed from a dramatic increase in the federal debt due to World War I and changes in the source of revenues for the federal government—namely, the decline in tariffs and the rise in corporate and personal income taxation. This interest in economy had great potential to conflict with the long-standing Senate tradition of upping amounts in the bills that were referred to it. MacNeil (1963, 394–395) argues that the creation of the Budget Bureau and the restoration of all appropriations bills to HAC were an attempt by the House to reassert itself against the Senate, which had dominated the appropriations process since the decentralization of 1885. These steps were viewed as a way for the traditionally more frugal chamber to cut back on profligate spending, consistent with the mood of economy that prevailed at the time. The desire to impose spending discipline in the 1920s might have led to floor conflict if SAC had increased appropriations in the allegedly fiscally conservative House bill. If the increases in appropriations happened at the SAC stage, then economy-minded non-SAC senators might have tried to alter bills when they had a crack at them at the floor stage.

While anecdotally the Senate appears to have long been the more generous chamber when it came to spending decisions, we do not know the extent to which this was the case systematically. The existing literature is also silent on whether the deference to SAC extends either back in time or to the committees that obtained part of SAC's jurisdiction from 1899 to 1922. We examined the dynamics of both intra- and interchamber conflict over alterations to regular appropriations bills. Our data include the percentage change in the bill reported by the relevant appropriations committee and the bill that passed on the floor in each chamber, as well as the difference between the initial bills passed by the House and the Senate (i.e., before their differences were worked out in conference).

Although there is substantial variation across appropriations types, one pattern that is evident is that the final bill that passes the Senate typically has a larger amount than the House bill, but the final bill hews closely to that reported by the relevant Senate committee (see figure 10.2 in Wawro and Schickler 2006). Consistent with what Fenno found in the mid-20th century, appropriating was done almost entirely in committee and not on the floors of the chambers. The difference between the bills passed by the chamber and the bills reported out of committee rarely departs from zero. The increases in House bills that occurred in the Senate appear to have largely been the result of committee deliberations. It was unusual for major changes to happen on the Senate floor, as the recommendations of the appropriating committees were for the most part accepted despite the lack of rules that would have restricted amendments. It is important to note that this does not mean that obstruction on the floor by senators who were upset about being stiffed by the committee over funds they sought was not an issue. Fenno (1966, 520) quotes a SAC staffer who suggests that this was indeed a concern of appropriating committees:

> You can do a lot of things in the House that you can't do in the Senate. If you get up to speak on appropriations there, they can shout you down. But over here, you got to listen to what a senator has to say no matter who he is. If you don't, he'll filibuster you and hold up an appropriation bill for three days.

The openness of the Senate committee and the interlocking memberships that existed appeared to have enabled the committee to anticipate the trouble noncommittee members could have caused on the floor and to modify bills in ways that preempted moves to change the bills through floor amendments.

Cloture and Appropriations Deadlines

The discussion in the previous section sets the stage for a quantitative analysis of the impact of cloture on the ability of the Senate to process appropriations bills by deadlines established by the end of Congress and the beginning of the fiscal year. The analysis includes all regular appropriations bills that were considered from 1890 to 1946, which is essentially the same period covered by the data on significant legislation previously discussed.[21] The dependent variable in our analysis takes on a value of 1 if the Senate *failed* to pass a bill for a given appropriations category by the relevant deadline and is 0 otherwise. The key explanatory variable we are interested in is a dummy variable that equals 1 for bills considered before the adoption of cloture and equals 0 for postcloture bills. If our hypotheses regarding the effectiveness of the cloture rule are correct we should observe a positive coefficient on this variable. This is an admittedly crude measure and could account for numerous changes that occurred around the time that cloture was adopted. As discussed in the previous section, the most important changes that happened proximate to the cloture rule concerned the recentralization of the jurisdiction over appropriations in HAC and SAC and the Budget Act of 1921. While we could model the effects of these changes with their own dummy variables, such variables would obviously be highly correlated with each other and the dummy variable, indicating the existence of a cloture rule. Including all of these dummies in our model would make it difficult to sort out the effects of the change in budget rules versus the change in floor procedure. Fortunately, we can do better by including more precise measures that capture theoretically relevant features of the institutional changes.

A key change under the Budget Act was to centralize in the Bureau of the Budget the processing of agency requests for funds before they were submitted to Congress. This was intended to bring about efficiency in the process as well as to promote fiscal discipline by reining in agencies who submitted overly large spending requests. The centralization should have reduced the amount of time that it took to process the spending bills, which would have made it easier for the Senate to have met appropriations deadlines. It also would have given senators more time to resort to the cloture procedure if they thought it necessary. One measure that indicates increased efficiency following passage of the Budget Act is the average number of days between important junctures in the process and the deadline. Post–Budget Act, there were on average more days between the deadline and the reporting of bills from HAC, their passage on the House floor, and the reporting of bills by SAC. The process before the bill reached the Senate floor moved more quickly after 1921, which gave senators more time to consider bills on the floor.[22] Since we are mainly interested in the processing of bills on the Senate floor, we include in our specification the variable measuring the number of days between the reporting of the bill by SAC and the relevant deadline.[23] Including this variable allows us to account for one of the main ways the Budget Act induced efficiency. We expect this variable to have a negative coefficient, since the longer it takes to get through the committee stage in the Senate, the more difficult it should be to process the bill on the floor before either the Congress or the fiscal year expires. Note that by including this variable we are also accounting for the amount of time it took the bill to make its way through the House, since the Senate did not begin to consider appropriations bills until the House had passed them.[24]

Most alterations to House bills happened in SAC and not on the Senate floor. To the extent that these alterations might have provoked discord on the floor, it should show up in the differences between the bill that passed the House and the bill reported by SAC. That is, economy-minded senators in the post–Budget Act world may have taken issue with increases in spending that occurred in committee and might have tried to use their prerogatives on the floor to strip out spending that they viewed as wasteful. The exercise of their prerogatives would have inhibited moving the bill forward toward final passage. To capture this possible effect, we include in our model a variable measuring the difference between the amount in the bill reported by SAC and the amount that passed the House. The greater this difference, the more potential conflict there might be on the floor as the competing interests of economy allegedly embodied in the House bill clashed with the increases that SAC had historically made to bills.[25] We expect a positive coefficient on this variable, which would indicate that greater differences led to more conflict and more difficulty in passing bills in the Senate.

The other major institutional changes that are crucial to account for concern the changing nature of committee jurisdictions over appropriations. The larger the percentage of the Senate that sat on the relevant appropriating committees, the smoother the floor stage of the process should have gone. In particular, the recentralization in 1922 and the concomitant increases in SAC's effective size should have made it more likely that the Senate would have met the deadlines as floor and committee agreement would have increased. The variable in our model that captures this effect is the percentage of members of the Senate who sat either on SAC or the relevant legislative committee between 1899 and 1922. This variable should have a negative effect (i.e., increases in the percentage of the chamber serving on the committee should decrease the probability of a failure to meet the deadline).

Alternatively, one could argue that the recentralization might have had negative effects on the meeting of deadlines. Stewart (1989, 120) cites one of the reasons for the devolution of appropriations bills from HAC as being that members of Congress charged that the committee was "severely overworked, as indicated by the tardiness with which appropriations bills were reported in the 48th Congress." Reconstituting SAC's jurisdiction might have led to similar difficulties after 1922. We doubt that this is the case because, first, the Bureau of the Budget should have made life much easier for both HAC and SAC, and second, the enlargement of SAC meant that workload would have been distributed more widely for particular bills. Nevertheless, the sign of the coefficient on the committee-to-chamber ratio variable will settle this question.

The point about workload suggests another variable that should be included in our model. If the decentralization of appropriations was in part motivated by concerns about committee workload, then it may be the case that devolved bills were dealt with more expeditiously since this spread out the work at the committee stage. This, of course, assumes that the newly acquired jurisdiction could be handled along with the committees' other legislative duties. To account for possible effects of the decentralization (as opposed to recentralization), the model specification includes a variable that indicates whether a bill was considered by a committee other than SAC in a given fiscal year. The inclusion of this variable helps to allay concerns that the change in appropriations jurisdiction in 1922 is responsible for the observed impact of cloture.

We include several other variables to account for additional factors that might have affected the Senate's ability to process appropriations in a timely fashion. The amount of general legislative demands that were placed on the Senate is one such factor. We employ Binder's (1997, 218–219) measure of workload, which is a factor score produced by a principal-component analysis of the number of public laws enacted, the number of days in session, and the number of senators in each Congress.[26]

The partisan and ideological makeup of the Senate may also have effects on its efficiency. A partisan view of appropriations might hold that the more unified the majority party is, the better able they can enforce discipline and meet appropriations deadlines. Given the importance of spending decisions to the construction of a favorable party label, unity should be promoted and exploited to keep the appropriations process functioning as smoothly as possible and to the benefit of the majority party (cf. Cox and McCubbins 1993; Kiewiet and McCubbins 1991). There was substantial variation in the unity of parties in the Senate during the period we cover. The conventional wisdom is that parties became uncharacteristically strong at the end of the 19th and beginning of the 20th centuries (Rothman 1966), but then unity declined substantially as we moved into the 1910s and 1920s. Considering the timing of this decline, it seems essential then to attempt to account for this variation to make sure it is not causing spurious results for the pre- and postcloture indicators. With the usual caveats about the difficulties of measuring party influence, we include in our model the standard measure of majority-party unity, the Rice cohesion score.

Finally, we account for potential ideological conflict that would cause delays in processing appropriations bills. Binder (2003) argues that intrachamber dissension is an essential component to understanding whether Congress passes legislation on its agenda. The more ideologically polarized the chamber is, the harder it will be to forge agreements within the chamber and, by extension, the harder it will be to pass legislation in a timely fashion. To account for these possible effects, the model includes Binder's measure of moderation and polarization. Using first-dimensional DW-NOMINATE scores, this measure is a count of the number of senators who are closer to the chamber median than to the median in their party, weighted by the distance between the party medians. The more senators located in this interval, holding distance constant, the greater the number of moderates in the chamber, which should promote bipartisanship and less conflict on the floor.

Overall, about 3 percent of the bills in our sample failed to pass the Senate by the relevant deadline. By this measure, the Senate was fairly efficient at processing spending bills. If anything, though, this probably reflects the urgency that senators felt to meet fiscal deadlines. Seven percent of the bills in our sample were near misses, beating the deadline by less than 3 days.[27]

To account for potential correlation among appropriations, we estimate the model using generalized estimating equations (GEEs; Liang and Zeger 1986; Zorn 2001). GEEs relax assumptions about the independence of observations, which helps to account for possible unobserved correlation among particular bills.[28] The results of the GEE probit analysis are reported in equation 15.5.[29] The coefficient on the key variable of interest, the precloture indicator, is statistically different from 0 and has the expected sign. The marginal effect for this variable indicates that before adoption of the cloture rule, a bill was 3 percent more likely to fail, with 95 percent confidence bounds (0.008, 0.094). While this effect is not huge, it is important to keep in mind that it was fairly uncommon for spending bills to fail, but the potential for disruption was significant when they did.[30] After cloture the probability of failure is essentially zero.

Passage of Approp Measures, 1890–1946 = −4.744(2.207*)Constant
+ 0.932(0.501)*PreCloture Indicator*
− 0.011(0.005*)*Days between Committee Report Deadline*
+ 0.625(0.479)*Diff between House Senate Bills*
− 0.128(0.040**)*%Chamber on App Committee*
+ 0.070(0.264)*Non-SAC Bill* − 1.029(0.633)*Senate Workload*
+ 0.026(0.026)*Maj Unity* + 0.110(0.030**)*Polarization*
(N = 631, Wald χ^2 [8 degrees of freedom] = 22.86 [p = 0.003]) **(15.5)**

The results on the other variables support the position that the cloture rule worked in tandem with other reforms to address one of the main problems that obstruction presented for the Senate—the ability to fulfill its constitutional duty in funding the operations of the federal government. The 1921 Budget Act and the recentralization of appropriations both appear to have had effects on efficiency. The earlier a bill makes it out of committee (and by extension the faster it moves through the earlier stages of the process), the more likely it is to meet the deadline. This is also true as the percentage of the chamber that sits on the relevant appropriating committee increases. Neither the percentage difference between the House and the Senate bills nor the consideration of a bill by a legislative committee appears to affect the likelihood of missing the deadline.

Of the ideological measures, party cohesion does not appear to affect whether a bill meets the deadline, and the moderation measure has effects that are in the opposite direction of what was expected.[31] The coefficient on the workload variable also has a sign different from expectations, although it misses statistical significance at the 0.1 level. Although we are limited to the crude measure of a dummy variable for measuring the effects of cloture, the results on the other variables that we include in the model and the accounting for unobserved correlation among observations should allay concerns that the effects we find for cloture are spuriously generated by other institutional or contextual factors.

Conclusion

We have shown theoretically how the 1917 cloture reform would have reduced the uncertainty that legislative entrepreneurs faced when trying to pass legislation. The supermajority rule had the potential to increase the Senate's efficiency in passing legislation by providing a clear threshold for cutting off debate and bringing legislation to a final vote.

We have reported empirical evidence that is consistent with these theoretical conjectures. The reduction in variance of coalition sizes on significant legislation and the increased efficiency in the appropriations process both indicate that the adoption of the cloture rule had a substantive impact on the operation of the Senate, contrary to what many have argued.

While our primary concern is to understand Senate history, the generalizability of our model of cloture reform can be assessed by applying it to other legislatures. Supermajority procedures are commonly used in legislatures other than the Senate, and our model offers a general explanation as to why legislators choose to adopt such procedures. For example, the House of Representatives often conducts business under suspension of the rules, which requires a two-thirds coalition. The House resorts to this procedure, which bars amendments not included in the motion and limits debate to 40 minutes, to expedite the passage of legislation (S. Smith 1989, 37–40). One interpretation for why House members adopted this procedure is that it affords them protection from some of the uncertainty of the floor stage in exchange for compromising on the substance of legislation. Such compromise would be necessary to attract the broader coalitions required to invoke the procedure, which in turn makes legislation less susceptible to parliamentary mischief. The analysis in this chapter can be extended to investigate whether other legislative bodies in the United States and abroad have adopted supermajority procedures for the reasons articulated by our model.

Chapter 16

Candidates, Parties, and the Politics of U.S. House Elections Across Time

JAMIE L. CARSON AND JASON M. ROBERTS

Introduction

In this chapter we reexamine the robustness of Cox and Katz's (1996, 2002) argument concerning the incumbency advantage to see whether it coincides with a previously undetected quality effect in the context of late 19th- and early 20th-century House elections. We find insufficient evidence to support some tenets of their theory in this historical context. We also discuss the implications of our analysis chapter, particularly in terms of both the electoral and the institutional development of Congress during this important political era.

Historical Work on Congressional Elections and Institutional Development

Recent years have witnessed a resurgence in the literature examining the electoral and institutional development of the U.S. Congress. While this trend has partly been motivated by the availability of new sources of historical data (see, e.g., Martis 1989; Parsons, Beach, and Dubin 1986, 1990; Dubin 1998, 2002), it has also been influenced by scholars seeking to test the robustness of contemporary theories in a historical context. Bianco, Spence, and Wilkerson (1996), for instance, examine legislators' voting behavior in conjunction with the Compensation Act of 1816 and find evidence of an electoral connection outside the modern era. Carson et al. (2001) reexamine the congressional elections of 1862–1863 and show that the entry of experienced candidates, district-specific war casualties, and the timing of individual races in conjunction with changing national conditions affected a legislator's electoral fortunes.

Beyond investigating the incidence of an electoral connection in the 19th century, students of congressional history have examined the effects of electoral motivations on a variety of institutional changes. Katz and Sala (1996), for instance, analyze the emergence of property rights norms in the House by linking this development to the adoption of the Australian ballot laws beginning in the 1890s (see Rusk 1970). Basing their discussion on the assumption that even 19th-century legislators were motivated by reelection (Mayhew 1974b), they contend that the secret ballot created new electoral incentives for incumbent legislators. These incentives ultimately contributed to secure committee tenure in the House, further enhancing the prospect of careerism in Congress. In the context of the Senate, Lapinski (2000) finds similar evidence that electoral motivations such as the direct primary and the adoption of the 17th Amendment led senators to begin to put more emphasis on securing property rights in terms of their committee assignments.

More recently, Engstrom (2006) has offered a related explanation for the growing job security among legislators at the end of the 19th century—the politics involved in strategic redistricting. Recognizing that the rapid adoption of Australian ballot laws reduced the overall level of uncertainty about the electorate, parties began creating more "safe" seats for incumbents, which shifted attention away from defeating candidates of the opposing party.

In another recent paper focusing on congressional elections across time, Jenkins (2004) examines all contested-election cases in the U.S. House from 1789 to the present. He explains that the central focus of his paper is to assess the extent to which partisanship was the deciding factor in influencing the outcome of contested-election cases. While he finds evidence that the majority party was often victorious when close elections were contested, it does not appear as though they regularly contested elections in an attempt to pick up additional seats in the House. Nevertheless, Jenkins does demonstrate how the Republicans were able to employ this strategy after the Civil War in an attempt to maintain some presence in the congressional delegations of Southern states that were primarily controlled by the Democrats. Overall, his analysis offers evidence of the role played by parties in shaping electoral and legislative strategies and illustrates the critical importance of elections in affecting outcomes in Congress.

In addition to each of the preceding studies, several other students of congressional and electoral politics of the 19th century have weighed in on a number of related issues. Kernell (2003) reconsiders the role of institutional changes at the end of the 19th century in the growing degree of careerism among incumbent legislators and concludes that these factors offer only a partial explanation for the emerging trends of this era.[1] Moreover, Goodman (2003) examines the congruence between constituency preferences and a legislator's roll-call behavior during the Populist era in an attempt to demonstrate the relationship between district sentiment and incumbents' voting behavior.

Linking the Past and the Present—Candidate Quality and Incumbency Advantage

Our own work to date overlaps much of the preceding literature by exploring the extent to which ambition theory and Jacobson and Kernell's (1981) strategic politician theory explains electoral patterns in the late 19th and early 20th centuries. While the influential role played by strategic politicians in the post–World War II era is well documented (see Jacobson and Kernell 1981; Jacobson 1989), we have a much more limited understanding of their effects on electoral politics in a historical context. Indeed, the received wisdom concerning 19th- and early 20th-century congressional elections has emphasized their unimportance. Factors such as the predominance of presidential elections, the party ballot, rotation in office, and the general lack of voter information supposedly combined to suppress the salience of both congressional elections and candidates (Jacobson 1990; Bensel 2003).

Jacobson (1989, 787) contends that, in a non-candidate-centered era, "the quality of individual candidates would be of small electoral consequence." Indeed, for a number of reasons we might not expect modern theories to contribute to our understanding of late 19th- and early 20th-century congressional elections. Changes during the past century, including the rise of legislative careerism, televised congressional sessions, professional staff, efficient travel, and weakened electoral parties, have contributed to the emergence of candidate-centered campaigns and the development of plebiscitary politics within Congress (Jacobson 1989; Smith, Roberts, and Vander Wielen 2005).

Despite the differences between these two eras, there is reason to believe that late 19th- and early 20th-century politicians would be affected by strategic parameters such as likelihood of victory, value of the seat, and opportunity costs similar to those faced by modern-day candidates. We contend that the dynamics facing congressional candidates in the late 19th and early 20th centuries are more similar to those faced by modern-day candidates than previously thought. As Bianco, Spence, and Wilkerson (1996, 147) note and we agree, "It is one thing to argue that a congressional career was less attractive or less feasible in an earlier time than it is today, but another to conclude that members of the early Congress were unconcerned about the electoral consequences of their behavior."

While we do not question that the importance of strategic politicians and the emergence of candidate-centered politics are related for the postwar era, we think there is good reason to suspect a similar pattern of strategic emergence in all time periods, even without the presence of candidate-centered campaigns. We have shown elsewhere that the mechanism through which this behavior occurs is the strategic calculation of ambitious politicians and parties and is not necessarily a function of the emergence of candidate-centered campaigns (Carson and Roberts 2005). Political parties have an incentive to maximize the quality of candidates running under their label at all times, but we maintain that they should have an easier time convincing experienced candidates to seek election when the combination of national and local conditions makes success more likely. Moreover, before the advent of the direct primary, political parties could prevent weak candidates from seeking election under the party label.

The preceding discussion has notable implications for our ability to test the robustness of contemporary theories on electoral politics in a previously unexplored historical context. If the electoral milieu between the historical and modern eras is *not* as different as previously believed, then we can gain important analytical leverage by examining unanswered questions across time. Indeed, we believe that the absence of many contemporary features of Congress during the late 19th and early 20th centuries provides an ideal opportunity to examine a long-standing puzzle in contemporary politics: the sources of the incumbency advantage.

We think there is a great deal to be learned about congressional history by testing the predictive power of modern-day theories in a historical context. If candidate quality in fact has an independent effect on election outcomes in a non-candidate-centered era, this would suggest that a party-dominated electoral process does not temper ambition theory. Further, such a finding would lead us to question Cox and Katz's (1996) conclusion that the growth of the incumbency advantage can be attributed to the rising importance of candidate quality and the increasing candidate-centered nature of congressional elections. In this chapter we use five elections spanning a

30-year period to assess the effects of factors such as incumbency, challenger quality, and district partisanship in late 19th- and early 20th-century congressional elections.[2]

DATA AND METHODS

One of the biggest challenges to testing modern-day theories in a historical context is the difficulty of finding the necessary data. To test the validity of ambition theory in the context of 19th- and early 20th-century congressional elections, we have collected a considerable amount of historical election data. Thankfully, recent years have seen a number of new data sources become available that facilitate such research. More specifically, information on incumbent electoral margins was coded from Dubin's (1998) *United States Congressional Elections, 1788–1997*, the most comprehensive source for electoral data over time. From this, we were able to collect relevant information on the names of the incumbent and related challengers, the vote totals on which percentages of the two-party vote were computed, and partisan affiliation for each candidate. The latter was supplemented with information contained in Martis (1989) to fill in any gaps in party identification.

Since we are particularly interested in examining the likelihood of strategic candidate entry within a historical context as well as its effect on incumbent electoral performance, it was necessary to collect data on candidates' political backgrounds. Although traditional sources of challenger-quality data such as *CQ Weekly Report* and Project Vote Smart are not available for the period we are studying, we coded as much of this data as we could from historical sources.[3] In particular, our search was facilitated by use of the *Biographical Directory of the U.S. Congress*, which allowed us to obtain relevant background information on challengers who defeated congressional incumbents as well as challengers who served before or after the election in question. This information was supplemented with data from the Political Graveyard, a Web site with data on over 138,000 politicians,[4] and various other electronic and print sources (see Carson and Roberts 2005 for more details).[5]

Despite our success in collecting these data, some gaps remain that limit our ability to draw inferences. For example, a key variable in modern-day electoral research is campaign spending, yet as of this writing it seems impossible to be able to recover these data for the period we are studying. Further, even our data on candidate quality is incomplete to varying degrees in this period. The most time consuming, if manageable, problem for analysis of data from this era is that most available data are not in a machine-readable form. While this has the benefit of forcing researchers to get their hands dirty with the data, it often precludes scholars from being able to make sweeping conclusions across long times because of the time-consuming nature of the data-collection process. Yet despite these limitations, we think the analysis presented in the remainder of the chapter provides a useful starting point for addressing questions pertaining to the role of candidates and the advantages of incumbency in this important period in American political development.

RESULTS

We now briefly discuss summary statistics on several of our variables of interest. For example, we find that the proportion of incumbents seeking reelection gradually increases in our sample of elections and that the reelection rate among incumbents exhibited considerable variation, from a low of 51 percent during the tumultuous 1894 elections to a high of more than 80 percent in 1914. Our data also suggest that experienced candidates exhibited differences in their patterns of entry across each of the elections with respect to the two major parties. During the tumultuous elections of the 1890s, both parties ran a high proportion of quality candidates, while in the relatively uneventful 1904 election we see very few quality candidates emerge.

In considering the patterns for incumbent marginality, we see that marginal incumbents—defined as those who won with less than 55 percent of the vote—faced a quality challenger at much higher rates than "safe" incumbents for all five elections in our sample. This pattern is particularly stark in the 1904 election, when marginal incumbents were three times more likely to face a quality challenger than safe incumbents were. Thus, our summary statistics provide some evidence suggesting that historical elections are not all that different from contemporary elections—candidates responded to national tides, experienced candidates challenged weak incumbents, and incumbent reelection fluctuated from election to election; nevertheless, one important puzzle clearly stands out and remains unaddressed: *incumbents lost at a much higher rate than in the contemporary era.*

To assess the extent to which an incumbency advantage may have been present in this era, we mimic the approach of Cox and Katz (1996). Cox and Katz break the incumbency advantage into two components: a direct effect attributable to things such as professional staff, franked mail, and convenient travel and an indirect effect that is the product of the quality advantage held by the incumbent's party and the ability of an incumbent to scare off experienced challengers. The incumbency advantage (*IA*) is the sum of the direct effect (D) and the indirect effect, which is the product of the quality advantage (Q) and the scare-off effect (S), thus: $IA = D + (Q \times S)$.

We estimate the incumbency advantage by employing the two-equation approach suggested by Cox and Katz. Equation 16.1 regresses the Democratic Party's share of the two-party vote in a given district ($DTP_{i,t}$) on lagged Democratic vote ($DTP_{i,t-1}$), the party of the incumbent candidate at time t and $t - 1$ ($IP_{i,t}$, $IP_{i,t-1}$), whether an incumbent was running ($IR_{i,t}$), and the Democratic quality advantage in the election ($DQA_{i,t}$) and is estimated via ordinary least squares:[6]

$$DTP_{i,t} = \hat{\alpha} + \hat{\beta}_1 DTP_{i,t-1} + \hat{\beta}_2 IP_{i,t} + \hat{\beta}_3 IP_{i,t-1} + \hat{\beta}_4 IR_{i,t} + \hat{\beta}_5 DQA_{i,t} + \hat{\varepsilon}_i \quad \textbf{(16.1)}$$

where $\hat{\beta}_4$ is the estimated direct effect of incumbency (D) and $\hat{\beta}_5$ is the estimated indirect effect of quality advantage (Q). Equation 16.2 regresses the Democratic quality advantage ($DQA_{i,t}$) on lagged Democratic vote ($DTP_{i,t-1}$), the party of the incumbent candidate at time t and $t - 1$ ($IP_{i,t}$, $IP_{i,t-1}$), and whether an incumbent was running ($IR_{i,t}$) and is estimated via ordinary least squares:[7]

$$DQA_{i,t} = \hat{\alpha} + \hat{\beta}_1 DTP_{i,t-1} + \hat{\beta}_2 IP_{i,t} + \hat{\beta}_3 IP_{i,t-1} + \hat{\beta}_4 IR_{i,t} + \hat{\varepsilon}_i \quad \textbf{(16.2)}$$

where $\hat{\beta}_4$ is the estimated scare-off effect (S) due to an incumbent seeking reelection.

The results of the regression analysis reveal little evidence of a direct effect of incumbency in this period. Our estimates are positive for four out of five elections (1896 excluded), but these estimates do not appear to be substantively or statistically significant. Further, we actually find a negative direct effect of incumbency in 1896; all else equal, candidates lost an average of just under 2.7 percent of the vote if they were an incumbent seeking reelection. These results are not necessarily surprising, however, as many of the institutional features of the contemporary incumbency advantage were not in place during this era and the relatively low reelection rates do not suggest that incumbents were particularly adept at winning reelection in this period.

As we turn to the indirect effect of incumbency, our results get more interesting. In all five elections we find evidence suggesting that candidate quality was an important determinate of election outcomes. Substantively, candidates with a quality advantage received an additional 4.5 percent to 7 percent of the two-party vote, all else equal. These results are in keeping with the quality advantage in contemporary elections and suggest that individual candidates are an important part of the explanation of election

TABLE 16.1
Decomposing the incumbency advantage in U.S. House elections, 1884–1914

Year	Quality effect	Scare-Off effect	Total indirect effect	Direct effect
1884	5.94	0.31	1.84	0.57
1894	4.76	0.58	2.76	0.71
1896	6.34	0.71	4.5	−2.69
1904	4.65	0.4	1.86	0.65
1914	6.7	0.61	4.09	1.7
All years	6.61	0.56	3.7	−0.15

results in this period. Further, we find evidence in all five of our elections suggesting that the presence of an incumbent in the race may have scared off experienced challengers, all else equal. Thus even in this non-candidate-centered era of electoral politics, we have found evidence suggesting that experienced challengers were responding to the strategic environment and exhibiting an independent effect on congressional elections as early as 1884 and that these effects persisted in both midterm and presidential-year elections.

Table 16.1 presents our estimates of the incumbency advantage. These results reveal that the indirect effect of incumbency in this period was as large, if not larger, than that found by Cox and Katz for the contemporary era and that the indirect effect was the major component of the incumbency advantage. Taken as a whole, these findings suggest that the Cox and Katz assertion that growth in the quality and scare-off effects of incumbency are responsible for the growth of incumbency is incomplete. Incumbents in the late 19th and early 20th centuries benefited from a quality advantage and were apparently quite adept at scaring off quality candidates, yet their electoral status was tenuous compared to recent history. For example, we estimate that incumbency in 1894 gave a candidate a 2.7 percent vote boost, all else equal, yet 49 percent of the incumbents who sought reelection lost. Similarly, the indirect effect of incumbency in 1914 was just over 4 percent of the vote, considerably larger than what we see in the contemporary era, yet almost 20 percent of incumbents seeking reelection were not able to translate this advantage into victory. Our results suggest that strong quality and scare-off effects may be *necessary* conditions for incumbent success, but it seems that these effects are not *sufficient* for incumbent success.

Obviously, the results presented in the previous section leave us with a new puzzle: incumbents had a considerable indirect advantage over non-incumbents in the late 19th and early 20th centuries, yet were unable to translate this advantage into consistent electoral success. A conclusive solution to this puzzle awaits further data collection and analysis, but we do have several potential explanations worthy of speculation. First, given that parties controlled ballot access for much of this period, it could be the case that parties were able to convince incumbents to seek reelection even when both the incumbent and the party knew the odds were stacked against them. Thus, unlike today, incumbents may have sought reelection knowing that they were unlikely to be successful. Second, the increasing role of money in elections could explain the trend we uncover. Nineteenth-century incumbents were unlikely to have been able to use large war chests to scare off and outspend experienced challengers. Third, the role of strategic redistricting must be considered. As Engstrom (2006) has demonstrated, parties were not hesitant to continually alter district lines to gain more seats in a state's House delegation. This constant churning of district lines could have made it much more difficult for incumbents to develop a reputation within their district over time. Finally, we think our findings warrant a reexamination of the impact of the direct effect of incumbency on electoral outcomes. Given that we have shown that incumbents are losing at high rates despite a large indirect advantage, it may well be the case that we have underestimated the importance of the direct effect for the contemporary era.

Conclusion

In this chapter we have turned back the clock to examine the generalizability of Cox and Katz's (1996) argument concerning the incumbency advantage in a historical context. While Cox and Katz have previously found evidence of a quality effect contributing to the growing incumbency advantage in the post–World War II era, we find a similar effect in the context of late 19th- and early 20th-century House elections, even though we do not find evidence that incumbents were able to translate this advantage into electoral success. The preceding results cast some doubts on the conclusion reached by Cox and Katz that the quality effect is contributing to the growth in the incumbency advantage in the contemporary era. Indeed, while purely speculative at this time, it may be the case that the institutional advantages of incumbency may be more important than Cox and Katz and others have argued.

Additionally, conventional wisdom would suggest that we should observe differences in the incumbency and quality effects when comparing midterm versus presidential elections during this era. Without a presidential candidate at the top of the ballot in midterm election years, it is more reasonable to expect the quality of the candidate to be of greater importance in such elections. Interestingly, we do not find such an effect in our analysis. Thus, while we set out to cast light on a contemporary "puzzle"—the rise of the incumbency advantage—we seem to have only enlarged our puzzle as we now must eventually explain the lack of incumbent success in spite of a considerable incumbency advantage.

Chapter 17

Speaker David Henderson and the Partisan Era of the U.S. House

CHARLES J. FINOCCHIARO AND DAVID W. ROHDE

The Partisan Era of the U.S. House

While the speakership of Thomas B. Reed has garnered much attention over the years, that of his Republican successor, David B. Henderson, has been virtually overlooked. The historical literature on the period, as well as the scant writings focused on Henderson in particular, generally paint a picture of a weak, rather aloof figurehead standing in stark contrast to the largely efficacious leadership of Reed. This state of affairs is peculiar in that Henderson assumed the reins of leadership at a point in time in which centralized, effective leadership would appear to have been more necessary than ever. The Republican majority over the Democrats and a handful of Populists and prosilver third-party candidates had slipped to just 13 seats (Fuller 1909, 248), the smallest majority margin for either party since Reed first assumed the speakership in 1889. Thus, this interlude of the partisan era begs for explanation. Was Henderson the partisan that the general depiction of the era might lead us to believe? If not, then theories of parties in Congress would seem to be missing something in their ability to explain the centralizing and decentralizing tendencies of parties based on changes in coalitional politics. The conditions for strong leadership were ripe, and yet there seems to be little or no evidence of such initiative on the part of Henderson.

The theoretical perspective from which we approach the consideration of David B. Henderson is conditional party government, or CPG (Rohde

1991; Aldrich 1995; Aldrich and Rohde 2000b, 2001). This view argues that the strength of party organizations in the House depends in large part on how homogeneous the policy views of members are (particularly in the majority party) and on how divergent the policy positions of the parties are. The idea is that members are more willing to delegate power to leaders when they can expect that the leaders are likely to hold views similar to theirs, and when legislative victories by the opposition would be particularly unsatisfactory. The literature on congressional politics for the Reed-Henderson period shows widespread agreement that the parties were quite homogeneous and sharply divided from one another (Brady and Epstein 1997; Brady and Altoff 1974).

If this consensus picture of the policy views of the two parties is correct, then CPG theory would expect members of the majority party to be particularly willing to delegate power to their leadership and to support the exercise of that power to advance the party's legislative program. In the case of Reed's speakership, events seem to square well with the theory, as does the later period of Joseph G. Cannon's leadership. The Reed rules empowered the Speaker and the rest of the leadership, and Reed (and Cannon) used the procedural advantages vigorously. The speakership of Henderson is, however, more problematic. Thus, to assess fully the accuracy of CPG theory for this period, we must look more closely at Henderson with regard to both the willingness of his party to delegate power and how he exercised power.

The Speakership of David B. Henderson, 1899–1903

David Bremner Henderson was born in Scotland in 1840 to a family who immigrated to the United States when he was 6 years of age, settling initially in Illinois and shortly thereafter in Iowa (Hoing 1957). Henderson's Scottish roots are particularly important in that they disqualified him for the presidency, a point that was noted frequently during his rise to power and eventual assumption of the speakership. Many of his contemporaries harbored executive ambitions, and this facet of Henderson's life set him apart from the likes of Reed and Cannon. Whether it was a factor in his election to the speakership is a matter of some speculation.

Henderson's career in the House before assuming the speakership was one of marked distinction. Unlike his successor, Joseph G. Cannon of Illinois, who would "never author a major bill" throughout his service in Congress (Peters 1997, 75), Henderson had been involved in the drafting of significant legislation at various points in his career. He chaired a select committee that the Republican caucus established early in 1899 to put together a banking bill (Gold 1980, 170; Hoing 1957, 13), which was a centerpiece of President McKinley's agenda at the time. He played a hand in the Railway Safety bill and "fathered the first important bankruptcy bill passed by Congress" (Hoing 1957, 4). Henderson also sat as a member of the Appropriations Committee for a few Congresses and chaired the Committee on the Militia in the 51st Congress. His stock rose to an even greater degree when the Republicans reassumed control of the House in 1895, as he chaired the Judiciary Committee in the 54th and 55th Congresses while simultaneously holding a seat on the prestigious Rules Committee (Canon, Nelson, and Stewart 1998).

Henderson was elected Speaker after Reed's decision not to return for another term in the House. The competition among Republicans for the gavel involved many of the party's leading figures and contained tones of regional and even intrastate conflict. For example, there were multiple candidates from both Illinois (Albert J. Hopkins challenging Cannon) and New York (James S. Sherman and Sereno E. Payne).[1] Hoing (1957) presents what seems to be the most extensive discussion of the circumstances surrounding the election, in which he argues that the election was clinched in the closing days because of the support of the Wisconsin and Ohio delegations. Critical to Henderson's victory, at least in the eyes of some observers, was his tie to the party establishment and to Reed's policies. Hopkins, who was threatening to undercut Henderson's support in the middle and Western states, ran prominently on "promises of liberality" and sought to paint Henderson and many of the other more regular Republican candidates as likely to mirror the tactics and practices of Reed in the Speaker's chair. As Hoing (1957, 11) argues, such "remarks probably won Hopkins a few friends but must have turned Reed supporters away from him, no doubt helping Henderson, who was fairly close to Reed in some respects."

A second factor in Henderson's election, according to Schickler (2001), was his support from a number of powerful senators, including fellow Iowan William Boyd Allison and Nelson Aldrich of Rhode Island. As Schickler notes, however, the evidence regarding the Senate leadership's role in the election, and its motivations in particular, is "indirect" (302). Further, his conclusion that one of the primary effects of Henderson's tenure as Speaker was to weaken the House vis-à-vis the Senate is, in his own words, "tentative" (303). Our treatment of Henderson will focus not at all on the potentially important relationship between the House and Senate but will grapple with the other fundamental question raised by Schickler and the historical and political science accounts of the era more generally: does the era represent one of strong party government, and how can party theory help in explaining the observed pattern?

HENDERSON AS PARTY LEADER

Interestingly, while Henderson was clearly a member of the party's mainstream at the time he was tapped to lead the party in the House, by all accounts a party regular with strong loyalties to the GOP, his tenure as Speaker seems to indicate anything but czar rule, which is what we have come to expect and associate with this era of congressional history. Hoing's 1957 study of Henderson alludes to the possibility that his decision to step down in 1902 was based on a relative weakness when it came to organizational matters. Citing a "Comment" in *Harper's Weekly*, Hoing suggests that "others believed Henderson realized that he lacked the strong personality to control the popular branch of Congress, because the Reed rules, necessary to operate the House effectively, demanded a firm hand" (26). In a similar vein, Fuller's (1909) account maintains that Henderson was a "man of moderate ability and rather weak of will power, . . . dominated at all times by the members of the Committee on Rules, consisting of Payne, [John] Dalzell, and Cannon. Henderson as a Speaker betrayed his weak points" (248).[2]

Others offer more tempered assessments of Henderson's leadership. Chiu (1928, 293) posits that he made practically "no advance in the importance of the Speakership." In the words of Kennon (1986, 194), when contrasted with "the brilliant and often imperious Thomas Brackett Reed, Henderson became known as a popular, though not brilliant, Speaker. Where Reed had ruled the House like a czar, Henderson managed affairs in a straightforward, businesslike manner." As a final example, in his study of the speakership, Peters evaluates Henderson's service as "lackluster" (1997, 75).

A general consensus among those looking at the speakership of the purportedly partisan era of the House holds that there was variation in the centrality and power of the office during this time, but others disagree (Bolling 1974; Galloway and Wise 1976; Riddick 1949; Schickler 2001; Hoing 1957; Clark 1920). Interestingly, some sources seem to offer accounts evincing both strength and weakness on the part of Henderson. Yet it is reasonable to say that, at the individual level, many have claimed that Henderson paled in comparison to his Republican counterparts in Reed and Cannon. In the next few sections, we turn to some evidence that bears more directly on this thesis.

A VIEW OF HENDERSON THROUGH THE LENS OF CPG

As we discussed earlier, CPG theory rests on two related factors: intraparty agreement and interparty divergence. As parties become increasingly homogeneous internally and find themselves at odds with the other party on significant policy questions, the likelihood of strong party leadership increases. Thus, power is more likely to be delegated to party leaders, and those leaders are more likely to exercise that power in the interest of broad party goals. Since CPG has been developed and discussed at length elsewhere, our aim here is to employ this perspective during David B. Henderson's tenure in the Speaker's chair in ways that will allow for a test of CPG theory in a historical era. The product is a narrative that, we will argue, provides a more complete understanding of this period of House history.

THE DELEGATION OF POWER TO SPEAKER HENDERSON

The theory's expectations about delegating power to leaders of a homogeneous party do not require that new powers be granted. If the preceding leader had been granted substantial powers, the delegation may consist of simply ratifying the status quo. This appears to be what happened when Henderson took over from Reed. The Republicans had to decide whether to continue with the Reed rules or to move to a less centralized regime. The matter was first addressed in the Republican caucus before Henderson's ratification as Speaker by the full House. The leadership wanted to confirm the Reed rules, but there was dissent. William Hepburn of Iowa (who would later be a significant figure in the 1909 revolt against Cannon) sought to return to the old method of recognition in which the chair always recognized the first person to rise. He also wanted to make the Rules Committee independent of the leadership. Hepburn put these ideas in the form of an amendment to the proposed rules, but after debate made clear that there was little support for his views, he withdrew the amendment (*New York Times*, September 3, 1899, p. 2). Two days later, the proposed rules package came before the full House. John Dalzell, one of the Republican floor leaders, proposed the readoption of the rules of the previous Congress. Democrats protested and argued for drafting a different set of rules. Hepburn then rose and said that he, too, had favored modifications but that the Republican caucus had been opposed to him (*New York Times*, September 5, 1899, p. 5). Thus the members of the majority still favored delegation of strong powers to their leadership, and the minority objected to this, just as the theory would expect. There is no evidence here that the Republicans wanted a less centralized leadership or a figurehead as Speaker.

THE RULES COMMITTEE AND FLOOR AGENDA SETTING UNDER SPEAKER HENDERSON

A central component of majority-party leadership and agenda setting, in both the modern House and in the House as it functioned in the late 1800s and early 1900s, is the Rules Committee. This panel, more than any other, holds significant influence over the flow of legislation. Speaker Reed, in the 51st Congress, began to use the Rules Committee for partisan ends, and with Speaker Crisp's subsequent fine-tuning of the process, the committee was clearly a hallmark of the majority partisan machinery by the time Henderson assumed the Speaker's chair in 1899. Acting as chair of the committee, the Speaker was traditionally the one who set the agenda and provided leadership as to the course of business.

Under Henderson's leadership, the Rules Committee was central in the passage of at least two very significant pieces of legislation during his last term. On February 17, 1902, the House took up a bill to repeal war-revenue taxation. While there was broad bipartisan support for scaling back the increased tax burden, the issue demonstrated division not only between the parties but also within the Republican caucus over tariff revision. Hoing (1957, 25) notes that "when the bill came up the strong support of the Middle West and Northwest for revision was evident. The House machine resorted to introducing the bill with a rule prohibiting amendments, and the Democrats refused to debate the bill after [James D.] Richardson, the Democratic floor leader, was unable to get [Wisconsin Republican Joseph W.] Babcock's cooperation in opposing it."

In this case, while there was apparent controversy within the Republican caucus over the tariff issue, the leadership (under the direction of Henderson) successfully preempted a floor fight and the possibility of a host of amendments through their use of a restrictive rule. The minority leader attempted to skirt the debate restrictions contained in the resolution providing for floor consideration by offering a motion to recommit with instructions, which if agreed to would have modified the rule and allowed for amendments. Speaker Henderson sustained a point of order raised against the motion, and as both he and Richardson note, this went against prior rulings by Speaker Reed (*Congressional Record*, February 17, 1902, pp. 1834–1835). On appeal of the Speaker's ruling, Republicans voted in lockstep, as they did on adoption of the rule. There were no Democratic defections on the appeal vote, and there was only one defection on the rule. With the battle over the rule lost, Richardson asked for unanimous consent that debate on the bill be forgone and an immediate vote be taken on passage. The measure passed unanimously (*Congressional Record*, February 17, 1902, pp. 1836–1837).

The situation was no less confrontational when the leadership brought the Cuban reciprocity bill to the floor in April of 1902. In the words of Republican Cushman of Washington,

> It is with humiliation unspeakable that I rise in my place on this floor and admit to my constituents at home that in this House I am utterly powerless to bring any bill or measure, no matter how worthy or meritorious it may be, to a vote unless I can first make terms with the Speaker (*Congressional Record*, April 17, 1902, p. 4320).

Cushman was objecting both to the Republican machine in the House and to the approach by which this particular bill was called up—as a privileged measure relating to the jurisdiction of the Ways and Means Committee, based on its control of legislation affecting revenue. Yet in committee, all revenue-related amendments were ruled out of order on the grounds of nongermaneness. The same issue emerged on the floor, where according to Hoing (1957, 25–26), "An amendment to put hides on the free list was defeated by only sixteen votes. All other attempted amendments to the act were then arbitrarily ruled out of order by Speaker Henderson." Thus, in this instance as well, it appears that the Republican majority was successful in heading off amendments that would likely have been adopted on the floor if consideration had been allowed.

Yet Hoing's account tells only part of the story. This occasion also witnessed what was probably the most significant insurrection within the ranks of the House majority party during Henderson's tenure. Led by Majority Whip James Tawney of Minnesota and energized by Cushman's floor speech denouncing the heavy-handed leadership style of the Speaker, a number of Republicans friendly to the beet sugar industry bolted from the party. They voted to overturn the initial ruling of the chair regarding the nongermaneness of an amendment to repeal the differential tariff on refined sugar and voted with the Democrats in adding the amendment to the bill. While much of the attention given to the issue of reciprocity with Cuba focused at the time on this defection, all subsequent amendments were ruled nongermane, and the Republicans stood with the chair of the Committee of the Whole, despite his repeated rulings going against the prior sense of the House when it overruled him on the germaneness question.

Thus, while the leadership lost once on tariff issues relating to a particular constituency, the party was able to maintain control over the broader issue and maintain the status quo on broader tariff policy when it came to a number of other specific items and even wholesale tariff revision, as had been proposed by Babcock and supported by other members of the Republican caucus. Speaker Henderson's actions in light of this occasion also tell us something about his leadership. While the insurgents predicted that they would go on to further victories, Henderson seems to have preempted such action by sending a strong message to the insurgents through his sanctioning of Tawney, who was temporarily removed as party whip (Ripley 1967, 21).

While these accounts paint a picture of Henderson's leadership as it relates to setting the floor agenda on two specific bills, it is worthwhile to consider the role of the Rules Committee in the aggregate as well. Because we are interested in describing Henderson's tenure as Speaker in relation to the other, purportedly more partisan, Speakers of the era, an informative picture may be painted by examining the variation in both special rules and their amendment restrictions over the course of time. Of perhaps the most interest is this—the Speaker to take fullest advantage of special rules throughout the partisan era was neither Reed nor Cannon, but rather Crisp (in the 53rd Congress). Henderson's use of special rules in the 56th and 57th Congresses was on par with that of Reed's in the 54th and 55th, with a subsequent uptick during Cannon's tenure in the 58th to 61st Congresses. According to Roberts and Smith (2003b), Henderson's Rules Committee employed rules with amending restrictions as much or more frequently than all previous Speakers. Thus, at least in the aggregate, Henderson does not appear to have differed significantly from prior Speakers in terms of special rules usage.

The final point we wish to make in our discussion of Henderson's management of the House's floor agenda has to do with the broader question of party dominance. The two case studies we presented provide a flavor of the manner in which Henderson and the Republican leadership administered affairs on a couple of particularly salient pieces of legislation. However, we arrived at these two instances largely through a reading of secondary sources. Thus, a particularly important question remains. To what extent was such activity systematic? Our citation of two examples certainly does not preclude a picture of a generally weak Speaker on other issues that came before the 56th and 57th Houses.

In light of this, we conducted an exhaustive electronic search of the *New York Times*, examining each story in which David B. Henderson was mentioned in either the headline or the full text of an article during the period of his speakership. Between the stories resulting from this search and a reading of secondary sources such as Hoing (1957), we identified a number of additional occasions in which the Republican machine dominated the proceedings of the House. Perhaps of more importance is that beyond one case these searches provide no indication of leadership contrary to the strong-party picture that was typically painted during this era. That is, we found only one other case in which the leadership was defeated, and the discussion of this case is remarkable in that it focuses almost exclusively on how surprising the defeat was. A brief discussion of this incident will give an impression of the extent to which contemporaries viewed Henderson and his associates as the dominant center of power in the House.

The substance of the issue surrounded an amendment to the Naval Appropriations bill. The vote went contrary to the wishes of the leadership, and the postmortem discussion centered on the fact that before defeat on the beet sugar amendment to the Cuban reciprocity bill and the amendment in question here, "the Speaker and his aides were looked upon with an awe and dread which cannot be realized outside of Washington. The country has probably no adequate conception even yet of the courage it took to oppose the organization of the House." Henderson and his coterie of lieutenants "were regarded as invincible," and members were said to have great "dread of the Speaker" (*New York Times*, May 21, 1902, p. 8). By opposing the party machine, members believed they were risking their careers—and with good reason. For instance, Henderson was reported to have decided on recognition rights for members' bills dealing with local matters as a function of their support of the party. It was said that "Mr. Henderson has the reputation of not being a man to trifle with" (*New York Times*, April 1, 1902, p. 3). Furthermore, charges of arbitrary rulings on matters of even private legislation were not unheard of during Henderson's speakership (*New York Times*, February 10, 1900, p. 5). Months after the two defeats we identify here, and subsequent to Henderson's announcement declining renomination to Congress, the *Times* continued to discuss his methods, placing particular emphasis on the objections surrounding the manner in which he accorded recognition to members wishing to call up their bills for consideration (*New York Times*, September 21, 1902, p. 3).

COMMITTEE ASSIGNMENTS UNDER SPEAKER HENDERSON

An implication of CPG is that in periods of heightened partisanship, when the conditions of strong party leadership are increasingly met, the majority leadership will take steps to solidify their control of features of House organization such as the committee system. Thus, it is worthwhile to examine the appointments to committees made by Henderson to ascertain whether a similar pattern held true in this earlier time.

In the first place, it is evident that Henderson had no qualms with significant numeric deck stacking on the committees of central interest to the party's interest, such as Appropriations and Ways and Means. Despite the Republican Party's share of seats in the House having shrunk to much lower levels in the 56th House (their margin over the Democrats was only about one-third that of the 55th House), committee ratios were only slightly modified at the margins, with strong bias in favor of the majority party maintained on Appropriations (11–6 in the 55th, 10–7 in the 56th) and Ways and Means (11–6 in the 55th, 10–6 in the 56th). The Rules Committee throughout this time traditionally had only five members, three of whom were majority-party members (the committee was, of course, chaired by the Speaker). Other prominent committees such as Merchant Marine and Fisheries (8–5 in the 55th, 10–7 in the 56th), Rivers and Harbors (9–7 in the 55th, 10–7 in the 56th), Foreign Affairs (9–6 in the 55th, 10–7 in the 56th), and Military Affairs (9–6 in the 55th, 10–7 in the 56th) saw their majority margins either remain the same or increase, while the margins of Judiciary (11–6 in the 55th, 10–7 in the 55th), Banking and Currency (12–5 in the 55th, 10–7 in the 56th), Interstate and Foreign Commerce (12–5 in the 55th, 11–6 in the 56th) were decreased somewhat, with a strong majority bias remaining in effect.

At the start of the 56th Congress, two new, prominent committees were filled from the ground up. These were Census and Insular Affairs. In both cases, and perhaps not surprisingly, the ratios were set in favor of the majority party (10–7 on Insular Affairs and 8–5 on Census). Chosen to head each of these panels were leading members of the Republican Conference. Albert J. Hopkins (Ill.) assumed the chairmanship of the Census Committee, while Henry Allen Cooper of Wisconsin took the helm of Insular Affairs. Interestingly, the new Insular Affairs Committee was termed a "committee of Chairmen" in that the heads of a number of prominent committees were placed on this panel (*New York Times*, December 19, 1899, p. 7).

Beyond committee ratios, of at least equal consequence is the ideological composition of committees. That is, the majority party can see an advantage by appointing like-minded members, in addition to controlling a committee through greater numbers. The degree to which Henderson filled vacancies on the more notable committees with more conservative Republicans may tell us something about this dynamic, though it is important to bear in mind that a number of other factors are at play in the politics of committee assignments. In the future, we plan to conduct a more systematic analysis, along the lines of Lawrence, Maltzman, and Wahlbeck (2001), to more fully account for the competing forces at work in the assignment process.

At this juncture, we simply look at the DW-NOMINATE scores of newly appointed members to the committees identified in advance by the *New York Times* as having "important vacancies": Ways and Means, Appropriations, Judiciary, Banking and Currency, Rivers and Harbors, Foreign Affairs, and Military Affairs (*New York Times*, December 6, 1899, p. 8). We also look at Census and Insular Affairs, given their status as new committees in the 56th House. By and large, the pattern squares with general expectations based on the partisan import of each panel. Appropriations, Banking and Currency, and Ways and Means all saw a group of new members appointed who, in the aggregate, were more extreme than the party median. In contrast, traditionally constituency-oriented committees such as Rivers and Harbors, Merchant Marine and Fisheries, and Insular Affairs saw members of a more centrist orientation appointed to fill vacant positions. It is important to bear in mind that, in this Congress, the separation condition of CPG theory was fully met in the NOMINATE scores of the two parties—the most liberal Republican was still to the right of the most conservative Democrat.

In summary, we can say that Henderson appears to have filled committee seats on the control committees with loyal, conservative Republicans. This is further evidenced in the one vacancy he filled on the Rules Committee—Charles Grosvenor of Ohio was in the 76th percentile of his party—more conservative than fully three-quarters of his fellow partisans—and was the choice of Henderson for this sole vacancy on Rules, along with the chairmanship of Rivers and Harbors, of which Grosvenor had not even been a member in the previous Congress. It may not be a coincidence that Grosvenor was a leading member of the Ohio delegation, whose support was seen as integral in assuring Henderson's election to the Speakership. This latter case is suggestive of one of the bases for our interest in conducting a more systematic analysis of assignments in the 56th and 57th Houses.

HENDERSON'S RULINGS FROM THE CHAIR

Another area in which to look for influence on the part of the Speaker is his parliamentary rulings—the decisions offered from the chair as the House's presiding officer. While Henderson was by all accounts not the brilliant parliamentary tactician of his predecessor Reed, and likely did not need to be, observers have noted at least two rulings worthy of discussion. Further study of Henderson's rulings is warranted, and in the future we plan to extend our analysis in this area by examining the votes surrounding each instance in which a parliamentary question of order was settled during his tenure.

Riddick (1949, 113) notes that in the spring of 1902 members questioned the prerogative of the Rules Committee to report a special rule on the basis that, because such a resolution sets aside the House's standing rules, positive action would require a two-thirds vote. In his precedents, Hinds details Henderson's ruling, which was based on such an action having been undertaken repeatedly in the past and the question "is well settled" (Hinds 1907, vol. 4, § 3169).

A second ruling of perhaps more long-standing consequence owing to its original nature had to do with quorum counting. Champ Clark

(1920, 199–200), the Democratic successor of Joseph G. Cannon, identifies Henderson's "elaborate and well-considered opinion" on exactly what constitutes a quorum in the House. There had apparently been some longstanding debate as to how members-elect should be counted. In an era in which absenteeism was notoriously high, the mechanics of vote counting were of much importance (as evidenced in Reed's historic ruling that all members present in the chamber should be counted). In this instance, Henderson's ruling held that only those "members elect sworn in and living who have neither resigned nor been expelled" should be figured into a quorum count (Cannon 1936, vol. 6, § 638).

THE TWILIGHT OF HENDERSON'S SPEAKERSHIP

A final aspect of Henderson's terms in the Speaker's chair that merits attention occurred on the last day the 57th House spent in session. The traditional practice of the House had been to adopt a resolution of thanks for the Speaker's service, usually offered by the minority leader. Yet as Alexander (1916, 74–75) notes, "The passage of the resolution has occasionally needed the gag of the previous question." This was true of the resolution of thanks offered by Majority Leader Payne—apparently some members interested in speaking were so thwarted, and an attempt was made to have a recorded vote on the resolution but to no avail. Unfortunately, the cause of member resentment in this case cannot be known, and we are left to imagine just what may have been revealed should they have been allowed to speak.[3]

Summing Up Henderson

This preliminary look at David B. Henderson as Speaker of the House, while advancing our knowledge of a key intermediate figure of the partisan era of the House, has also raised a number of important questions. A more detailed look at his speakership is necessary before we can speak with greater certainty to the issue of partisan power. While it is evident that observers and participants viewed the House under his leadership as a body wholly controlled by the Republican machine headed by Henderson, because of his relative obscurity it is somewhat difficult to find accounts that lend significant credence to this view. Clearly, on a number of occasions, the influence of party power was evident, and the sentiment of the time indicates that this was likely the case across a broader range of issues. But the degree to which this was characteristic of his leadership in terms of systematic effects on the policy-making process remains an issue for further analysis.

Chapter 18

The Motion to Recommit in the House: The Creation, Evisceration, and Restoration of a Minority Right

DONALD R. WOLFENSBERGER

The fact is that a motion to recommit is intended to give the minority one chance to fully express their views so long as they are germane. . . . The whole purpose of this motion to recommit is to have a record vote upon the program of the minority. That is the main purpose of the motion to recommit.

—Speaker Frederick H. Gillett (R-Mass.)
October 7, 1919

Introduction

In 1909 House Speaker Joseph Gurney Cannon (R-Ill.) temporarily staved off an attempt by liberal Democrats and insurgent Republicans to dethrone him as chair of the House Rules Committee by secretly blessing a substitute package of internal House reforms offered by a conservative Democrat. One of the changes offered by Cannon's Democratic ally amended House rules to give an opponent of a bill a final opportunity to amend it by offering a motion to recommit with instructions just before the vote on final passage of the measure.

Under previous practice, the Speaker had discretion to recognize a member of his choosing to offer a motion to recommit, and this was often a supporter of the legislation and a member of the Speaker's own party. The new guarantee was enforced by a provision prohibiting the Rules Committee from reporting a special rule that denied opponents the first right to offer the motion to recommit.

The 1909 rule remained essentially intact for over a half century. In 1932 Speaker John Nance Garner (D-Tex.) issued a ruling that firmly established the right as belonging to a minority *party* opponent of a bill, as opposed to any opponent, regardless of party (Cannon 1936).

Although there were some instances in the 1970s in which the Democratic majority used special rules to proscribe the contents of instructions minority Republicans could offer in their motion to recommit, it wasn't until the 1980s that they began denying instructions altogether on selective bills. When Republicans began challenging the practice by raising points of order against such special rules, the chair would cite an obscure precedent from 1934 in which Speaker Henry T. Rainey (D-Ill.) overruled a point of order against a special rule that, in effect, prohibited a motion to recommit from including instructions to amend a specified title of the bill in question.

Republicans in the 1980s reacted angrily to this stripping of what they considered a basic minority right, challenging the consideration of such special rules with points of order and votes on appeals from the rulings of the chair. The abuse also prompted Republicans to push for a change in House rules to guarantee to the minority the right to offer a motion to recommit of its choosing. When they took control of the House in 1995, the new Republican majority included such a guarantee to the minority as part of their opening day House rules package for the 104th Congress, even though it would now benefit the freshly demoted Democratic minority.

As time went on, however, Republicans increasingly used special rules to restrict the amendment process on important legislation, often leaving minority Democrats with little recourse other than the motion to recommit to amend a bill. A rule of fairness had been converted into an excuse for unfairness. Because the House Rules Committee, since the late 1970s, is again considered the "Speaker's committee," many have likened the current Republican approach to procedural fairness to the age of czar Speakers like Cannon and Thomas Brackett Reed (R-Maine), both of whom used their positions as chair of the Rules Committee to impose their legislative agendas and ideas of procedural fairness.

Speaker Reed made clear in his 1890 rulings from the chair, abolishing various minority obstructionist devices, that "the object of a parliamentary body is action, not the stoppage of action" (*Congressional Record* 1890, p. 182).[1] He had earlier outlined in a national magazine his intentions to end gridlock and implement majority-party rule. "If the majority do not govern," he wrote in *Century Magazine* in March 1889, "the minority will; and, if tyranny of the majority is hard, the tyranny of the minority is unendurable. *The rules, then, ought to be arranged to facilitate the action of the majority*" (Strahan 1998, 50–51; emphasis added).

The speakerships of Reed and Cannon are bookends to a remarkable two-decade period of party government in the House, including 4 years under Democratic majorities (1891–1895). The adoption of a House rule by a bipartisan majority in 1909, just a year before the Republican Speaker was stripped of his control over the Rules Committee and Republicans lost control of Congress, provides a fitting endnote, if not antidote, to Reed's bold assertion that rules are made solely to facilitate the working of the majority's will.

While the development might be viewed as the dawn of a new era of bipartisanship, or at least an important nod in the direction of renewed minority rights and fairness, one should not forget that the rule change had the implicit blessing of the "tyrant" against whom the revolt was aimed. That is not to suggest it was a cynical ploy with more froth than fruit. After all, until 1971, there were no recorded votes in the Committee of the Whole, meaning the only chance for the minority to get a roll-call vote on its preferred alternative was in the motion to recommit back in the House. But viewed in the context of today's legislative floor process, the minority's right to recommit with instructions may be more symbolic than significant and ultimately a greater friend of anxious majorities than of frustrated minorities.

This chapter traces the history of the motion to recommit as an example of why rules are adopted, modified, waived, ignored, gored, and restored and how it all relates to institutional power relationships between the majority and minority parties in the House.

Origins and Purpose of the Motion

The motion to commit a matter to a committee has existed in the rules of the U.S. House of Representatives since the first Congress in 1789. The terms *refer*, *commit*, and *recommit* are nearly interchangeable, but their correct usage depends on the parliamentary situation.

There are three categories of motions to recommit: (1) a straight motion to recommit, which in effect kills a bill by sending it back to committee; (2) a motion to recommit with general instructions, which are nonbinding directives to a committee to do such things as hold further hearings or conduct a study; and (3) a motion to recommit with instructions "to report back forthwith" with an amendment specified in the motion. This automatic device dates back at least to an 1891 ruling by Speaker Reed upholding a motion by fellow Republican Joe Cannon with instructions to a committee to report back "forthwith" a substitute bill (Hinds 1907). It is the device most used in modern times.[2]

The motion to "commit" was listed as the second in priority of four motions contained in the first body of rules adopted by the House in 1789: "When a question is under debate, no motion shall be received, unless to amend it, to commit it, for the previous question, or to adjourn. . . . A motion for commitment until it is decided, shall preclude all amendment of the main question. Motions and reports may be committed at the pleasure of the House." In providing for the consideration and disposition of bills, the first House rules also provided that, "on the second reading of a bill, the Speaker shall state it as ready for commitment or engrossment, and if committed, then a question shall be whether to a select committee, or to a committee of the whole house" (Rules of the House). And finally, the 1789 rule on Committees of the Whole House provides that, after the committee of the whole has finished debating and amending a bill, it shall report the bill to the House, which would then further debate and amend the bill until the previous question was ordered to bring the bill to a vote on final passage. Early rulings by the Speaker held against a committal (or referral) motion after adoption of the previous question.

In the comprehensive House rules rewrite of 1880, however, this was changed to permit a motion to commit, with or without instructions, either before or after the previous question is ordered. According to House precedents, quoting from the Rules Committee's report on the 1880 revision, this rule change was authorized so as to afford "the amplest opportunity to test the sense of the House as to whether or not the bill is in the exact form it desires" (Hinds 1907).

There is a difference of opinion in the literature and the precedents as to the actual purpose and effect of the change. Was it to advantage the majority in cleaning up its own bill at the end of the process? Or was it to allow opponents of the bill a final chance to change it?

Speaker Reed, for instance, in the 1891 ruling previously cited held the former view. It could be, he said, that the House had adopted two conflicting amendments, "and that a majority of the House would not be in favor of both amendments together. It is to give opportunity to remedy this that the motion to recommit is permitted" (Cannon 1936, vol. 5, § 5545).

Speaker Joe Cannon (R-Ill.) also seemed to hold this view of the motion's purpose. On April 27, 1904, for instance, Representative Alfred Lucking (D-Mich.) asked to be recognized to offer a motion to recommit with instructions a bill relating to the use of vessels of the United States for public purposes. Speaker Cannon refused to recognize him for that purpose, whereupon Representative David H. Smith (D-Ky.) made a point of order that Lucking was entitled to recognition. Cannon informed Smith that he was recognizing instead the member in charge of the bill, Representative Grosvenor (R-Ohio) to offer the motion. As Cannon explained it,

TABLE 18.1
Party of House speakers and members recognized to offer motions to recommit, 1881–1909

Speakership	Party and state of speaker	Congress(es) (years)	Same party recognitions to offer motion to recommit	Other party recognitions to offer motion to recommit
J. Warren Kiefer	Republican-Ohio	47th (1881–1883)	0	1
John G. Carlisle	Democrat-Kentucky	48th–50th (1883–1889)	1	3
Thomas B. Reed	Republican-Maine	51st (1889–1891)	2	3
Charles F. Crisp	Democrat-Georgia	52nd–53rd (1891–1895)	3	3
Thomas B. Reed	Republican-Maine	54th–55th (1895–1899)	2	3
David B. Henderson	Republican-Iowa	56th–57th (1899–1903)	1	2
Joseph G. Cannon	Republican-Illinois	58th–61st (1903–1911)	0	4
Total number (90)			9 (32%)	19 (68%)

> The object of the rule was to give the House a chance to cure a mistake, if perchance any had been made in the engrossment of a bill, or mishap to it. . . . The present occupant of the Chair, the Speaker of the House, follows the usual rule that has obtained ever since he has been a Member of the House, that the Chair chooses whom he will recognize . . . [and] under the present conditions, in the closing hours, the Chair has the prefect right, following the parliamentary precedents of all parties, to prefer some one with whom, perchance, the Chair is in sympathy or upon the Chair's side of the House. (Hinds 1907, vol. 2, § 1456)

Later, in 1910, reflecting on the 1880 rule, Cannon offered a similar observation:

> The object of this provision was, as the Chair has always understood, that the motion should be made by one friendly to the bill, for the purpose of giving one more chance to perfect it, as perchance there might be some error that the House desired to correct. (Cannon 1936, vol. 8, § 2762)

As a result of these statements in the precedents, many (including this author in a previous paper) have assumed and written that between 1880 and the 1909 rules change, the motion to recommit operated as a majority-party prerogative to clean up legislation, or at least to block the minority from making last-minute changes. A review of House precedents on motions to recommit between 1881 and 1909, however, reveals quite another picture. Although the precedents examined involved issues other than recognition, it was easy enough to track the party of the Speaker and the person offering the motion to recommit. As table 18.1 reveals, Speakers were more inclined to recognize members of the minority party than members of their own party to offer the motion to recommit. Of the 28 bills surveyed in the precedents, Speakers recognized members of the other party 19 times (68% of the total) and members of their own party just 9 times (32%; *Hinds' Precedents of the House of Representatives*).[3]

Even in 1904, when Speaker Cannon had refused to recognize a Democrat (on April 4) to offer the motion on grounds it was the prerogative of those friendly to the bill, he had recognized Democrats to offer the motion on three other bills, in January, February, and March. Moreover, he recognized a Democrat to offer a motion to recommit the following year on March 1, 1905 (Hinds 1907, vol. 5, § § 5540, 5551, 5571, and 5541, respectively).

Further undergirding the case that the 1880 rule was intended to advantage opponents of legislation are early rulings by Speaker John Carlisle (D-Ky.) in 1884 and 1886, upholding the right to amend a motion to recommit before the previous question is ordered on the motion. In his 1886 ruling he explained that the right to amend the motion should be protected "for the very obvious reason that an advocate of the pending measure, and therefore an opponent of recommitment might offer a motion to recommit with such instructions as it was evident the House would not agree to, thereby preventing anybody who desired in good faith to recommit the measure from submitting such a motion." Carlisle said he considered it "a matter of simple justice to those on the floor who desired to recommit with substantial instructions that they should have an opportunity to propose amendments" (Hinds 1907, vol. 5, § 5582).

Finally, in explaining the context of the 1909 rule change discussed in the following, Clarence Cannon's precedents indicate that the latter modification "was occasioned by the practice which had grown up under which the Speaker recognized the Member in charge of the bill to make the motion to recommit, *in effect nullifying the purpose of the motion*." The purpose of the 1909 rule change, the precedents continue, "is to insure recognition of a Member actually opposed to the measure and afford the House a last opportunity to express its preference on the final form of the bill" (Cannon 1936, vol. 8, § 2757).

The 1909 Revolt

Cannon first became Speaker in 1903, and while he was well liked personally, he gradually alienated members of both parties with his arbitrary leadership style. Not only did he rule with an iron fist in appointing and removing members from committees to ensure the legislative results he wanted in committee and on the floor, but as a "regular" Republican, he resisted pressures to clear progressive legislation for floor consideration. He is often quoted as saying, "We don't need any new legislation; everything's just fine back in Danville," his hometown in Illinois. As chair of the five-member Rules Committee, the Speaker controlled the flow of legislation to the floor.

Discontent with Cannon's rule was especially acute among a group of about 30 progressive Republicans, known as the Insurgents, led by Representative George Norris of Nebraska. Consequently, on March 15, 1909, the opening day of the 61st Congress, the Insurgent Republicans joined with Democratic Minority Leader Champ Clark in defeating the previous question on the adoption of House rules for the new Congress. Under the terms of the rules, if the previous-question motion is defeated, the chair then recognizes a member opposed to the previous question who is recognized for an hour and given the opportunity to amend the pending resolution.

Cannon recognized Clark, who offered a substitute set of House rules that, among other things, enlarged the Rules Committee to 15 members; removed the Speaker as member, chair, and appointing authority of the Rules Committee; and removed the Speaker's power to appoint all but five other committees (Ways and Means being the only important one left under his appointment authority; Boinville 1982).

Rather than take another hour of debate, Clark promptly moved the previous question on his substitute set of rules, to bring it to an immediate vote. However, while 28 Republican Insurgents joined in supporting Clark on adopting the previous question, 22 conservative Democrats, led by Tammany Hall chief John J. Fitzgerald (D-N.Y.), joined with the regular Republicans to defeat the previous question, 180–203.

Fitzgerald, whose machine Democrats feared some of the progressive legislation favored by the Insurgents as much as Cannon did, had conspired with the Speaker to engineer a procedural countercoup against Clark and the Insurgents. Cannon consequently recognized Fitzgerald to offer his own substitute rules package. Fitzgerald's substitute only slightly curbed the Speaker's powers by establishing a Consent Calendar 2 days a month for minor bills of interest to individual members and by requiring a two-thirds House vote to set aside the Calendar Wednesday—a procedure by which committees could bypass the Rules Committee and Speaker to call up reported bills. Finally, the Fitzgerald rules substitute gave opponents of a bill the right of first recognition to offer a motion to recommit legislation and prohibited the reporting of special rules denying that right.

The new recommit rule provided specifically that, "after the previous question shall have been ordered on the passage of a bill or joint resolution, one motion to recommit shall be in order, and the Speaker shall give preference in recognition to a Member who is opposed to the bill or joint resolution." Moreover, the rule prohibited the Rules Committee from reporting "any rule or order that would prevent the motion to recommit from being made as provided in paragraph 4 of Rule XVI" (*Congressional Record* 1909).

In explaining his proposed recommit change, Fitzgerald observed that "the greatest legislative outrages that have been perpetrated in this country have been by means of special rules by which the majority has denied the minority the right to have a vote on its position upon great public questions."

Representative John Dalzell (R-Pa.), a Cannon ally, nevertheless supported Fitzgerald's claim about the abuse of the rule and underscored the rule's original intent:

> We all know that the motion to recommit, under existing practice, has been used not to secure recommittal, but to prevent recommittal. The custom has grown up to have a Member of the majority party move to recommit and then have his colleagues vote the motion down. Now, that is, without any doubt, an infringement on the rights of parties who under the rules are understood and were intended to have the right to test the sense of the House on a motion to recommit. (*Congressional Record* 1909)

Fitzgerald's rules ploy in 1909 saved Cannon's position on the Rules Committee for only a time. A year later, on March 19, 1910, the Democrats and Insurgents successfully carried out their own parliamentary coup by voting 191 to 156 for a resolution offered by Republican Representative Norris to remove the Speaker from the Rules Committee and enlarge and elect its membership, thereby removing from the Speaker's power the ability to appoint Rules Committee members (Boinville 1982).

Early Precedents on the Modern Rule

Following his loss on the Norris resolution, Cannon offered to entertain a motion offered by a Democrat that the speakership be vacated. Cannon prevailed on that vote and remained in the chair for the remainder of the 61st Congress. But Cannonism and public support for a more activist Congress led to a Democratic takeover of both chambers of Congress in the 1910 elections, and Champ Clark was elevated to the speakership by the new majority.

One might think that the majority Democrats in 1911 would feel no special obligation to retain the rule that gave the minority the motion to recommit since it was the product of a conservative Democrat who used it specifically to thwart Clark's more ambitious rules changes when he was minority leader. However, there was no effort at the beginning of 62nd Congress to repeal the rule. In fact, Speaker Clark had an early opportunity in May 1912 to uphold the minority's right to recommit. A point of order was raised against a special rule from the Rules Committee discharging a bill from committee, together with Senate amendments adopted to it, disagreeing to the Senate amendments, and appointing conferees, *without intervening motion*. In ruling on the point of order that the rule denied a motion to recommit, Clark quoted from *Jefferson's Manual* to the effect that rules are instituted as a check and control on the actions of the majority and a shelter and protection to the minority. "It is not necessary to go into the history of how this particular rule came to be adopted," Clark continued, "but that it was intended that the right to make the motion to recommit should be preserved inviolate the Chair has no doubt whatever" (*Congressional Record*, May 14, 1912, p. 6410).

However, later that year, on August 16, 1912, drawing on the Carlisle rulings from 1884 and 1886, Speaker Clark upheld the majority's right to trump a minority-sponsored recommittal amendment with its own substitute. Representative John A. Moon (D-Tenn.) had called up a post office appropriations bill. At the end of the bill's consideration, House Minority Leader James R. Mann (R-Ill.) offered a motion to recommit with instructions to eliminate one of the Senate amendments to the bill. Representative Moon countered by offering a substitute motion.

Representative George Norris raised a point of order against the Moon motion, arguing that it in effect deprived the minority of its right to move to recommit. Clark responded that "the Chair has given the minority a right to make a motion" and that, once the minority exercises that right, under the precedence given to it by the rule, "then the motion is in the hands of the House and subject to every rule of the House and to every rule of amendment." The majority substitute motion, concluded Clark, "does not take away from the minority the preferential right in the matter" (Cannon 1936, vol. 8, § 2759).

Another instructive incident occurred when Republicans retook control of the House in the 1918 elections. In October 1919 a point of order was made against a motion to recommit a tariff bill with instructions to report back a substitute on grounds that the substitute had the effect of altering an amendment already adopted by the House. Former Speaker Charles Crisp

(D-Ga.), spoke against the point of order, saying the purpose of the motion was to give the minority of the House "a chance affirmatively to go on record as to what they think this legislation should be, and if a motion to recommit does not permit that, the motion is futile" (Cannon 1936, vol. 8, § 2727).

Representative Finis James Garrett (D-Tenn.) concurred, arguing, "The motion to recommit is regarded as so sacred that it is one of the few things protected against the Committee on Rules by the general rules of the House." Garrett concluded that if the Speaker should uphold the point of order, "the practical effect would be to do by parliamentary decision that which the Committee on Rules and the House itself cannot do under the general rules of the House. It will practically destroy the efficacy of the motion to recommit with instructions" (Cannon 1936, vol. 8, § 2727).

In delivering his ruling, House Speaker Frederick Gillett (R-Mass.) agreed with Crisp and Garret, "The whole purpose of this motion to recommit is to have a record vote upon the program of the minority" (Cannon 1936, vol. 8, § 2727).

The 1934 Precedent

The first indication of an erosion in the minority's right to recommit occurred in 1934 when a special rule was called up from the Rules Committee providing for the consideration of an appropriations bill for the executive office and various independent agencies. The rule waived certain points of order against provisions in the bill and prohibited any amendment to title 2 of the bill "during the consideration" of the bill—meaning in either the Committee of the Whole or in the House. Since the motion to recommit is made in the House, after a bill is reported from the Committee of the Whole, Representative Bertrand Snell (R-N.Y.) made a point of order against the rule on grounds that it effectively prohibited a motion to recommit with amendatory instructions.

In making the argument for his point of order, Representative Snell said that it "has been the precedent for a great many years that under no circumstances will the minority be prohibited from making a motion to recommit. . . . In this way the minority is allowed to place its position before the Congress, and, if enough members approve of it, they are entitled to a roll-call vote" (*Congressional Record*, January 11, 1934, p. 480).

Representative William Bankhead (D-Ala.) responded, "There is nothing in this rule that would prevent any Member from offering a motion to recommit on any other phase of the bill except that covered by Title II."

Snell shot back that the interpretation being put on the rule "is contrary to the spirit of the rules of this House and to every precedent of the House in the last 20 years" (ibid.).

Nevertheless, Speaker Henry T. Rainey (D-Ill.) overruled the point of order, saying the special rule in question "does not mention the motion to recommit," and therefore any motion to recommit could be made under the general rules of the House. However, Rainey went on, since the general rules of the House prohibit instructions "that might not be proposed directly as an amendment," and since the rule prohibits amendments to title 2, "it would not be in order . . . to move to recommit the bill with instructions to incorporate an amendment in title II of the bill." Rainey thus concluded that the special rule "does not deprive the minority of its right to make a simple motion to recommit," but that "a motion that includes instructions to incorporate a provision which would be in violation of the special rule . . . would not be in order" (ibid.).

The precedent is incorporated in *Deschler's Precedents*, published in 1977, with the statement that, while a special rule may not deny the minority a motion to recommit as provided by rule 16, clause 4, "such restriction does not apply to a special rule which may prevent a motion to recommit with instructions to incorporate an amendment in a title to which the special rule precludes the offering of amendments" (Deschler 1977, vol. 7, chapter 23, § 25.9).

The same precedent also appears in volume 6 of *Deschler's* and includes the additional information that Speaker Rainey's ruling was appealed and upheld by a vote of 260 to 112. Moreover, a parliamentarian's footnote to the precedent contains the following further explanation:

> Normally, such resolutions only prohibit certain amendments during consideration in the Committee of the Whole, allowing a motion to recommit with instructions in the House to add such amendments. *This is apparently the only ruling by the Speaker on the authority of the Committee on Rules to limit, but not to prohibit the motion to recommit.* (Deschler 1977; emphasis added)

Rainey's Ghost Rising

For whatever reason, Rainey's ruling did not open a floodgate of majority-party abuses of the minority's right to recommit with instructions. Rainey was a one-term Speaker, and his successor, William Bankhead of Alabama, was not forced by the Rules Committee to test the limits of the Rainey ruling. According to House precedents, it was not until 1975 that Rainey's ruling came to haunt the House. A special rule for a tax reform bill had been reported from the Rules Committee, which with certain exceptions, prohibited amendments to the bill either in the House or the Committee of the Whole. A motion to recommit the bill was offered that would have sent the bill back to the Ways and Means Committee with the instructions that it not report the measure back to the House until an amendment was included that provided that any revenues raised by the bill could not exceed governing expenditures over a specified level—in effect, an attempt to impose a cap on government spending.

The precedent on this incident (published in the 1982 *Procedure in the U.S. House of Representatives*, by Deschler and Brown) says, "No point of order was made against the motion," the implication being that one might have been raised on grounds that the motion was attempting to do indirectly what the special rule had directly prohibited in the way of amendment (Deschler and Brown 1982, chapter 23, § 14.13).

The same Deschler and Brown volume cites several other instances in which the motion to recommit a bill could not alter amendments already adopted by the House unless the special rules had specified that the motions to recommit could be "with or without instructions." And, in fact, standing practice is, whenever the Rules Committee makes in order a committee amendment in the nature of a substitute as an original bill for amendment purposes, for it to include in the special rule the guarantee of instructions that would otherwise be subject to a point of order for attempting to amend a bill that has already been amended in its entirety (Deschler and Brown 1982).

However, the Deschler-Brown precedents also contain the first modern instances in which special rules have directly placed limits on motions to recommit. The first such instance occurred on April 1, 1976, when a special rule mandated the precise form that the motion to recommit with instructions must take to a pending campaign-reform bill (thus leaving the minority no leeway in offering a different motion of its choosing; Deschler and Brown 1982).

The second instance cited occurred on April 4, 1977, and involved language in a special rule that permitted one motion to recommit, "which may include instructions if the House has not previously agreed to an amendment in the nature of a substitute." The Parliamentarian's note to this latter precedent explains the "unique language" in the most positive and charitable light, saying that the provision, added by way of amendment in the Rules Committee, "was intended to allow a motion to recommit with in-

TABLE 18.2
Special rules limiting and denying recommittal instructions (95th–103rd Congresses, 1975–1995)

Congress	Limiting rules	Denying rules	Total	Speaker
95th (1977–1979)	3	0	3	O'Neill
96th (1979–1981)	8	0	8	O'Neill
97th (1981–1983)	2	1	3	O'Neill
98th (1983–1985)	1	0	1	O'Neill
99th (1985–1987)	7	7	14	O'Neill
100th (1987–1989)	9	15	24	Wright
101st (1989–1991)	5	16	21	Wright/Foley
102nd (1991–1993)	0	5	5	Foley
103rd (1993–1995)	0	4	4	Foley

SOURCE: The data were compiled by the author from a rule-by-rule examination in each of the Congresses. An earlier version of the table was published in a paper written by the author while serving as the minority counsel on the House Rules Committee's Subcommitee on Legislative Process, "The Motion to Recommit in the House: The Rape of a Minority Right, November 12, 1990," and updated in an "Addendum to Motion to Recommit Paper," dated August 16, 1991. Both are included in U.S. Congress. House, Committee on Rules, Subcommittee on Rules of the House, "Roundtable Discussion on the Motion to Recommit," May 6, 1992, 93–175.

structions to amend a portion of the bill which had already been amended, except where an amendment in the nature of a substitute had been adopted. The rule thus permitted instructions to eliminate or amend certain amendments already agreed to" (Deschler and Brown 1982). Presumably the provision was intended to prevent the minority from having two bites of the apple if its substitute had earlier prevailed.

The instances cited in the preceding, while minor and relatively innocuous, helped lay the groundwork for a more substantive chipping away at the minority's right, beginning in the 95th Congress (1977–1978), the first term of Speaker Thomas P. "Tip" O'Neill Jr. (D-Mass.). It was under O'Neill that the experimenting began with limiting the minority's recommittal motion. And except for one instance in the 97th Congress (1981–1982), the special rules involved only limited exceptions but did not completely deny a motion to recommit with instructions. Table 18.2 compares special rules limiting and denying instructions in motions to recommit from the 95th Congress through the 103rd Congress (1993–1994).

The three rules in the 95th Congress and four of the eight in the 96th Congress that limited motions to recommit with instructions prohibited only one or two specific types of amendments per bill. All seven were special rules for appropriations bills and prohibited amendments dealing with such areas as abortion, federal pay, and the Federal Trade Commission (FTC; relating to providing a congressional veto for regulations).

The turning point in the Democratic leadership's crackdown on amendments in motions to recommit came with the last four rules granted in the 96th Congress (three in October of 1979 alone and the fourth in 1980). The first two were special rules that provided for consideration of continuing appropriations resolutions in the House. The first rule specified that the only amendment allowed was one dealing with federal pay; and the second rule permitted only one specified abortion amendment. Since consideration was in the House, the motion to recommit was also confined to the substance of the same amendments.

The third rule, for an FTC bill, allowed only three specified amendments, plus one substitute, "*in the House* and the Committee of the Whole" (emphasis added), thereby confining any amendments in recommittal instructions (which are made in the House) to those already made in order in the Committee of the Whole. Yet none of the three rules was contested.

That changed with the fourth and final special rule of the 96th Congress, which provided for consideration of the first-ever budget reconciliation bill—a proposal backed by the Carter administration. The Rules Committee reported a special rule that allowed for just three amendments "in the House and in the Committee of the Whole," one dealing with Superfund, a second with trade-adjustment assistance, and the third with cost-of-living adjustment reforms.

When Rules Committee Chair Richard Bolling (D-Mo.) called up the rule, Representative Del Latta (R-Ohio) complained about the severe limitation on amendments and argued for defeating the previous question on the rule so that he could make in order an additional amendment to eliminate a $3.1 billion spending increase in the bill as well as allow for a motion to recommit with instructions. "The way the motion is now, it is without instructions" (*Congressional Record*, September 4, 1980, p. 24191).

Bolling countered that "a motion to recommit with instructions enables the managers on that side to deal with all the political plums in town. Talk about politics, they could set up a Christmas tree alternative in either direction, either to save or to spend or a combination of the two that would be absolutely incredible" (ibid., p. 24192). Bolling prevailed on the previous question and the rule. But the battle set the stage for a series of future budget battles and rules restricting or denying minority rights of amendment and recommittal.

In 1981 the tables were turned on the Democrats as Republicans forged an alliance with "Boll Weevil" Southern Democrats in support of President Reagan's budget plan. When the Rules Committee reported a special rule for the Budget Committee's reconciliation bill, it made in order only portions of the requested Republican substitute (the sour without the sweet) and broke it into six separate amendments. Moreover, the special rule provided for two motions to recommit, one that could not contain instructions and another that allowed only for instructions that were identical to the butchered, six-part Republican substitute already made in order during the regular amendment process.

When the special rule was called up on the House floor on June 25, 1981, Republican outrage at the procedural abuse was palpable. Following the heated debate, the previous question for the rule was voted down, shifting recognition to Republicans to offer a substitute rule. The substitute called for the en bloc consideration of amendments to be offered by Latta (who was the ranking Republican on the Budget Committee) and for one motion to recommit, with or without instructions. The GOP's substitute rule eventually prevailed, 214 to 208, with 26 Democrats voting in favor.

When the Latta substitute for the bill was about to come to a final vote, the chair recognized a Republican member opposed to the package, Representative Claudine Schneider, who sought to restore the twice-annual cost-of-living adjustments for federal employees, which had been deleted in the Latta package. At that point Budget Committee Chair Jim Jones (D-Okla.) attempted to wrest control of the motion to recommit from Schneider by urging defeat of the previous question so that he could offer an alternative motion to recommit with instructions. But the House adopted the previous question on Schneider's motion, 215 to 212, then rejected her motion by voice vote, and proceeded to pass the Reagan reconciliation bill.

The ironic postscript to this episode occurred on July 31, 1981, on a rule providing for consideration of the reconciliation conference report plus a bill to be called up by Bolling to restore minimum benefits under Social Security that had been reduced in the reconciliation bill. The rule provided that the motion to recommit on the Social Security bill "may not contain instructions." This was the first instance of an outright denial of instructions. But because another Democrat was trying to defeat the previous question on the rule for purposes opposed by Republicans, Republicans supported the previous question and the rule. Nevertheless, that was the opening shot in what would lead to an escalation in special rules denying the minority's motion to recommit.

The Final Assaults

In the first four Congresses listed in table 18.2, there was only one, the 97th Congress, in which a special rule barred any instructions (on the Bolling bill just cited). However, as the table shows, the move to special rules that totally denied motions to recommit with amendatory instructions then began to grow in the 99th Congress, with 7 such rules, and peaked in the 101st at 16 before declining to 5 and 4 in the 102nd and 103rd Congresses, respectively.

In the 99th Congress all 7 rules that denied the minority's motion to recommit with a final amendment stated that the motion "may not contain instructions." Two of the 7 rules were on trade and budget sequestration bills and were adopted by voice vote. One was on a drug bill and was adopted by an overwhelming margin. The 4 other rules, on Central America, reconciliation, and 2 on immigration, were contested, and 1 was defeated (the first immigration rule).

In Representative Jim Wright's first (and only full) term as Speaker, the 100th Congress (1987–1988), 15 rules were reported that denied amendatory instructions. Of the 15, 3 were defeated, 7 were adopted with substantial opposition, 2 were adopted by voice vote (one of which barred instructions on two bills), and 2 were tabled. Wright's speakership became a lightning rod for Republicans' resistance and protest over what they saw as an innovative array of procedural abuses being visited on the minority. The denials of motions to recommit were but a small part of a larger pattern of procedural manipulation by the Speaker (Cheney 1989).

In October 1988 Republican Whip Trent Lott (R-Miss.), a member of the Rules Committee, inserted a special order in the *Congressional Record*, "Changing the Rules," in which he detailed the extent of procedural abuses, including comparative data on the increase in restrictive rules limiting the offering of amendments, self-executing rules, rules waiving the Budget Act, and rules prohibiting recommittal instructions. In discussing the motion to recommit, Lott said the history of the rule "makes clear that the intent was to permit the minority one final opportunity to get a vote on its position. . . . And yet, despite this clear legislative history and intent . . . the Rules Committee has dictated on 18 occasions in this Congress alone that the motion be rendered futile by prohibiting instructions" (*Congressional Record*, October 21, 1988, p. E3657).

In the 101st Congress, the procedural restrictions continued, even after Wright's resignation from the House under an ethics cloud in June 1989. All told, 5 special rules limited the motion to recommit with instructions while 16 denied recommittal instructions. Three of the denials were under Wright's speakership, but the remaining 13 fell on the shoulders of the new Speaker, Tom Foley. Four of the denial rules were adopted by voice vote, 6 others had substantial opposition, and 1 rule, for the crime bill, was defeated.

The rhetoric escalated on the Republican side as perceived procedural abuses mounted. On one bill, the Civil Rights Act of 1990, the special rule considered on August 2, 1990, allowed just one Republican substitute to be offered and denied a motion to recommit with instructions. Likewise, a campaign-reform rule in August 1990 allowed just one minority substitute and denied recommittal instructions. The omnibus crime bill rule in September 1990 allowed numerous amendments but denied a major amendment on habeas corpus requested by ranking Judiciary Committee member Henry Hyde (R-Ill.). The rule also denied a motion to recommit with instructions.

Rules Committee ranking Republican Jimmy Quillen recounted how he had asked in the committee why a motion to recommit with instructions was being denied: "I was told that a motion to recommit with instructions could not be allowed because it might be used to give the House a chance to consider the Hyde amendment." "Listen to that," Quillen continued. "How do you gang up on somebody like a respected member of this House, the gentleman from Illinois [Mr. Hyde]?" (*Congressional Record*, September 25, 1990a, p. H7999). Although an attempt to defeat the previous question and make in order the Hyde amendment was defeated, the rule was subsequently rejected by the House, 166 to 258. A subsequent rule made in order the Hyde amendment and three others but still denied a motion to recommit with instructions. It was adopted by voice vote.

The final showdown in the 101st Congress came on a reconciliation rule in October 1990 that denied a requested Republican substitute and denied any instructions in a motion to recommit. When the rule was called up, House Republican Leader Bob Michel raised a point of order against the rule on grounds that it denied the minority the right to offer instructions in the motion to recommit.

Michel argued that the key to the intent of the rule was Fitzgerald's rule that the motion to recommit could not be denied as provided by rule 16, which was adopted solely to give opponents the opportunity to offer a final amendment.

The Speaker pro tempore, Representative John Murtha (D-Pa.), overruled the point of order, citing Speaker Rainey's 1934 ruling as "the only precedent directly relating to the question at issue." Murtha said that precedent makes clear that "the Committee on Rules is not precluded . . . from specifically limiting motions to recommit bills or joint resolutions . . . to specific types of instructions. . . . Clause 4 of Rule XVI does not guarantee that a motion to recommit a bill may always include instructions. The Chair, therefore, overrules the point of order" (*Congressional Record*, October 16, 1990b, pp. H9933–9934). Representative Bob Walker (R-Pa.)

immediately rose to appeal the ruling of the chair, which Representative Butler Derrick moved to table. The appeal was tabled on a 251 to 171 party-line vote, with just one Democrat, Representative Charles Bennett of Florida, voting against tabling.

Turning the Tide

Two significant occurrences in the 102nd Congress began to turn the tide on the motion-to-recommit controversy. First, Representative Gerald B. Solomon (R-N.Y.), a second-term member on the Rules Committee, was elevated to the ranking minority slot on the committee by Minority Leader Michel (moving Quillen into second chair). Solomon considered himself a pit bull, a real fighter for minority-party rights in the House, and he made that his cause. One of his first acts as ranking member was to write a letter to Speaker Foley on the opening day of the new Congress and enclose a copy of a minority staff report (which I had written), "The Motion to Recommit in the House: The Rape of a Minority Right." In his letter Solomon summarized the document's history and arguments on the rule's original intent. He concluded his letter by saying it was his hope, "in light of this evidence, [that] the majority leadership and the Rules Committee will consider their past restrictions and denials of this minority right in the 102nd Congress, and thereby avoid future confrontations and points of order over such a fundamental guarantee" (*Congressional Record*, June 4, 1991, p. 3813).

Solomon sent copies of his letter and the paper to the House Republican leadership and the chair and members of the Rules Committee, making clear his intentions should the motion to recommit be denied in the future. Six months later, the Rules Committee issued a closed rule on a civil rights bill relating to employment discrimination. The rule also prohibited instructions on a motion to recommit, but Republicans did not challenge the rule because the GOP leadership and president supported the bill.

Less than 3 weeks later, however, the Rules Committee did report a special rule on campaign-finance-reform legislation that made in order three substitutes under a king-of-the-hill process (last substitute adopted wins) but failed to specify that instructions were permitted in the motion to recommit. That meant that if any substitute were adopted, as the majority's preferred substitute surely would be, then no further amendments would be in order in a recommit motion. As Michel had done before him, Solomon raised a point of order, repeating most of the same arguments. And predictably, the Speaker overruled the point of order, citing the 1934 precedent. Unlike Walker, though, Solomon took a diplomatic tack to begin with: "Mr. Speaker, out of respect for you, I will not appeal the ruling of the Chair, but I would hope that perhaps our Republican leader and you could sit down and discuss the long-range plans that deal with this particular subject." Solomon concluded, "We feel very strongly about it, but I do understand the Chair's ruling" (*Congressional Record*, June 4, 1991 pp. 3810–3811).

Notwithstanding the proffered olive branch, another procedural explosion, unrelated to the recommit issue, occurred 2 weeks later on a foreign-operations appropriations bill. The rule made in order only 11 amendments, even though the usual practice had been open rules on all appropriations measures. The outraged Republican reaction led to the threat of holding a series of dilatory votes. This in turn led to a bipartisan leadership summit meeting in the Speaker's office to which Solomon was invited. While the Republicans were not successful in changing the rule, they did extract a promise from Foley that the Rules Committee would reexamine procedures for considering appropriations bills as well as an examination of the minority's right to recommit.

This was the second major development in the new Congress on the recommittal issue. On July 22, 1991, Rules Committee Chair Joe Moakley (D-Mass.) wrote a letter to Representative Tony Beilenson, (D-Calif.), chair of the Subcommittee on Rules of the House, asking that his subcommittee "initiate a review of the issues and I would like to discuss the matter with you in the future" (Roundtable Discussion 1991, p. 176). After considerable delay and foot-dragging that required a pointed reminder from the Speaker, Beilenson finally convened a roundtable discussion on the motion to recommit on May 6, 1992, at which three parliamentary experts presented their views on the topic, and the subcommittee engaged in a dialogue on the matter.

As any congressional veteran knows, promises of hearings and studies can be nothing more than convenient excuses to delay and defer taking any meaningful action. It had already taken a year and a half from Solomon's first letter to the Speaker to move the issue to a subcommittee roundtable discussion.

In the meantime, two other special rules denying recommittal instructions were reported: one in February 1992 on the Economic Growth Tax Act, and the second in May (on the same day the roundtable discussion was taking place) on an omnibus rescissions bill. In both instances, Solomon raised points of order against the rules on grounds they violated the intent of the motion-to-recommit rule. In both instances he was overruled, and in both he appealed the rulings of the chair but lost on roll-call votes that tabled his appeals.

The final special rule of the 102nd Congress that denied recommittal instructions came in June 1992 on a voter registration bill from the Senate. Once again Solomon made his point of order and was overruled, forcing a vote on tabling his appeal of the Speaker's ruling. While the roundtable discussion had obviously not led to an immediate reconciliation between the parties on the issue, at least the number of denial rules had fallen to just 5 in the 102nd Congress—11 fewer than in the previous Congress.

The 103rd Congress (1993–1994) would witness a further de-escalation of the recommittal wars, with only four special rules denying a motion to recommit with instructions. Republican members of the Rules Committee challenged the first three (reconciliation, campaign finance reform, and an effective government bill) with points of order but did not appeal the chair's ruling on any of the three. The fourth rule, denying instructions on the legislative branch appropriations, was not challenged.

One of the main reasons for the new mood of accommodation was the prospect for real reform. Partially as a result of the procedural abuse protests in the preceding Congress, a Joint Committee on the Organization of Congress had been created in late 1992 to explore ways to improve the operations of the House and Senate. Representatives Lee Hamilton (D-Ind.) and David Dreier (R-Calif.) were the House cochairs. While the joint committee did not actually organize and begin its work until early in 1993, it did hold out the promise of giving Republicans a more significant forum than a subcommittee roundtable to vent their grievances and possibly even adopt some reforms they had long advocated.

Although Hamilton initially put forward only a bare-bones reform bill to begin the House markup process in November, he indicated an openness to including other reforms that had some bipartisan support. Since the House half of the joint committee was evenly divided between six Republicans and six Democrats, it would take at least one Democrat to adopt a Republican amendment and vice versa.

On November 18, 1993, Solomon offered his amendment to the reform bill to prevent the Rules Committee from reporting any rule or special order that "would prevent the motion to recommit from being made by the minority leader (or his designee) . . . including a motion to recommit with amendatory instructions." Representative David Obey (D-Wis.) questioned the need for such a minority right since they could now get recorded votes on their amendments in the Committee of the Whole—something that was prohibited before 1971. Solomon responded that

> the Democratic Leadership does not agree with you at all, because Speaker Foley and Majority Leader Gephardt and your Majority Whip Bonior, in a meeting with our leadership, have agreed to give us our motion to recommit and all I'm trying to do is to firm that commitment so that we don't run into situations where under certain political pressures they try to renege on it. And they support the motion to recommit for the minority down the line. (U.S. Congress 1993)

After further debate on the intent of some Democrats to link any concessions on minority rights in the House to changes in the Senate rules on holds and filibusters, the vote was postponed. Then, on November 21, after a perfunctory summation of arguments, Hamilton indicated that he intended to support the amendment. The vote was taken, and the Solomon recommit amendment was adopted, 10 to 2, with only Representatives Obey and Sam Gejdenson (D-Conn.) voting no.

Although the House contingent reported their bill to the House the following day by an 8 to 4 vote, the matter would not come to a vote in the Rules Committee until 10 months later. Significantly, the Solomon amendment had been retained in a substitute mark put forward by Rules Committee Chair Moakley, even though other provisions were omitted—a good indication that the leadership agreed with restoring the minority's right.[4] Nevertheless, the bill was pulled by the leadership in the middle of markup when it appeared a proxy voting ban and a committee reorganization amendment might be adopted (cf. Wolfensberger 2000).

A little over 3 months later, on January 4, 1995, the new Republican majority called up its resolution to adopt rules for the 104th Congress. While most of the focus was on the first eight House reforms that had been promised in the "Opening Day Checklist" of the Contract with America, the second title of the resolution contained another 23 House rules changes that Republicans had developed over their years in the minority. Section 210 of House Resolution 6 was titled "Affirming the Minority's Right on Motions to Recommit." The amendment added to the existing language prohibiting the Rules Committee from denying a motion to recommit with the words "including a motion to recommit with instructions if offered by the minority leader (or a designee)" (*Congressional Record*, January 4, 1995, p. H29). Title 2 was subsequently adopted by voice vote, and the minority's right to recommit with instructions was fully restored and enshrined in House rules by the new majority.

Postpartum Regression

The rebirth of the minority's right to recommit might be seen as analogous to the mythical phoenix, which burns and then rises from its own ashes to be born again. It would, that is, if we had ended the story on the opening day of the 104th Congress. However, viewed with the hindsight of five Republican-controlled Congresses, the rebirth of the minority right resembles more a Pyrrhic victory[5] in the battle for institutional fairness. And therein lies the rest of the story.

One of the things that has most puzzled political scientists who argue that rules are made to enable the majority to achieve its policy preferences, is why the new Republican majority would still support giving the minority party a final amendment in the motion to recommit. Two such political scientists, for instance, say of this rule change and a few others, "These developments are curious because they appear to run counter to the policy interests of majority party Republicans." They conclude that Republicans took these contrary moves because (a) they didn't want to be accused of being hypocritical; and (b) they were confident they could beat back any liberal Democrat amendments under an open process (Binder and Smith 1995).

As one who was heavily involved with this and other reform issues for Rules Committee and leadership Republicans over the years, I can attest that the Republicans who pushed to retain the recommit rule change when they moved to majority status genuinely believed it embodied a basic right of the minority that was so deeply embedded in institutional customs and values as to be practically sacrosanct in nature. To follow the Democratic majority's cynical manipulation of this right for narrow, partisan advantage, they reasoned, would be both hypocritical and wrong. There was never any serious discussion I was aware of about dropping the change.

Looking back on the restoration of the minority's right *today*, however, nearly a decade later, yields a different explanation and justification for the majority's retention of the right, one that is more compatible with rational choice theory that rules are designed to benefit the majority. As Republicans have become increasingly parsimonious in allocating floor amendments to Democratic members on important legislation, the motion to recommit has provided a convenient shield against charges that the majority is totally denying minority-party rights.

The data in table 18.3 on open versus restrictive amendment rules over the last several Congresses bear this out. In the 103rd Congress, the last and most amendment-restrictive of any Democratic Congress, only 44 percent of the special rules granted by the Rules Committee provided for a

TABLE 18.3
The amendment process under special rules, 103rd–107th Congresses

	103RD CONGRESS (1993–1994)		104TH CONGRESS (1995–1996)		105TH CONGRESS (1997–1998)		106TH CONGRESS (1999–2000)		107TH CONGRESS (2001–2002)	
Rule type	No.	%	No.	%	No.	%	No.	%	No.	%
Open/modified open	46	44	83	58	74	53	91	51	40	37
Structured	40	38	20	14	6	4	32	18	20	19
Modified closed	9	9	20	14	36	26	17	9	24	22
Closed	9	9	19	14	24	17	39	22	23	22
Totals	104	100	142	100	140	100	179	100	107	100

completely open amendment process; another 38 percent were structured rules, meaning they allowed only specified amendments; and 18 percent were equally divided between modified closed rules (usually allowing only one minority substitute), or closed rules, allowing no amendments. By the 107th Congress (2001–2002), their fourth consecutive Congress in power, the Republicans had far exceeded the Democrats' worst excesses in restricting floor amendments. Only 37 percent of the rules allowed an open amendment process, 19 percent were structured, and the remaining 44 percent were equally divided between modified closed and closed. Modified closed rules, permitting just one minority substitute, were rapidly becoming the rule of choice for House Republicans.[6]

The data for the 108th Congress's first session (2003) were even more stark in the contrast between openness and restrictiveness, with only 27 percent of the special rules open or modified open, 28 percent structured, 21 percent modified closed, and 23 percent closed.

At a November 12, 2003, luncheon address at a Library of Congress symposium, "Centenary of Cannon's Speakership," House Speaker Dennis Hastert proudly brandished the majority party's shield of protection for the minority's right to recommit as evidence of Republican procedural fairness. According to David Broder's account of Hastert's remarks,

> Hastert, whose personal qualities were praised by all of the Democrats, used the occasion to deliver his first extended response to complaints from Pelosi and other Democrats that they were routinely excluded from participating in House-Senate conference committees, are blocked from offering floor amendments, and are subjected to other restrictions on their legislative work. (Broder 2003, A29)

Broder goes on to quote Hastert as saying, "We take the job of fairness very seriously," adding that even when the number of amendments is limited, "we guarantee the minority the right to recommit the bill with instructions, giving them one last chance to make their best arguments to amend the pending legislation" (Broder 2003).

Conclusion

The modern-day motion to recommit has its origins in a perceived abuse of power by House Speaker Cannon who, among other things, had distorted the intent of the motion by recognizing members of his own party, rather than the minority, to offer the motion. The resulting House rules change of 1909 (offered and adopted with Cannon's approval) guaranteed the right of first recognition to offer the motion to opponents of a bill, and prohibited the Rules Committee from reporting special rules denying that right. The following year, House rules were changed to remove the Speaker as chair and member of the Rules Committee—a rule that remains in force today, though the committee is once again referred to as the Speaker's committee.

Seizing on a 1934 ruling by the Speaker that the Rules Committee could limit the type of amendments that could be offered in a motion to recommit, Democratic leaders began directing the Rules Committee in the late 1970s to limit the minority's right and, by the 1980s, to selectively deny any amendments in motions to recommit on major bills of importance to the majority party.

This practice was reversed when the Republican minority became a majority in 1995, fully restoring the minority's right to recommit in House rules. Today that guarantee is the fig leaf of fairness behind which the majority party attempts to justify ever-increasing restrictions on the floor amendment process. This development tends to reaffirm the rational-choice explanation that rules are made to advance the preferences of the majority and to guard against threats by the minority to defeat or distort those preferences. As has been seen from House history, such procedural abuses eventually have a way of coming back to bite the majority that perpetrates them.

Because special rules have become increasingly restrictive, often allowing for no amendments or just one minority substitute, the motion to recommit with instructions has in some ways become even more important as the minority party's final (or only) statement on a pending measure. Such a motion rarely passes because it is portrayed by Democratic and Republican leaders alike as an important party vote. The rule even institutionalizes this partisan usage by guaranteeing the motion to the minority leader or a designee. The question thus arises as to whether such motions are just one more platform for party position-taking in this age of permanent campaigns and message politics or whether they are still designed primarily to improve pending legislation.

While it is difficult to disentangle these two motives because both are often at work in the same motion, in an increasingly partisan and polarized House, with majority control hanging in the balance, both parties are anxious to highlight differences between themselves that may resonate with voters. Just as the majority party has the advantage of agenda control and issue-framing to advance its causes, the minority party has the motion to recommit to draw a sharp distinction between itself and the ruling regime. To that extent, the motion continues to serve the minority party well in an increasingly constricted legislative environment. Perhaps only Joe Cannon, who secretly blessed the 1909 rule, could fully appreciate how it now simultaneously serves the interests of both parties.

Chapter 19

The Motion to Recommit in the U.S. House of Representatives

GARY W. COX, CHRIS DEN HARTOG, AND MATHEW D. MCCUBBINS

Introduction

The motion to recommit (MTR), a procedure sometimes used in the House, is the subject of recent debate regarding whether the motion undermines the majority party's ability to manipulate outcomes in the House (Krehbiel and Meirowitz 2002; chapter 20 in this volume; Wolfensberger 2003; Roberts 2004). Most works in this debate suggest at least implicitly that the ability to use the motion confers some advantage on the minority party that it would not otherwise enjoy. Some of these works treat MTRs primarily as dependent variables whose use is to be explained (Wolfensberger 1991, 2003; Roberts 2004). Consequently, they are heavy on analysis of the minority's ability to offer (successful) recommittal motions; for the most part, however, they imply that the ability to offer MTRs benefits the minority party, without spelling out the nature of the benefit. Krehbiel and Meirowitz (2002) are an exception, arguing explicitly that the benefit that the minority party gains via MTRs is the ability to exert significant influence on the shape of legislative decisions.

To the extent that these studies of the motion's significance find that it weakens the majority party, they rely largely on theoretical arguments and anecdotal evidence to back up their claims. We examine various data in a more rigorous empirical evaluation than has heretofore been conducted of hypotheses following from the view that the MTR empowers the minority party to affect policy.[1] We show that these predictions are at sharp odds with observed behavior, suggesting that the MTR does not undermine the majority party as has been argued.

The Role of Recommittals

If offered, an MTR "with instructions" *and* with an order to "report forthwith" is essentially a proposal to substitute an alternative for a bill that is about to face a final-passage vote. If it passes, the alternative bill proposed by the MTR is then pitted against the status quo in a final-passage vote. If the MTR is rejected, then the final-passage vote on the original bill occurs just as it would in the absence of a recommittal motion. As discussed more later, a motion to recommit *must* have both instructions (which specify the alternative proposal) and a forthwith clause to work in the way just described.[2]

Proponents of the view that this motion undermines the majority party's control over the agenda argue that, regardless of whether the majority controls the agenda up to that point in the process, the MTR offers an opportunity for the minority to sneak in amendment proposals at the end of the process. This ability allows them to offer strategic proposals designed to split the majority party and produce outcomes that the minority party likes better than the majority party's proposed bill.

In contrast, we believe that this portrayal vastly overstates the importance of the motion. There are many means by which the majority party can (and often does) limit the minority party's ability to offer MTRs. In addition, even if offered, the motion would need to get a sincere vote from majority-party members to have the described effect. But we believe that MTR votes are akin to special-rules votes in the sense that majority-party members are strongly predisposed to support their leaders on recommittal votes.

Hypotheses and Evidence

FREQUENCY AND SUCCESS OF RECOMMITTALS

The first three hypotheses we test deal with the frequency with which MTRs are offered and are voted on. These hypotheses are the following:

> *Hypothesis 1*: Every final-passage vote is preceded, not just by a motion to recommit, but by a motion to recommit with instructions to amend and report forthwith.

Hypothesis 2: Every motion to recommit passes.
Hypothesis 3: The minority party never votes against a recommittal motion.

The reasoning underlying the first hypothesis is straightforward. A recommittal motion that does not include instructions is merely a motion to kill the bill under consideration, rather than to substitute an alternative. It therefore pits the bill against the status quo, which is exactly what would happen without the MTR. Similarly, if a recommittal motion does not contain a forthwith provision, then the motion does not have the effect of substituting an alternative proposal in place of the bill under consideration.

We rely heavily on Rohde's extensive House roll-call data (2003; see also Rohde 1991) to evaluate these hypotheses. We begin with hypothesis 1. Using Rohde's data, which covers the period from the 83rd through 105th Congresses (1953–1998), we find that there were only 27 percent (848 out of 3139) as many recommittal motions as final-passage votes in Congresses 83–105. This gives us a rough estimate that only about one-eighth of all final-passage votes in the House are actually preceded by the type of recommittal motion predicted in hypothesis 1, thus contradicting the hypothesis. Krehbiel and Meirowitz also present evidence that contradicts this hypothesis. They coded all recommittal motions that got roll-call votes in Congresses 80–104 and whether each included instructions or ordered that the bill be returned forthwith.[3] They report that there were 932 motions in this period, 695 of which included instructions. Of these 695 motions, 503 included an order to report forthwith. Thus, only 54 percent of the recommittal motions that Krehbiel and Meirowitz report are the type of recommittal motion on which their model relies. Krehbiel and Meirowitz do not tell us how many bills got roll-call final-passage votes in this period, but we can estimate a ballpark figure.

We turn now to hypothesis 2, that all recommittal motions pass. Turning again to Rohde's data, we find that, of the 848 recommittal motions, only 13 percent (109) passed. As before, this is inconsistent with the hypothesis.

To evaluate hypothesis 3, we use Rohde's data to calculate the rate the minority party opposes recommittal motions. To do so, we simply tabulate the votes on recommittal motions for which a majority of the minority-party members vote against them. Of the 848 motions, a majority of the minority party opposed the motion 160 times (19 percent). It is difficult for a model in which the MTR is a tool of minority-party agenda control to explain why a majority of the minority party opposes nearly one out of five recommittal motions.

The Policy Impact of Recommittals

In addition to examining how often MTRs are offered and voting patterns when they are offered, we also address the policy implications of recommittals. We do so by examining whether recommittals produce outcomes that the majority party dislikes, which we should expect to see if the minority party uses MTRs to undermine the majority party's control over outcomes. If the recommittal motion is really a significant weapon for the minority party, we might reasonably expect to see a number of instances in which a passing recommittal motion leads to the majority party being "rolled" on final passage of a bill (that is, the bill passes despite being opposed by a majority of the majority-party members).

To determine whether this is in fact the case, we gathered additional data about each of the 109 recommittal motions that passed in Rohde's data. For each, we used the Inter-university Consortium for Political and Social Research (ICPSR) roll-call-vote manuals to identify the measure that was recommitted by each motion. Using the manuals and House calendars, we then determined whether each measure received a final-passage vote after the recommittal motion. For those that received roll-call votes on final passage, we coded whether a majority of majority-party members opposed the bill on final passage.

We found that, of the 109 passed recommittal motions, 60 were motions to recommit House bills, 29 were motions to recommit conference reports,[4] 7 were motions to recommit House resolutions, 9 were motions to recommit House joint resolutions, 2 were motions to recommit House concurrent resolutions, and 1 was a motion to recommit a Senate joint resolution. Of the 70 recommittal motions on House bills or joint resolutions, 18 did not include instructions, 3 included instructions but did not order the measure returned forthwith, and 49 included instructions and an order to report forthwith. Of these 49 passing recommittal motions, *none* led to final-passage roll-call votes on which the majority party was rolled. Given this, we find it particularly hard to believe that the MTR is a tool that the minority party uses to undermine the majority party.

Conclusion

It seems clear that the minority party *does* value the right to make recommittal motions. This seemingly implies that they see recommittals as being valuable in some way. We have argued that, whatever the value is, it is *not* policy influence—but we have left open the question of why the motion is valuable to the minority party. We make no attempt here to provide a definitive answer to this question. However, we are inclined to believe the explanation suggested by Wolfensberger (1991) and Bach (1998a), which is that the motion is valuable to the minority for position-taking reasons. That is, it allows the minority party an opportunity to put forth its own alternative on the floor, and to force a recorded vote on the minority proposal.

We suggest three directions for future research on the motion to recommit. The first is an analysis of the just-mentioned possibility that recommittals present the minority party with valuable opportunities for position-taking. The second direction is to study the relationship between the MTR and the conditional-party-government model (Rohde 1991; Aldrich and Rohde 2000b). Roberts (2004) shows that MTRs are more successful when the majority party is more heterogeneous, suggesting that, whatever the value of MTRs to the minority party, it provides them with greater benefits when the conditions for strong-party government fall short of being met. The third direction is a comparative analysis of recommittals. In the Senate, for example, the MTR is an important prerogative of the majority party (Tiefer 1989; Oleszek 2001), as it was in the House until early in the 20th century. This indicates that recommittal motions can play different roles in different legislatures and suggests the importance of studying these motions in their broader contexts.

Chapter 20

The Motion to Recommit: More Than an Amendment?

D. RODERICK KIEWIET AND KEVIN ROUST

In 1909 the standing rules of the House of Representatives were changed to provide opponents of a bill with the final opportunity to amend it. Immediately before the vote on final passage, an opponent could offer a "motion to recommit forthwith," with instructions to amend the bill in a particular fashion. This motion would be subject to a simple majority vote, choosing whether the current bill or the bill as amended by the instructions should be put to a vote on passage. Through parliamentary rulings, particularly one by Speaker Rainey in 1934, it was established that the motion to recommit gave the minority party the opportunity to offer the last amendment, subject to the restrictions on amendments included in the special rule for the bill.

During their long years in the minority-party wilderness, Republicans frequently charged that restrictive amendment rules unfairly stifled their ability to influence legislation. Some of their most vociferous complaints were directed against restrictions on these amendatory motions to recommit (AMRs). Jerry Solomon's diatribe against a ban on AMRs to a 1990 child-care bill is illustrative: "This is the worst rule that has ever come before this House in the 12 years I have been a Member of this body. It is an abuse which is almost unbelievable. You know, democracy is breaking out all over the world; it is spreading all over the world; everywhere except in this House of Representatives" (quoted by Wolfensberger 1992, 127).

These remarks and others like them suggest that, for members of the minority party, being able to make an AMR is more valuable than being able to offer an amendment in the Committee of the Whole. An AMR, in other words, is worth more than an ordinary amendment. But is it? What is it about the AMR that would make it so?

In their characterizations of the AMR, House Republicans seemed to be of two minds as to why this motion was so important to them. On one hand, they often pointed to the AMR as allowing for a clear statement of the minority party's position on pending legislation. One of their leaders put it this way: "It is not merely an amendment. It is not merely a substitute. It is the Minority's alternative to what is being proposed" (Michel 1992, 87–88). This characterization of the AMR goes back to at least 1919, when Speaker Frederick Gillett noted that "a motion to recommit is intended to give the Minority one chance to express fully their views as long as they are germane" (quoted by Bach in Roundtable 1992, 18). Democrats argued that the rules that proscribed AMRs nevertheless permitted the Republicans to offer a substitute version of the bill as an amendment. As long as the rule permitted them to offer such an alternative once, what was the point of allowing them to do so twice—or, in the vernacular of the House, allowing a second bite at the apple?

But why would the minority party always want to use the AMR to stake out an official party position? This would seem to guarantee that such measures would rarely pass—the minority party is, after all, the minority. In 1909 John Fitzgerald, sponsor of the measure that made the AMR a minority-party prerogative, did not envision that the minority party's use of the AMR would be so constrained. He argued that "the minority . . . will have what it has never had before—an opportunity to move to recommit that bill, with instructions to report in any way the minority may determine" (*Congressional Record*, March 15, 1909, p. 25).

Republican critics of restrictions on AMRs also made what we see as the more cogent argument, that what made the AMR so important was that it occurred at the end of the regular amendment process. Anthony Beilenson, a Democrat on the Rules Committee in the late 1980s, would certainly agree with this. He blamed the passage of a Republican-sponsored crime bill in 1986 on the fact that it came as a "massive surprise," sprung at the last minute in the form of an AMR to a continuing resolution (Roundtable 1992, 73). Murray (in Roundtable 1992) also argues that a proposal has a better chance of success if made as an AMR instead of a substitute amendment: "I would take the motion to recommit because it has an element of last minute change and fluidity and sensing what is happening on the floor and picking up a few votes here or there or having a chance to win. It is better than having a substitute laid out for several days to be picked apart and to be criticized and to be demolished much more effectively" (40).

It is important at this point to understand that in describing AMRs as the last move in the amending process, we mean only that this is generally what turns out to be the case. AMRs would obviously be an invaluable asset for the minority party (or majority party, or any other subset of the House membership possessing the right to make them) if they were truly final, take-it-or-leave-it proposals. If an AMR were indeed the last possible amendment that could be considered, no counteramendment could be offered to undermine the coalition supporting it (see Weingast 1991). Anyone making an AMR would have proposal power analogous to that of the "setter" in Romer and Rosenthal's (1978) influential model.

In Congress, however, there never really is a last move. In the specific case of the AMR, majority-party leaders can take significant protective measures against a potentially successful AMR sponsored by the minority party. They can counter with their own AMR, which is in order if they succeed in defeating the call for the previous question on the minority-sponsored AMR. It is rare for this to happen, but it has happened (Roberts 2003, 6–7). Even if an AMR does pass over the objections of the majority leadership, other options remain. The House can either table or vote down the resultant final version of the bill. In such a case the impact of the minority's AMR would be limited to that of a killer amendment. Alternatively, the House can pass the amended bill and trust that the Senate will amend it further, in which case the House majority's conferees can see to it that the offending AMR is not included in the conference report (chapter 21 in this volume).

What we have so far are only arguments and anecdotes. The previous discussion, however, suggests a simple hypothesis. Let us express it in terms of the null hypothesis that there is no difference between an AMR and an ordinary amendment made in the Committee of the Whole, i.e., that they are perfect substitutes. Correspondingly, the counterhypothesis is that AMRs are more valuable than amendments, presumably because they are offered at the end of the amendment process.

One way to gauge the relative merits of these hypotheses is to examine the frequency with which AMRs are offered under different types of amendment rules. Under closed rules or highly restrictive rules AMRs may be the only game in town for the minority party. Assuming that AMRs are not similarly restricted, bills considered under restrictive amendment rules should receive AMRs at a relatively high frequency. For bills considered under open amendment rules, the null hypothesis implies that we should observe a lower frequency of AMRs. If an AMR is no more valuable than an ordinary amendment and there are no restrictions on amendments, then there is no point to waiting around to the end to offer an AMR. Why not just offer an amendment?

The counterhypothesis, that AMRs are more valuable because of the advantage that accrues from moving last, implies that there should be relatively more AMRs offered in unrestrictive, or open-rule, environments. It is in such settings, wherein previously made and approved amendments can significantly alter a bill, that moving last becomes particularly valuable. If this is the case, the consideration of legislation under open rules should lead to a higher frequency of AMRs. Or more weakly, if making an AMR is a particularly useful parliamentary prerogative, we should observe the minority exercising that right whenever and wherever they can, regardless of whether the rule governing consideration of a bill is restrictive or unrestrictive.

To examine these hypotheses, we calculated the frequency of AMRs offered under different rules governing bill consideration in the 103rd to 107th Congresses, from 1993 to 2002. The frequency of AMRs is strongly correlated with the nature of the rule governing consideration of the bills. Open-rule bills account for a large majority of all amendments offered (Kiewiet 1998), but they rarely encounter minority efforts to amend them via an AMR. Pooling across these Congresses, we find that only about 8 percent of open-rule bills and 17 percent of modified-open-rule bills encountered an AMR. In stark contrast, bills taken up under closed or modified closed rules are usually challenged by an AMR: 44 percent of the bills considered under a modified closed rule against 35 percent of the bills considered under a closed rule received an AMR. The differences in the AMR rate between open and modified closed rules, open and closed rules, and modified open and modified closed rules are generally significant within each Congress. For the 103rd through 107th collectively, those differences are all statistically significant.[1] These data reinforce the findings of Cox, Den Hartog, and McCubbins (chapter 19 in this volume) that the minority party forgoes most opportunities it would seem to have to offer this motion.

These findings imply that under general circumstances the ability to make an amendment at the last stage of the game is not, in and of itself, that big a deal—when the minority is free to offer amendments during consideration of a bill in the Committee of the Whole, they rarely propose an AMR. We can refine these findings, however, by exploiting a natural experiment created by a rule change in 1995.

Before and After 1995

Before the Republican takeover of the House in 1995, the Rules Committee sometimes restricted minority-sponsored AMRs and in some cases proscribed them entirely (Wolfensberger in Roundtable 1992). On taking control of the House in 1995, the Republicans strengthened the minority party's right to offer AMRs by prohibiting the Rules Committee from interfering with that motion, ostensibly guaranteeing that the Rules Committee would not have the authority to impose undue restrictions. While subject to the same restrictions that the standing House rules place on amendments in general (e.g., germaneness), an AMR cannot otherwise be prohibited.

This change provides a natural experiment to test the balance of power in the House of Representatives, because we can compare behavior between two distinct eras:

Pre-1995: Minority Republicans can offer amendments (subject to standing and special rules) and motions to recommit (subject to standing and special rules).

Post-1995: Minority Democrats can offer amendments (subject to standing and special rules) and motions to recommit (subject only to standing rules).

This leads to two natural hypotheses that we can test:

Hypothesis 1: In both eras, an AMR should be more valuable to the minority than an ordinary amendment (because an AMR is a take-it-or-leave-it offer).

Hypothesis 2: In the post-1995 era, an AMR should be even more valuable (because an AMR is subject to fewer restrictions than an amendment).

These hypotheses share a key underlying assumption: a party is rational and primarily interested in policy. This means that the minority party prefers passing an amendment (that they vote for) rather than proposing an amendment that fails. Hence, we compare the rate with which the minority can pass AMRs and can pass amendments that they like and the majority dislikes.

Our data on AMRs is drawn from David Rohde's roll-call dataset, supplemented by data from the Library of Congress (Thomas, http://thomas.loc.gov/) for recent Congresses. Being based on roll-call votes, the data do not include AMRs decided by voice vote or some other method. They also do not include motions to recommit made with respect to conference reports,

TABLE 20.1
Percentage of offered amendments that pass

Congress	Minority challenge amendments	Motions to recommit
93rd–98th (1973–1984)	16%	15%
99th–103rd (1985–1994)	11%	9%
104th–107th (1995–2002)	19%	2%

which are very common. The general form of the motion in such cases is that the conference report be recommitted and that the House delegation be instructed to insist on specific provisions of the House bill. We deem this language not to be amendatory and so do not include these motions in our analysis.[2]

For amendments, we follow Kiewiet (1998) and define a minority-party challenge amendment as one where at least two-thirds of the minority votes for an amendment while at least two-thirds of the majority votes against it. We use Kiewiet's data for 1973–1988 and data from Thomas for 1990–2002.[3] Table 20.1 summarizes the success rates.

Hypothesis 1 is thus not supported by these data. In the pre-1995 era, AMRs are as likely to pass as minority challenge amendments, supporting the null hypothesis of no difference. This suggests that the minority Republicans were proposing similar amendments through both channels and thus that they did not view the AMR as a much more valuable tool for changing policy. Since the AMR is essentially a take-it-or-leave-it offer, this suggests that the minority party is not solely policy motivated. It may well be that the minority uses the AMR as their "one chance to express fully their views" (in the words of Speaker Gillett) without attempting to directly influence policy by amending the bill with the AMR.

Hypothesis 2 is soundly rejected by this data, as is the null hypothesis of no difference. In the post-1995 era, AMRs are far less likely to pass than minority challenges posed in the form of ordinary amendments. This suggests that the minority Democrats were not using the AMR to change policy, choosing instead to use the usual amendment process. It is possible that the Republican and Democratic parties have fundamentally different preferences over parliamentary activity, leading the Democrats to always use the AMR for posturing while the Republicans occasionally use it like an amendment. Without an explanation of why the parties differ in this way, however, perhaps we should reassess hypothesis 2. If special rules were actually less restrictive than the standing rules, then the prediction would be reversed. Further, in recent Congresses, special rules have often included waivers of standing rules, permitting amendments that would not be acceptable otherwise.

Another explanation for the failure of hypothesis 2 can be derived from the notion of conditional-party government. It is possible that the preferences of the members of the post-1995 Republican majorities in the House have been extremely homogeneous, and thus they have acted very cohesively and have been very successful in turning away opposition to their legislation. It is also possible that the Republicans since 1995 have been unusually good at crafting legislation that anticipates and preempts potential opposition amendments. To drive down the success rate of minority-sponsored AMRs to zero, however, would hardly seem like an optimal strategy for the majority party. And if this were the case, why were they far less successful in warding off normal amendments backed by the minority? It would seem more fruitful to pursue an aggressive policy agenda and suffer a defeat on an AMR from time to time than to pursue an agenda that is so moderate that it is virtually inoculated against successful AMRs.

To possibly gain some additional insight into how the successful AMR became an endangered species, it might be useful to consider the three that did pass during this 9-year period. They are as follows:

The Communications Act of 1995 (HR 1555). The instructions in this AMR called for creation of a television rating system and required installation of the V-chip in all new televisions to filter shows on the basis of the rating system. These measures had originally been proposed as an amendment but were defeated by a substitute that merely called for further study of the issue. The AMR reproposed the amendment while leaving the substitute in place. It carried, 224–199, with 19 percent of the majority Republicans in favor along with 92 percent of the minority Democrats. The bill passed immediately afterwards, with the backing of 92 percent of the Democrats and 50 percent of the Republicans.

The Conservation and Reinvestment Act of 2000 (HR 701). The amendatory instructions prohibited any cuts in the benefit obligations of Social Security and Medicare. The motion carried with the support of 99 percent of the Republicans and all of the Democrats. The bill moved from the House and was placed on the Senate calendar, but never actually made it to the Senate floor before adjournment.

The Homeland Security Act of 2002 (HR 5005). The instructions in the AMR prohibited "enter[ing] into any contract with a subsidiary of a publicly traded corporation if the corporation is incorporated in a tax haven country but the United States is the principal market for the public trading of the corporation's stock." The motion passed with 50 percent support from the majority Republicans and 100 percent support from the minority Democrats, and the bill as a whole passed immediately afterwards.

By our reading, the second of these AMRs permitted members to go on the record as steadfastly opposing nefarious attacks on Social Security and Medicare and was of no consequence as far as policy was concerned. The first was of some policy consequence, as was the third, but it is obvious that the rules changes guaranteeing the minority party's right to propose AMRs have not been particularly injurious to the Republican policy agenda.

These minor amendments, moreover, were clearly not substantial alternative policies that one would normally associate with the standard minority substitute for a pending bill. More specifically, if a minority-sponsored AMR is to prevail, it must attract a requisite number of defectors from the majority party. For that reason those crafting the AMR, or any other amendment, must find weak spots in the majority-party coalition, as they were apparently able to do with the V-chip and anti-tax-haven measures previously described.

Conclusion

The present-day AMR is the product of two centuries of evolution in legislative practice in the House of Representatives. Viewed by Jefferson as an emergency mechanism for correcting problems that should have been detected and corrected earlier, it is now ensconced as a routine stage in the legislative process, wherein the minority party is provided a final chance to amend the bill pending before the House. The frequency with which AMRs are offered and the rates at which they are approved have been affected by recent changes in House rules, but not in the way one would expect. When the right to make AMRs was ostensibly restored in 1995, the frequency with which they were offered did increase. Success rates, however, fell precipitously. Between 1995 and 2003 only 3 of the 192 AMRs subjected to a roll-call vote secured passage in the House. In contrast, minority challenge amendments in the Committee of the Whole, which we consider to be similar to AMRs, continue to be reasonably successful. Future research on amendments, amendment rules, and AMRs we hope will help explain these puzzling empirical patterns.

Chapter 21

An Evolving End Game: Partisan Collusion in Conference Committees, 1953–2003

ROBERT PARKS VAN HOUWELING

Since the 1970s, members of the House and Senate have increasingly relied on political party organizations to perform important legislative tasks. The causes and consequences of this trend have been at the center of academic debates on the U.S. Congress for a decade. Some view this increasing activity as an outgrowth of changing electoral forces, albeit one with substantial policy consequences. To varying degrees, these scholars emphasize the role of party leaders as occasional disciplinarians of their rank and file (e.g., Rohde 1991; Aldrich 1995; Cox and McCubbins 1993; Deckard [Sinclair] 1995). Others have argued that the renewed prominence of parties and their leaders is largely window dressing and that party discipline that leads to substantially different policy than we would expect in its absence is largely a myth (e.g., Krehbiel 1993). Elsewhere, I offer an account that asserts parties are a consequential feature of the modern legislative process, but I place a strong emphasis on their role as enablers rather than disciplinarians (Van Houweling 2003).

Underlying my argument is a claim that legislators have an incentive to cede agenda and organizational power to party organizations when their personal policy preferences are more extreme than those they wish to reveal to their constituents. When vested with procedural control, parties are able to structure legislative agendas that produce policies in accord with their members' extreme preferences, while allowing the members to conceal those preferences from moderate constituencies. This logic suggests that growth in party-related activity in Congress over the past few decades is due to a widening gulf between the personal preferences of members of Congress—which I argue have become more bipolar, extreme, and cohesive since the 1960s—and the still moderate preferences of their constituents. In short, legislators have increased their reliance on political parties as it has become more difficult for them simultaneously to achieve the policy outcomes they desire *and* remain in office.

I have argued that policy consequences and voting patterns associated with agenda restrictions in the modern House of Representatives are consistent with what we should expect if its members increasingly prefer policies that are more extreme than those favored by the majority of voters in their districts (Van Houweling 2003). In doing so, I developed a model of special rules in the House that is unique in allowing for a divergence between public and private preferences. The practical implication of the model is that under specifiable circumstances legislation that reaches the House agenda under restrictive rules tends to generate outcomes nearer the House's ideological poles.

However, these House-specific findings leave the story incomplete. The majority party in the Senate does not have access to similar procedures that would allow it to prevent consideration of unsavory policy alternatives. Thus, even when senators in the majority party are unified in their personal support for an extreme policy, they often cannot avoid considering—and have little choice but to approve—moderate alternatives favored by their constituents. The conference-committee process that the House and Senate can employ to resolve their legislative differences offers a solution to senators in this predicament. When the two chambers sort out legislative particulars in conference, the resulting agreement returns to both chambers in an unamendable form. This allows majority-party senators to benefit from cover typically unavailable on the Senate floor. They can freely vote for constituency-pleasing amendments when they first pass legislation—trusting that their actions will be reversed in conference. The alternative procedure for sorting out House-Senate differences is passing amendments between the chambers. It does not afford cover to senators because under this procedure a measure is amendable in the Senate at every step along the way. With these institutional details in mind, I build on my model of rule choice in the House to generate expectations about when the House and Senate will choose conference to resolve legislative differences and what policy consequences will follow. I describe three broad implications of this extended model and evaluate them using data on conference outcomes between the 83rd and 107th Congresses.

I. An Example and Institutional Details

The passage of President Bush's tax cut in the House of Representatives serves to illustrate the intuition behind the model. For the purposes of this example, assume that every House Republican had a personal preference for a tax cut nearly as large as the one proposed by President Bush. Most evidence suggests that their constituents did not agree. A poll conducted the weekend before the vote on the first key measure indicated that only a bare majority of Americans preferred Bush's proposed tax cut to no tax cut at all. At the same time, the public's preference for the limited Democratic plan over the cut advocated by the president was not overwhelming, hovering around 55 percent.[1] In sum, it appears that the weight of opinion rested somewhere between the Republican and Democratic alternatives, allowing room for compromise that never materialized.

The first element of Bush's tax-cut package passed the House intact on March 8, 2001, under restrictive amendment procedures. In the days preceding the vote, Republican leaders indicated they were unlikely to propose a rule for consideration of the bill that would allow alternatives to the president's plan. In the end they relented, proposing a special rule that permitted a prespecified Democratic amendment with tax cuts weighted toward lower-income taxpayers and with an estimated cost half that of the Bush proposal. The rule did not allow any amendments in the substantial middle ground, however. House Republicans voted unanimously for the rule and unanimously for the Bush proposal over the Democratic alternative. By voting to place the middle ground off limits, Republicans from moderate districts were able to vote for the level of tax relief they preferred without revealing to their constituents that they actually favored the deep cut over more moderate alternatives.

Their rhetoric was consistent with this strategy—many claimed to have voted for the Bush bill because of the lack of a better alternative due to procedural limitations.[2] The president and the House leadership were common scapegoats for Republicans from moderate districts who uniformly supported the legislative procedures they criticized. Yet if they had truly wanted a more moderate alternative, they could have rejected or amended the legislative procedures. They chose not to do so.

There are explanations for the outwardly contradictory behavior of Republican representatives from moderate districts other than their personal desire for a large tax cut. The legislators often insinuate that they truly prefer a moderate alternative, but their party leaves them and other representatives with no choice but to vote against their better judgment. Theories of party organization that see legislators as bound together in pursuit of a collective good because of their similar electoral bases or their shared electoral fates (Cox and McCubbins 1993) offer a rationale for such behavior. In application to this case, the claim would be that the collective electoral interest of Republican lawmakers was served by the exercise of discipline over representatives from moderate districts. Enacting the more conservative policy enhanced the party's reputation and the prospective electoral success of its members. Moreover, representatives from moderate districts recognized this and willingly gave the party tools to enforce discipline. This perspective is certainly plausible but raises a question: how do majority-party members from moderate districts benefit from a party with a conservative reputation? There are answers to this question involving primary electorates, brand name distinctions, and voters who use informational shortcuts. But the more straightforward explanation is the one I focus on here: "moderate" Republican lawmakers preferred a large tax cut and agreed to the restrictive amendment procedure because it saved them from having to violate this preference by voting for moderate amendments favored by the majority of their constituents.

Rejoining the narrative, we turn to the Senate, which received the legislation from the House and passed a compromise that was around 15 percent smaller than the measure adopted by the House, seemingly blunting the efforts of the House majority. While Republican leaders in the Senate expressed displeasure with this compromise, they were unable to secure the votes of Republican senators from relatively liberal states on key amendments offered by moderate Democrats. Even if Republican senators from liberal states thought a large tax cut was the best policy, as we are assuming for this example, they did not buck their constituents on amendments that trimmed the cut. Conference was their only hope for salvation; if things went well, it would produce a bill with a bigger tax cut than they could safely vote for in the Senate the first time around.

Conference delivered. While the nominal figures hewed to the Senate line, creative accounting allowed the president to achieve nearly all of the cuts he desired. Most notable was a provision that key elements of the tax cut expired 1 year before the end of the 10-year budget window to keep its apparent costs down—a ruse so successful that it has now become standard operating procedure. Summing up the 2001 tax cut in an article about the remarkable effectiveness of Ways and Means chair Bill Thomas (R-Calif.), *CQ Weekly Report* noted, "It is hard to argue with results. Soon after taking over the chairmanship in 2001, Thomas helped deliver Bush's first tax-cut, a 10-Year plan that slashed revenue by $1.35 trillion principally by lowering individual income tax rates (PL 107-16). To fit almost all of Bush's proposed $1.6 trillion in cuts under a compromise ceiling, Thomas *joined* with Senate tax writers to limit cost by phasing in tax breaks" (emphasis added).[3]

When this conference report returned to the Senate in unamendable form, senators faced the same up or down vote that their copartisans in the House used for cover on initial passage. In response to any doubting constituents, they were able to respond that it was this cut or no cut and the economy needed a jump start. And in a bonus unavailable to their counterparts in the House, they were even able to say, Of course we all preferred a more moderate cut and I voted for it when I had the choice. Whether this was an intentional strategy with regard to the tax cut is an open question; whether there is evidence that legislators use it more regularly is a question I begin to explore here after considering the technical aspects of resolving differences between the chambers.

METHODS FOR RESOLVING DIFFERENCES

There are three ways to reconcile differences between the House and Senate and send legislation to the president for his signature. When there is disagreement, the chamber that acts second either passes a set of specific amendments to the bill passed by the first chamber or strikes everything but the enacting clause of the bill and replaces it with a substitute. In both of these cases, the chamber that acted first has three options: (1) insist on its bill, formally disagree with the amendment of the second chamber, and by majority vote proceed to conference; (2) concur in the amendment of the second chamber but offer a further amendment of its own; and (3) concur in the amendment of the second chamber, end the process, and send the bill to the president.

If the chambers formally disagree and choose conference, then each body appoints a set of conferees. It is typical practice in the House for the Speaker to appoint conferees with the advice of the chair of the committees that considered the legislation. In the Senate the conferees are usually appointed by unanimous consent on the advice of the bill managers, although the Senate can vote to elect conferees on an individual basis by majority vote if it chooses. In any case, by both Senate and House rules, the majority party holds a majority on conference delegations just as it does on substantive standing committees. In conference, each chamber has a vote (dictated by majority rule within its delegation) on disputed provisions, and the two chambers must agree on every provision they include in a conference agreement. Conferees are supposed to decide issues within the scope of the differences between the bills of the two chambers, although they have some flexibility on this when the legislation is qualitative instead of quantitative. Each chamber can instruct its conferees by majority vote. Only the chamber that considers the conference agreement first can move to recommit a bill to conference with or without instructions. However, instructions to conferees are not binding and are not grounds for a point of order in either chamber. As I have already mentioned, in both chambers conference reports are considered under what amounts to a closed rule with no amendments in order. While this is not an unusual procedure for the House, it is rare for the Senate and can offer the senators the type of restricted choices that closed and modified closed rules regularly create in the House (Bach 1996). In the context of the preceding tax-cut example, this procedure offered senators the protection from moderate amendments that they lacked when they initially considered the legislation.

Passing amendments between the chambers does not offer the same protection to senators. When the chambers disagree concerning legislation they have both passed, the chamber that acted first can choose to amend the bill passed by the chamber that acted second and send it back to the other side of the Capitol. Only two degrees of amending are allowed in this procedure, so the second chamber has the choice of agreeing and ending the process or sending one more amendment back to the first chamber. If agreement is still not reached at this point (or at any other stage of the process), either chamber can move to the stage of formal disagreement and request a conference (Bach 1996; Saturno 1999a, 1999b).

Amendments from the other chamber are considered under different rules in the House and Senate. In the House, the deck is stacked in favor of conference. Motions to disagree with the Senate amendment and go to conference are privileged over motions to consider or amend the Senate amendment. To get around this rule, the House managers can either ask for unanimous consent to consider the Senate amendment or the amendment can be considered under suspension of the rules or under a special rule. However, each of these procedures requires at least a majority; thus a majority will always have an opportunity to move to conference without ever entertaining the Senate amendment or being forced to explicitly cast a vote against it. If the House chooses to entertain a Senate amendment under a special rule, it usually restricts the alternatives available to its members (Saturno 1999a). If we apply these procedures to the preceding tax-cut example, we see that they allowed Republican members of the House from liberal districts to avoid an explicit vote against the moderate alternative that the Senate passed back to the House. The procedures instead allowed a quick move to conference.

In the Senate the procedure is more open and favors passing amendments between the chambers. Motions to consider House amendments are privileged and decided without debate. A motion to concur with the House amendments is advantaged, followed by a motion to concur and add an amendment, followed by a motion to reach the stage of disagreement and request a conference. Moreover, when the Senate debates whether to agree to an amendment passed from the House, amendments are always in order unless barred by a unanimous consent agreement (Saturno 1999a). To return to the tax-cut example one last time, this means that if the Senate had tried to reach consensus with the House by passing amendments between the chambers, Republican senators from liberal states would likely have faced additional votes on amendments to moderate the size of the cut. Consequently, they would have once again found themselves unable to secure the larger cut they preferred without explicitly violating the wishes of their constituents. In sum, passing amendments between the chambers would have provided little cover and they selected conference instead.

II. Returning to the Model for Guidance

When integrated into the model of rule choice that I have previously developed (Van Houweling 2003), these institutional details generate hypotheses about when the House and Senate will choose to resolve their difference through conference and how legislation will be altered in conference. The basic intuitions behind these hypotheses are seen by reexamining the prototypical situation in which the House majority proposes and adopts a restrictive rule to manipulate policy outcomes. To this end, the following example compares the House and Senate when they are controlled by the same party, and the public and private preferences of members of that party are arrayed such that the House will use a restrictive rule.

My original one-dimensional model of the House incorporates two players: one legislator with the power to propose policies and restrictive rules and a median legislator with the power to accede to the rules or reject them, offer amendments, and vote on final passage. The model allows legislators to have different personal preferences than those they wish to reveal publicly. The model is premised on the assumption that votes on final passage and amendments are visible to voters but votes on rule choice are not. This enables the median legislator to dodge responsibility when he or she supports an agenda that does not include the policy constituents prefer.

In the top panel of figure 21.1, the median legislator in the House is denoted by *H*, and a House bill proposer is denoted by *HP*. We can simplify

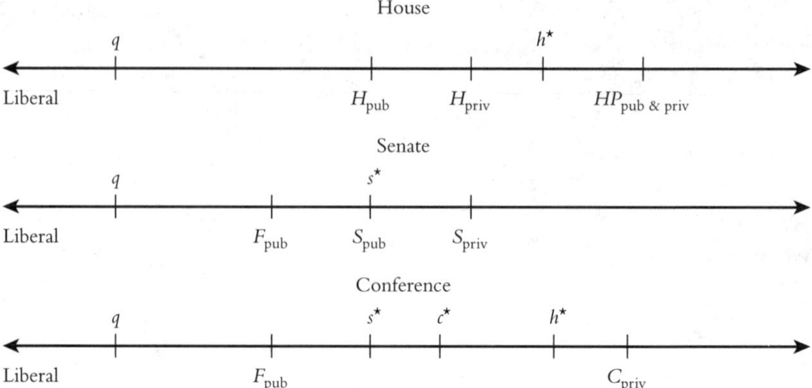

Figure 21.1 Models of legislative outcomes in the U.S. House, Senate, and conference committee

the treatment of the House by focusing on the median voter because voting is by simple majority rule. I usually refer to the proposer as a party leader when discussing applications of the model, but one could also think of the proposer as the median member of a committee, a committee chair, or a proposer selected in some other manner. In any case, the proposer is an exogenously specified member of the legislature.

Legislators' preferences have two components. The first component is legislators' electorally induced preferences, denoted as HP_{pub} and H_{pub} in the model. I assume that the primary goal of legislators is to win reelection. Voter behavior is not explicitly incorporated in the model. However, the model is based on the assumption that voters have single-peaked policy preferences in a unidimensional policy space. They vote for the incumbent unless a challenger can point to a specific instance in which the incumbent violated their preferences. There are only two actions in the model that can reveal legislators' preferences to challengers and voters. The first is votes on paired alternatives. To be reelected, legislators must always vote for the alternative that the median voter in their district prefers. The second is proposals the legislator makes. The second component of legislators' preferences is their personal policy desires, denoted as HP_{priv} and H_{priv} in the model. These are again single-peaked preferences in a unidimensional policy space, and the peaks can be located anywhere in the policy space. As I apply the model to the Senate and conference proceedings, I will add necessary players and specify their relevant ideal points. I begin by offering an example for the House.

First, consider the legislative process in the House (top panel) given the disparity between the median legislator's public and private ideal points, H_{pub} and H_{priv}, the extreme ideal point of the proposer, $HP_{pub\&priv}$, and a status quo policy located at q. This is a case in which the proposer will offer a closed rule, protecting a policy like h^* that diverges substantially from the median legislator's public ideal point. The median legislator will accept this rule and approve the new policy as long as he or she privately prefers it to the open-rule-policy equilibrium, which by assumption is at the legislator's public ideal point, H_{pub}. This is possible because his or her rule vote and its implications are not visible to constituents. Thus, in the House, the equilibrium outcome is h^*.

The equilibrium outcome in the Senate is different given a median legislator with the same preferences, S_{pub} and S_{priv}, and the same status quo policy. It is located at s^*, the public ideal point of the median member. While this pivotal senator would like to support a more extreme outcome, he or she cannot diverge from a public ideal point on final passage votes by assumption of the model. The proposer is not pictured in the Senate panel because that person plays no pivotal role. However, the public ideal point of the minority filibuster pivot, F_{pub},, is added and will become a limiting factor for the conferees. On passage the minority filibuster pivot does not filibuster because he or she publicly prefers s^* to q.[4]

These outcomes, s^* and h^*, leave the House and Senate with differences to resolve. Without the conference procedure, the resolution would proceed as follows. After the Senate passed its bill, which it would typically accomplish by amending the House bill, it would message the House with the modified measure. The House would then vote on whether to accept the Senate amendment to its bill. The amendment, aligned with the public ideal point of the median representative, H_{pub}, would succeed and the agenda manipulation at initial passage in the House would come to naught.

A conference like the one displayed in the third panel of figure 21.1 can prevent this outcome. The conference would be called by request of the House after receiving the Senate amendment and the Senate assenting to this request. Conference proceedings are difficult to follow; therefore, I assume the median private ideal points of each chamber's delegation are pivotal in determining the conference outcome.[5] House and Senate rules dictate that these will be members of the majority party, and I have assumed for the purposes of this example that they will have identical and relatively extreme private ideal points, denoted C_{priv}. The only limit placed on them by the chamber rules is that they must select a policy within the scope of the differences of those approved by the two chambers.[6] However, they can also be constrained by pivotal actors on the floor of either chamber, as is the case in the example illustrated. The conferees would like to adopt a proposal at the limit of the scope of the differences and identical to the one passed in the House. However, the public ideal point of the filibuster pivot in the Senate, F_{pub}, dictates that, without fear of electoral consequence, he or she would reject such a policy.[7] Thus, the conferees would settle for c^*, the reflection of the status quo policy, q, over F_{pub}. This proposal would then return to both chambers unamendable and pass with a comfortable majority. The final consequence is a policy shifted away from the one that would have resulted without a conference, but because of the supermajoritarian rules of the Senate, less extreme than the one the House was able to pass initially. In the following I evaluate two implications for conference procedures and outcomes over time.

III. The Evolution of Conferences between the 83rd and 107th Congresses

In this section, I examine how conference politics have changed since the early 1950s. My theoretical account implies that both the nature of conference disputes and the consequences of conference agreements for parties and chambers should have evolved substantially over the period. In particular, the partisan use of conference committees should have become more common as legislators have developed more polarized and extreme personal policy preferences over the past three decades. To refresh, I contend that the majority party in the House increasingly uses agenda restrictions to allow its members to secure the extreme policies they personally desire without having to explicitly reject policies favored by their more moderate constituents (Van Houweling 2003). The majority party in the Senate cannot rely on agenda restrictions at initial passage and presumably settles for more moderate policies even when its members might personally prefer more extreme ones. Thus, the frequent use of agenda restrictions in the House should create substantial and growing discrepancies between the measures the two chambers initially pass. One might expect this to provide fodder for traditional interchamber disputes with each chamber defending its position. Instead, I anticipate it will cause cross-chamber partisan cleavages in conference committees. My contention is that in recent Congresses majority-party members from each chamber tend to collude to produce conference agreements that tilt in the direction of the majority party—agreements that are protected from amendments that watered down the versions initially passed by the Senate.

To evaluate the plausibility of the account, I gathered data on conferences on "important legislative enactments," as identified by David Mayhew (1991), in odd-numbered Congresses between the 83rd and 103rd and all Congresses between the 104th and 107th.[8]

A. USE OF CONFERENCE AND CHAMBER CONTROL

My first expectation is that the chambers will be more likely to resolve disputes on important legislation through conference if they are controlled by the same party. When they are not, the incentive for the majority parties in each chamber to use conference is weakened because they will not be able to use conference to collude in protecting their private policy preference and repair the damage done to legislation during floor consideration in either chamber, most likely as a result of the Senate's open procedures.

Across these fifteen Congresses, a tendency for split chamber control leads to a reduced reliance on conference, with the divided Congresses in this era accounting for three of the four lowest conference usage rates in the entire sample. Over the entire period when there is divided control of the chambers, 65 percent of significant legislation is resolved with conference. When there is unified control of the chambers this fraction increases to 81 percent.[9] If one focuses on the 10 post-reform Congresses in the sample, the tendency strengthens: 87 percent of significant legislation was resolved with conference when chamber control was unified, while still only 65 percent was resolved with conference when chamber control was divided.[10] This analysis accords with my more general expectation that incentives for partisan collusion in conference have increased in recent Congresses owing to a growing divergence in the private policy preferences of legislators. These findings are, however, somewhat surprising given more traditional understandings of the role of conference committees in resolving interchamber disputes.

Typical accounts of conference politics might instead lead one to expect a positive relationship between divided chamber control and the use of conference (for a variety of accounts, see Ferejohn 1975; Strom and Rundquist 1977; Van Beek 1995; Vogler 1970). For example, on the view that conferences are tools for solving complex legislative differences, divided chamber control would be more likely to generate the divergent initial legislative outcomes that would dictate use of the procedure. The perspective that conference committees serve the informational interests of pivotal voters in both chambers (Krehbiel 1991) would also generate hypotheses inconsistent with my findings. In short, when the chambers are controlled by different parties, conference committees are more likely to be composed of two chamber delegations with heterogeneous preferences. By the tenets of informational theory, this should increase their propensity to reveal information to the chambers and lead the chambers to more readily grant them the de facto closed rules their agreements automatically receive.

To be clear, the findings presented do not provide evidence that conferences are not frequently employed to allow legislator-experts to resolve complex differences in ways that satisfy both chambers. The regular reliance on conference committees even during periods of divided chamber control may in fact be due to these advantages. However, the increased use of conference to resolve differences over important legislation during periods of unified party control is consistent with the view that conferences are an increasingly common venue for majority-party collusion.

B. PREVALENCE OF PARTISAN DISPUTES IN CONFERENCE

My second expectation is that conference-committee deliberations will be increasingly defined by partisan conflict. This follows from my argument that members of the House and Senate have acquired increasingly extreme and polarized personal preferences that they attempt to conceal from more moderate constituencies through agenda restrictions. When they utilize conference committees to this end, reporters should be more likely to cast the committees' deliberations and eventual agreements in partisan terms. To assess this expectation, I relied on the content analysis previously described and displayed in figure 21.2.

Over the past five decades, *CQ Weekly Report* postconference articles have become increasingly likely to mention partisan disputes and identify partisan winners and losers. In the pre-reform era, partisan cleavages were either nonexistent or not apparent to the reporters in around 80 percent of conferences on important enactments. Their prevalence increased consistently through the post-reform era to the point that reporters identified an interparty dispute in almost every conference in the 104th, 105th, and 106th Congresses. Of course, this overwhelming trend could simply be a by-product of the partisan tenor of recent Congresses, regardless of whether parties are manipulating conference proceedings. As the parties have taken ever more distinctive positions, it has become natural for reporters and others to describe debates and legislative alternatives in partisan terms. Nevertheless, it is a strong trend consistent with my expectations.

C. PARTISAN OUTCOMES

In this section, I examine how the majority party fares in conferences with clear interparty disputes. My general expectation is that, when the same

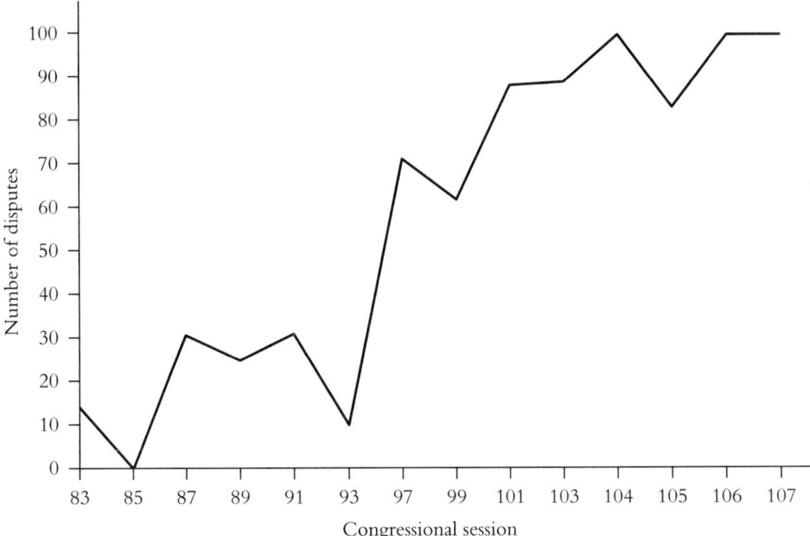

Figure 21.2 Reported partisan disputes in conference on significant legislation

NOTE: The number of pieces of significant legislation resolved by conference per Congress are as follows: 83rd, 7; 85th, 5; 87th, 13; 89th, 16; 91st, 16; 93rd, 20; 97th, 7; 99th, 8; 101st, 8; 103rd, 9; 104th, 12; 105th, 6; 106th, 6; 107th, 9.

SOURCE: Significant legislation identified by David Mayhew. Conference data gathered from CQ Weekly Report for the 83rd–91st Congresses and from http://thomas.loc.gov for the 93rd–107th Congresses.

party controls both chambers, conference agreements will tend to favor that party. To evaluate this hypothesis, I examine only legislation on which reporters identified a clear partisan dispute. Focusing on issues for which a central disagreement is cast in partisan terms helps minimize the possibility that any trends are due simply to reporters more easily identifying such disputes because party positions have become more distinctive on a range of issues.

Table 21.1 reports the cross-tabulation of the chamber control and the outcome of conferences for the entire sample of conferences where a partisan dispute was identified.

There are two findings to note. First, when either party controls both chambers of Congress, they clearly win in a majority of conferences and their opposition almost never wins. Second, when chamber control is split, most conferences do not lead to an outcome that is cast as a partisan victory.

TABLE 21.1
Congressional majority versus reported outcome

		CONFERENCE WINNER			
		Democrat	Mixed/unclear	GOP	*N*
Majority party	Democrat	60%	40%	0%	30
	Mixed	11%	68%	21%	19
	GOP	13%	38%	50%	24
	N	23	34	16	73

NOTE: The χ^2 for the cross-tabulation is 31.00, Pr = 0.000. The table includes all conferences in which a partisan dispute was mentioned.

One might anticipate such a finding given the numerical advantage chamber majorities hold in conference voting. As the frequency of mixed or unclear outcomes attests, however, this advantage does not make victory a foregone conclusion.

IV. Conclusion

This chapter applies a theoretical account of the partisan use of legislative procedure in the House that I develop elsewhere (Van Houweling 2003) to the resolution of interchamber differences. I present evidence about conferences on important enactments between the 83rd and 107th Congresses that is consistent with my expectation that bicameral congressional majorities use the conference procedure to provide cover for majority senators who favor extreme policies but were unable to vote for them under the bright light of the Senate's open floor procedures. To summarize, the axis of conference dispute is increasingly between the parties, and bicameral majorities are increasingly likely to win these disputes. Moreover, I find that the chambers are less likely to choose conference in the absence of a bicameral majority, when the procedure does not present an opportunity for partisan manipulation.

Chapter 22

Bicameral Resolution in Congress, 1863–2002

ELIZABETH RYBICKI

Introduction

The congressional conference committee is a remarkably successful institution. The House and Senate almost always disagree over the terms of major policy proposals; some argue such conflict is a necessary element of a bicameral system designed to promote conservative lawmaking and stability of outcomes (Hammond and Miller 1987; Riker 1992). Yet nearly all measures that pass both chambers arrive at the president's desk. Why have the House and Senate been so successful in resolving their differences? Are there conditions under which the House and Senate are less likely to reach agreement?

In this chapter I address these questions in three ways. I begin by tracing the development of selected bicameral resolution mechanisms to demonstrate that the House and Senate created and adapted very flexible procedures that encourage agreement rather than stalemate. Second, I argue that the long record of successful resolution of differences between the chambers is due partially to legislators' decisions about how best to expend their time and resources. In the final section, I discuss electoral and institutional conditions expected to affect the likelihood that the chambers will successfully resolve their differences. Flexible bicameral resolution procedures and knowledge about preference arrangements do not guarantee that measures will clear the legislative branch; each Congress, a small proportion of measures die because the chambers failed to resolve their differences. I present new longitudinal data on the failure of chambers to resolve their differences since 1877. At this stage of my analysis, I can discuss only possible causes of the variation in the rates of successful bicameral resolution over time. My only conclusion is that the effects of institutional change and electoral dynamics deserve further exploration.

Institutional Effects on Bicameral Negotiations

When the House and Senate disagree over the terms of a policy proposal, they often enter what economists term a distributional bargaining situation, where a gain for one side means a loss for the other. Although both sides may believe that a compromise policy exists that could gain sufficient support in both chambers, they do not know exactly what the other chamber will accept. Legislators naturally attempt to reach a compromise as close as possible to their version of the legislation. To reach an agreement, concessions must be made, but each side will concede only when it believes the other will not (Schelling 1956). Each chamber has an incentive to misrepresent to the other what it is willing to accept; in other words, both sides try to convince the other that it must concede or the bill will be lost.

Therefore, despite over 90 percent of bills and joint resolutions that pass both chambers making their way to the president's desk, the threat of failure is an inherent element of bicameral negotiations. In conference committee, House managers tell Senate managers that their proposed compromise will never pass the House; Senate managers apologetically explain to House managers that a threatened filibuster means a favored provision cannot be cut. Conferees from both the House and the Senate return to their respective parent chambers and regretfully report that they fought hard for their version of the measure, but the only other alternative to compromise was failure.

In short, both House and Senate negotiators try to capitalize on incomplete information about what will pass their chamber. Thomas Schelling (1956) identified and discussed several structures or institutions crucial to understanding outcomes in these kinds of bargaining situations. Essentially, he argued that the outcome can be heavily influenced by the existence of institutions that allow bargainers to credibly commit to a position. Negotiators can do this by reducing their power to do anything other than their preferred position. As Schelling explains, "in bargaining, weakness is often strength, freedom may be freedom to capitulate, and to burn bridges behind one may suffice to undo an opponent" (1956, 281).

While negotiators might create institutions to weaken their ability to concede in order to strengthen their bargaining position, such tactics carry a risk. If both sides commit to different positions, then agreement is not reached (Schelling 1956). Simultaneous commitment equals stalemate. The House and Senate therefore face a classic dilemma. Each chamber has an incentive to develop institutions that will allow it to credibly commit to a position to force the other chamber to concede. Yet if both chambers create these institutions, then both can credibly commit to different positions and cause stalemate, an undesirable result for both chambers.

The problem is not an easy one for the houses of Congress to solve, as is evident from the evolving nature of bicameral resolution mechanisms (McCown 1927; Rybicki n.d.). Over time, the chambers have created and, more importantly, adapted procedures that reduce uncertainty about the position of the other chamber. Through the development of conference-committee procedures, the chambers created a way that allows them to attempt to gain a bargaining advantage by communicating a position while minimizing the risk of stalemate.

In this chapter I describe the evolution of just two procedures, partial conference reports and motions to instruct conferees, to demonstrate how the chambers can adapt their institutions to facilitate communication and prevent stalemate. In the contentious decades following the Civil War, the chambers transformed conference-committee delegations into what Schelling (1956) terms "bargaining agents." By sending an agent to bargain, each chamber strategically weakened its ability to concede because agents can be forbidden to take certain actions. Both motions to instruct conferees and conference reports in partial or full disagreement served this purpose starting in the second half of the 19th century. Furthermore, post-floor procedures also evolved to ensure both chambers could reverse, or undo, a commitment. Partial conference reports permitted each chamber to go on record supporting or resisting a particular proposal, but these votes in no way prohibited further compromise. By the end of the 19th century, motions to instruct conferees were not binding in either chamber.

The history of these procedures, provided in the following, differs from other accounts in several respects. I argue that many of the institutions understood in other works to be mechanisms for the median legislator to control conference-committee delegations are actually means through which the chambers bargain. Partial reports and instructions are poor means to control conferees and, furthermore, seem to have been designed for the purposes presented here. Of course, institutions designed for one purpose are often used for many others. And it would be foolish to claim a single purpose for the evolution of any legislative institution; in fact, policy makers are likely to choose the rule or norm that best serves several goals. My primary goal is to explain the long history of successful resolution of bicameral differences. Regardless of what these institutions may also mean for party or committee power within each chamber, I seek to show how they evolved into devices that facilitated House and Senate agreement.

I selected partial reports and motions to instruct conferees as examples of the chambers' ability to adapt resolution mechanisms for several reasons. They are the most significant procedures to develop in the critical era following the Civil War. Before 1850, the chambers sent measures to conference committees far less frequently and resolution procedures did not involve a delegation of decision-making authority to an agent (Rybicki 2003). After the Civil War, conference delegations took on important characteristics of bargaining agents. While it was common in the antebellum period to select conferees from the standing committee of jurisdiction, by the 1870s nearly three-quarters of the managers came from the standing committee and by 1890 nearly all managers came from the committee. The gradual increase in the percentage of conferees appointed from the committee of jurisdiction coincided with the decrease in turnover in committee membership. In the decades following the war we also see systematic evidence of loyal partisans rewarded, in both chambers, with better committee assignments (Stewart and Canon 2002). Furthermore, by the mid-1870s, both chambers were no longer appointing new conferees to a second or further committee of conference. Instead, if a conference committee reported in partial or full disagreement, or even if a chamber rejected a conference report, the chambers frequently appointed the same managers to a further conference. In these decades, in short, conferees developed their own incentives to reach agreement—incentives different from those of the parent chamber but that nevertheless helped the chambers reach their goal of agreement. Conferees had incentives to preserve their reputation in expected future negotiations and to reap rewards for reaching a favorable agreement.

It addition, partial reports and motions to instruct conferees were not arcane procedures to members of Congress in this era. In the 19th century and indeed for most of the 20th century, it was not at all uncommon for bargaining between the chambers to involve both the ping-pong of amendments between the houses and the return of a measure to conference multiple times. Indeed, multiple conferences were held, on average, on 20 percent of measures sent to conference between 1867 and 1921.[1] As will be explained in full later, motions to instruct and partial conference reports were crucial elements of these lengthy bargaining negotiations. In sum, this is a study of the first major changes in bicameral resolution procedures after the development of the conference committee system.

Finally, before turning to the historical discussion, I must remind the readers that I describe the *emergence* of *19th-century* resolution mechanisms. Both partial reports and motions to instruct conferees are in order in the modern Congress, but contemporary Congress watchers may not recognize them as they are presented in these pages. Partial reports evolved in the 20th century, as McCown (1927) and Bach (1981) demonstrate, into tools for allowing full chamber action on amendments to appropriations bills that would not have been in order if offered on the House floor. In the House, motions to instruct conferees underwent considerable procedural evolution, and sometime after 1936 they became one of the few methods by which the minority party can secure floor time for debate.[2]

Emergence of Partial Reports, 1879–1895

After the Civil War, the chambers gradually began to rely on partial conference reports to communicate their policy positions to each other. A partial conference report recommends action on some amendments in disagreement but leaves other amendments before the chambers for separate action. For example, if the Senate amends a House bill in 10 places, the managers might compromise on 8 of those amendments but report the other 2 in disagreement. The House and Senate each then take action on the amendments, and they may request a further conference be held on unresolved differences.

Partial conference reports had been in order in both chambers long before they began to be used regularly in the 1880s. The 1860 edition of the *House Digest* cited an 1846 precedent as support for the assertion that conference committees "may report agreement as to some of the matters of difference, but unable to agree as to others" (Barclay 1860, 66; *House Journal*, 29 Cong., 1, August 10, 1846, p. 1302; *Senate Journal*, 29 Cong., 1, August 10, 1846, pp. 523–524). Later editions of the *House Digest* included additional precedents for partial reports, which were in turn cited by subsequent presiding officers. The Senate also occasionally relied on the work compiled by clerks from the other chamber. The president pro tempore, when a question arose over a partial report in 1880, cited precedents listed in the *Digest*, along with language from "Cushing's Manual" (*Congressional Record*, 46 Cong., 2, June 8, 1880, p. 4385). Both the 1856 and the 1863 editions of Cushing's privately published book on parliamentary procedures stated, "Sometimes, instead of a single point of difference between the two houses, there are several relating to or growing out of the same subject-matter; in which case, the two houses may agree upon different points at different stages of the proceedings" (Cushing 1856, 344).

Partial reports likely emerged at this time for several reasons. The first is that the chambers needed to replace an older, more time-consuming method of communicating their positions. Conference committees began to report in partial disagreement just as the House and Senate were moving away from floor consideration of second-acting-chamber amendments. For most of the 19th century, the House and Senate considered the amendments of the second-acting chamber on the floor. In other words, legislators debated the amendments of the other chamber, sometimes agreeing with, sometimes disagreeing with, and sometimes amending the changes of the other body. But by the second half of the 19th century, amendment exchanges both before and instead of sending a bill to conference committee had disappeared. The chambers were requesting and agreeing to meet in conference committee without any floor consideration of the second-acting-chamber amendments (McCown 1927; Rybicki 2003).

While moving directly to conference saved the time of the chamber, it also prevented the full membership from communicating their position through separate votes on second-chamber amendments. As a result, the chamber delegations in conference lacked information about what a majority in each chamber would accept. Partial reports allowed the chambers to send bills quickly to conference while preserving the possibility that a separate vote could be held later on amendments in disagreement to establish a position of the chamber on the issue. Conferees from both chambers, when reporting back amendments in disagreement, sometimes explained that they were seeking "some expression of the sense of the House" (*Congressional Record*, 46 Cong., 2, June 9, 1880, p. 4336) or "to obtain the vote of the Senate upon the question" (*Congressional Record*, 44 Cong., 2, March 3, 1877, p. 2151). The purpose of a partial report, according to one chair of a Senate delegation "was to come back to those who were competent to instruct us to learn whether or not they desired to still further insist" (*Congressional Record*, 46 Cong., 2, June 8, 1880, p. 4283).

Partial reports were not simply a more efficient method of bicameral communication. Allowing conferees to report back to the parent chamber portions of the legislation in disagreement became a mechanism through which the House and Senate could gain leverage in negotiations without increasing the risk of stalemate. If a parent chamber did not grant the conferees permission to concede, the bargaining agents—the conferees—could credibly claim to be restricted by the chamber vote. In other words, if the parent chamber voted to insist on its amendment (or on its disagreement to the amendment of the other chamber), the conference delegation could return to further negotiations armed with majority or even unanimous support for their chambers' position. The conferees could tell their counterparts from the other chamber that they could not possibly concede. Their parent chamber, as evident from the vote cast on an amendment in disagreement, would never agree to the proposed compromise.

If, on the other hand, the chamber granted the conference delegation the authority to back down, then the conferees retained their ability in future conferences to credibly claim they did not have the authority to back down (at least not without receiving explicit directions again). In several cases, the chambers made the very concessions the conferees felt they had not had the authority to make in committee. Sometimes the remaining differences were resolved through a further exchange of amendments, perhaps with one chamber receding from one amendment and the other receding from its disagreement to another amendment (*House Journal*, 29 Cong., 1, August 10, 1846, p. 1302; *Senate Journal*, 29 Cong., 1, August 10, 1846, pp. 523–524). In at least one instance, the House passed a resolution instructing House conferees to yield to the wishes of the Senate conferees (*House Journal*, 46 Cong., 2, June 9, 1880, p. 1436; *Congressional Record*, 46 Cong., 2, June 9, 1880, p. 4338).

Partial reports facilitated agreement even as they allowed the chambers to communicate their positions; they reduced the risk of simultaneous commitment because the positions taken on amendments in disagreement could always be undone. Just because a chamber has insisted on its disagreement (and requested a second conference) does not mean that it cannot reverse this position (by agreeing to a recommendation from the second conference committee that it recede from its disagreement and agree to the amendment—perhaps with an amendment). From 1879 to 1919, conference committees reported in partial disagreement at least once on 136 measures. On 110 of these measures, the chambers sent the bill back to conference after taking opposing actions on the amendments—yet the chambers ultimately reached agreement in 99 percent of these cases. Communicating a position in this fashion clearly did not irrevocably commit either chamber. The partial reports facilitate communication of chamber positions while minimizing the risk of stalemate.

Because they facilitated agreement, partial reports became an important element of bargaining strategies—particularly on the most contentious issues between the chambers. Many of the early reports in partial disagreement concerned not just policy disagreement but issues of chamber rights.

The conferees began to utilize this previously unfamiliar procedure, perhaps because agreement through the regular process seemed unlikely. For example, the chambers fought throughout the 1870s and into the 1880s over the payment of congressional employees. The Senate sometimes recommended higher wages for the clerks than the House did or proposed additional clerks for the Senate. Members of the House found it insulting that Senate proposed that its clerks be paid more than House clerks or that the Senate have more clerks than the House; senators found it insulting that the House interfered with administrative matters of the Senate. The controversy arose regularly over the approval of the legislative-, executive-, and judicial-branch appropriations bill. In both the 46th (1879–1881) and the 48th (1883–1885) Congresses, the conference committees on this appropriations bill reported amendments concerning employees of the chambers in disagreement.

The continuing conflict between the chambers over the separation of funding and policy decisions in the 1870s, 1880s, and 1890s also played out in the use of partial reports. During a time when Senate rules concerning the separation were stricter than House rules, conference committees often reported in disagreement the Senate amendments that struck out legislative provisions in the House bill. Reporting in disagreement allowed the Senate to discuss the legislative proposals and even suggest modifications that the conferees could propose as compromises in further negotiations (*Congressional Record*, 48, Cong, 2, March 2, 1885, p. 2385). When further institutional changes left the House with stricter procedures concerning legislation on appropriations bills, partial conference reports allowed the same consideration privileges to representatives (Bach 1981).

Motions to Instruct Conferees, 1863–1895

The emergence of the motion to instruct conferees in the same era contrasts with the development of partial reports. A comparison of the evolution of these two similar procedures illustrates the challenge to the chambers to independently adapt institutions to reduce the risk of stalemate. In some ways, motions to instruct seemed well suited to serve the same purpose as partial reports; in fact, at times members referred to directions on amendments left in disagreement as "instructions." Yet the content of motions to instruct and the ability of one chamber to instruct unilaterally led the chambers to use motions to instruct rarely and reluctantly in these decades, at least in comparison to partial reports. By the turn of the century, motions to instruct neither effectively communicated chamber positions to each other nor increased the risk of stalemate.

In the 1860s motions to instruct conferees were in order in both chambers. These motions were generally offered on the floor of the House or the Senate after a conference committee had met and reported.[3] The motions directed a chamber's conference delegation to take some action on amendments in disagreement, in some cases suggesting a policy compromise.

In the first decade during the Civil War, presiding officers of both chambers ruled instructions in order. In response to a point of order, Speaker Schuyler Colfax (R-Ind.) ruled the House had the power to instruct conferees, because "otherwise the whole power would be in the hands of a Speaker in appointing the committee" (*Congressional Globe*, 38 Cong., 1, March 1, 1864, p. 893). In the Senate, the vice president, Hannibal Hamlin, also ruled in order a motion to instruct the conferees. In addition, the 1867 edition of *Barclay's Digest* stated that "a committee of conference may be instructed like any other committee, but the instructions can only be moved when the papers are before the House" (Barclay 1867, 69).

Motions to instruct conferees, like partial reports, provided a new way for the full membership to vote on issues in disagreement, and their emergence coincided with the trend away from considering amendments of the other chamber on the floor before conference. Those in favor of passing instructions sometimes pointed out that the chamber had never directly voted on certain matters embraced in the amendments of the other chamber because the amendments had been disagreed to en bloc before conference (*Congressional Record*, 49 Cong., 1, July 23, 1886, p. 7404).

As in the case of partial reports, the House and Senate also used motions to instruct to increase the bargaining power of their conference delegation—either by restricting their ability to concede or by protecting their reputations in future negotiations by explicitly permitting them to concede. The Senate instructed its conferees three times in the 1860s, each time because the managers from a conference that failed to reach agreement requested guidance from the parent chamber. In two of these instances, the instructions directed the Senate delegation to concede. In March of 1865, the conference committee on the legislative, executive, and judicial appropriations bill reported an inability to agree, and the Senate recommitted the bill and instructed the committee to agree to one provision still in disagreement. The instructions directed the Senate managers to agree to the House position. The chair of the Senate delegation said the conference committee "did not feel themselves at liberty to depart from the action of the Senate" and desired "the instruction of the Senate" (*Congressional Globe*, 38 Cong., 2, March 1, 1865, p. 1225). Without the instructions, the conferees and most senators present on the floor seemed to agree, the delegation would not have had the authority to agree to the House provision. In 1866 the Senate instructed its conferees once again, because as the chair of the delegation claimed, the conferees did not feel "at liberty to accept" a compromise proposed by the House delegation (*Congressional Globe*, 39 Cong., 1, July 27, 1866, p. 4246).

There were important differences between motions to instruct and partial reports, however, and these differences had the potential to exacerbate conflict between the chambers rather than facilitate agreement. One problem was that instructions, unlike the motions in order following a partial report, could contain specific policy suggestions.[4] For example, in 1864, after two conference committees had failed to reach agreement on an internal revenue bill, the House instructed its conferees to agree to an additional duty on liquor between 20¢ and 40¢ a gallon (*Congressional Globe*, 38 Cong., 1, March 1, 1864, p. 892). When the partial report arrived in the other body, a senator moved that the Senate delegation be instructed to agree to a tax not exceeding 20¢ a gallon. The situation illustrates the problem of binding instructions. After some discussion, the full Senate rejected the motion to instruct and instead agreed to meet the House only in a further free conference. The House agreed to hold a free conference and the managers met without instructions from their chambers.

Furthermore, motions to instruct conferees were problematic because a chamber could act unilaterally. In the case of partial conference reports, both chambers are given the opportunity to make motions on the remaining amendments in disagreement. Motions to instruct, on the other hand, could be offered after the other chamber had acted on the first conference report. If they were made by the chamber that acted first on a conference report, then the other chamber had an incentive to either instruct its conferees in an opposing manner or to refuse to meet in conference at all. When conference committees report in partial disagreement, if the chambers want to send the measure back to conference, they must take opposing actions on an amendment; one chamber disagrees and the other insists. Because they are choosing to send the bill to conference, however, it is understood that both chambers want to reach agreement and one, or both, will have to back down from the motions taken to return the bill to conference. It was not at all clear in the 1870s, however, that managers need not follow motions to instruct.

Both the House and the Senate recognized the disadvantage of motions to instruct and took actions accordingly. In 1864 the House instructed its managers appointed to a further conference on the Montana Territory bill to adhere to the House position. In response, the Senate declined to agree to a committee of conference under the terms of the House. Because there was only one item in disagreement and the House had instructed its conferees to adhere to the House position, holding a committee of conference, according to some senators, would be absurd (*Congressional Globe*, 38 Cong., 1, April 15, 1864, p. 1640).

In 1868 the Senate instructed its delegation to recede from the Senate amendments except those relating to imported cotton (*Congressional Globe*, 40 Cong., 2, January 22, 1868, p. 675). When the House managers reported that the Senate managers "were unwilling to do anything except according to the instructions which had been given them by the Senate," the House rejected the conference report (*Congressional Globe*, 40 Cong., 2, January 24, 1868, pp. 742–743). A manager moved that the House ask for a further conference and instruct the delegation to adhere to the House position. Speaker Colfax said, however, that the practice had been against instructions, and the House followed his guidance.

The motion to instruct continued to be controversial into the 1880s and early 1890s. When the House passed what the Senate viewed as particularly egregious instructions in 1883, the Senate agreed by voice vote to a resolution that "it is the opinion of the Senate that the conference on House bill No. 5538 should be full and free, and that if the Senate conferees become advised that any limitation has been placed by the House upon the action of their conferees, the Senate conferees shall retire and report to the Senate for its consideration" (*Congressional Record*, 47 Cong., 2, February 27, 1883, p. 3376; McCown 1927).

In their early history, motions to instruct failed as a means of communication that would assist the chambers in reaching agreement. Yet neither chamber wanted to give up the right to instruct its own conferees because it would be putting itself in a weaker bargaining position. Instructions were ruled out of order in the Senate in 1873 not because they had the potential to cause stalemate but because a particular motion to instruct put senators in an awkward political situation.

In 1873 a majority of senators reversed a ruling of the presiding officer and made instructions out of order to avoid a direct vote on a congressional pay raise. The conference committee on the legislative-, executive-, and judicial-branch appropriations bill had reported in agreement. Senator George Wright (R-Iowa) moved that the report be recommitted and the conference committee be instructed to strike out the congressional pay raise.[5] Senator Lyman Trumbull (R-Ill.) made the point of order that the instructions were not in order. The presiding officer, George Edmunds (R-Vt.), overruled the point of order, relying on *Barclay's Digest*, which stated that a committee of conference could be instructed. Trumbull appealed the ruling, and the Senate debated the case. While many senators raised procedural issues, the main concern was the always politically sensitive issue of the congressional pay raise.[6] If the instructions were in order, then senators would have to vote on whether the conference committee should strike out the pay raise. Senator John Sherman (R-Ohio) asked senators to consider purely the question of order and "lay aside for the present consideration of the merits of the proposition, and only look to the question of order, because we are about to set a precedent which may bother us hereafter" (*Congressional Record*, 42 Cong., 3, March 3, 1873, p. 2173). The Senate instead overturned the ruling of the chair 47 to 11, deeming instructions to be out of order.

The initial reversal of a ruling was probably motivated by the desire to avoid a difficult vote, but the Senate continued to follow this precedent into the 1880s. At times, senators did wish to communicate their goals to conferees from both chambers, and they relied on other procedures to do so. In 1874, after the presiding officer said instructions would be out of order, a senator claimed he had received assurances from a manager that if they recommitted the conference report, the next report would be satisfactory (*Congressional Record*, 43 Cong., 1, June 22, 1874, p. 5369). In 1876 the Senate recommitted a conference report "upon such definitive ideas," as Senator Lot Morrill (R-Maine) said, "as that the committee might understand that they were in the way of instructions when they came to consider the question" (*Congressional Record*, 44 Cong., 1, February 17, p. 1876).

Although the Speaker never ruled the motion to instruct out of order in the House, representatives continued to express misgivings about the procedure and passed other kinds of motions in lieu of instructions. For example, in 1878 the House, after a conference committee failed to reach an agreement, adopted the resolution that "it is the opinion of this House that its conferees . . . should under the circumstances yield to the conferees on the part of the Senate" (*Congressional Record*, 45 Cong., 2, June 15, 1878, p. 4689). The following Congress, in 1880, Speaker Samuel Randall (D-Pa.) guided a representative "to change his resolution, so that it shall express an opinion on the part of the House, rather than be in the form of an instruction to the committee" (*Congressional Record*, 46 Cong., 2, June 9, 1880, p. 4337). Randall said he was aware of the assertion in *Barclay's Digest*, but he had "always doubted the propriety, in fact the power, to instruct, because it is an interference with the full and free conference of the two Houses. But the Chair admits there have been occasions when after various conferences the House has asserted the right to instruct conferees." In both of these examples, a majority agreed to pass resolutions short of actually instructing its managers.

Controversy over the motion to instruct conferees would last until the motion ceased to be a method through which the chambers could reach simultaneous commitment. In 1886, in response to a point of order against a report containing a recommendation contrary to instructions from the House, Speaker Carlisle ruled that, while the House could instruct its conferees, these instructions were not binding. As Carlisle explained, "while it is competent under the recent practice of the House to instruct conference committees, still the House in that case, as in the other, may ultimately recede from its disagreement to the very amendment in regard to which it had instructed its conferees to insist on a disagreement" (*Congressional Record*, 49 Cong., 1, July 23, 1886). Parliamentarians have interpreted the precedent to mean that reports cannot be ruled out of order for violating instructions (Hinds 1907, 705). After this ruling, the journal clerk of the House, Henry H. Smith, noted in the *Digest and Manual* that the decision "in relation to an alleged departure from instructions by the House by its conferees is so important, that it, together with the question raised, is given in full" (H. Smith 1887, 337).

It may be just as important that by the turn of the century it was established in House precedents that motions to instruct conferees should not be formally communicated to the other chamber.[7] In other words, they would pass in one chamber and be printed in the *Congressional Record*, but the other chamber would not receive an "official" message of instruction.

As these precedents and practices were established, motions to instruct ceased to be mechanisms that increased the chances of stalemate. By the 1890s motions to instruct were no longer controversial in the House. Speaker Thomas Reed wrote in his parliamentary handbook in 1894 that if a chamber wished to amend a conference report, its only recourse was to "reject the report, ask for another conference, and then instruct the committee to ask the conferees of the other body to agree to the proposed amendment to the report" (Reed 1952, 164).

Also by the mid-1890s, presiding officers were again ruling motions to instruct in order in the Senate. In 1887 the president pro tempore, John Sherman (R-Ohio), said he felt bound by the 1873 ruling of the Senate "and therefore is compelled to hold that the instructions are not in order" (*Congressional Record*, 49 Cong., 2, January 21, 1887, p. 663). Yet the following year the Senate passed a motion to instruct its conferees. John Sherman, no longer presiding, argued, "As a matter of course, either house can instruct its committees of conference as it can instruct any other committee at any time" (*Congressional Record*, 50 Cong., 1, September 21, 1888, p. 8824). Senator George Edmunds (R-Vt.), who had ruled against instructions in 1873, in this case also spoke in favor of instructions. The Senate voted on a motion to instruct its delegation again in 1890, the president pro tempore stating in response to a question, "It is within the power of the Senate to make the order" (*Congressional Record*, 51 Cong., 1, July 1, 1890, p. 6827).[8]

In sum, motions to instruct conferees emerged in both chambers at a time when the House and Senate no longer considered and voted separately on the amendments of the other body. While instructions served, in part, to allow the full chamber to express its opinion on individual amendments or compromise proposals, they also interfered with the full and free nature of conference committees. As a result, both chambers passed motions to instruct between 1861 and the mid-1890s amid controversy. Instructions were out of order entirely in the Senate for a time, and only became non-controversial after crucial House precedents established that they were non-binding and would not be formally messaged to the other chamber.

Anticipating the Arrangement of Policy Preferences

The evolution of selected bicameral resolution mechanisms just described demonstrates how, over time, the House and Senate have adapted procedures to help them resolve their legislative differences. But institutions alone do not explain the high rate of success in bicameral negotiations. Legislative outcomes, congressional scholars generally agree, depend on the interaction of institutional structures and legislators' goals. We therefore turn now to explanations for the outcomes of bicameral negotiations that focus on the policy goals of legislators.

Theories of legislative politics centered on preference arrangements and institutions predict legislators will reach agreement whenever both chambers prefer a compromise proposal over the status quo (S. Smith 1988; Riker 1992). In a unidimensional space, this means they will enact a policy whenever the ideal points of the chambers are on the same side as the status quo point. The conclusion has been generalized to apply to multiple dimensions (Tsebelis 1995).

The further apart the ideal points of the chambers, the more likely it is that the status quo point lies between them, and thus scholars generally claim that reaching a compromise agreement is more difficult when the House and Senate have distinct and distant positions on a legislative issue (Tsebelis and Money 1997; Binder 2003). The simple explanation of irreconcilable policy differences has also been suggested in case studies and contemporary accounts of bicameral disagreement (Paletz 1970, 408–409).

Theories emphasizing the policy preferences of key political actors often point to the possibility of a presidential veto or a filibuster as causes of legislative stalemate. Legislation successfully passed by a majority in each chamber may never make it to the president's desk because of these threats. Krehbiel's (1998) pivotal politics theory of lawmaking attributes policy gridlock to the policy preferences of key political actors. *Gridlock* is strictly defined to be any instance in which legislation preferred by a majority of legislators to the status quo does not become law. In the pivotal politics theory, the legislature is unicameral, but the basic premise can be extended to theories about bicameral resolution. According to the pivotal politics theory, the median legislators could send a bill to conference but could reach no compromise satisfactory to the filibuster pivot and either the president or the veto override pivot.

Empirical studies support the key conclusions of the pivotal politics theory. Clearly, the policy preferences of the chief executive affect the outcome, and the success, of bicameral negotiations (Longley and Oleszek 1989; Cameron 2000, 137–139). At the very least, legislators are aware of the potential of a presidential veto. The involvement of the executive branch often goes far beyond the negative power of a veto threat. In the modern Congress, administration officials meet with conferees on major measures and take part in crafting the compromise and trading policy provisions. Some historical evidence suggests the White House has played an active role in some conference negotiations since the first Congress. For this reason, it is likely that at times bills fail to be presented to the president because the House and Senate could not reach a compromise that could also satisfy the executive (or two-thirds of the legislators in both houses). The chambers might decide not to force the president to veto the bill for political or practical reasons, or they might run out of time trying to find a position that is acceptable to all players in the negotiations.

Similarly, there is no question that actual or threatened filibusters have killed measures after they passed both chambers.[9] For most of congressional history, Senators rarely mounted filibusters against conference reports (Paletz 1970; Longley and Oleszek 1989). Scholars attributed the infrequency of filibusters in the mid-20th century partially to the risk that an end-of-session filibuster would kill more than that single bill (Paletz 1970, 383–384). Others claim that Senate norms of comity precluded filibusters in the final stages of the legislative process, but Binder and Smith (1997) argue convincingly that the distribution of power in the Senate during the conservative coalition era explains the infrequency of filibusters in general (89–90).

This does not mean, of course, that threatened filibusters did not prevent conference reports from coming to the Senate floor at all. Although it is difficult to assess the effects of threatened filibusters over time, political scientists generally agree that in recent decades both actual and threatened filibuster have increased (Binder and Smith 1997; Deckard [Sinclair] 1989b). Senator Robert Byrd could claim without risk of ridicule in 1980 that "I do not recall a successful filibuster on a conference report since I have been in the Senate" (*Congressional Record*, 96th Cong., 2nd sess., April 30, 1980, p. S4358, quoted by Longley and Oleszek 1989). My review of articles in *Congressional Quarterly Weekly Report* revealed that in the last five Congresses (1993–2002), in contrast, the press blamed the threat of a filibuster for the death of 6 out of 20 measures that went to conference but did not clear the Congress.

If the arrangement of policy preferences of key political actors determines whether legislation is enacted, how can we explain the successful record of bicameral resolution? Few would argue the historically low rates of bicameral disagreement are due to the consistent election of key senators, key representatives, and presidents (or again, two-thirds of the legislators in each chamber) with policy preferences on the same side of the status quo on most issues.

It is far more likely that political actors have the ability to predict, given the structure of the political system, what issues stand a chance of becoming law. High rates of successful bicameral resolution are due in part to legislators' reluctance to embark on a major policy initiative if it is unlikely the House and Senate could ever agree on the same bill. Generally speaking, if the arrangement of member preferences on an issue precludes bicameral agreement, a bill on the issue is unlikely to reach the postpassage stage.

As a reminder, the historically high rates of bicameral resolution alluded to thus far are measured by the number of public measures *that passed both chambers* and were not presented to the president. A great number of measures die after passing just *one* chamber. Before 1945 approximately 20 percent of House public measures did not pass the Senate and 44 percent of Senate public measures did not pass the House. Since 1945 the percentages of House and Senate public bills that pass only one chamber have been higher, partially because of changes in the legislative process such as the increased use of omnibus bills and the practice of passing companion bills. Approximately 31 percent of House measures and 60 percent of Senate measures did not pass the other chamber between 1946 and 2000.[10] It seems likely that at least some of these bills did not pass the second-acting chamber because a sufficient number of legislators did not prefer the proposal—in any form acceptable to the other chamber—to the status quo.

A recent book by Binder (2003) provides circumstantial evidence for the argument that legislators know the preference arrangements of key actors and will abandon the pursuit of a hopeless major policy initiative early in the legislative process. Binder examined newspaper editorials from 1945 to 2000 to identify the most salient public policy issues facing each Congress. She was primarily interested in explaining the inability of the president and Congress to pass legislation on matters of national importance. One element of this study involved identifying at what stage of the legislative process measures die. She found that approximately 7 percent of the major issues identified died because of postpassage bicameral disagreement (Binder 2003, 48–49). A similar percentage died because the chambers failed to override a presidential veto, but most of the significant issues that died failed to achieve passage in both chambers.

Additional support for the notion that only those measures on which some zone of agreement exists among political actors pass both chambers can also be found in the observations of congressional scholars. Legislators do not go to conference looking to disagree; they believe some policy compromise is possible and they want to reach agreement (Fenno 1966; Pressman 1966). Conference negotiations have been described by congressional scholar and advisor Walter Oleszek as taking place in an "agreement-orientated context."[11]

In sum, an important reason few measures die after capturing majority support in both chambers is that few bills get to that stage if preference arrangements do not favor final enactment. Legislators have a number of information-gathering tools at their disposal, and not infrequently they abandon serious pursuit of an issue because they are fairly certain preference arrangements and institutional structures—including the veto and the filibuster—are working against them.

Unresolved Differences: Uncertainty, Institutions, and Strategic Disagreement

I have argued that much of the success of bicameral negotiations can be accounted for by flexible resolution mechanisms and the ability of legislators to anticipate what will clear both chambers. Yet each Congress the chambers fail to resolve their differences on some legislation pending before them. In other words, a small proportion of measures that a majority of legislators in each house supports do not become law. Sometimes one chamber amends a bill of the other chamber and action stops there; sometimes a bill dies after protracted negotiations in conference committee. Why do some bills fail late in the legislative process? Are there conditions under which failure is more likely?

Although I have contended here in the preceding that legislators predict with a high degree of accuracy what proposals can pass both chambers, some uncertainty still exists about the policy preferences of key actors, and this uncertainty can lead to unresolved differences. Legislators might sometimes mistakenly attempt to reach agreement on measures even when preference arrangements guarantee defeat.

It is more likely, however, that legislators might accurately predict that some compromise is possible yet be unable, because of uncertainty about the ideal points of legislators, to arrive at the compromise position. I argued in the preceding that over time the chambers have created and adapted bicameral resolution procedures that help to reduce uncertainty about the position of the other chamber without increasing the risk of stalemate. But the previously presented historical studies should have also made clear that the bargaining institutions are not perfect. Simultaneous commitment remains possible.

There is another important element of bicameral negotiations we have not yet discussed: the pursuit of goals other than the enactment of good public policy. Failure to resolve differences might not always be caused by the lack of a policy position acceptable to all political actors, or even to the inability, because of miscalculated posturing or poor negotiating skills, to arrive at the compromise position. Members of Congress sometimes choose to leave their differences unresolved to serve goals other than the enactment of the best possible public policy, such as the goal to put, or keep, a party in power. Gilmour (1995) calls it "strategic disagreement" whenever politicians choose political advantage over a policy compromise that would be an improvement over the status quo.

It is much easier to describe the factors expected to cause the breakdown of bicameral relations than to design a test of their effects. The status quo, the policy preferences of legislators, the political goals of legislators, and legislators' knowledge of their colleagues' preferences are all of course largely unobservable. But it may be possible to identify factors expected to increase uncertainty about policy-preference arrangements, such as the newness or complexity of an issue. Other issue-level factors, such as the results of public opinion polls, might be expected to increase the likelihood of strategic disagreement. In this way, it may be possible to model at the level of the individual issue the likelihood that the chambers would resolve their differences.

In this chapter, I am far less ambitious. I examine aggregate-level data and discuss some congressional-level electoral and institutional factors expected to influence rates of bicameral disagreement over time. I first present the aggregate-level data on the percentage of public measures that passed both chambers on which the chambers failed to resolve their differences. I offer some conjectures about the conditions expected to increase uncertainty about policy preferences and the conditions expected to favor strategic disagreement. I leave the challenges of measuring these conditions and constructing a multivariate test to future work.

The Frequency of Failure to Resolve Differences

To study bicameral resolution success rates over most of congressional history, I collected two kinds of data. The first set of data sacrifices breadth for depth; I collected data on every public measure that passed at least one chamber but only for every third Congress, or approximately every 5 years, since the 34th Congress (1855–1857). For every Congress, I collected data on public measures the chambers sent to conference committee. In the first dataset, there is some correlation between both the number (0.71) and the percentage (0.63) of measures that fail in conference and those that fail without ever being sent to conference. Some of the same factors affecting success rates of measures sent to conference seem to affect those that never make it to conference.

One other observation is necessary before proceeding to the analysis of the data. I am interested in the rates of failure of legislation, not necessarily the failure of individual legislative vehicles. For example, in the 100th Congress (1987–1988), 16 individual bills died in conference. However, all but 6 of these bills were general appropriations measures that were rolled into a single continuing resolution at the end of the session. The provisions of 2 other measures were likewise included in other omnibus bills. These instances of vehicle failure should be separated from, for example, the airline consumer protection bill of that Congress that, according to press reports, died when House and Senate conferees disagreed over requirements for random drug testing of transportation workers.

To identify instances where agreements reached in conference were ultimately rolled into alternative vehicles, I relied on both official congressional documents and press reports. Both the *House Final Calendar* and the index to the *Congressional Record* direct users to related bills. The *Calendar* and the *Congressional Record* index, however, do not describe how the measures are related, and they furthermore do not identify all instances where vehicles died but the legislation survived. I therefore also used press reports, largely from *Congressional Quarterly* but also from the *National Journal* and the *Washington Post*, to identify when measures that appeared to fail were actually added to other bills.

To be sure, the process of identifying failure was somewhat subjective. Sometimes the incorporation of measures into single vehicles is done precisely because as single measures they would fail to become law. Such instances were nevertheless categorized as a successful resolution of differences. Similarly, if the chambers chose to write and pass a new bill or joint resolution rather than report an old measure from the conference committee, this was not coded as an instance of bicameral disagreement. We are fundamentally interested in measures on which the differences were not resolved through any means. At this point, I have researched only secondary sources for the post-reform (1957–2002) era. The use of such packaging and other creative means to build coalitions increased considerably in the 1980s, and I extended the analysis farther back to confirm this well-reported characteristic of the post-reform Congress.

Conditions for High Uncertainty about Policy Preferences

Less than 10 percent of all public measures sent to conference fail to make their way to the president's desk. I argued in the preceding that the chambers resolve their differences on most measures that go to conference because the only measures that reach that stage are ones on which legislators are fairly certain agreement can be reached. When measures fail, one possible explanation is that it is because legislators were uncertain about preference arrangements.

I also argued in the preceding that bicameral resolution mechanisms reduced uncertainty about the chambers' positions. We might expect, therefore, that under certain institutional arrangements uncertainty about preference arrangements will be higher. We see some patterns in the data of change over time that correspond with known changes in the role of the standing committee system in the legislative process. In the middle of the 20th century, at least compared to the preceding era, there appears to be a reduction in the percentage of public measures on which differences were not resolved. Through the 1930s and 1950s, in only two Congresses did the percentage of failed measures rise above 5 percent. The era encompasses the textbook Congress, generally dated from the 1930s to the 20th-century reforms, in which strong norms of deference to the expertise of committee members prevailed in both houses of Congress.

Uncertainty about policy-preference arrangements might have been low in the mid-20th century for several reasons. With high deference to committees, resolution of differences became an agreement between a select few engaged in a repeated game. Communication of true preferences would be easier, both because conferees could be confident the other side spoke for their chamber and because the incentive to gain an advantage by misrepresenting one's position would be lessened by the prospect of meeting the same members in future negotiations. Another argument could be that this was a politically conservative era. New policy proposals, on which there is likely greater uncertainty about policy preferences, were likely to be stifled early in the legislative process.

The reforms of the 1970s brought an increase of measures on which the chambers did not resolve their differences. The rise in the number of measures left unresolved is only partially a by-product of the increased use of omnibus measures; the increase exists even when counting legislation, not vehicles, that were not resolved. The data confirms the work of others who have shown the effect of the reforms on bicameral relations (S. Smith 1989; Longley and Oleszek 1989). Again, a number of factors could arguably have contributed to a rise in uncertainty about preference arrangements. First, there were major changes in the composition of conference committees. Larger conference delegations, including junior and even some noncommittee members, made reaching agreement more difficult (Longley and Oleszek 1989; Deering and Smith 1997). As more members got involved, there was less certainty that conferees could accurately speak for the full chamber and less of an incentive to preserve good relationships for future negotiations. Of course, changes in the agenda, including the introduction of new and highly controversial issues, could also increase uncertainty and complicate the resolution of differences between the chambers. Finally, the rise in the use of filibusters and filibuster threats in the Senate, identified by Binder and Smith (1997), S. Smith (1989), and Deckard [Sinclair] (1989b), could have made reaching agreement less certain than it was in Congress at midcentury.

Conditions for Strategic Disagreement

Scholarly studies suggest that much more is involved in bicameral relations than structure and policy (Longley and Oleszek 1989; Pressman 1966; Fenno 1966). While uncertainty about acceptable policy positions might explain some instances of bicameral breakdown, it is also likely that in some situations legislators choose disagreement over compromise. As previously noted, John Gilmour (1995) defines *strategic disagreement* as any instance where politicians choose political advantage over a policy compromise that would be an improvement over the status quo. The advantages to be gained from not compromising are varied (Gilmour 1995, 24–47). Members of Congress sometimes find it difficult to explain to constituents why they voted for a policy far more moderate than the one they had supported on the campaign trail. It is also often advantageous to maintain a position of the party that attracts votes and is clearly different than that of your opponent—even if the position is unlikely to ever become law. Policy makers might also strategically disagree because they believe holding out will ultimately improve the final policy outcome of future negotiations.

Strategic disagreement might be expected to be more common under certain electoral conditions. For example, political actors can expect to gain more from strategic disagreement when they can blame the other party for the failure to enact a favored policy. Therefore, bicameral disagreement may be more likely under split party control of Congress. Similarly, we may expect party control of the presidency and Congress to affect incentives to compromise, although it is difficult to say how divided party control would affect bicameral agreement. On the one hand, the key actors might choose to kill a bill in conference to prevent the president from achieving a legislative accomplishment; on the other hand, they might deliberately send the measure to the president as "veto bait" (Gilmour 1995). The effect of divided party control also likely depends on the proximity of the next presidential election.

Chapter 23

The Electoral Disconnection: Roll-Call Behavior in Lame-Duck Sessions of the House of Representatives, 1879–1933

TIMOTHY P. NOKKEN

Introduction

In this chapter, I exploit a natural experiment that allows me to determine how severing electoral constraints influences roll-call behavior. I analyze the voting behavior of departing members in lame-duck sessions from the 46th to 72nd Congresses (1879 to 1933), and compare the behavior of members of Congress (MCs) in their final lame-duck session in office to behavior in previous terms to determine how electoral linkages affect their roll-call behavior. The time frame in this analysis is important and relevant for multiple reasons. First, and most notably, the time period is a long-standing and stable partisan era pitting Democrats against Republicans. I start with the 46th Congress because it was the first Congress elected after the Compromise of 1877, which ended Reconstruction with the removal of federal troops from the former Confederate states (Woodward 1966) and ushered in the post–Civil War party system. Second, starting in 1872 most states coordinated the timing of congressional elections to take place in November. Finally, the 72nd Congress serves as a natural end point because it was the last regularly scheduled lame-duck session convened before the implementation of the 20th Amendment.

The chapter proceeds as follows. In the next section I describe the regularly occurring pre–20th Amendment lame-duck sessions of Congress. I explain their theoretical utility for investigating the roll-call behavior of members of Congress and formulate a series of hypotheses regarding member behavior in the absence of constituent constraints. In the next section, I construct a series of tests to investigate both ideological and participatory shirking among departing members. I offer some final thoughts on the important implications of voting on legislation in sessions comprising lame-duck legislators in the last section.

Lame-Duck Sessions of Congress and Roll-Call Behavior

For much of our nation's history, Congress regularly convened lame-duck sessions, also referred to as short sessions, in the weeks following congressional elections. Workload in the House varied greatly across Congresses and from regular to lame-duck sessions. Lame-duck sessions are often marked by a high number of votes in which members worked on a substantive legislative agenda. A sizable number of the members who cast votes in the sessions did so in the absence of direct ties to constituents because they had decided to retire or because they had lost their reelection bids. The participation of departing members on substantive legislative prerogatives enables one to assess directly the role electoral forces play in shaping roll-call behavior.

Departing members who participated in lame-duck sessions did so in the absence of electoral concerns, which leaves open the possibility that lame-duck members made noticeable changes in their roll-call behavior during the lame-duck session in their last term in office. That possibility was not lost on members of Congress. Senator George Norris (R-Neb.), who ultimately penned the 20th Amendment, which eliminated the regularly occurring lame-duck session, argues,

> It was contrary to all reason and precedent that men who had been repudiated by their own people should continue to mold legislation as representatives of those people. This gave any President who desired to use it enormous power over legislation. On several occasions, it was revealed, many of these lame-duck members of Congress were willing to follow the command of the executive and to adopt legislation which he desired. For their subservience, they were given fat executive appointments. Not all defeated members of Congress were guilty of this subservience—many remained loyal to their conscientious convictions; but it had become quite common for men retired to private life by their people to do the bidding of the President of the United States in legislation of the gravest national importance. (1945, 332)

The recognition by members of the possible problems caused by lame-duck legislators provides further justification for using the roll-call-vote information from these sessions to study legislative shirking, whereby MCs alter their voting behavior to pursue personal goals or they simply exert less effort and participate in fewer roll calls.[1] First, lame-duck sessions were an institutionally defined component of the legislative calendar, making them an ideal "treatment" with which to study roll-call behavior in a member's last term. Second, they prove especially valuable because they allow analysis of the behavior of defeated members. That, in turn, allows me to assess whether voluntary exit leads to different behavioral consequences than involuntary exit. In sum, use of the lame-duck sessions improves on current studies of shirking by providing an institutionally defined time frame with which to evaluate member behavior and to expand the set of departing members to include defeated members.

In spite of such theoretically important qualities, roll-call voting in lame-duck sessions of Congress has received surprisingly scant scholarly attention.[2] In my analyses, I use members' roll-call behavior in the institutionally defined lame-duck sessions from the 46th to 72nd Congresses to revisit the question of whether departing members alter their behavior once the electoral connection is removed. These sessions provide me with an institutionally determined rather than arbitrarily created baseline to evaluate member behavior. Additionally, using the lame-duck sessions allows me to expand my dataset to include not only MCs who exited voluntarily but those who lost reelection bids. In the next section, I identify a series of hypotheses about members' roll-call behavior in lame-duck sessions of Congress.

Hypotheses of Lame-Duck Sessions and Legislative Behavior

The primary hypotheses I investigate center on the roll-call behavior of departing legislators in lame-duck sessions. Most broadly, the lame-duck hypothesis posits departing members would be expected to exhibit some sort of change in voting behavior in their lame-duck session. Behavioral changes could take place in either (or both) of two aspects of roll-call behavior: members could alter the ideological composition of their voting records, and members might exhibit differences in their roll-call participation. Expectations about participation are straightforward. Lame-duck MCs are expected to reduce their participation rates significantly in their final terms.[3]

For the reasons Senator Norris identifies (referred to subsequently as the Norris hypothesis), lame ducks from the president's party make ideological shifts consistent with what one would expect: Democrats move left, Republicans shift right. Control of the legislative agenda by the majority party suggests that the leadership schedules votes on matters of importance to the party, making it likely lame ducks cast roll-call votes on a strongly partisan agenda. Confounding such conjectures, however, is the possibility that different modes of exit might lead to different ideological reactions from retirees and losers. During much of the era I study, positions in state government were frequently viewed as more desirable than service in the House (see, for example, Stewart 1989). Retirees, however, may well have left the House with designs on winning positions at lower levels. Losers, on the other hand, may not have had jobs lined up, making them potentially more responsive to partisan cues, especially presidential influence. Following those cues may have enhanced the likelihood of receiving patronage positions.[4]

The expectations regarding participatory shirking for lame-duck MCs is clear: they are expected to vote less often. During their last days in office, lame ducks may reduce their levels of participation. Lame ducks do not, however, stop voting altogether. That fact leads to a refinement of the conjecture about participation in lame-duck sessions, namely, whether lame-duck members choose to participate on a certain types of votes and abstain on others. More specifically, one would expect even lame-duck legislators to respond to important considerations and to participate on those votes that serve to enhance a member's expected utility (Cohen and Noll 1991). The implication of an expected utility theory of roll-call participation is that vote-specific characteristics influence the likelihood of participation among both returning and lame-duck members.

The political dynamics of the time period also contribute to the difficulty in constructing a set of *ex ante* expectations about roll-call behavior in lame-duck sessions. First, unlike most of the post–World War II Congresses, partisan control of the chamber changed hands seven times during this time period. The lame-duck sessions of the 50th, 51st, 53rd, 61st, 65th, 71st, and 72nd Congresses convened with the knowledge that a new party would assume the majority at the beginning of the next Congress. Of course, changes in partisan control resulted from significant turnover in membership, with sizable numbers of retirements and defeats. The time period also includes emergence of the Reed rules in 1890, which ushered in the era of the strong Speaker. The exploits of Republican Speakers Thomas Reed (Maine) and Joe Cannon (Ill.) are legendary (Chiu 1928; Tuchman 1966; Jones 1968; Cooper and Brady 1981; Strahan 2002).[5] They controlled nearly every aspect of congressional proceedings, ranging from floor business to committee assignments (Lawrence, Maltzman, and Wahlbeck 2001). The reign of

Cannon ended in the 61st Congress when a coalition of Democrats allied with insurgent Republicans to pass a series of rules changes that sharply curtailed the Speaker's power (see, for instance, Riker 1986). Accounting for period-specific effects associated with each of these eras is an important concern for this analysis. The variation in the strength of parties and party leaders could have significant implications for time-specific behavioral consequences.

Data and Methods

In this section, I analyze roll-call-voting data to determine whether the elimination of electoral constraints caused changes in MCs' roll-call behavior. I specify a series of ordinary least squares (OLS) regression models to analyze individual-level roll-call behavior to determine whether members exhibited significant alterations in either ideology or participation. I then proceed to analyze aggregate abstention rates on individual roll-call votes to investigate the behavioral consequences of lame-duck sessions for both returning and departing members.

To measure member ideology, a colleague and I scaled roll-call votes from the 46th to 72nd Congresses to generate NOMINATE scores for regular and lame-duck sessions.[6] I used these NOMINATE scores to construct two variables to account for ideological change. The *IDEOLOGY1* variable is calculated by subtracting the lame-duck-session NOMINATE scores in Congress_{t-1} from the lame-duck-session NOMINATE scores in Congress_t for all members who served in those sessions.[7] *IDEOLOGY2* is measured as the difference between a member's lame-duck and regular-session NOMINATE scores for each Congress *t*.

An important quality of each of these ideological measures is that they capture both the direction and magnitude of ideological changes. Negative values for the *IDEOLOGY1* variable represent a liberal shift, and positive values represent a shift to the right. The effects are reversed for *IDEOLOGY2*, where negative values represent conservative shifts and positive values indicate liberal movement. The expectation for the direction of ideological changes is that Democrats and Republicans would, in all likelihood, move in opposite directions. If I were to estimate a pooled model, the countervailing shifts for the two parties would simply cancel out, masking any instances of meaningful ideological variation, hence I estimate separate models for Democrats and Republicans.

Turning next to individual-level participation rates, the two abstention-related dependent variables are similar to the ideological measures previously described. *ABSTENTION1* is generated by taking the difference between lame-duck-session abstention rates in Congress t minus the lame-duck-session abstention rates in Congress $t - 1$. *ABSTENTION2* measures the change in participation across sessions within a Congress, and it is calculated by subtracting a member's abstention rate from the abstention rate in the preceding regular session for a given Congress. The two participation variables are signed, which allows me to assess both the direction and magnitude of participatory changes. Positive values show increased abstention rates; negative values show increased participation in the lame-duck session.

Once again, using the roll-call information from lame-duck sessions in this manner allows me to make direct assessments of the behavioral consequences of both voluntary and involuntary departures from the House. Departing members no longer linked to the electorate may exhibit notable ideological shifts, and the particular mode of exit may lead to important types of behavioral changes. During much of the time frame I study, those who left voluntarily may well have had designs on political positions at the state or local level. Losers, on the other hand, may not have expected to be unemployed at the end of their congressional term, making post-congressional employment a matter of primary concern. Losers, then, would seem to comprise a pool of candidates seeking patronage positions from the president or their fellow partisans. To account for the effect of mode of exit, I include separate dummy variables to account for whether a member lost or retired.

Both ideological shifts and abstentions could be affected by certain partisan and institutional arrangements. Factors such as party status (majority or minority; Forgette and Sala 1999) or partisan control of the White House (as Senator Norris suggests) could influence the nature of business conducted during lame-duck sessions, which in turn might lead to modifications of members' roll-call behavior. A majority-party variable is coded 1 for members of the majority party, 0 otherwise. To ascertain how or whether the president influences roll-call turnout in lame-duck sessions, I included a variable coded 1 for those members who share the same party affiliation as the president, 0 otherwise. To gain further analytical leverage on the Norris hypothesis, I interact the *Lost* and *Member Pres Party* variables. Similarly, I interact the *Lost* and *Member Maj Party* variables to determine whether losers from the majority party tend to exhibit a greater likelihood of roll-call malleability. Changes in partisan control of the House may spur the outgoing majority to push through as much legislation as possible on the backs of their departing MCs. In previous work, Goodman and

Nokken (2002) found significant changes in roll-call behavior in the lame-duck session that preceded the change in majority-party control of the House. I include a dummy variable coded 1 for those Congresses that preceded a change in majority-party control, 0 otherwise.

While the time frame analyzed in this work comprises a long time line of a stable partisan system, it is important to account for important temporal effects, a series of distinct congressional eras, and important changes to key legislative institutions. First, I include a series of dummy variables for each Congress to account for Congress-specific effects.[8] The most notable institutional change is the rise of the strong Speaker era ushered in by the adoption of the Reed rules in 1890 under the Republican leadership of Thomas Reed, with the consequent domination of the House by Joseph Cannon's exploitation of those rules. I created a strong-Speaker variable coded 1 for those Congresses led by Republican Speakers Reed and Cannon (the 51st, 54th, 55th, and 58th–61st), 0 for others. I account for the post-Cannon-revolt era with variable coded 1 for the 62nd and each subsequent Congress, 0 for others. As length of service became an increasingly valuable factor in congressional service, I control for seniority with two variables. *Seniority* is coded as the number of Congresses in which a member served, and the square of *Seniority* is used to capture effects of long tenures in office.

Estimates of Ideological Changes

I specify a series of OLS models to estimate ideological changes in roll-call-voting behavior using two different dependent variables, *IDEOLOGY1* and *IDEOLOGY2*. I estimate separate models for Democrats and Republicans to assess the direction and magnitude of the ideological changes for lame-duck members. As noted, I include a series of Congress-specific dummy variables and use the cluster command in Stata to group members by their Inter-university Consortium for Political and Social Research (ICPSR) ID numbers to generate robust standard errors. I estimate two specifications for each dependent variable and do so separately for each party. The results for *IDEOLOGY1* are presented in equations 23.1 and 23.2; results for the *IDEOLOGY2* models appear in equations 23.3 and 23.4.[9]

$$\begin{aligned}
&\textit{IDEOLOGY1}, \text{Dems} = -0.34(0.05^{*})\text{Constant} + 0.02(0.02)\textit{Lost} \\
&\quad + 0.01(0.02)\textit{Retired} - 0.003(0.01)\textit{Seniority} - 0.00(0.001)\textit{Seniority}^2 \\
&\quad + 0.32(0.04^{**})\textit{Reed-Cannon Era} + 0.28(0.03^{**})\textit{Post-Cannon Revolt} \\
&\quad + 0.27(0.04^{**})\textit{Member Maj Party} - 0.20(0.03^{**})\textit{Member Pres Party} \\
&\quad + 0.16(0.03^{**})\textit{Change Maj Party} - 0.06(0.03^{*})\textit{Lost} \times \textit{Maj Party} \\
&\quad (R^2 = 0.34, N = 2{,}318) \qquad \textbf{(23.1)}
\end{aligned}$$

$$IDEOLOGY1\text{, Reps} = -0.12(0.04^{*})\text{Constant} + 0.03(0.03)\mathit{Lost} + 0.01(0.02)\mathit{Retired} - 0.002(0.005)\mathit{Seniority} - 0.00(0.001)\mathit{Seniority}^2 + 0.61(0.05^{**})\mathit{Reed\text{-}Cannon\ Era} + 0.42(0.13^{**})\mathit{Post\text{-}Cannon\ Revolt} - 0.74(0.04^{**})\mathit{Member\ Maj\ Party} + 0.43(0.03^{**})\mathit{Member\ Pres\ Party} - 0.09(0.04^{**})\mathit{Change\ Maj\ Party} - 0.003(0.04)\mathit{Lost} \times \mathit{Maj\ Party} \quad (R^2 = 0.36,\ N = 2{,}346) \tag{23.2}$$

Looking first at the *IDEOLOGY1* estimates, both of the Democratic and the Republican models are statistically significant. The variables of most interest are *Lost* and *Retired*. Statistically significant coefficients on these variables would indicate significant ideological changes resulting from lame-duck status. For the most part, the results provide strong support for the conventional wisdom of no significant changes. Turning to the interaction effects, though, Democrats exhibit statistically significant changes, while Republicans do not. When they are members of the majority and when they share the party label of the president, defeated Democrats make statistically significant leftward shifts in their voting behavior, consistent with the lame-duck and Norris hypotheses. Defeated Republicans, however, stand their ideological ground.

The effects of other partisan and institutional variables are mixed. Speakers Reed and Cannon successfully pulled both Republican and Democratic members to the right. The post-revolt Congresses also show significant positive coefficients, suggesting strong conservative tendencies for Republicans and moderating effects for Democrats. Lame-duck sessions that preceded a change in partisan control played a moderating role among both parties, evident by statistically significant positive coefficients for Democrats and significant negative coefficients for Republicans. The majority-party and presidential-party dummy variables also show different effects across parties. Majority-party status tends to have a moderating effect on both parties, while having one of their partisans in the White House leads to more extreme behavior, with Democrats shifting to the left and Republicans to the right.

The analyses of *IDEOLOGY1* provide evidence to indicate that defeated Democrats altered the ideological content of their roll-call behavior in response to specific partisan factors. While not an unequivocal proof of significant lame-duck effects across all members, it is an important finding that shows that removing the electoral connection did, indeed, play a significant role in the decision-making process of a certain category of MCs.

My second dependent variable measuring ideology, *IDEOLOGY2*, possesses a number of useful qualities for searching for lame-duck effects. First, the coding allows me to determine whether members make a significant shift over a much shorter period, from regular to lame-duck session. Second, it allows me to include a much larger number of members in the estimations. As in the previous set of estimates, I specify an OLS model with Congress-specific dummies, using the cluster command in Stata to group individuals and generate robust standard errors. Each specification of the model (displayed in equations 23.3 and 23.4) generates statistically significant *F* values. Once again, I find evidence of the existence of lame-duck-influenced shifts in voting behavior.

$$\begin{aligned} \textit{IDEOLOGY2}\text{, Dems} &= 0.33(0.03^{**})\text{Constant} + 0.04(0.02^{*})\textit{Lost} \\ &- 0.01(0.01)\textit{Retired} - 0.001(0.004)\textit{Seniority} - 0.00(0.00)\textit{Seniority}^2 \\ &- 0.53(0.04^{**})\textit{Reed-Cannon Era} - 0.30(0.02^{**})\textit{Post-Cannon Revolt} \\ &- 0.07(0.02^{**})\textit{Member Maj Party} - 0.14(0.01^{**})\textit{Member Pres Party} \\ &+ 0.09(0.01^{**})\textit{Change Maj Party} - 0.06(0.02^{*})\textit{Lost} \times \textit{Maj Party} \\ &(R^2 = 0.37,\ N = 3{,}819) \end{aligned} \tag{23.3}$$

$$\begin{aligned} \textit{IDEOLOGY2}\text{, Reps} &= 0.28(0.02^{**})\text{Constant} - 0.04(0.02^{*})\textit{Lost} \\ &+ 0.02(0.02)\textit{Retired} + 0.001(0.004)\textit{Seniority} - 0.00(0.00)\textit{Seniority}^2 \\ &- 0.11(0.03^{**})\textit{Reed-Cannon Era} + 0.36\ (0.032^{**})\textit{Post-Cannon Revolt} \\ &+ 0.25(0.03^{**})\textit{Member Maj Party} - 0.31(0.02^{**})\textit{Member Pres Party} \\ &- 0.02(0.02)\textit{Change Maj Party} + 0.03(0.02)\textit{Lost} \times \textit{Maj Party} \\ &(R^2 = 0.39,\ N = 3{,}926) \end{aligned} \tag{23.4}$$

These estimates show that defeated members from both parties make modest, but statistically significant, shifts in their voting behavior toward the ideological extremes of their respective parties. The interaction effects indicate significant behavioral implications for defeated members. Once again, the results provide evidence that lends support to both the lame-duck and the Norris hypothesis. Significant effects resulting from lame-duck status during lame-duck sessions generated behavioral shifts among certain subgroups of MCs.

Estimates of Changes in Participation

In the previous section, I found evidence to support the contention that lame-duck sessions influenced the ideological content of departing members. While those effects were not pervasive across all members, important subsets of MCs exhibited statistically significant modifications to their roll-call behavior. In this section, I specify a series of models to estimate changes in individual MCs' abstention rates. The one difference between these models and those from the previous section is that I pool all members in the abstention estimates since I have no *ex ante* expectations of opposing partisan effects on turnout.

The results for both abstention-related dependent variables are displayed in equations 23.5 and 23.6. All of the specifications across both dependent variables are statistically significant. The primary result of note is the sizable and statistically significant increase in abstention rates for departing members across each of the specifications in the two sets of models. Retirees exhibit a 10 percentage point increase in the *ABSTENTION1* estimates. Likewise, defeated members reduce their participation rates from 8 to 11 percentage points. The interaction effects yield few significant results. The take-home message, though, is clear: lame-duck sessions are marked by increased abstention rates among lame-duck MCs.

$$\begin{aligned} \textit{ABSTENTION1} = {} & 0.09(0.02^{**})\text{Constant} + 0.11(0.01^{**})\textit{Lost} \\ & + 0.10(0.01^{**})\textit{Retired} - 0.004(0.002)\textit{Seniority} + 0.000(0.000)\textit{Seniority}^2 \\ & + 0.03(0.02)\textit{Reed-Cannon Era} + 0.13(0.03^{**})\textit{Post-Cannon Revolt} \\ & - 0.02(0.01^{**})\textit{Maj Party Member} + 0.01(0.01)\textit{Member Pres Party} \\ & - 0.13(0.02)\textit{Change Maj Party} - 0.02(0.02)\textit{Lost} \times \textit{Maj Party} \\ & (R^2 = 0.14,\ N = 7{,}466) \end{aligned} \quad \textbf{(23.5)}$$

$$\begin{aligned} \textit{ABSTENTION2} = {} & -0.03(0.01^{**})\text{Constant} + 0.10(0.01^{**})\textit{Lost} \\ & + 0.06(0.01^{**})\textit{Retired} - 0.01(0.002^{**})\textit{Seniority} + 0.001(0.000^{**})\textit{Seniority}^2 \\ & + 0.05(0.01^{**})\textit{Reed-Cannon Era} + 0.01(0.01)\textit{Post-Cannon Revolt} \\ & + 0.01(0.004^{**})\textit{Maj Party Member} + 0.01(0.004^{**})\textit{Member Pres Party} \\ & - 0.03(0.02^{*})\textit{Change Maj Party} - 0.02(0.01)\textit{Lost} \times \textit{Maj Party} \\ & (R^2 = 0.10,\ N = 10{,}687) \end{aligned} \quad \textbf{(23.6)}$$

Looking at the changes in *ABSTENTION1*, I find weakly significant increases in abstention in the Reed-Cannon Congresses and large increases in the post-revolt era. Membership in the majority party leads to a modest increase in turnout in the *ABSTENTION1* estimates, while a change in majority-party control produces statistically significant increases in turnout.

Overall, the expectation of increased abstention among lame-duck members in lame-duck sessions holds. Other factors, however, serve to influence members' participation rates. While these effects are not uniform across the two sets of models, I do find evidence to suggest that certain settings create strong incentives for members to turn out and vote in lame-duck sessions. In the next set of estimates, I try to disentangle such affects and determine how different vote-specific factors influence aggregate turnout levels on individual roll-call votes.

Predicting Abstention Rates on Roll-Call Votes

The individual-level results lend some support to the contention that lame-duck sessions influence the ideological content of departing members' voting behavior and strong evidence that such sessions create strong disincentives for lame ducks to participate in roll-call votes. Departing members make relatively large and statistically significant reductions in their participation rates, even when one accounts for the different modes of exit. Lame-duck sessions are not marked by uniform changes across all members or across all Congresses. I now analyze the aggregate percentage of abstentions on each roll-call vote. The dependent variable for my two sets of models is the percentage of members abstaining on each non-unanimous roll-call vote.[10] I calculate the percentages separately for returning and departing members to discern how the groups respond to specific roll-call characteristics. The specifications include a number of the same institutional and partisan variables from the previous models. I also include variables to account for a series of vote-specific factors to gain analytical leverage on questions about strategic abstention and the effects of party leadership. Once again, I include a series of Congress-specific dummy variables, as well as dummy variables to account for lame-duck sessions preceding changes in party control, the strong Speaker era, and the post-Cannon-revolt Congresses.

The first vote-specific variable is a lame-duck dummy variable coded 1 for those roll calls held in lame-duck sessions, 0 for votes held in regular sessions. If lame-duck sessions are marked by an overall reduction in turnout, the coefficient will be positive and statistically significant. The *Percentage Margin* variable measures the perceived closeness of a vote and is coded as the difference between the total yea and nay votes as a percentage of total House membership. I include a variable (*Yea-Nay Distance*) that takes the value of the difference between the yea and nay NOMINATE positions for each scalable roll-call vote to measure the effect of ideologically extreme proposals on turnout.

As a way to evaluate the effect of party preferences on participation on individual roll-call votes, I include the observed Rice cohesion scores for each vote (Cox and Poole 2002). Higher values on the observed Rice score imply higher levels of partisan salience and, it is assumed, higher levels of pressure from partisan sources. The expectation is that increased party pressure leads to lower levels of abstention. Finally, the timing of votes could potentially influence participation. Congressional lore tells of a Tuesday-Thursday Club, in which important legislative business is scheduled during the middle of the week rather than on weekends to help facilitate member participation because members were able to reconcile campaign activities and roll-call voting (Nokken and Sala 2002). The *Tues-Thur* dummy variable takes a value of 1 for those votes held on Tuesday, Wednesday, or Thursday, 0 otherwise.

I use OLS to estimate two different specifications of the model. The results are displayed in equations 23.7 and 23.8. Both of the specifications have statistically significant *F* scores. Comparing the results from the two sets of estimates, some important differences emerge. The coefficient on the *lame-duck* variable is statistically significant, positive, but small (0.01) for departing members, suggesting that overall abstention rates among the lame-duck members creep up only slightly from regular to lame-duck sessions. Participation rates among returning members, however, actually increase in lame-duck sessions by 3 percentage points.

Percentage Lame-Duck Members Absent on House Votes, 46th–72nd Congresses
$$= 0.31(0.01^{**}) + 0.01(0.003^{*})\textit{Lame Duck} + 0.12(0.01^{**})\textit{Margin} + 0.04(0.01^{**})\textit{Unified Control} - 0.02(0.003^{**})\textit{Yea-Nay Distance} + 0.004(0.02)\textit{Reed Cannon Era} - 0.16(0.02^{**})\textit{Post Revolt} + 0.01(0.01)\textit{Rice Scores} - 0.01(0.02)\textit{Change Maj Party} - 0.01(0.003^{**})\textit{Tues-Thur}$$
$$(\text{Adj. } R^2 = 0.26,\ N = 5{,}960) \qquad \textbf{(23.7)}$$

Percentage Returning Members Absent on House Votes, 46th–72nd Congresses
$$= 0.24(0.01^{**}) - 0.03(0.003^{*})\textit{Lame Duck} + 0.17(0.01^{**})\textit{Margin} + 0.04(0.01^{*})\textit{Unified Control} - 0.03(0.004^{**})\textit{Yea-Nay Distance} - 0.05(0.02^{**})\textit{Reed Cannon Era} - 0.17(0.02^{**})\textit{Post Revolt} + 0.04(0.01^{**})\textit{Rice Scores} - 0.00(0.02)\textit{Change Maj Party} - 0.01(0.003^{**})\textit{Tues-Thur}$$
$$(\text{Adj. } R^2 = 0.30,\ N = 5{,}960) \qquad \textbf{(23.8)}$$

The take-home message from these analyses is that significant behavioral implications result from lame-duck status. Some sets of departing members of Congress do indeed exhibit significant ideological changes in roll-call behavior once their ties to the electorate are removed. They also sharply reduce their overall level of participation in their final terms in office, and those reductions hold for both voluntary and involuntary modes of departure. A couple of points are of particular interest. First, returning members who cast roll calls in lame-duck sessions respond to important political factors, namely, impending changes in majority control of the chamber. Furthermore, the aggregate-abstention results show that absenteeism actually goes down in lame-duck sessions of Congress. Lame-duck sessions of Congress are not defined solely in terms of increased levels of participatory shirking. It appears both departing and returning members respond to important partisan and institutional cues that provide them with strong incentives to participate on certain roll-call votes.

Conclusion

The data show that some departing members do change their ideological stripes in the lame-duck sessions of their final term in office. Certainly, members do tend to die in their "ideological boots" (Poole and Rosenthal 1997a, 8), but removing the electoral connection serves to alter the sets of constraints members face when deciding how to cast votes. When that electoral constraint is removed, members do exhibit some changes in their voting behavior, some of which, though, are rather subtle. Members do not suddenly move from one end of the ideological spectrum to the other. While such changes are relatively small, members may well make significant modifications to their voting behavior on a small number of important roll-call votes. Of particular interest is the possibility that members make dramatic reversals on particular roll-call votes or within specific policy categories. That possibility makes the analysis of specific votes an interesting and useful endeavor to help isolate the effects of particular variables thought to have a significant influence on vote choice (Bianco 1994, 158).

Part III

Policy

Although political scientists have devoted increasing attention to studying narrow aspects of congressional institutions or practice, the ultimate goal of this field of scholarship is to determine how the different structures of policy making affect the policies passed by Congress. The policy effects of the political process motivated many of the early congressional scholars (Wilson 1908; American Political Science Association 1950; Ranney 1951), and public policy is studied by the authors in this part of the volume. These chapters study how external conditions created an environment in which certain policy proposals were desirable and then consider how this demand for policy was enacted by politicians.

In "Measuring Significant Legislation, 1877–1948," Joshua D. Clinton and John S. Lapinski provide a measure of legislative output that can be used to characterize the lawmaking process across time. Clinton and Lapinski argue that a measure of legislation is important because if theories are relevant only for some types of lawmaking—such as consequential legislation—then testing those theories requires the ability to distinguish between legislative statutes and identify those for which our theoretical predictions are relevant.

Jeffrey Rogers Hummel and Barry R. Weingast argue in "The Fugitive Slave Act of 1850: An Instrumental Interpretation?" that the conventional wisdom that sees the Fugitive Slave Act of 1850 as a symbolic gesture is wrong. The act had two important features for its proponents. First, it was designed to control the slaves thought to be the most likely to run from a plantation. Second, the act served as a signal that allowed Northerners to reveal whether they were pro- or anti-South. This would prove critical to the South's evaluation of its ability to retain slavery as an institution. Their analysis suggests that the Fugitive Slave Act was not simply a hollow policy gesture, as previous authors have argued.

Erik Berglöf and Howard Rosenthal study the creation of a particular public policy in "Power Rejected: Congress and Bankruptcy in the Early Republic." They draw on a pivotal politics model in explaining how and when bankruptcy laws are enacted. They find that bankruptcy laws were enacted following severe macroeconomic downturns, were produced by unified government of the political right, and although enacted by political conservatives, were debtor friendly either by design or by practice.

Chapter 24

Measuring Significant Legislation, 1877–1948

JOSHUA D. CLINTON AND JOHN S. LAPINSKI

Introduction

In this chapter we provide a measure of legislative output that can be used to characterize outcomes of the lawmaking process across time. We summarize our efforts to assess the significance of the 21,741 public statutes passed between 1877 (45th Congress) and 1948 (80th Congress).[1] In so doing we collect both statute-level descriptive information and the assessments of several scholars and chroniclers who identify enactments of note during this time period. Using this massive data collection we can characterize and assess congressional lawmaking activity across a period spanning the Populist, Progressive, and New Deal eras as well as the two world wars.

We use a statistical model to integrate the information and estimate a statute-level measure of legislative output. Rather than relying on a single scholar's assessment of statutes' significance, we use an item-response model to aggregate the information contained in the nine assessments we collect. The statistical model provides the means for integrating the information in these assessments with statute characteristics—for example, the amount of attention the legislation received in Congress. Using several sources of information permits comparisons precluded by coarser characterizations. For example, we can compare the relative notability of the Pure Foods Act of 1906 and the Social Security Act of 1934 instead of treating the two statutes as equally significant.[2]

We develop the measure in several steps. First, we discuss the difficulties associated with defining *significant legislation* to situate the interpretation of our analysis. Having outlined the importance and the limits of the concept, we then describe the ratings and data we use to estimate legislative significance. The third section argues for a systematic means of combining the many existing assessments of legislative significance, and section four presents the item-response model we use to do so. Section five assesses the resulting statute-level estimates and characterizes lawmaking in the pre–World War II era. We conclude by discussing possible extensions of the measure and how the measure can be used to address fundamental questions.

Defining Significant Legislation

Defining precisely what is meant by the term *significant legislation* (or *important* or *landmark* legislation) is a very difficult task. Most scholars use established lists of important or landmark enactments for their empirical study, noting that they use others' definitions.[3] Although several lists of significant legislation exist, the bases on which the determinations of significance are made are largely unclear. Cameron (2000, 38) aptly characterizes the situation faced by every scholar seeking to construct such a measure when he notes that the pathways to significance "are so many and so varied that a tired but *apropos* phrase is irresistible: legislative significance is hard to define but easy to recognize."[4]

An attempt to precisely enumerate the conditions under which a statute may rightfully be considered significant quickly leads to a long list of conditions that prove difficult, if not impossible, to work with (see, for example, discussions by L. Chamberlain 1946; Mayhew 1991; Binder 1999, 2003; Coleman 1999; Edwards, Barrett, and Peake 1997; Howell et al. 2000; Light 2002; Peterson 2001; Stathis 2003). Furthermore, even if it were possible to specify what constitutes an important statute, it is likely impossible to make a determination based on such standards because of the difficulty of ascertaining whether the specified conditions are satisfied. The difficulty, if not futility, of such an exercise leads us to define *significant legislation* explicitly in terms of what is notable. Consequently, we refer to a statute or constitutional amendment as *significant* if it is identified as noteworthy by a reputable chronicler of the congressional session.[5] Likewise, legislation that was enacted but not mentioned during the period by a rater is treated as being deemed *insignificant*. Although our measure is more accurately described as a measure of notable legislation, we follow others and refer to "notable" legislation as "significant" legislation.

Focusing on notable legislation effectively compiles a list of high-stakes legislation. Although high-stakes legislation includes innovative and consequential legislation, it may also include controversial legislation that is neither innovative nor consequential. Insofar as political conflict is more likely on innovative and consequential legislation, however, probably very few banal or inconsequential statutes are notable. Although our measure is necessarily imperfect because of these caveats, it is difficult to conceptualize a less imperfect measure.

Measuring Legislative Significance

An evaluation of legislation is the result of the work of a "rater"—effectively, a set of standards as to whether a statute is noteworthy. A single individual may count as more than one rater if he or she uses different standards in assessing the legislation. For example, Peterson (2001) uses different sources and standards to produce his Sweep One and Sweep Two lists. Because our measure of legislative significance depends on whether the legislation is noteworthy, it is critical to identify appropriate raters.

We rely on nine raters for the period 1877 to 1948. Following Mayhew, we classify the raters according to the timing of the assessment: contemporaneous raters assess legislation at or near the time of enactment and retrospective raters rely on hindsight to determine noteworthiness given both prior and subsequent events. Some determinations combine both retrospective and contemporaneous assessments. Although we could compare the assessments that result from the three perspectives to examine how the perceived importance of individual statutes changes over time, our primary interest is in using the evaluations to construct a measure of legislative significance that reflects both contemporaneous and retrospective perspectives.

We use three contemporaneous raters for the period 1877 to 1948. The legislative wrap-ups of the *American Political Science Review* (*APSR*) and the *Political Science Quarterly* (*PSQ*) provide two sets of ratings. The wrap-up for each journal consists of a summary of the year's proceedings in Congress. *APSR* covers the years 1919 to 1948 in a section titled "The Legislative Record," and *PSQ* covers the years 1889 to 1925 in its annual "Record of Public Events." Each wrap-up was read by two coders, and all of the legislation mentioned in the wrap-up was recorded.[6] Peterson's (2001) Sweep One provides the third contemporaneous assessment. Although his replication of Mayhew's coding technique is inexact, Peterson identifies 213 statutes passed from 1881 to 1945 as significant according to contemporaneous sources.[7]

We also use five retrospective evaluations. Peterson's (2001) replication of Mayhew's Sweep Two for the period 1881 to 1947 using several policy area histories constitutes one rating. The nine period-specific volumes of the New American Nation Series provide a second list of significant legislation.[8] These period-specific historical accounts of U.S. political history were read twice in their entirety and content-coded for mentions of public enactments and policy changes. If a policy change was mentioned but the title of the statute associated with it was not, we searched the index of the *History of Bills and Resolutions* in the *Congressional Record* and the index of *Public Statutes at Large* for the associated statute. When necessary, we also searched the *Congressional Universe* and *Academic Universe* databases, as well as ProQuest's historical archives for the *New York Times*, *Washington Post*, and *Wall Street Journal*, using available information and clues (such as the date of enactment or legislative activity) to identify the public statute associated with the policy.

A third source of retrospective ratings comes from L. Chamberlain's *The President, Congress, and Legislation* (1946). In chronicling policy making in 10 issues from pre-1877 to 1940, Chamberlain identifies 105 monumentally important enactments. Reynolds's (1995) "mini-research report" culls from a textbook, *Enduring Vision*, mentions of important legislation to test for the effect of divided government on lawmaking before World War II, and he identifies 84 enactments for the period 1877 to 1948. A final source is Sloan's *American Landmark Legislation* (1984). Sloan compiles a selective list of laws on the basis of two factors: the important national significance they had at the time Congress passed them, and the bills' lasting effect on one dimension or another of American life.

The third type of rating, a hybrid of contemporaneous and retrospective sources, is based on previously compiled lists of important enactments drawn from both types of sources. We use one hybrid rater in this chapter: Congressional Research Service employees Dell and Stathis (1982) chronicle 200 years of congressional effort—from the 1st Congress in 1789 to the 96th in 1980—and identify 271 significant public enactments from 1877 to 1948.

In addition to these nine assessments, we also measure several characteristics of the statutes themselves. We collect information on when the legislation was introduced to control for the possibility that legislation introduced early in a session is more likely to be significant than legislation introduced later in the session (Neustadt 2001; Rudalevige 2002).[9] We count the total number of pages—including debate and general bill activity (such as committee referral or discharge)—relating to the statute in the *History of Bills and Resolutions* of the *Congressional Record* as a proxy for congressional attention to the legislation. Although imperfect, the page-count measure—which ranges from 4 to 4,024 pages—is available for the entire period and reflects an attempt to assess the importance of legislative debate and rhetoric (Bessette 1994). Our decision to include members' extended remarks is inconsequential; the page counts in randomly selected years correlate at greater than 0.95.

In every year we consider, between five and nine raters assess the enactments. Not surprisingly, the vast majority of legislation—nearly 96 percent (20,788 of 21,741)—is unmentioned by any rater. Furthermore, significant variation between raters is evident in the number of mentioned statutes. For example, both the New American Nation Series and Sloan's *American Landmark Legislation* implicitly consider every public statute between 1877 and 1948, but the former deems 305 enactments to be significant and the latter lists only 16.

Further evidence of rater differences are revealed by examining ratings from the 66th, 67th, and 68th Congresses. All nine raters evaluate the 1,832 enactments of this period: 1,729 statutes are unmentioned by any rater, 49 statutes are mentioned by one rater, 26 by two raters, 8 by three raters, 11 by four raters, 1 by five raters, 4 by six raters, and 4 by seven raters. No statute is mentioned by more than seven raters. The four statutes rated as significant by seven of the nine raters are the National Prohibition Act of 1919 (not mentioned by Sloan or Chamberlain), the Transportation Act of 1920 (not mentioned by Sloan or Reynolds), the Immigration Act of 1921 (not mentioned by Sloan or Reynolds), and the Immigration Act of 1924 (not mentioned by Sloan or Peterson, Sweep Two). Although heterogeneity is clearly evident, unanimous agreement exists in periods covered by fewer raters. For example, during the years when only eight raters are active, all eight mention the Securities Act of 1934, the Sherman Antitrust Act of 1890, the Pure Foods Act of 1906, and the Federal Trade Commission Act of 1906.

The preceding discussion demonstrates that any measure of legislative significance must confront the issue of rater heterogeneity: how should we interpret rater disagreement, and how should a measure of significance account for this heterogeneity?

There are three interpretations of rater disagreement. First, raters may differ because they use different criteria. For example, one rater may identify only the most important legislation sponsored by Southern legislators, whereas other raters may attempt to identify all important enactments. In this case, the selection criteria are not the same. We consciously selected raters to minimize this possibility; the raters we use all explicitly aim to identify either significant legislation or the major legislative events of the year or time period.

Second, raters may employ different standards—that is, the threshold that establishes legislative significance may differ among raters. For example, in its annual wrap-up the *APSR* may be more likely to identify a statute as an important policy change than a rater such as Sloan, who surveys an entire time period before making a determination. In other words, two raters may agree as to the dimension of interest but differ on the level that establishes significance.

A third, but related, possible difference is the issue of rater consistency across time. Because not every rater rates every statute, it is difficult to know how to compare ratings from different eras. For example, although Peterson attempts to extend Mayhew's Sweep One and Sweep Two ratings to an earlier era, it is impossible to determine whether they employ the same significance threshold and consequently how the two periods compare in terms of the number of significant enactments because Peterson and Mayhew use completely different sources in making their determinations and never rate a common set of statutes.

A further source of temporal inconsistency is the potential difference between contemporaneous and retrospective assessments. Being charged with reviewing the activity of a congressional session may cause a rater to artificially inflate the perceived significance of some legislation—particularly during periods of relative inactivity. For instance, a newspaper that summarizes every session may feel obliged to designate at least some legislation as significant in each session to provide content. Perhaps the standard used to identify significant legislation is not absolute (across all time, was any policy produced in this session particularly newsworthy?), but rather relative (of all the legislation passed in the session, which was the most newsworthy?). Depending on the amount of important legislation produced by a session and the standard used by the observer, standards may change from session to session owing to the pressures of publishing a story (and therefore mentioning legislation).

We cannot rule out this possibility, but available evidence suggests that this is not likely to be the case. Contrary to what we would expect if publishing needs artificially inflate the number of mentioned statutes relative to their true significance, the number of mentioned enactments varies considerably across years among the contemporaneous raters. For example, whereas *PSQ* mentions only 3 statutes in the 50th Congress and 5 in the 60th, it mentions 30 and 31 statutes in the 65th and 67th Congresses, respectively. The need to fill up column space does not result in a similar number of enactments being mentioned across time.

A final source of rater variation is the possibility that raters may make mistakes in their assessments. The process of culling through the legislative record is both exhausting and time-consuming. Raters may miss legislation that would have qualified as noteworthy according to their own standards.

The most prevalent response to rater heterogeneity is to adopt a "replication" strategy and determine whether substantive conclusions stand up to alternative measures. Howell and his colleagues (2000) employ this strategy in their replication of Mayhew's work on divided government. Although the replication strategy is used quite commonly in political science and is particularly pervasive in studies of lawmaking (see, for example, Krehbiel 1998; Coleman 1999), it effectively checks only whether the ratings are close enough to produce similar coefficient estimates when used in a regression structure.

A replication strategy is problematic because it fails to account for the information contained in the multiple ratings. Replication treats the 4 statutes identified as significant by seven raters (during the 66th, 67th, and 68th Congresses) identically to the 49 statutes rated significant by a single rater; and it ignores the plausible conclusion that rater agreement constitutes evidence of increased significance or certainty about the enactment's assessment. Likewise, rater disagreement suggests that we should be less certain about a bill whose significance is disputed relative to an enactment with complete rater agreement. Rater agreement and disagreement therefore conveys information about the magnitude and certainty of our assessment of legislative significance—information ignored by methods employing a replication strategy.

Two additional related problems arise. First, the dichotomous classification of landmark legislation versus everything else is extremely coarse. It is unlikely that every statue mentioned by Dell and Stathis (for example) is equally significant. Because we use the information in the multiple ratings to distinguish between more and less significant legislation, our measure allows us to make such distinctions. Second, existing measures of legislative significance tell us nothing about the certainty we have about the designated significance. That raters disagree in their determinations of the significance of legislation implies that uncertainty exists; although we may be quite confident that the 4 statutes identified as significant by seven raters during the 66th, 67th, and 68th Congresses are important, we may be less certain about the significance of the 49 statutes mentioned by a single rater.

It may be tempting to account for the information contained in the multiple ratings by using the average rating. However, aggregation requires strong assumptions. First, an additive aggregate measure such as the mean assumes that significance increases linearly—a statute rated significant by nine raters is nine times more significant than a bill so rated by only one. Second, it is not obvious how to account for missing evaluations. If only two raters evaluate a particular Congress and both designate a statute as significant, how should we compare the resulting significance to a statute rated significant by the same two raters but unmentioned by other raters? Is the first statute as significant as the second, as summing the number of mentions would suggest, or is the first statute more significant as the average number of mentions implies?

A third difficulty is that these possible aggregation strategies assume that rater determinations are equally informative—no rater is better able to determine the true significance of statutes than others. The presence of rater disagreement, however, suggests we should account for differences in how raters evaluate. There is no reason to assume that if two raters disagree in their assessment of the significance of two pieces of legislation, they must be equally significant; it is equally plausible that one rater is more likely to err in this determination.

Fourth, using a statistic from the ratings themselves does not provide an obvious way to incorporate additional information into the determination of legislative significance. Measuring significance using aggregated ratings alone ignores available information about the legislation. For example, significant legislation may be more likely to be introduced in the first congressional session, or it may be that the more attention is paid to the legislation (as measured through pages of coverage in the index of the *Congressional Record*), the more likely it is to be significant.[10] A convincing model of legislative significance would be one that exploits all available information.

A Statistical Model of Legislative Significance

Given the concerns noted in the previous section, we employ a statistical model to aggregate the information contained in the multiple ratings and the statutes' characteristics. The model assumes that raters' perceptions of the true underlying significance of legislation are subject to error and that their decision to rate legislation as significant depends on whether their perception of the legislation's true significance exceeds their threshold of what constitutes significance. We assume that all raters agree on what constitutes significant legislation (that is, they agree on what the significance dimension is), but raters may differ in their determinations either because they employ different significance thresholds (that is, they use higher or lower thresholds) or because idiosyncratic perceptual differences may obscure the true importance of the legislation to the rater. In the statistical literature, we employ what is known as the multirater model (see Albert 1999; Johnson and Albert 1999), which we estimate using Bayesian methods.

The measurement model we present improves on existing work in at least three ways. First, employing a statistical rather than a counting model yields estimates and standard errors of legislative significance that account for the information contained in the ratings of every rater while simultaneously recovering estimates of the relationship between the raters' determinations.

Second, although not every rater covers the entire time period, the overlap among the raters provides the required bridging observations to ensure that the scale is comparable across raters and across time. As long as the standards employed by each rater remain constant, we can use the relationship between the ratings on the 1,832 statutes passed in the 66th, 67th, and 68th Congresses (1919–1925) to recover rater characteristics that are directly comparable.[11] A second source of comparability results from relating the determinations of non-overlapping raters to a rater overlapping both. For example, if raters A and B contemporaneously rate legislation, then we can determine how their ratings relate using the set of commonly rated legislation. Similarly, the ratings of contemporaries B and C can also be determined. As long as B does not change the way he or she determines significance, knowing how the ratings of A and C relate to B's permits us to relate the ratings of A to C's even if A and C do not overlap.

Third, the statistical model we use allows us to incorporate information such as the amount of page coverage each statute receives in the *Congressional Record* and the session of Congress in which the legislation was proposed. Accounting for information besides the actual ratings is beneficial not only because the resulting measure accounts for this additional information but also because, if we are interested in the regression specification itself—as we would be if we were testing accounts predicting whether a statute is likely to be notable—then the estimated regression equation "controls" for the considerable uncertainty in the estimates of legislative significance.

THE BASIC MODEL

We assume that a true and unobservable value of legislative significance is associated with all legislation. For legislation $t \in 1, \ldots, T$ we denote the true latent significance as z_t. We assume that raters $i \in 1, \ldots, N$ of legislative significance (for example, *PSQ* and New American Nation Series) agree on what constitutes legislative significance and that z_t entirely determines a piece of legislation's true significance relative to other legislation. If the true significance were observable, all raters would agree on the relative legislative significance ranking even if they employ different thresholds in determining the significance of a bill—no rater would think that statute i is more important than statute j if $z_j > z_i$. Although raters may differ in the methods they use to assess significance, they all fundamentally agree on the unobservable determinants of legislative significance. Although there is no reason why significance must be a unidimensional concept, our investigation reveals no evidence of multiple dimensions—perhaps because the raters we use share a common aim of identifying important legislation.

Each rater "votes" on whether legislation t is significant (1) or insignificant (0) on the basis of the latent trait z_t. Let $\mathbf{Y}$ be the $T \times N$ matrix of ratings, with element y_{ti} containing the dichotomous choice of rater n with respect to legislation t. For the period we examine (the 45th through 80th Congresses), $T = 21{,}741$ and $N = 9$. Consistent with the observation that rater assessments may differ, we allow raters to imperfectly observe the true significance value z_t. Raters rely on the proximate measure $x_{ti} = z_{ti} + \varepsilon_{ti}$. In other words, for reasons such as the inherent difficulty of assessing legislative significance, the true significance of legislation is imperfectly observed by raters. Although we assume that rater perceptions are unbiased (that is, $E[\varepsilon_{ti}] = 0$), we permit raters to differ in the precision of their perceptions, perhaps because of different amounts of ambiguity in raters' standards. We denote the variance of ε_{ti} for rater i by δ_i^2.

Denoting the common distribution of ε by $F(\cdot)$, these assumptions imply that $\varepsilon_{ti} \approx F(0, \varepsilon_{ti}/\delta_i)$. To model the significance of legislation in a statistical model we impose some structure on raters' decisions. We assume that a rater's determination of whether an enactment is significant depends on whether the rater perceives the latent value of the legislation x_{ti} as exceeding the rater's threshold γ_i. Thus, $y_{ti} = 1$ if and only if $x_{ti} > \gamma_i$. In addition to allowing raters to differentially and imperfectly perceive the true significance of legislation, we also permit each rater to employ a different threshold when determining legislative significance. Consequently, raters may differ in their determinations either because of errors in their perception of statute significance or because they differ in the threshold they use. The model assumes that the discrepancy between the number of statutes (241) identified by Dell and Stathis (1982) and the number (16) identified by Sloan (1984) is due to Sloan employing a higher threshold rather than their evaluations being on different dimensions of legislation.[12]

Given this rating rule, the probability of observing rater i designating legislation t as significant is given by the probability that the rater's observed trait for t is greater than his or her threshold. Given the assumption that $\varepsilon_{ti} \approx F(0, \varepsilon_{ti}/\delta_i)$, this implies that

$$\begin{aligned} \Pr(y_{ti} = 1) &= \Pr(x_{ti} > \gamma_i) \\ &= \Pr(\varepsilon_{ti} > \gamma_i - z_t) \\ &= 1 - F[(\gamma_i - z_t)/\delta_i] \\ &= F[(Z_t - \gamma_i)/\delta_i] \end{aligned}$$

The expression $(z_{ti} - \gamma_i)/\delta_i$ can be reexpressed as $\beta_i z_t - \alpha_i$, where $\beta_t = 1/\delta_i$ and $\alpha_i = \gamma_i/\delta_i$. β_i measures the "discrimination" of rater i—how much the probability of a rater classifying a piece of legislation as significant changes in response to changes in the latent quality of the legislation. If $\beta_i = 0$, a rater's determination of legislative significance does not depend on the true significance of a statute z_t. If β_i is very high, then the rater's determination of significance is determined almost entirely by the underlying true significance of the legislation. The estimate of α_i is a function of the threshold used by rater i in determining significance. High (low) values of α_i indicate that a rater is more (less) likely to classify the legislation as significant for a given value of z_t.

Because not every rater evaluates every piece of legislation, we assume that the decision to not rate a piece of legislation is independent of both the significance of the legislation and rater qualities; if a rater fails to evaluate an enactment, this absence is uninformative about both the quality of the legislation and the rater. This assumption is unproblematic given that the missing data result not from the raters' conscious choice but rather from the fact that not all raters evaluate for the entire time period. Given this structure, the Bernoulli probability of y_{ti} is $\Pr(y_{ti} = 1 \mid z_t, \beta_i, \alpha_i) = F(\beta_i z_t - \alpha_i)^{y_{ti}} \times [1 - F(\beta_i z_t - \alpha_i)]^{(1-y_{ti})}$. Assuming that the ratings are independent across raters conditional on the true latent quality of legislation z_t and the rater parameters β_i and α_i imply that $\Pr(y_{t1}, y_{t2}, \ldots, y_{tN} = \mathbf{1} \mid z_t, \beta_i, \alpha_i) = \{F(\beta_1 z_t - \alpha_1)^{y_{t1}} \times [1 - F(\beta_1 z_t - \alpha_1)]^{(1-y_{t1})}\} \times \{F(\beta_2 z_t - \alpha_2)^{y_{t2}} [1 - F(\beta_2 z_t - \alpha_2)]^{(1-y_{t2})}\} \times \cdots \times \{F(\beta_N z_t - \alpha_N)^{y_{tN}} [1 - F(\beta_N z_t - \alpha_N)]^{(1-y_{tN})}\} = \prod_{i=1}^{N} F(\beta_i z_t - \alpha_i)^{y_{ti}} \times [1 - F(\beta_i z_t - \alpha_i)]^{1-y_{ti}}$. Further assuming that ratings are independent across legislation yields the likelihood function:

$$L(z, \alpha, \beta) = \prod_{i=1}^{N} \prod_{t=1}^{T} F(\beta_i z_t - \alpha_i)^{y_{ti}} \times [1 - F(\beta_i z_t - \alpha_i)]^{1-y_{ti}}$$

where only $\mathbf{Y}$ is observable.[13]

One might question whether the possibility that raters rely on similar sources in their evaluations violates the assumption of independent errors. It does not, because the assumption of independence is conditional on the rater parameters and the true significance of the legislation. In other words, that raters may use similar sources means that the rater parameters (that is, the significance threshold used and the amount of error in rater perceptions of true significance) are similar, not that raters' errors are correlated. An analogy to roll-call analysis might be helpful. Even though several roll-call votes may deal with a similar issue, we would not say that, conditional on the legislators' ideal points and the proposals being voted on, the errors in legislative voting are correlated. Instead, the similarity of votes on similar issues is reflected in the similarity of the resulting estimates for the bill item parameters.

Despite a different motivation and interpretation of the estimated parameters, the likelihood is identical to that used in roll-call analysis (see Clinton, Jackman, and Rivers 2004). This equivalence is most evident if we conceptualize pieces of legislation as "voting" on whether they are significant according to each rater (in other words, each of the 21,740 "legislators" may cast up to nine "votes").[14] Because everything except $\mathbf{Y}$ is unobserved, the scale and rotation of the parameter space are not identified by the likelihood (Rivers 2003). This means that $\mathbf{z}$ and $-\mathbf{z}$ yield equivalent values for the likelihood, as does $\mathbf{z}$ and $A \times \mathbf{z}$, where A is an arbitrary constant. As we estimate the model using Bayesian methods, we must specify prior distributions for the estimated parameters vectors $\mathbf{z}$, $\boldsymbol{\beta}$, and $\boldsymbol{\alpha}$. We have no prior information about the discrimination and difficulty of the raters so we adopt uninformative prior distributions and fix two statutes in the space.[15]

THE HIERARCHICAL MODEL

We can expand the basic model to accommodate additional information related to the latent significance of legislation using a hierarchical item-response model. A hierarchical model specifies a regression structure between observed characteristics and the latent significance $\mathbf{z}$. Instead of assuming that the prior distribution of legislation significance is identical and uninformative, for example, $z_t \approx N(0, 1)$, we assume that the prior of $\mathbf{z}$ is $N(\mu_z, \tau^2)$ and the prior mean μ_z is a function of additional observable information.

In our case, it is plausible that the length of time members of Congress spend on a statute (as measured by the number of pages devoted to it in the *Congressional Record*) is correlated with legislative significance. Some have also argued that legislation introduced in the first session of a Congress is more likely to be significant than legislation introduced in later sessions (Neustadt 2001; Rudalevige 2002).[16] A hierarchical item-response model allows us to account for such possibilities. Let $\mathbf{W}$ denote the $T \times d$ matrix of covariates. If we assume an additive and linear relationship, then estimating a hierarchical model assumes that $\mu_z = \mathbf{W}\boldsymbol{\kappa} + \boldsymbol{\zeta}$, where $\boldsymbol{\kappa}$ is a $d \times 1$ matrix of regression coefficients and $\boldsymbol{\zeta}$ is an independent and identically distributed error term. For example, in this chapter we posit that $\mu_z = \boldsymbol{\kappa}_0 + \boldsymbol{\kappa}_1 \log(\text{pages}) + \boldsymbol{\kappa}_2 I_1 + \boldsymbol{\kappa}_3 I_2 + \boldsymbol{\kappa}_4 I_3 + \zeta_t$, where I_1, I_2, and I_3 are indicator variables for whether legislation t was introduced in the first, second, or third session, respectively.

Imposing this linear regression structure and estimating a hierarchical model yields two benefits relative to the nonhierarchical model of the previous section. First, the hierarchical estimator of z_i "borrows strength" from the additional information. In other words, estimates of $\mathbf{z}$ account for information contained in the covariates $\mathbf{W}$. Because legislation with identical characteristics and covariates is assumed to share the same prior mean (although the prior variance permits legislation with identical covariates to differ in significance), the hierarchical estimator distinguishes between identically rated legislation on the basis of their characteristics (if those characteristics covary with legislative significance). This is particularly important when the problems associated with "chunky data" (Londregan 2000) result in few ratings.

Second, if we are interested in the determinants and covariates of legislative significance, adopting a hierarchical approach recovers estimates of $\boldsymbol{\kappa}$ that account for the substantial uncertainty in estimates of $\mathbf{z}$. Because the estimates $\mathbf{z}$ are effectively regressed on $\mathbf{W}$ at every iteration, as the estimates of $\mathbf{z}$ fluctuate across iterations, so too will the coefficients $\boldsymbol{\kappa}$ measuring the relationship.

Characterizing Legislative Significance

This section assesses the different significance scores we estimate for the period between 1877 and 1948. We compare the recovered parameter estimates from the nonhierarchical and hierarchical models, and we examine the resulting statute-level estimates of significance and estimates of aggregate lawmaking activity.

Comparing the nonhierarchical and hierarchical estimates to the mean rating for the 21,741 public statutes passed from the end of Reconstruction to the conclusion of World War II yields several conclusions.[17] First, if we compare the mean estimate to those of the nonhierarchical estimator, the estimated change in significance in moving from an average rating of 0 to 0.2 is much greater for the nonhierarchical estimates than the estimated change of moving from an average rating of 0.2 to 0.4; the marginal change of our estimate of legislative significance for the first rater's determination of significance is much larger than that of subsequent raters. Consequently, legislative significance is not simply a linear function of the number of raters who evaluate the legislation.

Second, incorporating additional information about the legislation using a hierarchical model refines our estimates of legislative significance. While the mean rating scores every nonrated statute with a significance of 0 (and the nonhierarchical item-response model recovers as small an estimate as possible given the lack of any information about those statutes), the hierarchical estimates permit covariates of significance to influence the recovered significance rating. The primary contribution of the hierarchical estimator is distinguishing among unrated legislation—we recover significance estimates for unrated statutes that range from 0 to 0.5 depending on the characteristics of the statute. Because the vast majority of statutes are unrated and unrated enactments are not equally unimportant, this is a valuable benefit.

As an illustrative example, consider public statutes authorizing bridge building. Passing legislation to build bridges is typical pork barrel politics. Although the appetite of members of Congress for pork is a well-established fact (Ferejohn 1974), not all pork is equivalent. From 1877 to 1948, Congress passed more than 3,100 bridge bills—a little more than 14 percent of all passed statutes. If we rely on the mean rating, all of these bills would receive the identical significance estimate of 0. The nonhierarchical estimator recovers similar estimates. However, the hierarchical estimator distinguishes between important and trivial bridge bills on the basis of the additional information that the hierarchical estimator employs. Because page coverage in the *Congressional Record* for bridge bills ranges from 4 to 57 pages, the hierarchical model distinguishes between significant and insignificant bridge bills using this information. For example, the bridge bill with the highest page count, passed in 1908, was the first omnibus bridge legislation ever enacted into law.[18] This bill included 23 bridges and faced unsuccessful attempts at obstruction. The posterior mean of the hierarchical estimate for this bill is 0.36, placing it in the top 8 percent of the distribution of all public bills according to the hierarchical estimator.

As further evidence, consider the top 1,000 significant statutes according to the hierarchical model. Of the top 1,000, 113 are not rated by a single rater as significant. Of these 113 statutes, over 90 address appropriation or tax-related measures. While these bills are clearly not as important as some of the legislation passed during the period (as evidenced by their lack of mention), they are certainly more important than most of the other unmentioned bills passed by Congress. These unrated enactments score high because several hundred pages of debate in Congress are recorded in the *Congressional Record* for each of them, a characteristic that corresponds to the likelihood of being rated given the regression structure we employ. These examples are typical of many other unmentioned statutes that are far from trivial.

Assessing Face Validity

Although the evidence thus far suggests that the hierarchical estimator performs reasonably well relative to available alternatives, it is useful to establish face validity for the hierarchical estimates by comparing the recovered estimates to conventional wisdom. The enactment with the highest estimated significance score is the establishment of the Federal Trade Commission (FTC) in the 63rd Congress.[19] The FTC dealt with the business trust issue first addressed by the Sherman Act of 1890.[20] Although we cannot be certain that the establishment of the FTC is *the* most important statute once we account for the considerable estimation uncertainty, what is notable is that the statutes we would expect to receive the highest significance scores actually do so. For example, the Pendleton Civil Service Reform Act (1883) receives a score of 0.866, while the National Industrial Recovery Act receives a statistically indistinguishable score of 0.865. Both statutes were tremendously influential, even though their policy content is distinct and they were passed in different eras. Also encouraging is the result that some Congresses do not produce legislation as significant as legislation produced by others. For example, the 45th Congress produced the Bland-Allison Silver Act (1878), which receives a score of 0.855, and the Timber and Stone Act (1878), which receives a score of 0.674, while the most significant statutes of the 46th Congress consisted of a sundry civil appropriation (0.486) and a military appropriation (0.471). The 54th and 58th Congresses were also not particularly memorable in terms of landmark legislation. The New Deal era, by contrast, especially the 73rd and 74th Congresses, produced loads of important enactments.

In addition to examining whether the statute-level estimates appear reasonable, we make a second check on validity: do the estimates aggregate to produce a time series of significant enactments that matches with historical understanding? To measure productivity, we follow Mayhew and count the

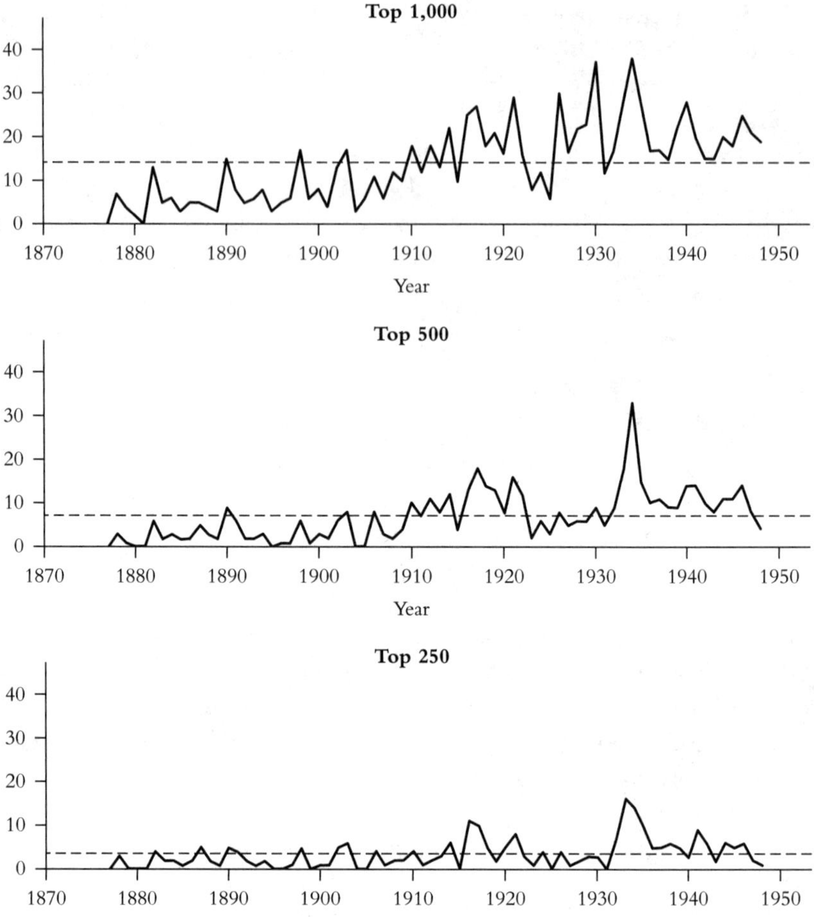

Figure 24.1 Number of statutes passed each year that are among the top 1,000, top 500, and top 250 statutes

number of significant statutes enacted during each year. A question arises: what gets counted? For a dichotomous measure of significance such as that employed by Mayhew, answering this question is straightforward: sum the identified bills. Because we can estimate a much finer measure, the question as to what is counted as a significant enactment is slightly more complicated. Consequently, we rank order the 21,741 statutes according to their estimated significance level and count the number of statutes each Congress passed that lie in some restricted set. Given this ambiguity, figure 24.1 presents the number of statutes passed each year that are among the top 1,000 (upper graph), top 500 (middle graph), and top 250 (lower graph) statutes.[21] The horizontal line denotes the number of statutes that would be passed if every Congress were equally productive.

A measure with face validity would capture important and known trends, such as the surges in legislative productivity during the Progressive and New Deal eras and the spikes during crises such as war. The expected surges, including solid bumps during World War I and World War II, are easy to identify. Capturing moments of inactivity is also important. The infamous 80th "Do Nothing" Congress produced only a single top-100 enactment (the Taft-Hartley Labor-Management Relations Act) and a well-below-average 12 top-500 enactments, but surprisingly, it also produced an above-average 40 in the top 1,000. Consequently, although the so-called Do Nothing Congress was inactive relative to the Congresses of the New Deal and World War II, it is actually near the middle of the distribution in terms of overall productivity. Such findings and trends are interesting in and of themselves in describing congressional productivity, but the true importance of the measure lies in offering a way to address substantive questions, such as the determinants of legislative productivity.

Conclusion

Improving our ability to identify high-stakes legislation is critical to assessing many of the questions that are fundamental to representative government. For example, our measure of significance can be used to explore how institutional rules affect collective choice outcomes. As Schickler (2001, 3) argues, "Congressional politics has depended crucially on such innovations as the 'Reed rules' of 1890, the Senate cloture rule adopted in 1917, the creation of congressional budget committees in 1974, the House breakaway from seniority rights to committee chairmanships in 1975, and the package of reforms adopted by the Republicans when they took over the House in 1995."

Because many of the most important reforms occurred before existing measures, scholarship has focused largely on the causes of institutional reform—for example, Binder's (1997) examination of the creation of minority and majority rights within Congress—rather than on the impacts of such reform on legislative productivity and lawmaking.[22] Given the number of important institutional (and electoral) reforms occurring before World War II—such as Reed's rules, cloture reform, committee reorganizations, and the direct election of senators—to the extent that the difficulty in measuring legislative output prevents investigations of the consequences of reform, the data and methodology we present offer the opportunity to examine the consequences of institutional changes. Although important and difficult questions are clearly raised by any such investigation (for example, how to control for both the demand for and the supply of high-stakes legislation), our data and measures enable us to begin to confront such questions.

By helping us understand how the configuration of preferences within an institutional structure affects legislative productivity, our measure gives us a way to begin answering questions such as Did "divided control" of the government make Congress unable to pass important legislation? Did the realigning elections of 1896 and 1932 produce periods of increased lawmaking? What has been the impact of a strong Speaker of the House (such as Reed and Cannon)? How has party polarization influenced Congress? Although all of these factors have received considerable attention, our ability to determine the actual impact of each on lawmaking has been inhibited by the difficulty to date of measuring policy output. Our estimates make it possible to conduct precisely such investigation.

Chapter 25

The Fugitive Slave Act of 1850: An Instrumental Interpretation

JEFFREY ROGERS HUMMEL AND

BARRY R. WEINGAST

Introduction

Why did Southerners seek a new fugitive slave act as part of the Compromise of 1850? The measure was so obviously pro-slavery, in a draconian fashion, that historians appear to believe that Southern demands require no explanation at all. Yet these same scholars usually dismiss the problem of runaway slaves as involving no serious losses. We are thus left with the paradox of slaveholders insisting on a measure that was simultaneously unnecessary and counterproductive. Why did they foist such an odious statute on Northerners with no major benefits at the risk of turning many against the South?

We argue that the Fugitive Slave Act of 1850 served an instrumental purpose in the face of political uncertainty: by forcing their Northern coalition partners to vote for a measure that was an obvious anathema in the North, Southerners could see whether a sufficient number of Northerners could support pro-Southern measures. If sufficient numbers of Northerners failed to do so in 1850, then it was also likely that too few Northerners would support Southerners when a future slave territory sought admission as a slave state. The Fugitive Slave Act was thus a form of signaling, allowing the Northern pivotal voters in Congress to reveal their type as pro- or anti-South. The willingness of sufficient Northerners to support the Fugitive Slave Act thus provided Southerners with critical information about the future of national politics and hence about the future security of slavery in the nation.

In sum, we contest the traditional view that the Fugitive Slave Act was an irrational measure sought by Southerners for symbolic reasons. We argue instead that this act served two separate instrumental purposes missed by most historians: one addressing the real problem of runaway males in the border states, the other enhancing the future security of slavery in the nation.

This chapter proceeds as follows. We discuss the background for the crisis in 1850, explaining the long-term sources of rational anxiety for Southerners. These sources help explain Southern motivation for seeking a new fugitive slave law. We then discuss our two hypotheses about the fugitive slave law, suggesting why it rationally fit the sources of Southern anxiety. Finally, we draw the wider implications of this approach for the rest of the decade and the Civil War.

Background to the Crisis

Two background issues are useful for understanding the role of the fugitive slave law in the Compromise of 1850: the problem of slavery's security within the nation, especially given Southerners' rational coalitional anxiety raised by the Wilmot Proviso, and the problem of runaway slaves.

SECURITY OF SLAVERY IN THE NATION

Throughout the antebellum era, property rights in slaves were potentially at risk. Nothing about U.S. political structure naturally sustained the nation as one protecting the interests of Southern slaveholders. A necessary condition for Southerners to participate in the Union was that Northerners and the nation provide a credible commitment that the national government would not act against slavery. True, long periods existed of relative quiescence with little agitation about slavery and little ostensible concern by slaveholders. But this occurred because slaveholders had demanded and received institutions that provided a credible commitment to protect slavery within the nation (see Weingast 1998, 2000).

The security of slavery was a concern during the Philadelphia convention of 1787 and helped shape a number of constitutional provisions (Finkelman 1987, 1996; North and Rutten 1987; Rakove 1996; Wiecek 1987). Beyond the Constitution, the country evolved a series of other protections for slavery, the most important of which became the balance between the number of free and slave states (Weingast 1998). This balance allowed both sections to retain a veto over national policy making through equal representation in the Senate.

Southern veto through the Senate had two big implications for antebellum history. First, the veto provided the national credible commitment to protect slavery. As long as their veto remained in place, Southerners could protect themselves against hostile Northerners. Moreover, it should be clear that this veto is not something that accumulates or that a party holding a veto comes close to (see Weingast 2000, chapter 2). Either a party has or does not have it. In voting institutions, there is no such thing as almost having a veto. Losing by 1 vote is no different than losing by 100. This implies that being 1 vote short of a veto is a far distance from actually holding a veto.[1]

Second, in an expanding country, the need to maintain the sectional veto generated a territorial imperative for the South. Three of the four principal antebellum crises (1820, 1846–1850, 1854–1861) occurred when members of one or the other section felt disadvantaged in this growth. When many Northerners feared Southern growth would lead to Southern dominance of national politics, they typically attacked slavery, as in 1819, creating the crisis over the Missouri, and again in 1846 with the Wilmot Proviso, creating the crisis over the Mexican cession. In both crises, Northerners attacked slavery. This strategy, in turn, reinforced Southerners' natural anxieties about the security of their slave property.

Southerners' territorial imperative created a dilemma during the crisis in 1850. Although Northerners could continue to expand into territories available to them under the Missouri Compromise, no territories existed for Southern expansion. Even worse, Northern insistence on the Wilmot Proviso prevented the organization of any new territories "without restrictions," that is, allowing slavery; so Southern territorial expansion could not match the ongoing Northern expansion. The Wilmot Proviso therefore dashed Southern hopes to expand into the territories obtained from Mexico.

At the same time, the discovery of gold in California drew so many people and resources that it demanded political organization. The absence of even a territorial government hindered all the normal processes of government, including those supporting property rights and contracts. Moreover, not organizing California risked having it seek independence to provide the normal benefits from governmental organization.

Unfortunately for the South, no comparable slave territory stood in the wings ready for admission to maintain sectional balance. The admission of

California alone threatened to tip the political balance permanently in favor of the North, and with it the demise of Southern veto over national policy making.[2]

In the wake of these difficulties, the survival of the nation depended on the ability of Southerners to obtain support from sufficient Northerners to pass pro-slavery laws, such as the organization of territories without restrictions and the admission of new slave territories. Indeed, nearly all pro-Southern measures passed with united Southern support and enough Northerners to make a majority, especially in the House of Representatives where Northerners held a majority. This coalition passed the pro-Southern components of the Missouri Compromise; the admission of slave states, such as Arkansas in 1836; the annexation of Texas in 1845; the fugitive slave law in 1850; and the Kansas-Nebraska Act in 1854 (see Weingast 1998).

From the Southern perspective, the Wilmot Proviso represented a critical defection by Northerners from the dominant Democratic Party coalition that was largely pro-Southern in its orientation. In the years 1846–1849 nearly all Northern Democrats voted with their section to maintain the Wilmot Proviso in the House of Representatives, where Northerners outnumbered Southerners. Many Southerners drew a lesson from this, as had John C. Calhoun of South Carolina in the 1820s after the Missouri crisis: a pro-Southern national party was insufficient to protect slavery within the nation because their Northern coalition partners could defect and did so at critical moments, as in 1819 and again in 1846–1850.

The crisis over the Wilmot Proviso was thus not simply about Southern honor—about Southerners demanding that Northerners give them symbolic respect by passing pro-slavery measures—but also about the nation threatening to tip permanently toward Northerners indifferent or hostile to slavery. Allowing the admission of California without admitting a slave state for balance permanently threatened the South. Had there been a viable slave territory waiting in the wings to balance California, this might have been a different matter, allowing a compromise as in 1820 that balanced California's admission with another slave state. But no such territory was available.

True, Northerners did retreat from the free-soil aspects of the Wilmot Proviso, agreeing to organize several territories without restrictions. Indeed, the Compromise of 1850 organized both the New Mexico and the Utah territories without restrictions. Nonetheless, organizing territories without restrictions is not equivalent to reinstating sectional balance. Although territorial organization allowed slaveholders to move into these territories, it did not guarantee that Northerners would, at a future date, support the admission of a slave state to balance California. Nor did it guarantee that sufficient slaveholders would move to the state to create a viable slave state.

The South's Northern coalition partners in the House defected from the coalition in the Wilmot Proviso in 1846 and in every vote on the proviso during the many times it arose in 1847–1849. This dangerous precedent boded ill for the long-term maintenance of a pro-Southern coalition. Slaveholders would rationally fear that, when the time came for their Northern partners to vote for something inimical to their section, their partners would again defect.

The main implication is that organizing a territory without restrictions was not nearly the same as voting in the future to admit a slave state to balance California. Because a current Congress cannot bind a future Congress, Southerners faced a dilemma in 1850—should they accept the compromise and hence the breaking of balance today, granting Northerners a numerical advantage that would allow them in the future to take advantage of the South were they opportunistically minded or, worse, fall prey to antislavery leadership? In exchange, Northerners were willing to organize two territories without restrictions and, through the Democratic Party, provide a "promise" that, at a future date, they would accept another slave state were one to apply for admission.

Yet nothing today could bind Northerners to this promise in the future. Northerners were clearly getting the better part of the deal.

THE RUNAWAY SLAVE PROBLEM

Southerners also faced a major economic problem with the slave system. Southerners constantly worried about runaway slaves. The U.S. censuses for 1850 and 1860 provide probably the most accurate glimpse of the problem of permanent runaways and—as several authors indicate (Hummel 2001, 268–271; Gara 1961, 38; 1964, 230n4)—a lower bound on its magnitude. The 1860 census (U.S. Census Office, p. 338) indicates that a minimum of about a thousand slaves fled per year, or more precisely, 1,011 in 1850 and 803 in 1860.

At first glance, these numbers seem small. The total U.S. slave population in 1850 was 3.2 million, meaning only 0.03 percent permanently escaped, while in 1860 slaves numbered nearly 4 million, with only 0.02 percent fleeing North. Slaveholders would tend to discount the value of any slave by a premium proportionate to the probability of losing their property. The higher the probability, the lower the price of the slave, other things equal. As a rough approximation (Hummel 2001, 406–411), if the annual risk of permanent escape remained constant at p and the annual interest rate was 10 percent, then a slave's price will fall from PV_0, its value with no risk of running away, to PV_p:

$$PV_p = (1 - p)PV_0(0.10)/(0.10 + p) \quad \textbf{(25.1)}$$

We estimate how changes in this probability affect the price of a prime male hand whose value was $1,200 without any risk of permanent flight ($p = 0$). If only 1 out of every 10,000 prime hands ran away permanently ($p = 0.0001$, or 0.01%), the impact on average price would have been negligible. PV_p would have fallen by merely $1. Raise the probability to 1 out of 1,000 ($p = 0.001$), and now average price will fall by $13, or a little over 1 percent. Assuming that 1 out of every 100 hands permanently ran off each year ($p = 0.01$), the effect becomes quite significant. PV_p falls to $1,080, or by 10 percent. When the annual probability went up to 1 out of 20 ($p = 0.05$), the price would have dropped to $760, or by 37 percent. And if the probability ever reached 1 of 10 ($p = 0.10$), the value of all remaining male hands would have plummeted by over half, to $540. Annual probabilities of permanent escape derived from the census figures (0.03% and 0.02%) appear so low as to have almost no effect. Historians have reasonably questioned whether there could be any tangible impacts on market prices of slaves.

Yet this first impression that these numbers are small is mistaken because the incidence of runaways was not uniform across all slaves but instead concentrated in two ways. First, not all slaves were equally likely to escape. Runaways were usually able-bodied, prime-age males, in other words, those slaves with the highest productivity. Infants, small children, their mothers, and the old and infirm rarely sought to escape. In the samples of Franklin and Schweninger (1999, 210; see also Genovese 1974, 648, 798), prime-age males constituted 70 to 80 percent of all runaways.

Second, location also mattered. A runaway heading north from Georgia faced hundreds of miles of unknown and hostile territory. In contrast, slaves living in the Upper South had to travel much shorter distances to free states. These slaves were therefore more likely to risk escape.

The census data bear out this hypothesis. The number of permanent escapes as a percentage of a state's slave population was highest in Delaware, Maryland, and Missouri (in that order); whereas South Carolina, Alabama, and Georgia were among those states having the smallest proportion of runaways in both 1850 and 1860. Although Delaware, Maryland, Virginia, Kentucky, and Missouri contained less than a fourth of the total slave population in 1860, runaways from these states combine to more than half of all runaways for either census year.

Let us reconsider the incidence of runaways given these two factors. The results suggest that the probability of a prime-age male permanently absconding from the border states was far higher than for the overall slave population. Delaware's probability was 5.68 percent in 1850 (or 1 chance out of 18) and 3.34 percent in 1860 (or 1 chance out of 30). For Missouri, the percentages were 0.34 in 1850 and 0.43 in 1860. Compare those rates with South Carolina's, which are lower than Delaware's by a magnitude of 1/100th: 0.02 percent in 1850 and 0.03 percent in 1860 (Hummel 2001, 304–305).

Slaveholders in both the border and Deep South were acutely aware of these differing probabilities, which were reflected in slave prices. The same prime-age male was worth more in the Deep South than in the Upper South. The best long-run time series on slave prices in different regions remains that compiled at the beginning of the 20th century by Phillips (1918, 368–377; 1929, 177) as converted from graphs to numbers by Evans (1962, 197–202), covering four trading areas for the period 1795–1860.

The data show that prices for prime-age male hands in Richmond were consistently below prices in Charleston, usually by about 10 percent. Between 1836 and 1840, the disparity peaked at 17.0 percent; whereas between 1856 and 1860 (under the new, harsher fugitive slave law) it fell to 6.5 percent. Consistent with our theory, these differences correspond roughly to those implied if we use the census probabilities in the preceding equation. Although Phillips and others have given us extensive time series for slave prices in New Orleans, we have none for St. Louis or for rural areas in Missouri and Kentucky. But a contemporary estimate by Seaman (1852, 619)—in a work that was the basis for the 1840 regional income estimates of Easterlin (1960)—suggests that, in the West also, the differential between slave prices in the Deep and Upper South was comparable.

These differences contributed to the out-migration of slavery along the border with the free states—at the very same time that the total number of American slaves was nearly doubling, from slightly more than 2 million in 1830 to nearly 4 million in 1860. During that interval, Delaware, Maryland, Kentucky, Missouri, and the western counties of Virginia witnessed a steady decline in the proportion of slaves out of their total populations, whereas the proportion for the South overall remained fairly constant at one-third. The percentage of slaves fell in Delaware from 4.28 to 1.61, in Maryland from 23.04 to 12.69, in Kentucky from 24.01 to 19.51, and in Missouri from 17.52 to 9.72.

Economic historians tend to lump North-South price differentials with the more commonly studied East-West ones. They attribute the entire difference to the greater productivity of the rich cotton lands of the Southwest. But the research of Yang and Friedman (1992, 263) suggests that the total differential of approximately 45 percent exceeded migration costs, such as transport and forgone earnings, by about 8 percent, no doubt because their price estimates capture both East-West and North-South gradients. Either running away or superior land would have affected a field hand's productivity, and the two would have interacted to draw slaves out of the periphery into the Southwest. For our purposes, the relative importance of the two effects does not matter. What matters is that both contributed to a decline of slavery in the Upper South.

But why does this risk of runaways, with its affect on the slave distribution within the South, matter to the Deep South where the price impact was trivial? To address this, we return to the political problem of the security of slavery within the United States. As noted, sectional balance was critical to maintaining Southern security through a veto over national policy. Yet this veto depended on not only a balance of free with slave states but also the nominal slave states remaining slave states and having a political commitment to slavery's future. Sectional balance could be upset *both* by adding more free than slave states and by a slave state losing its commitment to slavery.

The peculiar institution's steady decline in the upper tier of slave states implied that, every year, the economic commitment of these states to the institution declined. By 1860 the antislavery Republican Party was already a political force within the border slave state of Missouri. This epitomized the long-term risk of defections from the pro-slavery coalition and represented another potential threat to the Southern veto and to slaveholders' property. To forestall this threat, Southerners had to lower the probability of success for runaways. The answer was a revision of the fugitive slave law.

CONCLUSIONS

In 1850 slaveholders faced two risks to their principal source of long-term political security within the nation, their veto over national policy making through sectional balance. First, the admission of California without a slave state to balance it directly threatened the Southern veto. Second, the migration of slaves out of the border regions into the Deep South threatened to loosen the commitment of the peripheral slaveholders to slavery; again, threatening Southern veto through sectional balance. These risks set the stage for Southern behavior during the negotiations over the Compromise of 1850.

The Economic Effects of the Fugitive Slave Law

We argue that the purpose of the fugitive slave law was twofold. First, the law was designed to have a direct and instrumental effect on runaways, providing greater—if not complete—legal tools for slaveholders to recapture lost property. Second, and subtler, the law was designed to provide Southerners with critical information about their Northern coalition partners. We discuss these two effects separately.

REDUCING THE NUMBER OF PERMANENT RUNAWAYS

The law's instrumental purpose was to lower the probability of successful runaways. Congress had initially passed legislation enforcing the Constitution's fugitive slave clause in 1793. The recovery of runaways was put under joint supervision of national and state courts. At first, the free states willingly cooperated, and many of them allowed Southerners to bring along slaves on visits, sometimes for up to 9 months (Finkelman 1996, 1981; *Statutes at Large* 1:303–305).

Radical abolitionists attacked the first fugitive slave law during the 1830s and 1840s by challenging it in the courts and illegally evading it. The illegal evasion led to the underground railroad, while the legal challenges induced several Northern legislatures to pass personal liberty laws (see Drobak 1993 and Finkelman 1981). These laws tried to prevent the kidnapping and enslavement of Northern free blacks by granting alleged fugitives such rights as habeas corpus and trial by jury (Morris 1974).

One case arising under the personal liberty laws finally found its way to the Supreme Court in 1842. The Court's decision in *Prigg v. Pennsylvania* was a pro- and antislavery mixture. It granted slaveholders the right to recapture slaves using private force, without going through any legal process, state or federal. But Justice Joseph Story, rendering the Court's majority opinion, also conceded that the state governments were under no positive obligation to assist enforcement of the fugitive slave provision (Finkelman 1979).

Seven Northern legislatures responded with a new round of legislation that either prohibited state officials from participating in a recapture or forbade holding fugitive slaves in state or local jails. By the time of the Civil War, Illinois was the only free state that had not enacted a personal liberty law of some sort. Such hostile statutes could severely impede the slaveholder's legal privilege to head north and personally retrieve his chattel (Drobak 1993; Finkelman 1981). That is why Southerners demanded a tougher fugitive slave law. Preventing flight became of dire importance to the slave system. If blacks could simply obtain freedom by slipping across an open border, enforcement throughout the Upper South was compromised, and the lower South would feel the repercussions.

One Virginian who served in both his state legislature and Congress, Charles James Faulkner, understood quite well the implications of Pennsylvania's new personal liberty law. In a letter dated July 15, 1847, he wrote to Calhoun of South Carolina (as quoted in Boucher and Brooks 1929, 385–387),

> [It] has rendered our slave property . . . utterly insecure. . . . Slaves are absconding from Maryland and this portion of Virginia in gangs of tens and twenties and the moment they reach the Pennsylvania line, all hopes of their recapture are abandoned. . . . No proposition can be plainer than that the slaveholding interest in this country is everywhere one and the same. An attack upon it *here* is an attack upon it in South Carolina and Alabama. Whatever weakens and impairs it *here* weakens and impairs it *there*. The fanaticism of Europe and North America is embarked on a crusade against it. We must stand or fall together. (emphasis in original)

Although Faulkner undoubtedly exaggerated the number escaping to the free states, we can be certain that without fugitive slave enforcement the number would have increased.

Moreover, border South representatives had attempted to strengthen the first fugitive slave law almost from the moment of its passage. Senator William Vans Murray of Maryland introduced an amendment in 1793 that would have fined employers who hired fugitives $500, payable to the slave's owners. The Senate tabled his motion, but in 1801 Congressman Joseph Nicholson, also of Maryland, proposed a $500 fine on anyone "harboring, concealing or employing" a runaway, defined as any black person failing to show an official certificate of freedom. Nicholson's bill nearly passed the House. Again in 1817, James Pindall, a congressman from Virginia, wanted to transfer the legal onus for returning runaway slaves to the governors of the free states, just as in the case of fugitive criminals. Separate versions of his bill made it through both the House and the Senate, but the two chambers could not reconcile their differences. Although other measures were reported the next year and 3 years after that, both in response to Maryland resolutions complaining about the assistance that escaped slaves received in Pennsylvania, neither made much headway (Robinson 1971; S. Campbell 1970; McDougall 1891; Morris 1974).

In the end, Southerners obtained a new fugitive slave law only as a result of the Compromise of 1850. A petition from the Kentucky legislature had impelled Senator Andrew Pickens Butler of South Carolina to submit such a bill in 1848. But not until the territorial crisis over California's admission as a free state, 2 years later, was Congress ready to act. At the beginning of January, Senator James M. Mason of Virginia reintroduced Senator Butler's bill, which then went through a grueling spring and summer of round after round of debates and amendments. When the 73-year-old Henry Clay pleaded before the Senate for a comprehensive settlement of all outstanding controversies, the new fugitive slave bill was the only unequivocally pro-slavery provision of the Kentucky slaveholder's entire package. "I will go with the furthest Senator from the South," Clay promised, "to impose the heaviest sanctions upon the recovery of fugitive slaves, and the restoration of them to their owners" (*Congressional Globe*, 31st Cong., 1st sess. [February 5, 1850], appendix, p. 123).

Since the proposed law would apply retroactively, allowing the return of slaves who had escaped at any time in the past, Northern congressmen wanted to prevent the kidnapping of legally free blacks by requiring jury trials. To soothe these sensibilities, Clay himself was willing to provide the alleged fugitive with a jury trial, not in the free state where captured but in the slave state from which he or she had fled. Pro-slavery stalwarts in Congress, however, would have none of this, so jury trials of any sort were kept out of the final measure.

More hotly contested among Southerners was a proposed amendment from Senator Thomas George Pratt of Maryland. It would have required the U.S. Treasury to reimburse any slave owner for the value of the escaped slave plus all legal expenses whenever Northern hostility hindered return. Border South representatives tended to support this indemnity, but those from the Deep and Mid-South objected adamantly. Senator Jefferson Davis of Mississippi and others couched such objections in states' rights terms. Yet Hopkins L. Turney, senator from Tennessee, revealed the paramount concern (*Congressional Globe*, 31st Cong., 1st sess. [August 22, 1850], appendix, p. 1616). By weakening the incentives to prevent flight and to recover fleeing bondmen, the proposal's effect "will be to emancipate the slaves of the border States and to have them paid for out of the Treasury of the United States." Approaching outright compensated emancipation, Pratt's amendment would have hastened the very erosion of the peculiar institution that the fugitive slave bill was intended to forestall.

A final version of the Fugitive Slave Act, without either jury trial or indemnity, had passed both houses by mid-September of 1850 and was signed by President Millard Fillmore, a New Yorker. It had received the vote of every voting Southern representative, with Northern Democrats providing the margin for victory. Among free-state members of Congress, only 1 in 5 had supported the bill, but among the free-state Democrats, the vote had run 27 to 16 in favor. Easing passage had been the 39 Northern Congressmen and 15 Senators who had absented themselves from the vote, most lurking in the corridors.

One of the harshest congressional measures ever, the new act expanded a special category of federal court officials, called commissioners, to help slaveholders seize fugitives. The circuit courts appointed the commissioners, who had concurrent jurisdiction with the district and circuit court judges and were delegated broad police powers for the reclamation of fugitives. The commissioners could issue warrants, employ U.S. marshals, depose witnesses, and arrest and imprison offenders. All the slaveholder or his agent had to do to prove his case was present an affidavit from some legal officer in his home state. The alleged runaway not only had no right to a jury trial but could not even testify. Furthermore, commissioners had a financial incentive to rule against the fugitive. They received a $10 fee from the claimant for deciding that a black was an escaped slave but only $5 for not. To enhance enforcement, Congress empowered federal officials to conscript the physical aid of any private citizen. Anyone obstructing the law was subject to a $1000 fine, 6 months in prison, and $1000 civil damages for each escaped slave (*Statutes at Large*, 9:462–465).[3]

With this law, Southerners put the North on notice that nothing—not due legal process, not civil liberties, not even the cherished principle of state sovereignty—could stand in the way of masters recovering their human chattel. Whether the law would actually achieve its goal was another matter. Northern mobs ended up attacking slave catchers, broke into jails, and rescued fugitive slaves. The national government tried vigorously to prosecute these law breakers, but Northern juries refused to convict them. In some cases, the authorities had to rely on military force. The Fugitive Slave Act of 1850 also sparked stronger personal liberty laws. Beginning with Vermont, nine states either provided for legal defense of alleged runaways or openly defied the national government by requiring jury trial, habeas corpus, and other procedural safeguards.

Yet the fugitive slave law was far from a dead letter. The illegal rescues and legal obstructions received all the publicity, but the successful apprehensions and ultimate returns were more numerous. Stanley W. Campbell (1970, 110–147, 199–207) has tracked down details of 332 fugitive slave cases occurring in the 10 years after passage of the law. Over half, 191, went before a federal tribunal, while the other 141 involved slave owners or their agents seizing runaways without recourse to judicial process. In only 22 cases were blacks rescued from custody, only 1 escaped on his own, and another 11 were released. Thus, in almost 90 percent of the total cases, or 80 percent of the federal cases, the fugitive was hauled back South. Moreover, many private seizures were almost certainly unrecorded. Of course, that is also true of many permanent slave escapes, as we have already observed.

The evidence suggests that the fugitive slave law served its intended effect. We noted in the preceding that in the half decade from 1856 to 1860, the price differential between prime field hands in Charleston and those in Richmond had fallen for the first time below 10 percent. But the best indicator of the success of the Fugitive Slave Act of 1850 at deterring runaways is the census figures themselves. From 1850 to 1860, while the total slave population increased by more than 20 percent, the number of permanent escapes reported actually declined. If slaves had gotten away at the same rate as in 1850, the number in 1860 would have been 1,248, rather than 803, a hardly insignificant 50 percent greater. We can only agree with *National Anti-Slavery Standard*, which commented in 1861, "The falling off in the last decade *may* be owing to the imperfection of the returns; but if not, it is doubtless to be ascribed in part to the operation of the Fugitive Slave Law" (emphasis in original).

The Fugitive Slave Law and Sectional Balance

The Compromise of 1850 contained an implied promise for Northern support in the expansion of slavery in the form of future slave states. The promise was necessary because the compromise organized territories "without restrictions" but did not admit new slave states. Making good on the promise required that a future Congress vote to support this expansion. In the past, pro-Southern and pro-slavery measures, including the organization of new slave territories and the admission of new slave states, had passed with the support of nearly all Southerners in combination with sufficient Northerners (though typically a minority of that section) to comprise a majority in both houses.

The problem facing Southerners was the stalwart defection of the South's coalition partners to support the antislavery Wilmot Proviso. The Compromise of 1850 represented a promise to bury the sectional hostilities that had pervaded national politics since 1846 and return to politics as usual. For many Southerners, politics as usual meant expanding slavery in a fashion that paralleled the Northern expansion, so as to maintain their veto in the

Senate. Yet when the crunch came at some future date, would Southerners' Northern coalition partners act under their politics-as-usual incentives or under those that favored the Wilmot Proviso?

The choice facing Southerners was to accept the compromise and give up balance today to maintain the Union or continue hostile confrontation, possibly leading to civil war. As part of the compromise, Northern Democrats offered a promise that, if Southerners accepted the compromise, balance would be restored in the future. But could Northerners be trusted?

The risks of accepting the compromise, with its demise of balance today, depended on Southerners' expectations about Northerners' future behavior. Specifically, Southerners' dilemma concerned whether a sufficient number of rank-and-file Northerners—i.e., Northern Democrats—would cooperate in the future with the South by supporting a measure to reinstate balance. How were Southerners to know?

We argue that the fugitive slave law, to be voted on separately from the other provisions, addressed this issue. As a means of costly signaling, this measure allowed the pivotal Northern voters to reveal information about future behavior. By forcing their Northern coalition partners to support a pro-Southern measure today, Southerners would learn critical information about whether Northerners would cooperate in the future. An integral part of the measure's success for Southerners was that the fugitive slave issue was anathema to the North. From the late 1840s, and especially in the 1850s, this issue came to represent to both North and South the worst parts of the other.

This act served a particular purpose, one not simply about Southern honor but with a larger instrumental purpose involving acceptance of the larger compromise. A necessary condition for Southern acceptance of the compromise—breaking the balance today plus an uncertain promise to restore balance in the future—was that Northerners demonstrate that they had the ability to cooperate on pro-Southern measures onerous to the North.

Could Northerners be trusted to vote on a future measure dear to Southern hearts but costly for Northern constituents? Including the fugitive slave law as part of the compromise allowed Southerners to see whether sufficient numbers would vote for a hated measure. In technical terms, the question came down to, not the motives and intentions, but the willingness of Northern pivotal voters in the House to support measures benefiting the South but unpopular in the North.

The pivot is defined as follows. Virtually all Southerners voted for important pro-Southern measures. The pivotal voter is that Northerner sufficient to make a majority in Congress. In 1850 Southerners composed 38 percent of the House of Representatives. To form a majority, Southerners therefore needed the support of another 12 to 15 percent of the House, or approximately 20–25 percent of all Northerners.

But were 20–25 percent of Northerners willing to vote along with the South? Under the Wilmot Proviso, they had not been. If they were not willing to support the South in the future, today's promise to reinstate balance was vacuous.

What Southerners needed to know was whether sufficient Northerners would at some future date vote to reinstate balance. Yet this was unknowable with any certainty in 1850. But Southerners could learn a critical piece of information today about the future Northern willingness to support the South. If today's pivot were anti-South, then it is likely that tomorrow's pivot would be as well. Hence congressional leaders included the fugitive slave law in part to reveal information about the Northern pivot as either pro- or anti-South.

As with a future measure to admit a slave state, the fugitive slave law was costly for Northern members of Congress to support. The behavior of the Northern pivot on this measure would therefore provide something of a test of the pivot's future willingness to support the South. The Southerners' decision to participate in the compromise would be contingent on the Northerners' willingness to accept the Fugitive Slave Act. If sufficient numbers of Northerners would not support the act, then Southerners would know today that it was unlikely that a pro-Southern coalition would form in the future to admit a new slave state.

Signaling sometimes allows the uncertain player—here, the Southerners—to learn about the type of player they are facing—here, whether the Northern pivot is pro- or anti-South. Including the Fugitive Slave Act in the compromise provides such a test, giving pro-Southern pivots the opportunity to vote yes on the law, while anti-Southern pivots vote no. Southerners could then accept the compromise if and only if the pivot votes yes.

A pro-South pivot would behave differently from an anti-South one. The signaling test therefore provides Southerners with information about the Northern pivot. Only a pro-South pivot would vote yes for the fugitive slave law. Thus, observing the Northern pivot's choice on the Fugitive Slave Act affords Southerners critical information that they would not have without it. Without the vote on the fugitive slave law, Southerners would have to base their decision on the ex ante probability that the pivot was pro-South. Including the fugitive slave law as part of the compromise allowed Southerners to know today's pivot's type for sure.

Including the Fugitive Slave Act in the compromise therefore lowered the risk to the South of accepting the compromise. Similarly, had the pivot voted against the act, revealing it to be anti-South, Southerners would have known that the risks of accepting the compromise would have been greater. We argue, therefore, that Southerners in Congress would have supported the compromise if and only if the Northern pivot revealed its type as pro-South; that is, by voting for the Fugitive Slave Act.

The congressional debate surrounding the Fugitive Slave Act provides hints of the crucial signaling role of the 1850 compromise. Although the compromise was still in the form of a single, omnibus bill, Pierre Soulé, Democratic senator from Louisiana, proposed an amendment that required the following: "When admitted as a State, the said Territory, or any portion of the same, shall be received into the Union, with or without slavery, as their constitution may prescribe at the time of their admission." Senator Alexander H. Stephens of Georgia later identified passage of the Soulé amendment as "the turning point" in the debate over the compromise, and it eventually ended up in the final version of the compromise when passed as several separate acts (Fehrenbacher 1978, 171–172).

Legally the amendment was useless, since it could in no way bind a future Congress. According to our interpretation, Soulé himself claimed he wanted "to feel the pulse of the Senate" about a series of acts he believed to be "binding in the *future*." As the late historian Don E. Fehrenbacher (1978, 172) emphasizes, "He meant binding, not in law but as a pledge of honor, with the threat of disunion serving as the sanctional force. . . . Here . . . was a view of the compromise legislation as a set of pledges negotiated like an international treaty, the violation of which would lead to sovereign reprisals." But before Southerners would even enter such a treaty, they needed some assurance that Northerners could in fact uphold their promise to admit future slave states. Hence, the importance of their votes on the Fugitive Slave Act.

IMPLICATIONS

Given the pervasive uncertainty about the future of national politics, the South faced a difficult dilemma in 1850, and the fugitive slave law proved useful for reducing this uncertainty. The value of the law to the South was twofold. First, as noted in the previous section, the act served its ostensible purpose of facilitating the return of runaway slaves. Second, the act served an instrumental, signaling purpose of forcing the Northern pivot to reveal its type today. As a revelation mechanism, the act provided critical information to Southerners about the risks of supporting the compromise. By supporting the Fugitive Slave Act, the pivotal Northern member of Congress revealed his ability to support pro-Southern measures opposed by most Northerners.

Conclusion

Our analysis of the Compromise of 1850 and the Fugitive Slave Act focuses on Southern interests. We argue that Southerners received three benefits from the Compromise of 1850. First, historians have failed to understand that the Fugitive Slave Act served an important, instrumental purpose. Runaway slaves were in fact a big problem in the critical border states. Second, the compromise addressed the issue of sectional balance in several ways. Northerners agreed to recede from the Wilmot Proviso for the first time in 4 years. The compromise created the New Mexico and Utah territories "without restrictions" on slavery. We argue that the Fugitive Slave Act served a third instrumental purpose for Southerners in 1850. It provided a test for their Northern coalition partners. The act served as a signaling game—if the Southerners' Northern coalition partners could not vote to pass this measure today, they were unlikely to be able to withstand constituency pressure against voting to admit a slave state in the future.

In contrast to the traditional historical arguments, we disagree that the Fugitive Slave Act was principally about the psychology of Southern honor. Southern honor may well have been important, but so too were the instrumental aspects of including the act in the compromise.

Chapter 26

Power Rejected: Congress and Bankruptcy in the Early Republic

ERIK BERGLÖF AND HOWARD ROSENTHAL

Introduction

This chapter seeks some explanation of why the members of Congress chose to leave the nation without a federal bankruptcy law for much of American history. There are three important observations. First, bankruptcy laws were enacted following severe macroeconomic downturns. Second, the laws were produced by unified government of the political right. Third, although enacted by political conservatives, the laws were debtor friendly either by design or by practice. To understand these observations, we draw on formal theoretical developments in political science, most notably the pivotal politics approach of Krehbiel (1998; see also Brady and Volden [1998]). We also draw on the rapidly developing theoretical and empirical literature on the political economy of financial markets. We argue that the observations can be reconciled by acknowledging that the conservative political right in fact represents capitalists who are debtors as well as creditors. When the economy is in a funk, the debtors are likely to get more political weight. The political right was, moreover, generally eager both to extend the scope of the federal government and to obtain the relative impartiality of federal courts as opposed to state courts. To obtain the benefits of a national law, creditors were willing to make a political compromise on how bankruptcy law applied to debtors. This chapter traces the political economy that led to the absence of a federal bankruptcy law for most of the

110-year period from 1789 to 1898. We will focus on the federal response to debt crises in the 1797, 1819, and 1837 panics. The 1867 law remains largely uncharted territory.

The Political Economy of Bankruptcy

The economics part of the political economy starts with the observation that the early bankruptcy acts were responses to economic "panics." The 1800 act followed the Panic of 1797, while the 1841 act followed the Panic of 1837. In practice, these acts were not so much permanent procedures for handling the economic distress of individuals (recall that we are discussing a largely precorporate world) as a temporary expedient for writing off a wave of defaults.

The 1800 act, passed at the end of the 6th Congress, in fact had a 5-year sunset provision (Mann 2002, 248). After an unsuccessful effort at early repeal was made as soon as power shifted from the Federalists to the Jeffersonian Republicans in the 7th Congress, repeal was voted just 6 weeks into the first session of the 8th Congress.

Efforts to repeal the 1841 act were made on the heels of enactment, even before the act became effective. While the first attempts were aborted, the act was repealed in 1843 by, most unusually in the history of Congress, the enacting Congress, the 27th. In the year the act was in effect, the total number of bankruptcy filings reported by Warren (1935) represented 1 percent of the adult male white population of the United States. In an era when the nation was still demographically dominated by agrarian sole proprietors and laborers unlikely to file, the 1841 act represents a massive write-down of commercial debt.

After the intervening Panic of 1819, Congress voted a write-down of federal loans for land purchases.[1] This write-down amounted in economic terms to a *bailout* of private debt. The costs of a bailout fall on taxpayers. In contrast, a temporary bankruptcy law represents a partial *moratorium* on debt where the costs fall on private creditors. One might expect, therefore, the support for each measure to come from very different political coalitions (Bolton and Rosenthal 2002). These coalitions can vary in their political effectiveness, resulting in Congress being selective in the type of debt relief it allows in a macroeconomic crisis. Indeed, there was no bankruptcy law passed following the Panic of 1819. This observation leads to the politics piece of our political economy story.

Up through 1898, bankruptcy bills became law only when the Right (Federalists, Whigs, or Republicans) had unified control of the federal government. Otherwise, gridlock prevailed even when the necessary condition—panic—was provided by the economy. The Panic of 1819 occurred in the middle of 40 years of domination by Jeffersonian Republicans and Jacksonian Democrats. Only when this domination ended, some years after the Panic of 1837, was it possible to pass another bankruptcy act, under a unified Whig government.

The bankruptcy laws passed by the right-wing governments were generally debtor friendly in practice. Although the 1800 act was in large part copied from the British Statute of St. Anne and provided for only involuntary bankruptcy, Mann (2002) details how Americans innovated to use the statute to accomplish voluntary bankruptcy. For example, a father could be the creditor of a son. The son could have many other creditors. The father could initiate bankruptcy proceedings, to the potential displeasure of other creditors. Similarly, "vulture capitalism" Balleisen (1996, 2001) surrounded bankruptcy proceedings under the 1841 act. Part of the impetus for repeal came from the fact that debtors' assets were largely dissipated by various means, including collusion with friendly creditors to bid on the assets, fraudulent conveyance, and fees paid to court officials, printers, and so on. It was common for bankrupts, experienced with the process, to become bankruptcy lawyers who represented other bankrupts.

Bankruptcy acts also became debtor friendly not just because debtors became clever in using legislation on the books but also because the legislation was a compromise tilted toward debtors. Compromise was needed in 1800 because many, Virginians in particular, were concerned that land was an asset that could be seized (Mann 2002, 217). The concern over land initiated the homestead exemption debate that continues to this day (Posner, Hynes, and Malani 2001; Nunez and Rosenthal 2004). Debtors whose residences were remote from federal district courts were reluctant to accept federal jurisdiction. Even worse for debtors in 1800, creditors may have preferred that bankruptcy cases be decided by commissioners appointed by the president, outside the judicial process. Executive administration of bankruptcy was introduced by Napoleon in France and copied in the 19th century by the British, who processed debt default through the Board of Trade (Lester 1995). That bankruptcy was not processed by the executive branch was due to John Marshall's insisting that a jury trial be available before bankruptcy was imposed (Mann 2002, 218). Jury trials appear as a debtor-friendly compromise.

Debtor friendliness was also manifest in the 1898 act. This legislation was a compromise in which the creditor lobby ceded to the states the rights to define exemptions and priorities and to try cases of fraudulent conveyance. Grounds for involuntary bankruptcy set forth in the House bill were substantially weakened in conference, responding to the wishes of a more agrarian-centered Senate (Skeel 2001).

Why did the Right push for legislation that was in law and in practice debtor friendly? We believe there are two reasons. One turned around the Federalist, later Whig and postbellum Republican, push for a strong federal government. The second had to do with which debtors actually benefited from a bankruptcy law.

As to the first point, early America featured a debate between agrarianism and capitalism as outlined by Parrington (1927). The capitalists wanted a national government able to provide national defense, impose an external tariff, construct national roads and other infrastructure, and control monetary policy through a national bank. They wanted an expanded role for a federal judiciary. Mann (2002) indicates that Speaker of the House Theodore Sedgwick Sr., who cast a tie-breaking vote to pass the 1800 act in the House, was more concerned with the bill as a wedge for expanding the judiciary than for its effectiveness in dealing with defaulted debt.

Agrarians, in contrast, sought to maintain the prerogatives of state courts and legislatures, presumed more favorable to local debtors. There would be little need of a federal procedure to handle debtors in default if state legislatures could, as they did after the Panic of 1819 (Rothbard 1962; Bolton and Rosenthal 2002), vote "stay laws" that allowed all farm debtors to avoid repayment. Moreover, the agrarian insistence on states' rights would come, by the 1840s, to be reinforced by the debate on slavery.

The battle of states' rights versus federal jurisdiction could be influenced by how the courts changed the status quo on bankruptcy. In *Sturges v. Crowinshield* (1819) and *Ogden v. Saunders* (1827), the Supreme Court ruled that state laws were legal in the absence of a federal statute. The applicability of the laws was, however, sharply limited. The interstate commerce clause was used to judge the laws inapplicable to contracts between citizens of different states. The contract clause was used to deem the laws inapplicable to contracts concluded before the legislation went into force. The Court's use of the contract clause was not rigid insofar as the Court tried to strike a balance that extended flexibility to debtors. It did allow the states to modify legal remedies or methods of enforcing contracts. Consequently, the states freely enacted stay laws, which provided for debt moratoria or prolonged installment payments. Yet when these laws tilted too strongly against foreclosure, the Court, in *Baron v. Kinzie* (1843) intervened on the creditor side.[2] Over time, the Court appears to have constrained the ability of individual states to deal with private-debt default, particularly as interstate commerce developed. This change in the status quo may have favored a compromise on federal legislation.

Our second argument recognizes that the "capitalists" comprised both debtors and creditors. In economic downturns, the debtors would become more numerous and have more influence. The 1800 bill, moreover, was designed only for the relatively wealthy. Only someone with over $1,000 in debt could be held bankrupt, and only a creditor who owed more than $1,000 could initiate bankruptcy (Mann 2002, 222–223). Some Federalists, such as Theodore Sedgwick Jr., claimed the "rabble" of the masses were unworthy of benefiting from a bankruptcy law (Mann 2002, 258). Indeed, Shays's rebellion, undertaken by "little insurgents, men in debt, who want no law, and who want a share of the property of the others"[3] spurred the Constitutional Convention. Recent theoretical work by Ayotte (2002) and by Biais and Mariotti (2006) suggests that lenient bankruptcy procedures would tend to favor "high type" entrepreneurs to the detriment of "low type" who become credit rationed. A similar result with regard to debt collection in the courts was obtained by Jappelli, Pagano, and Bianco (2002). This recent work is echoed by empirical work for the United States by Gropp, Scholz, and White (1997) that shows that liberal state exemption laws for bankruptcy raise loan rates for the poor and lower them for the rich. A similar result, with regard to court efficiency, is obtained for Italian provinces by Fabbri and Padula (2003). So capitalist debtors may be quite favorable to government policies that keep creditors at bay.

An analysis of roll-call voting contains the evidence we present to support our arguments as to when and why the Right pushed through national bankruptcy laws. We will break the analysis into three major sections. We treat the brief triumph of Federalism in the passage of the 1800 Bankruptcy Act. Then we discuss democracy without bankruptcy and the congressional failure to enact a bankruptcy law between the 1803 repeal and the election of 1840. Finally, we cover the passage and repeal of the 1841 act, or the writing off of the Panic of 1837. We first pause to discuss methodological issues in our roll-call analysis.

Methodology

MEASURING LEGISLATOR IDEOLOGY

Our analysis relies on the widely used Poole and Rosenthal (1997a, 2006) two-dimensional DW-NOMINATE measures of ideology. The first dimension of DW-NOMINATE captures economic left versus right. At the very beginning of the Republic, this dimension was correlated with the regional division of the country. In the Second House, for example, the 19 leftmost representatives of the 63 scaled were from Maryland and southward while the 15 rightmost were from the North. Madison was the 13th leftmost. Sedgwick of Massachusetts, who as Speaker in 1800 played a critical role in passage of the first bankruptcy act, was 6th rightmost. By 1800 there is a well-formed two-party system with the Federalists on the right and the (Jeffersonian) Republicans on the left. By 1840, on the first dimension, Whigs have taken over on the right and Democrats on the left; the second dimension is the South-North division over slavery. DW-NOMINATE allows for shades of gray such that moderates are more likely to deviate from the majority of the party than are extremists.

PROBLEMS OF INTERPRETATION

Our analysis emphasizes not just ideological splits on bankruptcy legislation but also the effects of changes of partisan control of Congress and the presidency. In short, roll-call voting will reflect a mix of agenda control by the majority party, basic ideological preferences, and the mapping of policy choices onto the preferences.

1800: The Brief Triumph of Federalism

We now apply the political economy framework to legislation in the 1800s. Our ability to understand congressional action in this period is very much obligated to the superb treatment in Mann (2002). Our central conclusion is that support for a national law came from political conservatives, Federalists, and coastal districts. Although these variables are collinear, all had significant influences on roll-call voting. In particular, those Federalists who favored bankruptcy as part and parcel of a strong national government dragged an unenthusiastic party to support the legislation. There were important divisions among the Federalists, with only the more Right members strongly supporting the bill. After controlling for party and ideology, North-South regional differences have no effect. The relevance of the coastal variable anticipates the effect of national expansion. The coup de grace to a national bankruptcy law was brought about by the 1800 census, which shifted the balance in the House strongly in favor of Jeffersonian Republicans on the agrarian frontier.

The 1800 census was indeed the sole source of institutionally mandated change that would affect roll-call voting from the Fifth (1797–1799) through Eighth (1803–1805) Congresses. No new states were seated during Congresses 5–8, so the increase in representation of the frontier was largely a matter of differential population growth. The changes brought about by the 1800 census were first manifest in the elections of 1802 to the great benefit of the Republicans. The number of seats in the House rose from 106 to 137. Although the Federalists maintained their number of seats from the Seventh to the Eighth House, the Republicans increased their contingent dramatically and had a nearly 3:1 House majority. The Republicans further solidified their control of Congress by also gaining a 3:1 majority in the Senate, which was only narrowly controlled in the Seventh Congress. The Krehbiel (1998) pivotal politics approach suggests that repealing the 1800 bill, ceteris paribus, would have been much easier in the Eighth than in the Seventh Congress.

Results for House voting on the 1800 bill shows that voting was ideological (and on the first dimension). DW-NOMINATE outperforms a straight party-line voting model. On all the bankruptcy-related roll calls between 1789 and 1803, with the exception of roll call 86,[4] there are fewer classification errors in DW-NOMINATE than in a party voting model. The differences are small but consistent. Voting on bankruptcy is highly ideological, with high levels of proportionate reduction in error (PRE), except for the last roll call where the majority in favor of repeal was very lopsided.

The Senate is a different story. Throughout the Sixth and Seventh Senates, the spatial model does not improve on a model of party-line voting, perhaps because of the small sample size. The defections appear unrelated to spatial position or region. For example, the two defections on passage in 1800 (roll call 50) were James Hillhouse (Conn.) and Robert Goodhue (Mass.), both from the New England heartland of Federalism and both on the far right side of Federalist ideal points.

In the Eighth Senate, although the fit to the spatial model is modest, there is an improvement over the party-line model, but the votes are curiously along the second dimension. The second dimension is a weak dimension during this period (Poole and Rosenthal 1997a) and interpretation is not direct. Repeal was more narrowly voted in the Senate. As in the House, however, repeal was supported by Federalists as well as Republicans.

What led to the nonpartisan character of repeal? Presumably the larger Republican majorities themselves did not induce Federalists to support repeal. One suggestion, to anticipate our story for the 1841 bill, is that experience with the 1800 act played a role in abolishing the act before its legislated expiration. The "voluntary" involuntary bankruptcies may have been unanticipated; their occurrence may have strengthened creditor opposition. Another factor is that by 1803 the defaults from the bad times of the 1790s may have been worked out. In good times, creditors may have been able to argue for tougher terms. Repealing the bankruptcy law meant eliminating the discharge of debt and the fresh start that was available only in Federal law.

Let us make two further observations about the process surrounding the 1800 act. First, the bill did not generate enthusiasm, even among Federalists. On the critical passage vote in the Sixth House, the Federalists were able to obtain the votes of only 2 Republicans to pass the bill but they lost 7 of their own members. The Speaker's vote was needed for passage. In the Senate, the 10 Republican senators never flinched in their opposition to the bill in voting on passage and amendments, with the exception of two defections on roll call 37. In contrast, Hillhouse and Goodhue not only voted against passage but also voted with the Republicans on all the amendments.

The behavior of the two New England Republicans suggests a minor correction to Mann's work. Mann (2002, 218) places emphasis on Southern opposition, including Southern attempts to amend the bill. But on the Senate amendment that the act not extend to "farmers, graziers, doziers, or manufacturers" (roll call 31), the two defecting Federalists, Hillhouse and Goodhue, were Northern; the one Northern Republican, Langdon of New Hampshire, voted with his party; the one Southern Federalist, Read of South Carolina, also voted with his party; and Federalists from Kentucky and Maryland also voted with their party. Thus, opposition to the bill appears to be more partisan than regional. The parties were simply sharply split along North-South lines.

Similarly, the House did not divide solely on regional lines. It is true that the 2 Republicans who voted for the bill were non-Southern, representing Maryland and New York. It is also true that 5 of the 7 defecting Federalists[5] were Southern, 2 being the Georgia representatives, Jones and Taliaferro. They had ideal points in the middle of the Republican cluster, which indicates that they generally voted with the Republicans, and not just on bankruptcy. But 10 Southern Federalists voted for the law, as did 5 from the border states of Maryland and Kentucky.

Party, region, and ideology are all quite collinear. We have run a linear probability (regression) model with the Sixth House passage vote (1 for, 0 against) as the dependent variable. In comparison to the passage vote in the Fifth House, this vote presents a tougher test of the influence of ideology versus party membership since the cutting line now runs in the channel separating the Federalists and the Republicans.[6] Results are shown in equation 26.1. Nonetheless, ideology remains important for discriminating the likelihood of a defection from the party position. Indeed, after we control for the interactions of party with both ideology and the geographic position of the congressional district, party membership has only a weak effect on the vote. In the regression, the independent variables were *Party* (Federalist = 1, Republican = 0), *Region* (North = 1, Maryland or Kentucky = 0.5, South = 0), and the two DW-NOMINATE ideal-point coordinates. The *t* statistics are in parentheses.

$$\begin{aligned}
&\textit{House Vote on Passage of 1800 Bankruptcy Bill} \\
&\quad = 0.051(0.77) + 0.126(1.82)\textit{Region} + 0.439(3.33^{**})\textit{Party} \\
&\qquad + 0.464(3.03^{**})\textit{DW-NOM1} \\
&\qquad - 0.074(-1.231)\textit{DW-NOM2} \text{ (Adj. } R^2 = 0.718,\ N = 96) \qquad \textbf{(26.1)}
\end{aligned}$$

Democracy without Bankruptcy: 1803–1841

After the 1800 act was repealed in 1803, bankruptcy was not brought to a vote again in the House until 1818, during the Era of Good Feelings. But consideration of a bill in that year was postponed indefinitely despite strong support from the rump of the Federalist Party.

The Republicans did, however, soon have to deal with a major economic crisis, the Panic of 1819 (Rothbard 1962). Our main finding here is that this macroeconomic crisis did not result in a bankruptcy bill because of the opposition of Jeffersonian Republicans in the older states of the Union. Republicans from the frontier states supported a bankruptcy bill in the Senate, where they were critical to passage, but cast only one vote on the key roll call in the House.

In the wake of the panic, the Senate took up bankruptcy in 1820 but failed to pass a bill. Finally, in the lame-duck session of 1821, the Senate passed a bankruptcy bill. The major items of contention, as indicated by amendment voting, were whether voluntary bankruptcy would be allowed, whether bankruptcy would extend to individuals other than merchants, and whether a discharge would apply to debts owed to private individuals who were not the trade creditors of the debtor. Within this debate, Federalists appeared to support only merchant bankruptcy but allowed a full discharge for this class—once again, debtor friendliness to a segment of capitalists. Those Republicans who favored a bill wanted to democratize, that is, broaden the base of eligible individuals. When the bill passed 23–19, the Federalist votes were necessary. A majority of Republicans opposed. Nonetheless, the voting, in terms of PREs was only modestly ideological. Ideological differences were hard to pin down in the essentially one-party state of the Era of Good Feelings. Poole and Rosenthal (1997a, 38–40) show that 1815–1825 was one of two periods of American history where the spatial model gives a poor fit to roll-call voting behavior. Consequently, it is not surprising to find that bankruptcy votes in the Senate were not highly ideological at this time.

The House, however, failed to follow the Senate's lead when it received the bill near the end of the lame-duck session of the 16th Congress. Because nonvoting was rampant at this time, the outcome could be influenced by abstentions. When the dust settled, the bill was tabled. There was a clear regional split, however, with the South blocking consideration of the bill against the wishes of major urban centers.

We again use regression analysis to contrast ideology and region, which remain very collinear. The results for the motion to table are in equation 26.2. The variable definitions remain as in equation 26.1.[7] It can be seen that party and the two DW-NOMINATE coordinates are all significantly related to voting, with p values all below 0.037. Region is marginally significant with a p value of 0.073. Since the variables are collinear, region by itself is highly significant, with a t statistic exceeding 7.

$$\begin{aligned}\textit{House Vote 1821 Bankruptcy Bill}\\ &= 0.767(7.762) - 0.273(-1.811)\textit{Region} - 0.253(-2.307^*)\textit{Party}\\ &\quad - 0.425(-2.193^*)\textit{DW-NOM1}\\ &\quad - 0.150(-2.109^*)\textit{DW-NOM2}\ (\text{Adj. } R^2 = 0.384,\ N = 123) \qquad \textbf{(26.2)}\end{aligned}$$

The R^2 value is much lower than in 1800, echoing the preceding discussion of the limited applicability of the spatial model to roll-call voting during the Era of Good Feelings. Nonetheless, the negative signs on all estimates show that it was Southerners, Democrats, and the ideological left that favored tabling the bill. The second dimension is a North-South dimension, with the negative pole Southern at this time. The Southern pole supported tabling, but the second dimension was much less important than the first, even when region is not included as a variable.

Bankruptcy was brought up again in the 17th Congress, but the House, by a substantial majority, refused to order a third reading in a vote on March 12, 1822. During the same period, the federal government did deal with default on land debts to the federal government. Bolton and Rosenthal (2002) provide a brief analysis of the related roll-call votes. Frontier states were favorable to forgiving land debts and older areas were against. Because the frontier was tied to the Republicans, legislation passed that gave the land debtors a partial write-down or delayed repayment terms. Bolton and Rosenthal (2002) also looked at which state legislatures voted into effect stay laws or debt moratoria in this period. Those legislatures were also concentrated on the frontier and, to some degree, the North. The seaboard Southern states (Virginia, North and South Carolina, and Georgia), although Republican, had a conservative approach to debt that is echoed in opposition to bankruptcy legislation.

The fact that relief was given to land debt but not to bankrupt commercial debtors provides a clue as to why bankruptcy legislation cleared the Senate but failed to pass the House hurdle following the Panic of 1819. The demanders of bankruptcy legislation were concentrated in Federalists who remained in political eclipse. The demanders of land-debt relief were concentrated on the frontier, largely in Republican hands. Moreover, Southern Republicans, opposed to federal judicial intervention in private-debt contracts, could support a bailout that would maintain the inviolability of personal homesteads.

When frontier states were admitted, they had two seats in the Senate but just one in the House. The five most recently seated frontier states voting in the 16th Congress were Louisiana (1812), Indiana (1816), Mississippi (1817), Illinois (1818), and Alabama (1819).[8] (Maine, admitted in 1820, was of much older settlement; Missouri was admitted only in August 1821.) These states had a total of 10 of the 46 Senate votes but only 5 votes in the House. The 10 Republican frontier senators voted 7–3 on the passage of the bankruptcy bill in the Senate in 1821. Other Republican senators were heavily opposed, by a 16–9 margin. The frontier states and the 7 Federalists supplied 14 of the 23 votes in support of the bill.

In the House, in contrast, on the motion that tabled the bankruptcy bill, only one representative from the frontier states even voted (albeit to table). The remaining Republicans voted 62–43 to table, giving a margin larger than the total of 17 Federalists voting.

Two factors suggest why frontier Republicans broke with the party. First, the economic crisis was probably more severe on the frontier, leading to more political pressure for intervention. Second, these states had broader suffrage for white males than at least some of the older states. Freehling (1990) details, for example, how both Virginia and South Carolina had malapportioned state legislatures tilted toward the old planter groups. Thus, the frontier would be more willing to drop conservative inhibitions about debt discharge and more inclined to support fresh-start policies. In any event, the failure to pass a bankruptcy bill after the Panic of 1819 appears to reflect both the political weakness of the Federalists and the institutional differences inherent in the apportionment of the two Houses of Congress.

Writing Off the Panic of 1837

The quiescence of the years centered on Jackson's presidency was broken by the Panic of 1837. By the time of the panic, the Era of Good Feelings had given way to the sharp divisions between Democrats and Whigs. These divisions, as they pertained to bankruptcy, were largely a matter of the first, left-right DW-NOMINATE, dimension. A bankruptcy bill was passed only after a shift in party control with the Whig victory in 1840. The increased number of conservatives led to passage whereas bankruptcy bills were voted on, but not passed, before the shift in control. Controlling for ideology eliminates the effects of other variables, including party. Representatives from frontier states were, however, more supportive of bankruptcy insofar as they were relatively reluctant to vote repeal in 1843.

The Response of the Democratic Congress

As happened in the 1820s, the 26th Senate (1839–1841) took up and passed a bankruptcy bill that failed to be supported by the House. Bankruptcy indeed formed an important part of the agenda of this Senate, generating 26 of 334 roll calls. Some roll calls, on procedural matters or noncentral amendments, like the treatment of gambling debts, were not ideological. The more substantive votes were highly ideological, showing a sharp Whig-Democrat division, with the Whigs generally supporting a broader, more debtor-friendly law. On these roll calls, PREs were quite high. The roll calls included an amendment on the inclusion of banks (roll call 116, PRE = 0.69); eliminating the eligibility of merchants (121, 0.71); rights of married women, minors, and mortgagors (149, 0.63); involuntary bankruptcy for jailed individuals (150, 0.83); involuntary bankruptcy for fraud cases (151, 0.83); whether bankruptcy must be accepted by a majority (by value) of creditors (152, 0.75); no discharge in case of preferential treatment of creditors (153, 0.86); control of creditors by assignors (155, 0.75); and need to give notice to creditors (163, 0.68).

The bill was ordered to a third reading on June 24, 1840, by a one-vote margin and passed by two votes the next day, June 25 (165, 0.74). As was the case in the 1820s, votes of frontier senators were crucial. By 1840 the five previous frontier states were augmented by Missouri (1821), Arkansas (1836), and Michigan (1837). The eight frontier states voted passage by a

9–5 margin. The nine positive votes included the votes of all 4 frontier Whigs but also 5 Democrats. Elsewhere in the nation only 3 Democrats supported the bill against 14 opposed.

The Senate bill, then, was passed by a coalition of all 13 Whigs and defecting Democrats, largely from the frontier. The four votes from the cotton kingdom states of Louisiana and Mississippi, the richest part of antebellum America (Fogel and Engerman 1974, 248), were part of this coalition. In general, high per capita income portions of the country supported the bill.

The day after Senate passage, a motion to suspend the rules was made in the House. This failed on a tie vote. The frontier had less weight in the House and was slightly less favorable. The eight frontier states voted 10–7 to suspend. The closeness of the vote reflects the larger weight of the North, relative to the South, after the reapportionment of 1830. Two weeks later, however, the bill was tabled, by a much wider margin. Of those members voting on both occasions, there was a net change of 4 votes away from support of a bankruptcy bill. So the closeness of the vote to suspend is largely a matter of a very substantial number, 64, of nonvoters. When turnout was higher, on the table vote (only 49 nonvoters) the lack of support in the House was clearer. An attempt to revive the bill in the lame-duck session of 1841 also failed.

Although voting in the House, as in the Senate, was ideological with high PREs, the Whigs failed to replicate their Senate success in 1840. The Senate did continue, in two votes in the lame-duck session of 1841, to show strong support for bankruptcy legislation, but the matter was allowed to die. After all, the chances that a Senate bill would succeed in the House were slight. Bankruptcy would have to await the triumph of Tippecanoe and Tyler too.

The Whig Bankruptcy Act of 1841: Enactment and Repeal

The change that followed the elections of 1840 was purely a matter of a strong voter shift to the Whigs in the 27th Congress (1841–1843). No new states had been seated, and Congress was not reapportioned. The shift, nonetheless, was immense, leaving the Whigs with a nearly 3:2 majority in the House. In the Senate, however, the shift was less pronounced, given that the Senate was indirectly elected and had staggered terms. A bankruptcy bill secured final passage in August 1841. Although heavily Whig, the House voted repeal just 5 months later. Repeal, however, was blocked in the Senate when its proponents could not secure a two-thirds majority to bring the repeal bill to the floor. Thus, rapid repeal was blocked by majority-party agenda control. Repeal finally cleared Congress in early 1843. We now present a detailed account of votes in the 27th Congress, to see how bankruptcy law not only passed but also unraveled.

Perhaps because of the transfer of control from Democrats to Whigs in the elections of 1840, the 27th Congress convened unusually early, in March 1841, the earliest possible date under the Constitution. (In the 19th century it was common for a Congress to convene only in December of the year following its election. For example, the 26th House, elected in November 1838, took its first roll-call vote only in January 1840.) The Panic of 1837 had resulted in demand for bankruptcy legislation, but bankruptcy proponents, as we have shown, were previously blocked by the Democratic majority. The bill included provisions for voluntary and involuntary bankruptcy for individuals but no provisions for corporations, which were, at the time, chiefly banks. The major purpose of the bill was likely to have been debt relief for Whig merchants and traders.

The bill that passed was a Senate bill that was definitely a Whig Party bill with strong party whips on both sides. The votes on the bill up to passage were almost strict party-line votes, with no sharp regional differences. Whig unity was important, given their narrow majority in the Senate.

The bill went to the House after the House had taken a few votes on bankruptcy in June. In the House, the Whigs could tolerate defections from Southern representatives who, moreover, were subject to popular rather than indirect election. When the House passed the bill in August, the Whigs had 23 defections, most notably 19 from the South. In contrast, only 3 Democrats, 2 from Manhattan and 1 from King Cotton Louisiana, both "money" areas, defected to support the bill.

The 27th House was in fact preoccupied with bankruptcy, devoting 65 of 994 roll calls to the issue. The House votes on the bill fall into four natural groups:

1. Votes in June to August 1841, leading to passage
2. Votes in January 1842, leading to passage of repeal in the House. The Senate failed to pass repeal at this time
3. In the spring and summer of 1842, sporadic attempts at repeal or the inclusion of corporations under the law
4. A successful move to repeal in the lame-duck session. These votes took place between New Year's Eve and January 17, 1843

The entire period is characterized by a virtual absence of substantive amendments. Most of the votes are on procedural attempts to kill a bill or to delay action, a reflection of a bitter, close division, where turnout on a given day could influence the outcome. With the exception of attempts to maintain state debt-relief laws in force and to delay the effective date of repeal, members either manifested support or opposition to the bill. There was an absence of floor action aimed at reform or perfection. Positions were polarized.

The bill initially met strong opposition. In fact, the bill was tabled on August 17 by a vote of 110–99.[9] The Democrats were unified against, with only five defectors. These were all Wall Street Democrats (Roosevelt, Sanford, Ward, and Wood of New York and Plumer of Pennsylvania). Northern Whigs were just as unified in favor, with only six defectors. The swing votes were Southern Whigs, who voted 25–10 to table. The bill fit the spatial model quite well, with only 28 classification errors in 209 votes and a PRE of 0.72. Predicting straight party-line voting would have resulted in 36 classification errors.

Warren (1935) claims that passage was secured by a logroll engineered by Henry Clay that included distribution of government lands, a high tariff, and a national fiscal bank, with the bankrupt bill as a by-product. If this is the case, a deal must have been made with Southern Whigs. The Democrats were clearly not part of any logroll. When the bankrupt bill was reconsidered and then passed on August 18, there were even fewer Democratic votes for passage than there had been against tabling.[10] The bill passed 111–105 largely because it received majority (22–19) support from Southern Whigs. The spatial model makes only 18 classification errors with a PRE of 0.85. The straight party-line voting prediction would have resulted in 26 classification errors.

The vote to pass may have been more strategic than the vote to table. On the vote to table, members may have been expressing constituency interests on the legislation. On the logrolled passage vote, votes may have expressed strategic vote trades. Because party affiliation is an important determinant of location in the ideological space, a strategic, intraparty logroll classifies quite well.

Developing a logroll in this period involved influencing abstentions as well as simply switching votes. Opponents could be persuaded to abstain. The turnout of supporters could be increased. Between the motion to table and passage, the pro-bankrupt-law side lost one vote among Democrats voting both times[11] and gained three votes among Whigs.[12] The net gain was two votes. They needed a switch of six to swing the 110–99 defeat on tabling to a victory. The missing votes came from earlier nonvoters. In fact, the Whigs were able to increase their turnout by six voters while the Democrats could increase turnout by only one.

Of the many votes before passage of the act, there was only one substantive amendment. This amendment, by Nathan Clifford (D-Maine), a Northerner in the left wing of his party, manifests an important issue that divided proponents from opponents of the bill. On August 17, Clifford moved to amend, "adding that nothing in this act shall be construed to alter or repeal any state law for the relief of insolvent debtors, or any such law exempting certain goods and chattels from attachment, execution and distress."[13] With the amendment, debtors would have been allowed to use relatively friendly state laws as protection from creditors. Clifford's amendment passed 99–94. The vote on the amendment was perhaps the purest vote in terms of preferences. Democrats supported the amendment 73–4, Northern Whigs opposed 8–69. The amendment passed because of the division of Southern Whigs (17–21). There were only 19 classification errors and the PRE was 0.80. (Party-line voting implies 29 classification errors.)

Regression analysis of the Clifford amendment vote shows that left-right ideology was indeed the predominant variable. Equation 26.3 reports a regression with just the DW-NOMINATE dimensions, which had a higher adjusted R^2 than did using the same model from equations 26.1 and 26.2.

$$\textit{House Vote on Clifford Amendment} = 0.524(24.391^{**}) - 0.966(-18.624^{**})\textit{DW-NOM1} + 0.026(0.715)\textit{DW-NOM2} \ (\text{Adj. } R^2 = 0.65, N = 192) \quad \mathbf{(26.3)}$$

With the reappearance of a two-party system, fits return to the levels seen in votes on the 1800 bill. The more fine-grained DW-NOMINATE measure, however, captures all the information provided by party and provides additional discrimination. The *Region* variable has no bite as does an additional variable coded for *Frontier*. This variable was set to 1.0 for the eight frontier states previously identified. After their defeat on the Clifford amendment, the Whigs rallied before Congress resumed the next day, August 18. A motion was first made, and passed, to reconsider the tabling. Joseph Underwood (D-Ky.), who had moved to table on the 17th, so moved again. The motion failed. A motion was then made to reconsider the Clifford amendment. Clifford moved his amendment again. This time the amendment lost 91–119 on a nearly straight party-line vote. Democrats supported it by 79–1, Northern Whigs opposed it by 1–88, and Southern Whigs opposed it by 10–30. The spatial model has only eight errors and a PRE of 0.912. Of those voting both times on the amendment, 1 Democrat and 11 Whigs, including 8 from slave states, swung in favor of restricting state law. The House then passed the unamended bill.

The bill took effect February 1, 1842. Even before this date, there were roll-call votes in the Senate on motions to delay its implementation. A motion to move a repeal bill to third reading failed by one vote. Thomas Hart Benton (D-Mo.) was able to produce only a tie vote in July 1842 when he tried to obtain the two-thirds majority necessary to bring repeal to the floor.

In contrast, the House did vote to repeal at the end of a debate lasting from January 8 to January 17, 1842. There were a total of 27 roll-call votes, the large number reflecting efforts by the Whigs both to delay repeal and to include specie-issuing banks under the law. When repeal passed on January 17, the vote was 126–94, with Democrats favoring repeal by 85–7, Northern Whigs opposing by 9–76, and Southern Whigs being the swing vote in support, 30–12. The vote fits the spatial model well, with a PRE of 0.70 and 28 errors. The movement to repeal at this point reflects more the collapse of the logroll than a dramatic shift in preferences. Of those voting both on Underwood's original motion to table, which was thought to have killed the bill, and on repeal, only nine Whigs and four Democrats changed camps. Both parties had only a single individual who switched to the pro-bankruptcy-law side. The others switched against, including three New York and Pennsylvania Democrats and eight Southern and Western Whigs. The net gain of nine votes by the antibankruptcy side between the Underwood motion and repeal suggests only a mild shift in basic preferences. Since there had been no experience with the law in January, the first repeal effort was largely the unraveling of the logroll. As the Senate failed to act, however, the bill took effect.

Immediately before the repeal, the Whigs isolated the Southern Democrats by passing the Cushing amendment to maintain the law in effect for bankruptcies currently in progress in the courts. There were 34 spatial errors and a fairly low PRE of 0.452. Northern Whigs voted 80–1 to maintain current cases. Southern Whigs were nearly as solid, supporting the amendment 31–8. A substantial minority of Northern Democrats (25–30) also supported the amendment. Only Southern Democrats (11–23) were firmly against. (Another Whig amendment, which would have maintained the law for cases initiated before July, was easily defeated.) This vote demonstrates that Southern Democrats were the heart of opposition to a bankruptcy law.

The House voted to repeal, by a 140–71 vote, on January 17, 1843, less than 1 year since the bill took force. The Democrats voted for repeal unanimously. The Whig Party had become sharply divided. Southern Whigs voted for repeal by a more than 3–1 margin; even 20 Northern Whigs supported repeal. The swing against the bill was unambiguous. (Repeal was supported by all members who had been against passage and also voted on repeal.) The effect of experience with the bill is demonstrated by observing a gain of 15 more votes favorable to repeal in 1843 compared to the earlier repeal vote just before the bill's taking effect in 1842.

The spatial model is quite successful in finding those Whigs who voted for repeal. There are only 29 classification errors. (PRE drops to 0.594 because the roll call is more lopsided than the earlier votes.) In contrast, the party-line model has 52 classification errors, reflecting the split within the Whig Party.

The 27th House votes on bankruptcy reveal that party and region were both significantly related to support for a national bankruptcy law. Northern Whigs represent the core support for legislation, Southern Democrats the core of the opposition. This is basically the same alignment that takes place on major economic issues for the remainder of the 19th century, with the Republicans replacing the Whigs after the Civil War. (See Poole and Rosenthal [1993, 1994] for a similar story on votes on railroad regulation between 1874 and 1887.)

The North-South split on repeal is, however, largely captured by the DW-NOMINATE coordinates, as shown in equation 26.4. Like passage, the left-right split is again the variable that does the heavy lifting. The left votes for repeal. The second dimension, unlike the passage vote, is also significant. Positive values on this dimension, now identified with pro-slavery positions, are significantly related to repeal. The *Frontier* variable is now significant. The frontier, ridden with land debt, is against repeal, after controlling for ideology. The overall fit (both in adjusted R^2 and in the standard error of the estimate) on the repeal vote is lower than on the passage vote. We suspect that the reduction of fit reflects both a breakdown within the Whig party and a differential experience with the act across constituencies, and differential demands for debt relief across constituencies.

$$\begin{aligned}\textit{House Vote on Repeal, 1843}\\ &= 0.627(5.80^{**}) + 0.009(1.005)\textit{Region}\\ &\quad - 0.229(-2.711^{*})\textit{Frontier} - 0.004(-0.025)\textit{Party}\\ &\quad - 0.846(-4.75^{**})\textit{DW-NOM1} + 0.164(2.275^{*})\textit{DW-NOM2} \qquad \textbf{(26.4)}\end{aligned}$$

The House bill went to the Senate, which started debate on February 20 before voting repeal on February 25. Although the Whigs were able to maintain enough internal discipline to block consideration of the House bill by one vote on February 21, support for the bill quickly evaporated in a series of later votes. The Whigs had to acknowledge the bill's bad reputation by proposing an amendment "to modify the bankruptcy act to meet all the evils complained of, suitable to the wants and advantages of a great commercial nation." The amendment was solidly trounced. Repeal occurred by a large majority, 32–13, on February 25. Although the defenders of the bill were all Whigs, the party had become badly divided, splitting 13–13 with even the Northern Whigs voting against repeal only by an 11–7 margin.

Conclusion

The story of the 1841 Bankruptcy Act illustrates the instability of bankruptcy policy in the 19th century. Similarly, the 1800 act was cashiered before its scheduled sunset. On other occasions, bills were passed in the Senate only to fail in the House. Basic ideological preferences appear to be fundamental to the absence of bankruptcy law in the 18th and 19th centuries. The Left was always the motor for undoing the legislative accomplishments of the Right. The indirect preferences that result from the mapping of bankruptcy legislation onto ideology are conditioned by the state of the economy and public reaction to the effectiveness of the law. The distribution of preferences in Congress is determined by the volatile outcomes of national elections. It was, in the 19th century, also determined by the admission of new states, resulting in overrepresentation of the debt-ridden frontier in the Senate. Interests of the frontier states were an important addition to ideology in structuring roll-call voting. They were pivotal in the passage of two bills in the Senate that did not pass a House that reflected the more populous states. Thus, economics, elections, and ideology, themselves closely intertwined, produced legislative volatility.

AFTERWORD

DAVID BRADY AND MATHEW D. MCCUBBINS

The chapters in this volume give serious consideration to how politicians' choices affect the institution of Congress. The authors do not examine these choices in a vacuum but, rather, consider the role that other economic, social, and political circumstances had on the strategies of politicians. Thus, these chapters take the first steps toward creating a political economy of Congress.

Political scientists have used political economy approaches to understand a range of topics. For instance, Kalt and Zupan (1984, 1990) examine the interaction between a representative's ideology and his or her constituency in determining legislative voting. They find that representative ideology has an independent effect on how legislators vote on issues in Congress but that senators up for reelection are more constrained by their constituent's preferences. Other scholars have used political economy to study political business and spending cycles and have connected these cycles to the institutional structure of elections and politics in a country (Kramer 1971; Nordhaus 1975; Hibbs 1977; Tufte 1978; Alesina 1987, 1988; Beck 1987). Political scientists have shown that the design of electoral districts affects the incentives of politicians and, therefore, influences the mix of private- and public-regarding legislation (Katz 1980; Cain, Ferejohn, and Fiorina 1987; Cox 1990; Ramseyer and Rosenbluth 1993; Carey and Shugart 1995; Cox 1997; Mainwaring and Shugart 1997; Cox and McCubbins 2001). International relations scholars are increasingly focusing on the role that domestic factors play in international politics. For instance, scholars have studied how trade and security policy relate to a country's domestic interests (Rogowski 1987, and see Broz and Frieden 2001 for a review of the major arguments). Another strand of literature has connected the frequency of elections with shorter time horizons, which lead to less capital investment, less risk taking, and particularization of public policy (Cohen and Noll 1988).

This has been but a brief look at a number of the different uses of political economy to understand political institutions and public policy, and there are many other studies and topics that have used political economy approaches to understand how social factors interact with politics to produce policy outcomes.

Congressional scholarship can take a similar tack and develop theories that link changes in American society and economy to political developments within Congress and between the branches of American government. For instance, scholars have studied how increases in the caseload of the judiciary coupled with changes in party control lead to an increase in the size of the judiciary, particularly an expansion of Article I courts (Bond 1980; de Figueiredo and Tiller 1996; McNollgast 1995). However, scholars have not examined how these same causes can lead to changes in federal jurisdiction. This leaves open the question of whether changes in jurisdiction are purely a political response to new conditions or whether they are influenced by partisan politics, political ambition, and socioeconomic pressure.

Another issue central to American politics is the long-run expansion of the U.S. government. Political scientists have observed changes in the size and scope of the U.S. government (Lewis-Beck and Rice 1985); however, as historians point out (Higgs 1987), the government unfailingly grows during times of war and then never returns to its previous size. Once the political parties in power have this additional government capacity, regardless of their ideological attachments (or lack thereof), they bend government power to their other needs rather than relinquish it. As yet, no theory accounts for how and why political parties and politicians continue to expand the size and scope of government despite broad changes in social, economic, and political conditions.

Along similar lines, political scientists have yet to develop theories to explain the creation and growth of regulatory bodies, such as the Environmental Protection Agency. The current life-cycle approach (Kahn 1988) and its extension by Weingast (1981) provide a description of how regulatory bodies change. However, these approaches do not explain the creation of new regulatory agencies, their growth, or how politicians transform them. A compelling theory of regulatory power must take account of both the external conditions that seem to structure the opportunity set of politicians and the actions within Congress that determine the actual policies that are adopted. Political scientists have used political economy approaches for a number of important issues in the study of politics, but many topics remain that congressional scholars have yet to fully understand.

Political economy approaches force scholars to understand how economic and social factors interact with institutions to produce the political outcomes we observe. In American politics it requires a recognition that political outcomes have been profoundly shaped by the institutional structure of the Constitution and the long-standing division between the regions of the country. The chapters in this volume analyze the effects of political, economic, and social divisions on politicians, institutional rules, and policy outcomes. By integrating the external environment with political strategy, these scholars take an important step toward creating a political economy of Congress. And as history presents varied conditions to help test and refine theories of congressional organization and behavior, the political economy approaches used in this volume fit naturally with a historical perspective on institutional development. Often our theories are predicated on the implicit assumption that the past world looked the same as the current world. However, this volume shows that some theories are robust to historical changes while other theories are shown to be extremely sensitive to context and period. We will have more confidence in our theories of institutional development and, perhaps more importantly, better predictive power if we are able to offer explanations, not just for any particular historical period, but across historical periods.

NOTES

Notes to Chapter 1

1. It was indeed an omen when Charles Pinckney, leading the delegation from South Carolina, warned Madison at the Constitutional Convention that "South Carolina had already considered seceding from the Union" in anticipation of that meeting' attempts to "tamper with his state's right to keep importing slaves without limitation" (Cerami 2005, 113). Of course, South Carolina was constantly threatening to secede from the Union, as it did during the Nullification Crisis in 1832. In discussing the Virginia and New Jersey plans for the constitution, Madison remarked, "The great danger to our general government is the great southern and northern interests of the continent being opposed to each other" (Cerami 2005, 138).

2. According to the 1800 census, Virginia was considerably larger than New York in terms of population. If anything, this makes New York's leapfrogging of Virginia in terms of economic fortunes all the more impressive.

3. http://fisher.lib.virginia.edu/collections/stats/histcensus/.

4. For a visual presentation of election data see Dave Leip's Atlas of U.S. Presidential Elections at http://www.uselectionatlas.org/.

Notes to Chapter 2

Professor Ansolabehere and Professor Snyder thank the National Science Foundation for its generous financial support. We thank Gary Jacobson, John Huber, and seminar participants at the Columbia Political Economy Seminar (March 2, 2004) for their helpful comments.

1. On the adoption of primary election systems, see Merriam and Overacker (1928) and Ware (2002). Several other significant reforms followed a similar pattern of rapid adoption—e.g., on the adoption of the Australian ballot see Evans (1917).

2. See, for example, Jewell (1955); Clubb and Allen (1967); Brady (1972); Shade et al. (1973); Brady and Althoff (1974); Sinclair [Deckard] (1976, 1977); Clubb and Traugott (1977); Cooper, Brady, and Hurley (1977); Brady, Cooper, and Hurley (1979); Rosenthal (1981); Hurley and Wilson (1989);

Patterson and Caldeira (1988); Brady, Brody, and Epstein (1989); Cox and McCubbins (1991); Morehouse (1996); Snyder and Groseclose (2000).

3. Gubernatorial acceptance speech, August 8, 1900, quoted in Ranney 1975, 125.

4. Report to the New York Commission, quoted in Fanning 1911, 66.

5. Quoted in a news article, "The Remedy for the Evils of the Present System of Nomination," *Outlook* vol. 91, issue 3, January 16, 1909, p. 91.

6. Beard 1910, 187.

7. The exact dates are available from the authors. We used the following materials: Joint Committee of the Senate and Assembly of the State of New York (1910), Aylsworth (1908, 1912), Merriam (1908), Merriam and Overacker (1928), and various newspapers.

8. Another plausible view is that only a binding primary has teeth. When we drop the optional states, the results are virtually identical to those reported here.

9. We conducted alternative models for Democrats and Republicans, but to conserve space they are not shown. For the alternative specifications, contact the authors. In a separate analysis, not shown, we considered the U.S. Senate. The pattern is qualitatively similar to that in the House—indeed, for Republicans the estimated coefficients are even larger than those for the House—but the analyses are leveraged on only 30 cases, so we do not have much confidence in the estimates.

Notes to Chapter 3

We thank Gary Cox, Mathew D. McCubbins, Nathan Monroe, David Rohde, and James Snyder Jr. for helpful suggestions and comments. This research is generously supported by NSF (SES-0136260).

1. We also experimented with various dummy specifications of Senate-preference vote. None yielded statistically significant or otherwise suggestive results and so were left out of the final analysis.

2. The *Senate Preference* variable takes a value of 1 for states employing an Oregon-plan preference vote, in which voters expressed their choice for senator and the state legislature was then instructed to elect the candidate who received the largest number of votes.

3. If, for example, Democrats controlled both chambers, it was nearly assured that a Democratic senator would (eventually) be chosen. But exactly which Democrat, and from which faction of the party, would be selected often proved highly contentious.

4. In a separate analysis, we also estimated the model on elections from 1914 to 1940. The coefficient for party control of the state legislature was 1.41 (with a 0.19 standard error). This was significantly smaller than the coefficient for indirect elections, boosting our confidence that the results for the indirect era are not an artifact of some other statewide force.

5. In a separate analysis (not shown) we also included a lagged dependent variable. This variable was not significant, and its inclusion did not alter the pattern of results we get here. In addition, including the lagged variable would cause us to lose the first election immediately following the 17th Amendment.

Notes to Chapter 4

We thank Chuck Finocchiaro, Kristin Kanthak, Robert Grafstein, James Endersby, Keith Dougherty, Wendy Schiller, participants at the History of Congress Conference, University of California at San Diego, December 5–6, 2003, La Jolla, California, and participants at the annual meetings of the Southern Political Science Association, New Orleans, January 8–10, 2004, for comments on previous versions. We thank Michael Rocca for research assistance and the University of California at Davis Institute for Governmental Affairs for research support.

1. Formal statements, diagnostics, and data available on request. Contact Bernhard at Department of Political Science, 361 Lincoln Hall, University of Illinois, Urbana IL 61801. Contact Sala at Department of Political Science, One Shields Avenue, University of California, Davis CA 95616-8682.

2. We estimated the parameters (two per year) for the set of senators in each session-year who were in the 1st through 4th years of their respective terms—i.e., senators not yet up for reelection or in their lame-duck sessions. If late-term senators behave very similarly to early-term senators, excluding them would reduce our confidence in the precision of Groseclose, Levitt, and Snyder's adjustment factors, but it should not bias those parameter estimates. On the other hand, if late-term senators differ systematically from early-termers, including them would bias the calculation of the adjustment factors.

3. In performing this analysis we studied the number of reelection-seeking Senate incumbents who shifted by at least one standard deviation in the moderating or polarizing direction compared to the number moving less than a standard deviation, by election year. We also include the average standardized movement for the year within each category.

4. State legislative data are for the party shares of the *combined* (upper and lower chamber) seats. See Inter-university Consortium for Political and Social Research (ICPSR) study 16 (Burnham 1984).

Notes to Chapter 5

I would like to thank Amy Baumann, Rodrick Echols, Gail Hayworth, and Daniel Jacobson for their excellent research assistance and Andrea Campbell, Joseph Cooper, Dick Fenno, and Charles Stewart for their comments on a draft of this paper. In addition, I also thank the participants of seminars held fall 2003 at Rutgers, New York University, Columbia, and the University of California at San Diego as part of the History of Congress series.

1. The specific Congresses were selected in part because of data availability; the first comprehensive Senate-election returns were not published in the *Tribune Almanac* until the early 1880s. The men who reached the U.S. Senate during this era had extensive prior experience in the state legislature, Congress, or the governor's mansion. In this sample, 80% of senators ran for reelection at least once, with a 65% reelection rate.

2. There is a small body of literature on the impact of the 17th amendment on aggregate trends in the Senate. After direct elections were instituted, the partisan composition of the Senate shifted after 1913 toward the Democratic Party and away from a long period of Republican Party dominance, and senators typically had slightly longer tenures in office (Haynes 1938; Stewart 1992; King and Ellis 1996; Crook and Hibbing 1997).

3. Republican candidates were not confined to Northern or Western states. There are three Southern states in the sample, and only Louisiana failed to elect a Republican during this time. Both Kentucky and North Carolina had Republican candidates in repeated elections, and those states elected Republican senators during this time.

4. This model does not directly address the impact of sequenced, bicameral elections for senators during the period of indirect elections. But when a model is run with variables for the percentage of seats held by the senator's own party in the house and senate, respectively, it makes no difference whether the party holds more seats in one chamber or the other. The bicameral variables were insignificant, which shores up the argument that Senate elections were highly contentious within majority parties generally; holding a high percentage of seats in the house or senate did not guarantee a unified coalition of support within a party for one Senate candidate.

5. Model estimated via ordinary least squares. The numbers in parentheses are White-Huber robust standard errors.

6. For a discussion of the value of committees to House members during this time, see Wilson (1986).

7. For a long time, senators were assigned to committees only for a single session, so that within a Congress they would serve on two different sets of committees. That changed in 1886, when senators were appointed to serve on committees for entire Congresses (Canon and Stewart 2002b, 71).

8. Gorman also sat on the Rules, Pensions, Organization of Executive Departments committees, and Corporations Organized in the District of Columbia over the course of his career.

9. Speech at Charlotte, North Carolina, September 12, 1912 (see Rippy 1936, 154–155).

10. Cosponsorship was not practiced in the Senate during this time, and it was explicitly prohibited by a Senate ruling in 1913; however, in 1937 a senator was allowed to be named as a cosponsor of a resolution and cosponsorship was subsequently permitted (Riddick 1992, 233–234; Campbell 1982).

11. That is substantially higher than in the modern Senate, where senators introduce an average of about 30 public bills per session.

12. In this sample, separating out the effects of party affiliation from majority status is difficult because the Republicans controlled the Senate in each of the four Congresses—a model run with each of the variables produces the same result in that Republicans (majority) introduce more bills than Democrats (minority) do. In terms of types of bills, there is a clearer pattern in that Democrats introduce more relief bills and Republicans introduce more pension bills, which is understandable because most war-pension recipients lived in the North, which was heavily Republican.

13. However, being the senior senator within a delegation did not have a statistically significant effect on bill sponsorship.

14. In the case of primaries and nominating conventions, I would argue that the task at hand for an incumbent senator was the same but the arena in which the party determined its nominees differed.

Notes to Chapter 6

Thanks to Craig Goodman, Tim Nokken, Erik Engstrom, and Sam Kernell for sharing various data and to the many participants at the 2003 History of Congress Conference, held in San Diego, California, for their helpful suggestions.

1. For recent overviews and analyses of contested elections in the House and the Senate, see Jenkins (2004) and Jenkins (2005), respectively.

2. *Statutes at Large of the United States of America*, volume 9, chapter 11, pp. 568–570. See Jenkins (2005) for a more extensive discussion.

3. This would finally change in 1969 with the passage of the Federal Contested Election Act (FCEA), which updated and streamlined the mode of procedure in contested-election cases. See 2 *U.S. Code*, chapter 12, sections 381–396.

4. Sources used to code contested-election cases include Rowell (1901), which covers the 1st through 56th Congresses; Moores (1917), which covers the 57th through 64th Congresses; Dempsey (1956), which covers the 1st through 82nd Congresses; Deschler (1977), which covers the 65th through 92nd Congresses; and Welborn (2000), which covers the 73rd though 106th Congresses. Some coding discrepancies exist between the various works. For example, in identifying contested-election cases, with respect to Dempsey, Rowell differs on 5 occasions, Moores on 1, and Deschler on 10. To determine which coding scheme to use, I examined the debates in Congress, using the *Annals of Congress*, the *Register of Debates*, the *Congressional Globe*, and the *Congressional Record* as guiding materials.

5. Case in point: since the 67th Congress (1921–1923), only 5 of 128 cases (or 3.9%) have been decided in favor of the contestant.

6. This aggregate ratio is depressed by results since the beginning of the 20th century, wherein only 13.7% of contested-election cases were dealt with by roll call. This compares to 48.6% during the antebellum era and 39.4% during the late 19th century (see Jenkins [2004]).

7. Party affiliations for members of Congress, as well as contestees and contestants in election contests, are taken from Martis (1989) and Dubin (1998).

8. For additional evidence of party influence in election-contest roll calls, see Jenkins (2004).

9. The enforcement acts comprised five laws passed between May 1870 and June 1872 that, among other things, outlawed violence, fraud, and intimidation in the voting process; provided deputy marshals to oversee elections; and required that paper ballots be used in congressional elections.

10. For a discussion of the military withdrawal, political corruption, and Southern elections in the late 1870s, see Bensel (1990, 366–415).

11. For an argument that the enforcement of electoral laws continued into the 1880s, albeit at a significantly lower rate than during Reconstruction, see Valelly (1995).

12. In addition, the Republican pursuit of election contests in the South would be used as electoral fodder in the North, as coverage of Southern fraud and corruption would put Northern Democratic candidates on the defensive. See Bensel (1984, 87).

13. One Iowa Republican, Marsena Cutts, would be unseated in favor of a Democrat on the last day of the Congress, producing a net gain of five seats for the Republicans.

14. The Force Bill of 1890 would pass in the House but be bogged down in the Senate by a Democratic filibuster. The original force acts of the early 1870s would be repealed in 1893 during Grover Cleveland's administration. See Perman (2001, 38–47) and Golden (2001, 145–170).

15. This Arkansas case—*John M. Clayton v. Clifton R. Breckinridge*—was unusual, in that the Republican contestant was murdered before the taking of testimony had been completed. Nevertheless, the House continued with the investigation. In the end, a majority of the Committee on Elections held that fraud did in fact occur—a ballot box had been stolen—and once lost votes were counted, Clayton was the rightful occupant of the seat. Because of his death, the committee determined that the election should be voided. The House agreed by a 105 to 62 vote. For a full description of this case and the events surrounding Clayton's assassination while contesting his election defeat, see Barnes (1998).

16. In addition, one Democrat from Arkansas was unseated in favor of a member of the Labor Party.

17. In addition, two Democrats from the Deep South, one each from Alabama and North Carolina, were unseated in favor of Populists.

18. In fact, aside from the aforementioned areas and one district in Texas—the 14th, represented by Republican Harry M. Wurzbach from the 67th (1921–1923) through 71st (1929–1931) Congresses—the Republican Party would not capture another Southern district until the late 1950s.

19. This excludes cases involving U.S. territories.

20. These states include Alabama, Arkansas, Florida, Georgia, Louisiana, Mississippi, North Carolina, South Carolina, Tennessee, Texas, and Virginia.

21. These states include Delaware, Kentucky, Maryland, Missouri, and West Virginia. While these states were not "reconstructed," as were the former Confederate states, each had strong Democratic histories and Southern sympathies. Kentucky and Missouri, for example, elected rump governments during the Civil War, which were recognized by the Confederacy and provided representation in the Confederate Congress.

22. The Republicans would also void the election of Robert C. De Large (R-S.C.) in the 42nd Congress, but the seat remained vacant for the remainder of the Congress.

23. For examples of these various corrupt practices, see Kousser (1974), Argersinger (1985–1986), Perman (2001), and Summers (2001, 2004).

24. Henry Cabot Lodge (R-Mass.), a member of the Committee on Elections in the 50th Congress, echoed Reed's concerns, suggesting that contested-election cases consumed 30 to 60 days in each session of Congress (*New York Herald*, November 30, 1889).

25. Reed also had firsthand experience with election contests, having had his own seat contested in the 47th Congress (1881–1883). The contestant in the case, Democrat Samuel J. Anderson, leveled a number of charges, chief among them that a number of his would-be voters were intimidated by Reed's supporters and did not participate in the election. Filing a short brief with the Committee on Elections, Reed stated: "If I could scare them as easily as the contestant seems to think and by means as inadequate as he has proved, I have certainly been recreant in a plain duty. I ought to have scared more of them" (quoted in Robinson 1930, 75). Both the committee and the House found the evidence presented by Anderson flimsy and ruled in Reed's favor.

26. In fact, *one* candidate, William F. Aldrich (Alabama, Fourth District), won *three* successive election contests, in the 54th, 55th, and 56th Congresses.

27. For a similar breakdown, see Valelly (1995, 2003).

28. Both cases were from Florida, and both ended in dismissal.

Notes to Chapter 7

1. I am obliged to Keith Poole for providing these data, which may be found at http://voteview.com/ (October 8, 2003).

2. Poole and Rosenthal (1997a, 80–82) provide alternative measures of dispersion within the parties that display the same trends for the period under examination here.

3. Senate electoral coalitions are calculated from the moving average of the most recent three elections because only one-third of Senate seats are up for election in any single year.

4. Data for 2002 are omitted because the incoming members elected that year do not yet have voting records to compare with those of members remaining in or exiting Congress. The career DW-NOMINATE score is the average DW-NOMINATE over member's entire career in Congress.

5. The list of Republicans who are considered part of or allied to the Christian Right and who served between the 96th and 106th Congresses was kindly provided by John C. Green, a long-term student of the movement. Building on Green's list, I updated the data for the 107th Congress.

6. The proportion of House alumni from the Gingrich era (96th–106th Congresses) among Senate Republicans grew from 13% in the 101st Congress to 40% in the 107th Congress.

7. Calculated as 10 (trend coefficient) + 10 (terms coefficient).

8. I begin this analysis with the 96th Congress because data on one of the variables—ally of Christian Right—begin with this Congress.

9. *CQ Weekly Report* noted that the event "signaled a polarization between Democrats and Republicans that is likely to last for the remainder of the year" (Granat 1984, 1166).

10. After cloture, any amendments must be germane, so the minority party cannot get bills to the Senate floor as unrelated riders to legislation currently under consideration.

Notes to Chapter 8

Special thanks go to Jorge Bravo, Scott de Marchi, Giacomo Chiozza, Claire Kramer, Olga Shvetsova, participants of the Micro-Incentives Research Center Brownbag Lunch Group, and the participants at the two History of Congress conferences (University of California at San Diego, December 5–6, 2003, La Jolla, California, and Stanford University, April 9–10, 2004). Of course, this work would not have been possible without the generous lengths that Keith Poole goes to in making the DW-NOMINATE data available. All analyses here used Stata 8 (computer software, StataCorp LP, College Station, TX, 1985–2006). Additional tables and figures can be found at http://www.uwm.edu/~tofias.

1. This and the following few paragraphs are based on Aldrich and Rohde (2000a).

2. These one-dimensional measures differ from those reported in the earlier papers, because they are based on DW-NOMINATE, use the new measurement techniques described in the preceding, and are extended through the 107th Congress.

Notes to Chapter 9

The authors would like to thank Pamela Fiber, Gary Jacobson, and Charles Stewart for data provision. John Aldrich, David Brady, Jeff Jenkins, Mat McCubbins, Rose Razaghian, Alan Wiseman, participants of the 2004 History of Congress Conference at Stanford University, April 9–10, 2004, and participants at the 2004 Summer Workshop of the Yale University Center for the Study of American Politics are gratefully acknowledged for helpful comments.

1. The ADA chooses about 20 key votes per session to discern the degree to which members vote with them (100 as the most liberal score) or against them (0 as the most conservative score). Throughout the analysis here, we average the two session ADA scores for each member to generate a single ADA score per Congress. We rely on the raw ADA scores as opposed to ones that are scaled to be on a similar metric over time (Groseclose, Levitt, and Snyder 1999b) because the latter assume that members hold the same position in Congress over time, while the electoral marginality hypothesis and personal-vote perspective presume that the positions may vary as a function of electoral safety.

2. We excluded observations for which the member's seat was redistricted since the last presidential election, as those election results would not map to the member's district, thus generating an inaccurate district-based predicted ADA score.

3. Perhaps relatedly, members who vote consistently in line with their district have a better chance of becoming more senior members.

4. Running the analyses with a separate dummy variable for these committees generated coefficients that indicated they had a value of about 4 to 6 across the decades. A value of 5 is thus largely consistent with that alternative approach and is in line with the value that Groseclose and Stewart estimate for Appropriations (4.75) and Rules (4.55) in the earlier era.

5. We include only Democrats and Republicans in the following analyses. The handful of independents does not affect the results when included.

6. Another factor that could affect the degree to which members are willing to vote at ideological extremes is fund-raising. Before the creation of the Federal Election Commission in the mid-1970s, candidates were not required to publish detailed records of their fund-raising. Therefore, we lack data for the 1960s and 1970s on campaign contributions. To show consistent models over time, we here present the results without controls for fund-raising. We have, however, run analyses with such controls and found comparable results, which are available upon request.

7. We conducted a series of Hausman tests to determine whether the instrumental variable approach was needed instead of simple linear regressions. In addition to significance by decade, the test across the entire time period soundly rejected the null hypothesis that the coefficients of the instrumental

variable approach are the same as those from a linear regression [$\chi^2(6) = 40.8$, $p < 0.001$].

8. Assuming a set of member-specific effects, rather than district-specific ones, does not substantively change the results presented here nor does the use of fixed effects instead of random effects. Stata, version 8.0 (computer software, StataCorp LP, College Station, TX, 1985–2006).

9. To see this calculation, multiply the *Vote Share* variable's coefficient by the difference in vote share: $-177.9 \times -0.186 = 33.1$.

10. The 1983–1992 period contained the Republican presidencies of Ronald Reagan and George H. W. Bush, while 1993–2000 contained only the Clinton presidency.

Notes to Chapter 10

This chapter was originally prepared for presentation at the 1998 Annual Meeting of the American Political Science Association. This version was prepared for presentation at the History of Congress Conference, Stanford University, April 9–10, 2004. Some of the research in this paper was conducted in collaboration with Jeffery A. Jenkins of Northwestern University.

1. On the history and politics of early congressional printing see C. Smith (1977) and Jenkins and Stewart (2003).

2. Material from Clay's speakership is contained in the first three volumes of his *Papers*, and a small amount of material is in the fourth volume and the supplement.

3. Although the number of observations is small in this analysis, the result is borne out in other more detailed analysis that uses many more House members, though over shorter periods of time. See Jenkins and Stewart 2002.

4. It is ironic, on this score, that Clay's first nationally prominent legal client was Hamilton's murderer, Aaron Burr.

5. The one majority exception is Hatzenbuehler (1972, 1976).

6. Throughout this chapter, I rely on committee data drawn from the committee rosters in Canon, Nelson, and Stewart (2002). The Poole-Rosenthal D-NOMINATE scores used in this chapter were downloaded from Keith Poole's Web site, www.voteview.com. On the NOMINATE methodology generally, see Poole and Rosenthal (1997a). Even though Poole and Rosenthal note that their technique does not do especially well in classifying votes during the 1810s, the first-dimensional D-NOMINATE scores do an excellent job in predicting whether House members voted for or against declaring war with England. Therefore, I interpret these scores as tapping anti-English sentiment during the early 1810s.

7. The House had a select committee on Foreign Affairs each session of both Congresses. The Senate had no single Foreign Affairs Committee in the first session of the 11th Congress—legislative items were dispersed among several select committees. In the second session of the 11th Congress the Sen-

ate appointed a select committee to "Consider relations with Great Britain and France." A select committee by the same name was appointed again in the third session and in the first session of the 12th Congress. In the second session of the 12th Congress, the Senate appointed a select committee on "Relations with Great Britain and the Military Establishment."

8. In the reapportionment of 1811, New York gained seats in the House. The legislature chose to have two House members elected from Porter's former district in the 13th Congress. Therefore Porter had two immediate successors.

9. Even though the congressional literature has focused on the early evolution of the House committee system, the abrupt transformation of the committee system in the Senate is even more astounding. On the early evolution of the Senate, Swift remarks (1996, 131–133) on the "big bang" in Senate committees in 1816—the Senate added 11 legislative standing committees to its 2 minor housekeeping committees in one fell swoop—but the committee system itself is not her focus. See Canon and Stewart (2002c) for a recent review of new statistical evidence about the transformation of the Senate committee during this era.

10. Also see Rohde and Shepsle (1987) for the precursors to the Gamm-Shepsle argument.

11. The *Congressional Serial Set* (untitled, Serials 653–655, 32nd Cong., 1st sess.) contains an index to all private claims presented to the House from 1789 to 1851, including not only private petitions but memorials, government reports, and so on. That three-volume set lists about 59,000 private claims submitted to the House during this period, or about 1,900 per Congress. Because they were not introduced as bills, these petitions do not show up in bill-based workload statistics, even though a substantial fraction of the House was assigned to committees that processed these claims. It is significant that the first committee clerk ever provided for in an annual appropriations bill was for the House Committee on Claims. See *Statutes at Large*, 34th Congress, 2nd session, p. 644.

12. It is also important to keep in sight the principal-agent relationship that is the core of leader-follower dealings in the House. Clay was a bold, new Speaker who took a more active role in policy making. But he could not do it unilaterally: he needed the support of the membership, otherwise he would be voted out of power. If he was a stronger leader than previous speakers, then the membership must have wanted such (or at least showed a latent demand that Clay recognized and exploited). This point comes into sharper focus during periods of Clay's absence from the House, where the men chosen to be Speaker were perhaps less talented, leading to more costly and less seamless institutional arrangements to organize the House and more legislative friction along the way.

13. We can treat the division of the Commerce and Manufactures Committee into two during the 16th Congress as the creation of a single commit-

tee—Manufactures. That is because Manufactures was created in the opening days of the 16th Congress via a floor amendment to the House rules in which the jurisdiction of the Commerce and Manufactures Committee was left unchanged. Commerce and Manufactures had already been appointed, and none of the original members of the Manufactures Committee were taken from Commerce and Manufactures. Hence, Commerce was considered the successor committee to Commerce and Manufactures.

14. Although some scholars treat the 17th Congress as a continuation of the Clay era with a Clay surrogate in the Speaker's chair, evidence from speakership elections in the 16th, 17th, and 18th Congresses suggest otherwise (Leintz 1978, 70–72). When Clay left the House to attend to business back home, it took 3 days and 22 ballots to choose a successor. That succession fight developed into a regional battle (the Missouri Compromise was the looming political issue), tempered by regional politics and personal ambition. In the end a fierce opponent of slavery expansion, John W. Taylor (N.Y.), was elected Speaker. The political center of gravity shifted in the next Congress. Taking 2 days and 12 ballots to settle matters, the Virginian Philip P. Barbour eventually defeated Taylor for the speakership. Clay returned to the House in the 18th Congress, defeating Barbour for reelection, 139–142. Thus, over three Congresses the House deposed the incumbent Speaker twice, electing in turn a Northerner, Southerner, and Westerner. It is this sort of chaotic cycling, which also manifested itself in legislating, that has given rise to the observation that no natural majority existed in the House beginning in the late 1810s. On the issue of voting for Speaker during this period, see Stewart (1999) and Jenkins and Stewart (2003).

15. It was Tallmadge's amendment that Jefferson famously characterized as being "like a firebell in the night," tolling for the death of the Union itself.

16. Once the debate over Missouri ended, the House took up the bill to establish a territory of Arkansas out of the residual of the Missouri Territory not slated for statehood. Here, John Taylor moved to include the Tallmadge amendment to the Arkansas bill, and the House was off to debate the issue of slavery again. Eventually the Arkansas Territory bill was signed into law without having any slavery restrictions attached.

17. The first 12 elected to the committee had an average first-dimensional D-NOMINATE score of −0.207, compared to the next 11, whose average was 0.216 (t = 4.74). Remini (1991, 190) reports that Clay circulated a list of names beforehand, indicating whom he desired to serve on the committee. Although Remini—citing other sources in support of this view—takes this to be indicative of the wide-ranging support within the House for a resolution to the contest, its sectarian cast is betrayed by the pro-slavery elements still residing at the top of the committee as it was finally chosen. Furthermore, simple quantitative analysis reveals that the 101–155 vote to support the nam-

ing of this committee was strongly structured along ideological lines—ardent restrictionists opposed it, ardent pro-slavery representatives supported it, and the middle of the ideological space was moderately supportive. Thus, while a majority was being built in favor of a compromise on Missouri, it simply is not the case that the "growing temper of the representatives to resolve the problem" (191) was universal.

Notes to Chapter 11

For helpful comments on a previous draft, we thank David Brady, Gary Cox, Rod Kiewiet, Mat McCubbins, Kevin Roust, Wendy Schiller, and James Snyder.

1. The Rules Committee did not emerge as a control committee until the 1880s (Alexander 1916; McConachie 1898; Oleszek 1998; Roberts 2004; see also chapter 13 in this volume), and the Appropriations Committee was not created until 1865 (Galloway and Wise 1976). Before 1865 Ways and Means had jurisdiction over both revenue *and* spending, making it the locus of substantial power, and the most sought-after committee assignment (Canon and Stewart 2002a).

2. All data on committee appointments used in this chapter are taken from Canon, Nelson, and Stewart's (1998) *Historical Congressional Standing Committees, 1st to 79th Congresses, 1789–1947* data file. Data on party membership and majority-party status are from Martis (1989).

3. Note that, since we use the lag of loyalty and restrict our analysis to members who served but were not on Ways and Means in the previous Congress, our sample is restricted to nonfreshmen.

4. The analogy between a drug study and ours is limited, inasmuch as a drug study would also include a control group that did not receive the treatment; it is unclear that any such group exists for our study. We might treat new members of the House—who would have had no opportunity to exhibit loyalty in the prior Congress—as a control group. However, to the extent that Speakers' appointments are based on expected loyalty in Congress *t*, and past loyalty matters because it sends a costly signal about expected loyalty, the absence of such a costly signal does not have clear implications about the level of loyalty the Speaker expects from a new member. Indeed, treating new members as a control group with zero loyalty would imply that the Speaker expected zero loyalty from new members. In other words, this approach would entail a significant, and probably unrealistic, substantive assumption about expected loyalty of new members.

On the other hand, if the costly signal itself is the treatment, rather than expected loyalty, we might expect risk-averse Speakers to appoint returning members to Ways and Means at higher rates than new members. The data in our sample support this expectation. Using a simple difference-of-proportions test, we find that the proportion of returning majority-party members (who were not already on Ways and Means) that was appointed to Ways and Means (0.05) is significantly larger than the proportion of new majority-party members who were appointed to Ways and Means (0.02; the *p* value for the test is 0.0001).

5. We define key votes as those on which leading members from one party adopted a position that was opposed by leading members of the other party. See Den Hartog and Goodman (2004) for more details.

6. Though we do not show the results here, we have also estimated the model with unstandardized loyalty scores and fixed effects, unstandardized loyalty scores without fixed effects, and standardized loyalty scores without fixed effects. In each permutation, the direction and significance of the coefficient for $Loyalty_{it-1}$ is similar to what we report here.

7. $N = 787$; pseudo $R^2 = 0.0830$. Dummies for the 25th and 27th Congresses were omitted because they predict failure perfectly. See Den Hartog and Goodman (2004) for coefficients and standard errors of fixed-effect variables.

8. Standard errors were simulated using CLARIFY (King, Tomz, and Wittenberg 2000; Tomz, Wittenberg, and King 2001). All other variables are held constant at their means.

Notes to Chapter 12

This chapter is a revised version of the paper prepared for the History of Congress Conference, April 9–10, 2004, Palo Alto, California. A previous version of this manuscript was presented at the annual meeting of the American Political Science Association in Philadelphia. We thank David Brady, Christopher Deering, Rod Kiewiet, Mat McCubbins, and John Pitney for comments on previous versions of this paper. We also thank Keith Poole and Charles Stewart III for generously providing data. Any mistakes are the responsibility of the authors.

1. See Peters (1997), especially chapter 2, for detailed accounts of the exploits of Speakers Reed, Cannon, and a number of their Democratic counterparts. Riker (1986, chapter 12) provides an excellent account as well. He portrays the events that led to the adoption of the Reed rules and Cannon's overthrow through the lens of his notion of heresthetics.

2. When Crisp finally did order the count of Republicans in the chamber, Reed commented, "The House is about to adopt the principle for which we contended under circumstances which show its value to the country. I congratulate it upon the wise decision it is about to make." (Peters 1997, 72–73).

3. We identify the top 10 committees for each of the Congresses in question, using the Grosewart estimates of committee values.

4. *Abstention adjusted* simply means we treat abstentions as missing data, unlike some roll-call indexes that treat abstentions as "incorrect" votes.

5. We used the issue codes created by Poole and Rosenthal to identify the individual votes in question (see www.voteview.com for more details).

6. Ainsworth (1995) argues that support for Civil War pensions was not simply a partisan Republican position. Instead, support for Civil War pensions was a function of the size of the population of Civil War veterans and Grand Army of the Republic members in a congressman's district.

7. The complete set of results for these regressions is available upon request from the authors.

8. The fixed-effects model assumes any differences across units are captured by differences in the constant term (Greene 2000). In this case, the fixed effects capture any variation unique to a specific Congress.

Notes to Chapter 13

1. The Constitution does not require the Speaker to be a member of the House, but a nonmember has never been nominated for the post. Current House rule 19 provides for the motion for the previous question: "There shall be a motion for the previous question, which, being ordered, shall have the effect of cutting off all debate and bringing the House to a direct vote on the question or questions on which it has been ordered."

2. Our discussion of UCAs borrows heavily from Gamm and Smith (2000) and Smith and Flathman (1989).

3. The practice appears to have developed under Vice President John Nance Garner and Majority Leader Joseph Robinson. The precedent was noted by Garner in 1937 after Robinson died. Subsequent precedents extended the practice. In recognition priority, the majority leader is followed by the minority leader, majority bill manager, and minority bill manager whenever one of those senators seeks recognition (Riddick 1992, 1093).

Notes to Chapter 14

1. Entrepreneurs and parties are modeled as unitary actors for simplicity.

2. Another implication, not explored here, is that entrepreneurs can shape the direction of institutional change through their ability to set the reform agenda.

3. Binder and Smith (1997, chapter 6) stress the high transaction costs imposed on would-be reformers in the 20th-century Senate; consequently some senators who might prefer a revised cloture rule are deterred from supporting reform, and majority-preferred reforms are deterred or delayed. This is consistent with the *structure* of the model, in which majorities *can* achieve reform but may have to pay a steep price. This structure is intended to be diachronic and thus applicable to the 19th-century House, the 21st-century Senate, and other legislatures around the world in which the payments for majoritarian change may be negligible or even positive.

4. In this era, a conservative preferred limited government and low spending, while progressives sought government action to reform capitalism and address social inequities.

5. A legislative day ends when the Senate adjourns and thus may continue for several calendar days.

6. I compiled these statistics from the *Senate Journal* for the 62nd Congress. Another 1,590 bills not included in these statistics were reported from committee and incorporated into omnibus pension bills.

7. Beth stresses the limitations of this list of filibusters. The list was mostly compiled from secondary and historical sources and is used for illustrative purposes.

8. See, for example, Robert Owen's speech, *Congressional Record*, July 14, 1913, pp. 2407–2411.

9. This account draws from Burdette 1940, 97–101.

10. Senators reaffirmed this precedent on June 28, 1916, on a 42–25 vote. The implication of this vote is that, as senators argued at the time, the two-thirds threshold is itself subject to a simple-majority vote on the 1915 precedent *and can be overturned at any time.*

11. I base this on inspection of this vote in Voteview (software for manipulating legislative roll-call data; http://www.princeton.edu/~voteview/), Senate 63 Roll Call 486. The second dimension roughly corresponds to a progressive-conservative continuum.

12. ICPSR 0004, 63rd Senate, variables 528–530. On the motion to table, Democrats voted 41–7, Republicans 1–36 (La Follette bolting), Progressive 0–1. For the Democratic dissidents' varied motives, see *Congressional Record*, February 16, 1915, pp. 3843–3845; Link 1960, 153.

13. The Democrats passed a compromise shipping bill that was killed by a second filibuster when it emerged from a conference committee.

14. For James's statement, see *Congressional Record*, February 13, 1915, p. 3738. On Democratic strategy during the ship-purchase filibuster, see "Setback to Cloture," *Washington Post*, February 17, 1915, p. A2; "Democrats Gloomy Over Ship Bill," *Washington Post*, February 18, 1915, p. A5.

15. This formulation assumes that an entrepreneur can impose institutional preferences on the chamber or that all senators have uniform institutional preferences.

16. This finding is confirmed in a multivariate analysis (Koger 2004), which finds that the 1917 cloture rule had no significant effect once electoral patterns and workload effects are considered.

17. This includes both regular and supplemental appropriations. Source: U.S. Senate Documents 553 (64th Cong., 1st sess.), 744 (64th, 2nd), 303 (65th, 2nd), and 456 (65th, 3rd).

Notes to Chapter 15

Previous versions of this chapter were presented at the History of Congress Conference, Stanford University, April 9–10, 2004; at the Midwest Political Science Association Meeting, April 15–18, 2004; and the Politics Department Seminar Series at New York University. The authors gratefully acknowledge the comments and suggestions of David Brady, Charles Cameron, Ira Katznelson, Forrest Maltzman, Mathew D. McCubbins, Bruce Oppenheimer, David Rohde, Charles Stewart, and participants at the aforementioned conferences and seminar. Professor Stewart was particularly generous in his sharing of data for this project. We are also grateful to Ganesh Betanabhatla, Michael Kim, Mike Murakami, Kathryn Pearson, Vanessa Perez, John Sides, and Adam Zelizer for valuable research assistance.

1. For example, House rules provide that a majority can force a pending matter to a vote by approving a motion to call the previous question.

2. "Senate Votes Rule to End Filibusters," March 9, 1917, p. 1.

3. Or at least the utility he expected from this proposal appears to have been greater than what he would have obtained from pushing a majority cloture proposal, since the chances of such a proposal passing were much less.

4. The problem was that bill opponents could obstruct the motion to proceed to consideration of a bill, and the cloture rule did not apply to such motions.

5. See also Dion 1997 and Koger 2002.

6. For details on the proposals considered in the Democratic caucus, see "President Considers Convoying instead of Arming Merchantmen; Caucuses Approve Closure Rule," *New York Times*, March 8, 1917, p. 2.

7. Although Woodrow Wilson ([1885] 1956, 220) had a change of heart once he found himself on the business end of the filibuster, his view from the ivory tower on the absence of the previous-question motion from the Senate was positive: "that imperative form of cutting off all further discussion has fortunately never found a place there."

8. We also put to the side cases where ties occur. In these situations, the ties would be broken by the vice president, but this has little relevance for our main concerns.

9. To keep the model as simple as possible, we are "black-boxing" the various decisions and actions of senators that would determine the values of η and π.

10. For a graphical display of this trade-off, see figures 9.1 and 9.2 in Wawro and Schickler 2006.

11. Of course, the cloture rule would not have reduced uncertainty in the very last days of a Congress, since the procedure required 3 days for the cloture petition to "ripen" and allowed for some postcloture debate.

12. The nonparametric test is more appropriate for this sample than is the standard *F* test, which relies on asymptotic properties. Small sample sizes raise concerns about the power of statistical tests used with them, where *power* refers to the probability of rejecting the null when it is false. A small sample means low power (i.e., we would be unlikely to reject the null when it is false). Since we reject the null here, this should not be too great of a concern. While appropriate caution is necessary in drawing conclusions based on the sample we have, we wish to emphasize that the nonparametric approach is superior in this case to the parametric approaches that political scientists are more accustomed to.

13. If we treat voice votes as being near-unanimous (i.e., 0.9), the same results obtain.

14. Even though we see an increase in average coalition size after 1917 both early and late in a Congress, this does not mean we will also see changes in the variance for legislation passed early. The cloture rule created a sufficient but not necessary threshold for passing legislation. Earlier in a Congress, LEs can choose to resort to the cloture process, but it becomes more of a necessity late in a Congress. We might see LEs building bigger coalitions earlier on to avoid some potential problems, but they could still generally expect to get away with smaller coalitions because of costs and other constraints on obstruction. As a result, we might see an increase in the average coalition size earlier in a Congress, but we would not necessarily see a change in their variance.

15. Indeed, one of the reasons that the opposition to Jefferson Smith's filibuster in *Mr. Smith Goes to Washington* was so fierce was that his obstruction against the measure to expel him from the Senate for corruption was preventing the passage of an urgently needed appropriations bill.

16. Even-numbered fiscal years started on July 1 of odd-numbered calendar years.

17. See the preceding newspaper accounts of the consequences of missed deadlines.

18. The District of Columbia committee was also granted this right. The ex officio provision was in effect until 1974, when Congress again dramatically changed the appropriations process with the passage of the Budget and Impoundment Control Act.

19. This, of course, does not mean that all SAC members participate in committee deliberations to the same degree (cf. Hall 1996).

20. Committee overlap existed to a more limited extent before the creation of ex officio seats on SAC. In the five Congresses preceding the decentralization, the relevant legislative committees averaged between 0 and 1.8 members who also sat on SAC.

21. The appropriations amounts and data on the progress of bills were obtained from tables that appear in the Senate document *Appropriations, New Offices, Etc.* From 1890 on, this document regularly included tables compiled by

the clerks of HAC and SAC, which contain information about the amounts in and the progress of regular appropriations bills. We do not include deficiency appropriations bills in our analysis since these did not have the same kind of deadline requirements as regular appropriations bills.

22. The increased efficiency is not due to the elimination of lame-duck sessions in 1933 nor is it due to longer sessions in the 1930s. If we exclude Congresses after the 20th Amendment took effect, the average number of days between the important junctures and the deadline is greater across the board. Thus, it appears that the values for these measures increased after the Budget Act but then decreased after the 20th Amendment took effect.

23. In a few cases, the bill was reported from SAC after the deadline. These bills are dropped from the sample so that the floor is not penalized for the late action of SAC.

24. Including variables that measure the number of days between reporting or passage of the bill in the House produces essentially the same results as we report later.

25. One could argue that it was the Budget Bureau more than HAC or the House that sought fiscal discipline. Data on appropriations estimates from the executive are harder to come by for the period we examine. If we use data on estimates instead of what HAC reported, we obtain similar results, but our sample size is reduced by about half.

26. We also tried the number of requests for legislative action submitted to the Congress by the president (available in the Database of Congressional Historical Statistics compiled by Swift et al. [2000]). The general results we report later were unchanged when this variable was employed.

27. About 15% of the bills in our sample failed to be enacted into law by the deadline. More detailed data and a more complex model would be required to determine the effects of cloture on enactment of appropriations bills, since presidential vetoes and the conference procedure would need to be taken into account.

28. Because of the dichotomous nature of the dependent variable, we are limited in our attempts to account for observation-specific effects. For this analysis we cluster on bill title. We also tried clustering on fiscal year, but that washed out nearly all of the effects that we report later. This is not surprising since our key variables of interest mostly vary by fiscal year.

29. Unfortunately, we cannot conduct a similar analysis with the House to further assess the impact of cloture because the House passed all of the bills in our sample by the relevant deadlines. However, this reinforces the point that, apart from the House passing bills late in the game (but before the deadline), the problem with meeting the deadlines rested with the Senate.

30. The severity of problems caused by missing deadlines most likely varied across bills, although it is not clear for which bills missing deadlines would be most problematic. While failure to pass an army or navy appropriations bill

might endanger national security, the failure to pass a post office appropriations bill might provoke the most ire among constituents whose mail service would be disrupted. The GEE analysis should help to account for correlation induced by these kinds of unobserved factors.

31. Binder (2003, 8), who examines lawmaking in the post–World War II era, suggests that her measure may have different effects for earlier time periods. Political parties in Congresses of yesteryear may have had greater stakes in legislative accomplishments than do parties of today. Polarization might have led to (or been a symptom of) more disciplined parties that sought to establish substantive legislative records for an advantage in electoral competition.

Notes to Chapter 16

This is a revised version of the paper presented at the History of Congress Conference, December 5–6, 2003, in San Diego, California. We thank David Brady, Jeffery Jenkins, Mathew D. McCubbins, Nathan Monroe, and Barbara Sinclair for helpful comments and suggestions.

1. See also Anderson and Doherty (2003) for a discussion underlying the partisan motivations behind the adoption of the Australian ballot in the late 19th century.

2. In examining elections in this period we sought to choose a sample that was representative of elections in this period. This was complicated by the large number of "moving parts" in elections during this era. We see the gradual decline in the practice of rotation in office, the replacement of the party ballot with the Australian ballot, the party realignment of the 1890s, a gradual shift to the direct primary, and a gradual increase in legislative careerism. Thus, in selecting representative elections, we were chasing a moving target, and so we selected elections that reflected the diversity of the period. We have elections before and after the adoption of the Australian ballot, before and after the 1890s realignment, before and after the advent of the direct primary, and with wide variation in turnover and the proportion of incumbents seeking reelection. We also sought to minimize the effects of reapportionment by not choosing elections conducted in years ending in 2. Despite the diversity of the elections in our sample, our empirical results are remarkably consistent across the years we have chosen, which makes us reasonably confident that our sample selection is not driving our conclusions.

3. Note that we use a simple dichotomy of whether or not the challenger held previous elective office as our measure of challenger quality. We chose not to use more nuanced measures because the simple dichotomy performs as well as more sophisticated measures in other studies of challenger quality, thus the dichotomous measure makes inference more parsimonious without suffering any substantive loss. Further, it would be extremely difficult to construct a scale measure that would compare the "quality" of previous offices held in this period.

4. The Political Graveyard Web site can be accessed at http://www.politicalgraveyard.com.

5. In this chapter we followed the lead of Jacobson (1989) by assuming that candidates for whom we could not find candidate-quality information were nonquality. We have also estimated the reported models using three approaches: listwise deletion, assuming missing cases are nonquality, and multiple imputation. The substantive results are identical in all three approaches.

6. The party of incumbent is coded 1 for Democrats, −1 for Republicans. Incumbent running is coded −1 for Republican incumbents, 0 for open seats, and 1 for Democratic incumbents. Democratic quality advantage is coded −1 when the Republican party has a quality advantage (Republican is incumbent or quality challenger and opponent is neither), 0 if neither party has an advantage (incumbent vs. quality challenger, two quality opponents in an open seat, or two political novices), and 1 when the Democratic Party has a quality advantage (Democrat is incumbent or quality challenger and opponent is neither). Note that we are missing one variable in the Cox and Katz model (lagged-quality advantage) for all years but 1896. However, we find no substantive difference in our results for 1896 when we omit the lagged-quality measure, so we are reasonably confident that this omission does not affect our findings.

7. We also estimated this equation as an ordered probit model and found no substantive differences in the two models.

Notes to Chapter 17

We are grateful for the comments of Jennifer Merolla, Rick Wilson, and numerous participants at the 2003 History of Congress (San Diego, California) and the 2004 Southern Political Science Association (New Orleans, Louisiana) conferences. Portions of the data used in the analysis were generously provided by Keith Poole, Jason Roberts, and Charles Stewart.

1. A number of accounts attach great weight to the regional nature of the conflict (see, for instance, Peters 1997, 75).

2. Fuller's depiction is incorrect on the composition of the Rules Committee. The committee was composed of three majority-party and two minority-party members. In his two terms as Speaker, Henderson served alongside Dalzell and Grosvenor.

3. Interestingly, these resolutions of thanks were not only traditionally bipartisan enterprises but bipartisan even during Cannon's speakership.

Notes to Chapter 18

1. Speaker Reed, ruling from the chair, made his remark when overruling a point of order against his decision to count for a quorum those members present but not responding to their names—thereby eliminating the minority's disappearing quorum tactic.

2. While the Senate has the same range of motions to recommit available to it, including the motion to recommit with instructions to report back "forthwith" with an amendment, neither the Senate rule nor precedents give priority in recognition to a member of the minority party opposed to the pending legislation as is done in the House. Discretion in recognition lies with the chair. The motion may be offered at any time, has precedence over a motion to amend, and the Senate is not limited to a single motion to recommit. Moreover, the motion is not as important in the Senate as it is in the House given the openness of the regular amendment process in the Senate.

3. The source for this data is *Hinds' Precedents of the House of Representatives*, volume 5, from selected precedents found between sections 5526–5592, covering the years 1881–1909. Not counted were election cases or instances in which a member was not recognized because the motion was not considered to be in order at that point in the process. Only instances in which the Speaker recognized a member to offer the motion are counted.

4. Ironically, Moakley had earlier testified before the joint committee and suggested a compromise motion-to-recommit rule whereby instructions would be guaranteed to the minority if a special rule otherwise prohibited amendments to a bill. Republicans rejected his compromise out of hand because they said it would only encourage the majority to report more closed rules.

5. King Pyrrhus of Epirus, referring to the dearly bought victory at Asculum in 280 BC, is said to have remarked, "Another such victory over the Romans, and we are undone." Hence the term *Pyrrhic victory* (*Plutarch's Lives*, Pyrrhus, § 21).

6. I compiled the data for this table and for the 108th Congress (summarized in the paragraph following the table) over the years by a rule-by-rule examination. Only special rules providing for the initial consideration of bills, joint resolutions, and concurrent resolutions on the budget are counted.

Notes to Chapter 19

We thank Andrea Campbell, Clark Gibson, Peter Gourevitch, Phil Keefer, Rod Kiewiet, Skip Lupia, Nathan Monroe, Roger Noll, Sam Popkin, Jason Roberts, Kevin Roust, Ken Shepsle, Steve Smith, and Don Wolfensberger for insightful comments on an earlier draft. In addition, we thank Nathan Monroe for research assistance.

1. Some of the hypotheses (our hypotheses 1–3, discussed in the following) are implied by the Krehbiel-Meirowitz model; others are more general predictions about what we would expect to observe if the minority party uses recommittals to undermine majority-party agenda control.

2. For a fuller discussion of how MTRs work and the theory underlying this debate, see Cox, Den Hartog, and McCubbins (2004).

3. It is unclear whether Krehbiel and Meirowitz include motions to recommit conference reports in their data, though it appears that they do. They count 932 recommittal motions in Congresses 80–104, which is in line with the 848 found in Rohde's data for Congresses 83–105. As noted, the total of 848 recommittal motions in Rohde's data does include motions to recommit conference reports.

4. Conference reports can be recommitted with instructions, but the instructions *are not binding on conferees*; a conference committee, moreover, cannot be ordered to report forthwith. So recommittal with instructions of a conference report essentially constitutes an advisory statement about what the House would like conferees to do.

Notes to Chapter 20

We would like to thank Mike Alvarez, Gary Cox, Chris Den Hartog, Sam Kernell, Keith Krehbiel, Mat McCubbins, Tammy Roust, Barbara Sinclair, and Don Wolfensberger for their comments on an earlier draft of this chapter and David Rohde and Michael Crespin for making the newest version of the congressional roll-call dataset available to us. We also gratefully acknowledge the Dirksen Congressional Center for its financial support of this research.

1. For open vs. closed, open vs. modified closed, and modified open vs. modified closed rules, $p \ll 1\%$. Between modified open and closed rules, $p = 2\%$.

2. Roberts's (2003) series on AMRs is entirely consistent with ours. He also reports data on motions to recommit without instructions. The frequency of such motions is correlated with that of AMRs, but far fewer of them are made.

3. Amendments for 1989 were not collected, so the 101st House includes 2 years of MTR data but only 1 year (1990) of amendment data.

Notes to Chapter 21

1. "Public Supports Bush, Is Divided on His Tax-Cut Plan," *Los Angeles Times*, March 8, 2001, p. A1.

2. See, for example, "Castle Wary of Tax-cut Despite Vote for It," *Washington Post*, March 12, 2001, p. A15.

3. "A Rough but Steady Hand at Helm of Ways and Means," *CQ Weekly Report*, July 5, 2003.

4. The private ideal point of the filibuster pivot is also not depicted because it is not relevant. However, if private preferences are polarized, then it might well be the case that this legislator would have a private ideal point very close to the status quo. If this were the case, he or she would prefer to filibuster the s^*. However, I assume that the consequences of filibusters are publicly visible and legislators who engage in such behavior will only do so if it is consistent with their public ideal point.

5. This assumption is not crucial. If one were to assume that the conferees can be held accountable for their conference actions, then the majority party could simply take care to appoint members to the committees who can publicly take the positions the caucus privately favors.

6. This rule is often interpreted loosely because, as a point of order, it requires the support of a majority to be sustained in either chamber.

7. In this case the filibuster pivot places limits on the conference. Of course it could also face limits defined by other actors. For example, it could not enact a policy more extreme than the reflection of the status quo over the public ideal point of the median member of either chamber (though this would rarely bind because of the presence of the minority filibuster pivot).

8. Important legislative enactments are identified by David Mayhew in *Divided We Govern* (1991). A list is available at http://pantheon.yale.edu/~dmayhew/datasets.html. In the 14 Congresses in the sample, there were 183 conference-eligible significant enactments, of which 142 were considered by a conference committee. For each piece of legislation that received a conference, I gathered each article written in *CQ Weekly Report* about the conference agreements. In total, there were 209 articles in *CQ Weekly Report* that summarized the outcomes of the 142 conferences. Each conference was summarized by at least 1 article and some by as many as 6. Research assistants conducted content analysis on each article to determine five things: (1) Did the article mention a partisan dispute? (2) If so, did it indicate a partisan conference winner? (3) Did the article indicate which chamber won in conference? In the case of multiple articles, I based the summary coding on the articles that identified winners rather than those that failed to mention particular actors or did not clearly indicate the outcome. Fortunately, in no case did two articles about the same conference conflict when they identified a clear chamber or partisan winner.

9. The associated χ^2 statistic is 4.45 with a $p < 0.05$.

10. The associated χ^2 statistic is 8.14 with a $p < 0.01$.

Notes to Chapter 22

I am grateful to Steven S. Smith and Bill Heniff Jr. for their comments on drafts of this chapter and to Ida Brudnick and Elizabeth McAlpine for their excellent research assistance. The views expressed in this paper do not represent a position of the Congressional Research Service.

1. This figure is based on data from the 40th (1867–1869), 43rd (1873–1875), and 45th through 66th Congresses (1877–1921).

2. In the modern Congress, the Speaker will first recognize a minority-party member to offer a motion to instruct conferees after the House agrees to go to conference but before the appointment of conferees. The motion was not a minority-party prerogative at the time *Cannon's Precedents* was published in 1936.

3. In contrast to modern practice, early motions to instruct seem to have been offered only after a conference committee reported disagreement, but the practice varied as to whether the chambers formally passed a motion to recommit the report with instructions or passed the instructions and appointed a new conference committee. Although members sometimes, but inconsistently, objected when a motion to recommit was offered after one chamber had acted on a conference report and the conference committee was technically no longer in existence, whether the motion agreed to was to recommit or to reappoint the same managers to a new conference, the effect would be the same.

4. Reporting in partial disagreement leaves the amendments before the chambers just as they were when sent to conference. Therefore it is possible that specific policy instructions could be given after a conference committee reported in partial disagreement. A chamber could theoretically recede from its disagreement to an amendment and concur in the amendment with an amendment. In these decades, however, I saw no instances of this. The chambers chose, rather, to reassert their original motions and return to conference.

5. The amendment in disagreement between the chambers contained the pay raise, so the instructions directed the conferees to strike out that portion of the amendment.

6. Some procedural issues raised include that the conference committee had reported in agreement and, generally, instructions had been offered only after a conference committee reported an inability to agree. Others raised difficulties with motions to instruct conferees in general, such as what would happen if one chamber instructed the conferees one way and the other chamber instructed them the other way. The result would be a pointless meeting of the conference or simultaneous commitment.

7. A 1903 precedent is cited by Hinds (1907, vol. 5, § 6399).

8. Legislative practices change slowly. Four years after this ruling, the president pro tempore ruled specific instructions out of order but declined to rule on the broad question of the power of the Senate to instruct its conferees. Confusion over whether motions to instruct conferees were in order disappeared over time.

9. A filibuster could also be mounted postpassage but before going to conference. Such a filibuster, if made on each of the three motions necessary to go to conference and any number of motions to instruct conferees, is arguably insurmountable because cloture would need to be filed on each motion (Bach 2001a). The possibility that a single senator could prevent the resolution of differences in this way is not considered separately here because despite such a filibuster being possible procedurally that does not mean it is likely politically. For a discussion of why we do not see senators taking full advantage of their parliamentary rights, see Binder and Smith (1997, 111–115).

10. Percentages are based on data only from the following Congresses: the 10th (1807–1809), 13th (1813–1815), 19th (1825–1827), 25th (1837–1839), 28th (1843–1845), 30th (1847–1849), and every third Congress between the 34th (1855–1857) and the 106th (1999–2000) Congresses.

11. Dr. Oleszek, in addition to advising members of Congress on conference politics, regularly gives lectures to their staff on bargaining strategies and legislative procedures. This quote is taken from his outline distributed at one of these lectures.

Notes to Chapter 23

I would like to thank Scott Adler, Sarah Binder, Jamie Carson, Joe Cooper, Gary Cox, Mike Crespin, Chuck Finocchiaro, Brian Gaines, Scott Gates, Craig Goodman, Brian Humes, Jeff Jenkins, Rick Matland, Keith Poole, David Rohde, Brian Sala, and attendees of my presentation at the University of Minnesota for insightful comments and helpful suggestions. Amy Ware provided research assistance.

1. For additional studies on shirking, see Bender and Lott 1996; Carson et al. 2004; Lott 1990, 1987; Lott and Bronars 1993; Lott and Davis 1992; Rothenberg and Sanders 2000a, 2000b.

2. For example, see Loomis (1995), McArthur and Marks (1998), Rothenberg and Sanders (2000c), and Goodman and Nokken (2004).

3. An important assumption underlying this investigation is that the content of the legislative agenda remains relatively consistent from regular to lame-duck sessions. I find no evidence that the legislative agenda changes significantly.

4. One such example of apparent presidential influence in lame-duck-session voting behavior comes from Lincoln's efforts to win passage of the 13th Amendment in the lame-duck session of the 38th Congress. Despite sizable Republican gains in the House assuring its passage in the 39th Congress, Lincoln dispatched Secretary of State William Seward to offer Democratic members promises of patronage if they voted to support the amendment. Seward's effort is thought to have provided the margin of victory for the abolitionists (Cox and Cox 1963).

5. Reed served as Speaker in the 51st, 54th, and 55th Congresses, Cannon in the 58th through 61st Congresses.

6. There were an insufficient number of roll-call votes to generate NOMINATE scores for the lame-duck session in the 70th Congress.

7. *IDEOLOGY1* is comparable to the dependent variable used by Rothenberg and Sanders (2000a), allowing replication of their analysis. The one, slight difference between the two measures is that Rothenberg and Sanders use the last quarter of each Congress, while I use lame-duck sessions. To generate values for members of the 46th Congress, I used data from the 45th Congress but do not explicitly study roll-call behavior from the 45th.

8. I do not include a dummy variable for the 46th Congress, which serves as the reference. One might also use a fixed-effects model to estimate changes in ideology and abstention. Such models account for variation over time (over Congresses in my case) as well as variation within individuals (within MCs in my case). Given the tendency for individual MCs to maintain relatively consistent voting records over time, I choose simply to control for Congress-specific effects by including the dummy variables. I do, though, use the cluster command in Stata, grouping members by their ICPSR ID numbers to generate robust standard errors.

9. Stata version SE 9.2 (computer software, StataCorp LP, College Station, TX, 1985–2006). The large differences in sample size result from the use of the difference in lame-duck NOMINATE scores across Congresses. I am forced to drop members who served only one term (or who served nonconcurrent terms).

10. Members are coded as returning and lame duck for an entire Congress. I choose this strategy because it allows me to determine how lame-duck sessions influence the two different categories of members.

Notes to Chapter 24

The authors would like to thank David Brady and Mathew D. McCubbins, Ted Brader, Brandice Canes-Wrone, Charles Cameron, Gary Cox, Robert Erikson, Alan Gerber, Ira Katznelson, Jeffery Jenkins, Ken Scheve, David Mayhew, Nolan McCarty, Robert Mickey, Keith Poole, Rose Razaghian, Howard Rosenthal, Doug Rivers, Eric Schickler, Rob Van Houweling, and Greg Wawro. We also thank participants at the seminar at the Center for the Study of Democratic Politics at Princeton University, May 27, 2004; participants at the History of Congress Conference at Stanford University, April 9–10, 2004, Palo Alto, California; and participants in the American Politics Workshops held at Columbia University Institute for Social and Economic Research and Policy (March 8, 2005), Northwestern Department of Political Science (May 4, 2004), and University of Michigan Department of Political Science (May 7, 2004) for helpful criticisms of previous versions. We also would like to thank Eldon Porter and Melanie Springer for research assistance.

1. The *United States Public Statutes at Large* lists 21,758 public statutes passed during this period, including amendments to the Constitution. Of these statutes, we were able to identify 21,741 that became public laws. For 17 statutes listed in *Public Statutes at Large*, there is no corresponding information in the *Congressional Record*'s *History of Bills and Resolutions*, and they were dropped from the analysis. We are nearly finished extending the dataset through 2002 (107th Congress), covering a total of 39,630 public statutes.

2. For example, in his work on critical elections and lawmaking, Ginsberg (1972, 1973, 1976) notes that "clearly, some statutes are more important than

others, and statutes vary considerably in the magnitude of the policy objectives they attempt to achieve." However, he does not attempt to differentiate statutes by importance, and he concedes that "this analysis, which weights each statute equally, ignores important qualitative differences among statutes. . . . It is, however, difficult to conceive of any procedure which would permit systematic qualitative comparisons of the importance of laws" (Ginsberg 1976, 45). Personal communications with Ginsberg have confirmed that the statute-level data from his project are not available.

3. For example, Krehbiel (1998, 57) notes, "The dependent variable in the analysis are all forms of Congress-to-Congress *changes in legislative productivity*. Measurement of legislative productivity is a subject of an ongoing controversy about which a neutral stance is adopted here."

4. Cameron (2000, 38) lists some of these pathways as "changing people's lives, redistributing wealth, creating or destroying rights, limning partisan differences."

5. Mayhew (1991) sometimes substitutes *notable* for *significant*.

6. The authors of the records of political events were sometimes the same for *PSQ* and *APSR*. For example, Lindsay Rogers wrote the records for the *APSR* from 1919 to 1923 and also wrote the reviews for *PSQ* for 1923.

7. Peterson's sources vary across Congresses. For example, to identify legislation for the 47th Congress, he uses three sources that, in truth, do not meet Mayhew's criterion. See Peterson (2001) for a complete listing of his sources, which are too numerous to list here.

8. The series includes Garraty, *The New Commonwealth, 1877–1890* (1968); Faulkner, *Politics, Reform, and Expansion, 1890–1900* (1959); Mowry, *The Era of Theodore Roosevelt, 1900–1912* (1958); Link, *Woodrow Wilson and the Progressive Era, 1910–1917* (1954); Ferrell, *Woodrow Wilson and World War I, 1917–1921* (1985); Hick, *Republican Ascendancy, 1921–1933* (1960); Leuchtenburg, *Franklin D. Roosevelt and the New Deal, 1932–1940* (1963); and Buchanan, *The United States and World War II*, volumes 1 and 2 (1964).

9. The norm is two congressional sessions; however, several Congresses had special sessions.

10. Other sources of information of this type include the number of changes in the U.S. Code for each new public enactment (Young and Heitshusen 2002).

11. The argument is analogous to the means by which Poole and Rosenthal (1997a) estimate common-space scores across institutions. Assuming that individuals do not change their behavior across institutions (or across time in our instance) provides bridging observations that can be used to relate estimates in the two institutions (or across time).

12. We believe it is reasonable to assume that this is the basis for the difference for two reasons. First, we include only those raters who are consciously attempting to identify significant legislation. Second, estimating a

two-dimensional model of significance that permits rater assessments to correspond to different standards reveals no statistical support for this possibility.

13. To estimate the model, we assume that the errors are distributed logistically.

14. In other words, the same technology that is used to measure legislative inputs (legislator-induced preferences) can also be employed to measure legislative outputs.

15. The likelihood surface has many "flat spots" because of the small number of raters.

16. The norm is two congressional sessions; however, several Congresses have had special sessions.

17. For purposes of comparison, the posterior means of the hierarchical and nonhierarchical estimators have been rescaled to lie between 0 and 1. Given the scale invariance noted earlier, this rescaling is unproblematic.

18. One might think that important projects, including the building of the Golden Gate and George Washington bridges, would have been ranked as significant. Neither building project, however, was the direct result of action taken by Congress. The Reconstruction Finance Corporation played an important role in purchasing revenue bonds to finance the building of the Golden Gate.

19. The need for the FTC did not gain prominence as an issue until President Theodore Roosevelt repeatedly included messages about the dangers of trusts in his State of the Union addresses. Roosevelt made no progress, however, in regulating trusts during his administration (L. Chamberlain 1946). The trust issue was addressed through legislation during the 63rd Congress under unified Democratic control. Spurred by the Supreme Court decision over Standard Oil on May 15, 1911, Congress passed two bills that were signed by President Wilson, including the Clayton Act and the act establishing the FTC.

20. Interestingly, the Sherman antitrust bill receives one of the highest significance scores in our sample. The significance of this bill is certainly captured by the retrospective importance of the act.

21. Note that the uncertainty in the significance estimates necessarily produces uncertainty in our estimate of the number of significant statutes passed each year. Accounting for this uncertainty is straightforward, but this uncertainty does not affect our assessment of face validity and we have omitted it for presentational clarity.

22. Dion's *Turning the Legislative Thumbscrew: Minority Rights and Procedural Change in Legislative Politics* (1997) is another important book in this field.

Notes to Chapter 25

This paper began when Hummel was a National Fellow at the Hoover Institution. The authors thank Christopher Den Hartog for his helpful comments.

1. This is consistent with the economics literature, which shows that the economic stakes involved in the territorial expansion are too small to have motivated Southern demand for expansion. See Passell and Wright (1972).

2. On the other hand, working in favor of admission is that, for the near future, California's senators were likely to be Democratic.

3. Basinger (2003) provides the most thorough analysis of the enforcement aspects of the act.

Notes to Chapter 26

The authors thank Keith T. Poole; our discussant, Keith Krehbiel; and the editors for comments. We thank Professor Matthew Harrington of the New England School of Law for making available to us data on the location of federal district courts in the early 1800s.

1. Prompt repayment at 62.5¢ on the dollar was accepted, or alternatively, the full amount due could be repaid with a delay.

2. Our account of court action draws on Kelly and Harbison (1970).

3. The quote is from an *opponent* of the Constitution, Richard Henry Lee, cited by Parrington (1927, 295).

4. All the roll calls referred to in this chapter can be viewed using Voteview, a free software program available from voteview.ucsd.edu and ucdata.berkeley.edu:7101/new_web/VoteWorld/voteworld/vwpc.html. Viewing the ideological and geographic displays in Voteview complement reading of this chapter. Numbered roll calls in this chapter refer to the Voteview number of the roll call, in the House or Senate being discussed.

5. Mann (2002, 218) lists 11 Federalists as defecting. The difference may be in his coding of partisanship and our use of the Martis (1989) classifications.

6. The cutting lines for all roll calls in American history, including those discussed in this paper, can be viewed by downloading the Voteview software from voteview.com.

7. We did not run interactions with *Party* given the small number of Federalists. We did not include a *Frontier* variable (see the following discussion in the text) because only one frontier representative voted on the motion.

8. The state admitted before Louisiana was Ohio in 1803.

9. Warren (1935, 76) lists the margin as 110–97.

10. Roosevelt and Wood continued to support the bill, Plumer and Ward switched to opposition, and Sanford did not vote. J. B. Dawson of Louisiana switched to supporting the bill.

11. Two voted against and one switched his vote to for.

12. Four switched to vote for, one switched to vote against.

13. The source of the citation is the ICPSR codebook entry for the roll call.

REFERENCES

Abram, Michael, and Joseph Cooper. 1968. The Rise of Seniority in the House of Representatives. *Polity* 1:53–88.

Adams, John Quincy. 1875. *Memoirs of John Quincy Adams, comprising portions of his diary from 1795–1848*. Philadelphia, PA: J. B. Lippincott.

Ainsworth, Scott. 1995. Electoral Strength and the Emergence of Group Influence in the 1800s: The Grand Army of the Republic. *American Politics Quarterly* 23:319–338.

Albert, James. 1999. Criticism of a Hierarchical Model Using Bayes Factors. *Statistics in Medicine* 18:287–305.

Aldrich, John H. 1994. A Model of a Legislature with Two Parties and a Committee System. *Legislative Studies Quarterly* 19:313–339.

———. 1995. *Why Parties? The Origin and Transformation of Political Parties in America*. Chicago: Univ. of Chicago Press.

———. 1997. Does Historical Political Research Pose Any Special Methodological Concerns? *The Political Methodologist* 8(1): 17–21.

Aldrich, John H., Mark M. Berger, and David W. Rohde. 2002. The Historical Variability in Conditional Party Government, 1877–1994. In *Party, Process, and Political Change in Congress: New Perspectives on the History of Congress*, ed. David W. Brady and Mathew D. McCubbins, 17–35. Palo Alto, CA: Stanford Univ. Press.

Aldrich, John H., and David W. Rohde. 1997. The Transition to Republican Rule in the House: Implications for Theories of Congressional Politics. *Political Science Quarterly* 112(4): 541–567.

———. 2000a. The Republican Revolution and the House Appropriations Committee. *Journal of Politics* 62:1–33.

———. 2000b. The Consequences of Party Organization in the House: The Role of the Majority and Minority Parties in Conditional Party Government. In *Polarized Politics: Congress and the President in a Partisan Era*, ed. Jon Bond and Richard Fleisher. Washington, DC: Congressional Quarterly Press.

———. 2001. The Logic of Conditional Party Government: Revisiting the Electoral Connection. In *Congress Reconsidered*, 7th edition, ed.

Lawrence C. Dodd and Bruce I. Oppenheimer, 269–292. Washington, DC: Congressional Quarterly Press.

Alesina, Alberto. 1987. Macroeconomic Policy in a Two-Party System as a Repeated Game. *Quarterly Journal of Economics* 102:651–678.

———. 1988. Macroeconomics and Politics. *NBER Macroeconomics Annual.* Cambridge, MA: MIT Press.

Alexander, De Alva Stanwood. 1916. *History and Procedure of the House of Representatives.* Boston, MA: Houghton Mifflin.

Alford, John R., and John H. Hibbing. 2002. Electoral Convergence in the U.S. Congress. In *U.S. Senate Exceptionalism*, ed. Bruce I. Oppenheimer. Columbus: Ohio State Univ. Press.

Alston, Lee, 1983a. Farm Foreclosures in the United States During the Interwar Period. *Journal of Economic History* 43:885–903.

———. 1983b. Farm Foreclosure Moratorium Legislation: A Lesson from the Past. *American Economic Review* 74 (March): 445–457.

Anderson, Melissa, and Brendan Doherty. 2003. Parties under Siege or Parties in Control? Gauging Causal Inferences on Australian Ballot Reform Laws. Paper presented at the annual meeting of the American Political Science Association.

Ansolabehere, Stephen, David Brady, and Morris Fiorina. 1992. The Vanishing Marginals and Electoral Responsiveness. *British Journal of Political Science* 22:21–38.

Ansolabehere, Stephen, Alan Gerber, and Jim Snyder. 2002. Equal Votes, Equal Money: Court-Ordered Redistricting and Public Expenditures in the American States. *American Political Science Review* 96:4.

Ansolabehere, Stephen, and James M. Snyder Jr. 2000. Valence Politics and Equilibrium in Spatial Election Models. *Public Choice* 103:327–336.

Ansolabehere, Stephen, James M. Snyder Jr., and Charles Stewart III. 2000. Old Voters, New Voters, and the Personal Vote: Using Redistricting to Measure the Incumbency Advantage. *American Journal of Political Science* 44:17–34.

———. 2001a. The Effects of Party and Preferences on Congressional Roll Call Voting. *Legislative Studies Quarterly* 26(4): 533–572.

———. 2001b. Candidate Positioning in U.S. House Elections. *American Journal of Political Science* 45(1): 136–159.

American Political Science Association. 1950. *Toward a More Responsible Party System: A Report.* New York: Rinehart.

Argersinger, Peter. 1985–1986. New Perspectives on Election Fraud in the Gilded Age. *Political Science Quarterly* 100:669–687

———. 1992. *Structure, Process, and Party: Essays in American Political History.* Armonk, NY: M. E. Sharpe.

Arnold, Douglas R. 1990. *The Logic of Congressional Action.* New Haven, CT: Yale Univ. Press.

Arthur, W. Brian. 1994. *Increasing Returns and Path Dependence in the Economy.* Ann Arbor: Univ. of Michigan Press.

Atack, Jeremy, Fred Bateman, and William N. Parker. 2000. Northern Agriculture and the Westward Movement. In *The Cambridge Economic History of the United States*, vol. 2, ed. Stanley Engerman and Robert Gallman, 285–329. New York: Cambridge Univ. Press.

Austen-Smith, David, and John R. Wright. 1994. Counteractive Lobbying. *American Journal of Political Science* 38(1): 25–44.

Ayotte, Kenneth J. 2002. Bankruptcy and Entrepreneurship: The Value of a Fresh Start. Paper presented at the conference Understanding Financial Architecture: Financial Structure and Bankruptcy, Oxford, UK, September 13–14.

Bach, Stanley. 1981. Bicameral Conflict and Accommodation in Congressional Procedure. Paper presented at the annual meeting of the American Political Science Association, New York.

———. 1990. From Special Orders to Special Rules: Pictures of House Procedures in Transition. Paper presented at the annual meeting of the American Political Science Association, San Francisco, CA, August 30–September 2.

———. 1992. Statement of Stanley Bach. In *Roundtable Discussion on the Motion to Recommit.* Committee on Rules, House of Representatives. Washington, DC: Government Printing Office.

———. 1996. *Conference Committee and Related Procedures: An Introduction.* Report 96-708 GOV, July 29. Washington, DC: Congressional Research Service.

———. 1998a. Motions to Recommit in the House. CRS Report 98-383. Washington, DC: Congressional Research Service.

———. 1998b. Points of Order, Rulings, and Appeals in the House of Representatives. CRS Report 98-307. Washington, DC: Congressional Research Service.

———. 1999. *Conference Reports and Joint Explanatory Statements.* Report 98-382 GOV, January 27. Washington, DC: Congressional Research Service.

———. 2001a. CRS Report for Congress. Going to Conference in the Senate. Report RS20454. Washington, DC: Congressional Research Service.

———. 2001b. The Legislative Process on the House Floor: An Introduction. CRS Report 95-563. Washington, DC: Congressional Research Service.

Bach, Stanley, and Steven S. Smith. 1988. Managing Uncertainty in the House of Representatives: Adaptation and Innovation in Special Rules. Washington, DC: Brookings Institution.

Baker, John D. 1973. The Character of the Congressional Revolution of 1910. *Journal of American History* 60:679–691.

Baker, Richard Allan. 1985. The History of Congressional Ethics. In *Representation and Responsibility*, eds. Bruce Jennings and Daniel Callahan. New York: Plenum.

Balleisen, Edward J. 1996. Vulture Capitalism in Antebellum American: The 1841 Federal Bankruptcy Act and the Exploitation of Financial Distress. *Business History Review* 70 (Winter): 473–516.

———. 2001. *Navigating Failure*. Chapel Hill: Univ. of North Carolina Press.

Barclay, John M. [1860] 1867. *Constitution of the United States of America with the Amendments Thereto: To Which are Added Jefferson's Manual of Parliamentary Practice, The Standing Rules and Orders for Conducting Business in The House of Representatives and Senate of the United States and Barclay's Digest of the Rules of Proceeding in the House of Representatives of the United States*. Washington, DC: Government Printing Office.

Barfied, Claude E. 1970. "Our Share of the Booty": The Democratic Party, Cannonism, and the Payne-Aldrich Tariff. *Journal of American History* 57(2): 308–323.

Barnes, Kenneth C. 1998. *Who Killed John Clayton? Political Violence and the Emergence of the New South, 1861–1893*. Durham, NC: Duke Univ. Press.

Baron, David P., and John A. Ferejohn. 1989. Bargaining in Legislatures. *American Political Science Review* 83:1181–1206.

Barro, Robert, and Xavier Sala-i-Martin. 1995. *Economic Growth*. New York: McGraw-Hill.

Bartels, Larry M. 2000. Partisanship and Voting Behavior, 1952–1996. *American Journal of Political Science* 44:35–50.

Basinger, Scott J. 2003. Regulating Slavery: Deck-Stacking and Credible Commitment in the Fugitive Slave Act of 1850. *Journal of Law, Economics, and Organization* 19 (October): 307–342.

Bates, Robert H., Avner Greif, Margaret Levi, Jean-Laurent Rosenthal, and Barry R. Weingast. 1998. *Analytic Narratives*. Princeton, NJ: Princeton Univ. Press.

Beard, Charles A. 1910. The Direct Primary Movement in New York. *Proceedings of the American Political Science Association* 7:187–198.

———. 1924. *American Government and Politics*, 4th edition. New York: Macmillan.

Beck, Nathaniel. 1987. Elections and the Fed: Is There a Political Monetary Cycle? *American Journal of Political Science* 31:194–216.

Beck, Nathaniel, and Jonathan N. Katz. 1995. What To Do (and Not To Do) with Time-Series Cross-Section Data. *American Political Science Review* 89:634–647.

Bender, Bruce, and John R. Lott. 1996. Legislator Voting and Shirking: A Critical Review of the Literature. *Public Choice* 87:67–100.

Bensel, Richard Franklin. 1984. *Sectionalism and American Political Development, 1880–1980.* Madison: Univ. of Wisconsin Press.

———. 1990. *Yankee Leviathan: The Origins of Central State Authority in America, 1859–1877.* Cambridge, UK: Cambridge Univ. Press.

———. 2000. *The Political Economy of American Industrialization, 1877–1900.* New York: Cambridge Univ. Press.

———. 2003. The American Ballot Box: Law, Identity, and the Polling Place in the Mid-Nineteenth Century. *Studies in American Political Development* 17:1–27.

———. 2004. The American Ballot Box in the Mid-Nineteenth Century: Law, Identity, and the Polling Place. New York: Cambridge Univ. Press.

Berard, Stanley P. 2001. *Southern Democrats in the U.S. House of Representatives.* Norman: Univ. of Oklahoma Press.

Berelson, B. R., P. F. Lazarsfeld, and W. N. McPhee. 1954. *Voting: A Study of Opinion Formation in a Presidential Campaign.* Chicago: Univ. of Chicago Press.

Bernstein, H. Marvin. 1955. *Regulating Business by Independent Commission.* Princeton, NJ: Princeton Univ. Press.

Bernstein, Robert A. 1991a. Strategic Shifts—Safeguarding the Public Interest—United States Senators, 1971–86. *Legislative Studies Quarterly* 16(2): 263–280.

———. 1991b. Ideological Deviation and Support for Reelection: Party Differences in Senate Races. *Western Politics Quarterly* 44(4): 987–1003.

Bernstein, Robert A., Michael B. Berkman, and Gerald C. Wright. 1988. Controversy: Do U.S. Senators Moderate Strategically? *American Political Science Review* 82(1): 237–245.

Bessette, Joseph. 1994. *The Mild Voice of Reason: Deliberative Democracy and American National Government.* Chicago: Univ. of Chicago Press.

Beth, Richard S. 1993. The Motion to Proceed to Consider a Measure in the Senate, 1979–1992. Washington, DC: Congressional Research Service.

———. 1994. Filibusters in the Senate, 1789–1993. Washington, DC: Congressional Research Service.

———. 1995. What We Don't Know about Filibusters. Paper presented at the annual meeting of the Western Political Science Association.

———. 2001. The Discharge Rule in the House: Recent Use in Historical Context. CRS Report 97-856. Washington, DC: Congressional Research Service.

Biais, Bruno, and Thomas Mariotti. 2006. Credit, Wages and Bankruptcy Laws. Unpublished working paper, IDEI, Toulouse Univ.

Bianco, William T. 1994. *Trust: Representatives and Constituents.* Ann Arbor: Univ. of Michigan Press.

Bianco, William T., David B. Spence, and John D. Wilkerson. 1996. The Electoral Connection in the Early Congress: The Case of the Compensation Act of 1816. *American Journal of Political Science* 40:145–171.

Binder, Sarah A. 1995. Partisanship and Procedural Choice: Institutional Change in the Early Congress, 1789–1823. *Journal of Politics* 57(4): 1093–1118.

———. 1997. *Minority Rights, Majority Rule.* New York: Cambridge Univ. Press.

———. 1999. The Dynamics of Legislative Gridlock, 1947–1996. *American Political Science Review* 93(3): 519–533.

———. 2003. *Stalemate: Causes and Consequences of Legislative Gridlock.* Washington, DC: Brookings Institution.

Binder, Sarah A., and Steven S. Smith, 1995. Acquired Procedural Tendencies and Congressional Reform. In *Remaking Congress: Change and Stability in the 1990s*, ed. James A. Thurber and Roger H. Davidson, 69–70. Washington, DC: Congressional Quarterly Press.

———. 1997. *Politics or Principle? Filibustering in the United States Senate.* Washington, DC: Brookings Institution.

Biographical Directory of the American Congress, 1774–1996. 1997. Alexandria, VA: CQ Staff Directories.

Black, Earle, and Merle Black. 1987. *Politics and Society in the South.* Cambridge, MA: Harvard Univ. Press.

Bogue, Allan G., and Mark Paul Marlaire. 1975. Of Mess and Men: The Boardinghouse and Congressional Voting, 1821–1842. *American Journal of Political Science* 19 (May): 207–230.

Boinville, Barbara R. 1982. *Origins and Development of Congress*, 2nd edition. Washington, DC: Congressional Quarterly Press.

Bolling, Richard. 1974. *Power in the House: A History of the Leadership of the House of Representatives.* New York: Capricorn Books.

Bolton, Patrick, and Howard Rosenthal, 2001. The Political Economy of Debt Moratoria, Bailouts, and Bankruptcy. In *Defusing Default: Incentives and Institutions*, ed. Marco Pagano, 77–115. Baltimore, MD: Johns Hopkins Univ. Press.

———. 2002. Political Intervention in Debt Contracts. *Journal of Political Economy* 110(5): 1103–1134.

Bond, Jon R. 1980. The Politics of Court Structure: The Addition of New Federal Judges, 1949–1978. *Law and Politics Quarterly* 2:181–188.

Boucher, Chauncey C., and Robert P. Brooks, eds. 1929. *Correspondence Addressed to John C. Calhoun, 1837–1849.* Washington, DC: American Historical Association.

Bowers, Claude G. 1918. *The Life of John Worth Kern.* Indianapolis, IN: Hollenbeck Press.

Brady, David W. 1972. Congressional Leadership and Party Voting in the McKinley Era: A Comparison to the Modern House. *Midwest Journal of Political Science* 16:439–459.

———. 1973. A Research Note on the Impact of Interparty Competition on Congressional Voting in a Competitive Era. *American Political Science Review* 67(1): 153–156.

———. 1985. A Reevaluation of Realignments in American Politics: Evidence from the House of Representatives. *American Political Science Review* 79:28–49.

———. 1988. *Critical Elections and Congressional Policy Making*. Palo Alto, CA: Stanford Univ. Press.

Brady, David W., and Phillip Althoff. 1974. Party Voting in the U.S. House of Representatives, 1890–1910: Elements of a Responsible Party System. *Journal of Politics* 36:753–775.

Brady, David W., Richard Brody, and David Epstein. 1989. Heterogeneous Parties and Political Organization: The U.S. Senate, 1880–1920. *Legislative Studies Quarterly* 14:205–223.

Brady, David W., Brandice J. Canes-Wrone, and John F. Cogan. 2000. Out of Step, Out of Office: Legislative Voting Behavior and House Election Outcomes. In *Continuity and Change in House Elections*, ed. David W. Brady, John F. Cogan, and Morris P. Fiorina. Palo Alto, CA: Stanford Univ. Press / Hoover Institution Press.

Brady, David W., Joseph Cooper, and Patricia A. Hurley. 1979. The Decline of Party in the U.S. House of Representatives, 1887–1968. *Legislative Studies Quarterly* 4(3): 381–407.

Brady, David, and David Epstein. 1997. Intraparty Preferences, Heterogeneity, and the Origins of the Modern Congress: Progressive Reformers in the House and Senate, 1890–1920. *Journal of Law, Economics, and Organization* 13:26–49.

Brady, David, Judith Goldstein, and David Kessler. 2002. Does Party Matter? An Historical Test Using Senate Tariff Votes in Three Institutional Settings. *Journal of Law, Economics, and Organization* 18(1): 140–154.

Brady, David W., Hahrie Han, and Doug McAdam. 2003. Party Polarization in the Post WWII Era: A Two Period Electoral Interpretation. Paper presented at the annual meeting of the American Political Science Association, Philadelphia, August 28.

Brady, David W. and Mark Morgan. 1987. Reforming the Structure of the House Appropriations Process: The Effects of the 1885 and 1919–1920 Reforms on Money Decisions. In *Congress: Structure and Policy*, ed. Mathew McCubbins and Terry Sullivan, 207–234. New York: Cambridge Univ. Press.

Brady, David W., and Craig Volden. 1998. *Revolving Gridlock: Politics and Policy from Carter to Clinton.* Boulder, CO: Westview Press.

Broder, David. 2003. Hastert Defends His Leadership. *Washington Post*, November 13, 2003.

Brown, Everett S., ed. 1926. *The Missouri Compromises and Presidential Politics, 1820–1825.* St. Louis, MO: St. Louis Historical Society.

Brown, George Rothewell. 1922. *Leadership in Congress.* Indianapolis, IN: Bobbs-Merrill.

Broz, J. Lawrence, and Jeffrey A. Frieden. 2001. The Political Economy of International Monetary Relations. *Annual Review of Political Science* 4:317–343.

Buchanan, Russell A. 1964. *The United States and World War II.* 2 vols. New York: Harper & Row.

Burdette, Franklin L. 1940. *Filibustering in the Senate.* Princeton, NJ: Princeton Univ. Press.

Burnham, Walter D. 1975. Insulation and Responsiveness in Congressional Elections. *Political Science Quarterly* 90:411–435.

Burnham, Walter D., and Massachusetts Institute of Technology. 1984. *Partisan Division of American State Governments, 1834–1985.* Computer file. Ann Arbor, MI: Inter-university Consortium for Political and Social Research (ICPSR).

Busbey, L. White. 1927. *Uncle Joe Cannon: The Story of a Pioneer American.* New York: Holt.

Buthe, Tim. 2002. Taking Temporality Seriously: Modeling History and the Use of Narratives as Evidence. *American Political Science Review* 96:481–494.

Butler, Anne M., and Wendy Wolff. 1995. *Senate Election, Expulsion, and Censure Cases from 1793–1900.* Washington, DC: Government Printing Office.

Butler, D. E. 1951. *The British General Election of 1950.* London: Macmillan.

Byrd, Robert C. 1988. *The Senate: 1789–1989.* Washington, DC: Government Printing Office.

Cain, Bruce, John Ferejohn, and Morris Fiorina. 1987. *The Personal Vote: Constituency Service and Electoral Independence.* Cambridge, MA: Harvard Univ. Press.

Cameron, Charles. 2000. *Veto Bargaining: Presidents and the Politics of Negative Power.* New York: Cambridge Univ. Press.

Campbell, Angus, Philip Converse, Warren Miller, and Donald Stokes. 1960. *The American Voter.* Chicago: Univ. of Chicago Press.

Campbell, Stanley W. 1970. *The Slave Catchers: Enforcement of the Fugitive Slave Law, 1850–1869.* Chapel Hill: Univ. of North Carolina Press.

Campbell, James E. 1982. Cosponsoring Legislation in the U.S. Congress. *Legislative Studies Quarterly* 7:415–422.

———. 1991. The Presidential Surge and Its Midterm Decline in Congressional Elections, 1868–1988. *Journal of Politics* 53:477–487.

Canes-Wrone, Brandice, David W. Brady, and John F. Cogan. 2002. Out of Step, Out of Office: Electoral Accountability and House Members' Voting. *American Political Science Review* 96(1): 127–140.

Cannon, Clarence A. 1936. *Cannon's Precedents of the House of Representatives of the United States*. 5 vols. Washington, DC: Government Printing Office.

Canon, David, Garrison Nelson, and Charles Stewart. 1998. *Historical Congressional Standing Committees, 1st to 79th Congresses, 1789–1947*. Data file, http://web.mit.edu/17.251/www/data_page.html (accessed February 13, 1998).

———. 2002. *Committees in the United States Congress, 1789–1946*. 4 vols. Washington, DC: Congressional Quarterly Press.

Canon, David T., and Charles Stewart. 2001. The Evolution of the Committee System in Congress. In *Congress Reconsidered*, 7th edition, ed. Lawrence C. Dodd and Bruce I. Oppenheimer. Washington, DC: Congressional Quarterly Press.

———. 2002a. Committee Hierarchy and Assignments in the U.S. Congress: Testing Theories of Legislative Organization, 1789–1946. Paper presented at the annual meeting of the Midwest Political Science Association, Chicago.

———. 2002b. Parties and Hierarchies in Senate Committees. In *U.S. Senate Exceptionalism*, ed. Bruce Oppenheimer. Columbus: Ohio State Univ. Press.

———. 2002c. The Evolution of the Committee System in the U.S. Senate. In *U.S. Senate Exceptionalism*, ed. Bruce Oppenheimer. Columbus: Ohio State Univ. Press.

Caplin, Andrew, and Barry Nalebuff. 1988. On 64%-Majority Rule. *Econometrica* 56:787–814.

Carey, John, and Matthew Shugart. 1995. The Incentive to Cultivate the Personal Vote: A Rank Ordering of Electoral Formulas. *Electoral Studies* 14:417–439.

Carmines, Edward G., and Geoffrey C. Layman. 1997. Issue Evolution in Postwar American Politics: Old Certainties and Fresh Tensions. In *Present Discontents: American Politics in the Very Late Twentieth Century*, ed. Byron E. Shafer. Chatham, NJ: Chatham House.

Caro, Robert A. 2002. *Master of the Senate: The Years of Lyndon Johnson*. New York: Knopf.

Carson, David A. 1986. That Ground Called Quiddism: John Randolph's War with the Jefferson Administration. *Journal of American Studies* 20:71–92.

Carson, Jamie L., Michael H. Crespin, Charles J. Finocchiaro, and David W. Rohde. 2003. *Redistricting, Constituency Influence, and Party Polarization in*

Congress. Paper presented at the annual meeting of the Midwest Political Science Association, Chicago, April.

Carson, Jamie L., Michael H. Crespin, Jeffery A. Jenkins, and Ryan J. Vander Wielen. 2004. Shirking in the Contemporary Congress: A Reappraisal. *Political Analysis* 12:176–179.

Carson, Jamie L., Jeffery A. Jenkins, David W. Rohde, and Mark A. Souva. 2001. The Impact of National Tides and District-Level Effects on Electoral Outcomes: The Congressional Elections of 1862–63. *American Journal of Political Science* 45:887–898.

Carson, Jamie L., and Jason M. Roberts. 2005. Strategic Politicians and U.S. House Elections, 1874–1914. *Journal of Politics* 67:474–496.

Cerami, Charles. 2005. *Young Patriots: The Remarkable Story of Two Men, Their Impossible Plan, and the Revolution That Created the Constitution*. Naperville, IL: Sourcebooks.

Chamberlain, Gary A. 1980. Analysis of Covariance with Qualitative Data. *Review of Economic Studies* 47:225–238.

Chamberlain, Lawrence. 1946. *The President, Congress, and Legislation*. New York: Columbia Univ. Press.

Cheney, Richard B. 1989. An UnRuly House: A Republican View. *Public Opinion* January/February 1989, 41–44.

Chiu, Chang-Wei. 1928. *The Speaker of the House of Representatives since 1896*. New York: Columbia Univ. Press.

Clark, Champ. 1920. *My Quarter Century of American Politics*, vol. 1. New York: Harper.

Clausen, Aage. 1973. *How Congressmen Decide: A Policy Focus*. New York: St. Martin's.

Clay, Thomas Hart. 1910. *Henry Clay*. Philadelphia, PA: G. W. Jacobs.

Clinton, Joshua D., Simon Jackman, and Doug Rivers. 2004. The Statistical Analysis of Roll Call Data. *American Political Science Review* 98(2): 355–370.

Clinton, Joshua D., and Adam Meirowitz. 2003. Integrating Voting Theory and Roll Call Analysis: A Framework. *Political Analysis* 11(4): 381–396.

———. 2004. Testing Accounts of Legislative Strategic Voting: The Compromise of 1790. *American Journal of Political Science* 48(4): 675–689.

Clubb, Jerome M., and Howard W. Allen. 1967. Party Loyalty in the Progressive Years: The Senate, 1909–1915. *Journal of Politics* 29:567–584.

Clubb, Jerome M., and Santa A. Traugott. 1977. Partisan Cleavage and Cohesion in the House of Representatives, 1861–1974. *Journal of Interdisciplinary History* 7:375–401.

Cohen, Linda, and Roger Noll. 1988. Economics, Politics and Government Research and Development. In *Technology and Politics*, ed. Michael E. Kraft and Norman J. Vig. Durham, NC: Duke Univ. Press.

———. 1991. How to Vote, Whether to Vote: Strategies for Voting and Abstaining on Congressional Roll Calls. *Political Behavior* 13:97–127.

Coleman, John J. 1999. Unified Government, Divided Government, and Party Responsiveness. *American Political Science Review* 93(4): 821–835.

Conover, W. J. 1999. *Practical Nonparametric Statistics*, 3rd edition. New York: Wiley.

Cooper, Joseph. 1970. *The Origins of the Standing Committees and the Development of the Modern House*. Houston, TX: William Marsh Rice Univ.

Cooper, Joseph, and David W. Brady. 1981. Institutional Context and Leadership Style: The House from Cannon to Rayburn. *American Political Science Review* 75:411–425.

Cooper, Joseph, David W. Brady, and Patricia A. Hurley. 1977. The Electoral Basis of Party Voting: Patterns and Trends in the U.S. House of Representatives, 1887–1969. In *The Impact of the Electoral Process*, ed. Louis Maisel and Joseph Cooper. Beverly Hills, CA: Sage.

Cooper, Joseph, and Cheryl D. Young. 1989. Bill Introduction in the Nineteenth Century: A Study of Institutional Change. *Legislative Studies Quarterly* 14:67–106.

Cooper, Joseph, and Elizabeth Rybicki. 2002. Analyzing Institutional Change: Bill Introduction in the Nineteenth-Century Senate. In *U.S. Senate Exceptionalism*, ed. Bruce Oppenheimer. Columbus: Ohio State Univ. Press.

Cooper, Joseph, and Garry Young. 1997. Partisanship, Bipartisanship, and Crosspartisanship in Congress since the New Deal. In *Congress Reconsidered*, 6th edition, ed. Lawrence C. Dodd and Bruce I. Oppenheimer. Washington, DC: Congressional Quarterly Press.

Couch, Jim F., and William F. Shugart. 1998. *The Political Economy of the New Deal*. Northampton, MA: Edward Elgar.

Cover, Albert D. 1977. One Good Term Deserves Another: The Advantage of Incumbency in Congressional Elections. *American Journal of Political Science* 21:523–541.

Cox, Gary W. 1990. Centripetal and Centrifugal Incentives in Electoral Systems. *American Journal of Political Science* 34:903–935.

———. 1997. *Making Votes Count*. New York: Cambridge Univ. Press.

Cox, Gary, Chris Den Hartog, and Mathew McCubbins. 2004. Reconsidering Recommittals. Manuscript, Univ. of California at San Diego.

Cox, Gary W., and Jonathan N. Katz. 1996. Why Did the Incumbency Advantage in U.S. House Elections Grow? *American Journal of Political Science* 40:478–497.

———. 2002. *Elbridge Gerry's Salamander: The Electoral Consequences of the Reapportionment Revolution*. Cambridge, UK: Cambridge Univ. Press.

Cox, Gary W., and Mathew D. McCubbins. 1991. On the Decline of Party Voting in Congress. *Legislative Studies Quarterly* 16:547–570.

———. 1993. *Legislative Leviathan: Party Government in the House.* Berkeley: Univ. of California Press.

———. 1997. Toward a Theory of Legislative Rules Changes: Assessing Schickler and Rich's Evidence. *American Journal of Political Science* 41:1376–1386.

———. 2001. Institutional Determinants of Economic Policy Outcomes. In *Presidents, Parliaments and Policy*, ed. Stephan Haggard and Mathew D. McCubbins, 21–64. New York: Cambridge Univ. Press.

———. 2002. Agenda Power in the U.S. House of Representatives. In *Party, Process, and Political Change in Congress: New Perspectives on the History of Congress*, ed. David Brady and Mathew D. McCubbins. Palo Alto, CA: Stanford Univ. Press.

———. 2005. *Setting the Agenda.* New York: Cambridge Univ. Press.

Cox, Gary W., and Keith T. Poole. 2002. On Measuring Partisanship in Roll-Call Voting: The U.S. House of Representatives, 1877–1999. *American Journal of Political Science* 46(3): 477–489.

Cox, LaWanda, and John H. Cox. 1963. *Politics, Principle, and Prejudice, 1865–1866.* New York: Free Press.

Crook, Sara Brandes, and John R. Hibbing. 1997. A Not-so-distant Mirror: The 17th Amendment and Congressional Change. *American Political Science Review* 91(4): 845–853.

Crowe, B. M. 1969. The History of the Twentieth Amendment to the Constitution of the United States. Master's thesis, Univ. of Texas at Houston.

Cunningham, Noble E., Jr. 1963. Who Were the Quids? *Mississippi Valley Historical Review* 50:252–263.

Cushing, Luther Stearns. 1856. *Elements of the Law and Practice of Legislative Assemblies in the United States of America.* Boston, MA: Little, Brown. Repr., Shannon, Ireland: Irish Univ. Press, 1971.

Daynes, Byron W. 1971. The Impact of the Direct Election of Senators on the Political System. Ph.D. diss., Univ. of Chicago.

de Figueiredo, John M., and Emerson H. Tiller. 1996. Congressional Control of the Courts: A Theoretical and Empirical Analysis of Expansion of the Federal Judiciary. *Journal of Law and Economics* 39(2): 435–462.

Deckard, Barbara. 1989a. House Majority Party Leadership in the Late 1980s. In *Congress Reconsidered*, 4th edition, ed. Lawrence C. Dodd and Bruce I. Oppenheimer. Washington, DC: Congressional Quarterly Press.

———. 1989b. *The Transformation of the U.S. Senate.* Baltimore, MD: Johns Hopkins Univ. Press.

———. 1995. *Legislators, Leaders and Lawmaking.* Baltimore, MD: Johns Hopkins Univ. Press.

———. 1997. *Unorthodox Lawmaking: New Legislative Processes in the U.S. Congress.* Washington, DC: Congressional Quarterly Press.

———. 2000. Hostile Partners: The President, Congress, and Lawmaking in the Partisan 1990s. In *Polarized Politics: Congress and the President in a Partisan Era*, ed. Jon R. Bond and Richard Fleisher, 134–153. Washington, DC: Congressional Quarterly Press.

———. 2002a. Do Parties Matter? In *Party, Process, and Political Change in Congress: New Perspectives on the History of Congress*, ed. David Brady and Mathew D. McCubbins. Palo Alto, CA: Stanford Univ. Press.

———. 2002b. The 60-Vote Senate. In *U.S. Senate Exceptionalism*, ed. Bruce I. Oppenheimer. Columbus: Ohio State Univ. Press.

Deering, Christopher, and Steven S. Smith. 1997. *Committees in Congress*. 3rd edition. Washington, DC: Congressional Quarterly Press.

Dell, Christopher, and Stephen W. Stathis. 1982. *Major Acts of Congress and Treaties Approved by the Senate, 1789–1980*. Report 82–156 GOV. Washington, DC: Congressional Research Service.

Dempsey, John T. 1956. Control by Congress over the Seating and Disciplining of Members. Ph.D. diss., Univ. of Michigan.

Den Hartog, Chris, and Craig Goodman. 2004. Committee Representativeness of the Majority Party in the Antebellum House. Paper presented at the Southern Political Science Association annual meeting, New Orleans, LA.

De Santis, Vincent P. 1953. President Arthur and the Independent Movements in the South in 1882. *Journal of Southern History* 19:346–363.

———. 1955. President Hayes's Southern Policy. *Journal of Southern History* 21:476–494.

———. 1959. *Republicans Face the Southern Question: The New Departure Years, 1877–1897*. Baltimore, MD: Johns Hopkins Univ. Press.

Deschler, Lewis. 1977. *Deschler's Precedents of the United States House of Representatives*. 16 vols.. Washington, DC: Government Printing Office.

Deschler, Lewis, and William Holmes Brown. 1982. *Procedure in the U.S. House of Representatives*. Washington, DC: Government Printing Office.

Diermeier, Daniel, and Keith Krehbiel. 2003. Institutionalism as a Methodology. *Journal of Theoretical Politics* 15(2): 123–144.

Dion, Douglas. 1997. *Turning the Legislative Thumbscrew: Minority Rights and Procedural Change in Legislative Politics*. Ann Arbor: Univ. of Michigan Press.

Dion, Douglas, and John Huber. 1996. Party Leadership and Procedural Choice in Legislatures. *Journal of Politics* 58:25–53.

———. 1997. Sense and Sensibility: The Role of Rules. *American Political Science Review* 91:945–957.

Dowd, Kevin, 1999. Too Big to Fail? Long-Term Capital Management and the Federal Reserve. Washington, DC: CATO Institute briefing paper 52.

Downs, Anthony. 1957. *An Economic Theory of Democracy*. New York: Harper.

Drobak, John N. 1993. The Courts and Slavery in the United States: Property Rights and Credible Commitment. In *Political Economy: Institutions, Competition, and Representation*, ed. William A. Barnett, Melvin J. Hinich, and Norman J. Schofield. Cambridge, UK: Cambridge Univ. Press.

Dubin, Michael J. 1998. *United States Congressional Elections, 1788–1997: The Official Results of the Elections of the 1st through 105th Congresses*. Jefferson, NC: McFarland.

———. 2002. *United States Presidential Elections, 1788–1860: The Official Results by County and State*. Jefferson, NC: McFarland.

Easterlin, Richard A. 1960. Interregional Differences in Per Capita Income, Population, and Total Income, 1840–1950. In *Trends in the American Economy in the Nineteenth Century*. National Bureau of Economic Research. Studies in Income and Wealth Series, vol. 24. Princeton, NJ: Princeton Univ. Press.

Eaton, Clement. 1957. *Henry Clay and the Art of American Politics*. Boston, MA: Little, Brown.

Edwards, George, Andrew Barrett, and Jeffrey Peake. 1997. The Legislative Impact of Divided Government. *American Journal of Political Science* 41:545–563.

Engstrom, Erik. 2006. Stacking the States, Stacking the House: The Partisan Consequences of Congressional Redistricting in the 19th Century. *American Political Science Review* 100(3): 419–427.

Engstrom, Erik, and Samuel Kernell. 2001. The Effects of Presidential Elections on Party Control of the Senate under Indirect and Direct Elections. Paper presented at the annual meeting of the Midwest Political Science Association, Chicago.

Engstrom, Erik, and Samuel Kernell. 2005. Manufactured Responsiveness: The Impact of State Electoral Laws on Unified Party Control of the President and House of Representatives. *American Journal of Political Science* 49:547–565.

Epstein, David, and Sharyn O'Halloran. 1999. *Delegating Powers: A Transaction Cost Politics Approach to Policymaking Under Separate Powers*. New York: Cambridge Univ. Press.

Erikson, Robert S. 1971a. The Electoral Impact of Congressional Roll Call Voting. *American Political Science Review* 65 (December): 1018–1032.

———. 1971b. The Advantage of Incumbency in Congressional Elections. *Polity* 3:395–405.

———. 1972. Malapportionment, Gerrymandering, and Party Fortunes. *American Political Science Review* 66:1234–1245.

———. 2002. Explaining National Party Tides in Senate Elections: Macropartisanship, Policy Mood, and Ideological Balancing. In *U.S. Senate Exceptionalism*, ed. Bruce I. Oppenheimer. Columbus: Ohio State Univ. Press.

Erikson, Robert S., Michael B. MacKuen, and James A. Stimson. 2002. The Macro Polity. New York: Cambridge Univ. Press.

Erikson, Robert S., and Gerald C. Wright. 2000. Representation of Constituency Ideology in Congress. In *Change and Continuity in House Elections*, ed. David W. Brady, John F. Cogan, and John F. Ferejohn, 149–177. Palo Alto, CA: Stanford Univ. Press.

———. 2001. Voters, Candidates, and Issues in Congressional Elections. In *Congress Reconsidered*, 7th edition, ed. Lawrence C. Dodd and Bruce I. Oppenheimer. Washington, DC: Congressional Quarterly Press.

Evans, Cobb. 1917. *A History of the Australian Ballot in the United States*. Chicago: Univ. of Chicago Press.

Evans, C. Lawrence, and Walter J. Oleszek. 2002. Message Politics and Senate Procedure. In *The Contentious Senate: Partisanship, Ideology, and the Myth of Cool Judgment*, ed. Colton C. Campbell and Nicol C. Rae. New York: Rowman & Littlefield.

Evans, Robert, Jr. 1962. The Economics of American Negro Slavery. In National Bureau of Economic Research, *Aspects of Labor Economics: A Conference of the Universities—National Bureau Committee for Economic Research*. Princeton, NJ: Princeton Univ. Press.

Evans, Rowland, and Robert Novak. 1966 *Lyndon B. Johnson: The Exercise of Power*. New York: New American Library.

Fabbri, Daniella, and Mario Padula. 2003. Legal Institutions, Credit Markets, and Poverty in Italy. Paper presented at conference Credit Markets for the Poor, Princeton, NJ, May.

Fanning, Clara Elizabeth. 1911. *Selected Articles on Direct Primaries*. Minneapolis, MN: H. W. Wilson.

Faulkner, Harold U. 1959. *Politics, Reform, and Expansion, 1890–1900*. New York: Harper & Row.

Fehrenbacher, Don E. 1978. *The Dred Scott Case: Its Significance in American Law and Politics*. Oxford: Oxford Univ. Press.

Fenno, Richard. 1966. *The Power of the Purse: Appropriations Politics in Congress*. Boston, MA: Little, Brown.

———. 1973. *Congressmen in Committees*. Boston, MA: Little, Brown.

———. 1978. *Home Style: House Members in Their Districts*. Glenview, IL: Scott, Foresman.

———. 1996. *Senators on the Campaign Trail*. Tulsa: Univ. of Oklahoma Press.

Ferejohn, John. 1974. *Pork Barrel Politics: Rivers and Harbors Legislation, 1947–1968*. Palo Alto, CA: Stanford Univ. Press.

———. 1975. Who Wins in Conference Committee? *Journal of Politics* 37: 1033–1046.

———. 1977. On the Decline of Competition in Congressional Elections. *American Political Science Review* 71:166–176.

Ferrell, Robert H. 1985. *Woodrow Wilson and World War I, 1917–1921.* New York: Harper & Row.

Finkelman, Paul. 1979. *Prigg v. Pennsylvania* and Northern State Courts: Anti-Slavery Uses of a Pro-Slavery Decision. *Civil War History* 25 (March): 5–35.

———. 1981. *An Imperfect Union: Slavery, Federalism, and Comity.* Chapel Hill: Univ. of North Carolina Press.

———. 1987. Slavery and the Constitutional Convention: Making a Covenant with Death. In *Beyond Confederation: Origins of the Constitution and National Identity*, ed. Richard Beeman, Stephen Botein, and Edward C. Carter, II. Chapel Hill: Univ. of North Carolina Press.

———. 1996. *Slavery and the Founders: Race and Liberty in the Age of Jefferson.* Armonk, NY: M. E. Sharpe.

Fiorina, Morris P. 1974. *Representatives, Roll Calls, and Constituencies.* Lexington, MA: Lexington Books.

———. 1977. The Case of the Vanishing Marginals: The Bureaucracy Did It. *American Political Science Review* 71:177–181.

———. 1981. *Retrospective Voting in American National Elections.* New Haven, CT: Yale Univ. Press.

———. 1999. Whatever Happened to the Median Voter? Paper presented at Parties and Congress conference, Massachsetts Institute of Technology, Cambridge, MA.

Fiorina, Morris P., David W. Rohde, and Peter Wissel. 1975. Historical Change in House Turnover. In *Congress in Change*, ed. Norman J. Ornstein. New York: Praeger.

Fish, Carl Russell. 1904. *The Civil Service and the Patronage.* Cambridge, MA: Harvard Univ. Press.

Fleisher, Richard, and Jon R. Bond. 2000. Partisanship and the President's Quest for Votes on the Floor of Congress. In *Polarized Politics: Congress and the President in a Partisan Era*, ed. Jon R. Bond and Richard Fleisher, 154–185. Washington, DC: Congressional Quarterly Press.

———. 2000. Congress and the President in a Partisan Era. In *Polarized Politics: Congress and the President in a Partisan Era*, ed. Jon R. Bond and Richard Fleisher, 1–8. Washington, DC: Congressional Quarterly Press.

Fogel, Robert William. 1989. *Without Consent or Contract: The Rise and Fall of American Slavery.* New York: Norton.

Fogel, Robert William, and Stanley L. Engerman. 1974. *Time on the Cross: The Economics of American Negro Slavery.* Boston, MA: Little Brown.

Follett, Mary Parker. 1896. *The Speaker of the House of Representatives.* New York: Longmans, Green.

Foner, Eric. 1988. *Reconstruction: America's Unfinished Revolution, 1863–1877.* New York: Harper & Row.

Forgette, Richard, and Brian R. Sala. 1999. Conditional Party Government and Member Turnout on Senate Recorded Votes, 1873–1935. *Journal of Politics* 61(2): 467–484.

Franklin, John Hope, and Loren Schweninger. 1999. *Runaways Slaves: Rebels on the Plantation*. New York: Oxford Univ. Press.

Fredman, L. E. 1968. *The Australian Ballot: The Story of An American Reform*. East Lansing: Michigan State Univ. Press.

Freehling, William W. 1990. *The Road to Disunion*, vol. 1, *Secessionists at Bay, 1776–1854*. New York: Oxford Univ. Press.

———. 1994. The Reintegration of American History: Slavery and the Civil War. New York: Oxford Univ. Press.

Fritz, Harry W. 1977. The War Hawks of 1812: Party Leadership in the Twelfth Congress, vol. 5, Capitol Studies.

Frymer, Paul. 1995. The 1994 Aftershock: Dealignment or Realignment in the South. In *Midterm: The Elections of 1994 in Context*, ed. Philip A. Klinkner. Boulder, CO: Westview Press.

Fuller, Hubert Bruce. 1909. *The Speakers of the House*. Boston, MA: Little, Brown.

Galderisi, Peter F., and Marni Ezra. 2001. Congressional Primaries in Historical and Theoretical Context. In *Congressional Primaries and the Politics of Representation*, ed. Peter F. Galderisi, Marni Ezra, and Michael Lyons. Lanham, MD: Rowman & Littlefield.

Galderisi, Peter F., and Benjamin Ginsberg. 1986. Primary Elections and the Evanescence of Third Party Activity in the United States. In *Do Elections Matter*, ed. Benjamin Ginsberg and Alan Stone. Armonk, NY: M. E. Sharpe.

Galloway, George B., and Sidney Wise. 1976. *History of the House of Representatives*, 2nd edition. New York: Thomas Y. Crowell.

Gamm, Gerald, and Kenneth Shepsle. 1989. Emergence of Legislative Institutions: Standing Committees in the House and Senate, 1810–1825. *Legislative Studies Quarterly* 14:39–66.

Gamm, Gerald, and Steven S. Smith. 2000. Last Among Equals: The Presiding Officer of the Senate. In *Esteemed Colleagues: Civility and Deliberation in the United States Senate*, ed. B. Loomis, 105–136. Washington, DC: Brookings Institution.

———. 2001. The Dynamics of Party Government in Congress. In *Congress Reconsidered*, 7th edition, ed. L. Dodd and B. Oppenheimer, 245–268. Washington, DC: Congressional Quarterly Press.

———. 2002. The Emergence of Senate Party Leadership. In *Senate Exceptionalism*, ed. B. Oppenheimer. Columbus: Ohio State Univ. Press.

Gara, Larry. 1961. *The Liberty Line: The Legend of the Underground Railroad*. Lexington: Univ. of Kentucky Press.

———. 1964. The Fugitive Slave Law: A Double Paradox. *Civil War History* 10:229–240.

———. 1971. *The Liberty Line: The Legend of the Underground Railroad.* Lexington: Univ. of Kentucky Press.

Garraty, John A. 1953. *Henry Cabot Lodge.* New York: Knopf.

———. 1968. *The New Commonwealth, 1877–1890.* New York: Harper & Row.

Geddes, Barbara. 2003. *Paradigms and Sand Castles: Theory Building and Research Design in Comparative Politics.* Ann Arbor: Univ. of Michigan Press.

Gelman, Andrew, and Gary King. 1990. Estimating Incumbency Advantage without Bias. *American Journal of Political Science* 34:1142–1164.

Genovese, Eugene. 1974. *Roll, Jordan, Roll: The World the Slaves Made.* New York: Pantheon Books.

Geyl, Peter. 1961. The American Civil War and the Problem of Inevitability. Reprinted in *The Causes of the American Civil War*, ed. Edwin C. Rozwenc. Boston, MA: D. C. Heath, 1972.

Gillette, William. 1979. *Retreat from Reconstruction, 1869–1879.* Baton Rouge: Louisiana State Univ. Press.

Gilligan, Thomas W., and Keith K Krehbiel. 1987. Collective Decision-Making and Standing Committees: An Informal Rationale for Restrictive Amendment Procedures. *Journal of Law, Economics, and Organization* 3:287–335.

———. 1989. Asymmetric Information and Legislative Rules with a Heterogeneous Committee. *American Journal of Political Science* 33:459–490.

———. 1990. Organization of Informative Committees by a Rational Legislature. *American Journal of Political Science* 34:531–564.

Gilmour, John. 1995. *Strategic Disagreement: Stalemate in American Politics.* Pittsburgh, PA: Univ. of Pittsburgh Press.

Ginsberg, Benjamin. 1972. Critical Elections and the Substance of Party Conflict, 1844–1968. *Midwest Journal of Political Science* 16(4): 603–625.

———. 1973. Critical Elections and American Public Policy. Ph.D. diss., Univ. of Chicago.

———. 1976. Elections and Public Policy. *American Political Science Review* 70(1): 41–49.

Gold, Lewis L. 1980. *The Presidency of William McKinley.* Lawrence: Univ. of Kansas Press.

Golden, Robert M. 2001. *"A Free Ballot and a Fair Count": The Department of Justice and the Enforcement of Voting Rights in the South, 1877–1893.* New York: Fordham Univ. Press.

Goodman, Craig, and Timothy P. Nokken. 2002. *Lame Ducks and Roll Call Behavior in the US House of Representatives, 1869–1933.* Manuscript, Univ. of Texas at Houston.

———. 2004. Lame Duck Legislators and Consideration of the Ship Subsidy Bill of 1922. *American Politics Research* 32:465–489.

Gordon, Colin. 1994. *New Deals: Business, Labor and Politics in America, 1920–1935.* New York: Cambridge Univ. Press.

Granat, Diane. 1984. The House's TV War: The Gloves Come Off. *Congressional Quarterly Weekly Report*, May 19, p. 1166.

Gray, Lewis Cecil. 1933. *History of Agriculture in the Southern United States to 1860*, vol. 2. Washington, DC: Carnegie Institution of Washington.

Green, Matthew N. 2002. Institutional Change, Party Discipline, and the House Democratic Caucus, 1911–1919. *Legislative Studies Quarterly* 27(4): 601–633.

Greene, William H. 1990. *Econometric Analysis*, 2nd edition. Englewood Cliffs, NJ: Prentice Hall.

———. 2000. *Econometric Analysis*, 4th edition. Upper Saddle River, NJ: Prentice Hall.

Gropp, Reint, John Karl Scholz, and Michelle J. White. 1997. Personal Bankruptcy and Credit Supply and Demand. *Quarterly Journal of Economics* 112(1): 217–251.

Groseclose, Tim. 1994. Testing Committee Composition Hypotheses for the U.S. Congress. *Journal of Politics* 56:440–458.

———. 2001. A Model of Candidate Location When One Candidate Has a Valence Advantage. *American Journal of Political Science* 45(4): 862–886.

Groseclose, Tim, and David C. King. 2001. Committee Theories Reconsidered. In *Congress Reconsidered*, 7th edition, ed. Lawrence C. Dodd and Bruce I. Oppenheimer. Washington, DC: Congressional Quarterly Press.

Groseclose, Tim, Steven D. Levitt, and James M. Snyder Jr. 1999a. An Inflation Index for ADA Scores. *American Political Science Review* 93(1): 33–50.

———. 1999b. Comparing Interest Group Scores across Time and Chambers: Adjusted ADEA Scores for the U.S. Congress. *American Political Science Review* 93:33–50.

Groseclose, Tim, and James M. Snyder Jr. 1996. Buying Supermajorities. *American Political Science Review* 90(2): 303–315.

———. 2003. Interpreting the Coefficient of Party Influence: Comment on Krehbiel. *Political Analysis* 11:104–107.

Groseclose, Tim, and Charles Stewart III. 1998. The Value of Committee Seats in the House, 1947–91. *American Journal of Political Science* 42: 453–474.

———. 1999. The Value of Committee Seats in the United States Senate, 1947–91. *American Journal of Political Science* 43:963–973.

Hall, Richard L. 1996. *Participation in Congress.* New Haven, CT: Yale Univ. Press.

Hall, Richard L., and Bernard Grofman. 1990. The Committee Assignment Process and the Conditional Nature of Committee Bias. *American Political Science Review* 84:1149–1166.

Hall, Wallace Worthy. 1936. The History and Effect of the Seventeenth Amendment. Ph.D. diss., Univ. of California at Berkeley.

Hammond, Thomas H., and Gary J. Miller. 1987. The Core of the Constitution. *American Political Science Review* 81:1155–1174.

Harlow, Ralph Volney. 1917. *The History of Legislative Methods in the Period before 1825.* New Haven, CT: Yale Univ. Press.

Harvey, Anna, and Bumba Mukherjee. n.d. The Evolution of Partisan Conventions, 1880–1940. Manuscript, New York Univ.

Hasbrouck, Paul DeWitt. 1927. *Party Government in the House of Representatives.* New York: Macmillan.

Hatzenbuehler, Ronald L. 1972. Party Unity and the Decision for War in the House of Representatives, 1812. *William and Mary Quarterly* 29 (July): 367–390.

———. 1976. The War Hawks and the Question of Congressional Leadership in 1812. *Pacific Historical Review* 43 (February): 1–22.

Haynes, George H. 1906. *The Election of Senators.* New York: Holt.

———. 1938. *The Senate of the United States: Its History and Practice.* Boston, MA: Houghton Mifflin.

———. 1960. *The Senate of the United States: Its History and Practice*, vol. 1. New York: Russell & Russell. Repr., Boston, MA: Houghton Mifflin, 1938.

Heckman, James J., and James M. Snyder. 1997. Linear Probability Models of the Demand for Attributes with an Empirical Application to Estimating the Preferences of Legislators. *RAND Journal of Economics* 28: S142–189.

Helper, Hinton Rowan. 1857. *The Impending Crisis of the South: How to Meet It.* New York: Burdick Brothers.

Hibbs, Douglas. 1977. Political Parties and Macroeconomic Policy. *American Political Science Review* 71:1467–1487.

Hicks, John D. 1960. *Republican Ascendancy, 1921–1933.* New York: Harper & Row.

———. 1961 [1931]. The Populist Revolt: A History of the Farmers' Alliance and the People's Party. Lincoln: Univ. of Nebraska Press.

Higgs, Robert. 1987. *Crisis and Leviathan.* New York: Oxford Univ. Press.

Hinds, Asher C. 1907. *Hinds' Precedents of the House of Representatives of the United States.* 5 vols. Washington, DC: Government Printing Office. http://www.gpo.gov/congress/house/precedents/hinds/hinds.html.

Hirshson, Stanley P. 1962. *Farewell to the Bloody Shirt: Northern Republicans and the Southern Negro, 1877–1893.* Bloomington: Indiana Univ. Press.

History of the United States House of Representatives, 1789–1994. 1994. Washington, DC: Government Printing Office. House Document No. 103-324 (103rd Congress, 2nd session).

Hofstadter, Richard. 1955. *The Age of Reform.* New York: Knopf.

Hoing, Willard L. 1957. David B. Henderson: Speaker of the House. *Iowa Journal of History* 55:1–34.

Hood, M. V., III, Quentin Kidd, and Irwin L. Morris. 1999. Of Byrd(s) and Bumpers: Using Democratic Senators to Analyze Political Change in the South, 1960–1995. *American Journal of Political Science* 43 (April): 465–487.

Hoogenboom, Ari. 1988. *The Presidency of Rutherford B. Hayes.* Lawrence: Univ. of Kansas Press.

House, Albert V. 1935. The Contributions of Samuel J. Randall to the Rules of the National House of Representatives. *American Political Science Review* 29:837–841.

Howell, William, E. Scott Adler, Charles Cameron, and Charles Riemann. 2000. Divided Government and the Legislative Productivity of Congress, 1945–1994. *Legislative Studies Quarterly* 25(2): 285–312.

Huber, P. J. 1967. The Behavior of Maximum Likelihood Estimates under Nonstandard Conditions. *Proceedings of the Fifth Berkeley Symposium on Mathematical Statistics and Probability* 1:221–233.

Hummel, Jeffrey Rogers. 1996. *Emancipating Slaves, Enslaving Free Men: A History of the American Civil War.* Chicago: Open Court.

———. 2001. Deadweight Loss and the American Civil War: The Political Economy of Slavery, Secession, and Emancipation. Ph.D. diss., Univ. of Texas at Austin.

Hurley, Patricia A., and Rick K. Wilson. 1989. Partisan Voting Patterns in the U. S. Senate, 1877–1986. *Legislative Studies Quarterly* 14(2): 225–250.

Inter-university Consortium for Political and Social Research and Congressional Quarterly, Inc. (ICPSR). 1998. *United States Congressional Roll Call Voting Records, 1789–1996* (ICPSR 0004). Ann Arbor, MI: ICPSR.

Inter-university Consortium for Political and Social Research (ICPSR) and Carroll McKibbin. *Roster of United States Congressional Officeholders and Biographical Characteristics of Members of the United States Congress, 1789–1996: Merged Data.* ICPSR Study 7803. Ann Arbor, MI: ICPSR.

Jacobson, Gary C. 1987. The Marginals Never Vanished: Incumbency and Competition in Elections to the U.S. House of Representatives, 1952–1982. *American Journal of Political Science* 31:126–141.

———. 1989. Strategic Politicians and the Dynamics of U.S. House Elections, 1946–1986. *American Political Science Review* 83:773–793.

———. 1990. *The Electoral Origins of Divided Government: Competition in U.S. House Elections, 1946–1988.* Boulder, CO: Westview Press.

———. 2000a. Party Polarization in National Politics: The Electoral Connection. In *Polarized Politics: Congress and the President in a Partisan Era*, ed. Jon R. Bond and Richard Fleisher, 9–30. Washington, DC: Congressional Quarterly Press.

———. 2000b. The Electoral Basis of Partisan Polarization in Congress. Paper presented at the annual meeting of the American Political Science Association, Washington, DC, August 31–September 3.

———. 2000c. Public Opinion and the Impeachment of Bill Clinton. In *British Elections and Parties Review*, vol. 10, ed. Philip Cowley, David Denver, Andrew Russell, and Lisa Harrison. London: Frank Cass.

———. 2001. *The Politics of Congressional Elections*, 5th edition. New York: Addison-Wesley-Longman.

———. 2003. Partisan Polarization in Presidential Support: The Electoral Connection. *Congress and the Presidency* 30:1–36.

———. 2004. *The Politics of Congressional Elections*, 6th edition. New York: Longman.

Jacobson, Gary C., and Samuel Kernell. 1981. *Strategy and Choice in Congressional Elections*. New Haven, CT: Yale Univ. Press.

———. 1983. *Strategy and Choice in Congressional Elections*, 2nd edition. New Haven, CT: Yale Univ. Press.

James, Scott. 2000. *Presidents, Parties, and the State*. New York: Oxford Univ. Press.

Jappelli, Tullio, Marco Pagano, and Magda Bianco. 2002. Courts and Banks: Effects of Judicial Enforcement on Credit Markets, Working Paper 58. Salerno, Italy: CSEF, Dipartimento di Scienze Economiche e Statistiche Università di Salerno.

Jenkins, Jeffery A. 1998. Property Rights and the Emergence of Standing Committee Dominance in the Nineteenth-Century House. *Legislative Studies Quarterly* 23(4): 493–519.

———. 1999. Examining the Bonding Effects of Party: A Comparative Analysis of Roll-Call Voting in the U.S. and Confederate Houses. *American Journal of Political Science* 43:1144–1165.

———. 2004. Partisanship and Contested Election Cases in the House of Representatives, 1789–2002. *Studies in American Political Development* 18:113–135.

———. 2005. Partisanship and Contested Election Cases in the Senate, 1789–2002. *Studies in American Political Development* 19:53–74.

Jenkins, Jeffery A., Eric Schickler, and Jamie L. Carson. 2005. Constituency Cleavages and Congressional Parties: Measuring Homogeneity and Polarization across Time. *Social Science History* 28:537–573.

Jenkins, Jeffery A., and Charles Stewart III. 2002. Order from Chaos: The Transformation of the Committee System in the House, 1816–1822. In *Party, Process, and Political Change in Congress: New Perspectives on the*

History of Congress, ed. David Brady and Mathew D. McCubbins. Palo Alto, CA: Stanford Univ. Press.

———. 2003. Out in the open: The Emergence of *Viva Voce* Voting in House Speakership Elections. *Legislative Studies Quarterly* 28(4): 481–508.

Jewell, Malcolm E. 1955. Party Voting in American State Legislatures. *American Political Science Review* 49:773–791.

Johannes, John R., and John C. McAdams. 1981. The Congressional Incumbency Effect: Is It Casework, Policy Compatibility, or Something Else? *American Journal of Political Science* 25:520–542.

Johnson, Valen, and James Albert. 1999. *Ordinal Data Modeling.* New York: Springer-Verlag.

Joint Committee of the Senate and Assembly of the State of New York. 1910. *Primary and Election Laws of This and Other States*, vol. 1. Albany, NY: J. B. Lyon.

Jones, Arthur F., and Daniel H. Weinberg. 2000. The Changing Shape of the Nation's Income Distribution. *Current Population Reports.* P60-204. Washington, DC: U.S. Department of Commerce, Economics and Statistics Association. U.S. Census Bureau.

Jones, Charles, O. 1968. Joseph G. Cannon and Howard W. Smith: An Essay on the Limits of Leadership in the House of Representatives. *Journal of Politics* 30:617–646.

Josephy, Alvin M., Jr. 1979. *On the Hill: A History of the American Congress.* New York: Touchstone.

Kahn, Alfred E. 1988. *The Economics of Regulation: Principles and Institutions*, 2nd edition. Cambridge, MA: MIT Press.

Kalt, Joseph P., and Zupan, Mark A. 1984. Capture and Ideology in the Economic Theory of Politics. *American Economic Review* 74(3): 279–300.

———. 1990. The Apparent Ideological Behavior of Legislators: Testing for Principal-Agent Slack in Political Institutions. *Journal of Law and Economics* 33(1): 103–131.

Karoly, L. A., and Burtless, G., 1995. Demographic Change, Rising Earnings Inequality, and the Distribution of Personal Well-Being, 1959–1989. *Demography* 32(3): 379–405.

Katz, Jonathan N., and Brian R. Sala. 1996. Careerism, Committee Assignments, and the Electoral Connection. *American Political Science Review* 90:21–33.

Katz, Richard S. 1980. *A Theory of Parties and Electoral Systems.* Baltimore, MD: Johns Hopkins Univ. Press.

Keith, Robert. 1977. The Use of Unanimous Consent in the Senate. In U.S. Senate, *Committees and Senate Procedure.* 94th Congress, 2nd session. Washington, DC: Government Printing Office

Kelly, Alfred H., and Winfred A. Harbison. 1970. *The American Constitution: Its Origins and Development*, 4th edition. New York: Norton.

Kendall, M. G., and A. Stuart. 1950. The Law of Cubic Proportions in Election Results. *British Journal of Sociology* 1:183–197.

Kennon, Donald R. 1986. *The Speakers of the U.S. House of Representatives: A Bibliography, 1789–1984.* Baltimore, MD: Johns Hopkins Univ. Press.

Kernell, Samuel. 1977. Toward Understanding 19th Century Congressional Careers: Ambition, Competition, and Rotation. *American Journal of Political Science* 21:669–693.

———. 1997. *Going Public: New Strategies of Presidential Leadership.* Washington, DC: Congressional Quarterly Press.

———. 2003. To Stay, To Quit, or To Move Up: Explaining the Growth of Careerism in the House of Representatives, 1878–1940. Paper presented at the American Political Science Association meeting, Philadelphia, PA, August 28–31.

Kernell, Samuel, and Gary C. Jacobson. 1987. Congress and the Presidency as News in the Nineteenth Century. *Journal of Politics* 49:1016–1035.

Kernell, Samuel, and Michael P. McDonald. 1999. Congress and America's Political Development: The Transformation of the Post Office from Patronage to Service. *American Journal of Political Science* 43(3): 792–811.

Key, V. O. 1949. *Southern Politics in State and Nation.* New York: Knopf.

———. 1956. *American State Politics.* New York: Knopf.

———. 1964. *Politics, Parties, and Pressure Groups*, 5th edition. New York: Thomas Y. Crowell.

Kiewiet, D. Roderick. 1998. Restrictions on Floor Amendments in the House of Representatives. Paper presented at the Comparative Legislative Research Conference, University of Iowa, April 17–18.

Kiewiet, D. Roderick, and Mathew D. McCubbins. 1988. Presidential Influence on Congressional Appropriations Decisions. *American Journal of Political Science* 32:713–736.

———. 1991. *The Logic of Delegation: Congressional Parties and the Appropriations Process.* Chicago: Univ. of Chicago Press.

King, David C. 1997. *Turf Wars: How Congressional Committees Claim Jurisdiction.* Chicago: Univ. of Chicago Press.

———. 1998. Party Competition and Polarization in American Politics. Paper presented at the annual meeting of the Midwest Political Science Association, Chicago.

———. 1999. Party Competition and Polarization in American Politics. Manuscript, Harvard Univ.

King, Gary, Michael Tomz, and Jason Wittenberg. 2000. Making the Most of Statistical Analyses: Improving Interpretation and Presentation. *American Journal of Political Science* 44:347–361.

King, Ronald F., and Susan Ellis. 1996. Partisan Advantage and Constitutional Change: The Case of the 17th Amendment. *Studies in American Political Development* 10:69–102.

Kinsella, Kevin, and Victoria A. Velkoff. 2001. *An Aging World*. Washington, DC: U.S. Census Bureau, Series P95/01-1, U.S. Government Printing Office.

Klein, Jennifer. 2003. *For All These Rights: Business, Labor, and the Shaping of America's Public-Private Welfare State*. Princeton, NJ: Princeton Univ. Press.

Koger, Gregory. 2002. Obstruction in the House and Senate: A Comparative Analysis of Institutional Choice. Ph.D. diss., Univ. of California at Los Angeles.

———. 2003. The Majoritarian Senate. Paper presented at the annual meeting of the American Political Science Association, Philadelphia, PA.

———. 2004. Pivots For Sale: Endogenous Rules, Transaction Costs, and Pivotal Politics. Paper presented at the annual meeting of the American Political Science Association, Chicago.

Koopman, Douglas L. 1996. *Hostile Takeover: The House Republican Party, 1980–1995*. New York: Rowman & Littlefield.

Kousser, J. Morgan. 1974. *The Shaping of Southern Politics*. New Haven, CT: Yale Univ. Press.

Kramer, G. 1971. Short-Term Fluctuations in U.S. Voting Behavior, 1896–1964. *American Political Science Review* 65:131–143.

Krehbiel, Keith. 1990. Are Congressional Committees Composed of Preference Outliers? *American Political Science Review* 84:149–163.

———. 1991. *Information and Legislative Organization*. Ann Arbor: Univ. of Michigan Press.

———. 1993. Where's the Party? *British Journal of Political Science* 23: 235–266.

———. 1997a. Restrictive Rules Reconsidered. *American Journal of Political Science* 41:919–944.

———. 1997b. Rejoinder to "Sense and Sensibility." *American Journal of Political Science* 41:958–964.

———. 1998. *Pivotal Politics: A Theory of US Lawmaking*. Chicago: Univ. of Chicago Press.

———. 1999. Paradoxes of Parties in Congress. *Legislative Studies Quarterly* 24(1): 31–64.

———. 2000. Party Discipline and Measures of Partisanship. *American Journal of Political Science* 44(2): 212–227.

———. 2003a. The Coefficient of Party Influence. *Political Analysis* 11(1): 95–103.

———. 2003b. Asymmetry in Party Influence: Reply. *Political Analysis* 11:108–109.

Krehbiel, Keith, and Adam Meirowitz. 2002. Minority Rights and Majority Power: Theoretical Consequences of the Motion to Recommit. *Legislative Studies Quarterly* 27:191–217.

Krehbiel, Keith, Kenneth A. Shepsle, and Barry R. Weingast. 1987. Why Are Congressional Committees Powerful? *American Political Science Review* 81:929–945.

Krehbiel, Keith, and Alan Wiseman. 2001. Joseph G. Cannon: Majoritarian from Illinois. *Legislative Studies Quarterly* 26:357–389.

Kroszner, Randall S. 1999. Is It Better to Forgive Than to Receive? Repudiation of the Gold Indexation Clause in Long-Term Debt during the Great Depression. Photocopy, Univ. of Chicago.

Kuklinski, James H. 1977. District Competitiveness and Legislative Roll-Call Behavior: A Reassessment of the Marginality Hypothesis. *American Journal of Political Science* 21(3): 627–638.

Lambert, John R. 1953. *Arthur Pue Gorman*. Baton Rouge: Louisiana State Univ. Press.

Lapinski, John S. 2000. Representation and Reform: A Congress Centered Approach to American Political Development. Ph.D. diss., Columbia Univ.

Lawrence, Eric D., Forrest Maltzman, and Paul J. Wahlbeck. 2001. The Politics of Speaker Cannon's Committee Assignments. *American Journal of Political Science* 45:551–562.

Leintz, Gerald R. 1978. House Speaker Elections and Congressional Parties, 1789–1860. *Capitol Studies* 6 (Spring): 63–89.

Lester, V. Markham. 1995 *Victorian Insolvency: Bankruptcy, Imprisonment for Debt, and Company Winding-Up in Nineteenth Century England*. Oxford: Clarendon Press.

Leuchtenburg, William E. 1963. *Franklin D. Roosevelt and the New Deal, 1932–1940*. New York: Harper & Row.

Levitt, Steven D. 1996. How Do Senators Vote? Disentangling the Role of Voter Preferences, Party Affiliation, and Senator Ideology. *American Economic Review* 86(3): 425–441.

Levy, Frank, and Richard J. Murnane. 1992. U.S. Earnings Levels and Earnings Inequality: A Review of Recent Trends and Proposed Explanations. *Journal of Economic Literature* 30(3): 1333–1381.

Lewis-Beck, Michael S., and Tom W. Rice. 1985. Government Growth in the United States. *Journal of Politics* 47:2–30.

Liang, Kung-Yee, and Scott L. Zeger. 1986. Longitudinal Data Analysis Using Generalized Linear Models. *Biometrika* 73:13–22.

Liebman, Jeffrey B. 2002. Redistribution in the Current U.S. Social Security System. Working Paper 02-09, Center for Economic Studies, U.S. Census Bureau.

Light, Paul. 2002. *Government's Greatest Achievements: From Civil Rights to Homeland Defense*. Washington, DC: Brookings Institution.

Link, Arthur S. 1954. *Woodrow Wilson and the Progressive Era, 1910–1917*. New York: Harper & Row.

———. 1956. *The New Freedom*. Princeton, NJ: Princeton Univ. Press.

———. 1960. *The Struggle For Neutrality*. Princeton, NJ: Princeton Univ. Press.

Lipset, Seymour Martin. 1959. Some Social Requisites of Democracy: Economic Development and Political Legitimacy. *American Political Science Review* 53(1): 69–105.

Livermore, Seward W. 1966. *Woodrow Wilson and the War Congress, 1916–18*. Seattle: Univ. of Washington Press.

Loeb, Isador. 1910. Direct Primaries in Missouri. Proceedings of the American Political Science Association 7:163–174.

Londregan, John. 2000. Estimating Legislators' Preferred Points. *Political Analysis* 8(1): 35–56.

Longley, Lawrence, and Walter Oleszek. 1989. *Bicameral Politics: Conference Committees in Congress*. New Haven, CT: Yale Univ. Press.

Loomis, Michael. 1995. An Analysis of Legislator's Utility Function for Voting in the United States Congress. Ph.D. diss., Carnegie Mellon Univ.

Lott, John R. 1987. Political Cheating. *Public Choice* 52:169–186.

Lott, John R., Jr. 1990. Attendance Rates, Political Shirking, and the Effects of Post-Elective Office Employment. *Economic Inquiry* 28:133–150.

Lott, John R., Jr. and Stephen G. Bronars. 1993. Time Series Evidence on Shirking in the US House of Representatives. *Public Choice* 76:125–149.

Lott, John R., Jr. and Michael L. Davis. 1992. A Critical Review and Extension of the Political Shirking Literature. *Public Choice* 74:461–484.

Luce, Robert. 1922. *Legislative Procedure: Parliamentary Practices and the Course of Business in the Framing of Statutes*. Boston, MA: Houghton Mifflin. Repr., New York: Da Capo, 1972.

MacNeil, Neil. 1963. *Forge of Democracy: The House of Representatives*. New York: David McKay.

MacRae, Duncan, Jr. 1952. The Relation between Roll Calls and Constituencies in the Massachusetts House of Representatives. *American Political Science Review* 46:1046–1055.

Mainwaring, Scott, and Matthew Shugart, eds. 1997. *Presidentialism and Democracy in Latin America*. New York: Cambridge Univ. Press.

Maltzman, Forrest. 1997. *Competing Principles: Committees, Parties, and the Organization of Congress*. Ann Arbor: Univ. of Michigan Press.

Maltzman, Forrest, and Eric Lawrence. 2000. Why Did Speaker Henderson Resign? The Page 799 Mystery Is Solved. *Public Affairs Report* 41(4): 7–8.

Mann, Bruce H. 2002. *Republic of Debtors: Bankruptcy in the Age of American Independence*. Cambridge, MA: Harvard Univ. Press.

Margo, Robert A. 2000. The Labor Force in the Nineteenth Century. In *The Cambridge Economic History of the United States*, vol. 2., ed. Stanley Engerman and Robert Gallman, 207–245. New York: Cambridge Univ. Press.

Martin, Boyd A. 1947. *The Direct Primary in Idaho*. Palo Alto, CA: Stanford Univ. Press.

Martin, S. Walter. 1954. Charles F. Crisp, Speaker of the House. *Georgia Review* 8(1): 167–177.

Martis, Kenneth, 1989. *The Historical Atlas of Political Parties in the United States Congress: 1789–1989*. New York: Macmillan.

Matthews, Donald R. 1960. *U. S. Senators and Their World*. Chapel Hill: Univ. of North Carolina Press.

Mayer, George H. 1967. *The Republican Party, 1854–1966*. 2nd edition. New York: Oxford Univ. Press.

Mayhew, David R. 1974a. *Congress: The Electoral Connection*. New Haven, CT: Yale Univ. Press.

———. 1974b. Congressional Elections: The Case of the Vanishing Marginals. *Polity* 6:295–317.

———. 1991. *Divided We Govern*. New Haven, CT: Yale Univ. Press.

———. 1993. Let's Stick with the Longer List. *Polity* 25:485–488.

———. 2002. *Electoral Realignments*. New Haven, CT: Yale Univ. Press.

———. 2006. Lawmaking and History. In *The Macropolitics of Congress*, ed. E. Scott Alder and John S. Lapinski. Princeton, NJ: Princeton Univ. Press.

Mayo, Bernard. 1937. *Henry Clay: Spokesman of the Old West*. Boston, MA: Houghton Mifflin.

McArthur, John, and Stephen V. Marks. 1988. Constituent Interest vs. Legislator Ideology: The Role of Political Opportunity Cost. *Economic Inquiry* 26(3): 461–470.

McCarty, Nolan M., and Keith T. Poole. 1995. Veto Power and Legislation: An Empirical Analysis of Executive and Legislative Bargaining from 1961–1986. *Journal of Law, Economics, and Organization* 11:282–312.

McCarty, Nolan, Keith Poole, and Howard Rosenthal. 1997. *Income Redistribution and the Realignment of American Politics*. Washington, DC: AEI Press.

———. 2001. The Hunt for Party Discipline in Congress. *American Political Science Review* 95:673–687.

McClellan, George B. 1956. *The Gentleman and the Tiger: The Autobiography of George B. McClellan, Jr.* Philadelphia, PA: Lippincott.

McConachie, Lauros G. 1898. *Congressional Committees*. New York: B. Franklin.

McCormick, James M., and Michael Black. 1983. Ideology and Senate Voting on the Panama Canal Treaties. *Legislative Studies Quarterly* 8(1): 45–63.

McCown, Ada. 1927. *The Congressional Conference Committee*. New York: Columbia Univ. Press.

McCubbins, Mathew D., and Thomas Schwartz. 1988. Congress, the Courts and Public Policy: Policy Consequences of the "One Man, One Vote" Rule. *American Journal of Political Science* 32:388–415.

McDougall, Marion Gleason. 1891. *Fugitive Slaves (1619–1865)*. Boston, MA: Ginn.

McKenzie, Charles W. 1938. *Party Government in the United States*. New York: Ronald Press.

McNollgast. 1995. Politics and the Courts: A Positive theory of Judicial Doctrine and the Rule of Law. *Southern California Law Review* 68:1631.

McPherson, James M. 1988. *Battle Cry of Freedom: The Civil War Era*. New York: Oxford Univ. Press.

McSeveney, Samuel T. 1972. *The Politics of Depression: Political Behavior in the Northeast, 1893–1896*. New York: Oxford Univ. Press.

Meinke, Scott R. 2003. Vote Choice and Vote Change in the Antebellum House: Evidence from the Gag Rule, 1836–1845. Paper presented at the annual meeting of the American Political Science Association, Philadelphia, PA.

Merriam, Charles E. 1908. *Primary Elections*. Chicago: The Univ. of Chicago Press.

Merriam, Charles E., and Louise Overacker. 1928. *Primary Elections*. Chicago: The Univ. of Chicago Press.

Michel, Robert. 1992. Testimony by Robert H. Michel. In *Roundtable Discussion on the Motion to Recommit*. Committee on Rules, House of Representatives. Washington, DC: Government Printing Office.

Millspaugh, Arthur C. 1917. *Party Organization and Machinery in Michigan since 1890*. Baltimore, MD: Johns Hopkins Univ. Press.

Minutes of the U.S. Senate Democratic Conference, ed. Donald A. Ritchie. 1998. Washington, DC: Government Printing Office.

Moores, Merrill. 1917. *A Historical and Legal Digest of All the Contested Election Cases in the House of Representatives from the Fifty-Seventh to and Including the Sixty-Fourth Congress, 1901–1917*. House Document 2052, 64th Congress, 2nd session. Washington, DC: Government Printing Office.

Moraski, Byron J., and Charles R. Shipan. 1999. The Politics of Supreme Court Nominations: A Theory of Institutional Constraints and Choices. *American Journal of Political Science* 43(4): 1069–1095.

Morehouse, Sara McCally. 1996. Legislative Party Voting for the Governor's Program. *Legislative Studies Quarterly* 21:359–381.

Morgan, Dan. 1999. Bush Opposes Limiting Texas Bankruptcy Shelter, *Washington Post*, July 18, p. A06.

Morris, Thomas D. 1974. *Free Men All: The Personal Liberty Laws of the North, 1780–1861*. Baltimore, MD: Johns Hopkins Univ. Press.

Mowry, George E. 1958. *The Era of Theodore Roosevelt, 1900–1912*. New York: Harper & Row.

Murray, Hyde. 1992. House of Representatives in Changing Times: House Parliamentary Procedure. In *Roundtable Discussion on the Motion to Recom-*

mit. Committee on Rules, House of Representatives. Washington, DC: Government Printing Office.

Nadeau, Richard, and Harold W. Stanley. 1993. Class Polarization among Native Southern Whites, 1952–90. *American Journal of Political Science* 37 (August): 900–919.

National Anti-Slavery Standard, 22 (25 May 1861).

National Archives. 1987a. *Guide to the Records of the United States Senate at the National Archives*. Washington, DC: Government Printing Office.

———. 1987b. *Guide to the Records of the United States House of Representatives at the National Archives*. Washington, DC: Government Printing Office.

Neustadt, Richard E. 2001. The Presidential "One Hundred Days": An Overview. In *Triumphs and Tragedies of the Modern Presidency*, ed. David Abshire. Westport, CT: Praeger.

Nokken, Timothy P. 2000. Dynamics of Congressional Loyalty: Party Defection and Roll Call Behavior, 1947–1997. *Legislative Studies Quarterly* 25(3): 417–444.

Nokken, Timothy P., and Brian R. Sala. 2000. Confirmation Dynamics: a Model of Presidential Appointments to Independent Agencies. *Journal of Theoretical Politics* 12(1): 91–112.

———. 2002. Institutional Evolution and the Rise of the Tuesday-Thursday Club in the House of Representatives. In *Party, Process, and Political Change in Congress*, ed. David W. Brady and Mathew D. McCubbins. Palo Alto, CA: Stanford Univ. Press.

Nordhaus, William D. 1975. The Political Business Cycle. *Review of Economic Studies* 42(2): 169–190.

Norris, George W. 1945. *Fighting Liberal: The Autobiography of George W. Norris*. Lincoln: Univ. of Nebraska Press.

North, Douglass C. 1961. *Economic Growth of the United States, 1790 to 1860*. Englewood Cliffs, NJ: Prentice Hall.

———. 1990. *Institutions, Institutional Change and Economic Performance*. Cambridge, UK: Cambridge Univ. Press.

North, Douglass, and Andrew Rutten. 1987. The Northwest Ordinance in Historical Perspective. In *Essays on the Old Northwest*, ed. D. Klingaman and R. Vedder. Athens: Ohio Univ. Press.

North, Douglass C., and John Wallis. 1986. Measuring the Transaction Sector in the American Economy, 1870-1970. In *Long Term Factors in American Economic Growth*, ed. Stanley L. Engerman and Robert E. Gallman, chap. 3, 95–161. Chicago: Univ. of Chicago Press.

Nunez, Stephen, and Howard Rosenthal. 2004. Bankruptcy Reform in Congress: Creditors, Committees, Ideology, and Floor Voting in the Legislative Process. *Journal of Law, Economics, and Organization* 20(2): 527–557.

Nye, Russel Blaine. 1951. *Midwestern Progressive Politics: A Historical Study of Its*

Origins and Development, 1870–1950. East Lansing: Michigan State College Press.

Oleszek, Walter J. 1991. John Worth Kern: Portrait of a Floor Leader. In *First Among Equals: Outstanding Senate Leaders of the Twentieth Century*, ed. Richard A. Baker and Roger H. Davidson. Washington, DC: Congressional Quarterly Press.

———. 1996. *Congressional Procedures and the Policy Process*, 4th edition. Washington, DC: Congressional Quarterly Press.

———. 1998. A Pre-Twentieth Century Look at the House Committee on Rules. http://www.house.gov/rules/pre20th_rules.htm.

———. 2001. *Congressional Procedures and the Policy Process*, 5th edition. Washington, DC: Congressional Quarterly Press.

Oppenheimer, Bruce I. 1985. Changing Time Constraints on Congress: Historical Perspectives on the Use of Cloture. In *Congress Reconsidered*, 3rd edition, ed. Lawrence C. Dodd and Bruce I. Oppenheimer, 393–413. Washington, DC: Congressional Quarterly Press.

Ornstein, Norman, Thomas Mann, and Michael Malbin. 2002. *Vital statistics on Congress.* Washington, DC: Congressional Quarterly Press.

Overby, L. M., T. A. Kazee, and D. W. Prince. 2004. Committee Outliers in State Legislatures. *Legislative Studies Quarterly* 29(1):81–107.

Paletz, David Leon. 1970. Influence in Congress: An Analysis of the Nature and Effects of Conference Committees Utilizing Case Studies of Poverty, Traffic Safety, and Congressional Redistricting Legislation. Ph.D. diss., Univ. of California at Los Angeles.

Palmquist, Bradley. 1998. The Extended Beta Binomial Model in Political Analysis. Paper presented at the annual meeting of the Southern Political Science Association, Atlanta, GA.

Parrington, Vernon Louis 1927. *Main Currents in American Thought: Volume One 1620–1800, The Colonial.* New York; Harcourt, Brace & World.

Parsons, Stanley B., William W. Beach, and Michael J. Dubin. 1986. *United States Congressional Districts and Data, 1843–1883.* New York: Greenwood.

Parsons, Stanley B., Michael J. Dubin, and Karen Toombs Parsons. 1990. *United States Congressional Districts and Data, 1883–1913.* New York: Greenwood.

Passell, Peter, and Gavin Wright. 1972. The Effects of Pre–Civil War Territorial Expansion on the Price of Slaves. *Journal of Political Economy* 80:1188–1202.

Patterson, Samuel C., and Gregory A. Caldeira. 1988. Party Voting in the United States Congress. *British Journal of Political Science* 18(1): 111–131.

Perman, Michael. 1984. *The Road to Redemption: Southern Politics, 1869–1879.* Chapel Hill: Univ. of North Carolina Press.

———. 2001. *Struggle for Mastery: Disfranchisement in the South, 1888–1908.* Chapel Hill: Univ. of North Carolina Press.

Peters, Ronald M. 1997. *The American Speakership: The Office in Historical Perspective*, 2nd edition. Baltimore, MD: Johns Hopkins Univ. Press.

Peterson, Merrill D. 1987. *The Great Triumvirate: Webster, Clay, and Calhoun.* New York: Oxford Univ. Press.

Peterson, Eric. 2001. Is It Science Yet? Replicating and Validating the *Divided We Govern* List of Important Statutes. Paper presented to the annual meeting of the Midwest Political Science Association, Chicago, April 19–21.

Phillips, U. B. 1918. *American Negro Slavery: A Survey of the Employment and Control of Negro Labor as Determined by the Plantation Regime.* New York: D. Appleton.

———. 1929. *Life and Labor in the Old South.* Boston, MA: Little, Brown.

Pierson, Paul. 2000. Increasing Returns, Path Dependence, and the Study of Politics. *American Political Science Review* 94(2): 251–267.

Plutarch's Lives, Pyrrhus, sec 21.

Pollack, James K. 1943. *The Direct Primary in Michigan, 1909–1935.* Ann Arbor: Univ. of Michigan Press.

Polsby, Nelson W. 1968. The Institutionalization of the U.S. House of Representatives. *American Political Science Review* 62:144–168.

———. 2004. *How Congress Evolves: Social Bases of Institutional Change.* Oxford Univ. Press.

Polsby, Nelson W., Miriam Gallagher, and Barry S. Rundquist. 1969. The Growth of Seniority in the U.S. House of Representatives. *American Political Science Review* 63:787–807.

Poole, Keith T. 1998. Recovering a Basic Space from a Set of Issue Scales. *American Journal of Political Science* 42(3): 954–993.

———. 2003. Changing Minds? Not in Congress! http://voteview.com/chminds.pdf (accessed October 14, 2003).

Poole, Keith T., and Nolan McCarty. 1995. Veto Power and Legislation: An Empirical Analysis of Executive-Legislative Bargaining from 1961 to 1986. *Journal of Law, Economics, and Organization* 11(2): 282–312.

Poole, Keith T., and Howard Rosenthal. 1984. The Polarization of American Politics. *Journal of Politics* 46:1061–1079.

———. 1993. The Enduring 19th Century Battle for Economic Regulation: The Case of the Interstate Commerce Act Revisited. *Journal of Law and Economics* 26 (October): 837–860.

———. 1994. Railroad Regulation and Congress, 1847–1887. In *The Regulated Economy: A Historical Approach to Political Economy*, ed. Claudia Goldin and Gary Libecap, 81–120. Chicago: Univ. of Chicago Press.

———. 1997a. *Congress: A Political-Economic History of Roll Call Voting.* New York: Oxford Univ. Press.

———. 1997b. Multi-Dimensional Weighted Nominal Three-Step Estimation. Software. Pittsburgh, PA: Carnegie-Mellon Univ. http://voteview.uh.edu/W-Nominate.htm.

———. 2001. D-NOMINATE after 10 Years: A Comparative Update to *Congress: A Political Economic History of Roll-Call Voting. Legislative Studies Quarterly* 26:5–29.

———. 2006. *Ideology and Congress.* New Brunswick, NJ: Transaction.

Posner, Eric A., Richard Hynes, and Alup Malani. 2001. The Political Economy of Property Exemption Laws. Manuscript, Univ. of Chicago Law School.

Pressman, Jeffrey L. 1966. *House vs. Senate: Conflict in the Appropriations Process.* New Haven, CT: Yale Univ. Press.

Price, Douglas. 1975. Congress and the Evolution of Legislative Professionalism. In *Congress and Change*, ed. Norman J. Ornstein. New York: Praeger.

———. 1977. Careers and Committees in the American Congress: The Problem of Structural Change. In *The History of Parliamentary Behavior*, ed. William O. Aydelotte. Princeton, NJ: Princeton Univ. Press.

Rakove, Jack. 1996. *Original Meanings: Politics and Ideas in the Making of the Constitution.* New York: Knopf.

Rae, Nicol C., and Colton C. Campbell. 2001. Party Politics and Ideology in the Contemporary Senate. In *The Contentious Senate: Partisanship, Ideology, and the Myth of Cool Judgment*, ed. Colton C. Campbell and Nicol C. Rae. New York: Rowman & Littlefield.

Ramseyer, J. Mark, and Frances McCall Rosenbluth. 1993. *Japan's Political Marketplace.* Cambridge, MA: Harvard Univ. Press.

Ranney, Austin. 1951. Toward a More Responsible Two Party System: A Commentary. *American Political Science Review* 45:488–499.

———. 1975. *Curing the Mischiefs of Faction: Party Reform in America.* Berkeley: Univ. of California Press.

Ranney, Austin, and Willmoore Kendall. 1956. *Democracy and the American Party System.* New York: Harcourt, Brace & World.

Rector, Robert, and Rea Hederman. 1999. *Income Inequality: How Census Data Misrepresent Income Distribution.* CDA-9907. Washington, DC: Heritage Center for Data Analysis.

Reed, Thomas B. 1890. Contested Elections. *North American Review* 151: 112–120.

Reed, Thomas B. 1952. *Reed's Rules: A Manual of General Parliamentary Law with Suggestions for Special Rules.* Olympia, WA: State Printing Plant.

Reinsch, Paul S. 1907. *American Legislatures and Legislative Methods.* New York: Century.

Remini, Robert V. 1991. *Henry Clay: Statesman for the Union.* New York: Norton.

Reynolds, John. 1995. Divided We Govern: Research Note. Manuscript, Univ. of Texas at San Antonio.

Reynolds, John F. 1988. *Testing Democracy: Electoral Behavior and Progressive Reform in New Jersey, 1880–1920.* Chapel Hill: Univ. of North Carolina Press.

Riddick, Floyd M. 1949. *The United States Congress: Organization and Procedure.* Manassas, VA: National Capitol Publishers.

Riddick, Floyd. 1992. *Senate Procedure: Precedents and Practice.* U.S. Senate.

Riddlesperger, James W., Jr., and James D. King. 1982. Energy Votes in the U.S. Senate, 1973–1980. *Journal of Politics* 44(3): 838–847.

Riker, William H. 1955. The Senate and American Federalism. *American Political Science Review* 49(2): 452–469.

———. 1986. *The Art of Political Manipulation.* New Haven, CT: Yale Univ. Press.

———. 1992. The Justification of Bicameralism. *International Political Science Review* 13:101–116.

Ripley, Randall B. 1967. *Party Leaders in the House of Representatives.* Washington, DC: Brookings Institution.

Rippy, Fred J., ed. 1936. *F.M. Simmons: Statesman of the New South.* Durham, NC: Duke Univ. Press.

Rivers, Douglas. 2003. Identification of Multidimensional Spatial Voting. Paper presented to the conference on Measurement Modeling in Political Science, Stanford University, Palo Alto, California. http://polmeth.wustl.edu/working03.chron.html.

Roberts, Jason. 2003. Minority Rights and Majority Power: Conditional Party Government and the Motion to Recommit in the House. Paper presented at the annual meeting of the Midwest Political Science Association, Chicago.

———. 2004. Minority Rights and Majority Power: Conditional Party Government and the Motion to Recommit in the House, 1909–2000. *Legislative Studies Quarterly* 30 (May 2005): 219–234.

Roberts, Jason M., and Steven S. Smith. 2003a. Procedural Contexts, Party Strategy, and Conditional Party Voting in the U.S. House of Representatives, 1971–2000. *American Journal of Political Science* 47: 305–319.

Roberts, Jason M., and Steven S. Smith. 2003b. The Evolution of Agenda Setting Institutions in the House and Senate. Paper presented at the History of Congress Conference, University of California at San Diego, December 5–6.

Robinson, Donald R. 1971. *Slavery and the Structure of American Politics, 1765–1820.* New York: Harcourt Brace Jovanovich.

Robinson, William A. 1930. *Thomas B. Reed: Parliamentarian.* New York: Dodd, Mead.

Rogers, Lindsay. 1926. *The American Senate*. New York: Knopf.

Rogowski, Ronald. 1987. Trade and the Variety of Democratic Institutions. *International Organization* 41(2): 202–223.

Rohde, David W. 1991. *Parties and Leaders in the Postreform House*. Chicago: Univ. of Chicago Press.

———. 1995. Parties and Committees in the House: Member Motivations, Issues, and Institutional Arrangements. In *Positive Theories of Congressional Institutions*, ed. Kenneth A. Shepsle and Barry R. Weingast. Ann Arbor: Univ. of Michigan Press.

———. 2003. *Roll Call Voting Data for the United States House of Representatives, 1953–2000*. Compiled by the Political Institutions and Public Choice Program, Michigan State Univ., East Lansing, MI.

Rohde, David, and Kenneth A. Shepsle. 1973. Democratic Committee Assignments in the House of Representatives: Strategic Aspects of a Social Choice Process. *American Political Science Review* 67:889–905.

———. 1987. Leaders and Followers in the House of Representatives: Reflections on Woodrow Wilson's *Congressional Government*. *Congress and the Presidency* 14:111–133.

Romer, Thomas, and Howard Rosenthal. 1978. Political Resource Allocation, Controlled Agendas, and the Status Quo. *Public Choice* 33:27–44.

Romer, Thomas, and Barry R. Weingast, 1991. Political Foundations of the Thrift Debacle. In *Politics and Economics in the 1980s*, ed. Alberto Alesina and Geoffrey Carliner, 175–209. Chicago: Univ. of Chicago Press.

Rosenstone, Steven J., and John Mark Hansen. 1993. *Mobilization, Participation, and Democracy in America*. New York: Macmillan.

Rosenthal, Alan. 1981. *Legislative Life*. New York: Harper & Row.

Rosenthal, Howard, and Keith T. Poole. *United States Congressional Roll Call Voting Records, 1789–1990: Reformatted Data*. ICPSR Study 9822. Ann Arbor, MI: ICPSR.

Rossiter, Clinton. 1961. *The Federalist Papers*. New York: Mentor Books.

Rothbard, Murray, 1962. *The Panic of 1819: Reactions and Policies*. New York: Columbia Univ. Press.

Rothenberg, Lawrence S., and Mitchell S. Sanders. 2000a. Severing the Electoral Connection: Shirking in the Contemporary Congress. *American Journal of Political Science* 44:316–325.

———. 2000b. Legislator Turnout and the Calculus of Voting: The Determinants of Abstention in the U.S. Congress. *Public Choice* 103:259–270.

———. 2000c. Lame-Duck Politics: Impending Departure and the Votes on Impeachment. *Political Research Quarterly* 3:523–536.

Rothman, David J. 1966. *Politics and Power: The United States Senate 1869–1901*. Cambridge: Harvard Univ. Press.

Roundtable Discussion on the Motion to Recommit. 1991. *Congressional Record*, June 4, p. H 3813.

Roust, Kevin A. 2004. Minority Rights in the House of Representatives: Endogenous Rules and Minority Rights. Paper presented at the annual meeting of the Midwest Political Science Association, Chicago.

Rowell, Chester H. 1901. *A Historical and Legal Digest of All the Contested Election Cases in the House of Representatives from the First to the Fifty-Sixth Congress, 1789–1901*. House Document 510, 56th Congress, 2nd session. Washington, DC: Government Printing Office.

Rudalevige, Andrew. 2002. *Managing the President's Program: Presidential Leadership and Legislative Policy*. Princeton, NJ: Princeton Univ. Press.

Rules of the House of Representatives, April 7, 1789, reprinted by the First Federal Congress Project. http://www.gwu.edu/~ffcp/exhibit/p3/p3_1.html (accessed November 8, 2003).

Rusk, Jerrold G. 1970. The Effects of the Australian Ballot Reform on Split Ticket Voting: 1876–1908. *American Political Science Review* 64:1220–1238.

———. 2001. *A Statistical History of the American Electorate*. Washington, DC: Congressional Quarterly Press.

Rybicki, Elizabeth. n.d. The History of Bicameral Resolution Practices in the U.S. Congress. Ph.D diss., Univ. of Minnesota.

———. 2003. Resolving Bicameral Differences in Congress, 1789–2002. Paper presented at the annual meeting of the American Political Science Association, Philadelphia, PA.

Ryley, Thomas. 1975. *A Little Group of Willful Men*. Port Washington, NY: Kennikat Press.

Sait, E. 1938. *Political Institutions: A Preface*. New York: Appleton-Century-Crofts.

Sala, Brian R., William Bernhard, and Timothy P. Nokken. 2003. Strategic Shifting: Reelection Seeking and Ideological Adjustment in the U.S. Senate, 1952–98. Manuscript, Univ. of California at Davis.

Sanderlin, Walter S. 1947. Arthur P. Gorman and the Chesapeake and Ohio Canal: An Episode in the Rise of a Political Boss. *Journal of Southern History* 13:323–337.

Sapiro, Virginia, Steven J. Rosenstone, and the National Election Studies. 2002. *American National Election Studies Cumulative Data File, 1948–2000*. Computer file, 11th ICPSR version. Ann Arbor: Univ. of Michigan, Center for Political Studies (producer). Inter-university Consortium for Political and Social Research (distributor).

Saturno, James V. 1999a. *Amendments between the Houses*. Report 98-812, February 19. Washington, DC: Congressional Research Service.

———. 1999b. *Floor Consideration of Conference Reports in the House*. Report 98-736 GOV, February 19, 1999. Washington, DC: Congressional Research Service.

———. 2001. How Measures Are Brought to the Floor: A Brief Introduction. CRS Report RS20067. Washington, DC: Congressional Research Service.

Schelling, Thomas. 1956. An Essay on Bargaining. *American Economic Review* 46:281–306.

Schickler, Eric. 2000. Institutional Change in the House of Representatives, 1867–1998: A Test of Partisan and Ideological Power Balance Models. *American Political Science Review* 94:269–288.

———. 2001. *Disjointed Pluralism: Institutional Innovation and the Development of the U.S. Congress*. Princeton, NJ: Princeton Univ. Press.

Schickler, Eric, and Andrew Rich. 1997. Controlling the Floor: Politics as Procedural Coalitions in the House. *American Journal of Political Science* 41(4): 1340–1375.

Schickler, Eric, and John Sides. 2000. Intergenerational Warfare: The Senate Decentralizes Appropriations. *Legislative Studies Quarterly* 25:551–575.

Schiller, Wendy J. 1995. Senators as Political Entrepreneurs: Using Bill Sponsorship to Shape Legislative Agendas. *American Journal of Political Science* 1:186–203.

———. 2000. *Partners and Rivals: Representation in U.S. Senate Delegations*. Princeton, NJ: Princeton Univ. Press.

———. 2003. The Effects of Direct Senate Elections on Senate Delegations Dynamics. Paper presented at the annual meeting of the Midwest Political Science Association, Chicago.

Schurz, Carl. 1898. *Life of Henry Clay*. 2 vols. Boston, MA: Houghton Mifflin.

Seaman, Ezra C. 1852. *Essays on the Progress of Nations, in Civilization, Productive Industry, Wealth and Population*. New York: Scribner.

Senate Committee on Rules and Administration. 1988. *Senate Manual*. Washington, DC: Government Printing Office.

Shade, William G., Stanley D. Hopper, David Jacobson, and Stephen E. Moiles. 1973. Partisanship in the United States Senate: 1869–1901. *Journal of Interdisciplinary History* 4:185–205.

Shepsle, Kenneth A. 1978. *The Giant Jigsaw Puzzle*. Chicago: Univ. of Chicago Press.

———. 1979. Institutional Arrangements and Equilibrium in Multidimensional Voting Models. *American Journal of Political Science* 23:27.

Shepsle, Kenneth. 1989. The Changing Textbook Congress. In *Can the Government Govern?* ed. John Chubb and Paul Peterson, 238–267. Washington, DC: Brookings Institution.

Shepsle, Kenneth A., and Barry R. Weingast. 1981. Structure Induced Equilibrium and Legislative Choice. *Public Choice* 37:509–519.

———. 1987a. The Institutional Foundations of Committee Power. *American Political Science Review* 81:85–104.

———. 1987b. Reflections on Committee Power. *American Political Science Review* 81:35–104.

———. 1994. Positive Theories of Congressional Institutions. *Electoral Studies Quarterly* 19:149–179.

Silbey, Joel H. 1977. *A Respectable Minority: The Democratic Party in the Civil War Era, 1860–1868.* New York: Norton.

———. 1991. *American Political Nation, 1838–1893.* Palo Alto, CA: Stanford Univ. Press.

Sinclair, Barbara Deckard. 1976. Electoral Marginality and Party Loyalty in House Roll Call Voting. *American Journal of Political Science* 20:469–481.

———. 1977. Determinants of Aggregate Party Cohesion in the U.S. House of Representatives, 1901–1956. *Legislative Studies Quarterly* 2:155–175.

———. 1983. *Majority Leadership in the U.S. House.* Baltimore, MD: Johns Hopkins Univ. Press.

Skeel, David A., Jr. 2001. *The Rise and Dominion of Bankruptcy Law in America.* Princeton, NJ: Princeton Univ. Press.

Skaldony, Thomas W. 1985. The House Goes to Work: Select and Standing Committees in the U.S. House of Reprsentatives. *Congress and the Presidency* 12:165–188.

Skowronek, Stephen. 1982. *Building a New American Nation State: The Expansion of National Administrative Capacities, 1877–1920.* New York: Cambridge Univ. Press.

———. 1993. *The Politics Presidents Make.* Cambridge, MA: Belknap Press.

Sloan, Irving. 1984. *American Landmark Legislation.* 2nd series. Dobbs Ferry, NY: Oceana.

Sloan, Herbert E. 1995. *Principle and Interest: Thomas Jefferson and the Problem of Debt.* New York: Oxford Univ. Press.

Smith, Culver G. 1977. *The Press, Politics, and Patronage: The American Government's Use of Newspapers, 1789–1875.* Athens: Univ. of Georgia Press.

Smith, Henry H. 1887. *Digest and Manual of the Rules and Practice of the House of Representatives to Which Are Added the Constitution of the United States of America, with the Amendments Thereto, and so Much of Jefferson's Manual of Parliamentary Practice as under Rule XLIV Governs the House, the Standing Rules and Orders for Conducting Business in the House of Representative, the Joint Rules in Force at the Close of the 43rd Congress.* Washington, DC: Government Printing Office.

Smith, Steven S. 1988. An Essay on Sequence, Position, Goals, and Committee Power. *Legislative Studies Quarterly* 13:151–176.

———. 1989. *Call to Order: Floor Politics in the House and Senate.* Washington, DC: Brookings Institution.

———. 1999. *The American Congress*, 2nd edition. Boston, MA: Houghton Mifflin.

———. 2000. Positive Theories of Congressional Parties. *Legislative Studies Quarterly* 25:193–215.

Smith, Steven S., and Christopher J. Deering. 1990. *Committees in Congress*, 2nd edition. Washington, DC: Congressional Quarterly Press.

Smith, Steven S., and Marcus Flathman. 1989. Managing the Senate Floor: Complex Unanimous Consent Agreements Since the 1950s. *Legislative Studies Quarterly* 14(3): 349–374.

Smith, Steven S., and Gerald Gamm. 2001. The Dynamics of Party Government in Congress. In *Congress Reconsidered*, 7th edition, ed. Lawrence C. Dodd and Bruce I. Oppenheimer. Washington, DC: Congressional Quarterly Press.

Smith, Steven S., and Bruce A. Ray. 1983. The Impact of Congressional Reform: House Democratic Committee Assignments. *Congress and the Presidency* 10:219–240.

Smith, Steven S., Jason M. Roberts, and Ryan Vander Wielen. 2005. *The American Congress*, 3rd edition. http://congress.wustl.edu.

Smith, William Wolff. 1906. David Bremner Henderson. In *Twenty Years in the Press Gallery*, ed. O. O. Stealey. New York: Publishers Printing.

Snyder, James M., Jr., and Tim Groseclose. 2000. Estimating Party Influence in Congressional Roll-Call Voting. *American Journal of Political Science* 44(2): 193–211.

———. 2001. Estimating Party Influence on Roll Call Voting: Regression Coefficients versus Classification Success. *American Political Science Review* 95:689–698.

Socolofsky, Homer E., and Allan B. Spetter. 1987. *The Presidency of Benjamin Harrison*. Lawrence: Univ. Press of Kansas.

Spann, Edward K. 1957. John W. Taylor: The Reluctant Partisan, 1784–1854. Ph.D. diss., New York Univ.

Stanley, Harold W. 1988. Southern Partisan Changes: Dealignment, Realignment, or Both? *Journal of Politics* 50 (February): 64–88.

Stanwood, Edward. 1903. *American Tariff Controversies in the Nineteenth Century*, vol. 2. New York: Houghton Mifflin.

Stathis, Stephen. 2003. *Landmark Legislation: 1774–2002*. Washington, DC: Congressional Quarterly Press.

Statutes at Large of the United States of America, 1789–1873. 1850–1873. 17 vols. Washington.

Stewart, Charles H. 1989. *Budget Reform Politics: The Design of the Appropriations Process in the House of Representatives, 1865–1921*. New York: Cambridge Univ. Press.

———. 1991. Lessons from the Post-Civil War Era. In *Divided Government*, ed. Gary W. Cox and Samuel Kernell. Boulder, CO: Westview Press.

Stewart, Charles, III. 1992. Responsiveness in the Upper Chamber: The Constitution and the Institutional Development of the Senate. In *The Constitution and American Political Development: An Institutional Perspective*, ed. Peter Nardulli. Urbana: Univ. of Illinois Press.

———. 1999. The inefficient secret: Organizing for business in the U.S. House, 1839–1859. Paper presented at the annual meeting of the Midwest Political Science Association.

Stewart, Charles, III, and David Canon. 1996. *House Standing Committee Rosters, 1st to 46th Congress.* Manuscript.

———. 1997. *House Select Committee Rosters, 1st to 46th Congress.* Manuscript.

———. 2002. Committee Hierarchy and Assignments in the U.S. Congress: Testing Theories of Legislative Organization, 1789–1946. Paper presented at the annual meeting of the Midwest Political Science Association, Chicago.

Stewart, Charles H., III, and Barry R. Weingast. 1992. Stacking the Senate, Changing the Nation: Republican Rotten Boroughs, State-hood Politics, and American Political Development. *Studies in American Political Development* 6:223–271.

Stonecash, Jeffrey M., Mark D. Brewer, and Mach D. Mariani. 2003. *Diverging Parties: Social Change, Realignment, and Party Polarization.* Boulder, CO: Westview Press.

Strahan, Randall. 1994. Congressional Leadership in Institutional Time: The Case of Henry Clay. Paper presented at the annual meeting of the American Political Science Association.

———. 1998. Thomas Brackett Reed and the Rise of Party Government. In *Masters of the House: Congressional Leaders over Two Centuries*, ed. Roger H. Davidson, Susan Webb Hammond, and Raymond W. Smock. Boulder, CO: Westview Press.

———. 2002. Leadership and Institutional Change in the Nineteenth-Century House. In *Party, Process, and Political Change in Congress*, ed. David W. Brady and Mathew D. McCubbins. Palo Alto, CA: Stanford Univ. Press.

Strahan, Randall, Vincent G. Moscardelli, Moshe Haspel, and Richard S. Wike. 1998. Leadership and Institutional Development in the Early U.S. House: The Clay Speakership. Paper presented at the annual meeting of the Midwest Political Science Association, Chicago.

———. 2000. The Clay Speakership Revisited. *Polity* 32:561–593.

Strom, Gerald S., and Barry S. Rundquist. 1977. A Revised Theory of Winning in House-Senate Conferences. *American Political Science Review* 71:448–453.

Studenski, Paul, and Herman E. Kroos. 1952. Financial History of the United States. New York: McGraw-Hill.

Summers, Mark Wahlgren. 2000. *Rum, Romanism, and Rebellion: The Making of a President, 1884.* Chapel Hill: Univ. of North Carolina Press.

———. 2001. Party Games: The Art of Stealing Elections in the Late-Nineteenth-Century United States. *Journal of American History* 88:424–435.

———. 2004. *Party Games: Getting, Keeping, and Using Power in Gilded Age Politics.* Chapel Hill: Univ. of North Carolina Press.

Sundquist, James L. 1983. *Dynamics of the Party System: Alignment and Realignment of Political Parties in the United States*, revised ed. Washington, DC: Brookings Institution.

Swenson, Peter. 1982. The Influence of Recruitment on the Structure of Power in the U.S. House, 1870–1940. *Legislative Studies Quarterly* 7:7–36.

Swift, Elaine K. 1987. The Electoral Connection Meets the Past: Lessons from Congressional History, 1789–1899. *Political Science Quarterly* 102:625–645.

———. 1996. *The Making of an American Senate: Reconstitutive Change in Congress, 1787–1841*. Ann Arbor: Univ. of Michigan Press.

Swift, Elaine K., and David W. Brady. 1994. Common Ground: History and Theories of American Politics. In *The Dynamics of American Politics: Approaches and Interpretations*, ed. Lawrence C. Dodd and Calvin Jillson. Boulder, CO: Westview Press.

Swift, Elaine K., Robert G. Brookshire, David T. Canon, Evelyn C. Fink, John R. Hibbing, Brian D. Humes, Michael J. Malbin, and Kenneth C. Martis. 2000. Database of Historical Congressional Statistics. Ann Arbor, MI: Inter-university Consortium for Political and Social Research. http://webapp.icpsr.umich.edu/cocoon/ICPSR-STUDY/03371.xml.

Theriault, Sean. 1998. Moving Up or Moving Out: Career Ceilings and Congressional Retirement. *Legislative Studies Quarterly* 26:350–363.

Theriault, Sean M. 2003a. The Case of the Vanishing Moderates: Party Polarization in the Modern Congress. Manuscript, Univ. of Texas at Austin.

———. 2003b. Three Arguments to Temper Your View of Congressional Polarization. Manuscript, Univ. of Texas at Austin.

Theriault, Sean M., and Barry R. Weingast. 2002. Agenda Manipulation, Strategic Voting, and Legislative Details in the Compromise of 1850. In *Party, Process, and Political Change in Congress: New Perspectives on the History of Congress*, ed. David W. Brady and Mathew D. McCubbins. Palo Alto, CA: Stanford Univ. Press.

Thies, Michael F. 1998. When Will Pork Leave the Farm? Institutional Bias in Japan and the United States. *Legislative Studies Quarterly* 23(4): 467–492.

Tiefer, Charles. 1989. *Congressional Practice and Procedure: A Reference, Research, and Legislative Guide*. New York: Greenwood.

Tomz, Michael, Jason Wittenberg, and Gary King. 2001. CLARIFY: Software for Interpreting and Presenting Statistical Results. Version 2.0. Cambridge, MA: Harvard Univ.

Trelease, Allen W. 1971. *White Terror: The Ku Klux Klan Conspiracy and Southern Reconstruction*. New York: Harper & Row.

Tsebelis, George. 1995. Decision Making in Political Systems: Veto Players in Presidentialism, Parliamentarism, Multicameralism, and Multipartyism. *British Journal of Political Science* 25:289–326.

Tsebelis, George, and Jeannette Money. 1997. *Bicameralism.* Cambridge, UK: Cambridge Univ. Press.

Tuchman, Barbara. 1966. *The Proud Tower.* New York: Macmillan.

Tufte, Edward R. 1973. The Relationship between Votes and Seats in a Two-Party System. *American Political Science Review* 67:540–554.

———. 1978. *Political Control of the Economy*, Princeton NJ: Princeton Univ. Press.

Tulis, Jeffrey K. 1987. *The Rhetorical Presidency.* Princeton, NJ: Princeton Univ. Press.

Turner, Julius. 1951. *Party and Constituency: Pressures on Congress.* Baltimore, MD: Johns Hopkins Press.

U.S. Census Office. 1866. 1860 Census, *Statistics of the United States, (Including Mortality, Property, etc.) in 1860: Compiled from the Original Returns Being the Final Exhibit of the Eight Census.* Washington, DC: Government Printing Office.

U.S. Congress. Senate. 1985. Committee on Rules and Administration. *Senate Cloture Rule.* 99th Cong., 1st sess. Committee Print 99-95.

U.S. Congress. Senate. 1993. Joint Committee on the Organization of Congress. *Business Meetings on Congressional Reform Legislation, Meetings of the Joint Committee on the Organization of Congress.* 103rd Cong., 1st sess., Markup of Congressional Reform Legislation, November 18, 253–254.

U.S. House of Representatives, Amendments to the Constitution, http://www.house.gov/Constitution/Amend.html.

Uslaner, Eric. 1993. *The Decline of Comity in Congress.* Ann Arbor: Univ. of Michigan Press.

Valelly, Richard M. 1995. National Parties and Racial Disenfranchisement. In *Classifying by Race*, ed. Paul E. Peterson. Princeton, NJ: Princeton Univ. Press.

———. 2003. Congressional Modernization and the Federal Elections Bill of 1890. Working paper, Swarthmore College.

Van Beek, Stephen D. 1995. *Post-Passage Politics: Bicameral Resolution in Congress.* Pittsburgh, PA: Univ. of Pittsburgh Press.

Van Deuzen, Glyndon G. 1937. *The Life of Henry Clay.* Boston, MA: Little, Brown.

Van Houweling, Robert. 2003. An Evolving End Game: The Partisan Use of Conference Committees in the Post-Reform Congress. Paper presented at the History of Congress Conference, University of California at San Diego, December 5–6.

Vogler, David J. 1970. Patterns of One House Dominance in Congressional Conference Committees. *Midwest Journal of Political Science* 14:303–320.

Volden, Craig, and Elizabeth Bergman. 2006. How Strong Should Our Party Be? Party Member Preference over Party Cohesion. *Legislative Studies Quarterly* 31(1): 71–104.

Walker, Jack L. 1972. *Diffusion of Public Policy Innovation among the American States.* Computer file. Univ. of Michigan, Institute of Public Policy Studies. Ann Arbor, MI: Inter-university Consortium for Political and Social Research (producer and distributor).

———. 1991. *Mobilizing Interest Groups in America: Patrons, Professions, and Social Movements.* Ann Arbor: Univ. of Michigan Press.

Wallis, John, and Douglass North. 1986. Measuring the Transaction Sector in the American Economy, 1870–1970. In *Long-term Factors in American Economic Growth*, ed. Stanley Engerman and Robert Gallman. Chicago: Univ. of Chicago Press.

Walton, Gary M., and Hugh Rockoff. 1990. *History of the American Economy*, 6th edition. New York: Harcourt Brace Jovanovich.

Ware, Alan. 2002. *The American Direct Primary*. Cambridge, UK: Cambridge Univ. Press.

Warren, Charles, 1935. *Bankruptcy in United States History*. Cambridge, MA: Harvard Univ. Press.

Wattenberg, Martin P. 1991. The Building of a Republican Regional Base in the South: The Elephant Crosses the Mason-Dixon Line. *Public Opinion Quarterly* 55:424–431.

Wawro, Gregory, and Eric Schickler. 2004. Where's the Pivot? Obstruction and Lawmaking in the Pre-cloture Senate. *American Journal of Political Science* 48(4): 758–774.

———. 2006. *Filibuster: Obstruction and Lawmaking in the United States Senate.* Princeton, NJ: Princeton Univ. Press.

Weinberg, Daniel H. 2004. *A Brief Look at Postwar U.S. Income Inequality*. U.S. Census Bureau. May 13.

Weingast, Barry. 1981. Regulation, Reregulation and Deregulation: The Political Foundations of Agency-Clientele Relation. *Law and Contemporary Problems* 44(1): 147–177.

———. 1991. Fighting Fire with Fire: Amending Activity and Institutional Change in the Postreform Congress. In *The Postreform Congress*, ed. Roger Davidson. New York: St. Martin's.

———. 1998. Political Stability and Civil War: Institutions, Commitment, and American Democracy. In *Analytic Narratives*, ed. Robert H. Bates et al. Princeton, NJ: Princeton Univ. Press.

———. 2000. *Institutions and Political Commitment: A New Political Economy of the American Civil War Era.* Manuscript, Hoover Institution, Stanford Univ., Stanford, CA.

Weingast, Barry, and William Marshall. 1988. The Industrial Organization of Congress. *Journal of Political Economy* 96:132–163.

Welborn, Angie. 2000. *House Contested Election Cases: 1933 to 2000.* Congressional Research Service, Library of Congress, 98-194 A.

Welch, Richard E., Jr. 1965. The Federal Elections Bill of 1890: Postscripts and Prelude. *Journal of American History* 52:511–526.

White, William S. 1968. *Citadel: The Story of the U.S. Senate*. Boston, MA: Houghton Mifflin.

White, H. 1980. A Heteroskedasticity-Consistent Covariance Matrix Estimator and a Direct Test for Heteroskedasticity. *Econometrica* 48:817–830.

White, Lawrence J. 1991. *The S&L Debacle: Public Policy Lessons for Bank and Thrift Regulation*. New York: Oxford Univ. Press.

White, Leonard D. 1951. *The Jeffersonians: A Study in Administrative History, 1801–1829*. New York: Macmillan.

———. 1958. *The Republican Era, 1869–1901*. New York: Macmillan.

Wiebe, Robert. 1967. *The Search for Order: 1877–1920*. New York: Hill and Wang.

Wiecek, William W. 1987. The Witch at the Christening: Slavery and the Constitution's Origins. In *The Framing and Ratification of the Constitution*, ed. Leonard W. Levy and Dennis J. Mahoney. New York: Macmillan.

Wilson, Rick. 1986. What Was It Worth to Be on a Committee in the U.S. House, 1889 to 1913? *Legislative Studies Quarterly* 11:47–63.

Wilson, Woodrow. [1885] 1956. *Congressional Government: A Study in American Politics*. New York: Meridian Books.

Wirls, Daniel. 1999. Regionalism, Rotten Boroughs, Race, and Realignment: The Seventeenth Amendment and the Politics of Representation. *Studies in American Political Development* 13:1–30.

Wolfensberger, Donald. 1991. The Motion to Recommit in the House: The Rape of a Minority Right. *Roundtable Discussion of the Motion to Recommit*. Subcommittee on Rules of the House.

———. 1992. The Motion to Recommit in the House: The Rape of a Minority Right. In *Roundtable Discussion on the Motion to Recommit*. Committee on Rules, House of Representatives. Washington, DC: Government Printing Office.

———. 2000. *Congress and the People: Deliberative Democracy on Trial*. Baltimore, MD: Johns Hopkins Univ. Press.

———. 2002. Suspended Partisanship in the House: How Most Laws Are Really Made. Paper presented at the annual meeting of the American Political Science Association, Boston, MA, August 29–September 1. Tables updated November 2002.

Wolfensberger, Donald. 2003. The Motion to Recommit in the House: The Creation, Evisceration, and Restoration of a Minority Right. Paper presented at the History of Congress Conference, University of California at San Diego, December 5–6.

Wolff, Wendy, and Donald A. Ritchie, eds. 1999. Minutes of the Senate Republican Conference. Washington, DC: U.S. Government Printing Office.

Wolfinger, Raymond E. 1971. Filibusters: Majority Rule, Presidential Leadership, and Senate Norms. In *Readings On Congress*, ed. Raymond Wolfinger, 286–305. Englewood Cliffs, NJ: Prentice Hall.

Wood, B. Dan, and Angela Hinton Andersson. 1998. The Dynamics of Senatorial Representation, 1952–1991. *Journal of Politics* 60(3): 705–736.

Woodward, C. Vann. 1966. *Reunion and Reaction: The Compromise of 1877 and the End of Reconstruction*. New York: Oxford Univ. Press.

Wright, Gavin. 1974. The Political Economy of New Deal Spending: An Econometric Analysis. *Review of Economics and Statistics* 56:30–38.

Wright, Gerald C., and Michael B. Berkman. 1986. Candidates and Policy in United States Senate Elections. *American Political Science Review* 80(2): 567–588.

Wyman, Roger D. 1974. Middle-Class Voters and Progressive Reform: The Conflict of Class and Culture. *American Political Science Review* 68(2): 488–504.

Yang, Danghyu, and Gerald Friedman. 1992. Some Economic Aspects of the Southern Interregional Migration, 1850–1860. In *Without Consent or Contract: The Rise of American Slavery—Evidence and Methods*, ed. Robert William Fogel, Ralph A. Galantine, and Richard L. Manning. New York: Norton.

Young, Garry, and Valerie Heitshusen. 2002. Testing Competing Theories of Policy Production, 1874–1946. In *The Macropolitics of Congress*, ed. E. Scott Adler and John Lapinski. Princeton, NJ: Princeton Univ. Press.

Young, James Sterling. 1966. *The Washington Community: 1800–1828*. New York: Columbia Univ. Press.

Zaller, John. 1992. *The Nature and Origins of Mass Opinion*. New York: Cambridge Univ. Press.

Zorn, Christopher J. W. 2001. Generalized Estimating Equation Models for Correlated Data: A Review with Applications. *American Journal of Political Science* 45:470–490.

INDEX

Italic page numbers indicate material in figures or tables.